Wood Modification Technologies
Principles, Sustainability, and the Need for Innovation

Dick Sandberg

Professor of Wood Science and Engineering
Luleå University of Technology, Skellefteå, Sweden

Andreja Kutnar

Professor of Wood Science
University of Primorska, Koper and InnoRenew CoE, Izola, Slovenia

Olov Karlsson

Associate Professor of Wood Science and Engineering
Luleå University of Technology, Skellefteå, Sweden

Dennis Jones

Associate Professor of Wood Science and Engineering
Luleå University of Technology, Skellefteå, Sweden

CRC Press
Taylor & Francis Group
Boca Raton   London   New York

CRC Press is an imprint of the
Taylor & Francis Group, an **informa** business

A SCIENCE PUBLISHERS BOOK

Front cover: Lookout tower Pompejus in acetylated raiata pine, Fort De Roovere, Halsteren, The Netherlands.

The watchtower is also used as an open-air theatre, and an information point for tourists. The facade of the watchtower has been designed according to the principle of the Voronoi diagram, a mathematical design principle, which enables the triangles of the steel construction to be used to have windows and openings in the facade. By using this design principle, it allowed the facade to be divided into elements that could be prefabricated and transported, and at the same time, add an additional layer to the facade to break the dominance of the triangular steel structure.

Architects: RO&AD Architecten

Photographs © 2021 Dick Sandberg, Andreja Kutnar, Olov Karlsson and Dennis Jones.

First edition published 2021
by CRC Press
6000 Broken Sound Parkway NW, Suite 300, Boca Raton, FL 33487-2742
and by CRC Press
2 Park Square, Milton Park, Abingdon, Oxon, OX14 4RN

© 2021 Taylor & Francis Group, LLC

CRC Press is an imprint of Taylor & Francis Group, LLC

ISBN: 978-1-138-49177-9 (hbk)
ISBN: 978-0-367-76782-2 (pbk)
ISBN: 978-1-351-02822-6 (ebk)

Typeset in Times New Roman
by Radiant Productions

Preface

The forest sector and wood-based industries are challenged by changes in resource availability, energy supply and climate change. It is part of the continuing discussion between economics, ecology, and social welfare that can be summed up as sustainability. Wood is a natural, renewable, reusable and recyclable raw material that can play a major role in minimising the negative effects on the climate and environment, when it is sourced from sustainably managed forests. There is intense competition from the non-sustainably derived materials entering markets that have traditionally been dominated by timber products. Environmental concerns are leading to the phasing out of some traditional wood preservatives, which rely upon toxicity as their primary mode of action. Also, there are increasing quantities of plantation grown broad-leaved and conifer species being processed and such woods generally have inferior properties compared with timber sourced from natural forests. In order to maintain the competitiveness of wood, new approaches are needed. Research into wood modification is one way of meeting these challenges.

In his book *Wood Modification*, published in 2006, Professor Callum Hill gave a precise but also very general definition of the concept of wood modification:

Wood modification involves the action of a chemical, biological or physical agent upon the material, resulting in a desired property enhancement during the service life of the modified wood. The modified wood should itself be nontoxic under service conditions and, furthermore, there should be no release of any toxic substances during service life, or at the end of life following disposal or recycling of the modified wood. If the modification is intended for improved resistance to biological attack, then the mode of action should be non-biocidal (Hill, 2006, p. 20).

This work, together with the work performed in the European Thematic Network for Wood Modification[1] culminating with its first conference in Ghent 2003 (Van Acker and Hill, 2003), brought together different research and industrial activities in Europe in the area of wood modification. For almost two decades, wood modification research activities have been increasing around Europe and beyond. Besides intensified research, there were also increased volumes and new products of modified wood on the market. Among these were thermally modified, furfurylated and acetylated timber. Several networking activities related to wood modification have also been executed. Specifically, two activities within the frame of COST—European Cooperation in Science and Technology—have been central: COST Action FP0904 "Thermo-hydro-mechanical wood behaviour and processing" that ran from 2010 to 2014, chaired by Professor Parviz Navi from Ecole Polytechnique Fédérale de Lausanne (EPFL, Switzerland) and vice chaired by Associate Professor Dennis Jones, and COST Action FP1407 "Understanding wood modification through an integrated scientific and environmental impact approach—ModWoodLife" running from 2015 to 2019, chaired by Professor Andreja Kutnar (University of Primorska, Slovenia) and vice chaired by Associate Professor Dennis Jones. Although a considerable amount of research and development activities have taken place in the past two decades, we are still just at the beginning of a new era regarding the use of modified wood. The volumes of modified wood in Europe, but also in the rest

---

[1] A project entitled "Wood modification, the novel base, providing materials with superior qualities without toxic residue" funded by the European Commission, through its Fifth Framework programme.

of the world, is small compared to the volumes of wood products produced. A recent task within the framework of the COST Action FP1407 was to outline the current status of wood modification across Europe in terms of national inventories (Jones et al., 2019). Based on the reported production volumes and on subsequent investigations, it was estimated that in 2020 the annual production volume for modified wood in Europe will be slightly more than 700,000 m^3, which is, to say the least, a very modest volume.

However, modified wood, as defined by Hill, is not a new invention. Different modification methods can be traced back to ancient times (Navi and Sandberg, 2012; Ch. 2, Sandberg et al., 2017) and the industrial revolution, which resulted in highly industrialised production processes involving wood modification techniques for mass production of furniture, for example.

Wood modification is an all-encompassing term describing the application of chemical, mechanical, physical, or biological methods to alter the properties of the material. Such a definition of wood modification includes more or less everything that happens to the wood material after it has left the forest, and is more or less useless when one would like to simplify and give an overview of an area of interest. For this reason, the purpose of what would be achieved and the area in which the modifications are intended to be applied must be defined. This book focuses on industrial wood modification processes, i.e., processes that are applied on an industrial scale and deliver products to the market. Wood, is this case, is defined as solid wood and veneer, but of course, many of the processes described may also be applied to wood particles and fibres.

With this limitation in terms of wood modification, chemical treatments of wood that reach the core of cellulosic microfibrils, destroying the crystalline structure and eliminating most of the composite structure of wood, are in most cases, excluded from this book. Such subversive treatments radically modify the chemical components of the wood, and so the material produced lacks practically all the intrinsic characteristics of untreated natural wood. An example of a subversive treatment is the liquefaction of lignocelluloses (Jindal and Jha, 2016), typically to produce oil from biomass under very severe conditions.

There are already several good, fairly well-updated books in the field of wood modification, such as the already mentioned books by Hill, and by Navi and Sandberg, but also more chemistry-oriented presentations, such as *Chemical Modification of Wood* by a Professor at the University of Wisconsin (Madison, USA), Roger Rowell (Rowell, 2013). There are, however, only few, if any, overviews of the wood modification in the combined fields of sustainability, innovation, and industrialisation. This book aims to fill that gap.

The book is divided into six chapters. Chapter 1 gives an overview of wood modification with the aim of helping the reader to structure the field. A presentation of wood as a substrate for modification, and its response on a chemical and biological level, as well mechanical response upon loads before and after modification, is also presented within this chapter. For the reader that would need a deeper understanding in these fields, the chapter provides an extensive reference list of books covering the basic properties of wood as a material in detail. Wood modification has been divided into three main groups, each represented in their respective chapters (Chapters 2–4): (Chapter 2) chemical treatments, (Chapter 3) thermally-based treatments, and (Chapter 4) treatments with the use of electromagnetic irradiation, laser or plasma, for example. In Chapter 5, short presentations of different processes that are described in the literature or other places and that may be suitable to apply as wood modification processes are given. In general, these processes are not yet industrialised or may be well established in fields other than wood processing and modification. The intention with this chapter is to help the reader to sort out the potential of these processes, and find ways for further reading. The last chapter, *Modified wood beyond sustainability*, presents modified wood from a sustainability and circular economy perspective. Wood modification, its environmental impact and the use of modified wood in a healthy living environment are discussed. The potential role of wood and wood modification in achieving the ambitious targets of the European Green Deal are presented through discussion on recycling, up-cycling, the cradle to cradle paradigm, and end-of-life disposal options. The chapter concludes with the technical challenges identified in advancing Industry 4.0 in general and in wood modification processing.

The target audience for the book are students at high-school and university level, as well as researchers and people practiced in the industry. For the benefit of wood engineers and other people with an interest in this fascinating industry, we hope that the availability of this material as a printed book will provide an understanding of all the fundamentals involved in the processing of modified wood.

The authors hereby acknowledge COST—European Cooperation in Science and Technology— which enabled the authors of this book to meet many researchers from around Europe and develop great collaborations in the past several years. CT WOOD CoE at Luleå University of Technology and InnoReNew CoE are acknowledged for their financial support to the writing of this book. Furthermore, they give thanks to their supporters in the process of preparing this book, especially to Tatiana Abaurre Alencar Gavric, Gertrud Fábián and Chia-Feng Lin for helping them with the designs of the figures. A good graphic tells more than a hundred words.

Finally, they authors are dedicating this book to all young researchers from around the globe who are to take wood modification research to a new level, resulting in increased modified wood production and its use in the healthy built environments.

October 2020

Dick Sandberg
Andreja Kutnar
Olov Karlsson
Dennis Jones
Skellefteå, Koper, Neath

References

Hill, C.A.S. 2006. Wood Modification – Chemical, Thermal and Other processes. Wiley Series in Renewable Resources, Wiley and Sons, Chichester, UK.

Jindal, M.K. and M.K. Jha. 2016. Hydrothermal liquefaction of wood: A critical review. Reviews in Chemical Engineering 32(4): 459–488.

Jones, D., D. Sandberg, G. Goli and L. Todaro. 2019. Wood Modification in Europe: A State-of-the-art about Processes, Products and Applications. Florence University Press, Florence, Italy.

Navi, P. and D. Sandberg. 2012. Thermo-hydro-mechanical Processing of Wood. Presses polytechniques et universitaires romandes – EPFL Press, Lausanne, Switzerland.

Rowell, R.M. [ed.]. 2013. Handbook of Wood Chemistry and Wood Composites. CRC Press, Boca Raton, USA.

Sandberg, D., A. Kutnar and G. Mantanis. 2017. Wood modification technologies – A review. iForest 10: 895–908.

Van Acker, J. and C. Hill [eds.]. 2003. Proceedings of the First European Conference on Wood Modification: ECWM 2003, Ghent, Belgium.

Contents

Chapter 1

Wood and Wood Modification

1.1 Wood modification

As a natural renewable resource, wood is generally a non-toxic, easily accessible and inexpensive biomass-derived material. Since ancient times, wood has been used by mankind due to its inherent properties, where a specific part of a tree of a particular species that could be found locally was utilised to achieve the best performance when used in construction, for different types of tools or for purposes not included in the practical tasks of life. Apart from drying, modification of timber has been rare in historical terms. Nevertheless, since wood is a natural product that originates from different individual trees, limits are imposed on its use, and the material may need to be transformed to acquire the desired functionality. This has become increasingly evident in the modern and highly industrial era. Modification is thus applied to overcome weaknesses in points of the wood material that are mainly related to moisture sensitivity, low dimensional stability, low hardness and wear resistance, low resistance to bio-deterioration against fungi, termites, marine borers, and low resistance to UV radiation.

Nowadays, wood modification is defined as a process adopted to improve the physical, mechanical, or aesthetic properties of sawn timber, veneer or wood particles used in the production of wood composites. This process produces a material that can be disposed of at the end of a product's life cycle without presenting any environmental hazards greater than those that are associated with the disposal of unmodified wood.

The wood modification industry is currently undergoing major developments, driven in part by environmental concerns regarding the use of wood treated with certain classes of preservatives. Several fairly new technologies, such as thermal modification, acetylation, furfurylation, and various impregnation processes, have been successfully introduced into the market and demonstrate the potential of these modern technologies.

The main reasons for the increased interest in wood modification during the last decades with regard to research, the industry, and society in general can be summarised as:

1) a change in wood properties as a result of changes in silvicultural practices and the ways of using wood,

2) awareness of the limited availability of rare species with outstanding properties for modern use, such as durability and appearance,

3) awareness and restrictions by law of the use of environmental non-friendly chemicals for increasing the durability and reducing the maintenance of wood products,

4) increased interest from the industry to add value to sustainably sourced local sawn timber and by-products from the sawmill and refining processes further along the value chain,

5) EU policies supporting the development of a sustainable society, and

6) the international concern for climate change and related activities mainly organised within the frame of the United Nations (UN), such as the Paris Agreement under the United Nations Framework Convention on Climate Change (UNFCCC).

What is wood modification?

Wood modification is an all-encompassing term describing the application of chemical, mechanical, physical, or biological methods to alter the properties of the material. This definition of wood modification includes almost everything that happens to the wood material after it has left the forest and is more or less useless for simplifying and giving an overview of an area of interest. For this reason, it is necessary to define the purpose and the area in which the modification is intended to be applied. Such a purpose may, of course, change over time.

In the field of wood technology, wood modification includes any method or process that tends towards a better performance of the wood, where the term *wood* refers to roundwood (e.g., round timber, logs or other log-like products such as pit props, pylons, etc.), hewn timber, sawn timber, veneer, strands, chips and other types of wood particles used in wood composite products. In modern wood technology, it has become desirable for the modified wood to be non-toxic in service and that disposal at the end of life does not result in the generation of any toxic residues. This means that chemical treatments of wood that reach the core of the cellulosic microfibrils, destroying the amorphous and crystalline structures and eliminating most of the composite structure of wood, are in most cases excluded. Such subversive treatments radically modify the chemical components of the wood, and the material produced consequently lacks practically all the intrinsic characteristics of untreated natural wood. An example of a subversive treatment is liquefaction of lignocelluloses (Yao et al., 1994), which is mainly adopted to produce oil from biomass under very severe conditions.

Hill (2006) has provided a well-accepted definition of wood modification: *"Wood modification involves the action of a chemical, biological or physical agent upon the material, resulting in a desired property enhancement during the service life of the modified wood. The modified wood should itself be non-toxic under service conditions, and furthermore, there should be no release of any toxic substances during service, or at end of life, following disposal or recycling of the modified wood. If the modification is intended for improved resistance to biological attack, then the mode of action should be non-biocidal"*.

It should be noted that the above does not necessarily exclude the use of a hazardous chemical in the preparation of modified wood, provided that no hazardous residues remain in the wood when the modification process is complete.

In this book, the focus is on methods that have introduced a modified solid wood or veneer product or are introduced in large-scale wood preservation projects. This means that processes that are producing or are very near to being involved in the production of modified products are dealt with. The book does not focus on the following areas, however some are briefly described in Chapter 5, and readers are referred to other sources for an introduction to the field:

- treatments aiming to improve wood properties such as fire/flame stability (cf. Lowden and Hull, 2013; Visakh and Arao, 2015),
- preservation of ancient small artefacts (cf. Unger et al., 2001),
- wood particles or disintegrated wood mixed with other polymeric material, such as wood-plastic composites (cf. Jawid et al., 2017), or
- modification and derivatisation of extensively mechanically and chemically degraded wood constituents (cf. Huang et al., 2019).

The modification of wood can involve active modification, which changes the chemical nature of the material, or passive modification, in which the properties are changes without any alteration in the chemistry of the material. Most active modification methods investigated to date have involved a chemical reaction with the cell-wall polymer hydroxyl groups. These hydroxyl groups play a key role in the wood-water interaction while simultaneously being the most reactive sites. In moist wood, the water molecules settle between the wood polymers, forming hydrogen bonds between the hydroxyl groups and individual water molecules. A change in the number of these water molecules results in shrinkage or swelling of the wood. All possible types of wood treatment affect the wood-water interaction mechanism. The main wood-treatment interaction mechanisms that may be responsible for new wood properties are summarised in Figure 1.1.

Several wood-treatment interaction mechanisms tend to occur at the same time. For example, in thermal modification, parts of the cell-wall polymers are altered, which may lead to cross-linking, reduction of hydroxyl groups, and undesired cleavage of the polymer chains.

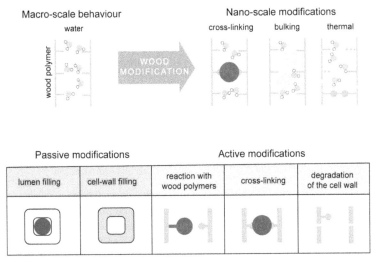

Figure 1.1 Schematic diagram illustrating the effect of active and passive modifications.

Most of the wood-modification processes that are being developed or under experimentation have full or partial origins in the pioneering research and seminal work of Alfred J. Stamm and his colleagues at the Forest Products Laboratory in Madison, Wisconsin, during the 1940s and 1950s (cf. Stamm, 1964). An early attempt to use chemical modification in industrial production was made by the Nobel family in their factory in St. Petersburg during the 1840s. To increase the durability and reduce the hygroscopicity of wood for wheel hubs, they impregnated the wood with a mixture of ferric sulphate and an acid, and dried it slowly in special boxes. Finally, they coated the hub with linseed oil and a varnish to further reduce moisture absorption. The trials were successful and they called the process "hardening wood". It was patented by Alfred Nobel's father Immanuel and his business partner Colonel Nikolai Aleksandrovich Ogarev, on 6 April 1844. The production was mechanised by a steam engine and 36 wheels a day were produced for the Russian army (Tolf, 1976; Meluna, 2009; Carlberg, 2019).

Wood modification processes[1]

To modify wood, four main types of process can be implemented: (1) chemical treatment, (2) thermally-based treatment, including thermo-hydro (TH) and thermo-hydro-mechanical (THM) treatment, (3) treatment with the use of electromagnetic irradiation, plasma or laser, and (4) other types of treatment, e.g., treatments based on biological processes (Figure 1.2).

---

[1] In this book, the different processes are denoted by their scientific denominations. When a trademark of a process is used in the text, it is marked with the ™ sign in general, regardless if the trademark is registered or not.

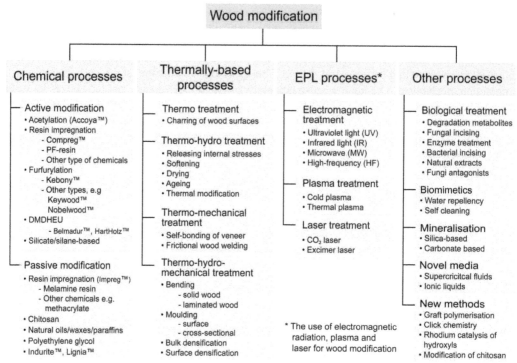

Figure 1.2 Classification of wood modification processes.

In the chemical modification of wood, a reagent reacts with a wood polymeric constituent (lignin, hemicelluloses, cellulose) to form a stable covalent bond between the reagent and the cell-wall polymer (Rowell, 1983). The reagent does not need to be environmental friendly itself, but the total process and the final product must be (i.e., the non-environmental reagent may just be used "indoors the process").

Chemical modification of wood can, therefore, in this sense be regarded as an active modification because it results in a chemical change in the cell-wall macromolecules. In this book, processes that only fill the lumen and/or cell wall are also included (Figure 1.1), as they follow the definition stated by Hill (2006). Currently, little is known about the general mode of action of chemically modified wood, but some hypotheses have been proposed by Hill (2006), specifically for biological degradation: (1) the equilibrium moisture content is lowered in modified wood, hence, it is more difficult for fungi to get the moisture required for growth and subsequent wood decay; (2) there is a physical blocking of the entrance of decay fungi to micro-pores in the cell walls; and/or (3) the action of specific enzymes is inhibited.

One group of emerging wood treatments involves the combined use of temperature and moisture through which force can be applied, i.e., thermo-hydro (TH) and thermo-hydro-mechanical (THM) processes (Navi and Sandberg 2012). In an orthodox definition, no additives are used in the processes except for water in combination with wood, heat, and, in THM, external forces to change wood properties or to shape the wood. Procedures including impregnation or gluing to lock a shape are usually also included in these modification processes.

In processes based on electromagnetic radiation, the aim will be to focus on processes that utilise the fact that wood at a high moisture content is capable of absorbing a large amount of electromagnetic energy. The amount of energy required to raise the temperature is determined by the specific heat capacity of the material. The specific heat capacity of wood is influenced by its moisture content, its dry density and the temperature. This type of modification process also includes changing the wood surfaces by laser or plasma treatment.

There is, of course, a wide range of processes which is not possible to describe in detail in this book, but which have been or may be of interest for the modification of wood. Some such processes are briefly described in Chapter 5, as a separate group of *other processes*. This chapter gives a short state-of-the-art description of processes that have been of interest in the wood industry but for some reason have not been further developed, or modification methods used (industrially or at least on a larger scale) in other industrial sectors than the wood sector (e.g., in the food or agricultural sectors, etc.) that may be of interest for the modification of wood.

The efficient modification of wood requires reactions at the molecular level and this requires an understanding of the fundamentals of organic chemistry which, together with other related areas of wood science, such as wood structure, wood-water relationship, wood biodegradation, weathering of wood, and stress-strain response of wood, are presented in this chapter.

1.2 Wood as a substrate for modification

A comprehensive knowledge of the characteristics of any material is essential for its optimal utilisation. This is especially true for wood because of its cellular nature, its complex cell-wall structure, and its variability. For the development and understanding of wood-modification processes, it is necessary to understand not only the principles of tree growth but also the macroscopic and microscopic features that determine wood quality in a broad sense. A wood modification process must, in general, be adapted to the species for which it is to be applied, and to the features and properties of the wood species in question.

Trees are major components of the biosphere and their wood is one of the most important renewable resources. Wood is the result of an evolutionary process over millions of years to perfectly meet three main functions: water transport, mechanical support, and storage of reserve nutrients for the living tree.

Wood is a material with a biological structure consisting of cellulose and lignin-based cells and the anatomy of a tree or a piece of wood requires a journey through several orders of magnitude. The structure of wood is multi-levelled and hierarchical, and it is possible to define more than ten different structural levels between the macroscopic (the trunk) and the molecular level, including cells and the grouping of cells into functional units and tissues of a characteristic size and shape. It is important to distinguish between the macro-structure, micro-structure and ultra-structure. The structure visible to the naked eye, or with a magnifying glass up to 10 times magnification is called the macro-structure, and macro-features such as grain and knots are readily apparent. A microscopic examination of the wood gives the overall information of the structure and the general character of the wood, showing the morphological characteristics of the woody plant. This is the most reliable method of wood identification, and microscopic examination is most important with conifers, where visual features of the wood are characterised more by similarities than differences. At the ultra-structure level, the cell-wall composition is in focus. Below this resolution lies the realm of individual chemicals. All these features must be considered when designing a wood modification process.

The tree

Everybody knows that a tree is a "large" plant with a stick (the trunk) in the middle to hold the crown with its foliage aloft. Trees generally produce wood during their growth, but do all trees produce wood? The answer is of a semantic nature and depends on how we define the concept of "a tree", i.e., must the central stick be of wood? Trees are among the largest organisms that have ever lived. A redwood (giant sequoia) tree growing in North America can, for example, have a weight 10 times that of a full-grown blue whale, but there are also very small trees like the Artic willow that reach a height of only a few centimetres. Many trees grow big when conditions are favourable and stay small when they are not. Foresters and other people have insisted that plants with several supporting stems should be called shrubs, but in nature such a definition is not easily pinned down. For example, in Brazil one particular species grows single-trunked trees where there is good availability of water, e.g., along the riverbanks, but multi-stemmed short shrubs where it is drier (Tudge, 2005). Trees may grow from ground level with several solid trunks of equal magnitude and the size of, e.g., a Scots pine tree. To divide species into trees and shrubs may be practical, but it is not really a distinction based on genetic differences. Nature is not designed to be easy for biologists and foresters!

In fact, there are many lineages of trees, separate evolutionary lines that have nothing to do with each another except that they are all plants (Tudge, 2005). A tree is not a distinct category—it is just a way of being a plant. Trees have dominated dry land for over 300 million years, which is far longer than both mammals and dinosaurs, and today forests cover about a third of the world's dry land. Trees are extremely diverse, with more than 80,000 species all over the globe—some of them evergreen, while others are deciduous. The accepted definition of a tree is that it is a plant with a more or less permanent shoot system supported by a single *woody* trunk, i.e., a plant where the cambium cells have the ability to undergo *secondary thickening*, i.e., the ability to produce both xylem tissue (wood) and phloem (bark). By such a definition, true wood comes only from conifer and broad-leaved trees.

Thus, evolution has resulted in two categories of tree, conifers (softwood) and broad-leaved (hardwood) trees, both originating from the so-called seed plants (Figure 1.3). Many lineages of seed plants have appeared during the long time of evolution, and most have long been extinct. Timber merchants label all conifers *softwoods* and all broad-leaved trees *hardwoods*, even though some conifers are a lot harder than many hardwoods, and the softest woods of all are in fact hardwood.

More than 360 million years ago, the first plants that reproduced not by spores but by seeds appeared. Seed plants, to which all trees belong, are divided into two categories: gymnosperms, i.e., plants with naked seeds, and angiosperms, i.e., plants with covered seeds. The gymnosperms consist of conifers, cycads (fern plants) and their relatives, ginkgos, and gnetales. Today, only one species of ginkgo remains: the maidenhair tree in western China. The gnetales group consists of about 70 distinct species, but the phylogenetic[2] position of the group is uncertain. It was sometimes placed close to the angiosperms, but is today associated with conifers.

The angiosperms include all other flowering plants. In contrast to the gymnosperms, the majority of angiosperm species are not trees but herbs. They are further divided into two categories: dicotyledons (dicots) and monocotyledons (monocots). The broad-leaved trees belong within the dicotyledon category. The most important structural difference between dicotyledons and monocotyledons is that the monocots have no ability to undergo secondary thickening, which means that monocot plants that look like trees, such as bamboo, palm trees and banana plants, are by definition not regarded as true trees.

The most important structural difference between gymnosperms and angiosperm trees is in their xylem fibre structure. Gymnosperm wood has only one type of cell, called tracheids, which

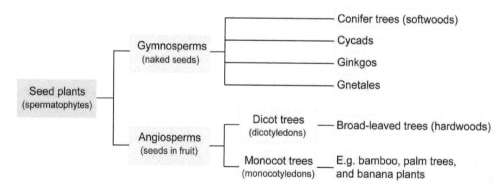

Figure 1.3 Conifer trees and broad-leaved trees are included in the botanical division of spermatophytes, i.e., seed plants.

---

[2] Phylogenetics—the evolutionary history and relationships among individuals or groups of organisms, e.g., species, or populations.

transport water up to the leaves and strengthen the trunk. The angiosperm wood has two main types of xylem cell for these functions: vessels which pipe water through the trunk, and fibres (libriform fibres and fibre tracheids) for the strength of the trunk.

Conifer trees are characterised by their needle-like leaves, and such trees are commonly considered to be evergreens because most of them remain green all the year around and annually lose only a portion of their needles. Most conifers also bear scaly cones, inside which seeds are produced. In contrast to conifers, broad-leaved trees bear "broad leaves" which generally change colour and drop in the autumn in temperate zones, and produce seeds within acorns, pods, or other fruit bodies.

Only a small fraction of a tree's biomass is capable of producing the sugars it needs to grow, i.e., most of the energy created by photosynthesis in the leaves is used for building up xylem in the stem, branches and root system as the tree grows. This strategy has been shown to be very successful in competition with other plants for the light, water and nutrients needed for survival.

Trees compete for the "light"[3] by holding their canopy of leaves high above the ground, and the permanent structure (the trunk) above the ground makes trees successful in that sense compared to, for example, non-woody herbaceous plants which die back every year. The single stem of a tree makes it competitive also to plants which typically branch near the ground and so have several narrow stems rather than a single trunk, i.e., shrubs. As a group of trees grow in height, they cast such a dense shade by their collective canopy that most of other plants die out and the area will become a forest. The disadvantage of the single-trunk tree strategy is the high energetic cost for the construction of the tall trunk-branch system, resulting in a slow growth compared with that of herbaceous plants.

The structure of trees

The structure of wood is a result of the requirements of the living tree. Xylem is the part of the tree that in everyday speech is called wood and consists of hollow tubes (cells) with a length of a few millimetres connected to each other (Figure 1.4). The majority of these cells within the living tree are dead, i.e., the protoplasm is absent, leaving hollow cells with rigid walls. Protoplasm is the living content of a cell that is surrounded by a plasma membrane, i.e., a biological membrane that protects the cell from its environment. The only living cells in a tree are located in the cambium, in the sapwood rays, and in the inner bark (phloem). Their functions are related to the growth of the tree (cambium cells) and to the storage of the nutrients produced by photosynthesis.

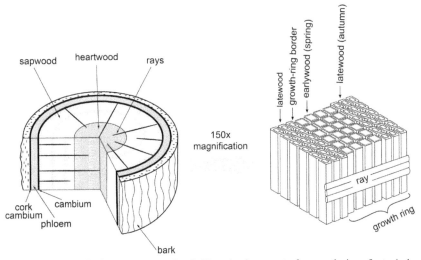

Figure 1.4 Major tissue types in the tree cross section (left), and enlargement of a growth ring of a typical conifer tree, showing the relative difference in size between earlywood and latewood cells (right).

---

[3] Light is defined by CIE in relation to the sensitivity of the human eye to wavelengths between 400 and 700 nm.

The vascular cambium is the main growth tissue in the stem and roots of a tree, sheathing the xylem tissue from roots to leaves. It is a single cell layer that generates tissue on both the inside and outside—the process of *secondary thickening*—so that the tree grows thicker year by year, always with fresh xylem and phloem tissue coming on line and guaranteeing the function of the tree. The cambium lays down xylem on the inside to strengthen the stem and increase its water transport capability. On the outside, the cambium produces a thinner layer of phloem, a tissue that transports sugars created by photosynthesis in the leaves down to the roots for use in producing new cells and for storage in the trunk and bark nutrient-storing cells.

After cambial division, each successive xylem cell undergoes enlargement, wall thickening, and lignification. The cells lose their living cytoplasm and are left as dead cells of cellulose stiffened with lignin. The rate of cell division and the final size are thought to be largely influenced by growth-regulating hormones (auxins). As time passes, the xylem cells lose their function as the conducting tissue and the inner structural part loses its ability to transport water (heartwood formation). Xylem tissue is formed in an aqueous environment and exists in a living tree in the maximum swollen state—*the green state*.

The bark usually refers to tree tissue outside the cambium, but it can be simply divided into the inner bark (phloem) and the outer bark (cork). A disadvantage for the tree is having vital phloem tissue in the outer parts of the trunk where there is a greater risk of damage. The outer bark protects the tree from drying out and from extreme temperature fluctuations, mechanical injury, fire, etc. The outer bark is compounded from formerly functional phloem and custom-built cork, highly evolved and adapted. The oldest vessels of the phloem are crushed as new phloem tissue is laid down inside them, so that their functions become redundant. The crushed phloem is incorporated into the bark, providing essential protection. Many trees have a layer of secondary cambium (cork cambium) outside the principal cambium layer, with the specific task of producing cork. Cork cells (like xylem cells) are born to die, they finish up small, with thick, impermeable cell walls.

Within the cross section of a stem, there is often a visible difference in colour between two broad divisions known as sapwood and heartwood. The sapwood portion of the tree is physiologically active, i.e., the sapwood is involved to the normal functions of the living tree, and the ray cells of the sapwood are in continuous communication with the cambium and the inner living bark (Figure 1.4). The sapwood acts as a nutrient- and water-storage reservoir and provides the function of sap conduction. Heartwood is usually found in the centre lower portion of mature stems and all its cells are dead. At one time, heartwood was sapwood, but it no longer has a physiological function.

The water-transport system in a tree

The conduction role of the tree starts with taking up water and minerals from the ground by the root system and continues up the xylem tissue, i.e., through the roots, stem and branches, to the leaves, where photosynthesis takes place. Sugars produced by photosynthesis are in return transported down the tree along the phloem tissue. Some trees may also take up water from the air; the redwoods of California get about a third of their water from the morning fogs that sweep in from the Pacific.

Over 90% of the wood cells are arranged along the axis of the trunk or branches. In conifers, the vast majority of these cells are the long (up to 10 mm) and narrow (about 30 μm) tracheid cells, which have the dual functions of water conduction and supporting the stem (see Table 1.1 for proportions and functions of different cell types). This dual function makes the tracheid cell non-optimal in its function; the water-transport is improved by having large-diameter cells, i.e., wide cells, whereas strength is improved by having long and narrow cells. The shape of the cells is a compromise between these two. Broad-leaved trees have long, narrow fibres (libriform fibres and fibre tracheids) which support the trunk, but also very wide and thin-walled vessel cells, which only have the function of water transport (Figure 1.5). The larger diameter of the vessels dramatically decreases the resistance to water flow through them. Broad-leaved trees therefore have a much better water transport than conifers, even though the vessels constitute only a small proportion of the total number of cells.

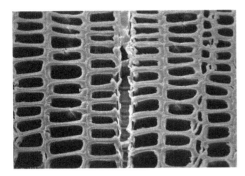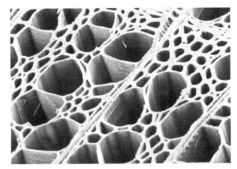

Figure 1.5 Cross-section view of tracheid cells in a conifer species, Swiss pine (left), and in a broad-leaved species, magnolia, containing both fibres and large-diameter vessels (right).

If a large air bubble gets into a wood vessel, the water column is broken by the tension in the water above and below it. The whole vessel then fills with air, forming what is called an embolism (Ennos, 2016). Once an embolism has formed, it is prevented from spreading through the whole length of the tree by sieve-like plates along the wood vessels which trap the air bubble. However, unless water is actively forced into the vessel again, the vessel remains empty and loses its conducting activity. Very dry conditions, but especially cold conditions increase the risk for embolism. Embolism is not common in conifers as the tracheid cells are much narrower than the vessels.

Regardless of the type of water-conducting cells in the tree, it is spectacular that water can rise from the root system to a height of 100 metres, to reach the leaves in their canopy. Several theories have been put forward over the years, such as the *positive root-pressure theory*, the *capillary force theory*, the *suction theory* and the *cohesion theory*. The positive root-pressure theory suggests that water is pumped up the trunk by the roots based on the osmosis effect, but it has only been possible to demonstrate this effect in birches and maple, and only in early spring (Ennos, 2016).

The capillary forces alone would be able to draw water to a height of only about 0.5 m in wood based on the dimensions of the different wood tissues, while the maximum height caused by the atmospheric pressure allows this capillary transfer to be only 10 metres or so. Cohesion theory, as defined by Boehm (1893) and Dixon and Joly (1894), is today the most accepted explanation for the water transport in trees. It is based on the fact that water is pulled up under tension when water is lost from the leaves by transpiration. If water is held in a narrow tube it can withstand large stretching forces without breaking. The cohesion-tension principles have been reviewed, particularly in terms of non-destructive testing (Bentrup, 2016). The strength of the water is due to cohesion between its molecules, and these forces can theoretically hold up a column of water nearly three kilometres high. These tensile forces acting upon the tree stem due to the water cohesion are sufficient to cause a measurable deformation in the shape of the stem.

The principal direction in trees and of wood

When discussing the structural features of wood, it is important to indicate which surface or direction is being referred to. Three distinctive planes exposing different views of the wood structure can be noted. A cut perpendicular to the longitudinal direction of stem is called a transverse or cross section, a cut in the radial plan is called a radial section and a longitudinal cut tangent to the growth rings is termed a tangential section. It is also necessary to distinguish between the three principal directions in wood; longitudinal or axial (L), radial (R) and tangential (T), which are the local directions responsible for wood anisotropy,[4] for its mechanical, physical and technological properties. Figure 1.6 illustrates schematically the principal axes and the corresponding radial, tangential and cross sections.

---

[4] Anisotropy is the property of being directionally dependent, which implies different properties in different directions, as opposed to isotropy. It can be defined as a difference along different axes in a material's physical or mechanical properties.

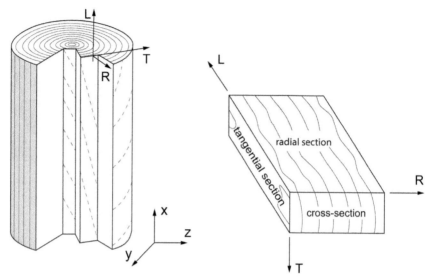

Figure 1.6 Schematic representation of the three principal axes and sections in wood. The stem section to the left show the principal axes, viz. longitudinal (L), radial (R) and tangential (T), and the rectangular piece of wood to the right shows the definition of the principal sections in sawn timber.

The macrostructure of wood

The main macroscopic parts of wood are, as shown in Figure 1.7:

- growth rings, earlywood and latewood,
- bark,
- pith,
- rays,
- resin canals of conifer wood,
- vessels of broad-leaved wood,
- sapwood and heartwood,
- knots,
- reaction wood,
- juvenile wood, and
- texture, colour and scent of wood.

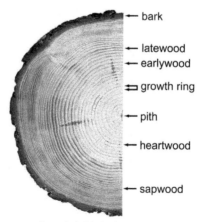

Figure 1.7 The macrostructure of wood visible in the cross section (un-dried disc) of Scots pine.

It is difficult to distinguish *juvenile wood* from *normal wood* by the naked eye, although it is here considered as a macroscopic feature due to its great importance for wood in use. For the same reason, features like texture, colour and scent of wood are briefly described in this section.

Growth rings, earlywood and latewood

In trees that grows seasonally, the addition of xylem and phloem is intermittent. In a typical tree growing in the temperate zone, the new xylem laid down in spring is wide but thin walled, while the later xylem is narrower but thick-walled. The difference can be seen in the cross section of a trunk as the presence of concentric layers. The layered arrangement of the xylem tissue in these growth rings is probably the most characteristic feature of wood. *False growth rings* may occur, and in some cases certain rings may be locally discontinuous. The growth rate and periodicity of trees growing in tropical forests—the forests located around the equator—are not the same as those of trees in temperate forests. Tropical trees in places where there are distinct wet and dry seasons also show growth rings, but trees growing where the climate is constant do not show growth rings. For these reasons, the term *growth ring* is preferred over *annual ring*.

In temperate regions, growth starts at the beginning of spring, continues in the summer and stops in the autumn. The part produced in the spring is called earlywood and that in the summer is called latewood. At the beginning of this vegetative growth, trees form a new layer of wood between the existing wood and the bark, the branches and the roots. The growth rings can often be easily distinguished because of differences in structure and colour between the earlywood and latewood. It is customary to divide the growth rings into three classes, conifers, ring-porous and diffuse-porous broad-leaved trees (Figure 1.8).

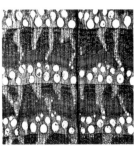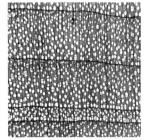

Figure 1.8 Cross-section view of a conifers species, Scots pine (left), a ring-porous broad-leaved species, oak (middle), and a diffuse-porous broad-leaved species, goat willow (right).

In temperate conifer woods, there is often a marked difference between latewood and earlywood (i.e., the growth-ring border), the latewood being denser than the earlywood, cf. Figure 1.9. The earlywood cells have thin walls (approximately 2 μm) and are mainly lumen, whereas the latewood cells have thicker walls (approximately 5 μm) with narrower lumen. The strength of the wood is in the walls, not the cavities. Hence, the greater the proportion of latewood, the greater is the density and strength. The width of a growth ring is less important for the density of a conifers as the proportion and nature of the latewood in the growth ring.

In contrast to the growth-ring border, the border between earlywood and latewood is diffuse, and the change in density and cell-wall thickness, for example, is gradual through this transition zone. There are numerous definitions to distinguish between earlywood and latewood, the most universally accepted definition being the one proposed by Mork (1928), who suggested that cells are classified as latewood when double the wall thickness is greater than the lumen diameter. Since then, more accurate definitions have been proposed, e.g., by Phillips et al. (1962) based on a β-particle method, and by Jagels and Dyer (1983) based on a digital image analysis of the shape of the cell cross section.

In ring-porous woods, each season's growth is always well defined, because the large vessels formed early in the season are on the denser tissue of the previous year, cf. Figure 1.8 middle.

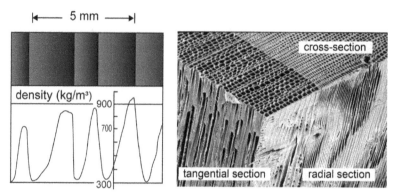

Figure 1.9 Density variation between earlywood and latewood in longleaf pine (left) after Phillips et al. (1962), and a 3D scanning electronic micrograph of Norway spruce (right).

In the case of the ring-porous broad-leaved woods, there seems to be a definite relationship between the rate of growth of timber and its properties. This may be briefly summed up in the general statement that the more rapid the growth or the wider the rings of growth, the heavier, harder, stronger, and stiffer is the wood. This, however, only applies to ring-porous woods, such as oak, ash, hickory, and others of the same group, and it is, of course, subject to exceptions and limitations.

In ring-porous woods of good growth, the thick-walled, strength-giving fibres are usually most abundant in the latewood. As the width of the ring diminishes, this latewood is reduced so that very slow growth produces relatively light, porous wood composed of thin-walled vessels and wood parenchyma. In good oak, these large vessels of the earlywood occupy 6 to 10% of the volume of the tree, whereas in inferior material they may make up 25% or more. The latewood of good oak is dark coloured, firm and consists mostly of thick-walled fibres which form one half or more of the wood. In inferior oak, this latewood is greatly reduced in both quantity and quality. Such a variation is largely due to the rate of growth.

In the diffuse-porous woods, the demarcation between growth rings is not always so clear and, in some cases, it is almost (if not completely) invisible to the naked eye. Conversely, when there is a clear demarcation there may be no noticeable difference in structure within the growth ring, cf. Figure 1.8 right.

In diffuse-porous woods, the vessels are uniform in size, so that the water-conducting capability is scattered throughout the ring instead of being concentrated in the earlywood. The effect of the rate of growth is not, therefore, the same as in the ring-porous woods, nearly approaching the conditions in the conifers. In general, it may be stated that woods give a stronger material when they grow at a medium rate than when they grow very rapidly or very slowly. In many uses of wood, total strength is not the main consideration. If ease of working is a requirement, wood should be chosen with regard to its uniformity of texture and straightness of grain, and this will, in most cases, occur when there is little contrast between the latewood of one season's growth and the earlywood of the next.

Radial growth begins first near the top of the tree and proceeds gradually downward in the stem, resulting in more earlywood and wider growth rings near the pith in the upper crown region. Transition to latewood occurs first near the base. Farthest from the source of the growth regulating hormones (auxins) and proceeds upwards. The density of an individual wood fibre is, therefore, determined by its position relative to the live crown and by the time of its formation.

Bark

The trunk has an outer covering, called bark, which protects the wood from extremes of temperature, drought, and mechanical injury. Bark constitutes, on average, about 10% of the volume of a tree, but this figure varies depending on tree species and age. The bark usually refers to tree tissues outside the cambium. It includes a number of different tissues, but bark can simply be divided into the inner bark (phloem and cork cambium) and the outer bark (cork layer). The relatively light-coloured inner bark is living tissue that conducts sugars downwards from the leaves. The dark-coloured and dry outer bark includes only dead tissue and is more or less impermeable to water and gases with an insulating function. The cell walls in the cork layer contain *suberin*, a waxy substance which protects the stem against water loss and the invasion of insects into the stem, and prevents infection by bacteria and fungal spores. The cork produced by the cork cambium is normally only one cell layer thick and it divides periclinally (parallel to the tissue surface) to the outside, producing cork. Like wood, bark is anisotropic with regard to dimensional stability and strength. Its thermal properties and heating value are similar to those of wood.

Pith

In the centre of the wood is the pith, which is formed during the first year of growth and becomes a storage area for impurities that are deposited from the active xylem during the growth of the tree. Pith consists of soft, spongy *parenchyma* cells, and is located in the centres of the stem, branches and roots. In some plants, the pith is solid, but in most cases it is soft. The shape of the pith varies between species and it varies in diameter from about 0.5 mm to 8 mm. Freshly grown pith in young shoots is typically white or pale brown, but it usually darkens with age. It may be inconspicuous, but it is always present at the centre of a trunk or branch. The roots have little or no pith and the anatomical structure is more variable.

Rays

Wood rays extend in the transverse direction from the bark toward the centre of the tree at a right angle to the growth rings. The first formed rays extend from the bark to the pith and are called primary rays, others extend from the bark to some later-formed growth ring outside the pith and are called secondary rays.

All the transverse cells found in any given wood are included in the wood rays, ribbon-like aggregates of horizontally oriented cells. The rays are formed by the cambium and extend in the radial direction in the xylem, cf. Figure 1.4. Rays consist of nutrient-storing cells and provide a route by which sap can be transported horizontally either to or from the inner bark (phloem).

Rays may contain ray parenchyma, ray tracheids and ray epithelial cells, but rays are usually composed predominantly of ray parenchyma cells, with ray tracheids forming one or more marginal rows of cells and an occasional row of cells in the body of a ray. When transverse resin canals are present, rows of epithelial cells and the resin canal cavity are also included in the ray.

The size of the rays is very different in different species. They can vary from being slightly visible to completely invisible to the naked eye. The variation between different species is great, and this means that they are useful for identification. In conifers, rays are usually one-cell or a maximum of two-cells wide in the tangential direction and 1 to 20 and sometimes up to 60 cells high. The rays in broad-leaved woods vary between one and several cells, depending on the species. These rays can always be observed in the tangential, radial and transverse sections.

Rays have a major influence on wood properties, not least the strength. The rays are the weakest zones in the wood, and they easily cause the wood to split. Rays are also one of the main causes of transverse hygroexpansion anisotropy, i.e., the rays restrain dimensional changes in the radial direction, and their presence is partially responsible for the fact that when wood is dried it shrinks less radially than tangentially. The mechanism of differential transverse hygroexpansion has been the subject of considerable controversy in the literature on wood science for many years, see for instance Skaar (1988).

Resin canals in conifer wood

A characteristic feature of some conifer woods is their resin content, which is often sufficient to give them a clear fragrance and make newly sawn timber sticky. Resin canals or resin ducts are tube-like intercellular spaces, which transport resin in both the longitudinal and horizontal directions

(Figure 1.10). The vertical and horizontal resin canals are interconnected and form a uniform network in the tree (Ilvessalo-Pfäffli, 1995). Transverse resin canals, that are located inside the rays, are seen in the tangential section. Resin is formed in epithelial parenchyma cells and can in some species be stored in special resin canal cavities, called resin pockets. These cells supply resin to the channels and pockets.

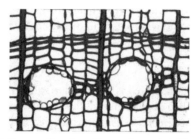

Figure 1.10 Cross-section view of two resin canals in Norway spruce.

Vessel elements in wood from broad-leaved trees

The fundamental anatomical difference between wood from conifer and wood from broad-leaved trees is that broad-leaved woods contain specialised conducting cells called vessel elements. These vessel elements are generally much larger in diameter than other types of longitudinal cells and the vessels are in general shorter than both broad-leaved and conifer fibres, cf. Table 1.1. A number of vessel elements are linked end-to-end along the stem to form long tube-like structures. Both the size and arrangement of the vessels in the cross-section of a wood sample are used to classify wood from different broad-leaved trees, cf. Figure 1.8.

Sapwood and heartwood

In most species, the difference in properties between sapwood and heartwood are substantial, especially regarding water and moisture transport, and they must be taken into consideration for most types of wood modification process. Some species, e.g., aspen, birch, beech, hornbeam and maple, do not normally develop heartwood, but these tree species may have discolouration around the pith due to microorganisms or frost, so-called *red core* or *false heartwood*. There are also differences in heartwood formation between species, especially between conifer and broad-leaved trees.

The sapwood is the outer, water-conducting part of the trunk that, in the living tree, contains living cells for the storage of reserve material (see rays). Young trees have only sapwood, but as they mature and no longer need the whole cross section of the xylem part of the trunk for fluid transport, they develop heartwood, i.e., the water-conducting function ceases, the remaining living wood cells die, and the cell walls are preserved and help to support the tree for many years to come. Heartwood is the inner and central part of the trunk, which, in the living tree, contains only dead and non-water-transporting cells and in which the reserve materials have been removed or converted into extractives. Heartwood can also be found in the roots of many species, especially in the region near the stem (Hillis, 1987). The new wood cells thus created are added to the sapwood, while the older cells adjacent to the heartwood gradually change to form new heartwood. The proportions of sapwood and heartwood vary according to species, the age of the tree, the position in the tree, the rate of growth, and the environment.

In some species, a zone usually comprising 1–3 growth rings can occur between the sapwood and the heartwood for a short period of time. This transition zone is described by Hillis (1987) as a narrow, pale-coloured zone surrounding some heartwood or injured regions, often containing living cells, usually devoid of starch, often impermeable to liquids, with a moisture content lower than that of the sapwood and sometimes also lower than that of the heartwood.

The volume percentage of living cells (parenchyma cells) in the sapwood varies between 5 and 40% of the total tissue volume (Hillis, 1987). The death of these cells and the transition of the sapwood to heartwood are accompanied by the secretion of oxidised phenols, which are often the origin of the pigmentation of heartwood. In trees in which heartwood and sapwood have the same colour, the death of these cells does not lead to pigmentation. The substances secreted by the trees are called extractives. They are typically toxic to wood-decaying organisms and help the wood to resist fungi and insects.

Figure 1.11 shows the difference in colour between sapwood and heartwood. Sapwood often has a clearer colour than the heartwood, but in many species this distinction between the sapwood and heartwood does not exist in colour but only in function and moisture content.

In contrast to heartwood, sapwood in the living tree has a very high moisture content. In Scots pine, there is also a large variation in moisture content in the sapwood between the earlywood and latewood, where the moisture is found mainly in the earlywood. In the heartwood, there is no difference in moisture content between earlywood and latewood (Figure 1.12).

During heartwood formation in a number of broad-leaved species, the vessels are filled with outgrowths of parenchyma cells called tyloses into the hollows of vessels, cf. Figure 1.13.

Tyloses are growths that partially or completely block the vessels in which they occur, a situation that can be either detrimental or beneficial depending upon the use to which the wood is put (Bosshard, 1974). The existence of tyloses in the heartwood vessels of white oak, and the relative

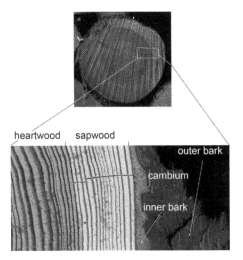

Figure 1.11 Cross section of a Scots pine log (upper) and a magnification of a portion of the same cross section, showing the inner bark, outer bark, cambium, and the sapwood/heartwood border (lower). The small dark dots in the lower image are resin, which has flowed out when resin canals were cut.

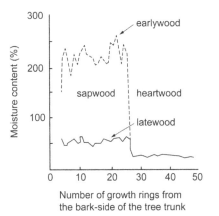

Figure 1.12 Moisture content of earlywood and latewood in sapwood and heartwood of Scots pine (Vintila 1939).

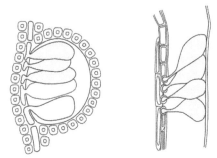

Figure 1.13 Tyloses in a broad-leaved tree vessel in transverse (left) and longitudinal (right) sections. The tyloses effectively prevent water transportation in the vessel.

lack of them in red oak, is the reason why white oak is preferred in the manufacture of barrels, casks and tanks for the storage of liquids. In contrast to this beneficial feature of tyloses, wood in which they are well developed may be difficult to dry or impregnate with chemicals (Bowyer et al., 2007).

Knots

As the trunk grows, old and new branches form junctions called knots. Where the cambium is alive at these points, there is a continuity of growth combined with a change in orientation and the knot is termed green or alive. On lower branches, the cambium is frequently dead, and the trunk grows around the branch enclosing its bark. These "black" or "dead" knots, are liable to fall out of sawn timber during sawing or during further processing. An important feature of knots is their deviant fibre orientation around and in the knot itself, which clearly affects both the appearance and properties of sawn timber.

Reaction wood

When a tree is growing on a sloping land surface or is exposed to a dominant wind direction, the load on the stem is unbalanced. The tree then starts to produce abnormal wood known as reaction wood to compensate for the unbalanced load. The formation of reaction wood is related to the process of straightening of leaning stems and the same happens in the branches and in the area where the branches join the stem.

Conifers and broad-leaved trees have adopted different strategies for the formation of reaction wood. The reaction wood of conifers is called *compression wood*, because it forms on the compression-stress side of leaning stems. In broad-leaved trees the reaction wood is called *tension wood* because the increased growth takes place on the upper or tension-stress side of the leaning tree, as shown in Figure 1.14.

In both conifer and broad-leaved trees, the wood formed on the side of the stem or branch opposite to the reaction wood is known as *opposite wood*, while that lying between the reaction wood and the opposite wood, is referred to as *lateral wood*. In comparison with wood production in a vertically growing stem with almost perfectly circular growth rings, compression wood and tension wood are usually produced in larger quantities, giving the stem a cam-shaped cross section with pronounced eccentricity with respect to the pith (Barnett and Jeronimidis, 2003).

Reaction wood has physical and mechanical properties different from those of normal wood and some of these properties are worth mentioning. The compressive strength of compression wood is greater than that of normal wood, however, compression wood is consequently very brittle. This brittleness can be a problem if the wood is subjected to bending. The tensile strength and Young's modulus of tension wood are greater than those of normal wood, and it also has a higher fracture toughness and impact resistance. Reaction woods have different shrinkage characteristics from those of the adjacent normal wood, due to a deviation in the micro-fibril orientation in the S_2 cell-wall layer, and this can result in warping and cracking of the wood during drying.

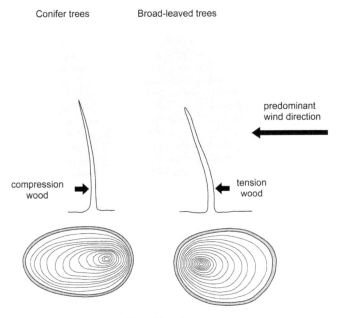

Conifer trees   Broad-leaved trees

predominant
wind direction

compression
wood

tension
wood

cross-sections of the stems

Figure 1.14 Formation of reaction wood in wood in conifer and broad-leaved trees as a result of a predominant wind direction over a long time.

Although it has not been generally recognised, reaction wood has many characteristics similar to those of juvenile wood (Zobel and Sprauge, 1998). In conifer wood, both juvenile wood and compression wood have short cells with flat micro-fibrillar angles and often a high lignin content; in broad-leaved woods, juvenile fibres of both the diffuse- and ring-porous wood types are short and broad-leaved woods have tension wood with a high cellulose content. When a tree is producing juvenile wood, it is especially susceptible to environmental forces that lead to the formation of reaction wood (Zobel and Sprauge, 1998).

Juvenile wood

Although it is not visible in the trunk cross-section, there is an important pith-to-bark gradient in density that is unique for each species. The fact that a relatively pronounced change in density often occurs in conifers during the first 15 to 30 years of growth gave rise to the term *juvenile wood* (Zobel and Sprauge, 1998). This term can lead to confusion, because this wood is found not just in young (juvenile) trees, but near the pith in every tree, regardless of age. However, the juvenile wood first laid down by the cambium near the centre of the tree has characteristics that differ from the wood formed at a large number of growth rings from the pith. This juvenile wood is sometimes referred to as *core-wood or crown-formed wood* and the mature wood as *outer-wood*. Although juvenile wood occurs in both conifer and broad-leaved trees, it is usually much less evident in broad-leaved woods. The source of juvenile wood is primarily in young plantations, thinnings, top wood, plywood cores and the harvesting of young stands.

Unlike heartwood that evolves in the lower parts of the trunk upwards, juvenile wood is formed nearest to the pith at all heights in young tress, and only in the top regions of mature trees (Figure 1.15). The most common characteristics used to identify the juvenile zone are density and cell length, although several other characteristics are also used. Each has a different curve of development from the pith outward so that the definition of the juvenile zone depends on the characteristic used. Bendtsen (1978) showed for hard pines (subgenus *Pinus*; soft pines has subgenus *Strobus*) that density, strength, cell length, cell-wall thickness, transverse shrinkage and latewood percentage increase from pith to bark, whereas the fibril angle, longitudinal shrinkage and moisture content

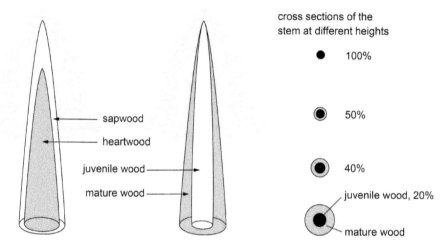

Figure 1.15 Juvenile wood occurs around the pith and roughly forms a cylinder up the tree. In contrast to heartwood, the proportion of juvenile wood increases towards the top of the tree.

of the same species decrease from pith to bark. Zobel and Talbert (1984) also conclude that the chemical composition of juvenile wood differs from that of mature wood. In most conifer woods, the lignin content is higher and the cellulose content lower in the juvenile wood. In wood from broad-leaved trees, Zobel and Talbert (1984) say that the proportion of and the chemical make-up of cellulose and lignin differ and that the holocellulose content is higher in juvenile wood than in mature wood.

The texture, colour and scent of wood

The texture of wood is material-dependent, i.e., the texture depends on the type of wood and on how the wood is built up. A piece of wood can show a great variation in hue depending, for example, on the type of wood, the content of extractive substances, heartwood or sapwood, and age. For most types of wood, the growth-ring orientation in the cross-section of the wood is important for the texture. A tangential surface with horizontal growth rings becomes mottled, whereas the radial surface with vertical growth rings has an even and harmonious pattern, as shown in Figure 1.16. Special patterns may result from uneven heartwood pigmentation, irregular growth-ring formation, deviations in cell and grain direction, or any combination of these.

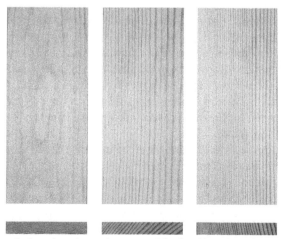

Figure 1.16 Influence of growth-ring orientation on the texture of the flat-side surface of Scots pine tangential section with horizontal growth rings (left), and radial section with vertical growth rings (right).

Colour is one of the most conspicuous characteristics of wood and, although quite variable, it is one of the important features used in identification as well as adding aesthetic value. Basic wood substances, i.e., cellulose and lignin, have little colour of their own, so any distinctive colour is associated with heartwood (Hoadley, 1990). A dark colour always indicates heartwood, whereas a light colour can be either heartwood or sapwood. Some wood also undergoes considerable colour change with age or on exposure to UV-radiation.

Certain woods have distinctive odours. Many conifer woods, as well as numerous tropical woods, are known for their aromatic character. The odour is due to volatile extractives or resins in the wood.

The microstructure of wood

The cellular structure of wood is generally classified as a *microstructure* because the structural units are on a millimetre to micrometre scale (Table 1.1), and some type of magnifying tool, such as a microscope, is needed for the study.

Table 1.1 Density, dimensions and volume percentages of various cells in different tree species from the temperate zones (Fengel and Wegener, 1984).

		Conifer wood		Broad-leaved wood		
	Fir	Nor. spruce	Scots pine	Eur. beech	Eur. oak	Poplar
Density [kg/m³]						
Minimum	320	300	300	490	390	
Average	410	430	490	680	650	400
Maximum	710	640	860	880	930	
Fibre[1] length (mm)						
Minimum	3.4	1.7	1.4	0.6	0.6	0.7
Average	4.3	2.9	3.1			
Maximum	4.6	3.7	4.4	1.3	1.6	1.6
Fibre[1] diameter (μm)						
Minimum	25	20	10	15	10	20
Average	50	30	30			
Maximum	65	40	50	20	30	40
Vessels length (mm)				0.3–0.7	0.1–0.4	0.5
Vessels diameter (μm)				5–100	10–400	20–150
Cell percentage (average values on volume)						
Tracheids	90	95	93	38	44/58	62
Vessels				31	40	27
Parenchyma	scarce	1.4–5.8	1.4–5.8	4.6	4.9	scarce
Ray cells	9.6	4.7	5.5	27	16.2/29.3	11.3

[1] Fibre – tracheids or libriform fibres. The following terminology misuse was pointed out by Zobel and Buijtenen (1989). The term "fibre" is commonly used for both the true fibres of broad-leaved woods and the tracheids of conifer woods. Although this is botanically incorrect, the general use of the term fibre must be recognised, since numerous publications refer to the fibre characteristics of conifer woods as well as to the real fibres of broad-leaved woods.

Microstructure of conifer wood

The wood of conifer trees consists of two types of cell: longitudinal tracheids and ray parenchyma, oriented both axially and horizontally. Most of the tracheids are longitudinal, while the parenchyma cells have a radial orientation. In addition to these two types of cell, other elements, such as epithelial

20   *Wood Modification Technologies: Principles, Sustainability, and the Need for Innovation*

cells, constitute longitudinal and horizontal resin canals. The transverse tracheids are not present in all species. The various types of conifer wood cells are presented in Table 1.2 and Figure 1.17.

The longitudinal or vertical tracheids constitute about 90–95% of the volume of conifer woods (Ilvessalo-Pfäffli, 1995). These are long, narrow cells with closed ends and bordered pits (Figure 1.18). The length of a tracheid varies from 2 to 6 mm and the width from 0.014 to 0.060 mm. The tracheids of latewood have a thick wall and a small lumen and are more suited to provide mechanical support than the tracheids of earlywood, whose function is mainly to conduct sap.

The length of a longitudinal tracheid, which is a closed unit, is very small compared to the height of the tree. To ensure the conduction of sap within the tree, it is thus necessary for each

Table 1.2 Different cell types and their functions in conifer wood.

Cell type	Function
Longitudinal tracheids	Support, conduction
Parenchyma	
Ray parenchyma	Storage
Longitudinal parenchyma	Storage
Epithelial parenchyma	Secretion of resin
Short tracheids	
Ray tracheids	Conduction
Strand tracheids	Conduction

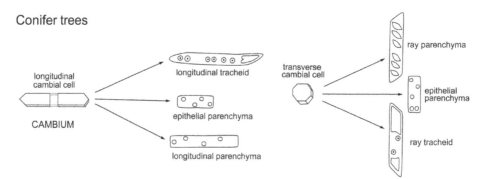

Figure 1.17 Diagram showing the anatomical elements in wood from conifer trees.

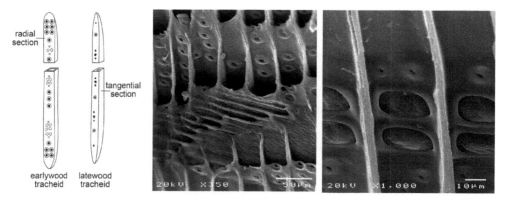

Figure 1.18 Diagrammatic representation of an earlywood and a latewood tracheid (left), and micrographs of the radial walls of Scots pine tracheids presenting bordered pits (middle), and (to the right) simple pits between tracheids and ray parenchyma cells (in the centre), and small bordered pits between tracheids and ray tracheids (above and below).

tracheid to be functionally connected to other tracheids. The conduction between tracheids, in both the lateral and vertical directions, takes place through pits, most of which are located in the radial walls. Pits also exist in the tangential walls of the tracheids, but they are much less numerous.

The pits of earlywood tracheids are large and circular, averaging about 200 pits per tracheid, whereas latewood tracheids have rather small, slit-like pits, and only 10 to 50 per tracheid (Trendelenburg and Mayer-Wegelin, 1955).

Pits have two essential parts, the pit *cavity* and the pit *membrane*, the cavity being open internally towards the lumen of the cell and closed by the pit membrane. Pits are of many shapes and sizes, but they are generally reduced to two basic types based on the shape of the cavity, viz. the *simple pit* and the *bordered pit* (Ilvessalo-Pfäffli, 1995).

In the simple pit, the cavity is almost straight-walled and only gradually widens or narrows toward the cell lumen. The lumen end of the cavity is known as the pit aperture. In the bordered pit, the cavity is constricted towards the lumen, forming a dome-shaped chamber, which is overarched by the pit border. The pits of adjacent cells are usually paired, forming three types of pairs (Figure 1.19).

A *simple pit pair* consist of two simple pits between parenchyma cells and in broad-leaved woods also between vessel elements and parenchyma cells. A *bordered pit pair* consists of two bordered pits between tracheids in conifers and between vessel elements in broad-leaved woods. A *half-bordered pit pair* consists of a bordered pit and a simple pit in the contact zone between the longitudinal tracheids and the rays and is, therefore, also called a *cross-field pit*. Their size, shape, and arrangement vary according to species and cross-field pitting is the most important feature in the identification of conifer species on a micro-structural level. Half-bordered pit pairs are also found between a vessel element and a parenchyma cell in broad-leaved woods.

In the bordered pit pairs of most conifer woods, the membrane has a thickening in the central zone called the *torus*, which is somewhat larger in diameter than the aperture and is impermeable to water. The membrane around the torus, the *margo*, is porous (Figure 1.20). When the torus is pressed against one of the apertures, the passage of water is prevented. The result of this phenomenon is called an *aspirated pit*, and it occurs when sapwood is transformed into heartwood or when the wood is dried. In heartwood, the pits are definitively blocked in this position (Figure 1.21).

The rays consist of radially oriented, brick-like and thin-walled parenchyma cells. The rays of conifers are composed either of parenchyma cells alone or of parenchyma cells and ray tracheids. In conifer trees, less than 25 parenchyma cells usually pile up to form a ray.

The ray tracheids are about the same size as the ray parenchyma cells. They are dead cells with small bordered pits leading to other ray cells and to longitudinal tracheids. The ray tracheids seem to be functionally limited to the occurrence of resin canals. Their functions are conduction, and the accumulation and storage of water and other substances in the radial direction.

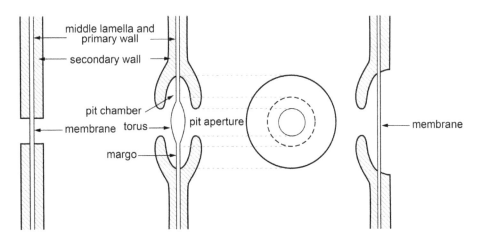

Figure 1.19 Three types of pit pair; simple pit pair (left), bordered pit pair (middle), and semi-bordered pit pair (right).

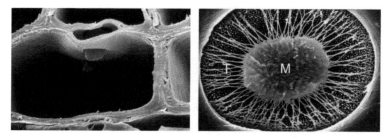

Figure 1.20 Cross-section view through a cell wall of European silver fir containing a pit (left), and membrane of a bordered pit showing the torus (T) and the margo (M) through which water passes from one cell to the next (right).

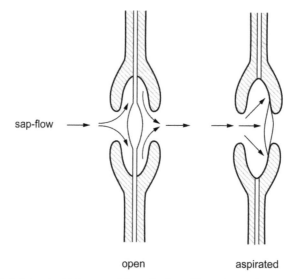

sap-flow →

open   aspirated

Figure 1.21 Aspiration of pits is involved in heartwood formation in conifers and may also occur when drying the sapwood.

Microstructure of wood from broad-leaved trees

The structure of broad-leaved wood is more complex than that of conifer wood and, during their evolution, broad-leaved wood have developed special types of cell from the tracheid: vessel elements for conduction and fibres for support. Wood from broad-leaved trees is made up of various types of cells which are very variable in dimension and form. The different types of cells constituting broad-leaved timber are presented in Table 1.3 and in Figure 1.22. Practically all broad-leaved

Table 1.3 Different cell types and their functions in wood from broad-leaved trees.

Cell type	Function
Vessel elements	Conduction
Fibres:	
Libriform fibres	Support
Fibre tracheids	Support
Parenchyma:	
Ray parenchyma	Storage
Longitudinal parenchyma	Storage
Tracheids:	
Vascular tracheids	Conduction
Vasicentric tracheids	Conduction

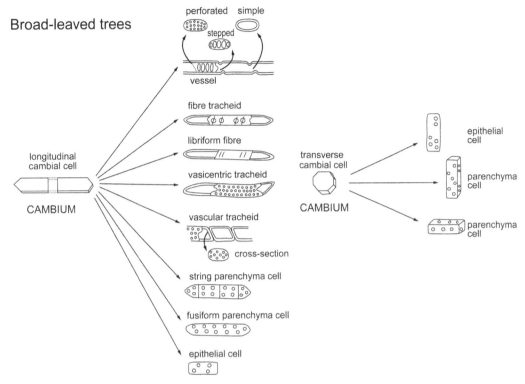

Figure 1.22 Diagram showing the anatomical elements in wood from broad-leaved trees.

wood contains longitudinal vessels, longitudinal fibres, and longitudinal parenchyma cell, as well as ray parenchyma cells. The broad-leaved wood rays, unlike those in conifers, consist exclusively of parenchyma cells.

Longitudinal cells

The longitudinal cells in broad-leaved trees consist of vessels, the tracheids, axial fibres, and axial parenchyma (Figure 1.22).

A vessel is a tube made of successive cell elements connected to form long continuous tubes in the tree. The volume of vessels in broad-leaved timber varies between 6 and 55%. Their diameter varies between 20 and 300 μm, and the passage of sap in the longitudinal direction is made possible by wide openings (perforations) at each end of the vessel elements. In addition, water and sap can transfer to adjacent vessels laterally through small pits in the vessel walls. The pits connecting two laterally adjacent vessels are different from the bordered pits, since they are primarily simple pits without a "torus" (Figure 1.19 left).

The fibres

The role of longitudinal cells is to provide mechanical support for the wood. They are long cells with thick and rigid walls varying between 0.8 and 2.3 mm. In wood from broad-leaved trees, the volume percentage of the fibres varies between 25 and 75%. Figure 1.23 shows a micrograph of wood from a broad-leaved tree with fibres, vessels and rays.

Wood from broad-leaved trees usually contains a greater volume percentage of longitudinal parenchyma than conifer wood. These cells fulfil a storage function for nutrients. The rays in broad-leaved woods consist of two or up to 40 radial cells in height, one to more than 20 in width, and sometimes in so great a number that the rays are visible to the naked eye.

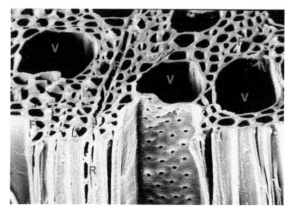

Figure 1.23 3D SEM micrograph of a broad-leaved wood structure showing vessels (V), fibres (F) and rays (R).

In summary, wood from broad-leaved trees is characterised by the presence of vessels, tracheids, fibres, longitudinal parenchyma and ray parenchyma. The vessels fulfil the role of conduction and the fibres with their thick walls ensure the flexible rigidity and mechanical support of the tree and often constitute most of wood volume, up to 60%. The radial and longitudinal parenchyma cells ensure that there is a reserve of nutrient substances in the tree.

Wood cell-wall structure and ultrastructure

With the help of a polarised, optical or electronic microscope, the various layers which form the cell wall can be observed. This wall consists of the primary wall (P) and the secondary wall (S). The *middle lamella* (M) is not an integral part of the cell wall but it interconnects the cells. The *middle lamella* and primary wall are however frequently treated as a single entity called the *compound middle lamella*. Figure 1.24 shows a representation of a segment of a longitudinal cell (tracheid) surrounded by other cells. The secondary wall is made up of three distinct layers: S_1, S_2 and S_3.

The middle lamella appears after the division of cambial cells and varies between 0.5 μm and 1.5 μm in thickness. The optical microscope shows the existence of an important quantity of lignin in this layer. This layer joins the cells together. To separate the cells (e.g., for anatomical study or for the manufacture of paper pulp), techniques involving maceration or chemical attack are used. These destroy the middle lamella and allow cells to be separated.

The primary wall is very thin and measures approximately 0.1 μm in thickness. Like the middle lamella, it contains a large quantity of lignin, but very little cellulose. It is often difficult to distinguish the primary wall from the middle lamella.

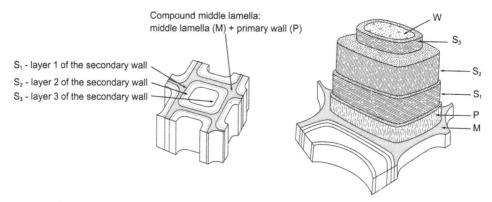

Figure 1.24 Diagrammatic representation of a longitudinal cell (tracheid) surrounded by six other cells (left), and representation of the various layers of the cell wall (right). M: middle lamella, P: primary wall, S: secondary wall with its S_1, S_2 and S_3 layers, W: warts layer.

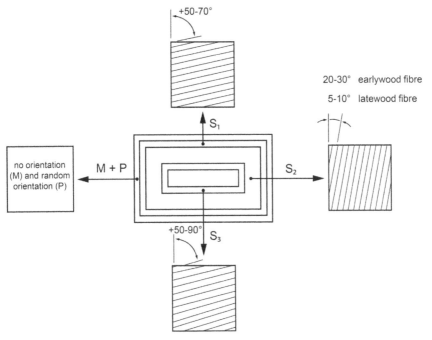

Figure 1.25 Schematic diagram of the microfibril-angle arrangements within the S_1, S_2 and S_3 layers. The angles are given with the longitudinal axis of the fibre as a reference.

A polarising microscope reveals that the secondary wall is made up of three layers (S_1, S_2 and S_3). In the latewood, the S_2 layer is the thickest part of the tracheid wall and there is little difference in thickness between the S_1 and S_3 layers. These layers consist of cellulose fibrils and microfibrils of different angles to the fibre axis.

The microfibril angle of the S_2 layer ranges between 5–10° (latewood) and 20–30° (earlywood), that of the S_1 between 50 and 70° and that of the S_3 layer between 50 and 90° (Figure 1.25). These layers, on the other hand, consist of concentric parallel laminae. The S_2 layer consists of 30 to 40 laminae in the cells of earlywood and more than 150 laminae in those of latewood. The S_2 layer is significantly thicker than its neighbours and, hence, contributes in a dominant way to the mechanical and physical properties of the cell wall.

1.3 The chemical composition of wood

Having established the basic structures within wood, it is necessary to consider their chemical composition. Wood consists mostly of carbon (50–53% in conifer wood and 47–50% in wood from broad-leaved trees) and oxygen (40–44%) together with 6% hydrogen, small amounts of nitrogen and other elements bonded together forming compounds with different elemental compositions, structures and weights (Tillman et al., 1981).

The main chemical components of wood are *cellulose, hemicelluloses* and *lignin*. In addition, there are other components called *extractives*, which, e.g., are deposited in the cell wall during the formation of heartwood. Table 1.4 gives the volumetric percentage of each chemical component, and its polymeric nature, degree of polymerisation and function, and Figure 1.26 shows their variation within different layers of the cell wall.

Brief introduction to covalent bonds

In any chemical compound, atoms strive towards distribution of valence (outermost) electrons corresponding to a stable noble gas state. Noble gases in group 8A in the periodic table of chemical

Table 1.4 Chemical components of wood, their polymeric natures and functions.

Component	Composition (% volume)	Polymeric nature	Degree of polymerisation	Basic monomer	Function
Cellulose	45–50	Linear molecule semi-crystalline	5,000–10,000	Glucose	Fibre
Hemicelluloses	20–25	Ramified amorphous molecule	150–200	Essential sugars, excluding glucose	Matrix
Lignin	20–30	Three-dimensional amorphous-bonded	-	Phenylpropane	Matrix
Extractives	0–10	Polymerised molecule	-	Polyphenol	A protection element
Ash	0–5	Minerals	-	-	-

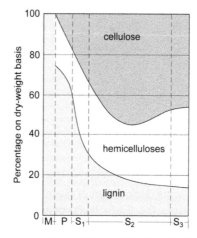

Figure 1.26 Distribution of cellulose, lignin and hemicelluloses within the cell-wall layers (after Panshin et al., 1964). For details of the different cell-wall layers, see Figure 1.24.

elements have this stable distribution of valence electrons and do not normally form chemical compounds (Figure 1.27). Most other atoms are satisfied with eight valence electrons and only the small hydrogen atom is satisfied with two valence electrons. Atoms in the upper left of the periodic table (Figure 1.27) are the most electropositive and wish to get rid of (donate) electrons, whereas those in the upper right corner are the most electronegative and wish take up (accept) electrons (except noble gases).

The position in the vertical group tells us how many electrons an atom can take up to achieve noble gas character; elements in groups 1A, 2A, 3A may lose one, two and three electrons, respectively, whereas elements in group 5A, 6A and 7A may take up three, two and one electrons, respectively. Adding electrons to such electronegative atom or withdrawal of electrons from electropositive atom leads to the formation of negative anions and positive cations, respectively. Ions with different charges are strongly attached to each other by electrostatic forces forming ionic bonds without sharing electrons, like the sodium cation (Na^+) and chloride anion (Cl^-) in table salt

	1A	2A	1B	2B	3B	4B	5B	6B	7B	8B	9B	10B	3A	4A	5A	6A	7A	8A
1	H																	He
2	Li	Be											B	C	N	O	F	Ne
3	Na	Mg											Al	Si	P	S	Cl	Ar
4	K	Ca	Sc	Ti	V	Cr	Mn	Fe	Co	Ni	Cu	Zn	Ga	Ge	As	Se	Br	Kr

Figure 1.27 Selected parts of the periodic table.

(NaCl). Since a carbon atom has four valence electrons (group 4A in the periodic table) and is neither electropositive nor electronegative, it can achieve noble gas character instead by sharing electron pairs with at most four atoms, whereas the small hydrogen atom (group 1A in the periodic table) can bind only one atom. Methane (CH_4) is the simplest stable organic molecule (neither electronegative nor electropositive) in which carbon is covalently bonded to four hydrogen atoms. Oxygen has six valence electrons (group 6A in the periodic table) and can share electron pairs with at most two atoms, which complete the octet of electrons in an oxygen atom. Multiple covalent bonds are not planar but tetrahedral to achieve a molecule with the lowest energy, so that molecules with such bonds have a three-dimensional structure. Single bonds are written as straight lines but to be able to draw such structures on paper, it is customary to print bonds pointing out of the paper plane as bold and those pointing back into the paper as dashed. Those in the plane of paper are printed as solid lines (Figure 1.28).

Single bonds such as the carbon-oxygen bond in the alcohol in Figure 1.28 can rotate. The hydrogen bonded to the oxygen atom can, therefore, point in the direction judged by the extent of rotation of the C-O bond. Rotation can, however, be restricted in more complicated structures due to interactions with other atoms within or between other molecules and rotation does not normally occur in double-bonded structures, as will be discussed later.

In dimethyl ether (CH_3-O-CH_3), the two carbon substituents called methyl groups (CH_3) are bonded covalently to the electronegative oxygen. The difference in electronegativity between those constituents is not so high that the bonding electron is not completely withdrawn towards the oxygen atom forming ions, but only polarises the bond so that the oxygen is partly negatively charged and the two carbon atoms partly positively charged (Figure 1.29). This leads to the formation of a dipole so that the angle between the two C-O bonds is tetrahedral, meaning that the dimethyl ether molecule has a net polar character. Note that compounds like tetrachloromethane are non-polar as the centre of gravity of charges coalesce at the same spot.

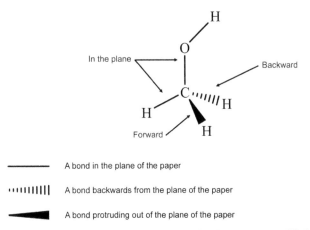

A bond in the plane of the paper

⋅⋅⋅⋅IIIIII A bond backwards from the plane of the paper

A bond protruding out of the plane of the paper

Figure 1.28 Drawing of molecules illustrating the three-dimensional structure exemplified with methanol.

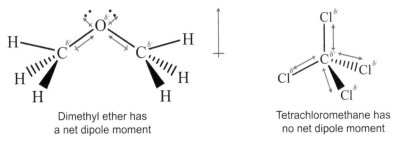

Dimethyl ether has a net dipole moment

Tetrachloromethane has no net dipole moment

Figure 1.29 Polar dimethyl ether and non-polar tetrachloromethane.

In wood, carbon and oxygen atoms can share not only one but two electron pairs (denoted as one or two solid lines in Figure 1.30), while nitrogen can share up to three electron pairs with carbon, resulting in a number of ways of forming different functional groups. Note that to simplify the drawings carbons are usually omitted in the phenolic rings and single bonds are not drawn between oxygen and hydrogen in hydroxyl groups. R denotes a compound group of C and H atoms.

The distance between the two hydrogen atoms in a hydrogen molecule (H_2) is 0.084 nm but the distance is greater between heavier atoms; 0.11 nm for a carbon-hydrogen bond and 0.15 nm for a carbon-carbon bond. Double bonds are shorter than single bonds; 0.13 nm for a carbon-carbon double bond in an alkene (Figure 1.30). A carbon-carbon double bond is stronger than a carbon-carbon single bond. The binding electrons are distributed equally between the two bonding atoms in the product and to homolytically cleave the bond requires 2.85 MJ/mol for $CH_2=CH_2$ and 1.59 MJ/mol for CH_3-CH_3 (Hart et al., 2003). A chemical structure with no carbon-carbon double bonds is saturated, but a structure with a carbon-carbon double bond is unsaturated. An

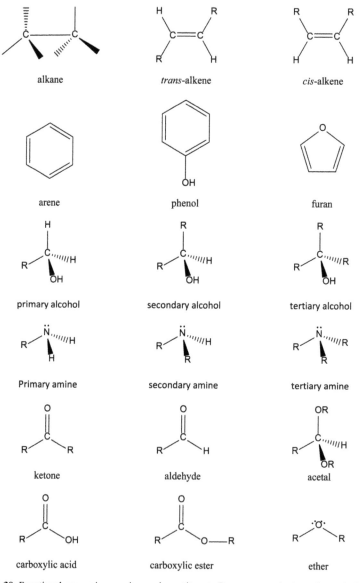

Figure 1.30 Functional groups in organic wood constituents. R represents a hydrocarbon substituent.

alkene in an unsaturated fat becomes saturated by reaction with hydrogen gas (-CH=CH- + H_2 → -CH_2-CH_2-). In the case of alternating single and double carbon-carbon bonds (so-called conjugated double bonds), the bond distance between carbons is between those of single and double bonds. In the symmetric arene in Figure 1.30, for example, the bond distance between the carbon atoms is the same, giving a stable aromatic character. Conjugated double bonds are thermodynamically more stable than isolated double bonds, since the electron cloud is distributed over a wider space, increasing the number of degrees of freedom and lowering the entropy of the system. The double-bonded structures are planar, i.e., not tetrahedral, and substituents are separated by 120 degrees, forming a flat structure.

The presence of functional groups influences the structure and the chemical, physical and biological properties of the compound. Important features of molecules are how they interact with other molecules by electrostatic forces or bonds. Such bonds are much weaker than covalent bonds and are usually written as dotted lines. These secondary forces are non-polar, polar and hydrogen bonds. Non-polar bonds act between non-polar compounds and are weaker (2−8 KJ/mol) than polar bonds (6−12 KJ/mol) which exist between polar compounds. Hydrogen bonds are the strongest secondary bonds (12−28 KJ/mol) existing between a hydrogen atom bonded to an electronegative atom (in wood oxygen or nitrogen) and another electronegative atom. Although these secondary forces are much weaker than covalent bonds, they are still of significant importance for the physical properties of the molecules. Non-polar bonds exist mainly between hydrocarbon structures such as non-polar alkanes, alkenes and arenes, whereas polar bonds exist between structures where carbons are bonded to oxygen, nitrogen or other strongly electronegative atoms, as in groups such as ethers, aldehydes, ketones, acetals, esters, amines and amides. Hydrogen bonds are found in alcohols, phenols, carboxylic acids, amines and amides. The hydrocarbon ethane (C_2H_6) which is a non-polar compound exists in a gaseous state at room temperature, whereas methanol (CH_3-OH), which has a molecular weight similar to that of ethane, is a liquid due to the formation of hydrogen bonds between the hydroxyl groups in the alcohol. Methanol can also form hydrogen bonds with water (H-OH) and is, therefore, miscible with water. The solubility of *n*-pentanol ($CH_3(CH_2)_3CH_2$-OH), however, is low. Alcohols with long hydrocarbon chains are insoluble in water because the weaker non-polar forces formed between long hydrocarbon chains in the alcohols counteract the forces between the hydroxyl groups of water and the alcohol, so that the alcohols mix with themselves instead, leading to separation of the mixture into two phases. The rule of thumb that "similar dissolves/interacts with similar" can often be used to roughly evaluate whether substances interact or are miscible with each other.

Chemical reactions of organic compounds

The polarisation of bonds and accessibility to bonds with high energy may indicate chemical reactions involving the breaking and formation of bonds. Those are mostly of a heterogeneous character, where electron pairs are involved, but reactions with single electrons are possible, such as when wood is subjected to UV-radiation and heating at high temperatures. In this section, we focus on reactions involving the heterogeneous breaking and formation of covalent bonds. Alkanes are non-polar and fairly unreactive, whereas one bond in the double bond in alkenes has higher energy and is more reactive than the other bond; ethene ($H_2C=CH_2$) can add water (H_2O) to form ethanol (CH_3-CH_2OH). The reaction rate increases in the presence of an acid catalyst, such as hydrochloric acid, which is totally dissociated into protonated water (H_3O^+) and a chloride anion. The proton will bind with the double bond in a first step, resulting in a high energy and reactive carbocation intermediate. A lone pair of electrons from the electronegative oxygen in water adds to the positively charged carbon, followed by a rapid deprotonation to give the alcohol, and the proton can be re-used as a catalyst in the first step of the reaction (Figure 1.31).

However, the reaction is reversible, which means that under certain conditions alkene can be formed as a result of the dehydration of the alcohol. Removal of the alcohol during hydration of the alkene favours the formation of new alcohol molecules in order to maintain the equilibrium, whereas

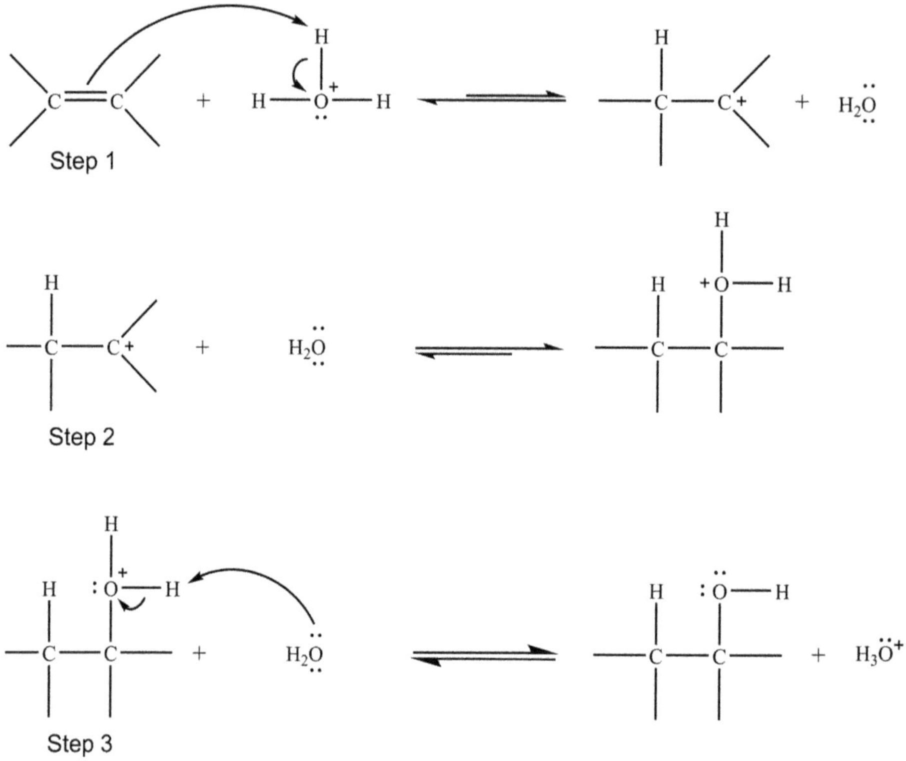

Figure 1.31 Hydration of alkene into alcohol catalysed by an acid (proton): Step 1: Protonation of the double bond to form a carbocation, Step 2: Nucleophilic attack by water, and Step 3: Deprotonation to form an alcohol.

removal of water favours the formation of alkene from alcohol. The stability and concentration of the reactants and products, their physical state (solid, liquid or gas) and the reaction temperature are also important for the outcome of the reactions and, in some cases, the reaction may take place in one direction. The reaction rates are generally lower for large and solid compounds than for small compounds in a liquid phase. The formation of ethers by condensation of two alcohol molecules is usually less favourable, but will result if the product is stabilised, as is the case when furfurals are formed by the heating of monosaccharides. Ethers (R-O-R) are fairly stable and need strong acids to be cleaved, but this may occur under milder acid conditions when the ether is activated, such as with the β-ether bond in the phenolic arylglycerol-β-aryl ether in some lignins (Figure 1.38).

Another reaction of importance in wood chemistry is the formation of acetals by the reaction of an aldehyde and two alcohol molecules catalysed by an acid (Hart et al., 2003). The lone electron pair from the oxygen atom in the alcohol (R^2OH) will bond to the electropositive carbon in the aldehyde ($R^1HC=O$) giving a hemiacetal which is normally not very stable and could reverse to the initial compound even under non-catalysed conditions. In the presence of an acid catalyst a new alcohol could react with the formed hydroxy group in the hemiacetal to give an acetal and water (Figure 1.32). As these reactions are reversible under those conditions, the removal of water moves the reaction towards the acetal, whereas the addition of water moves the reaction back towards the starting materials. Acetals are stable in strong alkaline conditions, as in the presence of NaOH (aqueous), whereas hemiacetals are not.

Ketals and hemiketals are formed in an analogous way by reaction with ketones ($R_2C=O$) and alcohols.

Aldehydes can also react with phenolic compounds, but the reaction with the phenolic hydroxyl group (PhOH, where Ph refers to the phenyl ring) results in fairly unstable products. The electron pair in the aromatic ring can instead bond with the electropositive carbon in the aldehyde by substituting

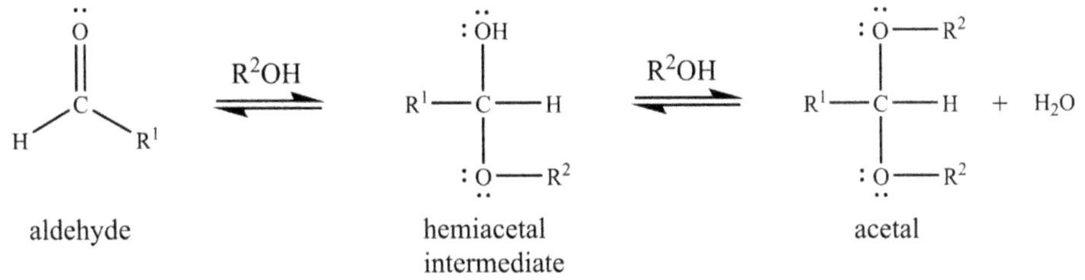

Figure 1.32 Reversibility of acid catalysed acetal formation (R^1 = H or hydrocarbon substituent, R^2 = hydrocarbon substituent).

with a hydrogen bonded to the ring (electrophilic aromatic substitution) (Hart et al., 2003). The reaction can be catalysed by both acid and alkali and a phenolic methylol ($HOPhCH_2OH$) group is formed by the reaction with formaldehyde (Figure 1.33).

As the aromatic structure is re-formed in the methylolated phenol (Hart et al., 2003), further reactions of formaldehyde with the methylolated phenol, unless blocked by other groups, may continue up to a maximum of three methylol groups. The phenolic methylol group ($HOPhCH_2OH$) can also react with the double bond in a vacant position in another phenolic unit, forming a more stable methylene bridge ($HOPhCH_2PhOH$). Examples of various coupling patterns are shown in Figure 1.33 (bottom). The reactions are condensation reactions, which means that a higher molecular weight compound and water is formed. In Figure 1.33, three possible dimers are shown and they

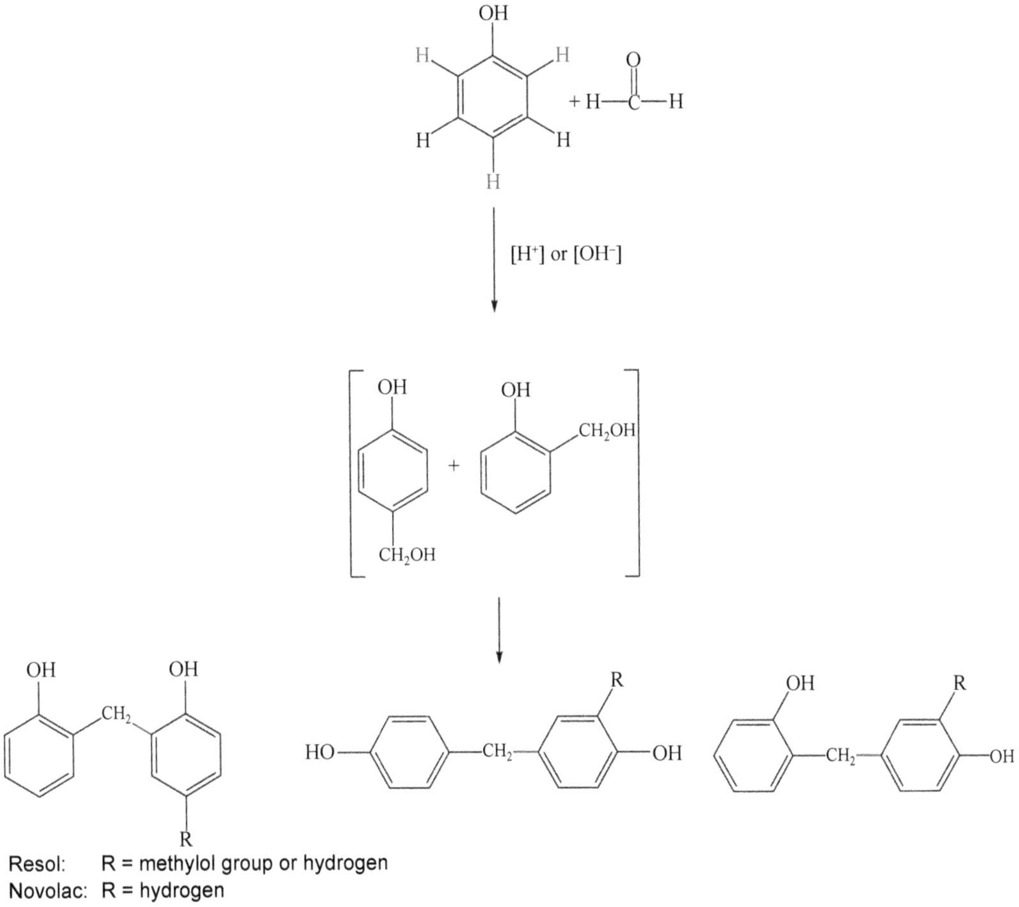

Resol: R = methylol group or hydrogen
Novolac: R = hydrogen

Figure 1.33 Examples of acid- and base-catalysed reactions of phenol and formaldehyde.

can continue to form higher molecular weight polymeric resol-type phenolic compounds when base catalysed via reactions with more phenolic methylol groups. During acid catalysis, novolac structures are formed with no methylol groups and formaldehyde needs to be added for achieving further condensation reactions. As a result of reactions with more extensively methylolated phenols, a less flexible cross-linked network structure can be obtained.

Structure and reactions of wood constituents

Almost all compounds in wood are organic molecules made up of carbon-based skeletons with straight, branched and ring structures in which atoms are held together by sharing electron pairs to form covalent bonds. Wood consists mainly of carbohydrates which basically consist of monosaccharides. In monosaccharides, hydrates (or hydroxyl groups) are covalently bonded to each carbon in a five- or six-carbon membered chain in which at least one of the hydroxyls is in the oxidised form, often as a terminal group (-CHO). Monosaccharides exist in the form of ring structures, such as β-D-glucose in the upper right part in Figure 1.34, essentially a ring-formed hemiacetal (Figure 1.32) in equilibrium with the open aldehyde form but also with the α-form of glucose in which the hydroxyl group at C1 points in the axial direction (upper left part in Figure 1.34). Glucose can be found mostly in the cambium where the biosynthesis of wood occurs. Nearly all carbohydrates in wood (except some mono- and oligosaccharides) are polymers consisting of covalently bonded monomers (monosaccharides or monosaccharide acids) forming linear and branched chains. Cellulose is the most abundant carbohydrate in wood, constituting 40–45% of the total wood mass in which the monomers (β-D-glucoside) are bonded in the same way; carbon 1 in one unit to carbon 4 in another unit via a glucosidic bond (1→4) into an extremely long straight back-bone chain, 10,000–15,000 monosaccharide units in the cell wall as shown in the lower part of Figure 1.34 (Goring and Timell, 1962). A glucoside is about 0.5 nm in size, so the maximal length of a cellulose chain is 5–7 μm, which is about the same as the cell wall thickness (Fengel and Wegner, 1989).

Water is formed in connection with formation of glucosidic bonds together with the growing chain during cellulose biosynthesis. However, the glucosidic bonds formed can be cleaved by reaction with water in the presence of a cellulose-degrading enzyme (cellulase), even under ambient

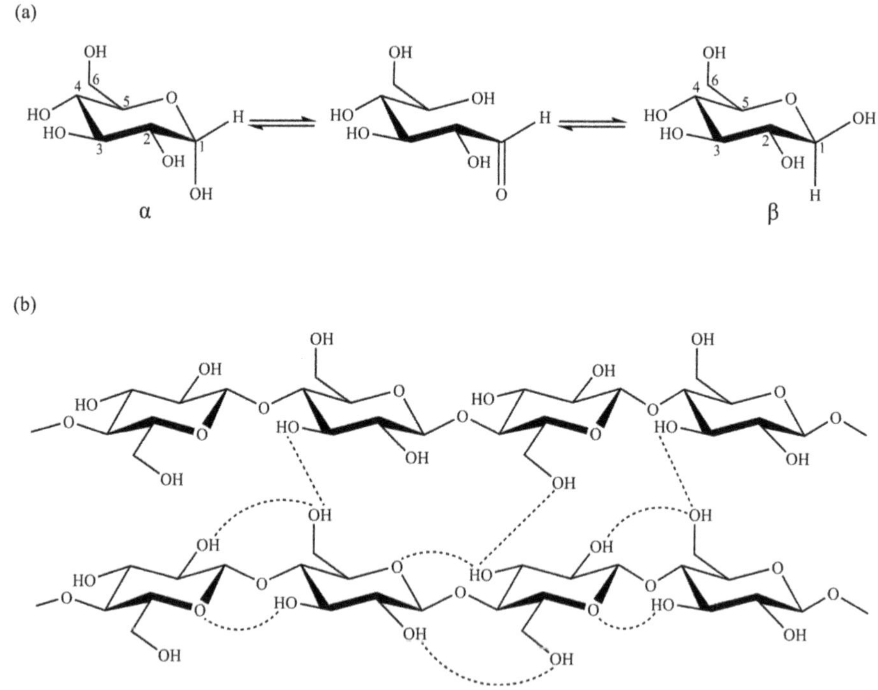

Figure 1.34 Equilibrium between β-D-glucose, open form and α-D-glucose (upper), and parts of two cellulose chains displaying hydrogen bonds within and between the chains (lower).

conditions. Acid catalysed hydrolysis (also consuming water) of the glucosidic bond in cellulose requires strong acid conditions and heat in contrast to the hydrolysis of many other polysaccharides (Figure 1.35). Homolytic cleavage of the glucosidic bond may take place, especially when wood is heated at high temperatures under neutral and dry conditions.

Why are such strong conditions needed when the formation of cellulose in the cell wall takes place under much milder conditions? This is because the cellulose chains in wood exist mostly in stable crystalline structures with a crystallinity of about 60% (Newman and Hemmingson, 1990). These crystalline structures are stabilised by forming hydrogen bonds (dotted lines in Figure 1.34) between hydroxyl groups and between hydroxyl groups and oxygen in neighbouring rings. Hydrogen bonds also exist between cellulose chains which are efficiently packed into three-dimensional crystalline fibrils joined into microfibrils 2–4 nm in width, as shown in Figure 1.36 (Donaldson, 2007). At the microcrystal surface, less ordered paracrystalline cellulose chains exist. Other molecules, such as hemicelluloses, water or similar polar compounds (preferentially those that can form hydrogen bonds) can also interact at the cellulose surfaces. Microfibrils are linked by more sensitive amorphous regions and aligned into thicker macrofibrils that can be up to 40 µm long, achieved by overlapping cellulose chains (Ek et al., 2009). Fibrils are oriented in various directions depending on their position in the cell wall. In the S_2 layers, the fibrils are almost aligned in the fibre direction, but they have other directions in other cell-wall layers (Figure 1.25 and 1.36).

Hemicelluloses are heterogeneous polysaccharides constituting 15–30% of the mass in wood and consist mainly of monosaccharides linked to each other by glucosidic bonds (Ek et al., 2009). The backbone chain in hemicelluloses consists of monosaccharides (β-D-glucose and β-D-

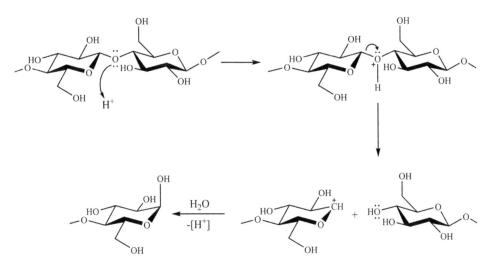

Figure 1.35 Acid catalysed hydrolysis of glucosidic bond in cellulose.

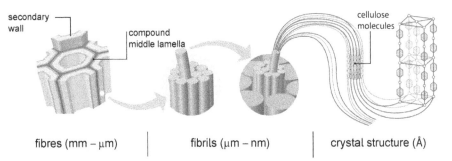

Figure 1.36 Elementary fibril, micro- and macrofibril of cellulose and their orientation in the cell-wall layers (Zimmermann et al., 2004).

mannose in glucomannans and β-D-xylose in xylans) with side groups (β-D-galactose in conifer glucomannans, α-L-arabinose in conifer xylans and acetyl groups in broad-leaved xylans as well as in conifer glucomannan) and ionising groups (4-O-methylglucuronic acid in xylans). The backbone is much shorter than the cellulose chains and consists of 100–200 monomer units (Figure 1.37).

This heterogeneous structure makes hemicelluloses amorphous with hydroxyl groups freer and more accessible to form hydrogen bonds with other compounds such as water. When wood is exposed to humid conditions, water molecules substitute with the hydrogen bonds mostly between

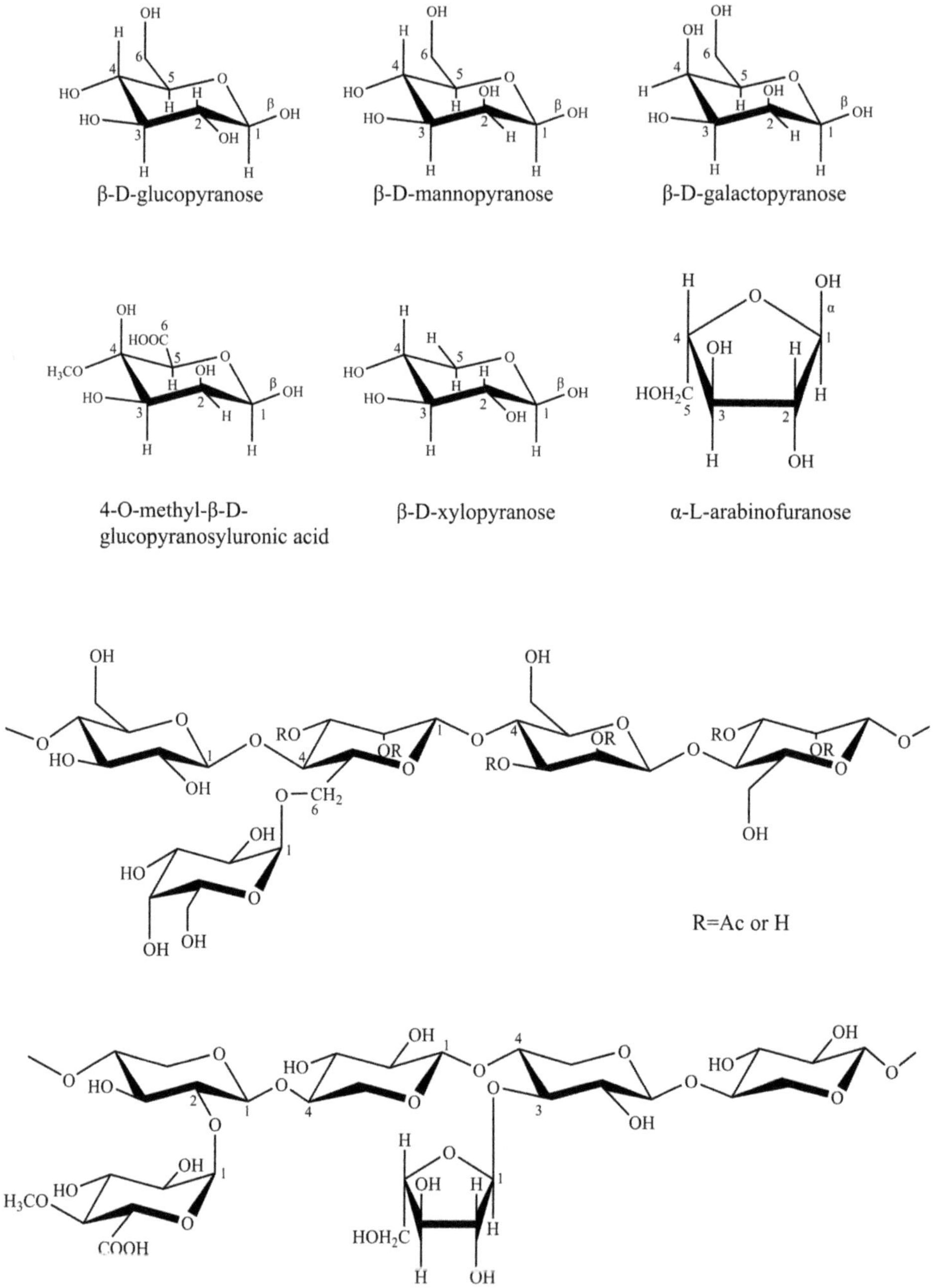

β-D-glucopyranose   β-D-mannopyranose   β-D-galactopyranose

4-O-methyl-β-D-
glucopyranosyluronic acid   β-D-xylopyranose   α-L-arabinofuranose

R=Ac or H

H₃CO

Figure 1.37 Hemicellulose structures: monosaccharides and uronic acid in hemicelluloses (upper two rows), galactoglucomannan in conifers (middle), and conifer xylan (lower).

carbohydrate chains and, therefore, require more space, resulting in a swelling of the cell wall up to a moisture content of 25–30% when the cell wall becomes saturated (at the so-called fibre-saturation point, FSP). The cell wall swells mostly outwards and the result is a macroscopic swelling of the wood, particularly in the transverse direction. Swelling also makes the wood more reactive and susceptible to microbial or other attacks. The wood constituents are also softened by the increase in moisture content and this occurs to a greater extent in the hemicelluloses than in the cellulose and lignin, especially at lower temperatures (Back and Salmén, 1982). To be able to selectively separate wood fibres during mechanical pulping, for example, softening at a high moisture content and sufficient high temperature of the lignin-rich middle lamella is necessary.

Polysaccharides are polymeric carbohydrates that are non-structural, but they still have important functions in wood, such as starch working as a nutrient, pectins which are constituents of the primary wall and pit membrane and galactan in tension wood. Further information on structures of polysaccharides has been published elsewhere (cf. Ek et al., 2009). Due to their carbohydrate origin, they are sensitive to acidic, alkaline and microbiological attacks and the pit membranes can be degraded by bacteria when wood is stored in water.

Lignin is also a polymeric compound, constituting 20–30% of the mass in wood. It has a higher C:O ratio and a higher calorific value than the carbohydrates and interacts with water to a lesser extent than hemicelluloses. The relative content of lignin is high in cell corners and the middle lamella but it is also present in the cell wall and assists in binding the wood cell together and in making the cell wall less sensitive to moisture. Lignins have a phenolic origin and, in wood, they are made up essentially of three phenylpropane units: H-type (*p*-hydroxyphenylpropane), G-type (guaiacylpropane) with one methoxyl (-OCH_3) group bonded to the aromatic unit dominant in conifers and S-type (syringylpropane) with two methoxyl groups. These last two types form the predominant GS-type of lignin in broad-leaved woods (Figure 1.38).

The presence of these units differs, depending on their position in the tree; compression wood has a higher lignin content and a higher content of H-units than the lignin in clear wood (Westermark, 1985). The middle lamella binds the wood cells together and has relatively more H-units than the secondary wall. The phenyl propane units in lignin polymers are linked to each other by ether and carbon-carbon covalent bonds in at least 10 different ways, the beta-ether bond (β-O-4) being the most common (Figure 1.38). The branching and phenolic content in cell-wall lignin are fairly low, but a lower content of uncondensed β-ether structures in the middle lamella has been suggested (Westermark, 1985) and this indicates more branching. In broad-leaved species, GS-lignin has more β-ether bonds than G-type lignin in conifers. The β-ether bonds are sensitive both to heating and to acidic and alkaline conditions (Westermark et al., 1995) and this is important for the delignification processes (Gierer, 1980). Such reaction will lower molecular weight and increase the phenolic content of lignin. Methoxyl groups bonded to aromatic rings are more stable than β-ether bonds under hydrolytic conditions. However, methoxyl groups in lignin could be degraded oxidatively by outdoor exposures (see Section 1.6). Thermal modification could lead to cleavage of β-ether bonds (Tjeerdsma et al., 1998; Windeisen et al., 2007). Most inter-unit carbon-carbon bonds are stable under hydrolytic conditions, but formaldehyde can be formed by splitting off the terminal methylol group in the propane chain during such heating. These reactions take place under acid-catalysed conditions at lower temperatures than thermal modification (i.e., below the threshold temperature of 150°C), especially in the presence of sulphuric acid (Lundquist, 1992). Under certain conditions, more stable condensed carbon-carbon structures may be formed (Figure 1.41). Lignin is, to some extent, mainly covalently bonded to hemicelluloses such as α-ether bonds (Karlsson et al., 2004; Balakshin et al., 2011). Galactoglucomannan in the lignin-hemicellulose matrix is considered to interact with cellulose fibril surfaces by hydrogen bonds (Ek et al., 2009). Thus, the ultrastructure of a conifer cell wall may be regarded as a series of interconnected layers consisting of cellulose, galactoglucomannan, lignin-xylan, galactoglucomannan and cellulose. Lignin-carbohydrate bonds can contribute to the (wet) stability of the matrix and explain the oxidative bleaching conditions needed to selectively remove residual lignin from pulps.

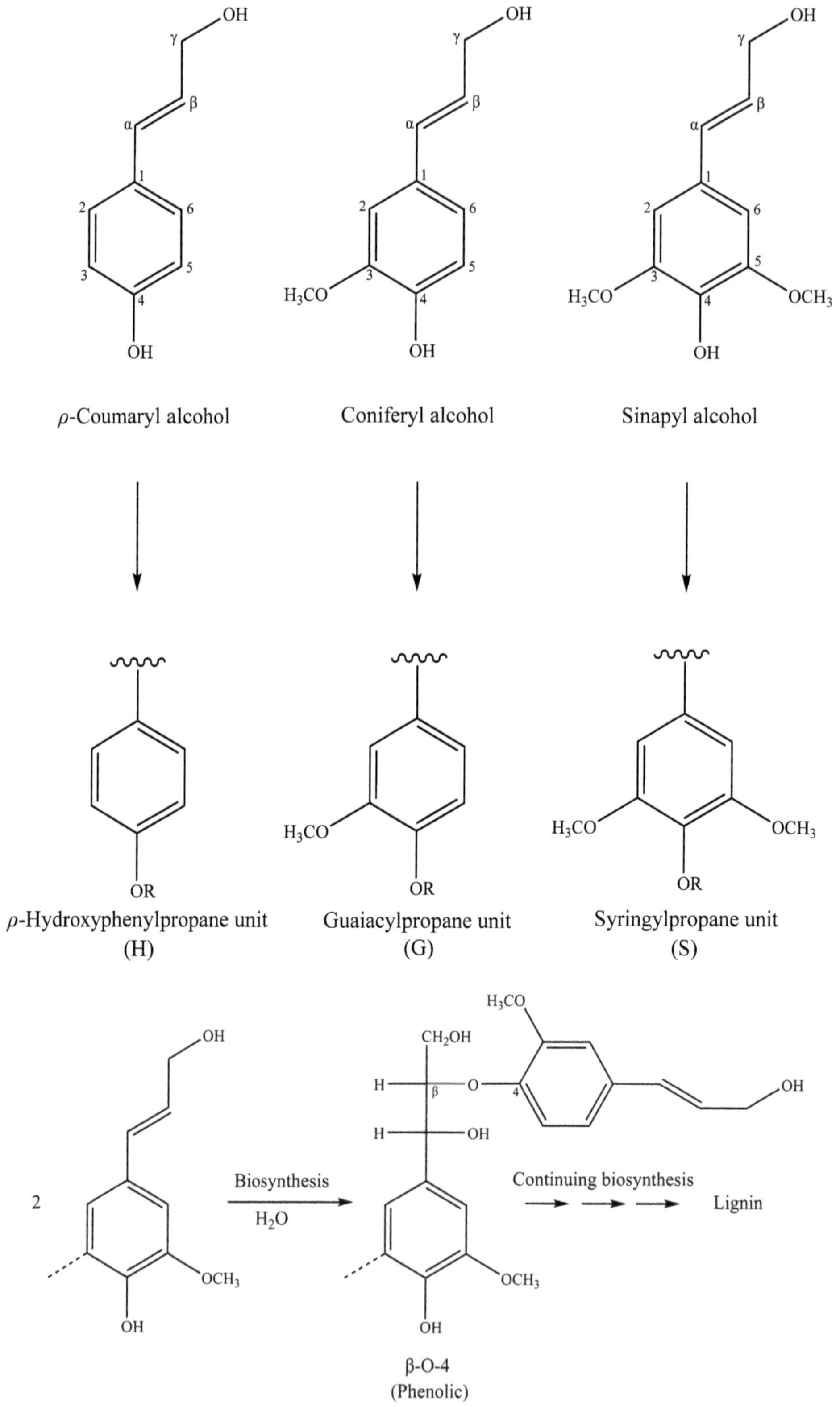

Figure 1.38 Building units in lignin and formation of arylglycerol-β-aryl ether (β-ether).

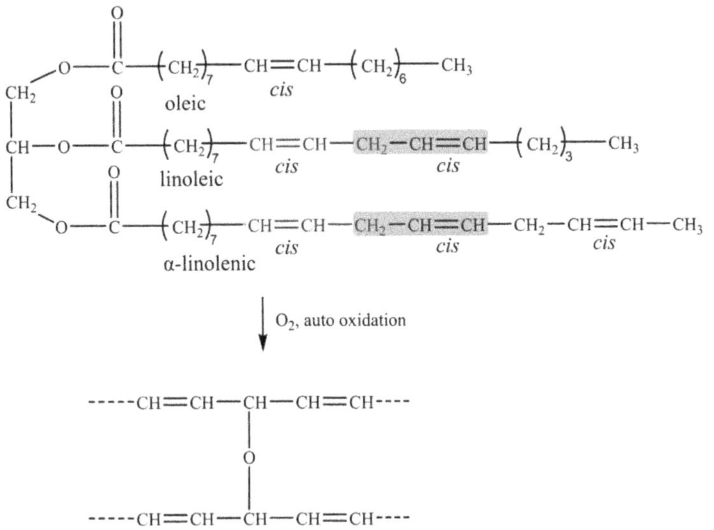

Figure 1.39 Reactions of unsaturated triglycerides during the curing of drying oils.

The non-structural compounds usually constitute a minor amount of the mass of wood and typically consist of low molecular hydrophobic extractives of various types and various solubilities, mono-, oligo- and polysaccharides, inorganic salts and small amounts of proteins and peptides. Basically, extractives obtained by extraction with organic solvents, such as acetone, are fats, waxes, fatty acids, terpenoids (resin acids, monoterpenes and sesquiterpenes, steroids) and stearyl esters, and phenols (lignans, tannins). They are considered to be used by the wood for protection (phenols, resin acids and terpenes, fatty acids), as nutrients (fats and sugars) and during biosynthesis (steroids, proteins, inorganics). These non-structural constituents have relatively little effect on the strength properties and the equilibrium moisture content (EMC) of wood, but they may consume some of the modifying reagents by reactions with reactive groups, such as hydroxyl groups in carbohydrates and phenolic compounds in tannins and lignans, etc. They may also hinder the efficient uptake and contact with the wood polymers by oxidative drying of migrated unsaturated oily resins in aspirated pits, resulting in ether cross-linking of the side-chains (Figure 1.39). Under alkaline conditions, ester bonds in fats, stearyl esters and waxes can be saponified, forming corresponding alcohols and ionisable fatty carboxylic groups which can have surfactant properties. Cleavage of ester bonds may also take place during acid conditions as well as by heating.

The chemistry of wood modification

When wood is modified, the aim is primarily to reduce the moisture uptake and thereby hinder biological degradation by changing the chemical structure instead of adding toxic substances (biocides) or using durable trees from, e.g., endangered tropical resources. The modification should be undertaken in a way to ensure there is no release of hazardous chemicals as a result of the treatment or during the service life of the product. Often, the modification results in a reduction in the interaction of the treated wood with moisture and water, so reducing its ability to swell and shrink, making the wood more dimensionally stable. Wood modification can be divided into two principles: *passive* and *active* modification (Hill, 2006). In Figure 1.40, various modification methods and their mechanisms of wood protection are presented.

The degradation of wood-polymer constituents involves a lot of possible reaction and reaction routes, some of which have already been presented. Degradation by the splitting of sensitive covalent bonds (glucosidic) in carbohydrate polymers increases with increasing temperature and, if water is present, it can be consumed during the splitting of these bonds (hydrolysis) catalysed by acid (cf.

Modification method	Principle		Commercialisation
Acetylation (Accoya™)			x
Phenol resin (Compreg™)			x
Furfurylation (Kebony™)			x
DMDHEU (Belmadur™)			(x)
Silicates/silanes			(x)
Resin impregnation (Impreg™)			(x)
Chitosan			
Natural oils/waxes/paraffins			x
Polyethylene glycol (PEG)			(x)
Thermal modification			x

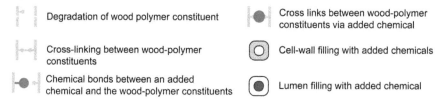

Degradation of wood polymer constituent

Cross-linking between wood-polymer constituents

Chemical bonds between an added chemical and the wood-polymer constituents

Cross links between wood-polymer constituents via added chemical

Cell-wall filling with added chemicals

Lumen filling with added chemical

Figure 1.40 Chemical- and thermal-modification methods, commercial and principle. X – available product, (X) – introduced or used in large-scale experiments.

Figure 1.35). Glucoside bonds in hemicelluloses are degraded more easily than cellulose during heating and by hydrolysis in the presence of acid. Bonds to hemicellulose side groups, like arabinose, are more sensitive to acid hydrolysis than the backbone chain as suggested by Mäki-Arvela et al., 2011 (Figure 1.37). Greater losses of carbohydrates were observed with birch than with pine even at a slightly lower temperature during thermal modification in open systems (Zaman et al., 2000). The formation of soluble xylose-rich carbohydrates during thermal modification was greater in closed systems saturated with steam than in an open system (Karlsson et al., 2012). The degradation of wood polymers leads to shrinkage of the wood cell wall and, thus, to the dimensions of the wood and a small reduction in wood density occurs when degraded materials are removed during the heating. Under high pressure conditions, the steam pressure had a greater influence than the peak treatment temperature on the degradation of European beech wood (Willems et al., 2015). During thermal modification, which is considered to start at ca. 150°C, the degradation reactions are dehydration of hydroxyl groups, increasing C:O ratio and the hydrophobicity of the material, although some volatile dehydration products, such as furfurals, may be removed during the thermal treatment (Figure 1.41). Acetic acid, formed by the hydrolysis of acetyl groups of acetylgalactoglucomannans in conifers, for example, together with other acids lower the pH and may further catalyse degradation reactions.

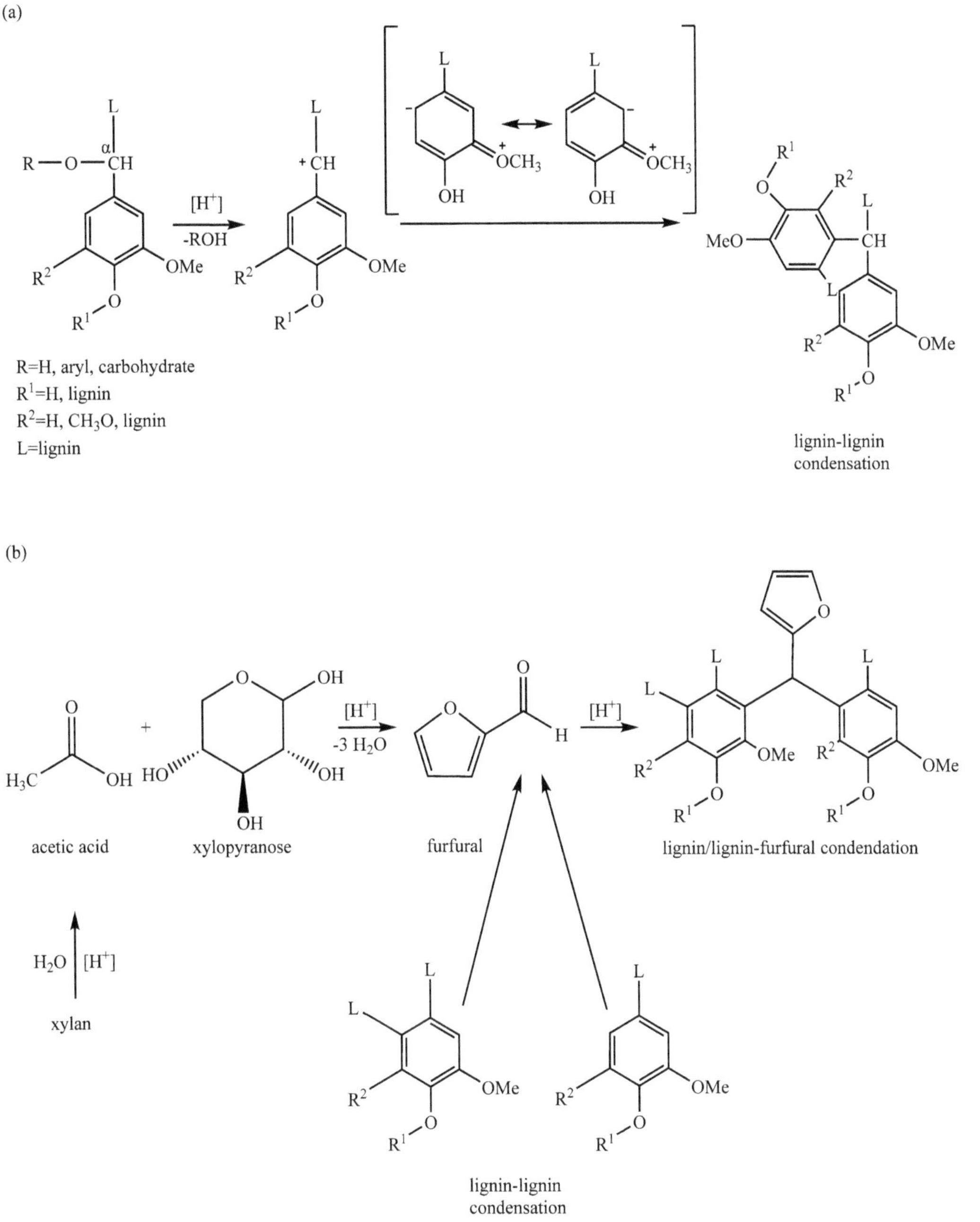

(a)

R=H, aryl, carbohydrate
R^1=H, lignin
R^2=H, CH$_3$O, lignin
L=lignin

lignin-lignin
condensation

(b)

acetic acid   xylopyranose   furfural   lignin/lignin-furfural condendation

H$_2$O | [H$^+$]

xylan

lignin-lignin
condensation

Figure 1.41 Examples of possible condensation products from lignin (upper), and degradation products of hemicelluloses during heating (lower).

Thermal modification under closed water-saturated conditions leads to an even lower pH, as has been found with birch sp., which has an acetyl content of about 3% (Torniainen et al., 2011; Rowell, 2012). As a consequence of the formation of more acidic modified-wood products, acid-resistant fasteners have to be used in constructions. It appears that there is a difference in the moisture uptake capacity of thermally modified wood during remoistening cycles, depending on whether the modification has been carried out in the presence of absence of water (Obataya and Tomita, 2002) and it has been suggested that this is due to the formation of reversible hydrogen bonds between hemicelluloses in the dry systems (Willems et al., 2020). The degradation can lead not only to a decrease in strength properties in wood but also to a less elastic material when the amorphous and flexible carbohydrate polymers are degraded.

The colour intensity increases with the intensity of treatment, this may be due to degraded lignin and also to lignin-like material formed from carbohydrate degradation products. Particularly in closed processes, moisture and acids can catalyse the modification reactions and a lower treatment temperature can be chosen than in an open process, such as the ThermoWood™ process, to get similar browning, although there being some differences in the reactions which occur. High strength and durability cannot be achieved by these processes. The material is quite durable but the treated wood is more sensitive to in-ground contact than wood from the acetylation and furfurylation processes.

In the presence of oxygen, the rate of degradation of wood is increased and alkali-labile oxidation structures may form. Sensitive bonds in lignin, such as β-ether bonds, may be cleaved, increasing the amount of phenols (Windeisen et al., 2007), while α-ether bonds (which are more sensitive than β-ether bonds) may result in free carbohydrates as a result of cleavage of lignin-carbohydrate structures. During heating, the formation of combustible gases may be sufficient to start a chain reaction and initiate combustion of the material. However, oxidative conditions are believed to have minor importance during the thermal modification of wood due to the inert atmosphere existing during the treatments.

Cross-links may occur between wood polymers when wood is heated (Tjeerdsma et al., 1998; Boonstra and Tjeerdsma, 2006). Condensation of lignin with itself (upper reaction in Figure 1.41) and together with some dehydrated carbohydrate compounds like furfural seems possible (lower reaction in Figure 1.41) especially under acidic conditions. Other aldehydes, such as formaldehyde, may lead to condensation products with lignin.

Since reactions with wood constituents on the cell-wall surface of the lumen or with pit membranes do not, in the long run, protect moisture from entering into and swelling the cell wall, the modifying chemicals need pores in the wood in order to be able to reach inner parts of the cell wall (Hill, 2006). Nano-pores exist in the cell wall when the wood is in a swollen state, but it is uncertain whether they are present in dry cell walls. They are either absent or very small. The modifying chemical and any solvent used must be able to find or create voids large enough to permit entry into the cell wall, and the covalently bonded penetrated material with low attained solubility still requires a greater volume when the solvents and reaction by-products have been removed at the end of process. This increases the cell-wall dimensions in the dry state and also the volume of the wood. Since wood swelling then becomes more restricted, the cell wall retains less water than untreated wood and this lowers the equilibrium moisture content in modified wood and reduces the dimensional changes upon drying and wetting. Under certain conditions, however, the swelling during treatment is so great that the wood starts to undergo irreversible cracking.

The acetylation of wood (Figure 1.42) is a chemical modification process in which the electrophilic reagent (acetic anhydride) is forced by the application of an external pressure to migrate through the wood pits, to react with accessible nucleophilic hydroxyl groups in the wood and to diffuse and react deeper into the cell wall (Rowell, 1983). Thus, bulking of the cell wall and loss of hydrophilic hydroxyl groups reduces the moisture uptake, and increases the resistance to swelling and the decay of wood (Hill and Jones, 1996; Hill, 2006). So far, radiata pine has mostly been used commercially due to its low density and open pore structure, but fibres in acetylated fibreboards can be more easily reacted than the solid wood products, and this can favour the use of other species.

As the anhydride is reactive with water, any moisture present will consume the reagent. The reactivity of the resulting acetic acid is not high and it will not further react with hydroxyl groups to any significant extent although it may work as a solvent (Rowell, 2012) and also assist in the degradation of wood constituents, especially if the temperature becomes too high due to the exorthermic nature of the acetylation reaction. Removal of the residual reaction solution at the end of the process leaves a bulked cell wall with increased wood dimensions, but also an essentially

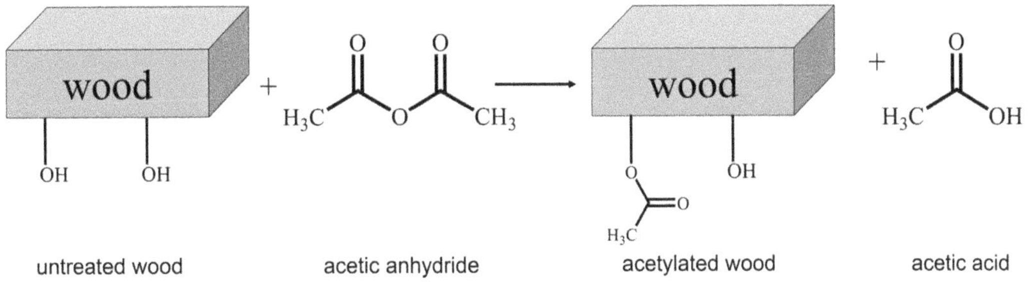

Figure 1.42 Acetylation of wood by acetic anhydride.

empty lumen with only small amounts of residual acetic acid. This and the extent of acetylation depend on several factors and is discussed together with other aspects of acetylation in Section 2.2.

The cross-linking of wood constituents by forming a bridge structure with the added chemical may also restrict the uptake of water by the cell wall, so that the total volume of the swollen wood cell wall at a given relative humidity is lowered (Figure 1.43 and Figure 1.44). Such reactions may be difficult to verify, especially if they are less prevalent, for example, during furfurylation (Figure 2.21). The formation of cross-linked structures can be supported if the modifying chemical contains more than one functionality or reactive group, if there is sufficient reactivity to form stable bonds with wood, if the size of the molecule is suitable for cross-linking and if the polarity of the molecule is appropriate for it to be mixed with the wood polymers.

Formaldehyde (HCHO) is known to react with phenols (Figure 1.33) and also with urea and melamine, forming synthetic adhesives. It seems also to react with wood polymers, especially in the presence of strong acid catalysts (Tarkow and Stamm, 1953) as the treatment gives a material with high resistance to swelling at low percentage weight gain. Formaldehyde itself has a low molecular weight, however, and a fairer comparison of the degree of reaction might be to consider the number of moles reacted. Nevertheless, formaldehyde may work as a cross-linker between lignin units but to a lower extent than when it reacts with phenols to form phenol-formaldehyde (PF) resin. The small formaldehyde molecule is not as flexible as larger aldehydes, such as glutaraldehyde, and this results in a brittle material. Formaldehyde itself is a gas and is seldom used due to its hazardous effects on human health. When used in the formation of PF and other formaldehyde-containing resin systems, it is applied as formalin (typically a 40% solution of formaldehyde in water).

Phenolic or resorcinol (PF or RF respectively) resins, formed from phenols or resorcinol (1,3-benzenediol) and formaldehyde, can be used as adhesives for wood products and also to modify and stabilise wood if an appropriately low molecular weight resin is used (Stamm and Seborg, 1939).

As they fill up lumen, the resin reacts/condenses with itself into larger more stable thermoset fragments when heated under alkaline conditions (Figure 1.43).

When an aqueous resin with relatively low viscosity and low molecular weight is used, a bulking effect is usually noted, and impregnation of the cell wall leads to a softening of the wood (Shams and Yano, 2011). Chemical bridges (like stable methylene) can form between reactive sites (activated aromatic carbons) in lignin and methylol groups ($-CH_2OH$) in PF-resin when wood is treated and cured with such a resin (Yelle and Ralph, 2016). The treatment leads to an increase of density which can be further increased by the application of pressure and heat during the curing of the softened wood in the Compreg™ process. Phenolic reagents may need careful handling and are based on fossil fuels, but they are included in this presentation as phenols may be replaced by bioderived alternatives.

An attractive wood modifier is 1,3-dimethylol-4,5-dihydroxyethyleneurea (DMDHEU) originally developed as a stable anti-wrinkling agent for fabrics, it has more recently been proposed and tested as an agent for wood modification. A stable bulking effect is seen when permeable wood

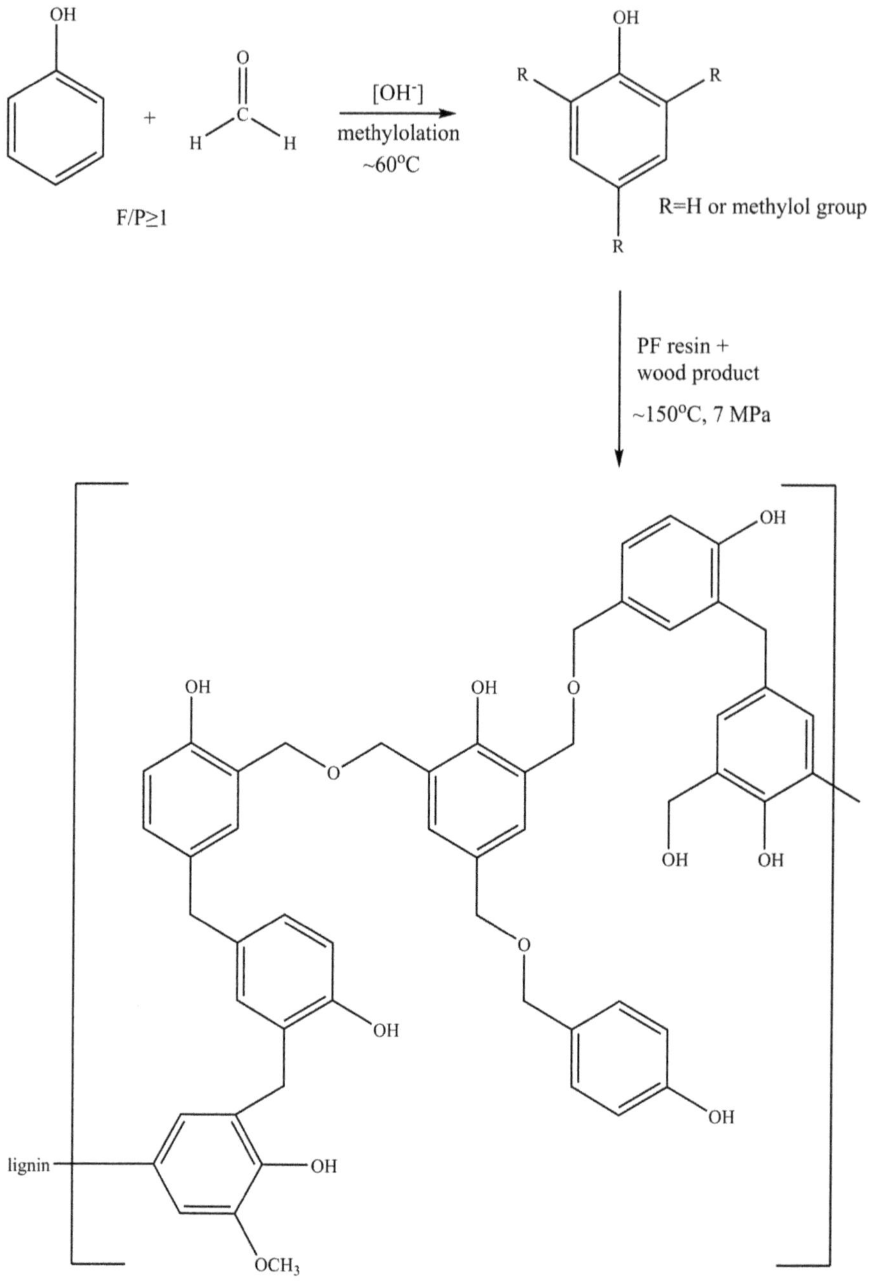

Figure 1.43 Curing of phenolic resin.

species are treated with aqueous DMDHEU (Militz, 1993; Emmerich et al., 2019). It may react with itself forming larger condensation products and at high treatment levels it can start to fill the lumen.

DMDHEU can also react with hydroxyl groups in wood constituents in the cell wall, forming new chemical bonds to these constituents (Figure 1.44). DMDHEU has two or more reactive functional groups and it has been suggested that cross-linked structures are formed in wood (Emmerich, 2019). Wood constituents may degrade due to high contents of added Lewis acid catalysts, and unreacted DMDHEU may lose formaldehyde during the process.

Treatment containing silicate/silane agents involves several types of more or less reactive compounds which may penetrate and swell the cell wall by reacting with hydroxyl groups in the

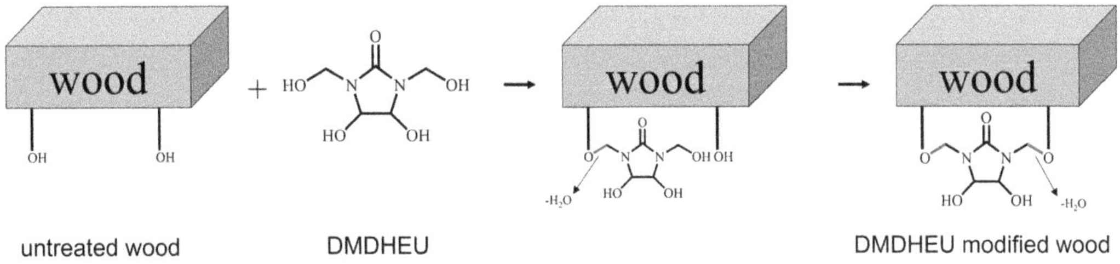

Figure 1.44 Reaction of dimethylol dihydroxy ethylene urea (DMDHEU) during wood modification.

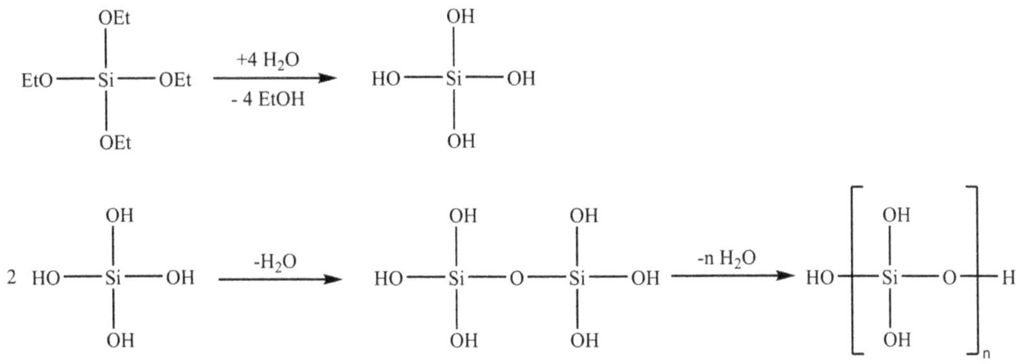

Figure 1.45 Reactions of silyl ether, tetraethyl-orthosilicate (TEOS) in presence of water (Mai et al., 2003).

wood constituents or by filling up the lumen in a more passive way, involving polymerisation reactions with the reagent itself. Treatment with water glass (sodium silicate) involves penetration into the wood but not into the wood cell wall, as bulking does not normally occur. Such alkaline silicates may need to be fixed to the wood to avoid leaching when the wood is exposed to water. There are numerous silanes and many of them are silyl ethers which will be hydrolysed in the presence of moisture to a silanol releasing the corresponding alcohol before reacting with itself (Figure 1.45) or with hydroxyl groups in the wood constituents (Mai et al., 2003).

The stability of the formed products may be influenced by the reacted silica-based compound itself, as well as by conditions such as the presence of acid together with moisture and heat.

Furfuryl alcohol or a similar agent reacts via condensation reactions, forming methylene and ether bridges, usually in the presence of an organic acid catalyst (Figure 1.45). Formaldehyde may be released during the treatments but could condense leading to a branched and cross-linked structure (Figures 1.46c and 1.46e, respectively).

Based on studies using model compounds of lignin, it has been suggested that bonds are formed between the furfuryl alcohol and the lignin but this is probably only to a minor extent (see the furfurylation section in Chapter 2). The cell wall is bulked by treatment and the percentage weight gain after hardening of the alcohol can be quite high. The lumen will, therefore, also start to be filled and that leads to the second type of treatment – *passive modification.*

Passive modification involves lumen filling and/or cell wall filling without a reaction with the wood constituents. Oils, waxes and paraffins can penetrate, if the viscosity is suitable through wood pits and more or less fill the larger pores (lumen) in the wood. Oils and waxes are mostly non-polar fatty esters and paraffins (Figure 1.47) and the latter may be heated to achieve a suitable viscosity. It may be more difficult for products like solid *carnuba oil* to penetrate into wood, but if they can be made less viscous (by heating or as an emulsion) they can be favourable because of less exudation during use.

The hydrophobic nature and fairly large molecular size of compounds, such as waxes and triglycerides, are often cited as the reasons for their not entering the hydrophilic cell wall when

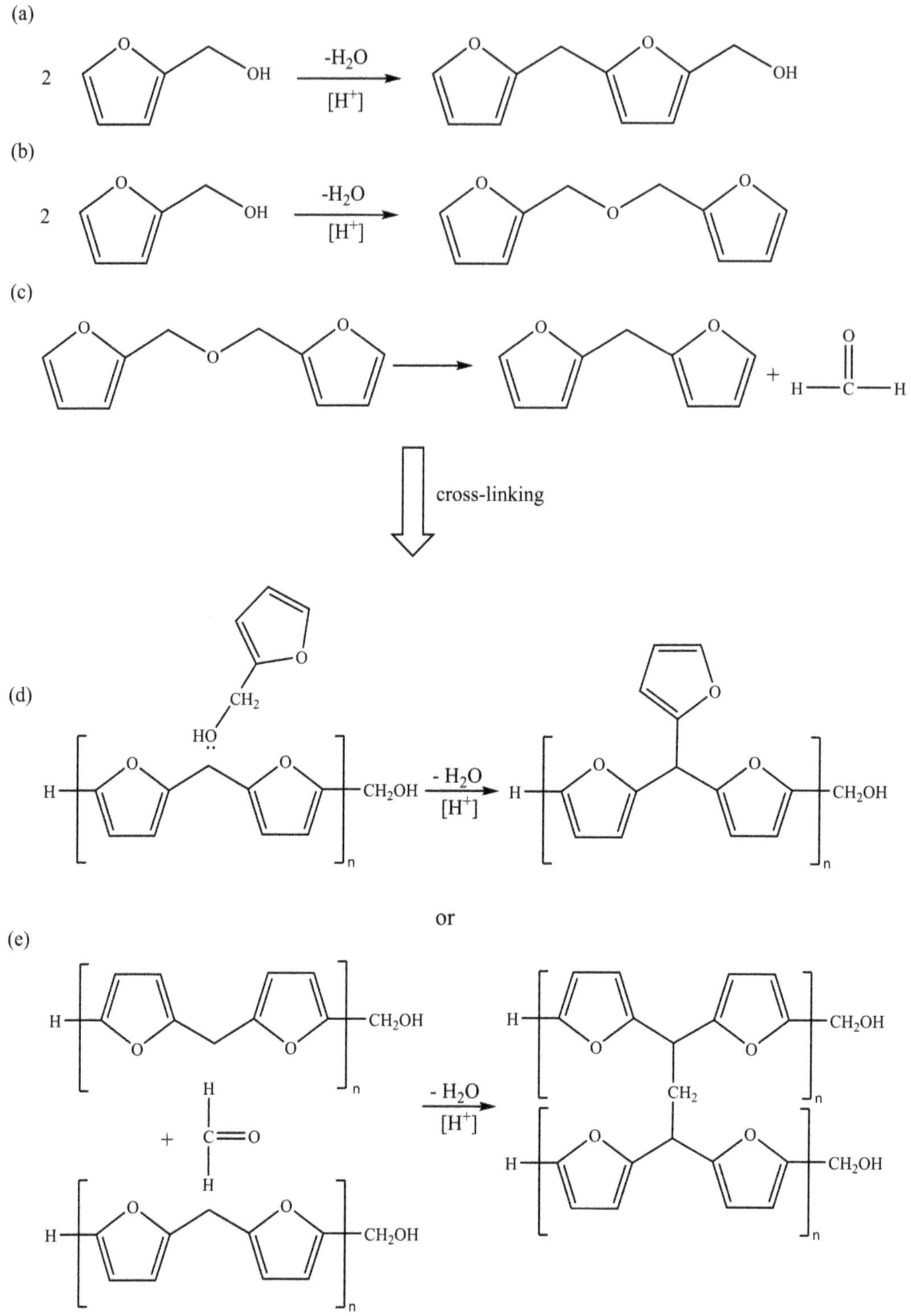

(a)

(b)

(c)

cross-linking

(d)

or

(e)

Figure 1.46 Reactions of furfuryl alcohol (FA): (a) condensation reaction forming a dimer of FA, capable of further reaction to trimer, etc., (b) condensation reaction with termination of polymerisation, (c) loss of formaldehyde during polymerisation of termination products, (d) cross-linking of methylene-bridged furfuryl alcohols with furfuryl alcohol, and (e) reaction of two methylene-bridged furfuryl groups with formaldehyde.

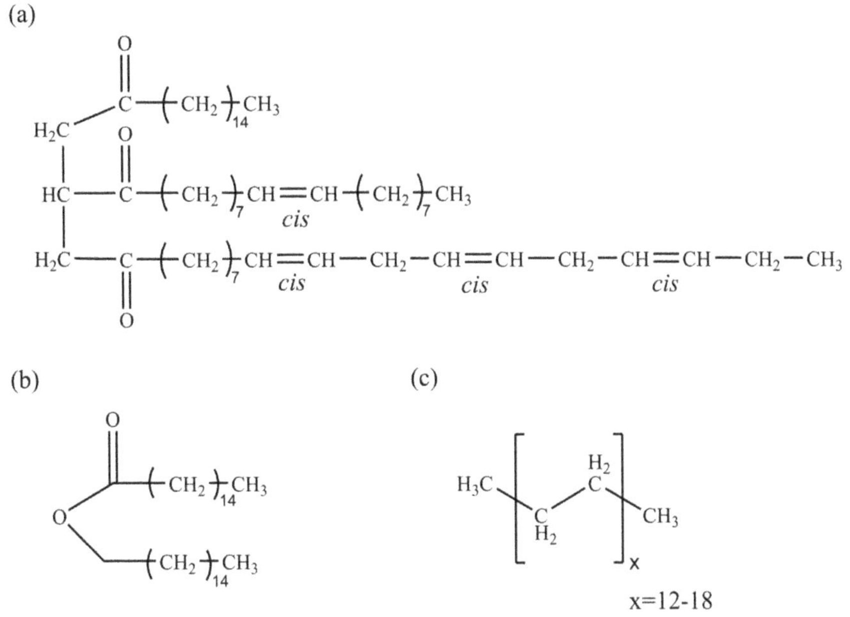

(a)

(b)   (c)

x=12-18

Figure 1.47 Chemical structure of: (a) triglycerides, (b) waxes, and (c) paraffins.

wood is exposed to such agents. Monomers, such as styrene and methyl methacrylate (often used in the plastic industries), may not efficiently penetrate into the cell wall either, despite their small molecular size, probably due to their more hydrophobic nature (Ermeyadan et al., 2014). Exudation from wood impregnated with oily substances may be a problem, especially when they are exposed to varying temperature conditions. This is because the drying/curing of oils (the formation of a cross-linked covalently bonded network between unsaturated hydrocarbon chains as shown in Figure 1.39) is slow due to limited access to oxygen inside the wood, as well as the presence of lignin (Salehi, 2012). Ester bonds are sensitive to both alkaline and acid conditions and to enzymes. Fats are known to be consumed under mild thermal wood modification conditions (Nuopponen et al., 2004). Creosote oils are coal distillates containing polyaromatic hydrocarbons and phenols, and they have been used to impregnate wooden poles and railway sleepers, but they will be phased out in many countries in the coming years due to their toxicity and are not considered in this book.

Polyethylene glycol (PEG) ($-CH_2CH_2O-$)$_n$ is basically a back-bone chain condensation product of ethylene glycol ($OHCH_2CH_2OH$) with various aliphatic chain lengths, producing a range of hydrophilic characters and solubilities. If a suitable molecular size of PEG is chosen, the cell wall can be impregnated. However, as it is applied in a water-soluble form, it will be leached out when exposed to weathering or other water-treatment conditions (Wahlström and Lindberg, 1999).

Chitosan is a polymeric product formed by de-acetylation and partially hydrolysis of the glucosidic bond of chitin, which is found in the shells of crabs, crayfish, shrimps and prawns. Chitosan consists of glucose amine and varying amounts of N-acetyl glucose amine units glucosidically bonded to each other β(1→4) (Figure 1.48).

The maximum size of a particle able to pass through a pit membrane is about 200 nm and into a cell wall 100 times smaller when the cell wall is in the swollen state. Commercial preparations of chitosan have a size in the range of 10–60 nm and it is therefore assumed that chitosan is deposited mostly in the lumen. The material has only a minor influence on wood swelling but it has fungicidal properties. It is possible that, when dissolved under acidic water conditions, the resulting protonated amino groups ($-NH_3^+$) in the chitosan will more easily interact with the cell walls of fungi, but also attach with ionising groups (carboxylic) in the wood constituents.

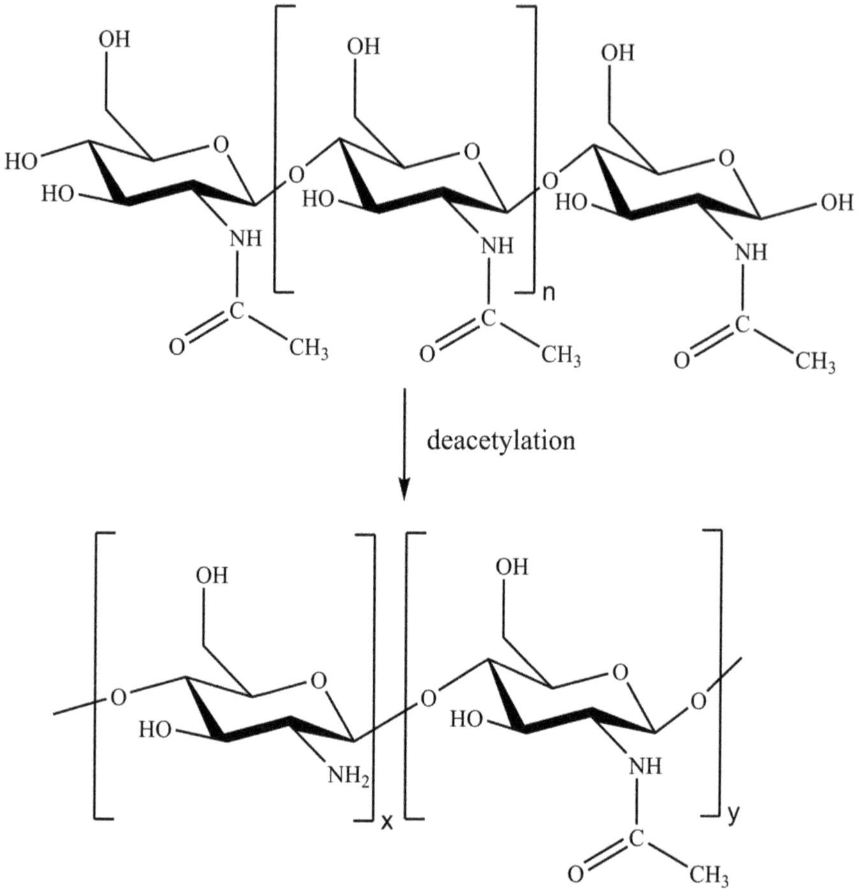

Figure 1.48 Deacetylation of chitin to chitosan.

Water-borne amino-plastic resins, such as melamine-urea-formaldehyde (MUF), can be used as adhesives but also as modifying agents in wood products (Hansmann et al., 2006), especially with low molecular MF-resin, such as metholylated melamines (Figure 1.49).

During impregnation, the resin fills the lumen and other larger pores and, if it is not too strongly cured, it can penetrate into the bulk of the cell wall where it can condense with itself forming a three-dimensional hardened structure (Norimoto and Gril, 1993; Lukowsky, 1999). In contrast to phenolic resins, melamine-urea formaldehyde (MUF) resin is not considered to react with wood components but it gives a rather brittle modified product. Careful control of the curing conditions is necessary to avoid the emission of formaldehyde.

Another commercial process, the Indurite™ process, involved the treatment of wood (radiata pine) with a mixture of starch and an amino-plastic resin. It can be considered to have been a passive process, although it was suggested that small amounts of cross-linker, such as formaldehyde or the dialdehyde glutaraldehyde (OHC-$(CH_2)_3$-CHO), needed to be added in order to improve the wood properties.

1.4 The wood-water relationship

As a biological material, a tree has an inherent need for water to facilitate its growth and sustenance. The same is true of wood-destroying mechanisms, which also depend on the presence of sufficient quantities of water to allow their bio-degradative mechanisms (Engelund Thybring et al., 2018). It is when felled timber is processed for use in construction that its usual natural parameters are changed.

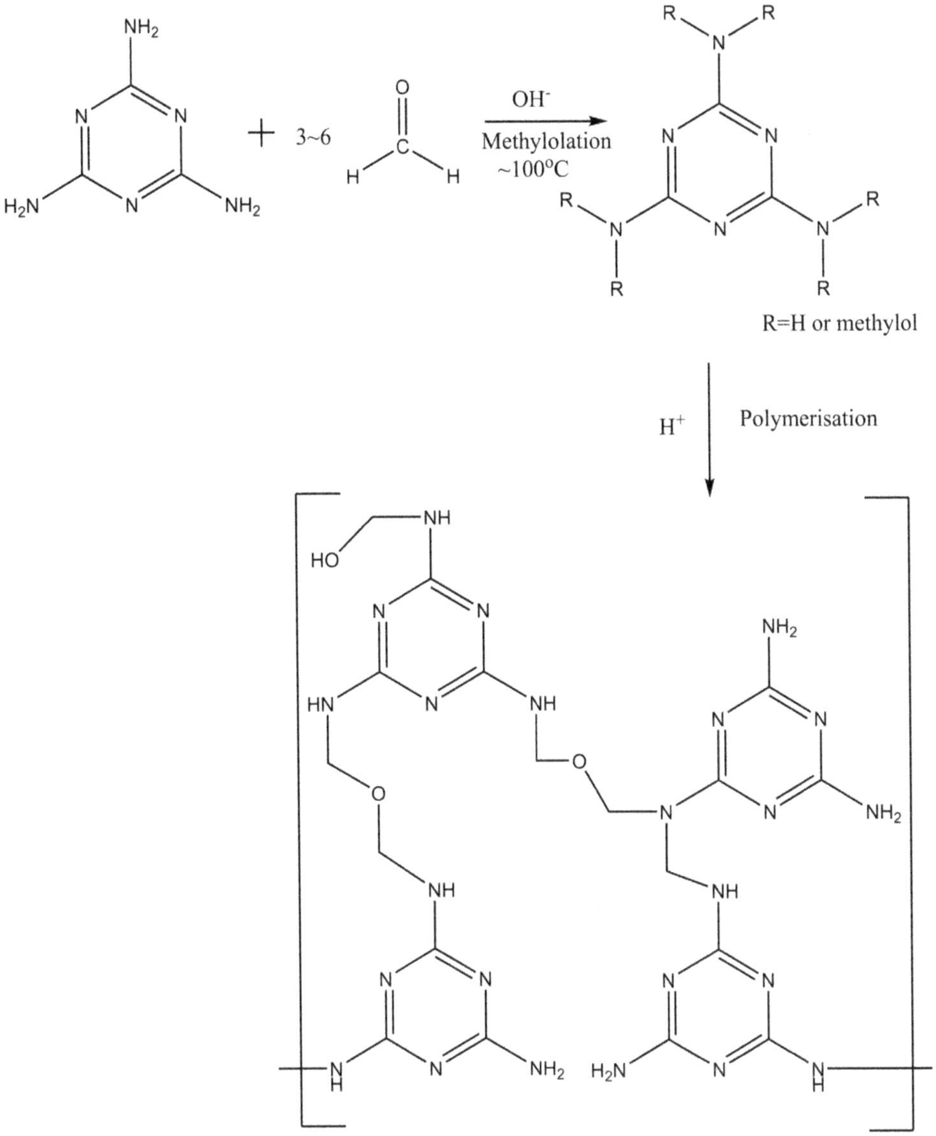

Figure 1.49 Melamine resin formation.

This section considers the relationship between wood and water in its natural and processed states, and how the performance of wood can be compromised through poor design. Methods for assessing the amounts of water present are also considered, together with the effects of wood modification on moisture levels.

Water in wood

The interaction of wood and water was clearly described by Skaar (1988):

Wood is a hygroscopic material, and its mass, dimensions and density, as well as its mechanical, elastic, electrical, thermal, and transport properties are affected by its moisture content. Wood is formed in a water-saturated environment in the living tree, but most of the water is removed prior to use. In use its moisture content and dependent properties change with changes in ambient conditions, particularly relative humidity. Wood is anisotropic with respect to most of its physical properties. The thermodynamics of moisture sorption, including enthalpy, free energy and entropy changes, are moisture dependent. Water sorption by wood is treated in terms of both surface and solution theories. Moisture transport in wood is also treated, particularly in relation to drying.

Within wood science, the moisture content is most commonly determined by the ratio:

$$\omega = \frac{m_w}{m_{dry}} \tag{1.1}$$

where ω (kg·kg^{-1} or often in %) is the moisture content, m_w is the mass of water, and m_{dry} is the dry mass. Since water in wood can be present both in cell walls and in the macro-void structure (i.e., mainly lumen), the maximum moisture content is the sum of the amounts of water present in cell walls and macro-voids.

Freshly cut and never-dried wood is usually known as "green" wood. In this state, the cell walls are water saturated and, in addition, water is found as a liquid, liquid–vapour mixture or vapour in cell lumens (Figure 1.50). The moisture state of green wood is not a unique quantity; it varies between tree species, within the tree, for example in the sapwood or heartwood, between seasons (if in a temporal zone) and possibly also with the time of day. This is clearly shown in Table 1.5, which gives an overview of a range of broad-leaved and conifer tree species (Glass and Zelinka, 2010).

The moisture content of the heartwood in conifers is typically much lower than that in sapwood. This is not always the case in broad-leaved trees, where the relation between moisture content in heartwood and sapwood depends not only on the species but on the season (Pallardy and Kozlowski, 2008).

As shown in Figure 1.50, when wood is dried, there is a reduction in the moisture content, and the cell walls eventually reach an unsaturated state. The moisture content at the transition point from saturated to unsaturated state, when all of the free water has evaporated is defined as the fibre saturation point (FSP). As the drying proceeds, the wood shrinks, and the reverse occurs if the wood is rewetted. The degrees of shrinkage depend upon the direction in relation to the direction of the grain, the shrinkage (swelling) being greatest in the tangential direction of the growth rings, and about half as much in the radial direction across the rings. The swelling is very low in the longitudinal direction. Tables of dimensional stability are available in the scientific literature (e.g., Glass and Zelinka, 2010), whilst reviews of moisture in wood (e.g., Engelund Thybring et al., 2013) provide details of studies and current understanding.

It is well known that the components of wood are capable of interacting with water through hydrogen bonding, the levels of which have been studied by several groups and compiled in Table 1.6 (Engelund Thybring et al., 2013; Engelund Thybring et al., 2020). The potential availability of OH groups is shown schematically in Figure 1.51, although maximum availability can never be achieved, especially when in situ within the wood cellular structure.

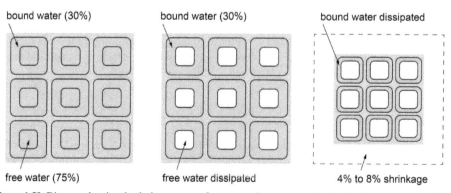

Figure 1.50 Diagram showing the drying process of green wood (green wood to the left, dry wood to the right).

Table 1.5 Average moisture contents of green wood mainly from North American species (based on data from: Glass and Zelinka, 2010). MC − moisture content, HW − heartwood, SW − sapwood.

Species	Broad-leaved trees	MC (%) in: HW	SW	Species	Conifer trees	MC (%) in: HW	SW
Alder	Red alder	-	97	Cedar	Eastern red cedar	33	-
Apple	Apple	81	74		Incense cedar	40	213
Ash	Black ash	95	-		Port Orford-cedar	50	98
	Green ash	-	58		Western red cedar	58	249
	White ash	46	44		Yellow cedar	32	166
Aspen	Aspen (Europe)	-	110	Cypress	Bald cypress	121	171
	Aspen (USA)	95	113	Douglas fir	Douglas fir (coast)	37	115
Basswood	American basswood	81	133	Fir	Balsam fir	88	173
Beech	American beech	55	72		Grand fir	91	136
Birch	Paper birch	89	72		Noble fir	34	115
	Silver birch	-	70		Pacific silver fir	55	164
	Sweet birch	75	70		White fir	98	160
	Yellow birch	74	72	Hemlock	Eastern hemlock	97	119
Cherry	Black cherry	58	-		Western hemlock	85	170
Chestnut	American chestnut	120	-	Larch	Tamarack	49	-
Cottonwood	Cottonwood	162	146		Western larch	54	119
Elm	American elm	95	92	Pine	Loblolly pine	33	110
	Cedar elm	66	61		Lodgepole pine	41	120
	Rock elm	44	57		Longleaf pine	31	106
Hackberry	Hackberry	61	65		Ponderosa pine	40	148
Hickory	Bitternut hickory	80	54		Red pine	32	134
	Mockernut hickory	70	52		Scots pine	35	134
	Pignut hickory	71	49		Shortleaf pine	32	122
	Red hickory	69	52		Sugar pine	98	219
	Sand hickory	68	50		Western white pine	62	148
	Water hickory	97	60	Redwood	Redwood	86	210
Magnolia	Magnolia	80	104	Spruce	Black spruce	52	113
Maple	Silver maple	58	97		Engelmann spruce	51	173
	Sugar maple	65	72		Norway spruce	37	133
Oak	California black oak	76	75		Sitka spruce	41	142
	Northern red oak	80	69				
	Southern red oak	83	75				
	Water oak	81	81				
	White oak	64	78				
	Willow oak	82	74				
Sweetgum	Sweetgum	79	137				
Sycamore	American sycamore	114	130				
Tulip tree	Yellow poplar	83	106				
Tupelo	Black tupelo	87	115				
	Swamp tupelo	101	108				
	Water tupelo	150	116				
Walnut	Black walnut	90	73				

Table 1.6 OH groups present in different wood polymeric components (Engelund Thybring et al., 2013).

Wood polymer	Formula unit	Molecular mass (g/mol)	OH-groups present	OH concentration (mmol/g)
Cellulose	$C_{12}H_{20}O_{10}$	324	6[f]	18.5[f]
Xylan[a]	$C_{33}H_{52}O_{24}$	833	12	14.4
Glucomannan[b]	$C_{30}H_{44}O_{24}R_6{}^{[g]}$	795–1,049	9–15	8.6–18.8
Lignin[c]	$C_{160}H_{178}O_{58}$	3,029	24	7.9
Lignin[d]	$C_{278}H_{300}O_{96}$	5,177	29	7.5
Lignin[e]	$C_{301}H_{335}O_{110}$	5,713	45	7.9

Formulae derived from (a) and (b) Sjöström, 1993, (c) Adler, 1977, (d) Sakakibara, 1980, and (e) Reid, 1995
[f] only 33% of cellulose OH groups are accessible to water. This gives a water-accessible OH concentration *in situ* of cellulose of 6.1 mmol/g
[g] R = CH_3CO or H

Moisture of wood in service

Moisture is more or less omnipresent in wood since water molecules can be absorbed from the surrounding air, but the relative humidity of the air may be affected *inter alia* by the season, daily temperature variations, heating regimes within buildings, etc. Wood in use can also become wet in direct contact with liquid water, as typified by precipitation in various forms, such as rain, hail or snow. Wood used outdoors without shelter is, therefore, frequently exposed to precipitation, which can be further intensified in the form of wind-driven rain (Nore et al., 2007; Abuku et al., 2009; Barreira and de Freitas, 2013) and splash water (Glass and TenWolde, 2007; Bornemann et al., 2014).

There is almost permanent wetting if the material is in direct contact with freshwater, sea water or moist soil. The European Use Class (UC) system according to EN 335 (CEN 2013) does not distinguish between exposure to fresh water and soil contact, although the Use Classes are defined by moisture conditions and potential degrading organisms in a specific use condition. According to EN 335, the Use Classes are defined as shown in Table 1.7.

Based on the definitions in Table 1.7 and experience in monitoring timber in use, Niklewski et al. (2017) suggested the following moisture content limitations for various Use Classes:

- UC2: the moisture content is occasionally > 20%, with a median of < 17.5%
- UC3.1: the moisture content is frequently > 20%, with a median of 20 ± 2.5%
- UC3.2: the moisture content is frequently > 20%, with a median of 25 ± 2.5%
- UC4: the moisture content is rarely or never < 20%, with a median > 27.5%

Decay risk

It is well known that the continued exposure of wood to high levels of moisture can increase the risk of biological decay, particularly due to fungal attack. Niklewski et al. (2017), showed that the decay risk for wood in different Use Classes can alter the overall performance of the wood component and risk its premature failure. The Use Classes, as defined by EN 335, refer to the decay risks associated with different wood-destroying organisms, and should be used in conjunction with Service Class definitions in EN 1995-1-1, i.e., Eurocode 5 (CEN, 2010), which define strength values and can be used to calculate deformations of structural timber members under defined environmental conditions, as shown in Table 1.8.

The decay risk is significantly affected by the macro- and micro-climate. The local influences can be seen in the Use Classes determined for various parts of a road bridge in Spain, showing how localised cover can have a significant effect on the observed Use Class (Figure 1.52). This study by Lorenzo (2016) indicated the variation in performance on either side of the bridge, emphasising the north-south variation in material service life.

Early work into better understanding these effects focused on conditions in the USA (Scheffer, 1971), where four different sites were initially evaluated in terms of the effects of temperature and

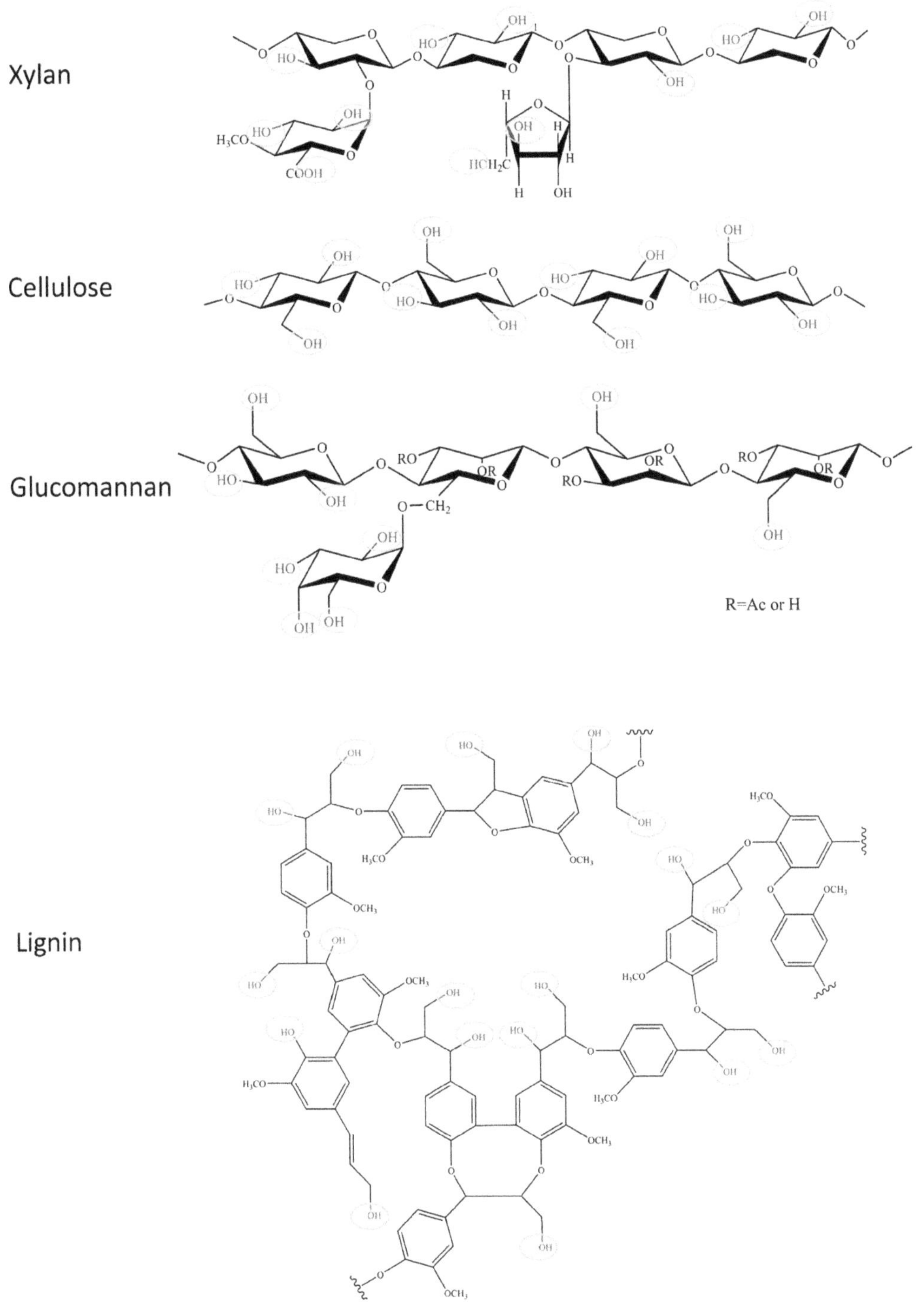

Xylan

Cellulose

Glucomannan

R=Ac or H

Lignin

Figure 1.51 Overview of potentially available OH groups (Engelund Thybring, 2014).

local rainfall on the hazard potential of timber and classified according to the Scheffer's Climate Index:

$$Climate\ index = \frac{\Sigma_{Dec}^{Jan}[(T-35)(D-3)]}{30} \qquad (1.2)$$

Table 1.7 Overview of Use Class classifications according to EN 335 (CEN, 2013).

Use Class	Definition according to EN 335
1	Situations in which the wood or wood-based product is inside a construction, not exposed to the weather and wetting. The attack by disfiguring fungi or wood-destroying fungi is insignificant and always accidental. Attack by wood-boring insects, including termites, is possible although the frequency and importance of the insect occurrence depends on the geographical region.
2	Situations in which the wood or wood-based product is under cover and not exposed to the weather (particularly rain and driven rain) but where occasional, but not persistent, wetting can occur. In this Use Class, condensation of water on the surface of wood and wood-based products may occur. Attack by disfiguring fungi and wood-destroying fungi is possible. Attack by wood-boring insects, including termites, is possible although the frequency and importance of the insect risk depends on the geographical region.
3	Situations in which the wood or wood-based product is above ground and exposed to the weather (particularly rain). Attack by disfiguring fungi and wood-destroying fungi is possible. Attack by wood-boring insects, including termites, is possible although the frequency and importance of the insect risk depends on the geographical region1). A large variety of in-use situations exist and, when relevant, Use Class 3 may be divided into two sub-classes Use Class 3.1 and Use Class 3.2.
3.1	In this situation, the wood and wood-based products will not remain wet for long periods. Water will not accumulate.
3.2	In this situation, the wood and wood-based products will remain wet for long periods. Water may accumulate.
4	A situation in which the wood or wood-based product is in direct contact with ground and/or fresh water. Attack by disfiguring fungi and wood-destroying fungi is possible. Attack by wood-boring insects, including termites, is possible although the frequency and importance of the insect occurrence depends on the geographical region.
5	A situation in which the wood or wood-based product is permanently or regularly submerged in salt water (i.e., sea water and brackish water). Attack by invertebrate marine organisms is the principal problem, particularly the warmer waters where organisms such as *Limnoria* spp., *Teredo* spp. and *Pholads* can cause significant damage. Attack by wood-destroying fungi and growth of surface moulds and staining fungi is also possible. The portion of certain components above water, for example harbour piles, can be exposed to wood-boring insects.

Table 1.8 Service Classes according to EN 1995-1-1 (CEN, 2010).

Service Class	Description
1	Characterised by a moisture content in the materials corresponding to a temperature of 20°C and the relative humidity of the surrounding air exceeding 65% for only a few weeks per year
2	Characterised by a moisture content in the materials corresponding to a temperature of 20°C and the relative humidity of the surrounding air exceeding 85% for only a few weeks per year
3	Characterised by climatic conditions leading to higher moisture contents than in Service Class 2

where T is the mean day temperature of the month (in Fahrenheit) and D is the number of days with more than 2.5 mm (0.1 inch) of rain per month. The original data showed that the decay hazard ranged from 0.0 for Yuma, Arizona to 137.5 for West Palm Beach, Florida, and that within continental USA three distinct climate zones were noted, indicating three levels of above-ground decay potential. The concept of the Scheffer's Climate Index has been further applied to a range of regions, including Europe, as shown in Figure 1.53.

As these studies have developed and expanded, the effect of wind-driven rain has become more apparent and this has led to its inclusion in hazard assessment. As a result, the relationships between total rain fall, rain fall intensity, wind speed, and wind direction have been assessed to

Figure 1.52 Examples of Use Classes from a road bridge in Spain (courtesy of David Lorenzo).

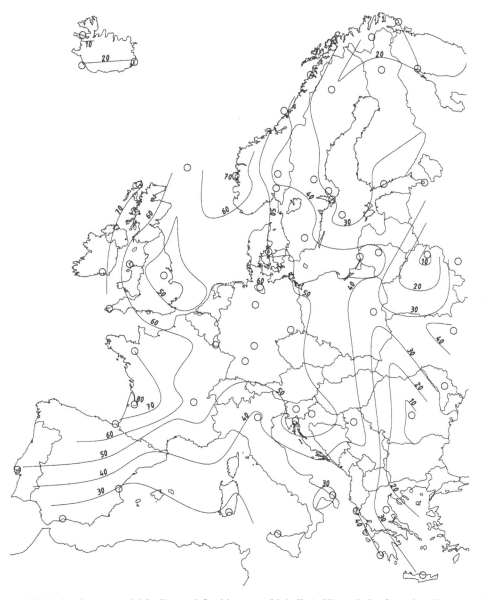

Figure 1.53 Relative decay potential for Europe defined in terms of Scheffer's Climate Index for various European sites (Brischke et al., 2011a).

create wind-driven rain maps. These studies are helping in developing better methods for assessing risks to timber components in use (e.g., cladding). A decay-risk model based on laboratory data was used to estimate wood decay across Europe (Viitanen et al., 2010). As a result, it was possible to determine the mass of Scots pine sapwood damaged as a result of brown rot decay related to the level of exposure to rain (Figure 1.54) and for similar wood samples protected from rain (Figure 1.55). Since the data in Figure 1.54 was based only on relative humidity and temperature data, no capillary uptake of moisture could be attributed via this model. The model appeared to deliver conservative results for sheltered wood. When wood was protected from rain—and provided there was no external moisture source—a lower loss of mass was expected from a biological viewpoint since the presence of liquid water inside wood was an essential requirement for degradation by fungi.

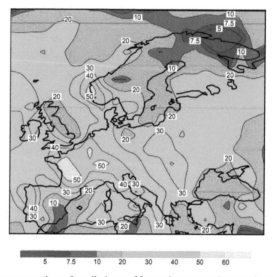

Figure 1.54 Modelled percentage mass loss of small pieces of Scots pine sapwood exposed to rain over a period of 10 years (1961–1979) in Europe (Viitanen et al., 2010).

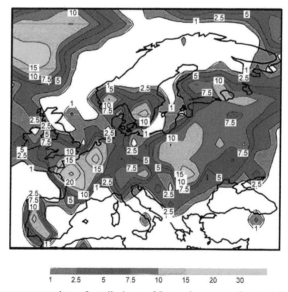

Figure 1.55 Modelled percentage mass loss of small pieces of Scots pine sapwood protected from rain over a period of 10 years in Europe (Viitanen et al., 2010).

Frühwald Hansson et al. (2012) developed a dose-based decay hazard map, further describing the relationship between wood moisture content and temperature and weather conditions, relative humidity, temperature and precipitation. The mapping was based on data collected from 206 sites across 38 European countries, standardised with respect to a fixed location, selected to be Uppsala in Sweden. Values below 1.0 were deemed to have a lower decay potential than Uppsala, and higher values a greater decay potential.

Comparison of data from different sites and different countries allowed for isoplethic mapping, as shown in Figure 1.56, where the dark red colour (e.g., western Ireland, north-west Spain) depicts

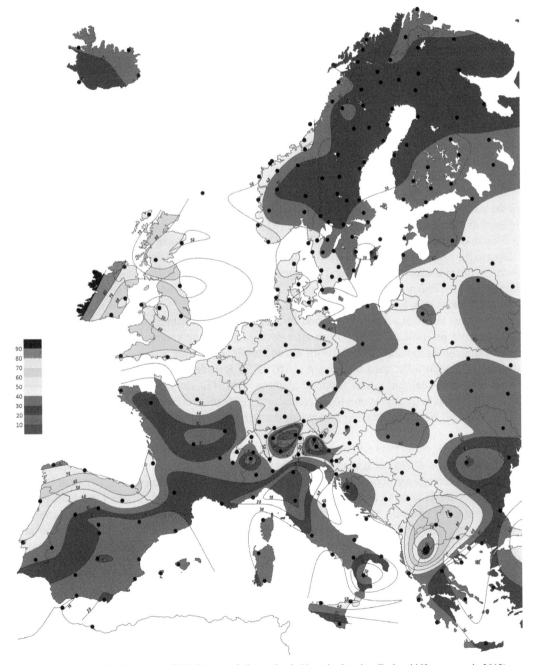

Figure 1.56 Relative decay potential in Europe relative to that in Uppsala, Sweden (Frühwald Hansson et al., 2012).

the areas of greatest decay risk and dark blue (e.g., most of Sweden and Finland) those of lowest decay risk.

Determining moisture in wood

It has already been pointed out that wood is a hygroscopic construction material. This means that the material constantly strives to remain in equilibrium with the local climate, i.e., the relative humidity (RH) and the temperature. The equilibrium moisture content (EMC) is defined as the moisture content of the wood when it is in equilibrium with the local climate conditions.

If the moisture content of the wood is higher than the equilibrium moisture content, the wood will dry out and if it is lower the wood will take up moisture. When the moisture content changes, below the fibre saturation point, the wood changes its volume, depending on whether moisture is being released or absorbed, the wood shrinks or swells. The dimension, strength and resistance to decay are key properties of wood that are affected by moisture.

The atmospheric content of water vapour, its vapour concentration, is usually stated in grams of water per cubic metre air and it varies throughout the year, depending on the climatic conditions in the particular region. For example in Sweden, the vapour concentration outdoors is at its highest in the summer (9–11 grams per cubic metre) and lowest in the winter (3–5 grams per cubic metre)— while the relative humidity and, thus, the wood's equilibrium moisture content in outdoor conditions is lowest in the summer (65–75% and 11–15% respectively) and highest in the winter (90–95% and 19–23% respectively).

Physically, the relative humidity is the ratio between the actual water vapour's partial pressure of the air and its saturation pressure at the temperature in question. The relative humidity of the air indoors in a heated room is highest in summer (45–60%) and lowest in winter (10–25%). The colder it is outdoors, the drier the air indoors. The moisture content in wood, both indoors and outdoors, adapts to the relative humidity and temperature of its surroundings. In heated Swedish homes in mid Sweden, the moisture content in wood averages out across the year at 7.5%, with the highest figures in summer (7–12%) and the lowest in winter (2–6%). On average, the indoor climate is drier in the north of Sweden than in the south during winter.

The most accurate yet simple method for measuring the moisture content in wood is through a gravimetric determination before and after drying. In the gravimetric method, which gives the mean value for the moisture content of the tested sample, the weight is first determined, after which the sample is then fully dried in an oven at 103°C, in accordance with EN 13183 (CEN, 2002a). Other more practical, but not as accurate methods exist. For exterior plywood, Van den Bulcke et al. (2009) mounted samples on a load cell and exposed them to climatic conditions, with variations due to rain and wind being taking in account through an inert material mounted onto an adjacent load cell.

Another indirect method of determining the moisture content is by measuring electrical resistance. Typically, wood is an electrical insulator, but the presence of moisture allows electrical current to be conducted. Readings are normally taken using stainless steel nails or screws attached to or inserted into the specimens to serve as electrodes. In some cases (Brischke et al., 2008), electrodes require a non-conductive covering whereby the tops need to be free to guarantee a top to top measurement, as shown in Figure 1.57. Resistive methods allow the moisture content to be determined at a certain position within a test specimen. The most common method used follows that outlined in EN 13183-2 (CEN, 2002b), where electrodes are hammered into the wood surface at a distance 300 mm from the end of a sample, to a depth of 0.3 times that of its thickness. The desire to undertake continual monitoring has, however, led to an increase in the use of the method reported by Brischke et al. (2008), and it has become a common method of analysis in many European research institutes and universities.

Instead of measuring the electrical resistance, it is also possible to determine the moisture content using a capacitance method, as outlined in EN 13813-3 (CEN, 2005). A capacitive electric field forms between the probes and the test material, and a higher moisture content leads to a high

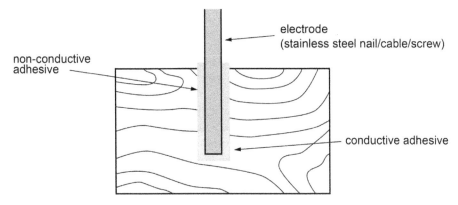

Figure 1.57 Method for connecting electrodes for continuous moisture monitoring of wood (Brischke et al., 2008).

dielectric constant, thus increasing the capacity. The capacitive method is a relative measurement, which means that the test result is given as the difference between the values for the dry and wet materials. Capacitive measurements suffer, however, from a strong relationship between permittivity and wood density, which is often unknown and may vary within a test object.

These methods are summarised in the work of Dietsch et al. (2015), together with other methods, some of which are gaining in popularity and are described below.

Sorption studies with dynamic vapour sorption (DVS) equipment

The rate at which wood adsorbs and desorbs water varies for each species. Never-dried wood, also known as green wood, has a desorption isotherm higher than the adsorption and desorption isotherms of oven-dried wood. The oven-dried desorption isotherm is always higher than the adsorption isotherm (Figure 1.58). The difference between desorption and adsorption curves is known as sorption hysteresis and this exists in many hygroscopic materials (Skaar, 1988). It is expressed as the ratio of the adsorption (A) to the desorption (D) moisture content at a given relative humidity. The A:D ratio ranges from 0.785 to 0.844 (mean value 0.812 ± 0.023) for conifer wood and 0.790 to 0.849 (mean 0.828 ± 0.018) for broad-leaved wood. Sorption hysteresis decreases with increasing temperature and disappears at a temperature of about 75°C (Skaar, 1988).

The theory behind the sorption process has been well documented (e.g., Engelund Thybring, 2013), and the thermodynamics of the process can be explained by the fact that any moisture change

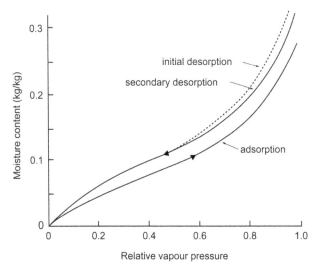

Figure 1.58 Typical adsorption and desorption isotherms for wood.

in wood is usually accompanied by an exchange of heat, heat being generated during adsorption via an exothermic process or consumed during desorption via an endothermic process (Zhao et al., 2013). The overall thermodynamic processes involved were described by Yang and Ma (2016) during their evaluations of the moisture sorption by a hybrid poplar.

Traditionally, one of the problems involved when undertaking sorption isotherm studies was the need to equilibrate samples to fixed relative humidities, using various salt solutions. This time-intensive method was made considerably easier in the 1990s through the development and commercialisation of *dynamic vapour sorption* (DVS) equipment. Since then, DVS has become an integral component of the equipment in most research facilities, whereby samples can easily be tested from one relative humidity to another as well as over a range of temperatures. Many studies of various timber species have been reported, e.g., Sitka spruce (Hill et al., 2010), radiata pine, black wattle and sesendok (Zaihan et al., 2009). Recent work by Uimonen et al. (2019) has demonstrated that it is possible to use DVS to ascertain the accessibility of hydroxyl groups using deuterium oxide as well as using alcohols as inclusion compounds.

X-ray computed tomography (CT)

X-ray computed tomography (CT) is a powerful method for the non-destructive evaluation of three-dimensional wood density and moisture content in wood and other bio-based materials. The density can be determined with an accuracy of about ±3 kg/m^3 for large specimens (sawn-timber dimension), and the accuracy in average moisture content below and above the fibre saturation point can be determined with an accuracy of about ±1 percent point. It is also possible to measure the density and moisture content in a randomly chosen volume element of say $1 \times 1 \times 1$ mm within the wood. CT scanning can also be used for evaluating:

- the development of fungal attack in wood,
- the development of attack by marine borers in wood,
- the distribution and rate of penetration of preservatives or wood modification chemicals into wood, and
- to evaluate wood drying after impregnation.

X-ray CT was introduced in the medical field in the early 1970s to obtain a density profile through a body following the same principle as in other radiographic technologies. The technique was developed by Hounsfield (1973) and Cormack (1963) and they were awarded the Nobel Prize in physiology and medicine in 1979 for their work. This technique is nowadays a standard medical examination method for investigating the possible presence and size of tumours in the brain, for example. This X-ray computed tomography scanning technology has recently been developed as an industrial tool for outer geometry assessment and internal feature detection in logs for the optimisation of the sawing/cutting processes in the sawmill and veneer industries. In wood science, CT is used mostly for steady-state studies of internal anatomical features of the wood material, but it is also possible to study processes such as drying, thermal modification, water absorption, internal and external cracking, and material deformation in a temperature- and humidity-controlled environment.

CT is an imaging technique that measures the amount of X-radiation sufficient to pass through a body of a given material, a property that is defined by the attenuation coefficient of the material. The working principle of an X-ray CT scanner is that X-rays are sent through a material and the intensity of X-ray photons that reach the detector at the other side per unit time is quantified. The X-rays are generated in the X-ray tube, which is in a fixed position in relation to the detectors at the opposite side. In general, the X-ray tube and the detector rotate around the scanned object, but in other CT scanners, the scanned object rotates while the tube and detectors remain stationary, which simplifies the mechanics of the device. After the rotation is completed, a computer can calculate the X-ray attenuation in small volume elements (voxels) within the entire scanned volume (Figure 1.59).

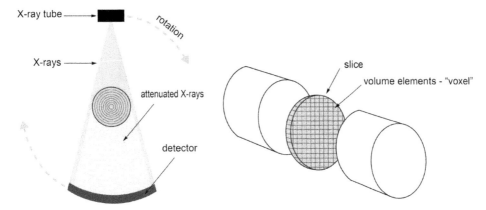

Figure 1.59 The working principle of a CT scanner (left), and voxels within a cross-section (right).

The theoretical background of CT lies within Lambert-Beer's law, which describe an exponential relationship between the intensity of the radiation and the attenuation coefficient:

$$I = I_0 e^{-\mu d} \tag{1.3}$$

where I is the intensity of the transmitted X-ray beam, I_0 is the intensity of the incident X-ray beam, μ is the linear attenuation coefficient of the material along the transmission path, d is the thickness of the body and e is Euler's constant.

CT images are presented in a grey scale and, for most biological materials, the grey scale values are almost linearly related to density, being darker for lower density and brighter for higher density.

The linear attenuation coefficient is normalised with respect to the linear attenuation coefficient of water, leading to the CT number or Hounsfield number, according to:

$$CT\ number = \frac{1000 \cdot (\mu_x - \mu_{water})}{\mu_{water} - \mu_{air}} \tag{1.4}$$

where μ_x is the linear attenuation coefficient of the scanned material, μ_{water} is the linear attenuation coefficient of water, and μ_{air} is the linear attenuation coefficient of air. The formula applies for CT scanners with an average photon energy of 73 keV. In Equation 1.4, a CT number of −1,000 is the attenuation value for air, and a CT number of 0 is the value for water.

The image reconstruction results in a map of the inhomogeneity of the cross section in a position perpendicular to the rotation axis. This map can be represented as a two-dimensional raster (also known as bitmap) image of the scanned cross section, formed by pixels with values of the X-ray linear attenuation coefficient. In a CT, one pixel represents a three-dimensional entity (voxel) of the material scanned with the dimensions of the pixel and the thickness of the scanning beam (the beam depth). After the processing, a CT scanner provides a raster image in which the value of each pixel is the average CT number of the voxel which it represents according to Equation 1.4. There is great variability in voxel dimensions and pixel size due to the type of CT, the specific device and the chosen settings.

Although the attenuation coefficient of a material is dependent on the effective atomic number, there is an approximately linear relation between the CT number and the density of wood (Lindgren, 1992), so that the greyscale of a CT image of wood can be interpreted as a density scale. CT images can be calibrated so that white represents water (1,000 kg/m³) and black represents air ($\approx$ 0 kg/m³). A water phantom is scanned with the specimen so that the density is defined by the greyscale, a model that is well suited for studying wood and wood-water relations. Figure 1.60 shows how sapwood in the green state is almost white because it is saturated with water, whereas dry wood has a darker grey hue.

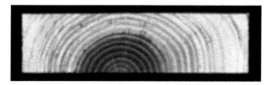

Figure 1.60 CT image of a cross section of Scots pine timber with heartwood (dark) and water filled sapwood.

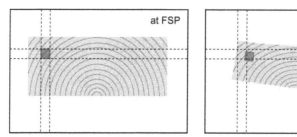

Figure 1.61 Deformation and displacement (exaggerated) relative to the pixel location of the voxel represented by one pixel when the wood piece is oven dried and re-scanned. FSP – fibre saturation point, MC – moisture content.

CT images are used to calculate moisture content by analogy with the gravimetric method. The estimation of the of the moisture content in wood using CT requires two images: one at the moisture content to be determined and another at a known reference moisture content, which here is, for practical reasons, always 0%. For pixel-wise distribution of the moisture content, image-processing algorithms are needed to compensate for the anisotropic distortion that wood undergoes as it dries. It is possible to determine the density of the material represented in any given pixel using the CT numbers of air and water as reference. The CT scanner settings establish the pixel size and scanning depth, and thus the voxel volume. It is then possible to calculate the mass of the material in the pixel and, if the mass is known, it is possible to calculate the moisture content.

Due to shrinkage anisotropy in the wood cross section, the region in a given pixel in the image at a certain moisture content is deformed when the wood is dried, and is then covered by more than one pixel because of the displacement (Figure 1.61). Since the voxels in the two images do not correspond to the same region in the specimen, the MC is determined as the average for the entire specimen. To quantitatively determine the moisture content in the local region, image processing must be performed to match the images (Couceiro, 2019). In the first applications of CT to wood drying, Lindgren (1992) attempted to take into account the swelling and shrinkage of cross-section images of timber by applying a linear transform combined with a bilinear and a non-linear transform to CT images of wood specimens at different moisture-content levels.

A considerable more accurate technique than X-ray to determine moisture in wood is to use neutrons for the detection. The neutron-based techniques are only used in research purposes, and are complicated to perform and require extremely expensive facilities, so they are not further discussed here.

Spectroscopy

Spectroscopy has become a valuable tool in the analytical arsenal of scientists, providing a means of identifying chemical bonds present as a result of their excitation at known frequencies. This technique has been further expanded through computer-aided deconvolution and processing, making identification much easier. Near-infrared (NIR) spectroscopy has applications in all facets of biological material assessments, given its non-destructive nature. NIR spectroscopic information on biological materials is particularly relevant given its ability to show water, which has specific absorption bands at 5,200 cm^{-1} (as a result of the combination of stretching and deformation vibrations for OH) and 6,900 cm^{-1} (due to the first overtone of the OH stretching vibration), and

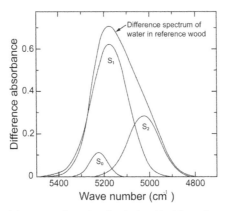

Figure 1.62 Difference and decomposed spectra of water in a hinoki wood sample (Inagaki et al., 2008).

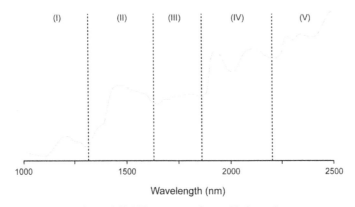

Figure 1.63 NIR spectrum of warty birch wood.

studies of these peaks can provide information on the amount of water present, as was demonstrated in work by Tsuchikawa and Tsutsumi (1998) for adsorptive and capillary-condensed water in wood, and further studies by Buijs and Choppin (1963) suggested that water molecules were classified into three components, free water molecules (S_0), molecules with one OH group engaged in hydrogen bonding (S_1), and molecules with two OH groups engaged in hydrogen bonding (S_2), as shown in Figure 1.62 for hinoki, whereby S_0, S_1 and S_2 components were separated (Inagaki et al., 2008). The effects of hydrogen bonding were found in subsequent work (Maeda et al., 1995) to be associated with two additional peaks (S_3 and S_4 respectively).

More detailed studies in the presence of moisture (Popescu et al., 2016) showed a range of spectral peaks (Figure 1.63) for untreated warty birch, which could be assigned the following chemical characterisations:

I) between 1,100–1,330 nm is mostly assigned to 1st and 2nd overtones of C-H stretching vibrations in methyl and methylene groups from carbohydrates and lignin;

II) between 1,330–1,640 nm is assigned to 1st overtone of the C-H combination bands, and 1st overtone of different O-H stretching vibrations;

III) between 1,640–1,850 nm is dominated by the 1st overtone of the aliphatic and aromatic C-H stretching vibrations and O-H combination bands in all wood components;

IV) between 1,850–2,210 nm is assigned mostly to C=O groups, O-H stretching and deformation vibrations and also to Car-H and C-H stretching vibrations, and

V) between 2,210–2,510 nm is assigned mostly to C-H stretching and deformation vibrations.

Wood modification and moisture

The ultimate aim of wood modification is to alter its performance and reduce the risks in service, particularly with regard to dimensional in stability and decay, both of which are strongly influenced by the presence of moisture. Wood in service in interior conditions is usually restricted to moisture contents below 10%, but design or exposure to high moisture conditions can significantly affect its performance. The same is true of wood in Use Classes 2 and 3, where the moisture content can often exceed 20% due to atmospheric conditions. The risk of decay is then increased, particularly if the exposure is over a prolonged period of time.

As was shown in Figure 1.51, the key components of wood contain large numbers of potentially accessible hydroxyl groups. These groups present a means by which modification can occur, either through direct chemical bonding or indirect bonding via hydrogen bonding of compounds that have been impregnated and subsequently polymerised, or as a result of a loss of functionality of the wood cell wall components. The mode of operation of the modifying agent can relate to one or more of these actions, as suggested in Figure 1.40. The key result of wood modification is, however, most often a decrease in the number of hydroxyl groups available for subsequent interaction with moisture in the environment. The higher the level of modification, the greater is the effect on the hydroxyl groups within the cell-wall components and hence on their potential interaction with moisture.

A comprehensive review by Engelund Thybring, 2013 has assessed the decay risk according to levels of moisture exclusion efficiency (MEE) and anti-swelling efficiency (ASE) and ASE* (an alternative measure of ASE, where the volume increase resulting from various wood modification methods has been deducted from the dry volume of the unreacted wood). Through the analysis of modification methods undertaken (Table 1.9), it was possible to estimate threshold levels for MEE, ASE and ASE* as well as the respective weight gain required for each treatment (a weight loss when considering thermal modification).

More detailed information on the effects on the moisture content of various modification methods is given in the sections on the respective modifications.

Table 1.9 Estimated threshold conditions for decay in various wood modifications (Engelund Thybring, 2013). WPG − weight percentage gain, MEE − moisture exclusion efficiency, and ASE − anti-swelling efficiency.

Modification	Threshold (WPG)	MEE	ASE	ASE*
Acetylation	20%	42%	63%	60%
Furfurylation	35%	40%	74%	-
DMDHEU	25%	43%	45%	43%
Glutaraldehyde	10%	24%	50%	48%
Glyoxal	> 50%	-	-	-
Thermal modification	−15%	42%	46%	-

1.5 Wood biodegradation

Wood can be decomposed by a wide variety of biological systems, provided suitable environmental conditions are present. Wood is inherently biologically degradable and may be attacked by fungi, bacteria, and insects individually or in combination, based on a variety of metabolism mechanisms linked to the individual components present within the wood. Wood in its natural environment is known to undergo colonisation by these microorganisms and insects, particularly when the bark, the external protection of the tree has become damaged, allowing more accessible attack and accelerating decomposition. The same is true of felled round timber lying on the forest floor, further assisted by the timber being exposed to super-saturation conditions. The cleavage of the main macromolecules present within wood—cellulose, lignin and hemicelluloses—leads to smaller oligomer or single unit components, which are easier to degrade as a food source, with such digestion leading to the basic components of all flora—carbon dioxide and water—whilst providing energy to the organism that has digested the wood material residue. While this degradation process is an important feature of forest regeneration, it is a problem when wood is used in the built environment, since such degradation in buildings can lead to premature failure. This has led to the need to protect wood in construction and in other applications through the use of correct detailing, coatings, wood preservation and, more recently, wood modification.

Wood as a substrate for microorganisms

As expected, the structural features of wood depend on the species in question. However, all wood cells are composed of cellulose, hemicellulose, and lignin in various ratios. In general, broad-leaved wood have a lower lignin content than conifers, and the type of lignin monomer in the woods is different. Both syringyl and guaiacyl units (Figure 1.38) are found in angiosperm lignin, whilst only guaiacyl-type lignin is present in gymnosperms. There are contrasting differences in the hemicelluloses of the respective tree groups, with galactoglucomannans (Figure 1.37, middle) dominating in gymnosperms and glucuronoxylans (Figure 1.64) in angiosperms.

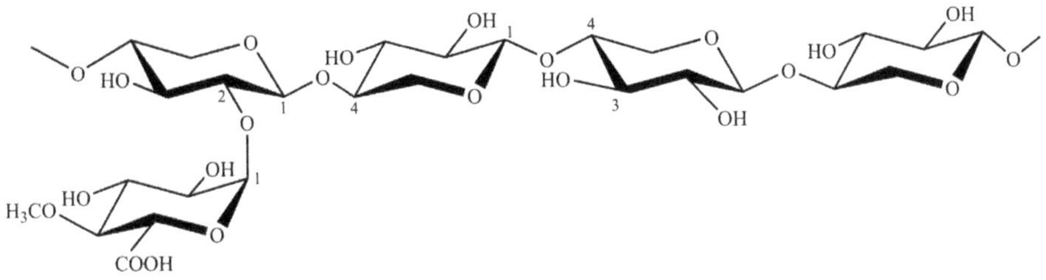

Figure 1.64 Structure of 4-O-methyl-D-glucurono-D-xylan in European beech (Strnad et al., 2013).

The greatest risk of germination and growth in fungal decay occurs when there is a suitable balance of five key factors: source of infection, suitable substrate (food), moisture, oxygen and temperature. The presence of the three main components of wood provide the necessary food for the attacking organism so that, if there is sufficient moisture and a suitable temperature, decay may be possible if colonisation occurs at sites of weakened resistance, such as damage to the bark of the tree. Many timber species produce a range of extractives as a natural protection against biological attack, but these are usually located within the heartwood of the tree, which can leave the outer sapwood more prone to decay. Preventing this has usually been undertaken with wood preservation, where a compound toxic to attacking organisms is introduced. However, wood modification is directed more to a reduction in the available moisture, so limiting one of the five key factors for decay.

Biological degradation of wood by fungi

The decomposition of wood by fungi is of two main types, often referred to as *brown rot* and *white rot*, together with the less common *soft rot* (Eriksson et al., 1990; Zabel and Morrell, 1992; Schmidt et al., 1996; Mohebby, 2003; Srivastava et al., 2013). There are also non-destructive fungi that result only in a discolouration of the timber, with no loss of mechanical strength. It has bed been suggested that these staining fungi help to provide channels of attack for wood-destroying fungal. In brown rot, the cellulose and its related pentosans are attacked while the lignin is more or less unchanged. This causes the attacked wood to darken in colour, undergoing shrinkage and cross-cracking into cubical or oblong pieces that can be readily broken and crumbled between the fingers into a brown powder. In white rot, all the components of the wood, including the lignin, may be decomposed and used by the growing fungus. White rot does not produce cross-cracking, but the wood becomes paler in colour, sometimes in pockets or streaks of various sizes and may eventually become a fibrous whitish mass. With some white rots, however, the cellulose may remain intact, while the lignin in the secondary wall and middle lamella is almost entirely removed. A graphical view of different rot-type fungi as well as moulds is shown in Figure 1.65 (Teacă et al., 2019).

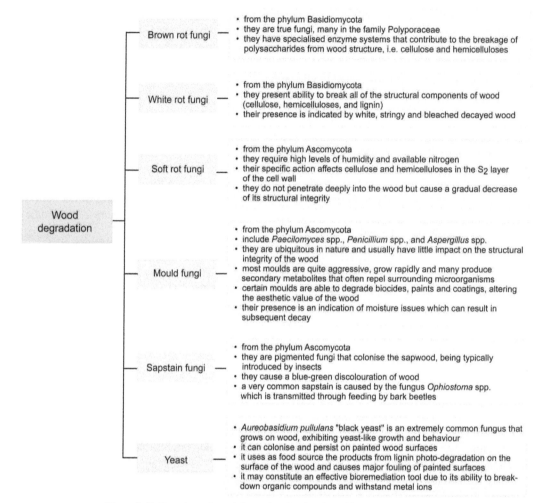

Figure 1.65 Overview of wood-destroying fungi and moulds (Teacă et al., 2019).

Since fungi do not contain chlorophyll, they are totally dependent upon extracting the necessary nourishment for growth and reproduction from their surroundings, i.e., from the timber under decay. When decay occurs in the core of a tree, it is in a zone where there is limited access to nitrogen and sulphur, essential components for growth (e.g., through enzymatic needs). This limitation to essential elements, in addition to the common increase in biologically restrictive chemicals as part of a species' natural durability, often limits the amount of decay which may occur the heartwood of a species.

As expected, decayed wood is less dense than sound wood and it usually exhibits a loss of strength, along with changes in firmness and the release of odours. Typically, the loss of weight resulting from brown rot is about 70%, since the lignin still remains, though its total destruction is possible in white rot. Even slight decay can reduce the toughness or shock resistance of wood and allow it to break easily under impact, although it may still appear hard and firm to the touch. Fungi that cause brown rot usually leads to a more rapid drop in most strength properties than those that cause white rot, although both types reduce the toughness of any wood that they attack. The fresh and resinous smell of sound wood is usually replaced by a distinctive mushroom odour as wood decays, and some wood-rotting fungi produce characteristic aromatic or sweet smells. Some examples of fungal species are given in Table 1.10.

Typically, the changes noted in wood as a result of fungal degradation can be summarised as in Table 1.11 (Blanchette, 1998).

Table 1.10 Examples of some discolouring and destroying fungi capable of attacking wood.

Destroying fungi		
Brown rot fungi	**White rot fungi**	**Soft rot fungi**
Basidiomycetes	**Basidiomycetes (ascomycetes)**	**Ascomycetes, deuteromycetes**
Coniophora puteana,[a,b] *Serpula lachrymans*, *Postia placenta*,[a,b] *Gloeophyllum trabeum*,[b] *Gloeophyllum sepiarium*, *Gloeophyllum abietinum, Antrodia Vaillantii*	*Trametes versicolor*,[a,b] *Donkioporia expansa*, *Schizophyllum commune*, *Phanerochaete chrysosporum, Pleurotus ostreatus*	*Chaetomium globosum*,[c] *Phialophora* spp., *Monodictys* spp., *Humicola grisea*,[c] *Petriella setifera*,[c] *Lechythophora mutabilis*,[c] *Trichurus spiralis*[c]
Staining fungi		**Surface moulds**
Blue stain fungi	**Other stain fungi**	
Ascomycetes, deuteromycetes	**Ascomycetes, deuteromycetes**	**Ascomycetes, deuteromycetes**
Aureobasidium pullulans, *Ceratocystis* spp., *Ophiostoma* spp., *Ceratocystiopsis* spp.	*Discula* spp., *Arthrographis cuboidea, Chlorociboria aeruginosa*	*Paecilomyces variotii*, *Aspergillus niger*, *Trichoderma* spp., *Bisporia* spp., *Penicillium* spp.

[a] Test fungus according to CEN/TS 15083-1 (CEN 2015)
[b] Test fungus according to EN 113 (CEN 1996)
[c] Test fungus according to ENV 807 (ENV 2001)

Table 1.11 Changes in wood due to degradation by fungi.

Decay	Wood characteristics	Strength loss	Cell-wall components	Morphology
Brown rot (dry rot)	Brown. Cracks and checks when dry, producing cubical fragments.	Large losses of strength in early stages of decay.	Cellulose depolymerisation and loss.	Porous and shrunken cell walls, skeleton of altered lignified wall material.
Soft rot	Brown. Often localised to wood surfaces. Cracks and checks when dry.	Loss in strength in late stages of decay.	Cellulose degraded.	Cavities present in secondary walls, or secondary walls eroded, leaving the middle lamellae.
White rot	Bleached appearance. Retains shape and composition until decay is advanced.	Major strength losses in intermediate to late stages of decay.	Lignin, cellulose and hemicelluloses degraded.	All secondary cell-wall layers and middle lamellae are eroded.
Fungal stain	Various discolouration in sapwood	No strength loss.	Free sugars, nutrients and wood extractives utilised, increase in melamin-like compounds and pigmented substances.	Preferential colonisation of ray parenchyma cells. No cell-wall degradation.
Surface moulds	Discolouration of wood surfaces only.	No strength losses.	Readily assimilated substances are removed.	Preferential colonisation of parenchyma cells. No cell-wall degradation.

Chemical and biochemical reasons for degradation

The general concepts of the chemical and biochemical reasons for degradation were covered in a comprehensive paper (Jeffries, 1987) considering wood as a whole as well as the constituent components.

White rot fungi use all the chemical components of wood cell walls. Bari et al. (2015) considered two of the more common fungi having differing modes of attack. *Pleurotus ostreatus* gains its nourishment from the breakdown and absorption of nourishment from dead and fallen trees (saprophytic means) as well as acting as a wounding parasite in living trees. On the other hand, *Trametes versicolor* causes extensive saprophytic degradation in dead and decaying wood. In a study by Riley et al. (2014), the range of secondary enzymes resulting from basidiomycetes attack were analysed, with particular emphasis on fatty acid synthases, non-ribosomal peptide synthases, polyketide synthases and terpene synthases. It was shown that the enzymes acting during white rot were more varied than those depicted for brown rot, though glucose–methanol–choline (GMC) oxidoreductase, a group comprising enzymes such as aryl-alcohol oxidoreductases, alcohol oxidases, cellobiose dehydrogenases, glucose oxidases, glucose dehydrogenases, pyranose dehydrogenases and pyranose oxidases (Sützl et al., 2019) was responsible for the highest levels of lignin degradation for both white and brown rot fungi. It is the activity of enzymes such as class II peroxidase, copper radical oxidase and laccase that provide the increased levels of degradation in lignin compared to the brown rot fungi.

The fungal biodegradation of wood may be utilised for industrial purposes and it has a great potential in the cellulose-producing and wood-processing industries. Fermentation with a selective white rot fungi can provide a route for the production of biofuel or cellulose-enriched forage for ruminants, and can serve as a delignifying pre-treatment to expose the polysaccharides to a subsequent hydrolytic digestion and increase the efficiency of biogas or bioethanol fermentation with bacteria or yeasts (Itoh et al., 2003; Amirta et al., 2005). Besides the fermentation of woody substrates using fungi which degrade or modify the different wood components, isolated oxidative enzymes from the same origin may be valuable tools for more specific and targeted chemical reactions in fibre bleaching and fibre modification and they have been tested for possible applications in the pulp and paper industries (Grönqvist et al., 2003; Maijala et al., 2008). It has long been noted (Leatham et al., 1990) that the use of enzymatic digestion can help for save energy in the pulping sector.

Brown rot fungi, on the other hand, have a unique ability to attack the cellulose fraction of wood while avoiding the surrounding lignin. It has been suggested that the fungi accomplish this by using a two-step process, first secreting chemicals and enzymes that open up the lignin framework and then releasing a second set of enzymes that break down the cellulose chains into sugars. The sugars are absorbed by the fungi to use as biofuel.

To accomplish this task, brown rot fungi generate highly reactive oxygen species that alter the chemical structure of the wood, working with enzymes that break down the cellulosic chains. However, reactive oxygen species might damage the fungal enzymes as easily as the wood structure, and it has long been hypothesised that the fungi spatially segregate the oxidant generation process from the secreted enzymes using chemical barriers. This is achieved through the enzymes incorporating the Fenton reaction, and generating highly reactive hydroxyl radicals:

$$H_2O_2 + Fe^{2+} \rightarrow OH^- + Fe^{3+} + \bullet OH \qquad (1.5)$$

Since the specificity of cellulosic attack negates the decay of lignin, brown rot decay typically occurs more rapid than white rot decay.

Decay mechanisms

Depending on the type of fungal species and the group to which it belongs, different mechanisms for the decay of wood are involved, although most of them involve enzymatic attack. Mahajan et al. (2012) reported that certain white rot fungi, such as *Trametes versicolor* and *Phanerochaete chrysosporium*, are capable of simultaneously degrading lignin, cellulose, and hemicelluloses. On the other hand, other white rot fungi, such as *Ceriporiopsis subvermispora*, appear to selectively degrade lignin and then only slowly to hydrolyse cellulose. The ability of fungi to selectively degrade lignin has been used to pre-treat and defibrillate wood in the production of mechanical pulp up to commercial production levels (Scott et al., 2002; Fackler et al., 2006; Mendonça et al., 2008).

The enzymes responsible for lignin decay have been reviewed by Abdel-Hamid et al. (2013), including the so-called class II secreted fungal peroxidases, all of which are extracellular heme peroxidases: lignin peroxidase (LiP), manganese-dependent peroxidase (MnP) and versatile peroxidase (VP). The mechanism by which they are understood to work is shown in Figure 1.66.

In order to describe the modes of action of these class II secreted fungal peroxidases, Abdel-Hamid et al. (2013) also described prokaryotic peroxidases (class I) and classical secreted plant peroxidases (class III), dye de-colourising peroxidase (DyP), copper-containing phenol oxidases (Laccase), and several oxidoreductases, which include glyoxal oxidase, aryl alcohol oxidase (veratryl alcohol oxidase), pyranose 2-oxidase (glucose 1-oxidase), cellobiose/quinone oxidoreductase and cellobiose dehydrogenase.

The catalytic cycle of MnP (shown diagrammatically in Figure 1.67) is similar to those of other heme-containing peroxidases. Activated through the initiation with hydrogen peroxide of a conventional ferric enzyme, it is unique in utilising Mn^{2+} as the electron donor to form Mn^{3+}. Abdel-Hamid et al. (2013) also suggest that MnP is capable of cleaving non-phenolic lignin substrates.

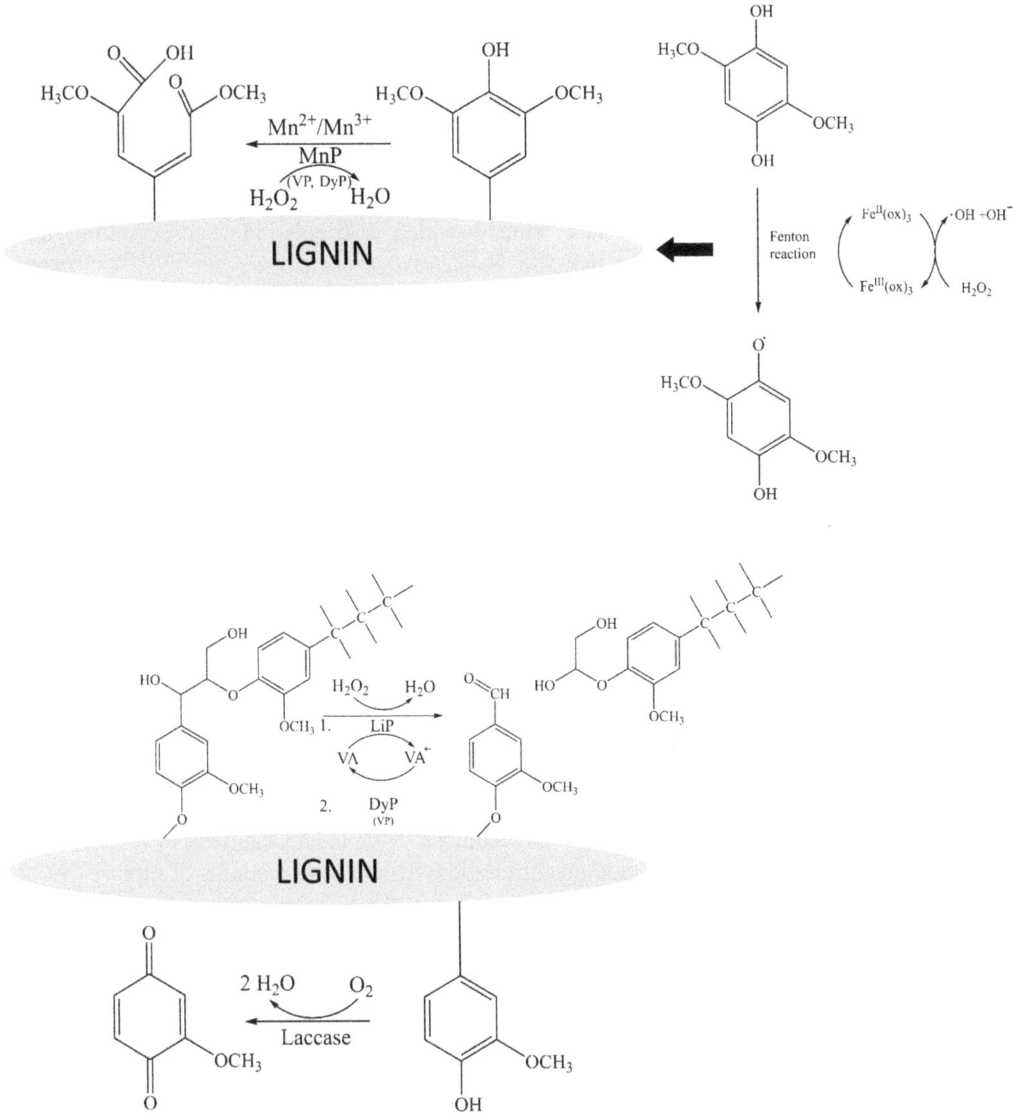

Figure 1.66 The reaction catalysed by lignin-degrading enzymes. LiP: lignin peroxidase, MnP: manganese peroxidase, VP: versatile peroxidase, AAO: aryl alcohol oxidase, GLOX: glyoxal oxidase (modified after Janusz et al., 2017).

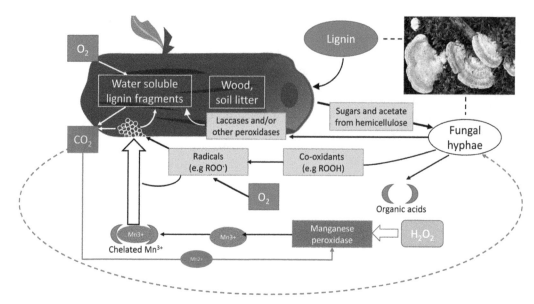

Figure 1.67 Diagram of lignin degradation by white rot fungi (after Zhou et al., 2013).

The white rot fungi also contain laccase, which is widely distributed in wood-degrading fungi, such as *Trametes versicolor, Trametes hirsuta, Trametes ochracea, Trametes villosa, Trametes gallica, Cerrena maxima, Phlebia radiata, Ceriporiopsis subvermispora*, and *Pleurotus eryngii* (Baldrian, 2006), although more than one iso-enzyme has been identified in many white rot fungal species. Typically, the laccases are monomeric proteins, although their structures often consist of two identical subunits. Baldrian (2006) presented a comprehensive list of substrates and inhibitors for fungal laccases.

It is known that brown rot fungi specifically attack the cellulose, leaving the lignin relatively intact, but it is not fully understood, since this would seem to restrict access to the polysaccharide food sources. This is thought to have developed during the evolution of brown rot fungi from an ancestral form of white rot fungi, a range of cellulose- and lignin-modifying enzymes being eliminated during its evolution.

Brown rot attack is initiated when germinated spores result in hyphae growth through the cell lumens to colonise ray cells and axial parenchyma. These are readily accessible sources of carbohydrate, providing the necessary nourishment for the hyphae to continue growing through pit membranes and accessing tracheid lumens. Growth is further aided by a glucan coating secreted during the growth process, which allows the hyphae to bind to the wood cell wall, and specifically to the S_3 layer (Illman and Highley, 1989). By linking onto the S_3 layer, the fungus can directly attack and severely degrade the S_2 layer, which has a lower lignin level than both the S_1 and S_3 layers respectively. This fairly rapid degradation of the cellulosic components can lead to a catastrophic strength loss, as much as 70% of the modulus of elasticity (MOE) and modulus of rupture (MOR) (Wilcox et al., 1974).

The mechanism for brown rot decay is understood to be based on the Fenton reaction, and the basic principles have been well reviewed by Arantes and Goodell (2014). Modified wood is still recognised as a possible nutrient source for fungal degradation, since fungi induce genes that are involved in cellulose degradation to even higher levels than in untreated wood (Alfredsen and Fossdal, 2010; Pilgård et al., 2012; Ringman et al., 2014). In some wood modifications, micro-pores are partly blocked, but it has been calculated that the low molecular weight molecules needed for oxidative degradation should be able to penetrate the modified wood (Hill et al., 2005). The next step is the diffusion of these low molecular weight molecules into the wood cell wall, though it has yet to be determined whether this occurs in modified wood. It is possible that the moisture levels inside the wood cell wall are too low to allow diffusion.

Recent work (Ringman et al., 2019) has emphasised the importance of moisture in the brown rot attacks on modified wood, with an emphasis on the *Fenton reaction* allowing hydrogen peroxide produced by the fungus to initiate the formation of hydroxyl radicals capable of degrading the hemicelluloses, although the mechanism of attack has still to be identified. The modes of action suggested to date (Zelinka et al., 2016) include (i) inhibition of diffusion through an increase in the glass-transition temperature of hemicelluloses (assumed to be the medium of transport); (ii) inhibition of diffusion by nano-pore blocking; (iii) no inhibition of diffusion but instead a lower rate of diffusion and/or inhibition of chemical reactions leading up to the Fenton reaction through alteration of the pH level, for example.

Moisture has been recognised as a key parameter in the infestation and decay of wood by wood destroying fungi. In addition to the supply of oxygen, a favourable temperature, and accessible nutrients, it is an essential factor in the fungal decay of wooden commodities and structures. For many decades, it was therefore essential to define the critical moisture content thresholds allowing the transport and activity of fungal enzymes in the wood cell walls leading to the degradation and severe rot of wooden elements. Nowadays, the wood moisture content is the most important input variable in many service life and performance prediction models, both in engineering and natural sciences (Brischke and Thelandersson, 2014).

Degradation models and service life

The group of wood-degrading organisms includes termites, wood-boring beetles, marine borers and various wood-destroying fungi and bacteria, all of which need to be considered when defining the natural durability of timber. In principal, this natural durability can be determined either in the field or in the laboratory by various standardised and non-standardised methods (Råberg et al., 2005; Brischke et al., 2011b; Curling, 2017). While laboratory tests require clearly defined conditions which give a high level of reproducibility, it is usually impossible to fully mimic real life conditions. On the one hand, there is a risk of creating a test scenario that is too severe in terms of moisture and temperature, which are ideal for the degrading organism and have been criticised as 'torture testing' (e.g., Brischke et al., 2011b). On the other hand, some parameters having an important impact on the degradation process cannot be considered adequately, for instance, the detoxification through so-called 'non-target organisms' or the limited number of test organisms considered in European test standards, which are not necessarily responsible for decay under real life situations.

It is generally accepted that field tests provide more realistic test conditions, but they often suffer from unacceptably long test durations. In-ground tests with buried stakes need at least five years to give an indication of the effectiveness of a wood preservative (Larsson-Brelid et al., 2011; Hansson et al., 2013), but the onset of decay in above-ground trials takes place significantly later, and service lives cannot be calculated before decades have passed (Wang et al., 2008; Brischke et al., 2012). For these reasons, the results of laboratory decay tests as well as field test data from in-ground graveyard tests are often presented, and natural durability studies with respect to above-ground exposure are rare, although they play a more important role in timber engineering. When considering moisture risk, the effects of mould and surface disfiguration must also be taken into account.

Three recent European projects—*PerformWOOD*, *Wood Build* and *Timber Bridges*—have attempted to determine issues related to moisture risk and the service of timber products. These projects have looked at a wide variety of timbers (both untreated and treated), but only in recent years has modified wood undergone a critical evaluation.

PerformWOOD: The objective of the project was to kick-start the development of new standards to make possible the service life specification of wood and wood-based materials for construction. This is critical to ensure the future sustainable use of European forests, to ensure that customers of wood products receive satisfactory and reliable products and to provide supplementary evidence of life cycle evaluations of construction products (e.g., Environmental Product Declarations).

Figure 1.68 Sneek bridge in The Netherlands, constructed using Accoya™.

Wood Build: The overall objective of the project was to raise awareness and to disseminate knowledge and expertise on damp proofing and, from the viewpoint of resistance, durable wood materials for the construction industry, in order to strengthen the competitiveness of timber as a building material. This will be achieved through the production of new knowledge that enhances our understanding of the link between climate exposure and the resistance of wood to biological attack.

Timber Bridges: The project considered the increased use of wood for bridge construction, emphasised by the building of some 650 timber bridges in Sweden alone in the past 15 years. Naturally, a strong emphasis must be placed on the durability and performance of the materials used, adopting best practice for the prevention of moisture uptake and the risk of decay. The construction of the Sneek bridge in The Netherlands using Accoya™ acetylated wood (Figure 1.68) has demonstrated how modified wood may help in overcoming some of the issues linked to premature failure.

Fungal testing of modified wood

The complexity of testing the durability of wood results from the different areas and exposure situations in which wood is used. Wood is used for constructions in the building sector ranging from simple constructions like range-land fences to more complex balconies and recently also roller coasters and multi-storey buildings. These different constructions and their specific components are accompanied by a wide range of different loads, where the decisive loads responsible for the risk of damage can be reduced to moisture, temperature and the presence of wood-destroying organisms. The first step in classifying a wooden component with respect to an expected load is to distinguish between in-ground and above-ground exposure. Numerous tests have been conducted all over the world and have been described in the literature referring to both of these exposure conditions (e.g., Fougerousse, 1976; De Groot, 1992; Fredriksson, 2010; Brischke et al., 2012). The ones referring to above-ground exposure have been less frequently used to determine durability and only a few have been standardised. The reason for this can be found in the long exposure periods for above-ground tests compared to in-ground tests. Testing wood durability exclusively in ground is however in contrast to the fact that most timber products in outdoor use are exposed above ground, e.g., façades, terrace decking, windows, balconies and carports (Blom and Bergström, 2005; Friese et al., 2009). A range of different standardised test methods have been drawn up and applied over the years (Table 1.12) but they have dealt exclusively with naturally occurring wood or material that has been subjected to a traditional wood preservation procedure.

To overcome this drawback a comparative study on the moisture performance and resulting decay response has been conducted (Meyer et al., 2013). Five different wood species were used in 27 different test set-ups representing a wide range of different exposure situations. The test set-up included established and standardised test methods (e.g., L-Joint test, decking test, ground proximity test) as well as some new test methods. Figure 1.69 shows schematic drawings of various tests conducted to date. A more comprehensive overview including the dimensions and details of the exposure conditions and specimen compositions of all the test methods is given by Meyer et al. (2013). This work expanded the methodologies and data available for exposed wood, which

Table 1.12 Standardised tests involving fungal decay of wood (modified from Brischke et al., 2013).

Standard	Title of standard
CEN/TS 15083-1	Durability of wood and wood-based products. Determination of the natural durability of solid wood against wood-destroying fungi, test methods. Basidiomycetes
CENT/TS 15083-2	Durability of wood and wood-based products. Determination of the natural durability of solid wood against wood-destroying fungi, test methods. Soft rotting micro-fungi
EN 113	Wood preservatives - Method of test for determining the protective effectiveness against wood destroying basidiomycetes - Determination of the toxic values
ENV 807	Wood preservatives - Determination of the effectiveness against soft rotting micro-fungi and other soil-inhabiting micro-organisms
TS 12404	Durability of wood and wood-based products - Assessment of the effectiveness of a masonry fungicide to prevent growth into wood of dry rot *Serpula lacrymans* (Schumacher ex Fries) F.S. Gray
EN 15457	Paints and varnishes - Laboratory method for testing the efficacy of film preservatives in a coating against fungi
EN 152	Wood preservatives - Determination of the protective effectiveness of a preservative treatment against blue stain in wood in service
CEN/TS 839	Wood preservatives - Determination of the protective effectiveness against wood destroying basidiomycetes - Application by surface treatment
AWPA E 10	Standard method of testing wood preservatives by laboratory soil-block cultures
ENV 12038	Durability of wood and wood-based products - Wood-based panels - Method of test for determining the resistance against wood-destroying basidiomycetes
JIS K 1571	Wood preservatives - Performance requirements and test methods for determining their effectiveness

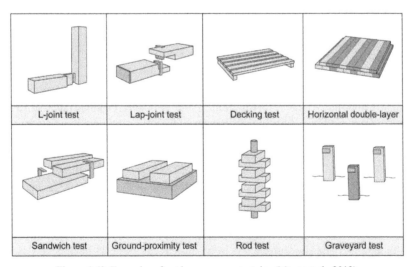

Figure 1.69 Examples of outdoor exposure test rigs (Meyer et al., 2013).

are being further applied to modified wood are developing the understanding of decay in both laboratory and field trials, as previously reported by Alfredsen and Westin (2009).

Minimum moisture thresholds and other physiological requirements of decay fungi were sought in field tests (Scheffer, 1971; Van den Bulcke et al., 2009; Meyer-Veltrup et al., 2017) as well as in experiments under laboratory conditions (Viitanen, 1997; Viitanen et al., 2010). The general consensus is that water availability in the cell walls is critical, but not necessarily in the cell lumens (Schmidt, 2006; Stienen et al., 2014).

Understanding the decay mechanisms due to fungal attack is essential in helping to predict building performance and the durability of wood components. The use of modified wood has the potential to provide additional durability. While the use of existing methods and standards provides a comparative performance factor against reference material, the modes of attack used in a particular standard may differ for modified wood compared to that suitable for untreated or preservative-treated materials. It has been suggested by several research groups at previous European Conferences on Wood Modification that modified wood should be considered as a new wood species. Since there may be issues to the means by which material-moisture interactions occur, and the fact that degradative pathways are blocked due to the inability of a decay organism to recognise the matrix means there is the need to undertake a systematic programme of research at laboratory and field study levels to determine how to correctly access the service life of modified wood products.

Biological degradation of wood by invertebrate organisms

Lignocellulosic materials, such as wood, are often used by insects for food, shelter and breeding, the most common lignocellulose-destroying insects belonging to Coleoptera (beetles) and Blattodea: Isoptera (termites) orders. They are referred to as wood-eating (xylophagous) insects, which means that they cannot live without wood or other lignocellulosic materials. Attack is not limited to above or in- or above-ground cases. Marine decay also occurs through the attack of worms or gribble.

Wood-boring insects

All insects have a similar structure. They have three pair of legs (gr. *Hexapoda*) and segmented bodies supported by exoskeletons, the hard outer covering being mostly chitin. The segments of the body are organised into three distinctive but interconnected units or tagmata: a head (the caput), a chest (the thorax) and the posterior (the abdomen). The insects pass through a metamorphic transformation during their life span. Beetles undergo four developmental stages (holometabolism), egg, larvae, pupa and adult (imago). Eggs are laid within the wooden structure, and they hatch and the subsequent larval and pupal stages are spent within the wood structure, from which nourishment is obtained. Most beetles are defined by having part of the hardened exterior forming the front wings (elytra), defining them within the family Coleoptera

The powderpost beetles are members of the *Lyctinae* subfamily within the *Bostrichidae* family, of which over 20 species have been identified, including *Lyctus brunneus* (brown powderpost beetle). Whilst it now has a global distribution, it was probably originally native to Central and South America. The common furniture beetle (woodworm, *Anobium punctatum*) spread from Europe to areas with similar climatic conditions, mainly as a result of colonisation over the past 300 years. In the larval stage, it bores into seasoned sapwood between 12–16% moisture content and feeds upon it. The adults are between 3.0 and 4.5 mm in length and have brown ellipsoidal bodies with a prothorax resembling a monk's cowl. Because of the risk to sapwood, some building regulations state that timber with more than 25% sapwood may not be used, in order to limit the risk of loss of structural integrity through wood-borer infection. The death watch beetle, *Xestobium rufovillosum*, is a species of wood-boring beetle that sometimes infests the structural timbers of old buildings, although its natural occurrence is in broad-leaved trees that have been dead for around 60 years. It has been suggested that this is due to fungal decay with an associated softening of the wood constituents and increased digestibility. Infestation in European oak has been associated with its colonisation by the fungus *Donkioporia expansa*. The death watch beetle originated in regions in Europe, but is now also present in USA. The house longhorn beetle (*Hylotrupes bajulus*) originated in Europe, and has been spread in timber and wood products as colonisation and emigration have progressed, so that it now has a practically world-wide distribution, including southern Africa, Asia, the Americas, Australia, and much of Europe and the Mediterranean. *Hylotrupes bajulus* preferentially attacks freshly produced sapwood of timber, though there have been cases of attack of the sapwood of certain broad-leaved species such as oak. In conifers such as Norway spruce, it also attacks the heartwood. An excellent summary of the attack by various wood-boring insects

Table 1.13 Some common wood-boring insects (modified from Blanchette, 1998).

Insect	Wood	Distinguishing characteristics
Common furniture beetle, *Anobium*	Sapwood of conifers and broad-leaved woods. May attack heartwood if fungal decay is present	Meandering tunnels 1–2 mm in diameter, often in direction of grain, filled with frass consisting of oval pellets and wood powder.
Lyctus, powderpost beetle	Sapwood of broad-leaved woods with large vessels, such as oak and elm	Damage in sapwood with high starch content. Circular tunnels 1–2 mm in diameter, usually parallel to the grain, filled with fine powder.
Bostrychid powderpost beetle	Sapwood of tropical timbers	Convoluted tunnels 3–6 mm in diameter, packed with fine powder.
Wood-boring weevil	Decayed conifer and broad-leaved woods	Tunnels 1 mm in diameter, orientated in the direction of the grain, with fine, granular powder.
Ptilinus beetle	Sapwood of broad-leaved woods	Meandering tunnels 1–2 mm in diameter, packed with fine bore dust.
Death watch beetle	Sapwood and heartwood of decayed broad-leaved woods	Tunnels variable in diameter from 0.5–3 mm, randomly orientated but common in the direction of the grain. Bore dust consists of fine, disc-shaped pellets.
House longhorn beetle, cerambycid beetle	Sapwood of conifers	Tunnels 6–10 mm in diameter with similar-sized oval emergence holes. Bore dust contains cylindrical pellets with fragments of wood. Most of the sapwood may be consumed, with just a veneer of surface wood left.

Figure 1.70 Common adult wood-boring beetles that can damage wood, from the left: True powder-post beetle (*Lyctus brunneus*), Woodworm or common furniture beetle (*Anobium punctatum*), Death watch beetle (*Xestobium rufovillosum*), and House longhorn beetle (*Hylotrupes bajulus*) (Wikipedia Commons, and BioLib.cz.).

was provided by Blanchette (1998), and it is shown in Table 1.13, with some examples of beetles in Figure 1.70.

Termites

Termites (Blattodea; formerly Isoptera) are consumers of cellulose and lignocellulose found in dead wood, grass, microepiphytes, leaf litter, and sometimes cultivated fungi. Some 3,000 species of termites have been described, most having a tropical and temperate distribution across the USA, central America, most of South America, southern Europe, Africa, Middles East, Southern Asia, Japan and Oceania. Figure 1.71 shows the global distribution of the three species most responsible for structural damage, namely *Coptotermes formosanus*, *Coptotermes gestroi* and *Cryptotermes brevis* (Rust and Su, 2012). Of these 3,000 species, only 83 are considered to present a risk to wooden structures and furniture (Rust and Su, 2012).

As can be seen in Figure 1.71, Europe lies on the border of traditional termite presence, but there are concerns as to how global warming may affect their distribution and spread then into more northern areas. A more detailed European distribution is shown in Figure 1.72 (Kutnik et al., 2020),

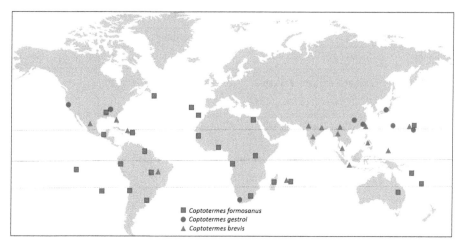

Figure 1.71 Distributions of the three most economically important and widely distributed termite pest species: *Coptotermes formosanus*, *Coptotermes gestroi*, and *Cryptotermes brevis* (Rust and Su, 2012) (Global map downloaded from www. presentationgo.com).

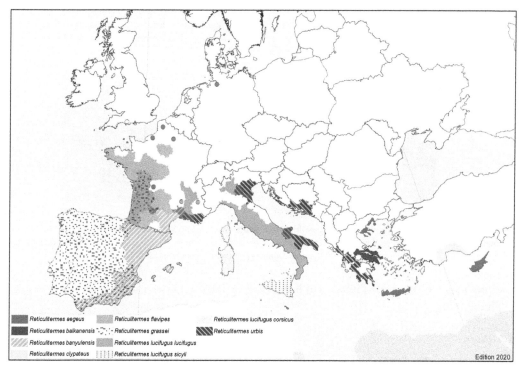

Figure 1.72 European distribution of termite species (courtesy of Magdalena Kutnik).

which shows the traditional range of a variety of *Reticulitermes* species. Additional sites outside these ranges have however occurred as a result of human activity and the importation of infected timber. This was the case with the infestation of *Reticulitermes flavipes* in Hamburg, Germany, a common termite in the eastern part of the USA, which established a colony in the city in the 1930s, taking advantage of the warm, moist conditions in the district heating system. Another species, *Reticulitermes grassei*, normally found in south-western France, Spain and Portugal, was identified in infested timber in Devon, England in the 1960s, but it has been suggested that this was a case of natural colonisation from France.

Traditionally, termites are classified into lower and higher termites, where the higher termites have undergone more evolutionary changes and live in more advanced social structures and colonies. Lower termites include eight families (*Mastotermitidae, Archotermopsidae, Hodotermitidae, Stolotermitidae, Kalotermitidae, Stylotermitidae, Rhinotermitidae,* and *Serritermitidae*), whereas higher termites belong to a single family, *Termitidae* (Engel, 2011). A detailed description of the types of termites and their economic and environmental impacts is available (e.g., Govorushko, 2019).

Termites are highly effective at processing biomass and are estimated to process up to 35% of dead wood in the tropics (Verma et al., 2009), and another study of tropical and subtropical areas has suggested that termites account for 10% of animal biomass and 95% of soil insect biomass (Donovan et al., 2007). Their activities create favourable conditions for primary producers, including maintaining soil pH, increasing water retention, mediating decomposition and nutrient cycling, and creating surface areas suitable for microbial colonisation. However, the desire to source suitable feedstocks has led to problems where timber has been used in construction and our built environment. Some species of termites feed on plant material and timber used by humans, necessitating expensive repairs, prevention and control efforts. Termites may also damage materials adjoining or close to timber that is being attacked for food, and this can create problems with items such as electrical and telephone wiring, cables, dams and farming equipment. One study (Jones et al., 2015) has suggested that a colony of 200,000 termites can consume up to 5.9 kg of cellulose per year. It is estimated that worldwide the costs for termite control and repair are round $30 billion (Rust and Su, 2012), most of these costs (80%) being associated with subterranean termites.

Marine wood borers

Marine wood borers have long been recognised for the damage the caus to wooden boats and infrastructures in maritime conditions. The marine wood borers are known to include *Bivalvia* (*Teredinidae* and *Xylophagaidae*), *Isopoda* (*Limnoriidae* and *Sphaeromatidae*), and *Amphipoda* (*Cheluridae*) Treu et al. (2019). Some examples of these are shown in Figure 1.73. In Europe most wood boring bivalves belong to the *Teredinidae* class, but species of the *Xylophagaidae*, such as *Xylophaga dorsalis*, have also been reported near the sea-bed in Europe (Santhakumaran and Sneli, 1978). Attack by *teredinids* is difficult to detect with the naked eye, but a magnifying glass can easily reveal entrance holes of larvae. The degree of attack is usually analysed by X-ray computer tomography, when a non-destructive evaluation is required (Charles et al., 2018), but it can also be investigated by density measurements or strength determination as well as by wood sample preparation and borer species identification (Turner, 1966).

The European wood boring *Crustacea* belong to the *Limnoriidae* and *Cheluridae* families. Their attack pattern is shaped by their tunnelling activities on the wood surface and it is usually easier to detect with the naked eye than shipworm attack. In combination with wave action in the tidal zone, wooden piles develop an hour-glass shape. More recent reviews of the potential attack by wood borers in a marine environment have been given for *Limnoriidae* by Cookson (1990) and Cragg (2003) and for *Teredinidae* by Distel (2003) and Voight (2015), where the authors provide the current state of knowledge of the biogeography, competition and predation among wood borers and the role of bacterial endosymbionts.

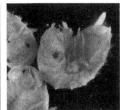

Figure 1.73 Examples of marine wood borers, from the left: *Limnoria quadripunctata* (courtesy of Graham Malyon), *Neoteredo reynei* (courtesy of Reuben Shipway), and *Sphaeroma terebans* (All images printed with permission of University of Portsmouth, U.K.).

Mechanism of decay due to insects

Many wood-destroying insects use wood not only as a food source but also as a home, in some cases for the adult insects but more commonly for juvenile (larval) growth. Very few of these insects can digest wood with their own enzymes and even then they are not very effective in their action. For this reason, it seems that most wood-boring insects have evolved a complex symbiosis with micro-organisms specialised in the degradation of wood components (Battisti, 2001).

In the case of *Hylotrupes bajulus*, early studies suggested that the secretion of cellulase allowed the enzymatic digestion of about 20% of the cellulose and hemicelluloses of the wood that was attacked the remaining indigestible 80%, including all the lignin components, being expelled with the faeces (Falck, 1930). Further studies at that time suggested that there were no micro-organisms in the gut and, therefore, that the cellulose is endogenous (Mansour and Mansour-Bek, 1934; Müller, 1934). With more sensitive analytical methods, however, the presence of glucosidase and carboxy methylcellulases (CMC-ase) activity throughout the whole *Hylotrupes* gut was demonstrated (but more pronounced in the foregut), with only a small number of bacteria being present in the midgut, suggesting the endogenous nature of the cellulolytic enzymes (Cazemier et al., 1997). The presence of beta-glucans in the faecal matter was interpreted as proof that starches did not form part of the nutritional needs of the insects (Höll et al., 2002). Since the lignin components remain intact during the colonisation and growth of *Hylotrupes baljulus* larvae, it has been suggested that the composition of the lignin and the presence of terpenoid extractives as a result of tree maturity increase the resistance to insect attack (Venäläinen et al., 2003). In order to gain access to the genetics and physiology of uncultured micro-organisms, the use of metagenomics, which enables the isolation of bacterial genomic DNA from an environment followed by its direct analysis, has emerged as a powerful identification technique (Handelsman, 2004).

In the case of *Anobium punctatum*, it was found (Baker, 1969) that 26–29% of the wood consumed by the larvae was digested. This is slightly higher than for *Hylotrupes bajulus*, but the more significant fact was that the levels of nitrogen was more than double the level available in the digested timber. The mechanism for this is still not fully understood, but it has been suggested that the mechanism involves atmospheric nitrogen, although more recently the presence of gut symbionts has been suggested. The level of decay of the timber also plays a significant role in this mechanism, particularly for *Anobium punctatum*, where the nitrogen within the fungal decay enzymes provides the required level. The role of microbial symbionts within insects has been evaluated in terms of biological nitrogen fixation within terrestrial ecosystems (Nardi et al., 2002). A review of a range of symbiotic mechanisms for different woodboring insects has been published (Chiappini and Aldini, 2011), covering ectosymbiosis, extracellular endosymbiosis and endocytobiosis.

As has been suggested for *Anobium punctatum*, fungal decay can contribute significantly towards the ease of digestibility for insects. Historically, this could pose a problem for timber used in high moisture conditions, as demonstrated in Table 1.14, where temperature and moisture thresholds have been identified (Brischke and Unger, 2017). However, the increase in central heating and more controlled moisture levels in buildings have led to a reduction in the risk of insects such as *Anobium punctatum*.

Many termites feed exclusively on wood, despite its low nutritional level and poor nitrogen content. This can be overcome through a symbiotic relationship with gut protists or flagellates, providing the bacterial capability to break down the wood components, and thus helping the overall

Table 1.14 Typical survival conditions for some wood-boring insects (Brischke and Unger, 2017).

Species	Moisture content (%)			Temperature (°C)			
	Min.	Optimum	Max.	Min.	Optimum	Max.	Lethal
Anobium punctatum	10–12	28–30	50–57	12	21–24	29	50–57
Hylotrupes bajulus	9–10	30–40	65–80	16–19	28–30	35	55–57
Lyctus brunneus	7–8	14–16	23	18	26–27	30	49–65

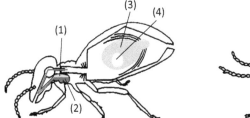 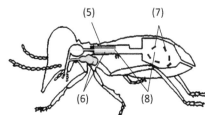

Figure 1.74 Comparison of degradative pathways of lower termites (left) and higher termites (right). Modified after Tokuda (2019). Lower termites (flagellate-harbouring): (1) Endo-β-1,4-glucanases (EGs) that primarily hydrolyse amorphous cellulose. (2) β-glucosidases (BGs) that hydrolyse cellobiose into glucose. (3) Protistan cellulases, hemicellulasesand cellobiohydrolases that actively hydrolyse crystalline cellulose, xylanases, and mannanases that participate in hemicellulose degradation. (4) Cellulose and hemicellulose digestion (in the midgut lumen and protistan cells). Higher termites (flagellate-free): (5) Endo-β-1,4-glucanases (EGs) that primarily hydrolyse amorphous cellulose are secreted in the midgut. (6) β-glucosidases (BGs) that hydrolyse cellobiose into glucose are secreted both in the salivary glands and the midgut. (7) Hindgut bacteria producing cellulases and hemicellulases; xylanases and cellulases are predominantly expressed in the fibre-associated bacterial community. (8) Cellulose and hemicellulose digestion (in the midgut and hindgut lumen).

digestion process, since termites often have their own endemic enzymes, such as endoglucanases and cellobiases. Lower termites harbour flagellated cellulolytic protists in the hindgut, whereas the higher termites have lost the protists but have a greater range of gut microbes. The digestive mechanisms of lignocellulose are, thus, differentiated between lower and higher termites in a way that higher termites can also feed on soil and a wider range of plant materials. The differences in indigestion processes between lower and higher termites are shown in Figure 1.74 (Tokuda, 2019).

These are not however sufficient alone and many termite species depend on the flagellate relationship to survive. If these are present within the gut systems, they must be transferred to the larvae, which is done through the larvae eating faecal matter containing these flagellates. The symbiotic relationship has been reviewed elsewhere, e.g., by Brugerolle and Radek (2006) who indicated that two lineages of protozoa exist in termites: the Oxymonadida and the Parabasalia, with more than 400 species identified in total. A more detailed breakdown of the major flagellate protist groups has been given by Duarte et al. (2017).

The flagellates work by breaking down the cellulose and hemicellulose via enzymatic pathways in order to release glucose and other sugar oligomers. These can then undergo secondary conversions (e.g., to pyruvate) or be used directly as energy and food sources. Since each flagellate has a distinct biochemical process, a thorough understanding of these and how certain enzymatic digestion can be limited or even inhibited can in principle offer routes to new biochemical processing for biorefining or even for developing new termiticides. Tartar et al. (2009) have also suggested that for some termites (e.g., *Reticulitermes flavipes*) there is laccase activity present in the foregut and salivary glands and that this aids the digestion of lignocelluose, as has been demonstrated through phenoloxidase activity.

In the case of marine borers, the levels of attack depend on the species and location. In a study of European marine borer activity (Borges, 2014), it was noted that in northern Europe, *Teredo navalis* was the species that posed the highest borer hazard, whereas *Lyrodus pedicellatus* was the most destructive species in the Atlantic coast of southern Europe, with the exception of two sites in Portugal. In those sites, *Limnoria tripunctata* was more destructive than *L. pedicellatus*. In the Mediterranean, both *T. navalis* and *L. pedicellatus* posed very high borer hazards to wooden structures. It has been well documented that the *Limnoria* genus is one of the few animals that can feed on wood without having any gut enzymes present to allow its digestion. Instead it has been suggested that the digestion process is assisted by the presence of hemocyanin, a copper-containing protein thought to be derived from phenoloxidases, recreating the activity of phenoloxidases via a loosening of the tertiary structure, enabling access to the copper-complexed active site. In addition,

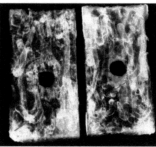

Figure 1.75 Evidence of teredinid attack on wood: the white arrows (left) show the extent of Limnoriid attack, and the red arrows (right) show the presence of shipworms within the wood structure (Borges, 2014) (courtesy of Luisa Borges).

it has been shown (Besser et al., 2018) that glycosyl hydrolases (GHs) are present, and in particular GH7 and GH9, which account for over 50% of the soluble GHs in the gut fluids.

Shipworms, such as *Teredo navalis*, have historically caused major problems for wood immersed in sea-water, as can be seen in Figure 1.75. As with *Limnoriids*, they have been found to be devoid of symbiotic microbres assisting in the enzymatic digestion of wood, but have a variety of carbohydrate active enzymes produced by endosymbiotic bacteria housed in specialised cells (bacteriocytes) in the animal's gills. The range of these glycosyl hydrolases is much wider than those found in *Limnoriids*. Earlier work by Hashimoto and Onoma (1949) showed the presence of cellulase, alginase and xylanase activity in the "liver" of Teredo worms, and Mawatari (1950) also reported the presence of amylase, cellulase, cellobiase, saccharase and maltase in the midgut.

Test methods for the risk of insect attack and the use of modified wood

Until recently, the main method for preventing insect damage to timber in constructions and in the built environment has been through the use of wood preservatives. This is clearly demonstrated by the test methods currently employed, as shown in Table 1.15, a thorough description of these methods being given by Curling (2017).

Table 1.15 Typical test methods used in the analysis of insect attack on wood.

Standard	Title of standard
EN 117	Wood preservatives: Determination of toxic values against *Reticulitermes* species (European termites)
EN 118	Wood preservatives: Determination of preventive action against *Reticulitermes* species (European termites)
ASTM D3345	Standard test method for laboratory evaluation of wood and other cellulosic materials for resistance to termites
AWPA E1	Standard field test for evaluating the termite resistance of wood-based materials: Choice and no-choice tests.
JIS K 1571	Test methods for determining the effectiveness of wood preservatives and their performance requirement
EN 46	Wood preservatives: Determination of the preventive action against recently hatched larvae of *Hylotrupes bajulus* (L.)
EN 47	Wood preservatives: Determination of the toxic values against larvae of *Hylotrupes bajulus* (L.)
EN 370	Wood preservatives: Determination of eradicant efficacy in preventing emergence of *Anobium punctatum* (De Geer)
EN 49	Wood preservatives: Determination of the protective effectiveness against *Anobium punctatum* (De Geer) by egg-laying and larval survival
EN 20	Wood preservatives: Determination of the effectiveness against *Lyctus brunneus* (Stephens)
EN 275	Wood preservatives: Determination of the protective effectiveness of preservatives against marine borers

Although there is a standard test for marine borers (EN 275), the testing of marine borers is generally based on design specifications put forward by whoever is conducting the test. EN 275 is a field trial method limited by the need to have active marine borers present, and this limits the number of sites that can be used for this test. The limnoriids *L. quadripunctata* or *L. tripunctata* and the teredinid *L. pedicellatus* are suitable for laboratory tests focused on wood for use in temperate to warm-temperate marine climate. Meaningful results can be gained within a month of experimentation. Tests using individual *Limnoriids* allow sufficient biological replication for determining optima in treatment variables. It has, however, been found that tests using feeder blocks with a colony of *Limnoriids* do not have a well-defined or easily replicated level of borer activity, and, although it has been suggested that laboratory tests can detect differences between experimental treatments relative to the level of attack on control blocks, such tests cannot be used to predict service life. Hence, for marine borers, it is necessary to undertake marine trials, under the caveat that only treatments causing the greatest mortality or reduction in feeding are valid.

The use of modified wood in limiting insect decay

As the production of modified wood has increased, its range of possible uses has also expanded, and it has become necessary to undertake a range of evaluations to see whether the material is fit for use and can provide the necessary service life. Given that wood modification has the ability to alter the chemical constituents of the wood as well as to reduce the equilibrium moisture content, it is logical to expect that wood modification techniques are capable of reducing insect decay by rendering the material inedible and/or by reducing the level of moisture needed for enzymatic processing. Evaluations are still ongoing, but known results relating to each modification method are given in their respective chapters. Attack by termites is still a matter of study, given that tests are often carried out on only small colonies and these may give incorrect results. It has been suggested (Kutnik et al., 2009) that such methodologies are not always relevant, especially when the tests are performed under laboratory conditions, since the reported mortality rates in isolated groups of termites do not reflect the behaviour of a termite colonies in natural field conditions. Mortality rates in field conditions are always worse than under laboratory conditions. Above ground resistance tests or laboratory tests performed on larger colonies could provide more reliable results. Another concern is that laboratory results based only on insects' mortality cannot provide information about the service life expectations, such as the impact of aesthetic damage, maintenance and expected durability of wooden construction components.

Insect attack, whether on land (above or below soil level) or in water (marine conditions), poses major problems to the use of wood in construction. The test methods currently advocated by testing bodies show that the prevention of attack has to date mainly been limited to the use of preservatives, although naturally durable species have been used in the past. These naturally durable species often come from tropical regions, and this makes their continued use a contentious issue. In addition, the leachability of preservatives into the surroundings has raised concern over the use of many historically effective treatments.

The use of modified wood continues to gain market acceptance in many cases, and there is a growing amount of data supporting its performance against insects. Further improvements in testing methodology may help increase these opportunities, or at least ensure that the correct treatment and usage has been ascribed to a particular wood product.

1.6 Weathering of wood

As a bio-based material, wood will eventually break down into its constituent components. In its natural environment, wood is protected from exterior forces by bark, but when it is exposed outdoors in typical construction uses above ground, it undergoes a series of bio-degradative processes linked to its exposure to chemical, mechanical, and light energy factors, resulting in what is known as weathering. Weathering should not however be confused with decay, which results from decay organisms, such as fungi which are able to attack and ultimately destroy wood in the presence of excess moisture and air over an extended period of time. A thorough overview of weathering of wood has already been published (Williams, 2005).

Factors contributing to weathering

Light – Photochemical degradation due to sunlight occurs fairly rapidly on exposed wood surfaces, with the effect increasing with the intensity and duration of exposure. It has been suggested by Tolvaj et al. (2001) that fluctuations in the ozone layer have increased the effects of UV-B irradiation, and this in turn has influenced the use of mercury lamps for artificial weathering tests. The initial effect of UV exposure is a colour change where wood become more yellow as a result of radical-initiated photodegradation of lignin components (Evans et al., 1992; Müller et al., 2003; Turkoglu et al., 2015). These compounds can be further degraded, resulting in compounds with a carbonyl bond conjugated to double bonds, resulting in an FT-IR spectral peak at $1,615$ cm^{-1} (Cogulet et al., 2016). These compounds may be leached with rain/moisture to eventually leave the grey appearance due to the birefringence of cellulose, the optical characteristics of the cellulose having a refractive index which relies on the polarisation and propagation direction of light. Cogulet et al. (2016) used Raman spectroscopy to show that the α and β carbons in lignin are photosensitive, and tend to undergo radical degradation, although there is a noted photoresistance of 5–5′ linkages between diaryl moieties within lignin. These studies also showed that holocellulose undergoes various degrees of photodegradation, although the results were all based on artificial ageing.

The colour variations resulting from photodegradation are caused by surface effects and reactions, and are species dependent. Oberhofnerová et al. (2017) undertook the simultaneous testing of the photodegradaticy of multiple species in an outdoor weathering experiment in Prague, Czech Republic. The results (Table 1.16) show that the lowest degree of discolouration was observed for English oak and the highest for Norway spruce. The depth of the colour changes was relatively similar among the conifers, but greater variations were noted with the broad-leaved woods. The values given in Table 1.16 are calculated as:

$$\Delta E = \sqrt{\Delta L^2 + \Delta a^2 + \Delta b^2} \tag{1.6}$$

where ΔL, Δa and Δb are, respectively, the differences in the L*, a* and b* coordinates of the CIELAB colour system.

When wood has a high content of extractives, the chemical processes leading to the colour changes tend to take place fairly quickly, wheres those with a low extractives content tend to be slower but more consistent in overall speed. It has been suggested that the initial increase in b* value indicates the degradation of lignin (Evans et al., 1992; Müller et al., 2003; Turkoglu et al., 2015).

Table 1.16 Colour variations from photodegradation. Mean values and standard deviation (in parentheses) for 24 measurements.

Wood species	1 month		3 months		6 months		12 months	
	ΔE*	gloss	ΔE*	gloss	ΔE*	gloss	ΔE*	gloss
Black alder	6.4 (2.5)	5.9 (1.2)	7.0 (2.5)	5.8 (1.9)	20.9 (2.5)	7.6 (2.2)	27.0 (2.8)	5.9 (2.1)
Black locus	8.8 (0.9)	6.9 (1.1)	12.5 (1.6)	7.0 (1.3)	16.0 (1.5)	9.0 (1.3)	29.6 (2.0)	6.3 (1.2)
Douglas fir	10.5 (0.8)	6.4 (0.8)	10.9 (1.4)	6.3 (1.0)	16.0 (1.3)	8.5 (1.3)	28.1 (1.6)	7.3 (1.2)
English oak	3.2 (0.7)	6.9 (0.7)	4.0 (1.5)	8.0 (1.4)	12.7 (1.5)	11.4 (2.0)	23.0 (1.2)	5.6 (0.8)
European larch	11.3 (2.9)	5.7 (1.2)	12.7 (3.8)	5.5 (1.5)	17.9 (2.7)	8.9 (2.4)	30.5 (2.6)	7.0 (1.6)
Norway spruce	11.4 (0.7)	12.9 (2.1)	13.9 (0.9)	12.7 (2.7)	18.3 (0.8)	16.3 (1.5)	34.1 (0.9)	9.3 (1.7)
Poplar	7.5 (1.3)	10.5 (0.8)	7.8 (2.8)	10.7 (1.1)	18.9 (5.9)	12.1 (2.1)	33.6 (2.5)	7.3 (1.5)
Scots pine	8.3 (2.1)	8.5 (0.9)	10.8 (1.8)	9.4 (1.7)	15.8 (2.4)	14.3 (2.3)	28.9 (2.3)	9.5 (1.9)
Sycamore maple	5.2 (0.7)	10.4 (2.1)	2.9 (0.6)	11.9 (1.2)	11.7 (2.1)	15.8 (2.1)	28.5 (1.6)	9.3 (1.5)

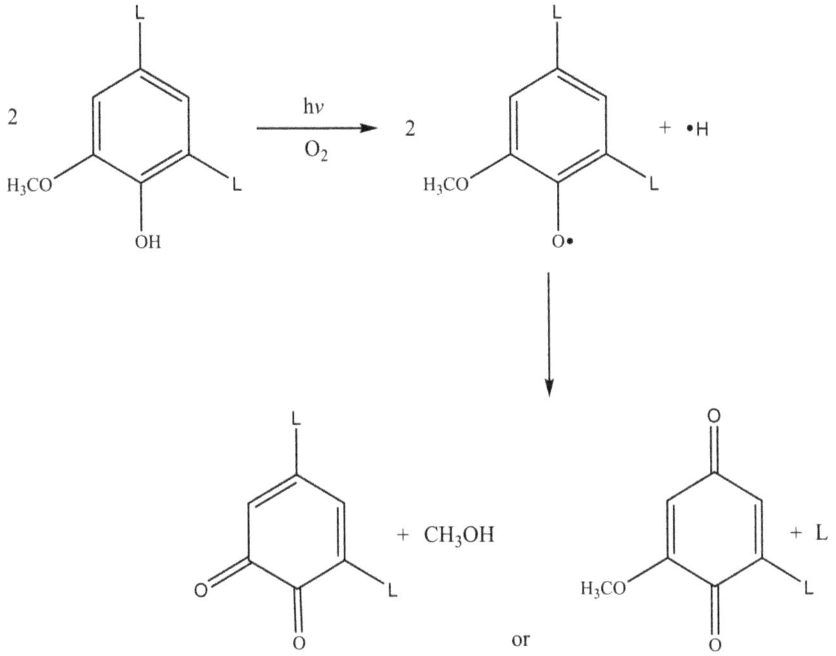

Figure 1.76 Proposed lignin photo-degradation mechanism by Anderson et al. (1991).

The subsequent decrease in yellowness may be attributed to the leaching by water of decomposed lignin and extractives (Turkoglu et al., 2015). The changes in a* values are determined mainly by the changes in the chromophore groups in the extractives. The results confirmed that in the early stages of weathering, dark woods tend to become light and light woods to become dark or turn into the silver grey colour (Dawson et al., 2008; Saei et al., 2015).

These photodegradative changes were initially thought (Hon and Ifju, 1978) to be limited to the outer 75–200 μm of the wood, but subsequent work (Kataoka and Kiguchi, 2001) has shown evidence of photo-induced degradation with extended exposure time at depths of around 500 μm. Figure 1.76 shows one example of a lignin photo-degradation mechanism given by Anderson et al. (1991), which suggested that lignin fragments can be activated via quinone methide intermediates which then undergo attack by light-induced radicals. It has also been proposed that, as a result of further photochemical cleavage of the C-C bonds adjacent to carbonyl groups, small, water-soluble, and leachable chemical compounds can be generated and removed during wetting cycles.

Moisture – One of the principal causes of weathering is the frequent exposure of the wood surface to rapid changes in moisture content. Indoor climates tend to be fairly constant in terms of their moisture content, except for areas with high moisture or liquid water (e.g., bathrooms, saunas, kitchens) or as the result of water leakage. In exterior use, wood is more prone to exposure to great variations in moisture, particularly if exposed in Use Class 3 situations, when direct rain or dew falling upon an unprotected surface is quickly absorbed by capillary action into the surface layer of the wood, followed by adsorption within the wood cell walls. The penetrative effect of the rain and moisture depends on the severity and time during which the wood undergoes the wetting process, and the dimensions of the wood element also contribute to the overall effect of wetting through the cross section of the material. The adsorptive uptake and release of water by the wood results in swelling and shrinkage, accentuated by changes in the climatic conditions, particularly when a wetting episode is immediately followed by exposure to direct sunshine. This results in stresses between the surface and the (often) drier interior, which can result in distortion or checking. The grain can rise as a result of poor wood processing, and differential swelling and shrinkage of the earlywood and latewood subsequently occur when the wood is wetted. The wetting process can also result in lifting of the grain, which also increases the level of leaching from the surface as a result of the UV-degradative process due to exposure to light. As the surface becomes more stressed, cracking leads to moisture ingress below the surface layers where photodegradation has occurred, opening up new sites for photodegradation as well as creating sites for possible colonisation by staining and decay fungi.

Building location – The position of a building and the exposure of its wooden elements can have a significant role on the weathering (micro-climate), degradation and performance of the material. The major factor is whether materials are in direct sunshine. This is further aggravated by the direction of the prevailing wind (and thus wind-driven rain). Further complications can be created by the channelling effects of surrounding mountains, ridges, tall buildings, etc. Typically, materials such as uncoated timber cladding will become grey over a relatively short period of time, with surfaces having unfavourable orientations undergoing a more rapid and variable weathering. Those having a less severe orientation (e.g., northern facing in the northern hemisphere), weather at a slower rate and more uniformly.

The orientation of a building and its components with respect to prevailing weather conditions significantly influence the periods of wetting experienced by products such as cladding. The ISO 15927-3 (ISO, 2009) standard describes how to determine the hygrothermal performance of buildings and more specifically their vertical surfaces and takes into account factors such as terrain, topography, wind sheltering and the presence of obstructions within close proximity. Many of these factors were also considered within the European-funded WoodBuild project, which considered the performance of a wooden material in terms of decay risks (Isaksson et al., 2015) and factors relating to weathering can be similarly applied.

Building design – In addition the location of a building, its design can also affect the weathering of wood components. The traditional design in a specific region often considers performance and modern design methods may pose a great stress on the performance of the materials. The use of eaves can help protect timbers from weathering from sunshine and excessive wetting (and ultimately from decay) but at the risk of creating different degrees of photodegradation and staining on a surface. This can be seen as unsightly by some, although over time all materials tend to achieve a uniform greying. The design should not only take into account how the material can be protected from the effects of exposure, but also how the material recovers after a weathering episode. When exposed to wind-driven rain, this means how long it will take for the material to dry back to normal conditions (i.e., to below the moisture threshold associated with fungal degradation). With timber cladding, ventilation has been shown to provide a better reduction than non-ventilated boards of the risk associated with wetting as shown in Figure 1.77 (Isaksson et al., 2015).

In a similar way, exposure at ground level tends to pose additional problems, not only from increased exposure to sunshine but also increased wetting as a result of splashing. Therefore, it is important to design the construction so that wood products are maintained at a height above ground level. There may also be regions which, due to the design of the building, are subject to splashing— and this can lead to the wood weathering faster. For wooden products, such as cladding, keeping the material at least 250 mm above the ground level is considered to be a practical means of limiting the risk of wetting.

Temperature – Although it is not as critical as UV irradiation or water, the temperature increases as a result of solar exposure and this affects both photochemical and oxidative reactions. Exposing wood to a high temperature after a wetting episode can lead to the rapid drying of the surface creating stresses that increase the risk of splitting and checking, which in turn can accelerate weathering and decay. Similarly, the expansion and contraction of water as a result of freezing and thawing may lead to similar degrees of wood checking.

Other climatic conditions – The effect of wind or wind-driven particles (such as sand) can accelerate the weathering process, and weakened surfaces may suffer fibre losses. This is often noticed as increasing weathering and degradation risk

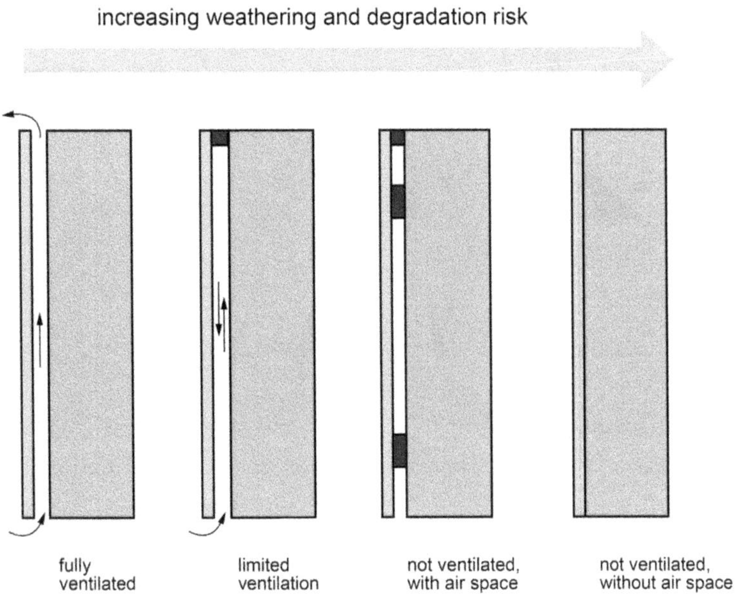

| fully ventilated | limited ventilation | not ventilated, with air space | not ventilated, without air space |

Figure 1.77 The way in which ventilation can alter the performance of timber cladding (modified from Isaksson et al., 2015).

raised grain on a wooden surface, as well as if the timber is coated with a deeply dark colour, which can cause extreme heating of the wood surface when exposed to intensive sunshine.

Human wear and tear – As with climatic abrasion, human use, such as walking on decking, can loosen fibres on surfaces that have undergone a period of weathering.

Effects of weathering

If left untreated, wood will suffer irreversible surface damage due to weathering. This damage can be divided into structural effects and aesthetic effects, both of which often necessitate physical replacement with significant financial implications (Figure 1.78).

Structural effects: the effects of weathering from the microscopic to the macroscopic level can be summarised thus:

Molecular level – UV-initiated degradation of selected bonds (e.g., $-CH_2$, $-CH$ or $-OH$) within the lignin and the generation of carbonyl-containing extractives (Hon and Chang, 1984). In addition, there is evidence (Pandey, 2005) that cellulose can undergo a reduction in the degree of polymerisation, even though the crystalline zones are the most stable.

Cellular level – As the molecular degradation proceeds, there is an increasing effect on the surface of the wood, the degradation being followed by leaching and colonisation of staining fungi (Ghosh et al., 2009), with surface cracking increasing the available sites for such colonisation.

Tissue level – The degree of weathering has been shown to be more rapid in the less dense earlywood than in the latewood, as this leads to an uneven and rougher surface (Williams et al., 2001). In addition, surface cracks can occur on the radial section at the growth-ring border as a result of density variations in the transition zone (Sandberg, 1999).

All these factors contribute towards the overall ageing of the wood leading to a grey appearance when the material exposed over a period of time.

Although the aesthetic aspects of a material are subjected to individual opinions, it is generally accepted that wood has a "feel-good" factor and has links to health and well-being (Burnard and Kutnar, 2015). The most obvious way of evaluating the aesthetic appearance of wood is by visual

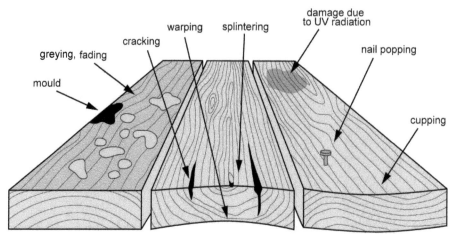

Figure 1.78 Examples of structural and aesthetic damage due to weathering.

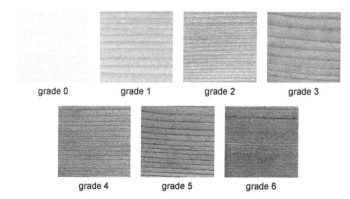

Figure 1.79 A proposed grading system for the degree of weathering of a wood surface (Sandak and Sandak, 2017).

assessment, but this can have a high level of variability, and the conditions under which an evaluation is undertaken can have an impact on the assessment, e.g., the amount of sunshine and dryness of the surface. An attempt to define conditions and provide some degree of quantification has been devised (Osgood et al., 1957), which for a material such as wood depends on the observed colour (or its greyness), surface cracking, checking, erosion, etc. For consistency, it is prudent to undertake evaluations by persons with some degree of training, and preferably to repeat evaluations carried out by the same person. In a recent overview of aesthetics, a grading system for evaluating the degree of weathering on wood was recommended, as shown in Figure 1.79 (Sandak and Sandak, 2017).

One of the key methods for limiting the weathering of wood has been by the application of a coating, such as paint. Here, it suffices to recognise the importance of this topic, and the reader is directed to several key reviews on this subject (Evans et al., 2015; Petrič, 2017; Teaca et al., 2019).

Monitoring weathering

When studying weathering, it is important to consider whether studies have been made under artificial conditions (e.g., by using a climate chamber) or on natural weathering (outdoor exposure). With artificial weathering, specimens are exposed to fixed periods of exposure to UV and driven water to correspond to conditions associated with natural outdoor weathering. However, these methods do not account for wind effects, or for erosion by particulates. Different regions have different climatic conditions, as indicated by the Scheffer Climate Index (Scheffer, 1971). This has been demonstrated with the establishment of several accredited test sites worldwide for the outdoor weathering of various materials, including wood. Table 1.17 shows the different climatic conditions,

Table 1.17 Overview of some accredited weathering test sites, showing the variation in exposure to radiation (McGreer, 2001).

Location	Latitude	Longitude	Elevation (m)	Average ambient temperature (°C)	Average ambient RH (%)	Annual mean rainfall (mm)	Annual mean total radiation exposure (MJ/m²)
Lochem (The Netherlands)	52°30' N	6°30' E	35	9	83	715	3,700
Hoek van Holland (The Netherlands)	51°57' N	4°10' E	6	10	87	800	3,800
Sanary (France)	43°08' N	5°49' E	110	13	64	1,200	5,500
Chenai Airport (Singapore)	1°22' N	103°59' E	15	27	84	2,300	6,030
Melbourne (Australia)	37°49' S	144°58' E	35	16	62	650	5,385
Townsville (Australia)	19°15' S	149°46' E	15	25	70	937	7,236
Ottawa (Canada)	45°20' N	75°41' W	103	6	73	1,910	4,050
Sochi (Russia)	43°27' N	39°57' E	30	14	77	1,390	4,980
Dharan (Saudi Arabia)	26°32' N	50°13' E	92	26	60	80	6,946

but more importantly the annual mean radiation exposure for timber at these sites (McGreer, 2001). Naturally, these conditions can vary on a year-by-year basis, depending on local weather during the timeframe of the exposure trial.

In addition to the test sites listed in Table 1.17, there are a number of other test sites capable of undertaking evaluations according to national and international standards.

The variation in annual mean total radiation exposure shown in Table 1.17 also demonstrates the difficulty in establishing a direct correlation between artificial weathering data and outdoor weathering. According to the European standard EN 927 Part 6 (CEN, 2018), a standard artificial weathering cycle takes a total of 12 cycles each of 1 week. Given these variations, there is no direct correlation between artificial and natural weathering, and the standard EN 927 Part 3 (CEN, 2000) states that the results of this test do not necessarily correlate with those from natural weathering. Both these standards relate to coated wood, but similar concepts apply to uncoated wood. Attempts were made within the WoodExter project (Jermer, 2011) to determine the exposure risks leading to overall decay of wood, taking in account sunshine, temperature, rainfall and prevailing wind conditions, all based on climatic data that could be processed through the computer software Meteonorm. This showed (Figure 1.80) a range of exposure risks across Europe, ranging from 0.6 in northern Scandinavia to 2.1 on the Atlantic coast in southern Europe. It is prudent to acknowledge that the effect of sunshine bleaching the wood surface will be much greater in areas such as southern Europe than in northern Europe, for example, but the overall weathering effect maybe reduced by the limited rainfall and subsequent less leaching of photodegraded components.

Although the monitoring of prevailing conditions can provide an indication of the weathering of a material, accurate results can be obtained only through the actual observation of timber in service. A number of methods have been used to determine the effects of weathering, on a variety of sample sizes. Microtensile testing of microtomed samples has been investigated (Derbyshire et al., 1995; Turkulin et al., 2004) and this initially demonstrated that the method gave a reliable means for determining the photostability of wood, and later how moisture increased the strength loss of the thin strips, although this was sometimes after an initial increase in strength, which was attributed to changes in the cellulose. Further studies of the microtensile strength (Klüppel and Mai, 2018) demonstrated a greater loss of finite-span tensile strength on exposure to sea water, but not of zero-span tensile strength. Furthermore, FTIR of these samples showed higher levels of lignin than in conventionally weathered samples, presumably as a result of the deposition and crystallisation of salt within the cell-wall nanopores, which in turn inhibited lignin photodegradation. Diffuse

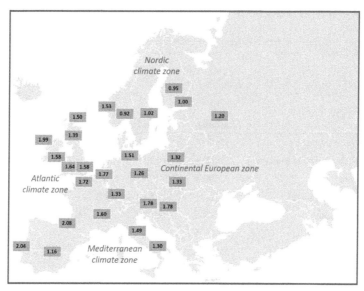

Figure 1.80 Exposure risk for wood product according to Meteonorm data (Jermer, 2011).

Reflectance Infrared Fourier Transform (DRIFT) Spectroscopy (Faix and Nemeth, 1988) used reflectance spectra instead of the conventional transmissive spectra in FTIR. Spectral equipment has now become portable, and handheld systems have made it possible to make field measurements to be taken.

More recently, the use of Near Infrared (NIR) Spectroscopy has gained in popularity and has been used (Sandak et al., 2016) to determine the kinetics involved in the weathering process based on lignin measurements, and thus to suggest weathering index rates for different wood samples. The use of NIR was part of the toolbox of evaluation methods, together with colour measurement, gloss measurement, and the spectral and statistical analysis of artificially weathered samples (Petrillo et al., 2019), showing the potential of a multi-sensor approach.

Although most spectroscopic methods have focussed on an analysis of the photodegradation of lignin, X-ray diffraction in association with FTIR has been applied to assess the cellulose crystallinity in weathered wood (Lionetto et al., 2012). Turkulin (2004) reported the use of scanning electron microscopy (SEM) for evaluating the natural and artificial weathering of wood. For unweathered wood, the mechanical properties of latewood dominated the tensile behaviour of the strips, with tension failure beginning in the latewood via a brittle-like mode (Figure 1.81, left), and spreading to the earlywood zones in an interlocked, ductile mode. Weathered wood were however more prone to brittle failure (Figure 1.81 right).

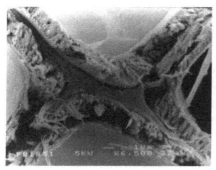 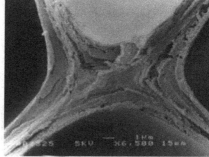

Figure 1.81 SEM analysis of conifer earlywood tracheids at their corner joint. Unweathered samples (left), and samples naturally weathered for 14 days (right).

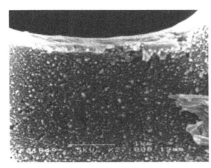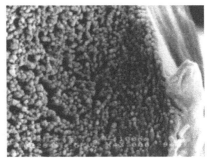

Figure 1.82 High resolution SEM microscopy of conifers. Unweathered wood showing S_2 and S_3 layers (left), and S_2/S_3 layers of a weathered earlywood tracheid with micro-voids between the fibrils due to delignification (right).

This work also reported that the breakdown of the middle lamella during weathering often causes the detachment of surface cells, while the thinning of the cell walls (Figure 1.81, right) was attributed to the breakdown of the lignin in the S_2 layer of the cell wall. Higher resolution microscopic images (Figure 1.82) further emphasise the photodegradative delignification, with the exposed fibrils being loosely packed and lacking radial agglomeration (Figure 1.82, right).

Wood modification and weathering

The aim of wood modification is to provide a more stable substrate for use in products exposed to various Use Classes. Many of the modification processes occur with chemical bonding other than that directly affected by the UV-degradation process, so that the weathering may occur at a rate different from that of the unmodified material. Some overviews of early studies into the effects of chemically modified wood have been published (Plackett et al., 1992; Evans et al., 2000; Williams, 2005), together with some studies into thermal modification (Nuopponen et al., 2005; Yildiz et al., 2011; Srinivas and Pandey, 2012). Recent studies into the effects of the various wood-modification techniques are reported in the relevant sections of this book.

1.7 Stress-strain response of wood: Considerations in wood modification

A structure is often defined as "any assemblage of materials which is intended to sustain loads", such as an airplane, a bridge, or a building. Only a minority of structures are made by human beings; the rest are products of biological design. The majority of living tissues have to carry mechanical loads of one kind or another. Plants, such as trees, are structures, designed to grow tall and stand up to strong winds. Biology places a great premium on strength and metabolic efficiency. In fact, trees are very efficient structures indeed. Nowadays, with modern knowledge, we tend to shy away from making too sharp a division between structure and material, at least in sophisticated structures. In biology, the distinction is often not possible.

The mechanical or strength properties of wood determine its fitness and ability to resist an applied or external forces, an external force being any force outside a given piece of material that tends to alter its size or shape or to deform it in any manner. Deformation may also be brought about by forces acting entirely within a piece, such as those which arise in wood due to changes in its moisture content, but these forces are concerned chiefly with the physical properties of wood other than those strictly pertaining to strength (Wangaard, 1950).

The English natural philosopher, architect and polymath Robert Hooke (1635–1703) studied the effects of forces on different materials and structures. He took a considerable variety of wires, springs, and wooden beams and loaded them progressively by adding weights to scale-pans, and measured the resulting deflections. When he plotted the variation in load against the deflection he found in each case that the graph was a straight line, and when the load was progressively removed the recovery was also linear, and the specimens returned to their original dimensions when they were unloaded. Thus, Hookean behaviour of a material or a structure was discovered, and Hooke concluded:

"It is very evident that the rule or law of Nature in every springing body is that the force or power thereof to restore itself to its natural position is always proportionate to the distance or space it is removed therefrom, whether it be rarefaction, or separation of the part from one another, or by condensation, or crowding of these parts together. Nor is it observable in those bodies only, but in all other springy bodies whatsoever, whether metal, wood, stone, baked earth, hair, silk, bones, sinews, glass and the like."

Hooke was saying that a solid can resist an external force only by changing its shape: by stretching if it is subjected to a tensile force, or by contraction if it is compressed. There is, according to Hooke, normally no such thing as an absolutely rigid material or structure. His discovery was a logical consequence of Newton's third law. A perfect elastic material follows Hooke's law of 1678 which requires small deformations and states that the stress (σ) is directly proportional to the strain (ε) and independent of the strain rate:

$$\sigma = E\varepsilon \qquad (1.7)$$

The modulus of elasticity (E) is a material dependent constant, corresponding to the inclination of the straight line in the stress-strain plot. Nowadays, it is known that materials in general do not show soley Hookean behaviour under load, and that some materials behave in a fully elastic manner but not linearly elastic as Hooke suggested for all materials. The basic nature of this complex behaviour of materials under load is exemplified in Figure 1.83:

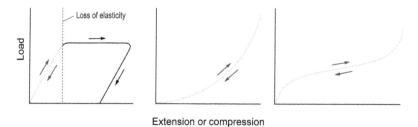

Figure 1.83 Examples of general stress-strain responses of different types of materials and structures.

Left: The elastic or plastic behaviour shown by a ductile metal. Under small loads the extension or compression increases linearly with increasing load (Hookean), but when a certain load is reached, the metal yields, undergoing a large additional extension or compression, that is mostly irreversible when the load is removed.

Middle: Fully elastic J-curve behaviour shown by many animal tissues. The greater the load, the smaller the additional extension or compression, and when the load is removed the material return to its original dimension.

Right: Fully elastic S-curve behaviour shown by many synthetic rubbery solids. Most extension or compression occurs over a relatively narrow medium load range. Such solids may be brittle under higher loads, i.e., when reaching the region of steep increase in load to the right of the curve.

Wood is a material with a complex behaviour under load, that depends not only on the external load such as force, moisture or temperature, but also on its ultra-, micro-, and macrostructure, as well its chemical constituents. Wood is an "elasto-viscoelastic" material because its response to loads may be Hookean (linear elastic) but also shows a time-dependent deformation behaviour depending on the loading history, the temperature, and the moisture content, as well as on moisture variations (Navi and Sandberg, 2012). These parameters may interact together producing coupling effects. It is essential to understand the elasto-visco-plastic behaviour of wood during wood-modification processes such as steam-bending (the Thonét method, see Figure 1.92) and densification, where an understanding of the stress-strain response of the wood material is essential.

Elastic behaviour of wood

Wood has an anisotropic mechanical behaviour, the strength and rigidity of wood in its longitudinal (L) direction being much greater than in the transverse, radial (R) and tangential (T), directions, and strength and rigidity in the radial direction being different from that in the tangential direction. In a tree trunk, which is more or less cylindrical, the circular shape of the growth rings and the organisation of the longitudinal cells give the wood axis-symmetric mechanical properties. Apart from defects and natural growth imperfections, the similarity of the two local symmetry planes, i.e., longitudinal-radial (L-R) and radial-tangential (R-T) passing through any given point means that wood may be considered to be a cylindrical orthotropic material. Figure 1.84 shows an idealised cylindrical trunk and a close-up element with the principal directions R, T, and L corresponding to a given arbitrary point in the trunk.

Under a longitudinal tensile force, wood is typically elastic with a quasi-linear elongation up to a breaking point, as shown in Figure 1.85 (left). Breaking occurs by a brittle fracture, under controlled force conditions when the ultimate strain is 1−3%. Nevertheless, when the displacement is controlled, the response of a wood specimen to a simple tensile force, as shown in Figure 1.85 (right), is different. The force displacement curve shows a strain-softening behaviour after the peak, as a consequence of strain localisation (fracture with a damaged zone) in the wood.

When wood is subjected to a tensile force in the transverse direction, the force-displacement curve have features similar to those in the longitudinal direction, but the breaking and peak stresses are much lower.

Under a compression force, the deformation of wood depends on the direction of loading. Typical stress-displacement curves of poplar under compression in the three principal directions radial, tangential and longitudinal under controlled deformation are shown in Figure 1.86.

Under axial compression, the specimen shows an almost three segmented stress-strain curve: a quasi-linear segment followed by a non-linear second segment curve with a negative slope due to localised longitudinal buckling of the cell walls and/or local fracture. The third segment shows an increase in the modulus of the specimen with increasing compressive force.

Transverse compressive stress-strain curves (corresponding to the radial or tangential direction) also consist of three segments. The first segment shows a quasi-linear behaviour and is followed by a non-linear curve showing a decreasing modulus corresponding to a transverse flexural buckling of the cell walls. The third segment is a quasi-linear curve indicating a progressive increase in the modulus, which can reach a value higher than that of the first segment. During segments 2 and 3,

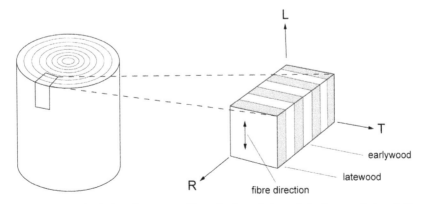

Figure 1.84 An idealised cylindrical trunk represented by a circular cylinder and circular growth rings (left), and a close-up view of a small element cut from the trunk where L, R and T are the local principal axes in the longitudinal, radial and tangential directions, respectively (right).

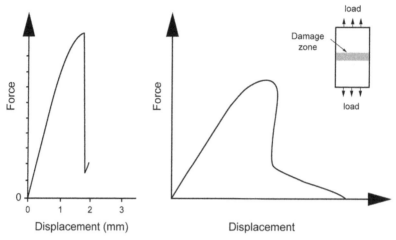

Figure 1.85 Typical force-displacement curve of a wood specimen subjected to a controlled longitudinal tensile force (left), and a controlled longitudinal tensile displacement (right) where the curve shows not only the linear region but also strain softening of the specimen after the peak force.

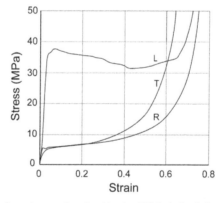

Figure 1.86 Stress-strain curves of specimens of poplar (density 350 kg/m³) of dimensions 25 × 25 × 5 mm subjected to compression in radial (R), tangential (T) and longitudinal (L) directions under controlled displacement at a rate of 1 mm/min (Roussel, 1997).

the strain can be greater than 50%, indicating a large transversal deformation, which leads to a densification of the wood cells.

Viscoelastic behaviour of wood

Wood behaves in a viscoelastic manner, where its anisotropic mechanical properties depend on time, temperature and moisture. In relative terms, at short times, low temperatures and low moisture content, wood exhibits glassy behaviour and can be characterised as stiff and brittle. At long times, high temperatures and high moisture contents, wood exhibits a rubbery behaviour and can be characterised as compliant. The temperature associated with the phase transition between these two distinct regions is called the glass-transition temperature T_g (Wolcott et al., 1994). The glass-transition temperature is also known as the softening temperature, since it characterises the softening behaviour of amorphous polymers. When wood is subjected to thermo-hydrous conditions, its amorphous components soften and become easy to deform and this opens the way to many industrial processes such as moulding, densification, large bending, shaping, surface densification, etc. Many properties of the amorphous constituents in wood change dramatically when the material passes the glass-transition temperature (Figure 1.87).

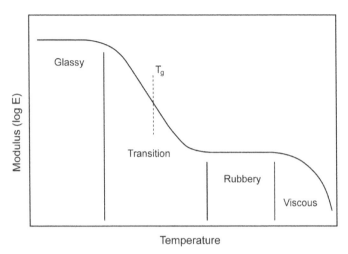

Figure 1.87 General behaviour of the relaxation modulus with temperature of an amorphous polymer (Lenth, 1999). T_g – glass-transition temperature.

The physical and mechanical properties of an amorphous polymer such as wood lignin, can be characterised as follows:

- In the glassy state, the physical properties are very similar to those of a solid phase whose values are not strongly sensitive to the chemical nature of the material like the topology of the polymeric network. The molecular movements which occur in this state are of low amplitude (movements of side groups or co-operative movements of a few monomeric units).

- In the rubbery state, the modulus of elasticity is 3,000 to 4,000 times lower than that of the glassy state, and the elongation at rupture is about 100 times greater. This high extensibility is due to the fact that thermal action decreases both the inter- and intra-molecular cohesion (Van der Waals forces, hydrogen bonds). Molecular movements of large amplitude (macromolecular movements) and the complete extension of the segments of the macromolecular chain are then possible, thanks to rotation around the covalent carbon-carbon (-C-C-) and carbon-oxygen (-C-O-) bonds.

Hillis and Rosza (1978) studied the influence of wood components on the softening of wood and suggested that moisture lowered the softening points of hemicelluloses and lignin, which are above 160°C when these two components are isolated. Hemicelluloses in the cell wall softened first (at 54–56°C), and this decreased the wood stiffness. This enabled wood fibres to adapt their cross-sectional shape to the applied forces. The softening of lignin (at 72–128°C) in the cell wall and middle lamellae permitted further cross-sectional movement within and between the fibres. Hillis and Rozsa (1985) investigated the softening of wood in different growth rings taken from young radiata pine trees. They reported softening points of about 80°C due to hemicelluloses and 100°C due to lignin, and based on the results of Hillis (1984), they attributed differences in the softening curves to the differences in the chemistry of the hemicelluloses in sapwood and heartwood. Baldwin and Goring (1968) have shown that T_g of the isolated components of wood differ from those in native wood, but the dependence of the T_g of wood components on the relative humidity is now fairly well known. Navi and Sandberg (2012) have presented thorough review of the glass-transition temperature of amorphous and semi-crystalline polymers.

The glass-transition temperature T_g of the amorphous components of wood decreases with increasing moisture content and vice versa (Figure 1.88). Östberg et al. (1990) showed that an increase in moisture content of Norway spruce and silver birch leads to a decrease in the softening temperature. Water molecules plasticise wood polymers, forming secondary bonds with the polar groups in the polymer molecules, and spreading them apart, thus reducing the secondary bonding

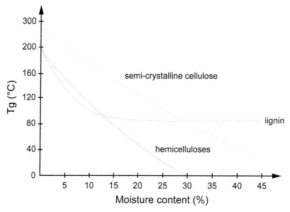

Figure 1.88 Glass-transition temperatures T$_g$ of the isolated components in wood as a function of moisture content (Salmén, 1982).

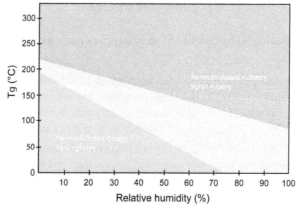

Figure 1.89 Glass-transition temperature for a matrix of native hemicelluloses-lignin as a function of the ambient relative humidity (Salmén et al., 1986).

between the polymer chains and providing more room for the polymer molecules to move around. Moisture thus increases the free volume of the system, the wood becomes more easily deformed and the glass-transition temperature is lowered.

Figure 1.89 shows the glass-transition temperature of the native matrix of hemicelluloses and lignin as a function of the relative humidity. It is, thus, essential to consider wood as a cellulose–hemicelluloses–lignin material whose three principal components are chemically linked together. Figure 1.89 shows that, at relatively high moisture content, the lignin has the highest glass-transition temperature, apart from crystalline cellulose. Therefore, the glass-transition temperature of lignin determines the limiting lowest temperature of the thermo-hydro-mechanical (THM) process for wood. The forming temperature must be selected according to two criteria. Firstly, the minimum temperature under which the wood can be formed, which is usually considered to be at least 25°C higher than glass-transition temperature of the lignin, i.e., approximately 110°C under moisture-saturated conditions and approximately 140°C at 80% relative humidity, and secondly, the maximum temperature, usually considered to be 200°C when air is saturated, to avoid thermal degradation of the wood components. The thermo-hydrous window for the forming of wood is thus limited to temperatures and relative humidity from respectively 110 to 140°C and 80 to 100%. Under these conditions, the lignin, hemicelluloses and the semi-crystalline cellulose are relatively mobile and can be deformed easily thanks to two molecular phenomena:

1) The inter- and intra-molecular interactions of the Van der Waals type in an amorphous or semi-crystalline polymer decrease strongly when their temperature is higher than their T_g.

2) The inter- and intra-molecular interactions of the hydrogen bond in an amorphous polymer which has functional hydroxyl (-OH) groups decrease strongly when its moisture content increases. The adsorbed water molecules are placed between the molecules, so they are by the hydroxyl groups. Consequently the average inter-molecular distance and the mobility of the molecules increase, and this lowers the T_g.

The water molecules act as a plasticiser by decreasing the interactions between the hemicelluloses and lignin macromolecules and the amorphous regions of the cellulose.

The semi-crystalline cellulose and hemicelluloses have many hydroxyl groups and are highly hygroscopic so that, when they are saturated with water, their T_g drops to a temperature lower than room temperature (Figure 1.88).

On the other hand, lignin contains fewer hydroxyl groups and water does not, therefore, have a great impact on its T_g which is approximately 85°C from about 15% moisture content to the saturation condition. The large number of hydrogen bonds in crystalline cellulose means that it has a compact and stable structure and that water is unable to penetrate into the crystal lattice. Only the hydroxyl groups on the surface of crystallites can adsorb water. Apparently the percentage of semi-crystalline cellulose is not really important. Consequently, the fibrils remain crystalline and very rigid at high temperatures and high moisture contents.

Various transitions in polymers are commonly studied by Dynamic Mechanical Analysis – DMA (Menard, 2007). DMA is a method based on sinusoidal tests that enable the characterisation of bulk properties directly affecting material performance. The DMA is a common method to decouple thermal activation from the time effect, characterising of materials that exhibit significant changes in their viscoelastic behaviour with changing conditions of temperature and the frequency of a dynamic force. It is often used to study the behaviour of polymers, e.g., to determine their glass-transition temperature.

DMA can be simply described as the application of an oscillating force to a material and the material's response to that force. DMA enables various properties of the material to be determined like the tendency to flow (viscosity) from the phase lag and the stiffness (modulus) from the recovery of the material. These properties are often described as the ability to lose energy as heat (damping) and the ability to recover from deformation (elasticity). The DMA also data relating to the relaxation of the polymer chains and the changes in the free volume of the polymer that occur. The storage modulus E', which is a measure of the material stiffness, the loss modulus E", which reflects the amount of energy that has been dissipated by the sample, and the ratio E"/E' = tan δ (δ is the phase angle), an index of material viscoelasticity, are calculated from the material response to the sine wave. These different moduli give a better characterisation of the material, since they show the ability of the material to return or store energy, its ability to lose energy, and the ratio of these effects, which is called damping. In a DMA test, where a specimen is heated stepwise and the three parameters are plotted as a function of temperature, a strong change in tan δ indicates a change in the material's viscoelastic properties, e.g., the transition from a glassy to a rubbery state. Since cellulose, hemicellulose, and lignin are polymeric, DMA can be used for the characterisation of wood. Depending on the environment (humidity, air, inert-gas), thermal degradation and/or reconfiguration of the constitutive polymers of wood can occur during a DMA test revealing its viscoelastic properties (Assor et al., 2009). Internal friction (tan δ) is particularly sensitive to the structure of the wood cell-wall "matrix" (lignin and hemicelluloses). Therefore, DMA data as a function of temperature simultaneously provide mechanical data and indications of chemical modifications (Laborie, 2006). Due to the hygroscopicity of wood, DMA tests on wood as a function of temperature are usually conducted either in a completely dry or in a saturated state. However, the versatility of DMA has seldom been applied to monitor the *in situ* changes occurring during thermal treatment processes involving several steps under different conditions.

Mechano-sorption

The variation in the viscoelastic behaviour of wood under varying climatic conditions is referred to as the mechano-sorptive effect, a phenomenon that is still not understood in detail. The term *mechano-sorption* is often used to express the effect under carrying conditions of the coupling between mechanical stress and moisture content in wood. It has been shown that a variation in the moisture content of a wood specimen subjected to a mechanical load can lead to important deformations. Under high load and extreme variations in moisture content, high deformation can lead to structural damage of the wood. Figure 1.90 illustrates the effect of cyclic variation in the relative humidity combined with a different stress level on the delayed deformation in bending of small clear specimens.

Phenomena observed under varying moisture conditions have been described by Grossman (1976). These phenomena are presented in Figure 1.91 which shows a typical mechano-sorptive creep curve after deduction of the free swelling or addition of the free shrinkage observed under zero loading.

The main features are:

- The deformation increases during drying, as has been shown by Armstrong and Kingston (1962), Hearmon and Paton (1964), Pittet (1996) and others.

- The first re-humidification lead to an increase in the deformation. Subsequent re-humidification leads to a minor reduction in deformation when the applied compressive load is low and an increase in deformation under high compressive loads (Armstrong and Kingston, 1962; Hearmon and Paton, 1964; Navi et al., 2002).

- The mechano-sorptive deformation is independent of time. It is determined by the degree of variation in the moisture content while it is below the fibre saturation point (Armstrong and Kingston, 1962; Leicester, 1971).

- When the stress level is less than 15–20% of the short-term ultimate stress, the deformation due to mechano-sorption seems to be linear.

- A constant flow of moisture through the wood without any local change in the moisture content does not lead to any mechano-sorptive effect (Armstrong, 1972).

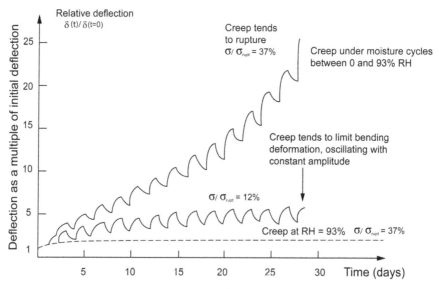

Figure 1.90 Creep in bending of small specimens of European beech with dimensions (2 × 2 × 60 mm) under cyclic variations in relative humidity (Hearmon and Paton, 1964).

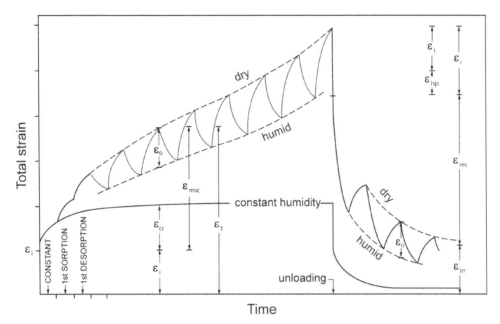

Figure 1.91 Typical curve showing the mechano-sorptive creep of wood (Grossman, 1976).

- After unloading and recovery of the instantaneous elasticity, most of the total deformation is irrecoverable. New humidification-drying cycles lead to a decrease the residual deformation. The recovery is greater during drying than during humidification (Armstrong and Kingston, 1962; Pittet, 1996).

It is important to note that the dimensions of the specimen have a considerable influence on the kinetics of the mechano-sorptive effect. This is partly related to the time to reach moisture equilibrium in the specimen. For example, in the case of two specimens, one $1 \times 1 \times 60$ mm and the other $20 \times 20 \times 900$ mm in size, the mechano-sorptive effect is similar, but the time necessary to reach moisture equilibrium in the thin specimen is only 2–3 hours, whereas about 50 hours are necessary for the thick specimen.

Stress-strain relationship under longitudinal deformation

The stress-strain relationship in the longitudinal direction of wood is of interest in bending after plasticisation. The reason for the difficulty in bending solid wood is the low extension of wood in tensile failure, see, e.g., Prodehl (1931a). Wood in its natural state exhibits elastic properties over only a limited stress range (Figure 1.92). When the stress is removed within this limited elastic range, the wood returns to its original shape. If the deformation in tension exceeds the limit stress in the longitudinal direction of wood, the wood remains bent. If the deformation strain exceeds the strength of the wood, it breaks.

However, when wood is plasticised it becomes *plastic shapable*. Its compressibility in longitudinal direction is then greatly increased, to as much as 30–40%, although its ability to elongate under tension is not appreciably affected (Figure 1.92). After plasticisation, a combination of bending and compression in the longitudinal direction of the wood can be used to limit the extension of the wood in tension and it is then possible to bend wood through a relatively sharp curvature. In practice, this means that the manufacturer has to control the length of the pieces during bending; to use some type of end stops (strap-and-stop) on the tensile side of the pieces being bent will prevent it from being streched by more than 1–2%.

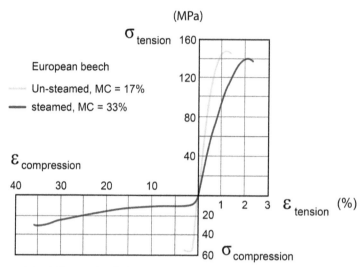

Figure 1.92 Stress-strain (σ-ε) diagrams for air-dry un-steamed beech and for steamed European beech. Note that the stress and strain axes have different scales to the right and to the left of the origin (after Prodehl, 1931a,b). MC – moisture content.

The theory of solid wood bending is relatively complicated, for the following reasons:

1) Wood is an elasto-visco-plastic material with no distinct yield point.

2) The yield points in tension and in compression are numerically very different, as shown in Figure 1.92, and the difference increases with increasing moisture content as well as with increasing temperature.

3) The strain to failure is much greater in compression than in tension.

Many researchers have studied the mechanisms of deformation of conifer and broad-leaved wood under compression at the cellular level (e.g., Kučera and Bariska, 1982; Gibson and Ashby, 1988; Hoffmeyer, 1990; Boström, 1992; François and Morlier, 1993; Gril and Norimoto, 1993; Roussel, 1997; Navi and Heger, 2005). In this section, only the large deformation of conifer wood is presented. In conifers at the cellular level, the microstructure is more simple and uniform than that of broad-leaved wood. In conifers, the longitudinal tracheids occupy approximately 90% of the volume and the remaining cells, the ray cells, are directed in the radial direction in the R–L plane (see Section 1.2 for details of the micro-structure of wood).

Physical mechanisms of deformations at the cell level under longitudinal tension

A tensile force tends to pull apart the material. This external force is communicated to the interior, so that each portion of the material exerts a tensile force on the remainder, due to the property of cohesion in the material. The result is an elongation or stretching of the material in the direction of the applied force. Wood exhibits its greatest strength in tension parallel to the fibres, i.e., in the longitudinal direction. A typical stress-strain response for a conifer specimen is shown in Figure 1.93. When a direct tensile load is applied, the strain is proportional to the stress up to the point of failure and there is no well-defined proportional limit. Wood is capable of only yielding a slight amount prior to ultimate failure in tension.

The strength of wood parallel to the fibre direction depends on the strength of its fibres and this is affected not only by the nature and dimensions of the wood elements but also by their arrangement. It is greatest in straight-grained wood with thick-walled fibres (high density), its strength is greatly reduced if the force is applied in a direction deviating from parallel to the fibres.

Failure of wood in tension parallel to the fibres practically always occurs when dry wood is subjected to bending. In tensile failure, the fibre walls are torn across obliquely and usually in a

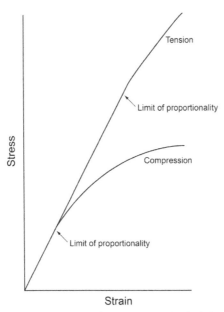

Figure 1.93 Stress-strain curves of wood subjected to tension and compression in the longitudinal direction under controlled displacement.

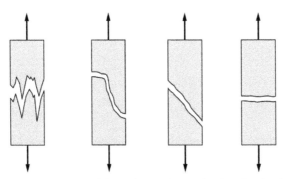

Figure 1.94 Failure types in clear wood stressed in tension parallel to the fibre direction in the wood. From the left: splintering tension, combined tension and shear, shear, and brittle tension failure.

spiral direction following the sprial-grain of the tree. There is practically no pulling apart of the fibres from each other, i.e., no separation of the fibres along their walls, regardless of their thickness. The nature of tensile failure is apparently not affected by the moisture content of the wood, at least not as much as the other strength values.

Figure 1.94 shows commonly occurring types of failure of wood loaded in longitudinal tension, such as splintering tension, combined tension and shear, shear, and brittle tension failure.

Earlywood and latewood zones of a conifer specimen loaded to failure in tension parallel to the longitudinal direction exhibit completely differing patterns as shown in Figure 1.95. The earlywood zone typically shows a brittle failure, with separation occurring across the tracheid walls. In latewood, the failure is typically a combination of shear and tension failure.

Physical mechanisms of large deformation under longitudinal compression at the cell level

In compression, the force acts on a body in the direction opposite to that in tension. As shown in Figure 1.96, the strain response of a low-density wood specimen to a uniaxial longitudinal compressive force can be divided into three distinct segments. The specimen behaves almost linearly up to a certain limit (B). The slope of the first segment of the curves (A–B) gives the

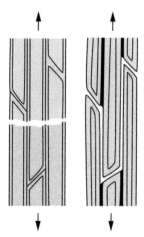

Figure 1.95 Most common failure of tracheids in tension parallel to the fibres: earlywood (left) and latewood (right).

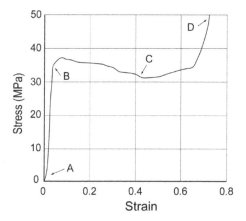

Figure 1.96 Stress-strain curve of a specimen of low-density wood subjected to compression in the longitudinal direction under controlled displacement.

effective Young´s modulus of the specimens in compression in the longitudinal direction. Above the linear limit, the specimen shows a smoothing or strain softening behaviour (B−C), followed by a rigidification or densification (C−D).

The softening behaviour can be explained by various mechanisms of deformation at the cellular level. Many researchers have observed this behaviour in various kinds of wood. For wood of low density (< 300 kg/m³), Easterling et al. (1982) showed that the cause of the wood softening was the collapse of fibres by rupture at the ends of the cells. This mechanism is shown schematically in Figure 1.97 (middle). In wood of higher density, Kučera and Bariska (1982) have shown that the softening of the wood can be due to a local Euler-type buckling in the walls of the cells, illustrated in Figure 1.97 (right), which generally leads to the formation of a shear band as shown in Figure 1.98 on the wood macro-level.

Stress-strain relationship under transverse compression

The stress-strain behaviour of wood loaded in the transverse direction is of interest mainly under compression, where the cells are greatly deformed and the cell-lumen volume decreases, resulting in an overall decrease in the volume of the compressed specimen. Since the amount of material in the specimen is unchanged, the density increases with increasing compression, and the process is called *wood densification.*

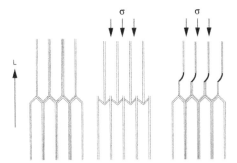

Figure 1.97 Diagrammatic representation of the mechanisms of local large deformations of wood cells under a longitudinal compression force. Wood before the application of the force (left), collapse of fibre by rupture (middle), and collapse by the buckling of cell walls (right). L is the longitudinal direction of wood.

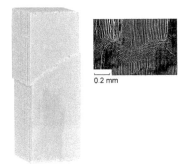

Figure 1.98 Collapse of the specimen by the buckling of fibre walls, which creates a shear band: observed at the macro-level (left), and at the cell-wall level (right).

Wood densification can be achieved in one or more directions, but wood is mostly densified along one of its orthotropic axes, diffuse broad-leaved wood being preferred to conifer wood for its anatomical structure. Primarily, wood and in particular conifer wood, is densified along the radial axis, as its latewood is much more dense than its earlywood. If it is tangentially densified, the latewood spreads into the earlywood forming waves or zigzags (Küch, 1951).

Densification in the transverse direction of wood flattens the cells without any noticeable damage on a macroscopic level, so that the strength increases with increasing density (Sandberg, 1998; Haller and Wehsener, 2004). Because of its viscoelastic nature, wood also exhibits rheological properties such as creep and relaxation. The strain-time curve of wood under a compressive load can be divided into four parts: initial elastic deformation, viscoelastic deformation, final elastic spring-back and time-dependent spring-back or creep recovery (Tang and Simpson, 1990). Wood densification can have both permanent and recoverable components, which together have a significant influence on the physical and mechanical properties of the material (Lenth and Kamke, 2001). The viscoelastic behaviour results in densification due to a permanent transverse compression of the cells.

During transverse compressive loading, a typical stress-strain curve of wood has three distinct regions (Bodig, 1963; Bodig, 1965; Kennedy, 1968; Wolcott et al., 1994; Uhmeier et al., 1998; Reiterer and Stanzl-Tschegg, 2001; Nairn, 2006), as shown in Figure 1.99. The initial part of the stress-strain curve for wood is a linear elastic region, in which the stress is directly proportional to strain. The second part is a "plastic" or collapse region, in which the stress is relatively constant even though the strain increases and the wood is deformed. After the plastic region, the stress increases strongly with little further strain. This region is termed the densification region (Tabarsa and Chui, 2000).

A yield point is found at the beginning of cellular collapse. When most of the cells have collapsed, densification begins (Wolcott et al., 1994). During densification, the stress rapidly increases as a result of the elimination of air voids and compression of the solid wood structure—consolidation

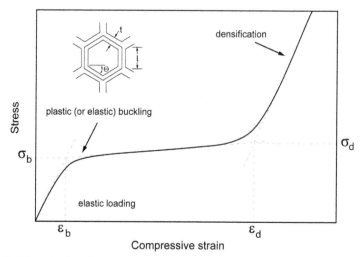

Figure 1.99 Schematic view of a transverse compressive stress-strain curve for wood (after Nairn, 2006).

of the collapsed cell walls. Cellular collapse occurs by elastic buckling, plastic yielding, or brittle crushing, depending on the test conditions and on the nature of the cell wall material (Wolcott et al., 1989).

The key details of the compression properties are dependent on various anatomical features of the wood specimen such as density, percentage of latewood, ray volume and loading direction (Nairn, 2006). Kunesh (1968) noticed that in the radial compression of solid wood, failure starts with the buckling of rays in an earlywood layer and results in progressive failure by buckling of the rays throughout the specimens. The first failure in earlywood was also found by Bodig (1965). Tabarsa and Chui (2000) found that earlywood primarily controlled the elastic and plastic parts of the stress-strain response for white spruce under radial compression. The first collapse of the cellular structure, which signified the onset of the plastic region, occurred in the cell layer with the lowest gross density in the earlywood. The initial part of the densification region was largely an elastic response of the latewood to the compressive stress, and collapse of latewood cells may not have occurred due to their large wall thickness. In broad-leaved woods, the first failure was initiated in the largest vessels surrounded by thin-walled paratracheal parenchyma cells (Tabarsa and Chui, 2001).

Several researchers have reported that wood responds differently to radial and tangential compression due to its anisotropic nature (Kennedy, 1968; Kunesh, 1968; Bodig and Jayne, 1982; Dinwoodie, 2000; Tabarsa and Chui, 2001; Wang and Cooper, 2005). In radial compression, the final consolidation stage is dominated by the elastic deformation of latewood, and in the tangential direction the final stage begins after readjustment of the latewood layer by buckling (Tabarsa and Chui, 2001). Reiterer and Stanzl-Tschegg (2001) studied the compressive behaviour of spruce wood under uniaxial loading at different orientations to the longitudinal and radial directions. Their results showed that the deformation pattern is highly dependent on the orientation. In the case of loading in the longitudinal direction, buckling deformation and cracks occurred, but no densification was observed, whereas loading in the radial direction resulted in plastic yielding and (gradual) collapse of the wood cells starting in the earlywood region of a whole growth ring and followed by densification at higher strains. Schrepfer and Schweingruber (1998) studied the anatomic structures of reshaped press-dried wood and found that earlywood cells were deformed more easily than latewood cells, which resulted in zones of compressed cells next to zones of uncompressed cells, in wave-like patterns. Kultikova (1999) also showed wave-like patterns of compressed and uncompressed cell zones in densified wood. The differences in compressibility of the wood tissue affects the distribution of void areas, and thus also the vertical density distributions and mechanical properties of compressed wood (Lenth and Kamke, 1996).

The type and amount of cell collapse have a great effect on the physical and mechanical properties of densified wood (Wolcott, 1989). The strength usually increases less than the density in relative terms, since uniaxial compression of solid wood results in a general collapse of the structure and possibly also in crushing and checking (Blomberg et al., 2005). This relation was found by Perkitny and Jablonski (1984) for bending strength and axial (parallel to grain) compressive strength. Blomberg et al. (2005) used a strength potential index to quantify how much the strength of densified wood increased relative to what could be expected for non-densified wood of similar density.

Hydrothermal treatment has a strong influence on the mechanical behaviour of wood during compression/densification. Softening and degradation occur depending on factors such as temperature, moisture, steam, and time (Morsing, 2000). The degree of improvement in the properties of densified wood due to hydrothermal treatment is affected not only by softening but also by the amount of thermal degradation induced by the compression process (Reynolds, 2004). Thermal degradation of amorphous wood components causes a weight loss of wood, and this can influence the mechanical strength properties (Jennings, 1993). For wet Norway spruce in radial compression, a thermal degradation process was observed between 150 and 200°C (Uhmeier et al., 1998).

Physical mechanisms of large deformations at the cell level under transverse compression

As shown in Figure 1.100, the stress-strain response of a specimen of poplar wood to uni-axial compressive force in the transverse direction has three distinct segments. The specimen behave almost linearly up to a certain limit which depends on the direction of the applied force. The slopes of the first segments of the curves (A–B) give the effective Young's modulus of the specimens in the radial and tangential directions, respectively. In the radial and tangential directions, unlike in the longitudinal direction, wood exhibits a typical plastic behaviour with a positive work hardening (B–C) followed by a rigidification or densification (C–D).

In the radial and tangential directions, the first zone represents a linear elastic behaviour, while the second zone (B–C in Figure 1.100) represents a plastic behaviour of the cell walls. In the third zone (C–D), a densification of the cells occurs.

Different researchers have explained these phenomena. Under the application of a compressive force in the radial direction, deformation occurs as a flexural buckling (or crushing) of the fibre walls starting in the weakest layer of the material. The cells of earlywood are the first to buckle because their walls are thinner (~ 2 μm) than the walls of latewood cells (~ 10 μm). This buckling leads to the densification of the fibres, the establishment of points of contact between the cell walls and increases the local rigidity so that this layer can support force sufficient to buckle the next layer which is the weakest one (Figure 1.101).

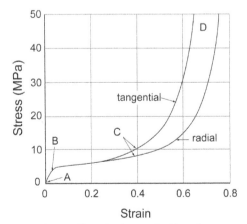

Figure 1.100 Stress-strain curves of specimens of low-density wood subjected to compression in the radial and tangential directions under controlled displacement.

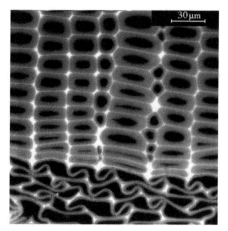

Figure 1.101 Micrograph of Norway spruce densified in the radial direction obtained with a confocal microscope. The contact points between cellular walls in the earlywood zone are shown by red dots.

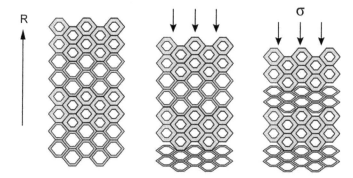

Figure 1.102 Diagrammatic representation of the compressive deformation of wood of the cellular level in the radial direction: wood before compression (left), localisation of the deformation and crushing of fibres in the weakest layer, partial densification (middle) and, crushing of fibres in the weakest layer followed by densification (right). R is the radial direction of wood.

These deformation mechanisms consisting of localisation, buckling and densification have been observed by, e.g., Gibson and Ashby (1988) and Navi and Heger (2005). A diagrammatic representation of this phenomenon is given in Figure 1.102. After the yielding of the first cellular row, the phenomenon is propagated progressively to the other rows of earlywood cells and later to the latewood cells.

In conifers compressed in the radial direction, the earlywood rows yield first, followed by the latewood rows, whereas in the tangential direction, thanks to the micro-structure of wood, buckling of the cell walls occurs at the same time in both latewood and earlywood cells.

The slope in the second segment of the curves increases with increasing compressive force, due to a closing of the lumens and multiplication of the points of contact between the walls of the cells of the initial wood. As the compression force increases, the thickness of these bands of buckled cells increases and others start to yield. When all the lumens are closed, the stress necessary to continue the deformation increases exponentially in the third segment. Wood densification starts in segment two and continues in segment three. As a result of this linear and non-linear behaviour, as shown in Figure 1.100, the wood can be deformed by more than 50%.

To model the behaviour of wood under compression deformation, constitutive equations of wood undergoing linear and non-linear deformation therefore become important.

Kutnar and Kamke (2013) studied the transverse compressive behaviour of Douglas fir wood and hybrid poplar at high temperature (170°C) and saturated steam conditions. They applied modified Hooke's law and modelled the compressive stress as a function of elastic modulus of cell wall substance and a non-linear strain function. They found that Douglas fir and hybrid poplar behave differently when subjected to transverse compression due to the different cellular structures of conifer woods versus broad-leaved woods. However, when the comparison was made on the basis of the relative density change, the transverse compressive responses of Douglas fir and hybrid poplar were remarkably similar. The relative density of a cellular material, defined as the ratio of the apparent density of the material to the real density of the solid of which it is made (Ribeiro and Costa, 2007), is a characteristic feature that significantly affect compressive behaviour of cellular materials.

The effect of the steam environment on the stress-strain response, non-linear strain function $\psi(\varepsilon)$, and relative density change can be studied by a modified Hooke's law based on the load-compression behaviour of flexible foams (Gibson and Ashby, 1988; Dai and Steiner, 1993; Wolcott et al., 1994; Lang and Wolcott, 1996; Dai, 2001; Zhou et al., 2009; Kamke and Kutnar, 2010) in the following form:

$$\sigma = E \cdot \varepsilon \cdot \psi(\varepsilon) \tag{1.8}$$

where σ is compressive stress, E is transverse compression Young's modulus of the cellular material, ε is compressive strain, and $\psi(\varepsilon)$ is a dimensionless non-linear strain function. The value of $\psi(\varepsilon)$ can determined (Wolcott, 1989; Lang and Wolcott, 1996) as:

$$\psi(\varepsilon) = \frac{\epsilon_y / C_2}{\varepsilon} \left[\frac{1 - \rho_r^{1/3}}{1 - \rho_r(\epsilon)^{1/3}} \right]^3 \tag{1.9}$$

where ε_y is yield strain, C_2 is a linear elastic constant, ε is the compressive strain, ρ_r is the relative density of the wood (a ratio of the bulk-wood density to the cell-wall density, assumed to be 1,500 kg/m³), and $\rho_r(\varepsilon)$ is the change in relative density under a compressive strain. A thorough development of (Equation 1.9) is provided by Gibson and Ashby (1988).

The change in relative density under a compressive strain $\rho_r(\varepsilon)$ at a given strain ε can be determined (Wolcott, 1989; Lang and Wolcott, 1996):

$$\rho_r(\varepsilon) = \frac{1}{\rho_r \left[1 - \varepsilon_p + \frac{2}{3} \mu \varepsilon_p - \mu \epsilon_p^2 \right]} \tag{1.10}$$

where ε_p is plastic strain ($\varepsilon_p = \varepsilon - \varepsilon_y$) and μ is the expansion ratio defined as the ratio of lateral strain to compressive strain in the nonlinear stress-strain region.

The Young's modulus of the cell wall (E_{cw}) can be determined by an expression given by Wolcott (1989), where the Young's modulus of any wood species can be calculated as a function of the cell-wall modulus and the relative density:

$$E = C \, E_{cw} \, \rho_r^3 \tag{1.11}$$

where C is a constant, E_{cw} is the cell-wall modulus, and ρ_r is the relative density, i.e., the density of the wood divided by the cell-wall density.

1.8 Conclusions on wood and wood modification

The aim of this chapter has been to lay the basis of how wood modification has been developed and where it has occurred, been commercially manufactured. To do this, it is necessary not only to understand the wood modification processes, but also the substrate being modified, i.e., wood. As can be seen from subchapters herein, it is necessary to understand the basics behind:

- the different wood species and their structures,
- the chemical composition of wood and how these chemicals can react,

- the reaction between wood and its components and water,
- the biological nature of wood and its susceptibility to degradation,
- the effects of exposing wood to outdoor conditions, and
- the effects of loads on the mechanical performance of wood.

The introduction to these areas will provide the reader with a sufficient entry knowledge to more detailed understandings of the wood modification methods described in the following chapters. Based on the information in these chapters, combined with the introductions provided in this chapter, it is hoped that the reader will increase their knowledge of wood modification processes to help in new research and applications of this expanding technology.

References

Abdel-Hamid, A.M., J.O. Solbiati and I.K.O. Cann. 2013. Insights into lignin degradation and its potential industrial applications. Advances in Applied Microbiology 82: 1–28.
Abuku, M., B. Blocken and S. Roels. 2009. Moisture response of building facades to wind driven rain: field measurements compared with numerical simulations. Journal of Wind Engineering & Industrial Aerodynamics 97: 197–207.
Adler, E. 1977. Lignin chemistry: Past, present and future. Wood Science and Technology 11: 169–218.
Alfredsen, G. and M. Westin. 2009. Durability of modified wood, laboratory vs field performance, pp. 515–522. In: Englund, F., Hill, C.A.S., Militz, H. and Segerholm, B.K. [eds.]. Proceedings of the 4th European Conference on Wood Modification, Stockholm, Sweden.
Alfredsen, G. and C.G. Fossdal. 2010. Postia placenta gene expression during growth in furfurylated wood. In: The Proceedings IRG Annual Meeting, Biarritz, France. International Research Group on Wood Protection IRG/WP 10-10734.
Amirta, R., T. Tanabe, T. Watanabe, Y. Honda, M. Kuwahara and T. Watanabe. 2005. Methane fermentation of Japanese cedar wood pretreated with a white-rot fungus, Ceriporiopsis subvermispora. Journal of Biotechnology 123(1): 71–77.
Anderson, E.L., Z. Pawlak, N.L. Owen and W.C. Feist. 1991. Infrared studies of wood weathering. Part I: Softwoods. Applied Spectroscopy 45(4): 641–647.
Arantes, V. and B. Goodell. 2014. Current understanding of brown-rot fungal biodegradation mechanisms: A review, pp. 3–21. In: Schultz, T.P., Goodell, B. and Nicholas, D.D. [eds.]. Deterioration and Protection of Sustainable Biomaterials. ACS Symposium Series, Vol. 1158.
Armstrong, L.D. 1972. Deformation of wood in compression during moisture movement. Wood Science 5: 81–86.
Armstrong, L.D. and R.S.T. Kingston. 1962. Effect of moisture changes on the deformation of wood under stress. Australian Journal of Applied Science 13: 257–276.
Assor, C., B. Chabbert, A. Habrant, C. Lapierre, B. Pollet and P. Perré. 2009. Concomitant changes in viscoelastic properties and amorphous polymers during the hydrothermal treatment of hardwood and softwood. Journal of Agricultural and Food Chemistry 57: 6830–6837.
Back, E. and L. Salmén. 1982. Glass transition of wood components hold implications for molding and pulping processes. Tappi 67: 107–110.
Baker, J.M. 1969. Digestion of wood by Anobium punctatum DeGeer and comparison with some other wood boring beetles, pp. 31–39. In: Wallace, W. and Smith, S.E. [eds.]. Proceedings of the Royal Entomological Society of London C 33.
Balakshin, M., E. Capanema, H. Gracz, H. Chang and H. Jameel. 2011. Quantification of lignin–carbohydrate linkages with high-resolution NMR spectroscopy. Planta 233: 1097–1110.
Baldrian, P. 2006. Fungal laccases—occurrence and properties. FEMS Microbiology Reviews 30: 215–242.
Baldwin, S.H. and D.A.I. Goring. 1968. The thermoplastic and adhesive behaviour of thermomechanical pulps from steamed wood. Svensk Papperstidning 71(18): 646–650.
Bari, E., N. Nazarnezhad, E.M. Kazemi, M.A.T. Ghanbary, B. Mohebby, O. Schmidt and C.A. Clausen. 2015. Comparison between degradation capabilities of the white rot fungi Pleurotus ostreatus and Trametes versicolor in beech wood. International Biodeterioration and Biodegradation 104: 231–237.
Barnett, J.R. and G. Jeronimidis. 2003. Reaction wood, pp. 118–136. In: Barnett, J.J. and Jeronimidis, G. [eds.]. Wood Quality and its Biological Basis. Blackwell Publishing, Melbourne, Australia.
Barreira, E. and V.P. de Freitas. 2013. Experimental study of the hygrothermal behaviour of external thermal insulation composite systems (ETICS). Building and Environment 63: 31–39.
Battisti, A. 2001. Insetti che attaccano gli alberi deperienti e il legno nelle prime fasi della lavorazione [Insects that attack perishable trees and wood in the early stages of processing.], pp. 91–104. In: Chiappini, E., G. Liotta, M.G. Reguzzi and A. Battisti [eds.]. Insetti e restauro. Legno, carta, tessuti, pellame e altri materiali. Calderini Edagricole, Bologna, Italia (In Italian).
Bendtsen, B.A. 1978. Properties of wood from improved and intensively managed trees. Forest Products Journal 28(10): 61–72.

Bentrup, F.-W. 2016. Water ascent in trees and lianas: the cohesion-tension theory revisited in the wake of Otto Renner. Protoplasma 254(2): 627–633.

Besser, K., G.P. Malyon, W.S. Eborall, G.P. da Cunha, J.G. Filgueiras, A. Dowle, L.C. Garcia, S.J. Page, R. Dupree, M. Kern, L.D. Gomez, Y. Li, L. Elias, F. Sabbadin, S.E. Mohamed, G. Pesante, C. Steele-King, E. Ribeiro de Azevedo, I. Polikarpov, P. Dupree, S.M. Cragg, N.C. Bruce and S.J. McQueen-Mason. 2018. Hemocyanin facilitates lignocellulose digestion by wood-boring marine crustaceans. Nature Communications 9: Article ID 5125.

Blanchette, R.A. 1998. A guide to wood deterioration caused by microorganisms and insects, pp. 55–68. *In*: Dardes, K. and Rothe, A. [eds.]. Proceedings of the Structural Conservation of Panel Paintings, Los Angeles, USA. The Getty Conservation Institute.

Blom, Å. and M. Bergström. 2005. Mycologg: a new accelerated test method for wood durability above ground. Wood Science and Technology 39(8): 663–673.

Blomberg, J., B. Persson and A. Blomberg. 2005. Effects of semi-isostatic densification of wood on the variation in strength properties with density. Wood Science and Technology 39: 339–350.

Bodig, J. 1963. The peculiarity of compression of conifers in the radial direction. Forest Products Journal 13(10): 438.

Bodig, J. 1965. The effect of anatomy on the initial stress-strain relationship in transverse compression. Forest Products Journal 15: 197–202.

Bodig, J. and B.A. Jayne. 1982. Mechanics of Wood and Wood Composites. Van Nostran-Reinhold, New York, USA.

Boehm, J. 1893. Capillarität und saftsteigen [Capillarity and sap transport.]. Berichte der Deutschen Botanischen Gesellschaft 11: 14–23.

Boonstra, M. and B. Tjeerdsma. 2006. Chemical analysis of heat treated softwoods. European Journal of Wood and Wood Products 64(3): 204–211.

Borges, L.M.S. 2014. Biodegradation of wood exposed in the marine environment: Evaluation of the hazard posed by marine wood-borers in fifteen European sites. International Biodeterioration and Biodegradation 96: 97–104.

Bornemann, T., C. Brischke and G. Alfredsen. 2014. Decay of wooden commodities—moisture risk analysis, service life prediction and performance assessments in the field. Wood Material Science & Engineering 9: 144–155.

Bosshard, H.H. 1974. Holzkunde. Band 1. Mikroskopie und Makroskopie des Holzes. [Wood science. Volume 1. Microstructure and Macrostructure of Wood.] Birkhäuser Verlag, Basel, Germany (In German).

Boström, L. 1992. Method for determination of the softening behaviour of wood and the applicability of a nonlinear fracture mechanics model. PhD. Thesis, Lund University of Technology, Sweden.

Bowyer, J.L., R. Shmulsky and J.G. Haygreen. 2007. Forest Products & Wood Science. (5th edn.), Blackwell Publishing, Ames, USA.

Brischke, C. and S. Thelandersson. 2014. Modelling the outdoor performance of wood products—A review on existing approaches. Construction and Building Materials 66: 384–397.

Brischke, C. and W. Unger. 2017. Potential hazards and degrading agents, pp. 188−203. *In*: Jones, D. and Brischke, C. [eds.]. Performance of Bio-based Building Materials. Elsevier, Amsterdam, The Netherlands.

Brischke, C., A.O. Rapp and R. Bayerbach. 2008. Measurement system for long-term recording of wood moisture content with internal conductively glued electrodes. Building and Environment 43(10): 1566–1574.

Brischke, C., E. Frühwald Hansson, D. Kavurmaci and S. Thelandersson. 2011a. Decay hazard mapping for Europe. *In*: The Proceedings IRG Annual Meeting, Queenstown, New Zealand. International Research Group on Wood Protection IRG/WP 11-20463.

Brischke, C., C.R. Welzbacher, L. Meyer, T. Bornemann, P. Larsson-Brelid, A. Pilgård, E. Frühwald Hansson, M. Westin, A.O. Rapp, S. Thelandersson and J. Jermer. 2011b. Service life prediction of wooden components – Part 3: Approaching a comprehensive test methodology. *In*: The Proceedings IRG Annual Meeting, Queenstown, New Zealand. International Research Group on Wood Protection IRG/WP 11-20464.

Brischke, C., L. Meyer, G. Alfredsen, M. Humar, L. Francis, P.-O. Flæte and P. Larsson-Brelid. 2012. Durability of timber products – Part 1: Inventory and evaluation of above ground literature data on natural durability of timbers. *In*: The Proceedings IRG Annual Meeting, Kuala Lumpur, Malaysia. International Research Group on Wood Protection IRG/WP 12-20498.

Brischke, C., L. Meyer and E. Suttie. 2013. Survey on "Moisture risk and Wood Durability Testing". Report, pp. 36, PerformWOOD.

Brugerolle, G. and R. Radek. 2006. Symbiotic protozoa of termites, pp. 243–269. *In*: König, H. and Varma, A. [eds.]. Soil Biology, Volume 6: Intestinal Microorganisms of Soil Invertebrates. Springer-Verlag, Berlin, Heidelberg, Germany.

Buijs, K. and G.R. Choppin. 1963. Near-infra-red studies of the structure of water. I. Pure water. The Journal of Chemical Physics 39(8): 2035–2041

Burnard, M.D. and A. Kutnar. 2015. Wood and human stress in the built indoor environment: A review. Wood Science and Technology 49(5): 969–986.

Carlberg, I. 2019. Den gåtfulle Alfred, hans värld och hans pris [The Mysterious Alfred, his World and his Prize.] Nordstedts, Stockholm, Sweden (In Swedish).

Cazemier, A.E., H.J.M.O. den Camp, J.H.P. Hackstein and G.D. Vogels. 1997. Fibre digestion in arthropods. Comparative Biochemistry and Physiology A, Physiology 118: 101–109.

CEN. 2000. EN 927-3. Paints and varnishes—Coating materials and coating systems for exterior wood – Part 3: Natural weathering test. European Committee for Standardization, Brussels, Belgium.

CEN. 2002a. EN 13183-1. Moisture content of a piece of sawn timber—Part 1: Determination by oven dry method. European Committee for Standardization, Brussels, Belgium.

CEN. 2002b. EN 13183-2. Moisture content of a piece of sawn timber—Part 2. Estimation by electrical resistance method. European Committee for Standardization, Brussels, Belgium.

CEN. 2005. EN 13183-3. Moisture content of a piece of sawn timber—Part 3. Estimation by capacitance method. European Committee for Standardization, Brussels, Belgium.

CEN. 2010. EN 1995-1-1: Eurocode 5: Design of timber structures—Part 1-1: General—Common Rules and Rules for Buildings. European Committee for Standardization, Brussels, Belgium.

CEN. 2013. EN 335:2013. Durability of wood and wood-based products—Use Classes: Definitions, application to solid wood and wood-based products. European Committee for Standardization, Brussels, Belgium.

CEN. 2018. EN 927-6. Paints and varnishes—Coating materials and coating systems for exterior wood—Part 6: Exposure of wood coatings to artificial weathering using fluorescent UV lamps and water. European Committee for Standardization, Brussels, Belgium.

Charles, F.K., J. Coston-Guarini, J.-M. Guarini and F. Lantoine. 2018. It's what's inside that counts: Computer-aided tomography for evaluating the rate and extent of wood consumption by shipworms. Journal of Wood Science 64(4): 427–435.

Chiappini, E. and R.N. Aldini. 2011. Morphological and physiological adaptations of wood-boring beetle larvae in timber. Journal of Entomological and Acarological Research, Ser. II 43(2): 47–59.

Cogulet, A., P. Blanchet and V. Landry. 2016. Wood degradation under UV irradiation: A lignin characterization. Journal of Photochemistry and Photobiology B: Biology 158: 184–191.

Cookson, L.J. 1990. Annotated check-list of the Limnoriidae. *In*: The Proceedings IRG Annual Meeting, Rotarua, New Zealand. International Research Group on Wood Protection IRG/WP 90-4160.

Cormack, A.M. 1963. Representation of a function by its line integrals, with some radiological applications. Journal of Applied Physics 34: 2722–2727.

Couceiro, J. 2019. X-ray computed tomography to study moisture distribution in wood. PhD. Thesis, Luleå University of Technology, Skellefteå, Sweden.

Cragg, S.M. 2003. Marine wood boring arthropods: ecology, functional anatomy, and control measures, pp. 272–286. *In*: Goodell, B., Nicholas, D.D. and Schultz, T.P. [eds.]. Wood Deterioration and Preservation. American Chemical Society, Washington DC, USA.

Curling, S. 2017. Test methods for bio-based building materials, pp. 385–481. *In*: Jones, D. and Brischke, C. [eds.]. Performance of Bio-based Building Materials. Woodhead Publishing, Duxford, UK.

Dai, C. 2001. Viscoelasticity of wood composite mats during consolidation. Wood and Fiber Science 33(3): 353–363.

Dai, C. and P.R. Steiner. 1993. Compression behavior of randomly formed wood flake mats. Wood and Fiber Science 25(4): 349–358.

Dawson, B., A. Singh, H.W. Kroese, M.A. Schwitzer, S. Gallagher, S.J. Riddiough and S. Wu. 2008. Enhancing exterior performance of clear coatings through photostabilization of wood. Part 2: Coating and weathering performance. Journal of Coatings Technology and Research 5(2): 207–219.

De Groot, R.C. 1992. Test assemblies for monitoring decay in wood exposed above ground. International Biodeterioration and Biodegradation 29: 151–175.

Derbyshire, H., E.R. Miller and H. Turkulin. 1995. Investigation into the photodegradation of wood using microtensile testing. Part 1: The application of microtensile testing to measurement of photodegradation rates. Holz als Roh- und Werkstoff 53: 339–345.

Dietsch, P., S. Franke, B. Franke, A. Gamper and S. Winter. 2015. Methods to determine wood moisture content and their applicability in monitoring concepts. Journal of Civil Structural Health Monitoring 5(2): 115–127.

Dinwoodie, J.M. 2000. Timber. Its Nature and Behaviour. (2nd edn.), E & P Spon, London, UK.

Distel, D.L. 2003. The biology of marine wood boring bivalves and their bacterial endosymbionts, pp. 253–271. *In*: Goodell, B., Nicholas, D.D. and Schultz, T.P. [eds.]. Wood Deterioration and Preservation. American Chemical Society, Washington D.C., USA.

Dixon, H.H. and J. Joly. 1894. On the ascent of sap. Annals of Botany 8: 468–470.

Donaldson, L. 2007. Cellulose microfibril aggregates and their size variation with cell wall type. Wood Science and Technology 41: 443–460.

Duarte, S., L. Nunes, P.A.V. Borges, C.G. Fossdal and T. Nobre. 2017. Living inside termites: An overview of symbiotic interactions, with emphasis on flagellate protists. Arquipelago Life and Marine Sciences 34: 21–43.

Ek, M., G. Gellerstedt and G. Henriksson. 2009. Wood Chemistry and Wood Biotechnology. 1. Pulp and Paper Chemistry and Technology. DeGruyter, Berlin, Germany.

Emmerich, L., S. Bollmus and H. Militz. 2019. Wood modification with DMDHEU (1.3-dimethylol-4.5-dihydroxyethyleneurea): State of the art, recent research activities and future perspectives. Wood Material Science & Engineering 14(1): 3–18.

Engel, M.S. 2011. Family-group names for termites (Isoptera), redux. ZooKeys 148: 171–184.

Engelund Thybring, E. 2013. The decay resistance of modified wood influenced by moisture exclusion and swelling reduction. International Biodeterioration and Biodegradation 82: 87–95.

Engelund Thybring, E. 2014. Introduction to moisture relationships in biobased materials. Presentation at the COST FP1303 meeting, 27–28 January, Paris, France.

Engelund Thybring, E., L.G. Thygesen, S. Svensson and C.A.S. Hill. 2013. A critical discussion of the physics of wood-water interactions. Wood Science and Technology 47(1): 141–161.

Engelund Thybring, E., M. Kymäläinen and L. Rautkari. 2018. Moisture in modified wood and its relevance for fungal decay. iForest – Biogeosciences and Forestry 11(3): 418–422.

Engelund Thybring, E., S. Piqueras, A. Tarmian and I. Burgert. 2020. Water accessibility to hydroxyls confined in solid cell walls. Cellulose 25(10): 5117–5627.

Ennos, R. 2016. Trees—A Complete Guide to their Biology and Structure. Comstock Publishing Associates, Cornell University Press, Ithaca, New York, USA.

Eriksson, K.E.L., R.A. Blanchette and P. Ander. 1990. Microbial and Enzymatic Degradation of Wood and Wood Components. Springer-Verlag, New York, USA.

Ermeyadan, M.A., E. Cabane, N. Gierlinger, J. Koetzd and I. Burgert. 2014. Improvement of wood material properties via in situ polymerization of styrene into tosylated cell walls. RSC Advances 4: 12981–12988.

Easterling, K.E., R. Harrysson, L.J. Gibson and M.F. Ashby. 1982. On the mechanics of balsa and other woods. Proceedings of the Royal Society A383(1784): 31–41.

Evans, P.D., A.J. Michell and K.J. Schmalzl. 1992. Studies of the degradation and protection of wood surfaces. Wood Science and Technology 26(2): 151–163.

Evans, P.D., A.F.A. Wallis and N.L. Owen. 2000. Weathering of chemically modified wood surfaces. Wood Science and Technology 34(2): 151–165.

Evans, P.D., J.G. Haase, A. Seman, B.M. Shakri and M. Kiguchi. 2015. The search for durable exterior clear coatings for wood. Coatings 5(4): 830–864.

Fackler, K., C. Gradinger, B. Hinterstoisser, K. Messner and M. Schwanninger. 2006. Lignin degradation by white rot fungi on spruce wood shavings during short-time solid-state fermentations monitored by near infrared spectroscopy. Enzyme and Microbial Technology 39(7): 1476–1483.

Faix, O. and R. Nemeth. 1988. Monitoring of wood photodegradation by DRIFT-spectroscopy. Holz als Roh- und Werkstoff 46(3): 112.

Falck, R. 1930. Apparent destruction of coniferous wood by larva of common beetle (*Hylotrupes bajulus*). Cellulosechemie 11: 89–91.

Fengel, D. and G. Wegener. 1984. Wood: Chemistry, Ultrastructure, Reactions. Walter De Gruyter, Berlin, Germany.

Fengel, D. and G. Wegener. 1989. Wood: Chemistry, Ultrastructure, Reactions. (2nd edn.), Walter de Gruyter, Berlin, Germany.

Fougerousse, M. 1976. Wood preservatives: Field tests out of ground contact – brief survey of principles and methodology. *In*: The Proceedings IRG Annual Meeting, Wildhaus, Switzerland. International Research Group on Wood Protection IRG/WP 269.

François, P. and P. Morlier. 1993. Plasticité du bois en compression simple [Plasticity of wood in simple compression.] Matériaux et Techniques 81(12): 5–14 (In French).

Fredriksson, M. 2010. Methods for determination of moisture conditions in wood exposed to high moisture levels. Licentiate Thesis, Lund University, Sweden.

Friese, F., E. Larnøy, G. Alfredsen, A. Pfeffer and H. Militz. 2009. Comparison between different decay assessment methods, pp. 85–92. *In*: Bergstedt, A. [ed.]. Proceedings from WSE Conference – Nordic Baltic Network in Wood Material Science & Engineering. September, Copenhagen, Denmark. University of Copenhagen.

Frühwald Hansson, E., C. Brischke, L. Meyer, T. Isaksson, S. Thelandersson and D. Kavurmaci. 2012. Durability of timber outdoor structures: Modelling performance and climate impacts, pp. 295–303. *In*: Quenneville, P. [ed.]. The Proceedings of the World Conference on Timber Engineering, Auckland, New Zealand. New Zealand Timber Design Society.

Ghosh, S.C., H. Militz and C. Mai. 2009. The efficacy of commercial silicones against blue stain and mould fungi in wood. European Journal of Wood and Wood Products 67: 159–167.

Gibson, L.J. and M.F. Ashby. 1988. Cellular Solids: Structure and Properties. Pergamon Press, Oxford, UK.

Gierer, J. 1980. Chemical aspects of kraft pulping. Wood Science and Technology 14: 241–266.

Glass, S.V. and A. TenWolde. 2007. Review of in-service moisture and temperature conditions in wood-frame buildings. General Technical Report FPL-GTR-4, U.S. Department of Agriculture, Forest Service, Forest Products Laboratory, Madison (WI), USA.

Glass, S.V. and S.L. Zelinka. 2010. Moisture relations and physical properties of wood, Chapter 4. *In*: Ross, R.J. [ed.]. Wood Handbook—Wood as an Engineering Material. General Technical Report FPL–GTR–190, U.S. Department of Agriculture, Forest Service, Forest Products Laboratory, Madison (WI), USA.

Goring, D.A.I. and T.E. Timell. 1962. Molecular weight of native cellulose. Tappi 45(6): 454–460.

Govorushko, S. 2019. Economic and ecological importance of termites: A global review. Entomological Science 22: 21–35.

Gril, J. and M. Norimoto. 1993. Compression of wood at high temperature, pp. 135–144. *In*: Birkinshaw, C. [ed.]. Proceedings of the COST 508 Wood Mechanics, Workshop on Wood: Plasticity and Damage, Limerick, Ireland. University of Limerick.

Grossman, P.U.A. 1976. Requirements for a model that exhibits mechano-sorptive behaviour. Wood Science and Technology 10(3): 163–168.

Grönqvist, S., J. Buchert, K. Rantanen, L. Viikari and A. Suurnakki. 2003. Activity of laccase on unbleached and bleached thermomechanical pulp. Enzyme and Microbial Technology 32: 439–445.

Haller, P. and J. Wehsener. 2004. Festigkeitsuntersuchungen an Fichtenpressholz [Mechanical properties of densified spruce]. Holz als Roh- und Werkstoff 62: 452–454.

Handelsman, J. 2004. Metagenomics: application of genomics to uncultured microorganisms. Microbiological Molecular Biology Revue 68: 669–685.

Hansmann, C., M. Deka, R. Wimmer and W. Gindl. 2006. Artificial weathering of wood surfaces modified by melamine formaldehyde resins. Holz als Roh- und Werkstoff 64: 198–203.

Hansson, E.F., S. Bardage and S. Thelandersson. 2013. Modelling the risk for mould growth on timber stored outdoors protected from rain. *In*: The Proceedings IRG Annual Meeting, Stockholm, Sweden. International Research Group on Wood Protection IRG/WP 13-20529.

Hart, H., L.E. Craine and H. Hart. 2003. Organic Chemistry—A Short Course. (11th edn.), Houghton Mifflin Company, Boston, New York, USA.

Hashimoto, Y. and K. Onoma. 1949. Digestion of higher carbohydrates by mollusca (*Dolabella scapula* and *Teredo* sp.). Nippon Suisan Gakkaishi (Bulletin of the Japanese Society of Scientific Fisheries) 15(6): 253–258.

Hearmon, R. and J. Paton. 1964. Moisture content changes and creep of wood. Forest Products Journal 14(8): 357–359.

Hill, C.A.S. 2006. Wood Modification—Chemical, Thermal and Other processes. Wiley Series in Renewable Resources, Wiley and Sons, Chichester, UK.

Hill, C.A.S. and D. Jones. 1996. The dimensional stabilisation of Corsican pine sapwood by reaction with carboxylic acid anhydrides. Holzforschung 50: 457–462.

Hill, C.A.S., S.C. Forster, M.R.M. Farahani, M.D.C. Hale, G.A. Ormondroyd and G.R. Williams. 2005. An investigation of cell wall micropore blocking as a possible mechanism for the decay resistance of anhydride modified wood. International Biodeterioration and Biodegradation 55: 69–76.

Hill, C.A.S., A.J. Norton and G. Newman. 2010. The water vapour sorption properties of Sitka spruce determined using a dynamic vapour sorption apparatus. Wood Science and Technology 44: 497–514.

Hillis, W.E. 1984. High temperature and chemical effects on wood stability. Part 1. General considerations. Wood Science and Technology 18: 281–293.

Hillis, W.E. 1987. Heartwood and Tree Exudates. Springer-Verlag, Berlin, Heidelberg, Germany.

Hillis, W.E. and A.N. Rozsa. 1978. The softening temperatures of wood. Holzforschung 32(2): 68–73.

Hillis, W.E. and A.N. Rozsa. 1985. High temperature and chemical effects on wood stability. Part 2. The effect of heat on the softening of radiata pine. Wood Science and Technology 19: 57–66.

Hoadley, R.B. 1990. Identifying Wood: Accurate Results with simple Tools. The Taunton Press, Newtown, Connecticut, USA.

Hoffmeyer, P. 1990. Failure of wood as influenced by moisture and duration of load. PhD. Thesis, State University of New York, Syracuse, New York, USA.

Hon, D.N.-S. and G. Ifju. 1978. Measuring penetration of light into wood by detection of photo-induced free radicals. Journal of Wood Science 11: 118–127.

Hounsfield, G.N. 1973. Computerized axial scanning tomography. The British Journal of Radiology 46: 1016–1022.

Huang, J., A. Dufresne and N. Lin. 2019. Nanocellulose: From Fundamentals to Advanced Materials. John Wiley & Sons. Wiley-VCH Verlag GmbH & Co. KGaA, Weinheim, Germany.

Höll, W., M. Frommberger and C. Strassl. 2002. Soluble carbohydrates in the nutrition of house longhorn beetle larvae, *Hylotrupes bajulus* (L.) (Col., Cerambycidae): From living sapwood to faeces. Journal of Applied Entomology 126: 463–469.

Illman, B. and T.L. Highley. 1989. Decomposition of wood by brown rot fungi, pp. 465–484. *In*: O'Rear, C.E. and Llewellyn, G.C. [eds.]. Biodeterioration Research Vol. 2: General Biodeteriorations, Biodegradation, Mycotoxins, Biotxins and Wood Decay. Perseus Books, Basic Books, New York, USA.

Ilvessalo-Pfäffli, M.-S. 1995. Fiber Atlas, Identification of Papermaking Fibers. Springer Verlag, Berlin, Heidelberg, Germany.

Inagaki, T., H. Yonenobu and S. Tsuchikawa. 2008. Near-infrared spectroscopic monitoring of the water adsorption/ desorption process in modern and archaeological wood. Applied Spectroscopy 62(8): 860–865.

Isaksson, T., S. Thelandersson, C. Brischke and J. Jermer. 2015. Service life of wood in outdoor above ground applications: Engineering design guideline. Background document. Report TVBK-3067, Lund University, Sweden.

ISO. 2009. ISO 15927-3. Hygrothermal performance of buildings: Calculation and presentation of climatic data. Part 3: Calculation of a driving rain index for vertical surfaces from hourly wind and rain data. European Committee for Standardization, Brussels, Belgium.

Itoh, H., M. Wada, Y. Honda, M. Kuwahara and T. Watanabe. 2003. Bio-organosolve pretreatments for simultaneous saccharification and fermentation of beech wood by ethanolysis and white-rot fungi. Journal of Biotechnology 103: 273–280.

Jagels, R. and M.V. Dyer. 1983. Morphometric analysis applied to wood structure. 1. Cross-sectional cell shape area change in red spruce. Wood and Fiber Science 15(4): 376–386.

Janusz, G., A. Pawlik, J. Sulej, U. Świderska-Burek, A. Jarosz-Wilkołazka and A. Paszczyński. 2017. Lignin degradation: Microorganisms, enzymes involved, genomes analysis and evolution. FEMS Microbiology Reviews 41(6): 941–962.

Jawaid, M., M. Sapuan Salit and O.Y. Alothman. 2017. Green Biocomposites: Design and Applications. Springer International Publishing AG, Cham, Switzerland.

Jeffries, J.W. 1987. Chapter 24: Physical, chemical and biochemical considerations in the biological degradation of wood, pp. 213–230. *In*: Kennedy, J.F., Phillips, G.O. and William, P.A. [eds.]. Wood and Cellulosics: Industrial Utilisation, Biotechnology, Structure and Properties. Ellis Horwood Ltd. Chichester, West Sussex, UK.

Jennings, C.M. 1993. Bonding densified wood I. ASC/CASS Undergrad. Research Report. Center for Adhesive and Sealant Science, Virginia Tech, Blacksburg (VA), USA.

Jermer, J. 2011. WoodExter—Service life and performance of exterior wood above ground—Final report. Report 2011:53, SP Technical Research Institute of Sweden.

Jones, R., P. Silence and M. Webster. 2015. Preserving History: Subterranean Termite Prevention in Colonial Williamsburg. Colonial Williamsburg Foundation, Williamsburg, USA. museumpests.net/wpcontent/uploads/2015/03/Preserving-History-SubterraneanTermite-Prevention-in-Colonial-Williamsburg1.pdf (2020-03-01).

Kamke, F.A. and A. Kutnar. 2010. Transverse compression behavior of wood in saturated steam at 150 to 170°C. Wood and Fiber Science 42(3): 1–11.

Karlsson, O., T. Ikeda, T. Kishimoto, K. Magara, Y. Matsumoto and S. Hosoya. 2004. Isolation of lignin-carbohydrate bonds in wood. Model experiments and preliminary application to pine. Journal of Wood Science 50: 142–150.

Karlsson, O., P. Tornianinen, O. Dagbro, K. Granlund and T. Morén. 2012. Presence of water soluble compounds in thermally modified wood: Carbohydrates and furfurals. Bioresources 7(3): 3679–3689.

Kataoka, Y. and M. Kiguchi. 2001. Depth profiling of photo-induced degradation in wood by FT-IR microspectroscopy. Journal of Wood Science 47: 325–327.

Kennedy, R.W. 1968. Wood in transverse compression. Forest Products Journal 18: 36–40.

Klüppel, A. and C. Mai. 2018. Effect of seawater on the weathering of wood. European Journal of Wood and Wood Products 76(3): 1029–1035.

Kultikova, E.V. 1999. Structure and Properties Relationships of Densified Wood. M.Sc. Thesis, Virginia Tech, Blacksburg (VA), USA.

Kunesh, R.H. 1968. Strength and elastic properties of wood in transverse compression. Forest Products Journal 18: 36–40.

Kučera, L.J. and M. Bariska. 1982. On the fracture morphology in wood. Part 1: A SEM study of deformations in wood of spruce and aspen upon ultimate axial compression load. Wood Science and Technology 16(4): 241–259.

Kutnar, A. and F.A. Kamke. 2013. Transverse compression behavior of Douglas-fir (*Pseudotsuga menziesii*) in saturated steam environment. European Journal of Wood and Wood Products 71: 443–449.

Kutnik, M., I. Paulmier, F. Simon and M. Jequel. 2009. Modified wood versus termite attacks: What should be improved in assessment methodology? pp. 69–76. *In*: Englund, F., Hill, C.A.S., Militz, H. and Segerholm, B.K. [eds.]. Proceedings of the 4th European Conference on Wood Modification, Stockholm, Sweden.

Kutnik, M., I. Paulmier, D. Ansard, M. Montibus and C. Lucas. 2020. Update on the distribution of termites and other wood-boring insects in Europe. *In*: IRG Webinar 2020. International Research Group on Wood Protection IRG/WP 20-10960.

Küch, W. 1951. Über die Vergütung des Holzes durch Verdichtung des Gefüges. [Improvement of wood properties by compression of the cell structure.] Holz als Roh- und Werkstoff 9(8): 305–317 (In German).

Laborie, M.-P.G. 2006. The temperature dependence of wood relaxations: a molecular probe of the woody cell wall, pp. 87–94. *In*: Stokke, D.D. and Groom, L.H. [eds.]. Characterization of the Cellulosic Cell-wall, Blackwell, Ames, Oxford, Victoria, UK.

Lang, E.M. and M.P. Wolcott. 1996. A model for viscoelastic consolidation of wood-strand mats. Part II: Static stress-strain behaviour of the mat. Wood and Fiber Science 28(3): 369–379.

Larsson-Brelid, P., C. Brischke, A.O. Rapp, M. Hansson, M. Westin, J. Jermer and A. Pilgård. 2011. Methods of field data evaluation – time versus reliability. *In*: The Proceedings IRG Annual Meeting, Queenstown, New Zealand. International Research Group on Wood Protection IRG/WP/11-20466.

Leatham, G.F., G.C. Myers and T.H. Wegner. 1990. Biomechanical pulping of aspen chips: Energy savings resulting from different chemical treatments. Tappi Journal 73: 117–123.

Leicester, R. 1971. A reological model for mechano-sorptive deflection of beams. Wood Science and Technology 5(3): 211–220.

Lenth, C.A. 1999. Wood material behavior in severe environments. PhD. Thesis, Virginia Tech, Blacksburg (VA), USA.

Lenth, C.A. and F.A. Kamke. 1996. Investigations of flakeboard mat consolidation. Part I: Characterizing the cellular structure. Wood and Fiber Science 28(2): 153–167.

Lenth, C.A. and F.A. Kamke. 2001. Equilibrium moisture content of wood in high-temperature pressurized environments. Wood and Fiber Science 33(1): 104–118.

Lindgren, O. 1992. Medical CT-scanners for non-destructive wood density and moisture content measurements. PhD. Thesis, Luleå University of Technology, Skellefteå, Sweden.

Lionetto, F., R. Del Sole, D. Cannoletta, G. Vasapollo and A. Maffezzoli. 2012. Monitoring wood degradation during weathering by cellulose crystallinity. Materials 5: 1910–1922.

Lorenzo, D., J. Fernández, M. Touza, M. Guaita, A. Lozano, J. Benito and T. de Troya. 2016. The problem of exterior structures built in northern Spain climates in fir and spruce due wood destroying Fungi attacks. The example of a wood exterior structure in Pontevedra, Spain and the importance of design in the performance, pp. 49–50. *In*: de Troya, T.,

Galván, J. and Jones, D. [eds.]. The Proceedings of the COST FP1303 Performance of Bio-based Building Materials Meeting. Designing with Bio-Based Building Materials—Challenges and Opportunities. Madrid, Spain.

Lowden, L.A. and T.R Hull. 2013. Flammability behaviour of wood and a review of the methods for its reduction. Fire Science Reviews 2(4): 1–19.

Lukowsky, D. 1999. Holzschutz mit Melaminharzen. [Wood protection with melamine resins.] M.Sc. Thesis, University of Hamburg, Germany (In German).

Lundquist, K. 1992. Acidolysis, pp. 289–300. In: Lin, S.Y. and Dence, C.V. [eds.]. Methods in Lignin Chemistry. Springer Series in Wood Science, Berlin, Heidelberg, Germany.

Maeda, H., Y. Ozaki, M. Tanaka, N. Hayashi and T. Kojima. 1995. Near infrared spectroscopy and chemometrics studies of temperature-dependent spectral variations of water: relationship between spectral changes and hydrogen bonds. Journal of Near Infrared Spectroscopy 3(4): 191–201.

Mahajan, S., D. Jeremic, R.E. Goacher and E.R. Master. 2012. Mode of coniferous wood decay by the white rot fungus *Phanaerochaete carnosa* as elucidated by FTIR and ToF-SIMS. Applied Microbiology and Biotechnology 94(5): 1303–1311.

Mai, C., S. Donath and H. Militz. 2003. Modification of wood with silicon compounds, pp. 239–251. In: Van Acker J. and C. Hill [eds.]. Proceedings of the first European Conference on Wood Modification, Ghent, Belgium.

Maijala, P., M. Kleen, O. Westin, K. Poppius-Levlin, K. Herranen, J.H. Lehto, P. Reponen, O. Mäentausta, A. Mettälä and A. Hatakka. 2008. Biomechanical pulping of softwood with enzymes and white-rot fungus *Physisporinus rivulosus*. Enzyme and Microbial Technology 43: 169–177.

Mansour, K. and J.J. Mansour-Bek. 1934. The digestion of wood by insects and the supposed role of micro-organisms. Biological Reviews 9: 363–382.

Mawatari, S. 1950. Biological and industrial study of marine borer problem in Japan. Suisan Dobutsu Nokenkyu 1(l): 45–124.

McGreer, M. 2001. Weathering Testing Handbook. Atlas Electric Device Company, USA.

Meluna, A.J. (ed.). 2009. Documents of Life and Activity of the Nobel Family 1801–1932. Volume 1. J.S.C. Humanistica, St. Petersburg, Russia (In Russian).

Menard, K. 2007. Dynamic Mechanical Analysis: A Practical Introduction. (2nd edn.), CRC Press, Boca Raton, USA.

Mendonça, R.T., J.F. Jara, V. González, J.P. Elissetche and J. Freer. 2008. Evaluation of the white-rot fungi *Ganoderma australe* and *Ceriporiopsis subvermispora* in biotechnological applications. Journal of Industrial Microbiology and Biotechnology 35(11): 1323–1330.

Meyer, L., C. Brischke and J. Rieken. 2013. Testing the performance of timber using 27 different field test methods. In: The Proceedings IRG Annual Meeting, Stockholm, Sweden. International Research Group on Wood Protection IRG/WP 13-20517.

Meyer-Veltrup, L., C. Brischke, G. Alfredsen, M. Humar, P.-O. Flæte, T. Isaksson, P. Larsson Brelid, M. Westin and J. Jermer. 2017. The combined effect of wetting ability and durability on outdoor performance of wood–development and verification of a new prediction approach. Wood Science and Technology 51: 615–637.

Militz, H. 1993. Treatment of timber with water soluble dimethylol resins to improve their dimensional stability and durability. Wood Science and Technology 27(5): 347–355.

Mohebby, B. 2003. Biological attack of acetylated wood. PhD. Thesis, Göttingen University, Germany.

Mork, E. 1928. Die Qualität des Fichtenholzes unter besonderer Rücksichtnahme auf Schleif- und Papierholz [The quality of spruce wood, with special consideration for pulpwood and paper.] Der Papier-Fabrikant 48: 741–747.

Morsing, N. 2000. Densification of wood—The influence of hygrothermal treatment on compression of beech perpendicular to the grain. PhD. Thesis, Technical University of Denmark, Copenhagen, Denmark.

Müller, W. 1934. Untersuchungen über die Symbiose von Tieren mit Pilzen und Bakterien. III. Mitteilung: Über die Pilzsymbiose holzfressender Insektenlarven [Studies on the symbiosis of animals with fungi and bacteria. III. Message: About the symbiosis of fungi in wood-eating insect larvae.] Archiv für Mikrobiologie (Archives of Microbiology) 5(1): 84–147 (In German).

Müller, U., M. Rätzsch, M. Schwanninger, M. Steiner and H. Zöbl. 2003. Yellowing and IR changes of spruce wood as result of UV-irradiation. Journal of Photochemistry and Photobiology B: Biology 69(2): 97–105.

Mäki-Arvela, P., T. Salmi, B. Holmbom, S. Willför and D.Y. Miurzin. 2011. Synthesis of sugars by hydrolysis of hemicelluloses—A review. Chemical Reviews 111(9): 5638–5666.

Nairn, J.A. 2006. Numerical simulations of transverse compression and densification in wood. Wood and Fiber Science 38(4): 576–591.

Nardi, J.B., R.I. Mackie and J.O. Dawson. 2002. Could microbial symbionts of arthropod guts contribute significantly to nitrogen fixation in terrestrial ecosystems? Journal of Insect Pathology 48: 751–763.

Navi, P. and F. Heger. 2005. Comportement Thermo-Hydromécanique du Bois [Behaviour of Thermo-hydro-mechanical Processed Wood.] Presses Polytechniques et Universitaires Romandes, Lausanne, Switzerland (In French).

Navi, P. and D. Sandberg. 2012. Thermo-hydro-mechanical Processing of Wood. Presses Polytechniques et Universitaires Romandes, Lausanne, Switzerland.

Navi, P., V. Pittet and C.J.G. Plummer. 2002. Transient moisture effect on wood creep. Wood Science and Technology 36(6): 447–462.

Newman, R.H. and J.A. Hemmingson. 1990. Determination of the degree of crystallinity of cellulose in wood by carbon-13 NMR spectroscopy. Holzforschung 44: 351–355.

Niklewski, J., T. Isaksson, E. Frühwald Hansson and S. Thelandersson. 2017. Moisture conditions of rain-exposed glue-laminated timber members: The effect of different detailing. Wood Material Science & Engineering 13(3): 129–140.

Nore, K., B. Blocken, B.P. Jelle, J.V. Thue and J. Carmeliet. 2007. A dataset of wind-driven rain measurements on a low-rise test building in Norway. Building and Environment 42: 2150–2165.

Norimoto, M. and J. Gril. 1993. Structure and properties of chemically treated woods, pp. 135–154. *In*: Shiraishi, N., Kajita, H. and Norimoto, M. [eds.]. Current Japanese Materials Research. Elsevier, Japan.

Nuopponen, M., H. Wikberg, T. Vuorinen, S.L. Maunu, S. Jämsä and P. Viitaniemi. 2004. Heat-treated wood softwood exposed to weathering. Journal of Applied Polymer Science 91(4): 2128–2134.

Nuopponen, M., T. Vuorinen, S. Jämsä and P. Viitaniemi. 2005. The effects of a heat treatment on the behaviour of extractives in softwood studied by FTIR spectroscopy. Wood Science and Technology 37(2): 109–115.

Obataya, E. and B. Tomita. 2002. Hygroscopicity of heat-treated wood II. Reversible and irreversible reductions in the hygroscopicity of wood due to heating. Mokuzai Gakkaishi 48(4): 288–295.

Oberhofnerová, E., M. Pánek and A. García-Cimarras. 2017. The effect of natural weathering on untreated wood surface. Maderas. Ciencia y tecnología 19(2): 173–184.

Osgood, C.E., G.J. Suci and P.H. Tannenbaum. 1957. The Measurement of Meaning. University of Illinois Press, Champaign (IL), USA.

Östberg, G., L. Salmén and J. Terlecki. 1990. Softening temperature of moist wood measured by differential calorimetry. Holzforschung 44: 223–225.

Pallardy, S.G. and T.T. Kozlowski. 2008. Physiology of Woody Plants. (3rd edn.), Elsevier, New York, USA.

Pandey, K.K. 2005. A note on the influence of extractives on the photo-discoloration and photo-degradation of wood. Polymer Degradation and Stability 87(2): 375–379.

Pandey, K.K. and T. Vuorinen. 2008. Comparative study of photodegradation of wood by a UV laser and a xenon light source. Polymer Degradation and Stability 93(12): 2138–2146.

Panshin, A.J., C. de Zeeuw and H.P. Brown. 1964. Textbook of Wood Technology. Volume I: Structure, Identification, Uses, and Properties of the commercial Woods of the United states. (2nd edition) McGraw-Hill Book Company, New York, San Francisco, USA.

Perkitny, T. and W. Jablonski. 1984. Zur Beurteilung der mechanischen Eigenschaften vor Pressvollholz. [For assessing the mechanical properties of densified wood.] Holz als Roh- und Werkstoff 42: 81–84 (In German).

Petrič, M. 2017. Coatings and hydrophobes, pp. 217–227. *In*: Jones, D. and Brischke, C. [eds.]. Performance of Bio-based Building Materials. Woodhead Publishing, Duxford, UK.

Petrillo, M., J. Sandak, P. Grossi and A. Sandak. 2019. Chemical and appearance changes of wood due to artificial weathering—Dose-response model. Journal of Near Infrared Spectroscopy 27(1): 26–37.

Phillips, E.W.J., E.H. Adams and R.F.S. Herman. 1962. The measurement of density variation within the growth rings in thin sections of wood using beta particles. Journal of the Institute of Wood Science 10: 11–28.

Pilgård, A., G. Alfredsen, C.G. Fossdal and I.C.J. Long. 2012. The effects of acetylation on the growth of *Postia placenta* over 36 weeks. *In*: The Proceedings IRG Annual Meeting, Kuala Lumpar, Malaysia. International Research Group on Wood Protection IRG/WP 12-40589.

Pittet, V. 1996. Etude expérimental des couplages mécanosorptifs dans le bois soumis à variations hygrométriques contrôlées sous chargements de longue durée [Experimental study of mechano-sorptive effect in wood subjected to moisture variations under controlled loads of long duration.] PhD. Thesis, Swiss Federal Institute of Technology in Lausanne (EPFL), Switzerland (In French).

Plackett, D.V., E.A. Dunningham and A.P. Singh. 1992. Weathering of chemically modified wood. Holz als Roh- und Werkstoff 50: 135–140.

Popescu, C.-M., C.A.S. Hill and M.-C. Popescu. 2016. Water adsorption in acetylated birch wood evaluated through near infrared spectroscopy. International Wood Products Journal 7(2): 61–65.

Prodehl, A. 1931a. Zur Holzbiegetechnik [About the wood bending technology.] Zeitschrift des Vereines deutscher Ingenieure 75(39): 1217–1222 (In German).

Prodehl, A. 1931b. Untersuchungen über das Biegen gedämpften Holzes [Studies on the bending of steamed wood.] PhD. Thesis, Sächsischen Technischen Hochschule zu Dresden (Dresden University of Technology), Germany (In German).

Reid, I.D. 1995. Biodegradation of lignin. Canadian Journal of Botany 73: 1011–1018.

Reiterer, A. and S.E. Stanzl-Tschegg. 2001. Compressive behaviour of softwood under uniaxial loading at different orientations to the grain. Mechanics of Materials 33: 705–715.

Reynolds, M.S. 2004. Hydro-thermal stabilization of wood-based materials. M.Sc. Thesis, Virginia Tech, Blacksburg (VA), USA.

Ribeiro, H.A. and C.A.V. Costa. 2007. Modelling and simulation of the nonlinear behaviour of paper: A cellular materials approach. Chemical Engineering Science 62: 6696–6708.

Riley, R., A.A. Salamov, D.W. Brown, L.G. Nagy, D. Floudas, B.W. Held, A. Levasseur, V. Lombard, E. Morin, R. Otillar, E.A. Lindquist, H. Sun, K.M. LaButti, J. Schmutz, D. Jabbour, H. Luo, S.E. Baker, B. Henrissat, F. Martin, D. Cullen, D.S. Hibbet and I.V. Grigoriev. 2014. Extensive sampling of basidiomycete genomes demonstrates inadequacy of the white-rot/brown-rot paradigm for wood decay fungi. Proceedings of the National Academy of Sciences of the United States of America 111(27): 9923–9928.

Ringman, R., A. Pilgård and K. Richter. 2014. Effect of wood modification on gene expression during incipient *Postia placenta* decay. International Biodeterioration and Biodegradation 86: 86–91.

Ringman, R., G. Beck and A. Pilgård. 2019. The importance of moisture for brown rot degradation of modified wood: A critical discussion. Forests 10(6): Article ID 522.

Roussel, M.O. 1997. Conception et caractérisation d'un bois reconstitué pour absorbeur d'énergie [Design and characterization of a reconstituted wood for absorber the energy.] PhD. Thesis, University of Bordeaux I, France (In French).

Rowell, R.M. 1983. Chemical modification of wood: A review. Commonwealth Forestry Bureau, Oxford, England 6(12): 363–382.

Rowell, R.M. 2012. Handbook of Wood Chemistry and Wood Composites (2nd edn.). CRC Press, Boca Raton, USA.

Rust, M.K. and N.Y. Su. 2012. Managing social insects of urban importance. Annual Review of Entomology 57: 355–375.

Råberg, U., M.-L. Edlund, N. Terziev and C.J. Land. 2005. Testing and evaluation of natural durability of wood in above ground conditions in Europe—An overview. Journal of Wood Science 51: 429–440.

Saei, A.M., B. Mohebby and M.R. Abdeh. 2015. Effects of oleothermal treatment and polydimethylsiloxane (PDMS) coating on natural weathering of beech and fir woods. Maderas: Ciencia y tecnología 17(4): 905–918.

Sakakibara, A. 1980. A structural model of softwood lignin. Wood Science and Technology 14: 89–100.

Salehi, M. 2012. Chemical interactions between fatty acids and wood components during oxidation process. M.Sc. Thesis, Royal Institute of Technology (KTH), Stockholm, Sweden.

Salmén, N.L. 1982. Temperature and water induced softening behaviour of wood fiber based materials. PhD. Thesis, Royal Institute of Technology (KTH), Stockholm, Sweden.

Salmén, N.L., P. Kolseth and M. Rigdahl. 1986. Modelling of small-strain properties and environmental effects on paper and cellulose fiber, pp. 211–223. *In*: Salmén, N.L., de Ruvo, A., Seferis, J.C. and Stark, E.B. [eds.]. Composite System from Natural and Synthetic Polymers. Elsevier Science Publisher, Amsterdam, The Netherlands.

Sandak, A. and J. Sandak. 2017. Aesthetics, pp. 285–294. *In*: Jones, D. and Brischke, C. [eds.]. Performance of Bio-based Building Materials. Woodhead Publishing, Duxford, UK.

Sandak, A., J. Sandak, I. Burud and L. Ross Gobakken. 2016. Weathering kinetics of thin wood veneers assessed with near infrared spectroscopy. Journal of Near Infrared Spectroscopy 24: 549–553.

Sandberg, D. 1998. Inverkan av isostatisk komprimering på cellstrukturen [The influence of isostatic compression on the cell-wall structure of wood.] Report TRITA-TRÄ R-98-35, Royal Institute of Technology (KTH), Stockholm, Sweden.

Sandberg, D. 1999. Weathering of radial and tangential wood surfaces of pine and spruce. Holzforschung 53(4): 355–364.

Santhakumaran, L.N. and J.A. Sneli. 1978. Natural resistance of different species of timber to marine borer attack in the Trondheimsfjord (Western Norway). *In*: The Proceedings IRG Annual Meeting, Peebles, Scotland, UK. International Research Group on Wood Protection IRG/WP 435.

Scheffer, T.C. 1971. A climate index for estimating potential for decay in wood structures above ground. Forest Products Journal 21: 25–31.

Schmidt, O. 2006. Wood and Tree Fungi: Biology, Damage, Protection, and Use. Springer-Verlag, Berlin, Heidelberg, Germany.

Schmidt, O., W. Liese and U. Moreth. 1996. Decay of timber in a water cooling tower by the basidiomycete *Physisporinus vitreus*. Material und Organismen 30: 161–178.

Schrepfer, V. and F.H. Schweingruber. 1998. Anatomical structures in reshaped press-dried wood. Holzforschung 52(6): 615–622.

Scott, G.M., M. Akhtar, R.F. Swaney and C.J. Houtman. 2002. Recent developments in biopulping technology at Madison, WI. Biotechnology Progress 21: 61–71.

Shams I. and I. Yano. 2011. Compressive deformation of phenol formaldehyde (PF) resin-impregnated wood related to the molecular weight of resin. Wood Science and Technology 45: 73–81.

Sjöström, E. 1993. Wood Chemistry—Fundamentals and Applications. (2nd edn.) Academic Press, San Diego, USA.

Skaar, C. 1988. Wood-Water Relations. Springer-Verlag, Berlin, Heidelberg, Germany.

Srinivas, K. and K.K. Pandey. 2012. Photodegradation of thermally modified wood. Journal of Photochemimstry and Photobiology B: Biology 117: 140–145.

Srivastava, S., R. Kumar and V.P. Singh. 2013. Wood Decaying Fungi. Lambert Academic Publishing, Germany.

Stamm, A.J. 1964. Wood and Cellulose Science. The Ronald Press Company, New York, USA.

Stamm, A.J. and R.M. Seborg. 1939. Resin-treated plywood. Industrial & Engineering Chemistry 31(7): 897–902.

Stienen, T., O. Schmidt and T. Huckfeldt. 2014. Wood decay by indoor basidiomycetes at different moisture and temperature. Holzforschung 68: 9–15.

Strnad, S., N. Velkova, B. Saake, A. Doliška, M. Bračič and L.F. Zemljič. 2013. Influence of sulfated arabino- and glucuronoxylans charging-behavior regarding antithrombotic properties. Reactive and Functional Polymers 73(12): 1639–1645.

Sützl, L., G. Foley, E.M.J. Gillam, M. Bodén and D. Haltrich. 2019. The GMC superfamily of oxidoreductases revisited: Analysis and evolution of fungal GMC oxidoreductases. Biotechnology for Biofuels 12: 118.

Tabarsa, T. and Y.H. Chui. 2000. Stress-strain response of wood under radial compression. Part I. Test method and influences of cellular properties. Wood and Fiber Science 32(2): 144–152.

Tabarsa, T. and Y.H. Chui. 2001. Characterizing microscopic behavior of wood under transverse compression. Part II. Effect of species and loading direction. Wood and Fiber Science 33(2): 223–232.

Tang, Y. and W.T. Simpson. 1990. Perpendicular-to-grain rheological behavior of loblolly pine in press drying. Wood and Fiber Science 22(3): 326–342.

Tarkow, H. and A.J. Stamm. 1953. Effect of formaldehyde treatments upon the dimensional stabilization of wood. Forest Products Journal 3: 33–37.

Tartar, A., M.W. Wheeler, X. Zhou, M.R. Coy, D.G. Boucias and M.E. Scharf. 2009. Parallel metatranscriptome analyes of host and symbiont gene expression in the gut of the termite *Reticulitermes flavipes*. Biotechnology for Biofuels 2: Article ID 25.

Teacă, C-.A., D. Roşu, F. Mustaţă, T. Rusu, L. Roşu, I. Roşca and C.D. Varganici. 2019. Natural bio-based products for wood coating and protection against degradation: A review. Bioresources 14(2): 4873–4901.

Tillman, D.A., A.J. Rossi and W.D. Kitto. 1981. Wood Combustion: Principles, Processes and Economics. Academic Press, Orlando, USA.

Tjeerdsma, B.F., M. Boonstra, A. Pizzi, P. Tekely and H. Militz. 1998. Characterisation of thermally modified wood: Molecular reasons for wood performance improvement. Holz als Roh- und Werkstoff 56: 149–153.

Tokuda, G. 2019. Plant cell wall degradation in insects: Recent progress on endogenous enzymes revealed by multi-omics technologies. Advances in Insect Physiology 57: 97–136.

Tolf, A.W. 1976. The Russian Rockefellers: The Saga of the Nobel Family and the Russian Oil. Publ. No. 158, Hoover Institution Press, Stanford University, Stanford (CA), USA.

Tolvaj, L., E. Preklet, E. Barta and G. Papp. 2001. Dependence of light sources on the artificial photodegradation of wood. *In*: Proceedings of the COST E-18 High Performance Wood Coatings, Paris, France.

Torniainen, P., O. Dagbro and T. Morén. 2011. Thermal modification of birch using saturated and superheated steam, pp. 43–48. *In*: Larnøy, E. and Alfredsen, G. [eds.]. The Proceedings of the 7th meeting WSE conference—Nordic Baltic Network in Wood Material Science & Engineering, Oslo, Norway.

Trendelenburg, R. and H. Mayer-Wegelin. 1955. Das Holz als Rohstoff [Wood as raw material.] (2nd edn.) Carl Hanser Verlag, München, Germany (In German).

Treu, A., K. Zimmer, C. Brischke, E. Larnøy, L. Ross Gobakken, F. Aloui, S.M. Cragg, P.-O. Flæte, M. Humar, M. Westin, L. Borges and J. Williams. 2019. Durability and protection of timber structures in marine environments in Europe: An overview. BioResources 14(4): 10161–10184.

Tsuchikawa, S. and S. Tsutsumi. 1998. Adsorptive and capillary condensed water in biological material. Journal of Materials Science Letters 17(8): 661–663.

Tudge, C. 2005. The Tree: A Natural History of what Trees are, how they live, and why they matter. Three Rivers Press, Random House Inc., New York, USA.

Turner, R.D. 1966. A Survey and Illustrated Catalogue of the Teredinidae (Mollusca: Bivalvia). The Museum of Comparative Zoology, Cambridge, Massachusetts, Harvard University, USA.

Turkulin, H. 2004. SEM methods in surface research on wood. *In*: COST E-18 final seminar, 26–27 April 2004. http://virtual.vtt.fi/virtual/proj6/coste18/turkulinpaper.pdf (2020-03-18).

Turkulin, H., H. Derbyshire and E.R. Miller. 2004. Investigations into the photodegradation of wood using microtensile testing. Part 5: The influence on moisture rates. Holz als Roh- und Werkstoff 62: 307–312.

Turkoglu, T., E. Baysal and T. Toker. 2015. The effects of natural weathering on color stability of impregnated and varnished wood materials. Advances in Materials Science and Engineering 2015: 1–9.

Uhmeier, A., T. Morooka and M. Norimoto. 1998. Influence of thermal softening and degradation on radial compression behavior of wet spruce. Holzforschung 52(1): 77–81.

Uimonen, T., S. Hautamäki, M. Altgen, M. Kymäläinen and L. Rautkari. 2019. Dynamic vapour sorption protocols for the quantification of accessible hydroxyl groups in wood. Holzforschung 74(4): 412–419.

Unger, A., A.P. Schniewind and W. Unger. 2001. Conservation of Wood Artifacts—A Handbook. Springer-Verlag, Berlin, Heidelberg, Germany.

Van den Bulcke, J., J. Van Acker and J. De Smet. 2009. An experimental set-up for real-time continuous moisture measurements of plywood exposed to outdoor climate. Building and Environment 44: 2368–2377.

Venäläinen, M., A.M. Harju, P. Kainulainen, H. Viitanen and H. Nikulainen. 2003. Variation in the decay resistance and its relationship with other wood characteristics in old Scots pines. Annals of Forest Science 60: 409–417.

Verma, M., S. Sharma and R. Prasad. 2009. Biological alternatives for termite control: A review. International Biodeterioration and Biodegradation 63: 959–972.

Viitanen, H. 1997. Modelling the time factor in the development of mould fungi—The effect of critical humidity and temperature conditions on pine and spruce sapwood. Holzforschung 51: 6–14.

Viitanen, H., T. Toratti, L. Makkonen, R. Peuhkuri, T. Ojanen, L. Ruokolainen and J. Räisänen. 2010. Towards modelling of decay risk of wooden materials. European Journal of Wood and Wood Products 68: 303–313.

Vintila, E. 1939. Untersuchungen über Raumgewicht und Schwindmass von Früh- und Spätholz bei Nadelhölzern [Studies on density and shrinkage of earlywood and latewood in conifers.] Holz als Roh- und Werkstoff 2(10): 345–357 (In German).

Visakh, P.M. and Y. Arao. 2015. Flame retardants: Polymer blends, composites and nanocomposites. Springer International Publishing, Cham, Switzerland.

Voight, J.R. 2015. Xylotrophic bivalves: Aspects of their biology and the impacts of humans. Journal of Molluscan Studies 81(2): 175–186.

Wahlström, L. and H. Lindberg. 1999. Measurement of cell wall penetration on wood of water based chemicals using SEM/EDS and STEM/EDS technique. Wood Science and Technology 33(2): 111–122.

Wang, J.Y. and P.A. Cooper. 2005. Effect of grain orientation and surface wetting on vertical density profiles of thermally compressed fir and spruce. Holz als Roh- und Werkstoff 63: 397–402.

Wang, C.-H., R.H. Leicester and M.N. Nguyen. 2008. Decay Above Ground. Manual No. 4. CSIRO Sustainable Ecosystems, Urban Systems Program, Highett, Victoria, Australia.

Wangaard, F.F. 1950. The Mechanical Properties of Wood. John Wiley & Sons Inc. Chapman & Hall, Ltd, London, UK.

Westermark, U. 1985. The occurrence of p-hydroxyphenylpropane units in the middle-lamella lignin of spruce (*Picea abies*). Wood Science and Technology 19: 223–232.

Westermark, U., B. Samuelsson and K. Lundquist. 1995. Homolytic cleavage of the β-ether bond in phenolic β-O-4 structures in wood lignin and in guaiacylglycerol-β-guaiacyl ether. Research on Chemical Intermediates 21(3/5): 343–352.

Wilcox, W.W., N. Parameswaran and W. Liese. 1974. Ultrastructure of brown rot in wood treated with pentachlorophenol. Holzforschung 28: 211–217.

Williams, R.S. 2005. Weathering of wood, Chapter 7. *In*: Rowell, R.M. [ed.]. Handbook of Wood Chemistry and Wood Composites. CRC Press, Boca Raton, USA.

Williams, R.S., M.T. Knaebe and W.C. Feist. 2001. Erosion rates of wood during natural weathering. Part II. Earlywood and latewood erosion rates. Wood and Fiber Science 33(1): 43–49.

Willems, W., M. Altgen and H. Militz. 2015. Comparison of EMC and durability of heat treated wood from high versus low water vapour pressure reactor systems. International Wood Products Journal 6: 21–26.

Willems, W., M. Altgen and L. Rautkari. 2020. A molecular model for reversible and irreversible hygroscopicity changes by thermal wood modification. Holzforschung 74(4): 420–425.

Windeisen, E., C. Strobel and G. Wegener. 2007. Chemical changes during the production of thermo-treated beech wood. Wood Science and Technology 41: 523–536.

Wolcott, M.P. 1989. Modelling viscoelastic cellular materials for the pressing of wood composites. PhD. Thesis, Virginia Tech, Blacksburg (VA), USA.

Wolcott, M.P., B. Kasal, F.A. Kamke and D.A. Dillard. 1989. Testing small wood specimens in transverse compression. Wood and Fiber Science 21(3): 320–329.

Wolcott, M.P., F.A. Kamke and D.A. Dillard. 1994. Fundamental aspects of wood deformation pertaining to manufacture of wood-base composites. Wood and Fiber Science 26(4): 496–511.

Yang, T. and E. Ma. 2016. Moisture sorption and thermodynamic properties of wood under dynamic condition. International Journal of Polymer Science 2016: Article ID 2454610.

Yao, Y., M. Yoshioka and N. Shiraishi. 1994. Soluble properties of liquefied biomass prepared in organic solvents. I. The soluble behavior of liquefied biomass in various diluents. Mokuzai Gakkaishi 40(2): 176–184.

Yelle, D.J. and J. Ralph. 2016. Characterizing phenol-formaldehyde adhesive cure chemistry within the wood cell wall. International Journal of Adhesion and Adhesives 70: 26–36.

Yildiz, S., U.C. Yildiz and E.D. Tomak. 2011. The effects of natural weathering on the properties of heat-treated alder wood. BioResources 6(3): 2504–2521.

Zabel, R.A. and J.J. Morrell. 1992. Wood Microbiology. Academic Press, New York, USA.

Zaihan, J., C.A.S. Hill, S.F. Curling, W.S. Hashim and H. Hamdan. 2009. Moisture adsorption isotherms of *Acacia mangium* and *Endospermum malaccense* using dynamic vapour sorption. Journal of Tropical Forest Science 21(3): 277–285.

Zaman, A., R. Alén and R. Kotilainen. 2000. Thermal behavior of Scots pine (*Pinus sylvestris*) and silver birch (*Betula pendula*) at 200–230°. Wood and Fiber Science 32(2): 138–143.

Zelinka, S.L. R. Ringman, A. Pilgård, E. Engelund Thybring, J.E. Jakes and K. Richter. 2016. The role of chemical transport in the brown-rot decay resistance of modified wood. International Wood Products Journal 7: 35–43.

Zhao, T., E. Ma and W. Zhang. 2013. Moisture and temperature changes of wood during adsorption and desorption processes. Wood and Fiber Science 45(2): 187–194.

Zhou, C., G.D. Smith and C. Dai. 2009. Characterizing hydro-thermal compression behavior of aspen wood strands. Holzforschung 63(5): 609–617.

Zhou, X., W.-R. Cong, K.-Q. Su and Y.-M. Zhang. 2013. Ligninolytic enzymes from *Ganoderma* spp.: Current status and potential applications. Reviews in Microbiology 39(4): 416–426.

Zimmermann, T., E. Pöhler and T. Geiger. 2004. Cellulose fibrils for polymer reinforcement. Advanced Engineering Materials 6(9): 754–761.

Zobel, B.J. and J. Talbert. 1984. Applied Forest Tree Improvement. John Wiley & Sons, New York, USA.

Zobel, B.J. and J.P.v. Buijtenen. 1989. Wood Variation: Its Causes and Control. Springer-Verlag, Berlin, Heidelberg, Germany.

Zobel, B.J. and J.R. Sprauge. 1998. Juvenile Wood in Forest Trees. Springer-Verlag, Berlin, Heidelberg, Germany.

Chapter 2
Chemical Modification Processes

2.1 Introduction

Chemicals and natural products have been used to change the properties of wood since ancient times, but such treatments relate mostly to changes in the wood surface. Methods of modification of the whole or significant parts of the wood started to develop in the Twentieth Century, although the commercialisation of such processes did not become apparent until the 1990s with the growing awareness of the negative influence of wood preservatives on the environment. These preservatives had the effect of hindering the decay of wood by microorganisms and insects. After modification, the uptake of moisture in the wood cell wall is lowered and the resistance to decay enhanced. In contrast to water-based wood preservatives, chemically-modified wood shrinks and swells less, which is beneficial, reducing the formation of stresses as well as reducing blisters in coated products. The influences of the various processes on the properties of the wood are described herein.

The aim of this chapter is to describe the modification processes currently in use to produce wood products with improved and new desirable properties by the addition of chemicals. Other treatments are described to put these processes into perspective. Further definitions and the choice of modification process are referred to in Chapter 1.3. A list of common modification methods is given in Figure 2.1.

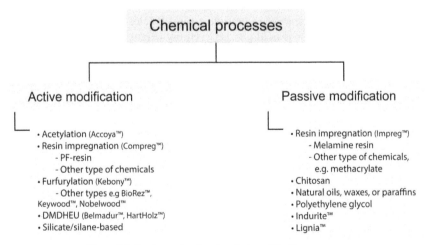

Figure 2.1 Passive and active chemical modification processes.

As discussed in Chapter 1, chemical treatments can be divided into: *active* and *passive* modification processes. In *active modification*, wood constituents and preferably the dominant ones, hemicellulose, lignin and cellulose, can be chemically altered. *Passive modification* involves the filling lumen and/or cell wall without any reaction with the main wood constituents in the cell wall (see Figure 1.1), but it may involve condensation reactions with the added chemical itself increasing its molecular weight (see Figure 1.46).

The formation of new chemical bonds between added chemicals and reactive groups in the wood is probably the most characteristic feature of an active modification process, such as acetylation (see Figure 1.42). This can only be efficiently done by allowing chemicals to diffuse into the cell wall and not just react with the cell wall surfaces, such as those facing the lumen in a tracheid and other micro-voids. Cross-linking of constituents in the cell wall to form a connecting bridge structure is also possible, especially if more than one bonding position exists in the active modifying chemical (see Figure 1.43). Cross-linking without the addition of chemicals and/or chemical degradation of wood constituents may take place, depending on the applied reaction conditions and the wood materials used (see Figure 1.41). Chemical structures and their formation during wood modification processes are identified on the basis of an analysis of physical, microstructural and chemical data, but detailed information of the resulting structures varies.

By studying macroscopic changes in the wood during the modification process and the subsequent exposure of the final material to various conditions, it is possible to understand what occurs on a microscopic level and even down to the molecular level. The fibre wall in wood is elastic and can absorb and desorb moisture, the moisture content (MC), being defined by:

$$\omega = \frac{m_w - m_d}{m_d} \tag{2.1}$$

where ω is the MC, m_w is the mass of wet wood and m_d is the mass of oven-dry wood.

At a MC higher than the fibre saturation point (FSP), wood cannot swell further. Drying and removal of moisture causes the material to shrink rather linearly with decreasing MC to an extent which depends on the direction (tangential < radial << longitudinal) within the wood and on the wood species. The density of a dry cell wall is close to that of cellulose and, if voids exist, they must be extremely small. A dried fibre wall (below FSP) may however start to take up moisture and swell although to a somewhat less extent at a given relative humidity of the surrounding air than during the drying cycle, exhibiting a hysteresis phenomenon (see Section 1.4). If wood is exposed to water or other chemical, solution or mixture, it may also absorb such fluids. The efficiency of such a process is basically related to the permeability of the wood, the properties of the modifying fluid and the process conditions. A porous, low-density wood can be easier to impregnate than wood with low permeability such as heartwood with its aspirated (closed) pores, whereas the presence of window-like (fenestriform) cross field pits between ray parenchyma and longitudinal tracheids in Scots pine but not in Norway spruce contributes to the higher permeability of its sapwood. The presence of extractives, the MC and the drying conditions/history, cracks, board dimensions, etc. also influence the permeability of wood. Furthermore, it is usually easier to impregnate wood with a modifying agent prepared under diluted conditions and with a lower molecular weight than with a more viscous fluid. Longitudinal penetration has long been known to be much faster than penetration in the transverse direction due to the open structure in the cross-section of the wood. The presence of rays in the radial direction favours flow along this pathway compared to tangential flow, especially when these are small pits in this direction, as is the case with Norway spruce. Using vacuum and pressure favours the penetration of liquids into wood as well as the heating of the fluid as it usually reduces viscosity, as long as components in the fluid do not start to react or polymerise before entering into the wood. After impregnation, the process often ends with a drying/curing step to stabilise the modifying agent and to remove solvents and, depending on the process used, any remaining reactants. The weight percentage gain (WPG) indicates how much wood has increased in dry weight as a result of the treatment.

$$WPG = \frac{m_{dm} - m_d}{m_d} \tag{2.2}$$

where m_{dm} is dry mass after modification and m_d is the dry mass before modification.

There are basically two ways by which a modifying chemical can be deposited in wood: in the pores such as the lumen and/or inside the cell wall. Filling the lumen will basically not change the dimensions of the wood and the mass increase will result in a higher density of the modified material at a given MC and an increase in associated strength parameters such as the compressive strength. The filling of the lumen will also lower the porosity of the material and the possibility for the uptake of other compounds or liquids.

The cell wall can absorb liquids other than water as long the properties of the liquid are not too different. A nano-pore in fully swollen wood is estimated to be 2–4 nm in size (Hill, 2006), while that of a water molecule is about 0.15 nm and that of furfuryl alcohol is about 0.6 nm, and molecules with a relatively low molecular weight have a greater chance of diffusing into the fibre wall. Furthermore, a polar and protic compound/solvent will interact better than a hydrophobic one with the hydrophilic cell wall and its components. This is typified by the easier spreading of a water droplet than an oil droplet on a fresh wood surface and a greater absorption of water into wood, resulting in swelling of a cell wall. This also means that a stable emulsion, with particles larger than the swollen nano-pores in the cell wall but small enough to penetrate through pit membranes, cannot enter into the cell wall even if the molecular weight of the chemical itself is relatively low. The middle lamella, however, consists mostly of lignin which is less hydrophilic than the carbohydrate polymers and this may absorb more hydrophobic compounds, possibly via pit openings where the middle lamella is more exposed. After drying and curing, compounds may remain in the cell wall, leading to a swollen or bulked structure, but also to an increase in the dimensions of the wood, as porous materials tend to swell outwards. The bulking coefficient (BC) is defined as:

$$BC = \frac{V_{dm} - V_d}{V_{dm}} \tag{2.3}$$

where V_{dm} is the volume of the dry modified wood and V_d is the volume of the dried unmodified wood.

The cell wall contains several layers, with the microfibril angles in the S_1 and S_3 layers counteracting the swelling of the thicker S_2 layer, where the microfibril angle is almost longitudinal (Skaar, 1988), but this effect seems to be of minor importance in most wood species, and the formation of a smaller lumen is less easy to understand and to study experimentally. Volume changes are usually studied in order to determine BC, but the wood cannot swell more than the fibre saturation point, and it is difficult to bulk the cell wall more than this without causing damage to the wood. That means that to achieve a WPG over 25%, the modifying substance must start to fill up the lumen instead.

An observed bulking effect indicates that the modifying chemical stays in the cell wall during the drying stage, when solvents such as water in the cell wall are evaporated whereas the modifying agent remains due to its lower volatility or because it reacts with the wood components or with itself. It has been speculated that the increase in bulking of the cell wall can be enhanced with a fluid-filled lumen, because the capillary flow of a liquid solvent during drying will take place earlier than that of cell-bound water and, as a result, will increase the concentration gradient favouring the further uptake of modifying compound in the wood cell.

It is difficult to decide whether or not a reaction with the wood polymers occurs by measuring the outer dimensions of wood, but exposing the material to moisture or water or some other solvent may be of great help. Soaking or extraction with water or other appropriate solvent shows whether a modifying chemical has reacted with the cell wall components and with itself or whether the chemical is un-bonded, soluble and can be leached out from the treated wood product. Such treatments are repeated with intermittent drying, as a single extraction may not be sufficient. To decide whether a modifying chemical has become bonded to wood components, chemical analysis or microscopy together with spectroscopic investigation may be undertaken. If the wood cell wall is filled with modifying agent, the uptake of water and swelling and shrinking are reduced, which means that the dimensional changes and stresses due to moisture changes are reduced. This is calculated as the anti-shrinking or anti-swelling efficiency (ASE), based on the swelling of modified and non-modified wood. The swelling (S) of wood is defined as:

$$S_w = \frac{V_s - V_d}{V_d}$$

(2.4)

where V_s is the volume of water-swelled wood, and the swelling of modified wood S_m is given by:

$$S_m = \frac{V_{sm} - V_{dm}}{V_{dm}}$$

(2.5)

where V_{sm} is the volume of water-swollen modified wood and V_{dm} is the volume of dry modified wood. ASE is defined as:

$$ASE = \frac{S_w - S_m}{S_w}$$

(2.6)

When the wood is in equilibrium with the moist air, an equilibrium moisture content (EMC) can be determined.

$$EMC = \frac{m_{we} - m_d}{m_d}$$

(2.7)

where m_{we} is the mass of moisture in the equilibrated wood. The moisture content of wood is determined by the relative humidity and temperature of the surrounding air and these must be specified. In general, 1–2 weeks are sufficient to achieve a stable moisture content in northern softwoods like Norway spruce and Scots pine, but modified wood and tropical wood may take longer due to the influence of their altered chemistry and lower porosity. EMC_r is sometimes used, but the moisture uptake is then related to the mass of wood before modification, so the moisture uptake is related not to the extent of the modification but to the initial weight of the wood (Hill, 2006).

The moisture exclusion efficiency (MEE) can be calculated by comparing the equilibrium moisture contents of the modified and unmodified wood.

$$MEE = \frac{EMC_m - EMC_{um}}{EMC_{um}}$$

(2.8)

where EMC_{um} is the EMC of the original wood and EMC_m that of modified wood. A filled cell wall resulting from modification will lower the MEE, especially when hydrophobic components have been introduced.

Reactions involving the degradation of wood polymers, such as hydrolysis or dehydration, those leading condensation with the possibility of cross-linking in the material, may occur, especially if the temperature and acid content are high (see thermal modification in Chapter 3). Cross-linking may also occur if the cross-linking agent or suitable modification substance is added. It has been suggested that the extent of cross-linking can be elucidated by using ASE′ (Hill, 2006):

$$ASE' = \frac{S_w - S_{m'}}{S_w}$$

(2.9)

where

$$S_{m'} = \frac{V_{ms} - V_d}{V_d}$$

(2.10)

and where V_{ms} is the volume of swollen modified wood.

By applying repeated extractions and studying the volume changes, further information can be obtained regarding the modification reactions. If soluble wood degradation products are removed by repeated extraction with water, the dry volume of the wood as well as the volume of water-swollen material will decrease. If both the modification agent and the wood cell wall are degraded, an increase in swollen volume will be seen together with a decrease in the dry volume of the modified wood (Hill, 2006).

2.2 Acetylation

Cellulose acetate was one of the first plastic materials produced by mixing cellulose with acetic anhydride and it has been used in many products (cigarette filters, films, etc.). Attempts to develop an efficient acetylation process for wood started more than ninety years ago at the Forest Products Laboratory (FPL), United States Department of Agriculture, in Madison (WI), USA, and later in many other sites around the world (Japan, New Zealand, Russia, Sweden, The Netherlands, UK) by both industry and academia.

In the acetylation process, hydroxyl groups in wood constituents are converted into more hydrophobic acetyl groups which increase the hydrophobicity of the treated material. In fact, some of the hemicelluloses in wood are already acetylated (see Section 1.3), which influences the ability of many hydrolytic enzymes to degrade the hemicellulose, due to the steric effect of the acetyl groups blocking the enzymes (Pawar et al., 2013). Undertaking acetylation will further increase this blocking effect, so that the decay rate is severely reduced, with the lowered uptake of moisture by the acetylated wood appearing to play an important role. As swelling is restricted by the wood structure, the bulky acetyl group will also hinder moisture uptake and give a decay resistant and more dimensionally stable material with good mechanical strength. Acetic acid is produced as a by-product in the acetylation process which could be converted back to acetic anhydride by the removal of water with the possibility of achieving a more or less closed chemical process, except for the chemicals consumed by the wood. Currently, the company Accsys Technologies in Arnhem (The Netherlands) industrially produces acetylated wood. This wood material is marketed under the commercial name Accoya™; radiata pine is the predominant species used in current treatment schedules. On average, Accoya™ wood attains an acetyl weight gain of approximately 20% and about 60,000 m^3 acetylated wood was produced in 2018. The main uses of Accoya™ wood include: exterior windows and doors, decking, cladding, and other civil construction applications.

Material selection and preparation

The acetylation process has been applied to solid wood, but the treatment of flakes allows further processing to wood fibres aimed for MDF products. Many different types of wood have been acetylated using a variety of procedures, including beech (Militz, 1991a,b), Norway spruce, Scots pine (Larsson-Brelid and Simonson, 1994) poplar, radiata pine (Bongers and Beckers, 2003), black locust (Németh et al., 2010), Southern yellow pine, ponderosa pine (Goldstein et al., 1961), red oak and sugar maple (Dreher et al., 1964), walnut, elm, cativo, eucalyptus (Rowell, 1984; Ozmen, 2007), rubberwood (Rafidah et al., 2006), poplar sp., willow sp. (Ozmen, 2007), and oriented strand boards (OSB) (Rowell and Plackett, 1988) as well as other lignocellulosic resources such as bamboo (Rowell and Norimoto, 1987), bagasse fibre (Rowell and Keany, 1991), jute (Callow, 1951; Andersson and Tillman, 1989), kenaf (Rowell and Harrison, 1993), wheat straw (Gomez-Bueso et al., 2000), pennywort, and water hyacinth (Rowell and Rowell, 1989). Nevertheless, the acetylation of wood is not applicable to every species, red oak and teak, for example, had a low ASE despite having a high WPG (Rowell, 1984). Norway spruce and Douglas fir are difficult to impregnate with the acetylating reagent (Bongers and Uphill, 2019). Acetylation of selected wood and lignocellulosic species is summarised in Table 2.1. Heartwood in thicker solid wood boards can be more difficult than sapwood to impregnate efficiently and to react with the anhydride reagent; this can mean a lower overall durability. According to Accsys Technologies, fast-grown and easily impregnated radiata pine sawn timber, initially shipped from New Zealand with a low proportion of heartwood, and to some extent alder sp., are species which are mostly acetylated.

Not only hemicellulose and lignin, but also extractives, e.g., sugars and pectin, are acetylated making them more hydrophobic and soluble in the reaction anhydride media. Heartwood and, to a

Table 2.1 Acetylation of some wood and lignocellulosic species.

Species	Acetylation	Reference
Small-medium scale		
African locust bean	acetic anhydride or acetic acid/CaCl$_2$, heating at 120°C for 3 hours	Azeh et al. (2013)
Caucasian alder, Oriental beech	acetic anhydride, soaking for 24 hours, heating at 120°C for 90 or 360 minutes	Akhtari and Arefkhani (2016)
Bagasse fibre	acetic anhydride heating at 120°C for less than 4 hours	Rowell and Keany (1991)
Beechwood	acetic anhydride or acetic acid/CaCl$_2$, heating 120°C for 3 hours	Azeh et al. (2013)
African baobab	acetic anhydride or acetic acid/CaCl$_2$, heating 120°C for 3 hours	Azeh et al. (2013)
Corsican pine	acetic anhydride/pyridine, vacuum for 1 hour, heating 120°C	Hill and Jones (1996)
River red gum, populus spp., white willow	acetic anhydride/dimethylacetamide heating at 100°C for less than 6 hours	Ozmen (2007)
European beech	acetic anhydride vacuum/pressure, heating at 120°C for 9 hours, drying at 105°C for 12 hours	Militz (1991a)
European white birch	acetic anhydride heating at 110°C, various time	Popescu et al. (2014)
Dark-bark spruce	various methods (catalysed and uncatalysed)	Obataya and Minato (2009)
Jute cloth	acetic anhydride, heating at 120°C for 2 hours	Andersson and Tillman (1989)
Japanese cedar	acetic anhydride/supercritical carbon dioxide at 10–12 MPa, heating to target temperature of 120–130°C for less than 63 hours	Matsunaga et al. (2010)
Maritime pine	acetic anhydride 100°C pyridine, or vinyl acetate 90–110°C, potassium carbonate catalyst	Jebrane et al. (2011)
White cedar, sugi	acetic anhydride treatment for 24 hours, heating at 120°C for 24 hours	Hadi et al. (2015)
Norway spruce, Scots pine	acetic anhydride, vacuum for 1 hour, impregnation at 10 bar for 1 hour, heating at 120°C for 6 hours	Larsson and Simonson (1994)
Obeche	impregnation with acetic anhydride, heat 120°C for 1–5 hours	Adebawo et al. (2019)
African oil palm	acetic anhydride: xylene heating at 140°C for 4 hours, or acetic anhydride:toluene, heating at 135°C for 1 hour	Subagiyo et al. (2017)
Rice straw fibre	acetic anhydride/various catalysts, heating at 100°C for 0.5 hour	Sun R.C. and Sun (2002), Sun, X.F. and Sun (2002)
Radiata pine	acetic anhydride, vacuum, heating at 110°C	Beck et al. (2018)
Rubberwood	acetic anhydride/pyridine, heating at 100°C for less than 27 hours	Rafidah et al. 2006
Norway spruce, Scots pine	acetic anhydride, vacuum, impregnation at 10 bar for 2 hours at 20°C and microwave heating	Larsson-Brelid and Simonsson (1999b)
Southern yellow pine	acetic anhydride, vacuum, heating at 140°C	Zelinka et al. (2020)
Southern yellow pine, ponderosa pine	acetic anhydride/xylene, heating vacuum, oven heating	Goldstein et al. (1961)
Wheat straw	immersion/drain, 120°C at BP chemicals, UK	Gomez-Bueso et al. (2000)
Industrial conditions		
European beech, European alder, linden, maple	acetylated in the plant of Accsys Technologies in Arnhem, the Netherlands	Bollmus et al. (2015)
European hornbeam	acetylated in the plant of Accsys Technologies in Arnhem, the Netherlands	Fodor et al. (2017)

Table 2.1 Contd. ...

...Table 2.1 Contd.

Species	Acetylation	Reference
Norway spruce, Douglas fir	acetylated in the plant of Accsys Technologies in Arnhem, the Netherlands	Bongers and Uphill (2019)
Radiata pine	acetylated in the plant of Accsys Technologies in Arnhem, the Netherlands	Bongers and Beckers (2003)
Southern yellow pine	Eastman Perennial wood 21% acetyl content	Wålinder et al. (2013)
Fibres from European aspen, European beech	immersion/drain, 120°C at BP chemicals, UK	Gomez-Bueso et al. (2000)

greater extent, knots containing a high content of extractives such as phenolic pinosylvins in Scots pine can consume reagent, but for commercially used species like radiata pine, the amounts of knots and heartwood portion are low in the sawn timber being processed. Dissolved extractives can make the residual reaction with anhydride/acid liquor more complex, and this influences the reuse of reaction liquid. In the acetylation process, the moisture content in wood cannot be too high, as the moisture will consume the anhydride reagent, reducing the efficiency (and increasing the cost) of the acetylation process (see below). Drying of wood is often the bottle-neck in a sawmill. A higher drying temperature and thereby faster drying rate will increase the capacity in the process but may lead to crack formation which is a critical issue in wood drying. A somewhat greyish surface can be observed in acetylated wood but this may be removed by planing. The origin of this is not known, but it may be due to the drying conditions, forcing extractives to migrate towards surface and react according to a Maillard reaction, as has been shown to occur in the drying of radiata pine (McDonald et al., 2000).

The modification process

Commercially, acetylation is undertaken using acetic anhydride. Penetration into the material is important, especially in timber with large dimensions and where the wood structure is more closed. Heterogeneous impregnation can result in a gradient of acetylation that can influence the moisture uptake and dimensional stability, leading to distortion of the material during processing and in end-used products.

The use of gaseous anhydride is less attractive due to an induction period (Nishino, 1991) as well as low permeability (Rowell et al., 1986a). The use of more reactive reagents, such as acetyl chloride, results in the formation of strong acid catalysts (e.g., hydrochloric acid) during the treatment that are difficult to remove and which may catalyse the degradation of the wood material. A potassium acetate-catalysed acetylation of wood at low temperatures has been presented (Obataya and Minato, 2009).

The swelling of Corsican pine in pyridine followed by a reaction with acetic anhydride has been reported by Hill and Jones (1996). Acetic acid itself is not capable of reacting with wood to any significant extent under the used conditions, but carboxylic acids may react with cellulose to some extent at a higher temperature than that used in the acetylation process, especially when alpha-hydroxy- or keto-acid groups are present (Pantze et al., 2008). A process has been designed using mixing acetic anhydrides with fatty acids, where it is believed that acetic anhydride forms new fatty anhydrides in an equilibrium reaction. The resulting anhydride can react with the wood components, introducing a more stable substitution of fatty compounds which increase the water repellence and dimensional stability of wood (Peydecastaing, 2008). The Wood Protect™ product was considered for market entry based on such chemistry. The acetylation of wood with vinyl acetate and acetic anhydride has also been reported (Jebrane et al., 2011). Carboxylic acids like citric acid together with sorbitol can also be used to modify wood, probably via a trans-esterification mechanism, but it is not clear whether this is via an active or passive mode (Larnøy et al., 2018). Under laboratory conditions, various catalysts such as pyridine and magnesium dichloride have been tried when using liquid acetic anhydride (e.g., Tarkow et al., 1946; Rowell, 1983). Cyclic anhydrides have been used alone (Matsuda, 1987) and with a hypophosphite catalyst (Kim et al., 2019). In laboratory conditions, vacuum treatments have mostly been used for the impregnation of wood with liquid (Rowell, 1986). By using vacuum and a pressure of 10 bar for 2 hours at room temperature, Norway spruce and Scots pine blocks have been homogeneously acetylated under laboratory conditions using microwave heating (Larsson-Brelid and Simonsson, 1999b).

In the commercial acetylation process, wood is impregnated in a pressurised autoclave, so that the reagent penetrates through the porous wood and further into the wood cell wall. The removal of moisture from the wood before the introduction of acetic anhydride is crucial, as water will consume reagent and produce acetic acid in a reaction that is enhanced by a high temperature. As can be seen in Figure 2.2, acetic acid can to a certain extent help the acetylation by swelling the wood, making it easier for the reagent to reach reactive groups (Rowell et al., 1990). It is considered to be important to impregnate a thicker solid wood with the anhydride under cold conditions to prevent the early formation of large amounts of acetic acid which will dilute the reagent (Rowell, 1986). It should be noted that, under dilute aqueous conditions, the content of acetic anhydride was reduced to half within 5 minutes at 23°C (Kovač Kralj, 2007).

In the Accoya™ process, radiata pine is imported and dried at a high temperature and then re-equilibrated to a moisture content of 5–7% prior to acetylation, which produces a material that has a durability matching that of some of the most durable tropical wood species, as well as that of conventional pressure-impregnated sawn timber with conventional preservatives. In pressure-impregnated sawn timber with conventional preservatives, it is however only the sufficiently impregnated wood parts that have these properties; heartwood and less permeable wood species are difficult or impossible to treat (Rowell et al., 1986a; Becker and Militz, 1994). It can be noted that the reactivity of solid radiata pine heartwood and sapwood are similar from studies of wood flakes (Rowell, 1990).

Figure 2.3 shows the scheme of the acetylation process. During this process, the impregnated wood is heated (100–180°C) allowing the reagent to react with hydroxyl groups in the wood (Minato and Ito, 2004; Rowell, 2006; Obataya and Minato, 2009).

Under laboratory conditions, it was found that the rate of increase in WPG was highest in the early stages of the acetylation process and that it levelled off when a high WPG had been achieved (Figure 2.4).

WPG is a good indicator of properties of the products, such as moisture uptake, swelling and decay. The WPG of industrial products is obtained by determining the amount of ester-bonded acetyl groups with alkali titration. When titrating using sodium hydroxide, however, the presence of any initial acetyl groups, acids and other alkali cleavable bonds may lead to an overestimation

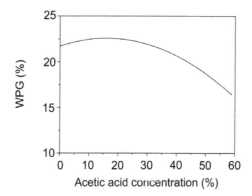

Figure 2.2 Influence on weight percentage gain (WPG) of the acetic acid concentration during acetylation of wood with acetic anhydride at 120°C for 5 hours (Rowell, 1990).

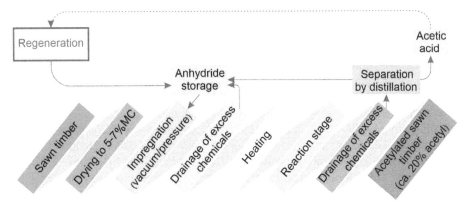

Figure 2.3 Scheme of the acetylation process (Larsson-Brelid, 2013).

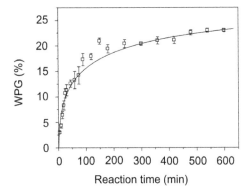

Figure 2.4 Influence on weight percentage gain (WPG) of reaction time during the acetylation of wood with acetic anhydride (Hill, 2006).

of the extent of acetylation (Beckers et al., 2003; Hill, 2006). Other methods, such as infrared spectroscopy (FTIR), liquid chromatography (HPLC) and mass detection (TOF SIMS), have also been studied (Beckers et al., 2003). The Månsson method (Månsson and Samuelsson, 1981), in which only bonded and not free acetyl groups are determined, has been used in lignocellulosic materials, and may be used for acetylated wood.

The acetylation reaction is exothermic, and it is important to control the reaction temperature, since an increase in temperature not only increases the reaction rate but may also result in a degradation of wood material leading to a loss of strength of the material. After the reaction, residual chemicals are drained off and removed from the wood.

Any remaining reagents in the material may reduce its suitability for use in interior installations due to emissions of the acid and to degradation of materials and metallic fastenings. Residual acetic acid is difficult to remove, especially from sawn timber with large dimensions, and various methods have been studied, including heating in vacuum followed by oven heating (Goldstein et al., 1961), a heated vacuum treatment followed by water washing and oven drying (Beckers and Militz, 1994), vacuum heating using microwaves (Larsson-Brelid and Simonsson, 1999a,b), azeotropic distillation using ligroin or mineral spirit (Goldstein et al., 1961), organic vapour stripping in xylene (Goldstein et al., 1961) and steam post-treatment (Bonger and Beckers, 2003). The formation of acetic acid, its removal during the treatment and the possibility of purifying and converting residual acetic acid back to the anhydride are all key steps in the process and these latter steps require large amounts of heat.

Although acetylation is more complicated than other methods, e.g., thermal modification, it gives a material that is more stable under a variety of conditions (ground contact or in load-bearing conditions) than these other methods.

The influence micro- and chemical structure of wood

The aim of acetylation is to reduce the uptake of moisture in the cell wall and thereby to increase the dimensional stability and durability of the wood while maintaining its strength. This is done by the reaction of acetic anhydride with those hydroxyl groups responsible for the uptake of moisture and not with those which form the strong crystalline cellulose structure in wood.

In general, for a chemical to be able to react with wood constituents in a quantitative manner, it needs to penetrate into the wood and the structure which needs to be modified should therefore preferentially be in a swollen state. In fact, the presence of nano-pores in dry wood is low or more likely non-existent. The size of an acetic anhydride molecule can be assumed to be 0.7 nm, whereas a pore in the fully swollen cell wall is considered to be 2–4 nm in size (Hill, 2006). However, acetic anhydride can react at low moisture contents even though it does not then swell the cell wall to any appreciable extent (Rowell, 1983). At higher moisture contents, the increased formation of acetic acid can be beneficial due to the increased swelling it imparts, but the moisture content should not be significantly high as it will then dilute the anhydride (Figure 2.2). In the industrial process, the wood is fairly dry and the reagent gradually swells the wood as the anhydride diffuses into the fibre cell wall and reacts by substitution of a proton in the hydroxyl groups in wood with the larger acetyl group (CH_3CO). One hypothesis is that acetylation near the lumen increases the swelling of the cell wall and reduces the hydrophilicity of the acetylated wood constituents.

The number of accessible hydroxyl groups in dry wood has been calculated to be 8.6 mmol/g, assuming that crystalline cellulose does not react, and the total amount was estimated to be 14.9 mmoles. It has been estimated that at a WPG of 25%, 5.9 mmoles of hydroxyl groups would be substituted per gram of oven-dried Corsican pine wood (Hill and Jones, 1996; Hill, 2006). Hydroxyl groups, like those found inside the crystalline cellulose, are not accessible to further derivatisation under uncatalysed conditions, but accessible hydroxyl groups may exist in the amorphous parts of the cellulose structure. As the acetylation and swelling of the cell wall proceeds, new hydroxyl groups may become accessible and changes in X-ray crystallography at WPG above 25% of cellulose have been observed (Zhao et al., 1987).

When a proton is replaced by a larger acyl group, the cell wall increases in thickness. It has been suggested that the porosity of the wood does not change, and this has been confirmed by studies with CT at 0.8 μm (Moghaddam et al., 2017). The wood dimensions increase with an increase in the WPG after treatment, but lumen could actually decrease in size as a result of bulking of cell wall at high WPG (Evans et al., 2000; Hill and Ormondroyd, 2004). Volume changes in the cell wall do not always correlate well with changes in the outer dimensions, as has been reported with Corsican pine (Kwon et al., 2007). When a high WPG of acetylation is achieved, as in the presence of pyridine, which is a known swelling solvent and catalyst, (micro) cracks may influence the outer dimensions of wood (Hill, 2006).

It seems impossible that cross-links are formed with acetylating agent and wood constituents during acetylation and a more thorough examination of the position of acetylation needs to be undertaken in order to fully understand the reactions. However, such type of bonds between wood constituents can not be ruled out.

Rowell et al. (1991) used chlorinated acetic anhydride and found indications that penetration occurred both into the wood fibre and later from the lumen side. Studies on isolated wood constituents indicated that lignin was slightly more reactive than hemicellulose (Callow, 1951; Rowell et al., 1994). Figure 2.5 shows the reactivity of wood and wood components during acetylation with acetic anhydride. Phenolic hydroxyl groups react faster than alcoholic groups, but the content of the former in wood is relatively low. Studies using NMR suggest that, in wood, hemicelluloses are more easily acetylated than lignin (Ohkoshi and Kato, 1997; Ohkoshi et al., 1997).

It is possible that acetylation of the phenolic and alcoholic groups in the compound middle lamella influence the interactions between wood constituents and the strength properties of wood processed at a high temperature, as in the case of wood-pulp refining processes. In groundwood pulp, acetylation was found to occur first on the primary hydroxyl groups of the polysaccharides and

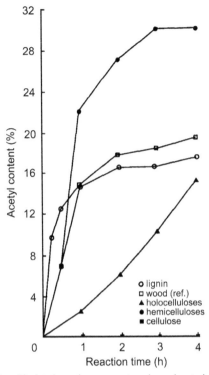

Figure 2.5 Reactivity of isolated wood components and wood material during acetylation.

lignin, followed by the secondary hydroxyl groups of the polysaccharides, and finally the hydroxyl groups at the α-position of phenylpropane units of lignin. Results suggest that the acetylation is instantaneous compared to the diffusion of the acetyl reagent and that it is related more to the accessibility of hydroxyl groups than to their reactivity. With longer hydrocarbon chains in the anhydride, the situation seems to be more complex (Hill and Hillier, 1999; Hill, 2003).

If done properly, acetylation leads to an increase in the dimensions of the wood by bulking of the cell wall that reduces the ability of the wood to take up moisture from the air because of the reduced ability of the cell wall to swell further. It can be seen in Figure 2.6 that the fibre saturation point (FSP) and equilibrium moisture content (EMC) of acetylated wood decreases the WPG of

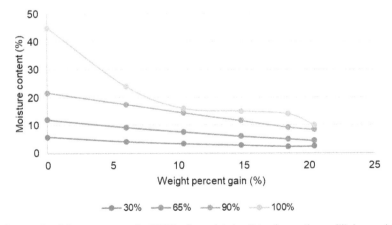

Figure 2.6 Influence of weight percentage gain (WPG) of acetylated radiata pine on the equilibrium moisture content at different relative humidities.

acetylated radiata pine (Strømdahl, 2000; Hill, 2006; Rowell, 2012). A similar behaviour has been reported for aspen (Rowell, 2014).

The acetylated wood is stable, and repeated cycles of wetting and drying do not alter the WPG nor the dimensions in the final dry or conditioned state (Rowell, 2012). Not only is the EMC reduced by the acetylation, but the moisture uptake to reach the EMC is much slower, illustrating the effect of the increased hydrophobicity of the material.

Sorption curves for acetylated spruce fibres are presented in Figure 2.7, showing that an increase in the extent of acetylation will considerable lower the moisture uptake in the wood.

The accessible hydroxyl groups available in wood after acetylation have been studied by treatment with heavy water (Figure 2.8) and have been found to correlate with WPG data (Popescu et al., 2014).

By increasing the length of hydrocarbon chain of anhydrides, the maximum WPG is achieved at a corresponding lower extent of substitution of accessible hydroxyl groups (Hill and Jones, 1999). It has been suggested that the most probable reason for the reduction in moisture uptake is the bulking of the cell wall that hinders the uptake of moisture (Papadopoulos and Hill, 2002; Papadopoulos,

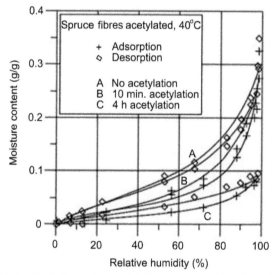

Figure 2.7 Sorption isotherms for acetylated Norway spruce fibre (Strømdahl, 2000).

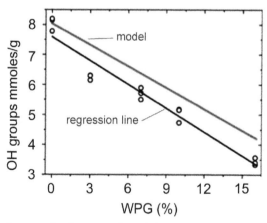

Figure 2.8 Accessible hydroxyl groups related to extent of acetylation measured as the weight percentage gain (WPG) using deuterated water and theoretically calculated.

2010) rather than a decrease in the number of hydroxyl groups that can adsorb moisture by hydrogen bonding or some other mechanism (Beck et al., 2018).

It is, however, interesting that the capillary uptake of water is high in acetylated radiata pine, which means that the wood may contain water even though the moisture content in the cell wall is relatively low.

The modified product

The acetylation process currently applied by the Accsys Technologies company yields chemically modified timber and improves many physical, chemical, mechanical, and biological material properties.

Physical and chemical properties

The substitution of a proton of a hydroxyl group by an acetyl group leads to a weight increase as well as to a swelling of the cell wall (Table 2.2). Anisotropy during acetylation is also seen and the tangential increase (2.2%) is higher than the radial increase (0.7%).

Commercial products like Accoya™ focus mostly on a fairly high extent of modification and this results in an increase in density for radiata pine from 466 kg/m³ to 512 kg/m³ at a temperature of 20°C and 65% RH (SHR, 2007).

Acetylated wood absorbs less moisture than normal wood and it is known that the EMC is related to the extent of acetylation, but moisture absorption may not be fully hindered even with high levels of treatment and WPG (see Figure 2.6). The acetylation process also lowers the FSP of the wood (see Figure 2.7). An FSP of 10% was obtained at a WPG of 19.2% (Strømdahl, 2000). Commercial acetylated products have a fibre saturation point below 15%, thus, the cell wall has a high moisture exclusion efficiency (Hill, 2006). The acetylated wood is porous and liquid water can still be transported through its pore system despite the lower moisture absorption in the cell wall.

The dimensional stability of acetylated wood is related to the extent of acetylation or WPG (Figure 2.9). The swelling and shrinkage properties are reduced by as much as 70–75%, compared

Table 2.2 Changes in dimensions of radiata pine during acetylation. WPG – weight percentage gain.

WPG	Increase in wood volume[1]	Calculated volume of added chemical[2]
17.5	3.0	2.9
22.8	3.9	4.0

[1] Difference in oven-dry volume between reacted and non-reacted wood
[2] Density used in volume calculations: acetic anhydride 1,049 kg/m³

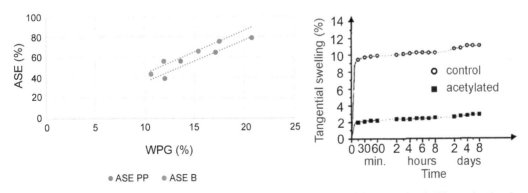

Figure 2.9 Dimensional stabilisation of wood: ASE of ponderosa pine (PP) and European beech (B) acetylated under laboratory conditions at 100°C for 2 hours at 0.3 MPa (left) (Rowell 2014), and tangential swelling of acetylated Scots pine sapwood (right) (Larsson Brelid, 2013).

to untreated wood (Jones and Hill, 2007; Rowell, 2014). Tangential swelling can be greatly reduced by acetylation (Figure 2.9).

The stability of the anti-shrink efficiency (ASE) value was studied by repeated wetting and drying cycles (four cycles) and found to be stable under those conditions with a weight loss of less than 0.2% (Table 2.3).

Table 2.3 Stability of acetylated of solid radiata pine wood during four wetting cycles in water (Rowell, 2012). WPG – weight percentage gain, ASE – anti-shrink efficiency.

	WPG	ASE	ASE2	ASE3	ASE4	Weight loss after test
Acetic anhydride	22.5	70.3	71.4	70.6	69.2	< 0.2

The use of supercritical carbon dioxide increased the rate of WPG and increased the ASE somewhat compared to liquid-state treatment at low levels of modification, but it gave a similar ASE at high WPG (Matsunaga et al., 2010). The acetic anhydride changes light wood into a slightly darker colour, whilst dark wood is slightly bleached by a similar treatment (Swedish Wood, 2015).

The acetylation process may result in discolouration, typically to a depth of 5 mm, with sticker marks up to 6 mm in depth and, due to natural wood variations, these may occasionally be deeper. The timber quality purchased for the manufacture of Accoya™ may exhibit certain visual defects after being processed, such as distortion, internal cracks, bark and resin pockets. Planed acetylated timber has been found to be less susceptible to initial greying than untreated sawn timber, but, acetylation to 5–10% WPG increased the tendency of the timber to change colour when exposed to external conditions and only at a high level of acetylation (20%) was the tendency to change colour reduced. A modification of the compound middle lamella could be the reason for this behaviour, as free hydroxyl groups in lignin seem to be relatively easily modified. Erosion is greatly reduced (by as much as 50%), and the depth of weathering in acetylated wood is also reduced (Rowell, 2012). Table 2.4 shows that acetylation at typical levels protect the lignin and delay weathering during artificial weathering tests, although some of the acetyl groups were lost.

Acetic acid is a by-product in the reaction and it will remain in the wood if steps are not undertaken to remove it. It is not, however, practically possible to remove all the acetic acid and, as a result, acetylated products have been mainly used outdoors. The hydrolysis of acetylated wood during use is slow and acetic acid is always present in acetylated wood, although at a low level (1.8 % acetyl content), which is controlled before the product is sold (Accoya, 2018).

Table 2.4 Acetyl group and lignin analysis before and after 700 hours of accelerated weathering of aspen fibreboards made from acetylated fibres (Rowell, 2012). WPG – weight percentage gain.

	Before weathering		After weathering	
WPG	Surface (%)	Remainder (%)	Surface (%)	Remainder (%)
		Acetyl		Acetyl
0	4.5	4.5	1.9	3.9
19.7	17.5	18.5	12.8	18.3
		Lignin		Lignin
0	19.8	20.5	1.9	17.9
19.7	18.5	19.2	5.5	18.1

Mechanical properties

Acetylation has only a low impact on the mechanical (strength) properties of wood (Rowell, 2012; Larsson-Brelid, 2013). The hemicellulose and lignin are acetylated but probably not the cellulose, and certainly not its major crystalline part under the industrial acetylation conditions used. The

Table 2.5 Dry and wet strength and stiffness of untreated and acetylated radiata pine. MOR − modulus of rupture, MOE − modulus of elasticity.

Sample	Dry strength MOR (MPa)	Dry stiffness MOE (MPa)	Wet strength MOR (MPa)	Difference (%)	Wet stiffness MOE (MPa)	Difference (%)
Untreated	63.6	10,540	39.4	−62	6,760	−36
Acetylated	64.4	10,602	58.0	−10	9,690	−8.6

modulus of rupture (MOR) has been reported to increase in conifer woods but decrease in broad-leaved woods (Dreher et al., 1964; Minato et al., 2003). The modulus of elasticity (MOE) of acetylated radiata pine was similar or slightly less than that of normal radiata pine wood, but under wet conditions the MOR was considerably higher than that of the control (Table 2.5).

Crystalline regions are more separated in the dried state as the hemicellulose-lignin matrix becomes acetylated with a greater bulk. The presence of hydrogen bonds between hydroxyl groups is reduced, whilst the presence of water and its interactions with water, which normally acts as a softening agent in wood, are inhibited. The impact strength of acetylated wood has been found to be similar (Koppers, 1961), but studies with acetylated pine have indicated a reduction. The cross-cut area is larger than that of the unacetylated material, though this is sometimes not reported.

The hardness of wood has also been found to increase by up to 30% after acetylation, with a lower EMC probably contributing to this value (Larsson-Brelid and Simonsson, 1994; Rowell, 2012). Wet and dry compressive strength also increases as a result of the acetylation treatment (Koppers, 1961; Dreher et al., 1964). The fibre stress at the proportional limit, and the work to proportional limit have been reported to increase as a result of acetylation (Dreher et al., 1964; Rowell, 1983). The shear strength parallel to the grain decreases in acetylated wood (Dreher et al., 1964). Strength grading of acetylated wood has been reported (Bongers and de Meijer, 2012), and the use of acetylated Scots pine as a construction material is currently being studied within a project in Sweden, which started in 2018.

Biological properties

Wood is a material that is exposed to nature's life cycles, especially when it is used in tougher outdoor regimes. This means that it often degrades and loses some of its attractive properties. Mould, bacteria and discolouring fungi consume the surface nutrients and are known to be early colonisers of wood surfaces. Sap stains are followed by rot fungi which start to degrade the structural wood components. In parallel, insects such as termites, beetles, etc., can attack wood, and under maritime conditions, marine borers quickly degrade the wood. Under certain conditions, certain bacterial attack can also lead to degradation.

It has been suggested that the wood substrate and the redistribution of extractives are the reasons where wood is susceptibile to moulds. Even though the EMC of acetylated wood is much lower than that of the untreated wood, the wood can still be susceptible to staining and mould fungi (Gobakken and Westin, 2008; Gobakken and Lebow, 2010; Gobakken et al., 2010). Although the moisture uptake is reduced, acetylated material requires protection from water and moisture during storage, application and end-use since the uptake of capillary water can still occur.

Moulds and sap-stain fungi do not attack the structural wood polymers. Decay occurs when wood is exposed to rot fungi and this leads to a degradation of the wood, a loss of material and a reduction in mechanical strength. In acetylated wood, these decay processes are substantially slower and the material's durability at a WPG of around 20% or higher can, in this respect, be compared to that of a durable tropical wood, as well as to that of wood treated with commonly used synthetic biocides. As stated in Chapter 1, many methods to test the decay resistance of wood are available, such as pure culture tests, sterile and non-sterile laboratory soil burial tests, and long-term outdoor exposure tests. Each test method has its strengths and its weaknesses and a threshold WPG of modified wood as a way to estimate decay resistance can be difficult to establish, due to the fact that fungi are living cultures with specific strains and varying virulence.

Several studies have pointed out that acetylated wood material exhibits a high biological resistance (Larsson-Brelid et al., 2000; Papadopoulos and Hill, 2002; Rowell et al., 2007; Hill, 2009; Mohebby and Militz, 2010; Larsson-Brelid, 2013), and the biological durability of acetylated wood reaches the highest durability class (Class 1), similar to that of extremely durable tropical species such as teak and ipé (Sandberg, 2017). This means that it can even be used in ground contact conditions and that it competes with traditional biohazard treatments (Figure 2.10).

The improvement in the durability of wood due to WPG was clearly demonstrated by Hill et al. (2003) in the case of Corsican pine exposed to *Coniophora puteana* brown rot fungi (Figure 2.11).

The threshold of acetyl weight gain for in-ground contact has been estimated to be 18–19% (Larsson-Brelid and Westin, 2010). With white rot fungi, degradation is usually slower than with brown rot fungi and a lower threshold WPG value has been estimated (WPG ca. 13%) (Hill, 2006). This means that, in order to degrade wood, white rot may require a higher moisture content and more extensive swelling of the cell wall than the more aggressive brown rot. On the other hand, it will, in contrast to brown rot, also degrade the more hydrophobic lignin.

Several theories to explain the high durability of acetylated wood have been proposed, but bulking of the cell wall by reducing the cell wall void volume seems to be crucial. Non-recognition of the acetylated wood component by the enzyme, micropore blocking and a smaller number of OH groups and absorbed water may also be important (Ringman et al., 2014). However, moisture may be transported by the fungus, and this complicates the interpretation of brown rot decay (Zelinka

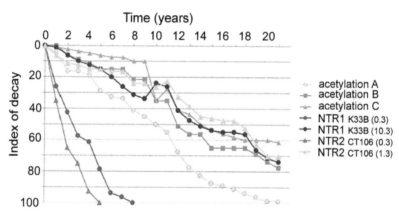

Figure 2.10 Rot index after soil-buried test of acetylated wood: A (high WPG), B (medium WPG), C (low WPG) and CCA-types of preservative treated ones: K33B (low charge), K33B (high charge), CT 106 (low charge), CT 106 (high charge).

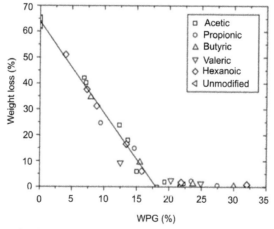

Figure 2.11 Weight loss of acetylated Corsican pine sapwood exposed to brown rot *Coniophora puteana* (Hill et al., 2003).

et al., 2020). White rot fungi have enzymes and mediator systems that can degrade both lignin and carbohydrates, whereas brown rot can only modify the lignin possibly via Fenton-like oxidation chemistry and it degrades the carbohydrates via specific enzymatic systems. It has been proposed that brown rot degradation starts with the middle lamella compound and S_1 layer, in which reactive mediators can be used so that the fungal organism in the lumen is protected from the harsh oxidative conditions existing in the reaction zone. With removal of acetyl groups and oxidation of lignin and other wood polymers, it is likely that the EMC of the material will rise and that more suitable conditions for decay will be obtained. Later in the process, when the structure is more porous, larger cellulases can penetrate and begin degrading the cellulose further.

Marine aqueous conditions, especially in tropical waters, are usually tougher than those on land and in fresh water. At treatment levels (> 20% acetyl content), Accoya™ wood has been found to possess excellent resistance to attack by marine borers even after 16 years of exposure on the Swedish west coast, to levels similar to that of CCA-treated Scots pine wood (Westin et al., 2016). In another study, acetylated wood with an acetyl content of 22% showed moderate attack after 10 years exposure on the Swedish west coast (Larsson-Brelid and Westin, 2010). Marine trials in Italy showed no attack on acetylated wood whereas untreated material was degraded after 2 years of exposure (Bongers et al., 2018). The mechanism of protection needs to be further studied, but non-recognition of the acetylated wood by the enzymes in the attacking organisms has been suggested (Westin et al., 2006).

Acetylation improves the resistance of wood to termites, and probably also to other insects. Acetylated wood has been proven to be very resistant to subterranean and Formosan termites (Alexander et al., 2014). Pine sapwood acetylated to 22% WPG exposed for 1 year at an outdoor test site in Indonesia showed a weight loss of only 2% due to termite attack, whereas unmodified controls lost 93% of their weight in the same period (Westin et al., 2004).

Technological aspects

The machinability of acetylated radiata pine is comparable to that of broad-leaved woods but, as the product is slightly acidic, there is a risk of corrosion of metal fasteners and machining tools, especially if high moisture contents are prevalent.

The type of adhesive used influences the adhesion of acetylated wood (Vick and Rowell, 1990; Vick et al., 1993; Frihart et al., 2004). The glueability of acetylated radiata pine is reported to be good if polyurethane (PU), emulsion-polymer-isocyanate (EPI), epoxy or phenol-resorcinol-formaldehyde (PRF) adhesives are used (Accoya, 2018). Adhesive bonding performance is, however, reduced if casein adhesives, PVAc or urea-formaldehyde resins are used, probably because the treated wood surface is more hydrophobic due to the loss of OH-groups which effects the absorption of adhesive into the wood. Residual acetic acid may influence the glueability of acetylated wood if acid-catalysed binders are used. Other parameters, such as applied pressure, open and closed press time, and temperature, also need be considered.

A high level of acetylation makes wood more stable to photodegradation, but the product will eventually grey on extended outdoor exposure (Evans, 2009), probably due to the deacetylation of phenolic units in lignin catalysed by the presence of residual acetic acid in the wood. Although the surface of acetylated wood usually has a more hydrophobic character than the untreated wood, water-borne paints, such as acrylates, penetrate sufficiently to achieve a good adhesion to the surface of the acetylated wood (Larsson-Brelid and Westin, 2007; Bonger and Meijer, 2012). As the dimensional stability increases as a result of the acetylation, the moisture-assisted movements in wood are reduced, and tensions in the film-forming surface treatments are reduced. Less flexible film-forming alkyd paints were not affected, however, possibly due to the presence of residual acetic acid.

Care should be taken during the storage of acetylated products and effective cross-grain sealing of coated wood may be necessary, as the uptake of capillary water by radiata pine can be high, its subsequent removal by drying being relatively slow. The uptake depends, however, on the wood species, capillary uptake by acetylated European beech was slower than that by radiata pine

(Sehlstedt-Persson, 2020). It may therefore be necessary to determine the moisture content of the wood prior to further processing such as glueing and coating. Sanding in between coating with water-borne paints is not necessary, since there are no raised fibres on the hydrophobic acetylated wood. Oils are absorbed easily and more oil may be required than on untreated wood. The service life of surface treated decking with a translucent non-film-forming coating and an oil-based stain will depend on the exposure conditions and has been found to be similar to that of untreated wood.

High quality stainless steel, corrosion-resistant aluminium or naval brass products may be used in areas exposed to moisture or condensation. Wood plastic composites (WPCs) with acetylated fibres are even more durable than those containing untreated wood.

Acetylation also improves the acoustic properties of wood, due to a small increase in the density, leading to a reduction in both sound velocity and sound absorption by nearly 5% compared with untreated wood (Rowell, 2014). Due to its improved acoustic properties, acetylated wood has been suggested as a material for musical instruments. The low moisture uptake also increases the resistance of acetylated wood to thermal (electrical) transport.

Environmental aspects

The formation of anhydride from acetic acid by fermentation, the removal of water and the removal of acetic acid from the product all require heat, which may be provided by the combustion of residual waste products from nearby industries, such as sawmills. Some loss of acetic acid or anhydride may occur during production, but this does not seem to be a problem. Combination with other industrial applications that use the modifying agents could be beneficial.

There is a high potential for the incorporation of acetylated wood in composite products, and the lack of any added toxic chemicals allows the disposal of material at the end of its service life for energy conversion, for example. The environmental performance of Accoya™ has been tested and published as a Life Cycle Analysis (LCA following ISO 14040/44) and an Environmental Product Declaration (EPD following ISO 14025).

Industrial use and application

Having established the principles of acetylation, the potential of commercial production has been developed and modified over recent decades, and several commercially produced materials are now available.

Commercial industrial processes

One of the first attempts to acetylate wood was made by Stamm and his colleagues using wood veneers and acetic anhydride (Tarkow et al., 1946; Stamm and Tarkow, 1947). Trials using various acetylating reagents, catalysts and gaseous ketene followed (Baird, 1969; Karlson and Svalbe, 1972; Kumar and Agarwal, 1982). In the 1960s, Goldstein presented a way of acetylating sawn timber by impregnation with a mixture of acetic anhydride and xylene without using a catalyst (Goldstein et al., 1961) in a vacuum/pressure process at 100–130°C under pressurised conditions. Acetic acid, as a by-product, and excess acetic anhydride were afterwards removed from the wood by vapour drying. This process was ended by an additional evaporation phase under vacuum. For several years, this method of acetylating the timber was carried out by the Koppers Co. in Pittsburg, USA on a pilot-plant scale (Koppers, 1961). Unfortunately, high solvent recovery costs weakened interest in this method and the pilot-plant scale project was stopped. A simplified procedure for the acetylation of sawn timber with a thickness up to 30 mm was proposed by Rowell et al. (1986b), where only a limited amount of acetic anhydride was used during the acetylation treatment. For thicker timber, a vacuum/pressure process with cold acetic anhydride followed by heating was developed by Rowell (2014). No catalyst was used in this simplified procedure, where the crystalline strength of cellulose and thereby the stability of the product was retained.

In the late 1980s in Japan, Daiken started commercial production of acetylated wood for flooring called *Alpha-wood*. In the early 1990s, a commercial attempt to acetylate fibres was made by a collaboration of British Petroleum (BP), A-Cell acetyl cellulosics AB (A-Cell), and the BioComposites Centre (Sheen, 1992). For technical and economic reasons, these attempts were commercially unsuccessful. Based on previous studies, a continous acetylation process was established in 2007 in Arnhem by Accsys Technologies PLC with an annual capacity of 30,000 m³. SHR Rimber Research (Wageningen, The Netherlands) made a large contribution to the scaling up of what was formerly called TitanWood™ through the characterisation of various properties of the product. The product name was changed to Accoya™ and the product was taken over by the Accys Technologies company. The process is based on an uncatalysed acetylation process using liquid acetic anhydride in pressurised heated autoclaves. The facility was established alongside an already existing industry producing acetylated cellulose product, and this made the scaling up an easier process while also providing access to an existing industrial infrastructure. About 40,000 m³ acetylated timber was produced by the Accsys company in 2016, and this was increased to ca. 60,000 m³ in 2018. Attempts have been made in other countries but to date these have not reached the scale of the plant in Arnhem.

The acetic acid content of Accoya™ timber is measured as part of the quality-control procedure and within the KOMO™ Quality System, by sampling from every batch produced to ensure that the residual acetyl content is not higher than 1.8%. Eastman Chemical Co. in USA produced acetylated timber, Perennial Wood™, but decided to close production in 2014, a lack of resources being suggested as one possible reason (Deckmagazine, 2020). A process has been developed for producing MDF using acetylated wood fibres, to achieve dimensionally stable and decay-resistant panels for exterior use marketed as Tricoya™. Construction of a new commercial facility for producing Tricoya™ is ongoing in Hull, England.

Applications of acetylated wood

Acetylated timber is mainly intended for above ground applications, such as bridges and structural, decking, marinas, shutters and louvres, cladding, sidings, facades, windows and doors, where preservative-treated timber is used today. The road bridge of acetylated radiata pine built in 2008 at Sneek in The Netherlands shows the potential of the acetylated material (Figure 2.12) (Tjeerdsma and Bonders, 2009). The Accoya™ products aim for service lives of 50 years in above-ground uses (Use Classes 1, 2 and 3 as defined in EN 335 (CEN, 2013)). Even though moisture uptake is low and the dimensional stability is good, capillary water is still absorbed by the acetylated radiata pine, and mould growth may be a problem in outdoor claddings and window frames. Independent inspection of 17 projects with acetylated wooden doors, windows, cladding, and decking built between 2007 and 2016 in The Netherlands showed that the use of acetylated wood increases the lifetime of timber products and decreases the intensity of maintenance (Klaassen et al., 2018), but special attention is needed in order to avoid rapid water uptake in outdoor as well as indoor (condensation) conditions by using appropriate design and application practices. The expected life of an acetylated product in ground or fresh water is 25 years (Use Class 4 as defined in EN 335 (CEN, 2013)). This does not mean that it may not withstand marine water conditions as described above, but more studies are required before this is confirmed.

To date, there have been various products manufactured and tested using acetylated wood, this being summarised in Table 2.6.

Figure 2.12 Application of acetylated wood: Sneek bridge in the Netherlands (left), windows and facades in a passive house in Rinkhout, Zele (middle), and swimming pool decking, Italy (right).

Table 2.6 Applications of acetylated wood divided into Use Classes, see Table 1.7.

Product type/Use Class	Interior		Exterior		
	1	2	3	4	5
Indoor furniture	x				
Floor and non-structural interior uses	x	x			
Exterior joinery			x		
Cladding			x		
Decking			x		
Fencing			x		
Outdoor furniture			x	x	
Construction elements			x	x	
In-ground timber				x	
Products exposed to water				x	(x)

where: x = products have been produced by companies using the modified wood
(x) = products may be produced, based on pre-commercial trials, research, etc.

2.3 The Compreg™ process

Phenoplastic polymers were among the first commercially successful synthetic polymeric products. Although many phenoplastic materials have now been replaced with less brittle thermoplastic polymers, they are still used to create water-resistant bonding in plywood, hardboards and other panel products, as well as being an active component of modified wood products. Hard and dense products can also be created by curing wood impregnated with a thermoset resin similar to the Impreg™ process (see Section 2.4), but wood can be compressed in Thermo-Hydro-Mechanical processes to an even higher density, giving improved product properties. Hot compression (Compreg™) during the curing of an impregnated wood (typically with PF-resin) gives a product with extreme dimensional stability, very low spring-back and set-recovery, good hardness and a high decay-resistance material (Stamm and Seborg, 1939; Stamm and Seborg, 1955; Stamm and Bachelor, 1960; Stamm, 1959; Stamm, 1964). Applications, such as speaker cabinets, storage tanks, industrial floors and bullet-proof materials, have been produced. The hazardous chemicals, phenol and formaldehyde, are based on fossil fuels and must be handled with care when producing the resin but not when they have been adequately hardened.

Material selection and preparation

Only easily penetrated wood species should be used for the production of Compreg™ type products. European beech is a common species and is in this respect suitable for impregnation. Veneers are mostly used, as dimensional sawn timber is more difficult to impregnate and, if the timber is too thick, the exothermic reaction leads to a reduction in the product properties. The preparation of veneers is similar to the processing of plywood and laminated veneer lumber (LVL) with drying and grading before further treatment with resin. As the PF molecules do not react with water, it is less important to control the moisture content as it is in the acetylation process, for example (Section 2.2). Green timber takes up less resin, but it can still be used.

European beech is a tough and a relatively hard type of wood, but it can still be impregnated. Its homogeneous structure, ideal cell structure and purity provide excellent mechanical and electrical properties. Nevertheless, species such as Japanese cedar and cypress have been proposed for products in Japan, while Norway spruce, Japanese white birch and oil palm have been tried in laboratory studies (Yano et al., 2000; Yano et al., 2001a; Bakar et al., 2013).

The modification process

In 1936, Stamm and Seborg started studies on the impregnation of wood with various resins, including phenol formaldehyde (PF), urea- and thiourea-based resins and furfural. PF resins were found to be the best, especially for the wet strength of the compressed product (Stamm and Seborg, 1939). Compreg™ is nowadays an established process for making densified wood products and they are manufactured by a number of producers (Figure 2.13).

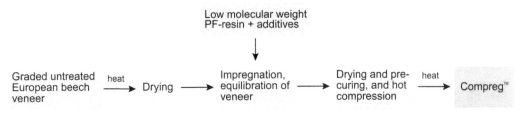

Figure 2.13 Outline of the Compreg™ process based on wood veneer.

Stamm and Seborg (1939) listed three essential criteria for the effective resin treatment of wood:

- The molecular size of the resin molecules must be sufficiently small to allow penetration into the cell wall, requiring that the resin should be unpolymerised or only slightly polymerised.
- The molecules of the resin should be soluble in polar solvents, so that the cell wall is in a swollen state to allow for diffusion into the interior of the cell wall.
- The resin molecules should exhibit sufficient polarity so that they exhibit a high affinity with the cell wall macromolecular components.

For a good result, pressure treatments are used to force the resin to enter into the wood structure to the desired extent. Stamm found out in his early trials (Stamm and Seborg, 1939) with water-soluble resin that it was beneficial to soak the veneers before impregnation. Veneers are used in most compressed wood applications, to avoid the premature setting of the resin that tends to occur during the drying of the impregnated timber when larger dimensions are used (Stamm, 1964). The use of many veneers may however induce an excessively high curing temperature, as the reaction is exothermic which can lead to a detoriation in product properties. For a product with a density of 1,300 kg/m^3, a charge of at least 30% dry weight of resin is needed (Stamm, 1964). At lower product densities, cured Compreg™ pieces may need to be glued with a suitable phenolic or similar adhesive to achieve the desired product thickness. The moisture content should be under control to avoid the formation of checks (Stamm, 1964). In the corresponding Impreg™ process, a vacuum pre-treatment is not really necessary before the veneers are pressure impregnated in order to ensure that the resin (around 30% on dry weight) can freely penetrate into the veneer during the pressure treatment. The impregnation time for the Compreg™ process may be anything from 10 minutes to six hours at pressures from 0.1 to 1.4 MPa depending on wood species and thickness of the veneers (Stamm, 1964). This is followed by equilibration of the resin-treated sample for 1–2 days after the impregnation (Figure 2.13). Low molecular weight phenolic resin (LMW-PF) has been used to impregnate veneers and this leads to significant softening of the cell walls, reducing the Young's modulus of the material before hardening. The veneer materials can be arranged either in parallel or crosswise and then compressed in a heated press (open system), causing water to be evaporated. The veneers can be pre-cured at a medium temperature before being finally compressed at a high temperature and pressure depending on the targeted product properties. For a density of 1,200–1,350 kg/m^3, a pressure of about 7 MPa and a temperature of 125–150°C seem to be necessary (Kollmann et al., 1975). Once pressed, the products are conditioned to the appropriate moisture content.

The influence of the micro- and chemical structure of wood

As a result of the force applied during the hot curing stage, the cell wall collapses, but the resin filling the cavities in the material and being cured gives a composite material with a low porosity and high density. It is important to consider the viscosity of the impregnating solution and the molecular weight of the resin molecules with regard to penetration into the wood and its cavities. A low rather than a high molecular PF resin was found to contribute to dimensional stabilisation and decay resistance. Improvements in dimensional stability have been found to correlate strongly with the mono-methylol phenol content of the PF resin (Goldstein, 1959). The importance of the penetration of PF-resin into the cell wall was deduced using a *meta*-brominated phenol resin (Furuno et al., 2004) (Figure 2.14, left). With a low molecular weight PF-resin, almost all the resin seemed to penetrate the cell wall before starting to fill up other larger cavities. In the case of a PF resin having a molecular weight of 820 g/mol, only a displacement in the lumen was observed (Figure 2.14).

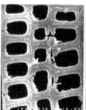  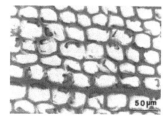 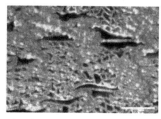

Figure 2.14 Photomicrographs showing wood impregnated with phenolic resin: low molecular weight meta-brominated PF of latewood and Br-L X-ray maps (left, Furuno et al., 2004), transverse section of sugi sapwood with high molecular weight resin (middle, Ryu et al., 1991), and safranin-stained and fluoresced 10% WPG specimen (right, Ryu et al., 1991).

Using a more elaborate hot-pressing technique, a relatively high molecular weight PF-resin gave good dimensional stabilisation of wood (Gabrielli and Kamke, 2010).

During the formation of the PF-resin, phenol is allowed to react with formaldehyde, giving mostly monomeric methylolated phenolics of monomers. Further heating leads to the formation of ether and methylene bridges together with water by condensation reactions (see Figure 1.33). Methylene bridges are more stable than ether bridges (which can form methylene bridges by splitting off formaldehyde during a curing process). Since there are still reactive positions left in the phenolic ring, as well as methylol groups, further heating under hot compression will remove water and cure the resin, forming a cross-linked network structure (see Figure 1.43). A higher concentration of methylol groups ($-CH_2OH$) in the methylolated phenol favours a more cross-linked structure.

Hill (2006) proposed two mechanisms that are responsible for preventing the loss of the cell wall impregnant once curing has taken place.

- Polymerisation within the complex cell wall micro-pore geometry effectively 'locks' the resin in place due to entanglement of the resin network structure with the cell wall polymeric constituents.

- The formation of chemical bonds between the resin components and the cell wall polymers is also a distinct possibility. Wellons (1977) considers this to be a certainty.

Using nuclear magnetic resonance (NMR) techniques Yelle and Ralph (2016) have found covalent bonds between PF-resins and lignin constituents caused by methylene bridges. The exudation of hardened resin from the structure is, thus, hindered not only by size and polarity but also by chemical bonds in the wood polymer structure.

Regardless of the mechanism, it is essential that the bonds formed, whether intramolecular within the resin network or intermolecular between the resin and the cell wall polymers, are stable to hydrolysis; otherwise, the resin may leach out and the cell wall bulking effect will be lost.

Dimensional stabilisation of delignified cedar wood can also be achieved by impregnation with PF-resin of wood and compressing at comparatively low pressure at 140°C (Shams and Yano, 2011).

The removal of lignin leads to a softening and cell-wall collapse, as well as creep deformation of the resin-impregnated wood under low pressure. Yano et al. (2001b) concluded that the specific bending strength of wood could be increased two-fold by a combination of (a) a pre-treatment to remove matrix substances such as lignin and (b) resin impregnation and compression. The addition of urea was found not only to reduce formaldehyde emission and the use of a lower concentrations of LMWPF resin, but also to reduce the dimensional stability. Using glyoxalated alkali lignin and PF resin, the emission of formaldehyde was also reduced, but in this case no dimensional stabilisation was achieved (Ang et al., 2018).

The modified product

As expected, the modification of wood with a resin system yields products with properties considerably different from those of the untreated wood.

Physical properties

The product is dark and dense, probably due to the formation of conjugated quinone methides. When a resin of neutral pH was used, a brighter but less stable product was obtained (Furuno et al., 2004). When the product is exposed to weathering, it eventually turns grey. Depending on the extent of compression, different densities can be achieved, up to 1,400 kg/m^3. For applications in transformers, an accurate oil uptake is important, and the more hydrophobic structure should be favourable, but the complete closure of cavities may be avoided. As the porosity is low in the Compreg™ product, the uptake of liquid water is also low; the water uptake by a compressed laminated PF-treated beech veneer (Panzerholz™) in water for 24 hours was reported to be only 3.5%. Phenol–formaldehyde resins with an appropriate molecular weight were shown to be able to penetrate and bulk the cell wall (Stamm and Seborg, 1936; Rowell and Banks, 1985; Furuno et al., 2004). Anti-swelling efficiency (ASE) values of 75 and 95% at weight percent gains of 35 and 30% for Impreg™ and Compreg™, respectively, have been reported (Stamm, 1959a). Ohmae et al. (2002) obtained anti-shrink efficiencies (ASE) up to 74 at a 30% weight percent gain using a low molecular weight PF and suggested that the effect is due to both bulking and cross-linking of the cell wall. Ryu et al. (1991) observed little change in ASE with resin loadings above 40% with a PF resin treatment (Table 2.7).

PF resin, when cured in hardboard products, normally releases only small amounts of formaldehyde. Formaldehyde emission class E1 according to European standard EN 13986 + A1 (CEN, 2004) is claimed for the Delignit-Fineply™ D product. A low molecular weight PF resin could give a higher emission of formaldehyde in Compreg™ products. The addition of urea as a formaldehyde catcher to PF was able to reduce the formaldehyde emission from Compreg™ material (Rabi'atol Adawiah et al., 2013). The resin itself should be handled with care due to the presence of unreacted starting materials.

Table 2.7 Mechanical properties of Compreg™ products. Values represent the average of 10 replicates, standard deviations in parentheses. WPG – weight percentage gain, WPG$_E$ – estimated weight percent gain TS – thickness swelling, ASE – anti-swelling efficiency, ASE$_N$ – normalised anti-swelling efficiency, IS – irreversible swelling, MOE – modulus of elasticity, and MW – molecular weight.

Treatment	Conc.	WPG (%)	WPG$_E$ (%)	TS (%)	ASE (%)	ASE$_N$	IS (%)	MOE (%)
PF high MW	5	3.6 (0.7)	9.1 (0.9)	21.8 (4.3)	70.6 (5.4)	20.3 (3.6)	2.1 (4.4)	159 (24)
	10	11.3 (2.2)	17.2 (2.8)	19.0 (4.1)	74.7 (5.0)	6.8 (1.2)	1.5 (3.0)	150 (17)
	20	23.0 (2.6)	32.6 (4.6)	9.2 (4.8)	86.1 (6.5)	3.8 (0.6)	2.4 (7.7)	-
PF low MW	5	4.1 (1.4)	17.1 (2.8)	39.7 (5.6)	50.3 (6.6)	13.8 (6.0)	20.6 (10.2)	131 (31)
	10	5.8 (1.2)	16.2 (1.8)	33.1 (5.0)	56.8 (5.4)	10.1 (2.0)	9.3 (6.0)	154 (23)
	20	16.5 (2.1)	32.9 (2.8)	25.8 (3.5)	66.5 (4.3)	4.1 (0.5)	7.5 (6.7)	138 (21)
Control	-	-	-	76.2 (11.5)	-	-	20.3 (10.8)	208 (19)

Mechanical properties

In commercial laminated-veneer-lumber type Compreg™ products, flexural strength (MOR) up to 200 MPa parallel to the grain and a modulus of elasticity of 17 GPa at a density of 1,200–1,300 kg/m³ can be achieved. Similarly, hardness values around 230 MPa and impact strengths between 20 and 50 KJ/m² according to DIN 53453 (DIN, 1975), depending on the impact direction for densities between 1,350 and 1,400 kg/m³, can be achieved (Delignit, 2020). Kajita et al. (2004) reported that highly alkaline phenolic resin caused a decrease in the modulus of elasticity in treated wood.

Biological properties

The PF modification of wood has been shown to enhance the resistance against white rot and brown rot fungi (Ryu et al., 1991). Stamm and Bachelor (1960) studied the microbial resistance of wood modified by five different techniques, including impregnation with PF resin, and found that the weight loss due to decay became negligible when the ASE was 70% or higher, which was probably related to efficient bulking of the cell wall. Ryu et al. (1993) undertook an extended study of the influence of the molecular weight of the PF resin from 369 to 1,143 g/mol. High molecular weight resins imparted a lower degree of decay resistance at lower resin loadings, although the differences in efficacy became less apparent as resin loadings were increased. With an alkaline resin, very good durability of wood could be achieved against the brown rot *Tyromyces palustris* and the white rot *Coriolus versicolor* at even moderate resin loadings (11.8%) and after leaching in water (Furuno et al., 2004). In general, broad-leaved woods required much higher resin loadings than conifer wood, which was attributed to differences in cell wall penetration by the resin (Takahashi and Imamura, 1990; Ryu et al., 1991). Stabilisation against termites and white rot were achieved by compression of oil palm wood treated with low molecular weight PF resin (Bakar et al., 2013). Deka and Saikia (2000) also reported that resin-treated wood was resistant to attack by termites.

Technological aspects

Difficulties similar to those found in the processing of high-density hardwoods are found with Compreg™ products, such as the wearing of saw blades. Most of the resins used are alkaline, so that corrosion of metallic fasteners, which occurs with other wood products modified with an acidic pH, such as acetylated, furfurylated and thermally modified wood, is not a problem.

As modification with PF results in a less porous structure, the efficiency of adhesives can be affected due to a decrease in adhesive penetration into the porous network of cells. Where a PF-resin with a concentration of 25% was used for impregnation and subsequent curing, a decrease in adhesion was found when using PVAc but not with a PRF resin under dry conditions (Adamopoulos et al., 2012).

The surface treatment of Compreg™ materials is less common. The surfaces of Compreg™ products are more or less hydrophobic, so water-based paints need more work to spread evenly on the material, and the lack of pores makes it more difficult for binders to penetrate into the wood structure and adhere to wood surfaces. Non-water-borne paints, such as a two-component polyurethane, work better than thermoplastic polymers and they are also favoured by the higher dimensional stability of the treated wood due to less movement during cycling moisture conditions.

The thermal and electrical conductivities are low, partly due to the lower moisture content in the Compreg™ material. The high density of the hardened resin imparts a high resistance to wear and abrasion. Compreg™ materials have a high oil absorption and they are used as a base material in transformers.

Environmental aspects

PF resins are based on fossil fuels and the main components, formaldehyde and phenol, are classed as hazardous compounds, but if they are correctly cured, the emission of these compounds is low. For many of the wood products in the EU today, the wood is taken from certified forests. Delignit™

is taken from PEFC certified forests (Delignit, 2020). PF resin is a thermoset type that cannot easily be re-used in new polymeric applications, but it may be used as a filler after milling in wood-plastic composites. Energy production by the combustion of PF-resin-impregnated wood is favoured because it has a higher carbon-oxygen ratio than untreated wood.

Industrial use and application

Phenolic resin was one of the first commercially successful plastics, such as the stiff, black and brittle material Bakelite™ developed in 1907. It was later found that it could be formulated as an adhesive and also to stabilise wood structures. Compreg™, based on phenolic-resin-impregnated veneers cured under high pressure, was developed in the USA during the early 1940s and it immediately found a use as a replacement for stainless steel in certain niche applications, e.g., pitch propellers and connector plates in the World War II allied air fleet.

The Compreg™ process is nowadays fairly well established, beech veneers are still used and the use of thicker dimensions is avoided. Production is also found globally, but not in the Nordic countries. Compared to other modified materials, Compreg™ products are among the best in terms of reduced moisture uptake, dimensional stability, improved decay resistance, bending strength and especially hardness. However, its high density and the difficulty in producing thick material may hamper further applications for Compreg™.

Applications

A few examples of applications of Compreg™ are given in Figure 2.15. Panzerholz™ compressed wood, produced by the German company Delignit Aktiengesellschaft (Delignit AG), is an extremely hard multi-layered sheet material, manufactured from beech veneers and synthetic adhesives under heat and high pressure. Under these conditions, the veneers are compressed to half their original thickness. The material is used for security panels, tooling, jigs, moulds, transformer parts, support for liquid natural gas tanks, neutron shielding and audio component cases. Other products from Delignit AG include Feinholz™, Carbonwood™, obo-Festholz™ and VANyCARE™. Another product produced in Germany by Deutsche Holzveredelung is Dehonit™, a compressed laminated wood manufactured from selected high-quality European beech veneers coated or impregnated with a special synthetic phenolic adhesive. The veneers are pressed under high pressure and temperature to form a laminate material. Another use for densified adhesive-impregnated veneer is in storage containers for liquid natural gas and associated support structures (such as wear plates for machinery and transportation vehicles, machine pattern moulds, bullet-proof barriers and some structural building components). Permawood™, also known as Lignostone™, is produced in France and is a densified material made of beech veneers laminated together using a synthetic adhesive that hardens under pressure and heat to give a material for transformers, fuel tanks and vessels, with formaldehyde emissions achieving class E1 (corresponding to the regulations of the Chemicals Ordinance). In the United States, densified wood is on the market under the trade names Permali™ and Insulam™ (Insulam, 2018). These materials are densified, phenolic-resin-impregnated and laminated products made from beech veneers, laminated with cross-directional fibres. The veneers are impregnated under vacuum and then densified with heat and pressure. The result is a homogeneous material with high strength and toughness and excellent dimensional stability and dielectric properties, used for

Figure 2.15 Compreg™ products, from the left: gym rings (Lignit™), bullet-resistant panel (Lignit™), screws (Dehonit™), and plywood (Dehonit™).

electric power equipment, structural supports in cryoenvironments and electrical insulation for rail transportation vehicles. In Australia, Insulcul Services Ltd produces densified wood manufactured from beech veneers, impregnated with a synthetic adhesive and densified under high pressure at 90°C, resulting in a material with uniform strength and stability. The product is used by the electrical power industry. In Italy, a laminated and densified beech product (RANPREX™) is produced by Rancan Srl. The product is impregnated with a special thermosetting adhesive and densified at high pressure and temperature. The product is an excellent electrical and thermal insulator, with good physical and mechanical characteristics under compression and bending loads and with good impact resistance. The material is also self-lubricating and extremely resistant to wear. It is used for many different applications; in the electrical power distribution industry, for support beams, treaded rods, compression blocks and pressure rings. Adhesive-impregnated laminated densified wood products are also produced in India by Surendra Composites Private Ltd, for example. They produce laminates of adhesive-impregnated veneer, which are used for electrical power transmission equipment and machine parts. In Japan, Olympus Corp. has developed a three-dimensional process for moulding wooden materials, where the density of a piece of cypress wood can be increased from approximately 450 kg/m^3 to more than 1,000 kg/m^3. The resulting material is thin enough to be used as a casing material for electronic products, but it is much harder than ABS plastics and polycarbonate-adhesive-based engineering plastics, for example, that are normally used in such applications. MyWood2™ Corporation (Iwakura, Aichi, Japan) manufactures densified solid cedar wood products for flooring in Japan and China, and the products are also sold for use in furniture. The MyWood2™ product is a wooden product impregnated with a polymer to provide resistance to water, and compressed to approximately 50% of its original volume.

Although the final products meet emission standards, such as European standard E1 according to EN 13986 (CEN, 2004), formaldehyde is emitted during production, and reductions in formaldehyde release are of interest. Phenol is obtained from fossil fuel sources and substitutes such as furfuryl alcohol have been tested (Westin et al., 2009). The replacement of phenol in PF resins using mono-phenols derived from lignin has also been studied (Biziks et al., 2020). Substitution with natural phenols, such as lignins or tannins, have been of interest mostly as bio-based adhesives (Hemmilä et al., 2017) but they may be used at least partly in Impreg™ and Compreg™ processes if similar properties of the products can be attained. Materials other than beech veneers, such as oil palm, may be of interest.

Table 2.8 summarises where products have been made using Compreg™.

Table 2.8 Applications of Compreg™ wood divided into Use Classes, see Table 1.7.

	Interior		Exterior		
Product type/Use Class	**1**	**2**	**3**	**4**	**5**
Indoor furniture	x	x			
Floor and non-structural interior uses	x	x			
Exterior joinery			x		
Cladding			(x)		
Decking			x		
Fencing					
Outdoor furniture					
Construction elements			x		
In-ground timber					
Products exposed to water					

where: x = products have been produced by companies using the modified wood
       (x) = products may be produced, based on pre-commercial trials, research, etc.

2.4 Impreg

Impreg™ and Compreg™ were developed during the first half of the 20th century (Stamm and Seborg, 1943; Stamm and Seborg, 1944; Stamm et al., 1946). In the Impreg™ process, wood is impregnated with resin then cured and dried. The resin may be phenol-, melamine- or urea-based, cured under mild acidic or alkaline conditions, and incorporating a monomer such as methyl methacrylate or styrene, which harden by a stepwise polymerisation mechanism. The latter are mostly odorous and difficult to handle, and their hydrophobicity does not allow them to easily penetrate cell walls or to subsequently increase material properties, such as dimensional stability. Urea-based resins are less likely to be used, because they are less stable under moist and outdoor conditions. Epoxy resins are restricted due to the necessary dilution of the high viscosity resins and their use is, therefore, more attractive as an adhesive (Moore et al., 1983). PF resins and heated compression have, however, found applications in several various stable and high-density products, as described in Section 2.3. Melamine-based resins give hardness and a clear wood colour and are found mainly in indoor products such as furniture and handicrafts (see below).

Material selection and preparation

As the migration of melamine resin, especially at high concentrations, is rather slow, large dimension sawn timber is seldom used for Impreg™ products (as long as penetration is not an issue). Melamine-resin-treated papers applied to panels are commonly used and melamine-treated veneers glued together into laminated products are typical examples. Extensively dried and extractive-rich wood should be avoided.

The modification process

Impreg™ was originally described as a process using a thermosetting fibre-penetrating resin which was impregnated into wood and cured without compression (Figure 2.16).

The wood is soaked in the aqueous resin solution or, if air dry, impregnated with the solution under vacuum (pressure) until the resin content reaches to 25–35% of the weight of dry wood. Depending on the product, the treated wood may be allowed to stand under non-drying conditions for 1–2 days to permit a uniform distribution of the solution throughout the wood. The resin-containing wood is then dried at a moderate temperature to remove the water and finally heated at 60–150°C to cure the resin. Very high drying rates should be avoided in order to prevent excessive migration of the resin to the surface. Resins based on phenol, resorcinol, melamine- and urea-formaldehydes, phenol-furfural, furfuryl-aniline and furfuryl alcohol have been found to successfully polymerise within the cell walls (Stamm and Seborg, 1939). Developments of the process have since then focused mainly on melamine resins, which combines physical improvements with the maintenance of the natural appearance of the solid wood (Hagstrand, 1999).

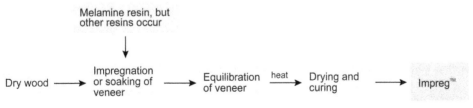

Figure 2.16 The Impreg™ process.

The influence of the micro- and chemical structure of wood

The ability of melamine resins to penetrate wooden cell walls to give a high degree of dimensional stabilisation was described by Stamm (1964). This is classified as a passive (impregnation) modification, where the chemical is deposited in the cell wall without any chemical reactions with the matrix polymers (Norimoto and Gril, 1993). The stabilisation effect is based on the formation of a three-dimensional network within the cell wall, which is believed to provide a mechanical fixation, rather than on a covalent bonding to the wood matrix (Lukowsky, 1999). This means that the resin must have a low molecular weight and methylolated melamines are usually a dominant constituent of the resin (see Figure 1.49). To achieve such a low molecular weight resin, the level of free formaldehyde in the mixture needs to be relatively high, which means that the emission of formaldehyde may cause health issues, although the addition of urea can reduce such emissions. Solubility can also hamper the application of the resin when high loads are required. Moisture and content of extractives are also of importance for the penetration of resin into the wood structure (Rapp et al., 1999; Gindl et al., 2002).

The modified product

During curing, the thermoset resin shrinks, and this may influence the strength of the material. The conditions during curing influence the hardening of the resin. The formaldehyde emission from the material and the work in bending depend on the relative humidity during processing. A high relative humidity gives a material that is less brittle with lower formaldehyde emissions (Behr et al., 2018a). The moist hardening process gave a higher resin concentration in the cell wall and fewer micro-cracks than the dry process (Behr et al., 2018b).

Because of the penetration of melamine resin into the cell wall (Rapp et al., 1999; Gindl et al., 2002) the water uptake is reduced, and the dimensional stability increased (Stamm, 1964; Pittman et al., 1994). Melamine-treated wood showed a resistance to wood-decaying fungi (Lukowsky, 1999; Rapp et al., 1999; Gsöls et al., 2003; Kielmann et al., 2016) and lower flammability (Pittman et al., 1994; Hagstrand, 1999). The fire-resistant properties are due to the nitrogen contained in melamine, which is released as a gas upon exposure to high heat and can extinguish a flame. Melamine is also a heat sink, and this is beneficial because it can absorb a large amount of heat energy. This helps the fire-resistant properties because, once exposed to flame, melamine forms a layer of char on the wood substrate and this protects the more combustible groups of the wood and of the polymer. Melamine resin was found to improve the stability of fire-retardant impregnated wood against water leaching (Lin et al., 2019).

A distinct improvement in strength and hardness was observed for solid wood (Inoue et al., 1993; Miroy et al., 1995; Rapp, 1999; Gindl et al., 2003), and this has been confirmed at the cellular level by nano-indentation (Gindl and Gupta, 2002). A lower impact bending strength was, however, found, i.e., an embrittlement, which has been attributed to the incorporation of cured resin inside the wood matrix (Pittman et al., 1994; Epmeier et al., 2004). With regard to natural and artificial weathering, melamine-treated wood showed less discolouration than untreated wood (Inoue et al., 1993; Pittman et al., 1994; Rapp and Peek, 1999). The increase in surface hardness obtained by impregnation with low molecular weight melamine resin with a low methylol content was essentially retained after long periods of artificial weathering and the crack formation was less than in untreated wood (Hansmann et al., 2006). Aqueous solutions of methylated N-methylol melamine (NMM) were used to fixate a metal-complex dye and were found to improve the material against outdoor exposure (Kielmann et al., 2012) as well as the water-related properties of the Impreg™ wood (Kielmann et al., 2016). High molecular weight resins deposited in cell lumens can block the access of moisture or water to the cell walls, thus inhibiting short term dimensional changes in wood (Cai et al., 2007).

Industrial use and application

Melamine resins have not been widely applied industrially to solid wood because they cost more than methyl methacrylates, styrenes, or phenol resins, for example (Stamm, 1964; Schneider, 1994). Impreg™ products from laminated veneer products can be bent into various shapes using metal tension bands, an inflated flexible rubber hose or a metal strap, for example. Resin-impregnated paper is used to protect the surfaces of various kinds of particleboard, fibreboard and laminated

Figure 2.17 Applications of resin-impregnated materials and products: Impregnated wood for knife handle (left), rot wood impregnated with clear resin and phosphorescent powder (middle), and plywood foliated with phenolic resin paper (right).

products. Aesthetics and constructional possibilities are enhanced by impregnation with resins and additives, such as coloured pigments, for products such as tables and knife handles (Figure 2.17).

The impregnation of methyl methacrylate and its subsequent polymerisation in wood has also attracted industrial application. Poly(methyl methacrylate) (PMMA) has attracted interest as an impregnation–polymerisation process due to the adhesive properties of the resin, which can hold the cellulose fibres together during weathering. Given that weathering is a surface phenomenon, it may be possible to simply surface treat the finished wood product. Furthermore, the increase in density, as demonstrated by the work of various research groups (e.g., Ding et al., 2008; Hadi et al., 2013), whereby densities of various timber species increased between 45 to 130% depending on the species. Such improvements in densities can improve surface hardness, making such material suited for flooring applications. Commercial production of wood treated with PMMA has been carried out since the 1950s. The USA company Grammapar commercialised the production of acrylic impregnated parquet flooring in 1963. Grammapar was taken over in 2001 by Nydree, who subsequently took over the product PermaGrain™ in 2003. Nydree flooring is still sold as an acrylic infused wood made with superior toughness over untreated products. The flooring product also includes a polymeric coating capable of incorporating pigments in marine-grade plywood to impart higher levels of water resistance and is marketed as being benzophenone free.

PMMA has been used in conjunction with nanoparticles for the development of novel properties. The work of Gan et al. (2017) showed that the impregnation of γ-Fe_2O_3@YVO_4:Eu^{3+} into delignified Cathay poplar allowed for the compound's magnetic and luminescent properties to be incorporated into the hierarchal wood structure, it being bound within the PMMA resin used as the co-impregnant. The resulting product had high transparency, unique luminescence, moderate magnetism, good thermal properties, dimensional stability, and excellent mechanical properties, which indicated that wood modified in this manner could be developed as green LED lighting equipment, luminescent magnetic switches, and within anticounterfeiting facilities.

Comparison between Impreg™ and Compreg™

As the name suggests, the main difference between Impreg™ and Compreg™ is the application of compressive forces before and during the curing process. An excellent overview of the properties of these two products was given by Ibach (2010), which is summarised in Table 2.9.

The use of Impreg™ wood and its equivalents in products is given in Table 2.10.

2.5 Furfurylated wood

Furfuryl alcohol is a liquid produced from agricultural wastes, such as sugar cane and corn cobs. Furfurylation is a process in which a material is impregnated with furfuryl alcohol (or its derivative/ prepolymer) in the presence of a mild acid catalyst. This is followed by a heat-curing step and drying including recycling of chemicals, where the heating results in a hard and resistant product. The resin contributes to the dark (brownish) colour of the product but, when exposed to direct solar radiation, greying occurs. The first commercial plant for the furfurylation of wood was the Kebony™ AS company which started in 2009 in Skien outside Oslo in Norway (Kebony, 2020). It can produce

Table 2.9 Comparison of Impreg™ and Compreg™ processed timbers (Ibach, 2010).

Property	Impreg™	Compreg™
Density	15% to 20% greater than untreated wood	Usually 1,000 to 1,400 kg/m³
Equilibrium swelling and shrinking	1/4 to 1/3 that of untreated wood	1/4 to 1/3 that of untreated wood at right angle to direction of compression, greater in direction of compression but very slow to attain
Spring-back	None	Very small when properly made
Face checking	Practically eliminated	Practically eliminated for a density less than 1,300 kg/m³
Grain raising	Greatly reduced	Greatly reduced for uniform-texture woods, considerable for contrasting grain woods
Surface finish	Similar to untreated wood	Varnished-like appearance for densities greater than about 1,000 kg/m³; cut surfaces can be given this surface by sanding and buffing
Permeability to water vapour	About 1/10 that of untreated wood	No data, but presumably much less than Impreg™
Decay and termite resistance	Considerably better than untreated wood	Considerably better than untreated wood
Acid resistance	Considerably better than untreated wood	Better than Impreg™ because of impermeability
Alkali resistance	Same as untreated wood	Somewhat better than untreated wood because of impermeability
Fire resistance	Same as untreated wood	Same as untreated wood for long exposures, somewhat better for short exposures
Heat resistance	Greatly increased	Greatly increased
Electrical conductivity	Conductivity 1/10 that of untreated wood at 30% RH; 1/1,000 that of untreated wood at 90% RH	Slightly more than Impreg™ at low relative humidity values due to entrapped water
Heat conductivity	Slightly increased	Increased about in proportion to density increase
Compressive strength	Increased more than proportional to density increase	Increased considerably more than proportional to density increase
Tensile strength	Decreased significantly	Increased less than proportional to density increase
Flexural strength	Increased less than proportional to density increase	Increased less than proportional to density increase parallel to grain, increased more perpendicular to grain
Hardness	Increased considerably more than proportional to density increase	10 to 20 times that of untreated wood
Impact strength		
• Toughness	About 1/2 of value for untreated wood, but very susceptible to the variables of manufacture	1/2 to 3/4 of value for untreated wood, but very susceptible to the variables of manufacture
• Izod	About 1/5 of value for untreated wood	1/3 to 3/4 of value for untreated wood
Abrasion resistance (tangential)	About 1/2 of value for untreated wood	Increased about in proportion to density increase
Machinability	Cuts cleaner than untreated wood, but dulls tools more	Requires metal-working tools and metal-working tool speeds
Mouldability	Cannot be moulded but can be formed to single curvatures at time of assembly	Can be moulded by compression and expansion moulding methods
Glueability	Same as untreated wood	Same as untreated wood after light sanding or in the case of thick stock, machining surfaces plane

Table 2.10 Applications of Impreg™ wood divided into Use Classes, see Table 1.7.

Product type/Use Class	Interior		Exterior		
	1	2	3	4	5
Indoor furniture	x	x			
Floor and non-structural interior uses	x	x			
Exterior joinery			x		
Cladding			x		
Decking			x		
Fencing					
Outdoor furniture			x		
Construction elements			x		
In-ground timber					
Products exposed to water			x	x	

where: x = products have been produced by companies using the modified wood
(x) = products may be produced, based on pre-commercial trials, research, etc.

20,000 m³/year and another plant has recently been established in Antwerp, Belgium. Foreco Dalfsen in The Netherlands also produces furfurylated solid wood products named Nobelwood™ (1,000 m³) from radiata pine using prepolymerised furfuryl alcohol resin (Jones et al., 2019).

Material selection and preparation

Although furfurylated wood products manufactured today are made from Scots pine and radiata pine, several other wood species have been evaluated, such as Southern yellow pine, and broad-leaved woods such as maple. European beech and silver birch have also been studied (Lande et al., 2004). A summary of furfurylation treatments of various wood species is given in Table 2.11.

Furfurylation of permeable radiata pine gives a homogeneous, highly impregnated and dense product with a low content of unimpregnated heartwood (Kebony Clear™). The absorption of moisture by the product is low and it is more dimensionally stable than untreated wood, the stability increasing with increasing content of furfuryl alcohol. In the case of Scots pine, a lower WPG is achieved giving a product, Kebony Character™, with only slightly improved moisture resistance, and dimensional stability (Figure 2.18). The bending strength is, however, similar to that of the Kebony Clear™ product and both types can be used above ground for facades, decking, etc.

The modification process

The furfurylation process has been extensively studied since its development as a potential wood modification process (Goldstein, 1959), and a thorough overview has been presented (Lande et al., 2008), the details of which are summarised below.

Process description
The process is similar to the Impreg™ process (cf. Figure 2.16), in which dried wood is impregnated with a resin, usually as an aqueous emulsion, together with a catalyst and a buffer (Lande et al., 2004). Initially, an organic solvent such as ethanol was proposed but, since it is desirable to have a high level of recycling and re-use of chemicals, water is now used to regulate the WPG of the product. Mild organic catalysts and buffers were introduced into the process in order to reduce hydrolysis and increase the strength of product. The timber is dried to a certain extent and is then impregnated in an autoclave with the treatment solution in a vacuum step, a pressurised step and a short post-vacuum step (Figure 2.19). As the chemicals penetrate into the cell wall, the wood is swollen allowing cavities in the wood to absorb the resin. The batch is then transferred to a curing

Table 2.11 Furfurylation treatment of wood species.

Specie	Process condition	Reference
European beech, European birch, Scots pine	Furfuryl alcohol resin (BioRez)/vacuum for 45 min, pressure at 12 bar for 2 hours. warming at 20–40°C for 4 hours, heating at 103°C for 16 hours	Lande et al. (2004)
Scots pine (sapwood)	Vacuum, 7–12 bar, and drying at 130°C for 16 hours	Hoydonckx et al. (2007)
Rubberwood, kelempayan, sena (*Pterocarpus indicus* Willd.), European beech, Scots pine sapwood	Furfuryl alcohol/maleic anhydride or furfuryl alcohol/citric acid. Vacuum, 12 bar, and drying at 130°C for 16 hours	Venås and Wong (2008)
European beech, European ash, radiata pine, Southern yellow pine, Scots pine	Furfuryl alcohol/citric acid, cyclic anhydride, Kebony (TM) process for outdoor level	Puttman et al. (2009)
Maritime pine boards	Furfuryl alcohol/additives, vacuum/pressure stage, curing, vacuum drying	Esteves et al. (2009)
European beech, European ash, radiata pine, Southern yellow pine	Furfuryl alcohol (30%), full-cell impregnation, vacuum drying, steam cure, drying	Pilgård et al. (2010)
Scots pine (sapwood)	Furfuryl alcohol/citric acid, vacuum, preeure at 13 bar for 2 hours, heating at 130°C for 0.5–24 hours	Thygesen et al. (2010)
Chinese white poplar, Cunninghamia, swamp mahogany, Masson's pine	Furfuryl alcohol/additives vacuum 30 minutes, 12 hours soaking, and 100°C for 12 hours	Dong et al. (2016)
Masson's pine	Furfuryl alcohol/citric acid/oxalic acid/sodium borate, vacuum, curing at < 115°C for up to 8 hours, drying 60–103°C	Li et al. (2016)
Scots pine (sapwood)	40% furfuryl alcohol (full-cell impregnation)	Alfredsen et al. (2016)
European beech	Furfuryl alcohol/various catalysts, vacuum for 5 minutes, 12 bar for 5 minutes, drying for 10 hours at 20°C, heating < 120°C for up to 24 hours	Sejati et al. (2017)
Poplar	180°C water, furfuryl alcohol /maleic anhydride, borate, vacuum for 1 hours, heating at < 103°C for 3 hours, then at 60–80°C for 4 hours, drying at 103°C	Yang et al. (2019)
Radiata pine	Furfuryl alcohol/additives, soaking for 15 days, heating at 120°C for 16.5 hours.	Skrede et al. (2019)
Southern yellow pine (sapwood)	Furfuryl alcohol/various catalysts, vacuum for 45 min, pressure at 12 bar for 2 hours. warming at 20–40°C for 4 hours, heating at 103°C for 16 hours	Ringman et al. (2020)

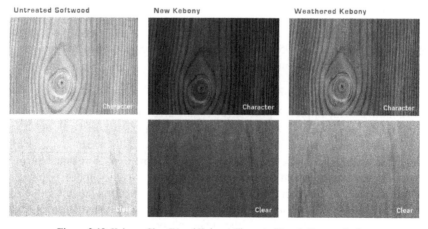

Figure 2.18 Kebony Clear™ and Kebony Character™ and after weathering.

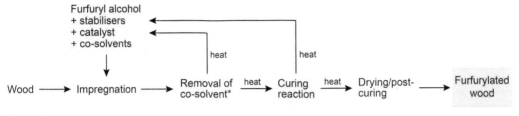

Figure 2.19 Diagram of the Kebony™ process for solid wood.

chamber so that the formation of volatiles is controlled. The curing chamber is heated with a direct injection of steam, and the temperature achieved depends on the product and on their intended use. The chamber is operated as a closed system during the curing period, except for a ventilation period at the end. The ventilation gas is cooled and the condensate is separated from the gas and returned to the condensate tank for re-use together with fresh furfuryl alcohol, water, buffer, catalyst, etc. The final treatment of the product is performed in a kiln dryer, which is essential to minimise emissions and obtain a desirable final moisture content. The emissions during the process are taken care of by cleaning the ventilated gases.

As the starting material could be toxic if it were leached out from the product, it needs to be reacted completely without degrading the material at too high a curing temperature. The heating efficiently cures the resin, leading to a hard and durable modified wood material. The material showed low toxicity when exposed to leaching tests (Pilgård et al., 2010). Initial studies of a combination of curing and drying were not successful, sticky chemicals being deposited on the machinery.

Transfuran chemicals company (Belgium) developed a process which uses a prepolymerised furfuryl alcohol resin (BioRez™) to modify wood with curing additives to yield products similar to those given by the Kebony process (Hoydonckx et al., 2007). A product named KeyWood™, which resembles furfurylated wood, has been developed within the EU-funded project *Ecobinders* (Larsson-Brelid, 2013). The reactant, which contains small amounts of tri-hydroxy-methyl furan (THMF) and furfuryl alcohol, is more soluble in water than furfuryl alcohol itself, and easily penetrates the cell wall. After curing the impregnated wood, the polymer formed within the cell wall resembles the polymer formed in the Kebony™ process, but, unlike furfurylated wood, no covalent bonds to the cell wall constituents were detected within the Ecobinders project. Due to the higher quantity of residual hydroxyls in the polymer as well as the lack of bonds to the lignin, the KeyWood™ product has a higher equilibrium moisture content than furfurylated wood at a given relative humidity. Kiln drying temperatures of 125°C were necessary for sufficient curing, but this temperature can cause problems with cracking and brittleness. The technology was sold to the Arch SA company in 2009, but production volumes seem to be very small. Meanwhile, the present market developments of the KeyWood™ process are not clear and have not been disclosed publicly (Sandberg et al., 2017).

The influence of micro- and chemical structure

As with many other impregnation processes, the extent and penetration depth during furfurylation are related to the permeability of the wood and to the process conditions. The heartwood in Scots pine is more difficult to impregnate while the sapwood of pines such as radiata, and Southern yellow pine is more easily treated. As cavities in wood start to fill up during impregnation, especially with a higher loading of furfuryl alcohol, the density of the treated wood increases. Wood furfurylation is considered to be an impregnation modification process, in which the properties of the furfurylated material appear to be more like those of a polymer-filled cell wall rather than of a reacted cell wall (Rowell, 2012; Larsson-Brelid, 2013). During the furfurylation treatment, the wood swells and, after curing, the "bulking" of the cell wall and swelling of cells is permanent. It is believed that the cured furfuryl alcohol inside the cell wall occupies some of the space that is normally filled with water

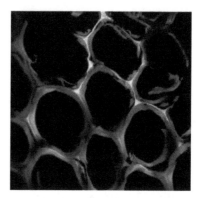

Figure 2.20 Cross section of radiata pine wood with cell walls containing furan polymer (in reddish areas), image through fluorescence microscopy.

molecules when wood swells under humid conditions (Lande et al., 2008). Fluorescence microscopy has shown that the resin penetrates into the cell wall (Figure 2.20) (Thygesen et al., 2010).

In fact, the penetration seems to reach the middle lamella and reactions with lignin may be possible. An increase in the hydrophobicity of the cell wall due to the cured resin may also contribute to a lower uptake of moisture. Recent nanoindentation studies have indicated that improvements in the indentation modulus and hardness of furfurylated wood cells may show indirectly that furfuryl alcohol penetrates the wood cells during the modification process (Li et al., 2016).

The wood is impregnated with furfuryl alcohol or a prepolymer (BioRez™ by Transfuran chemicals) in the presence of a mild acid catalyst such as maleic anhydride or citric acid (Transfuran chemicals, 2010). Recent studies indicate that tartaric acid may be an even better acid catalyst than citric acid (Sejati et al., 2017). The extent of degradation of hemicelluloses should be limited, as such reactions normally takes place at higher temperatures (170°C for softwood under saturated steam conditions, such as the WTT™ process), since only mild acid catalysts are used and thermal modification also produces mild acids.

The polymerisation of furfuryl alcohol in wood is a complex chemical reaction, and the question of whether furfurylation is a distinct chemical process remains unanswered. The furfuryl alcohol reacts with itself forming a polymeric structure and possibly with the lignin in the cell walls (Lande et al., 2008; Nordstierna et al., 2008; Gérardin, 2016; Li et al., 2016). Furfuryl alcohol condenses with itself forming water (Figure 2.21) and a furan condensed product in which the furan units are held together by methylene bridges, although dimethyl ether bridges are sometimes formed (see Figure 1.46) (Lande et al., 2008).

Figure 2.21 Reactions during the furfurylation of wood: (a) self-condensation of furfuryl alcohol, forming a methylene bridge, and (b) condensation of furfuryl alcohol to phenolic compounds via methylene bridging.

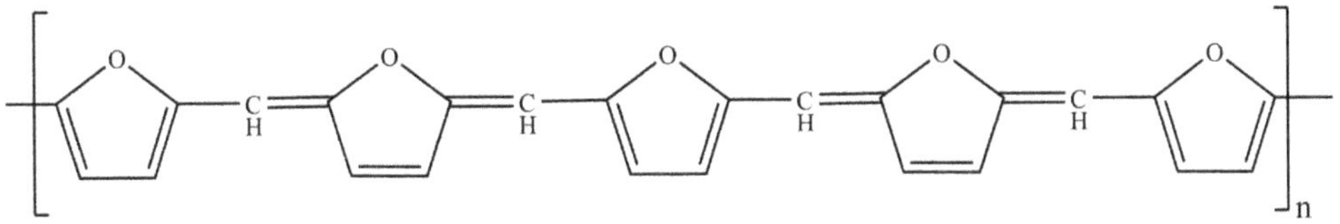

Figure 2.22 Conjugated carbon-carbon double bonds in condensed furfuryl alcohol.

An acid catalyst assists the removal of water from the furfuryl alcohol and catalyses the polymerisation process. The mechanism has not been described in detail, but activation of furfuryl alcohol by the formation of an ester adduct with maleic anhydride is possible (Nordstierna et al., 2008). Cross-linking reactions also seem to occur and contribute to a harder material. It is possible that formaldehyde is liberated during the heating of the ether-bonded structures and that it reacts further forming more thermodynamically stable methylene bridges as the main cross-links (see Figure 1.46). Other reactions also seem to occur, such as cyclic reactions, oxidations reactions and reactions leading to extended conjugated structures (Figure 2.22), which may contribute to the brownish colour of the product.

The interaction of furfurylated wood with moisture has been found to be lower than in untreated wood with increasing relative humidity up to 99% (Fredriksson, 2019). Low field nuclear magnetic resonance (NMR) showed a greater relaxation of lumen water in furfurylated wood than in untreated wood at WPG of 63%, and this was interpreted as being due to the formation of a more hydrophobic cell wall (Thygesen and Elder, 2008).

The modified product

The furfurylation process results in a wood product that in many aspects has distinctly improved properties (Lande et al., 2004; Lande et al., 2008; Rowell, 2012; Larsson-Brelid, 2013; Mantanis and Lykidis, 2015), which may be summarised as follows:

Physical and chemical properties

The density of Kebony Clear™ is 670 kg/m³ compared with a density of 480 kg/m³ for untreated radiata pine. For Kebony Character™ a density of 570 kg/m³ has been reported compared with 490 kg/m³ for untreated Scots pine.

As expected for a product with a large uptake of resin, the furfurylated product absorbs less moisture (4–8%) under normal outdoor conditions (Kebony Clear™). The lower furfurylated product Kebony Character™ has a lower degree of hydrophobicity, with moisture levels between 7–13%. This variation in uptake can at least in part be explained by a variation in the proportion of heartwood in the commercial Scots pine product, which is more difficult to impregnate than sapwood. Capillary suction tests showed that the uptake of water by furfurylated wood was greatly reduced at 40% WPG, and that the effect of a further increase in WPG was small (Bastani et al., 2015). The furfurylated wood also had a greater hydrophobicity.

The moisture uptake by furfurylated wood is related to the WPG (Epmeier et al., 2004; Epmeier et al., 2007). Thybring proposed that the decay resistance of modified wood was related to a threshold MEE, a 40% MEE being obtained at a WPG of 35% for furfurylated wood (Thybring, 2013). The dimensional stability increases with increasing WPG but levels off at a WPG above 30–40% corresponding to an ASE of 75% due to filling the lumen (Figure 2.23). Values of the anti-shrinking efficiency of 50% and 25% respectively for the commercial Kebony Clear™ and Kebony Character™ products, respectively have been reported.

The colour of furfurylated wood is brownish and the product with larger amounts of furfuryl alcohol seems to be deeper in colour. Discolouration of furfurylated wood was delayed to some extent compared to untreated wood, and it can be further delayed using UV-stable oils, although the timber eventually becomes grey on outdoor exposure. Crack formation was also delayed by furfurylation.

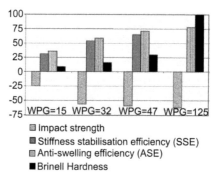

Figure 2.23 Strength properties of furfurylated wood (Lande et al., 2004).

Recent studies regarding the ecotoxicology of furfurylated wood and leachates from furfurylated wood showed no significant ecotoxicity, and its combustion did not release any volatile organic compounds or polyaromatic hydrocarbons above the normal levels when wood is combusted (Pilgård et al., 2010).

Mechanical properties

Furfurylated wood has a greater hardness, elasticity, and rupture modulus than untreated wood; but it is also more brittle (lower impact resistance) when the wood is treated with a furfuryl-alcohol polymer (Larsson-Brelid, 2013). As can be seen in Figure 2.21, the hardness increases and the impact strength decreases with increasing WPG (Lande, 2004).

Biological properties

The resistance to fungal decay of wood can be significantly improved by furfurylation and the biological durability has been upgraded to "Class 1" (Gérardin, 2016). Furfurylated wood of moderate loading (30–35% weight percentage gain) had a resistance to decay comparable with that of Scots pine wood impregnated with copper chromium arsenate (CCA), as shown in Figure 2.24 (Larsson-Brelid, 2013). The heartwood of Scots pine is more difficult to modify and Kebony™ products are recommended for above ground applications. Studies in a tropical termite field showed very low mass losses with a high or medium WPG of chemicals, whereas untreated samples were almost totally consumed (Lande et al., 2004; Hadi et al., 2005). Even at a WPG of 29%, furfurylated wood samples survived Swedish marine conditions for four years whereas CCA samples were degraded.

The cured furfuryl alcohol resin is leached from the wood with difficulty and is difficult to hydrolyse especially if methylene bridges are formed holding the furan units together. Gene expressions of furfurylated timbers exposed to the brown-rot fungus *Postia placenta* showed high levels of oxidative metabolites, but the levels of some of the genes related to enzymatic degradation

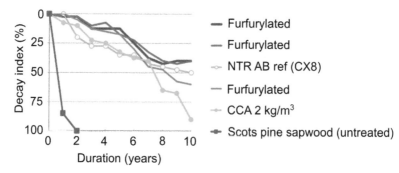

Figure 2.24 Decay resistance of furfurylated wood in ground (EN 252) and preservative impregnated (Kebony, 2014).

varied, some endoglucanase and β-glucanase enzymes being reduced (Alfredsen et al., 2015). Gene regulation in modified wood before any significant mass loss can be detected may be more complex than an overall up-regulation of chelator-mediated Fenton reaction (CMF) genes related to the oxidative degradation phase (Ringman et al., 2020). A potential threshold for the lower mass loss due to the high furfurylation treatment has been suggested (Skrede et al., 2019).

Technological aspects

For the Kebony Clear™ grade, machining could be compared to that of broad-leaved woods, so that profiling and planing are possible, but the same is not true with Kebony Character™, as it is not sufficiently homogeneously treated.

Phenol-resorcinol-formaldehyde (PRF) and epoxy systems may be used as adhesives for furfurylated wood. Furfurylated European beech has been glued satisfactorily with emulsified polymeric isocyanate (EPI) and melamine-urea-formaldehyde (MUF), even though the percentage bond-line failure increased under wet conditions (van der Zee et al., 2007). In maple and beech, the wood was more stable than the bond-line, but for Southern yellow pine the situation was reverse. The shear strength of aspen, radiata pine and Southern yellow pine was reduced, and the reduction increased with increasing extent of treatment with furfuryl alcohol. A decrease in shear strength when using PUR, EPI and polyvinyl acetate (PVAc) adhesives was found in the case of furfurylated Scots pine, probably due to the increased brittleness of wood rather than to a weak bond-line (Bastani et al., 2017).

Furfurylated wood may be painted, stained or coated. Wood oils and water-based acrylic paints are recommended. Alkyd and acrylate can be used, but a somewhat lower adhesion was obtained with high solid contents paints (van der Zee et al., 2007).

Acid-proof fasteners, such as stainless-steel fasteners are recommended to avoid staining (Jermer et al., 2017). Leaching from the furfurylated wood may discolour copper and zinc materials. Pre-drilled holes are recommended and, for Kebony Character™, cross-cut ends should be protected.

Environmental aspects

Seventy per cent of raw material comes from FSC- or PEFC-certified forests and is controlled by the EU Timber Regulation (EUTR). Quality control scanners are used to follow the development of the wood product. The furfurylated wood products, the chemicals used, and the overall process have obtained the Nordic Swan Eco-label. The carbon footprint (cradle-to-grave, including energy recovery) for furfurylated Southern yellow pine obtained in 2010 was 660 kg CO_2/m^3, and this value is used in Environmental Product Declarations (EPDs). With good maintenance, cleaning with a soft brush and household detergent, the service life expectancy will be over 30 years.

Industrial use and application

The potential of commercial modification with furfuryl alcohol has been established and modified, particularly since the 1990s.

Commercial industrial processes

Research relating to the modification of wood with furfuryl alcohol was initiated by Stamm and Goldstein (Goldstein, 1959; Stamm, 1977), but using cyclic carboxylic anhydrides as catalysts, furfurylated wood with superior properties was provided by Schneider (1995) in Canada. Westin and his collegues (Westin et al., 1998; Lande et al., 2010) in Sweden subsequently developed a technology based on stable solutions with better impregnating capacities and promising properties, like resistance to decay. Nowadays, Kebony AS, based outside Oslo in Norway, has an annual production of approximately 22,000 m^3, and it is increasing its production capacity by building additional facilities in Antwerp, Belgium (Mantanis, 2017; Jones et al., 2019).

Applications

Kebony AS company (Norway) currently produces two furfurylated wood products, Kebony Character™ and Kebony Clear™. The latter is highly furfurylated wood, dark and hard, and is mainly based on radiata pine but also on Southern yellow pine and maple used for flooring. Kebony Character™ produced from Scots pine is more lightly loaded and is presently used as decking, siding, roofing (where a waterproof membrane is said to be required) and outdoor furniture. Furfurylated wood can also be used in cladding, street furniture and marine applications, such as piers, walkways, and boat decks (Figure 2.25).

Following a series of extensive quality tests in Germany, furfurylated wood, which can be worked with as easily as with broad-leaved woods when using EPI, PRF and MUF adhesives, is presently recommended by the German Association of Windows and Facades (VFF).

Nobelwood™ is produced using a pre-polymerised furfuryl alcohol resin by the Foreco Dalfsen company, in The Netherlands. They also produce a product (FRX™) using fire retardants that is stable to outdoor conditions and reaches Euroclass B grading, the best fire rating possible for a timber product. The colourless FRX™ treatment is also said to maintain the natural appearance of the wood and to retard weathering.

To date, there have been various products manufactured and tested using furfurylated wood, this being summarised in Table 2.12.

Figure 2.25 Applications of furfurylated wood: (a) cladding and roofing, (b) walkway and barrier, (c) deckings, and (d) window profile.

Table 2.12 Applications of furfurylated wood divided into Use Classes, see Table 1.7.

| | Interior | | Exterior | | |
Product type/Use Class	1	2	3	4	5
Indoor furniture	x	x			
Floor and non-structural interior uses	x	x			
Exterior joinery			x		
Cladding			x		
Decking					
Fencing			x		
Outdoor furniture			x		
Construction elements			x	(x)	
In-ground timber				(x)	
Products exposed to water				x	(x)

where:　x = products have been produced by companies using the modified wood
　　　　(x) = products may be produced, based on pre-commercial trials, research, etc.

2.6 DMDHEU

Many wood modification techniques have their origins in other chemical processing technologies, particularly those for modifying cellulose. This is the case with treatments involving the cyclic N-methylol compound 1,3-dimethylol-4,5-dihydroxyethyleneurea (DMDHEU) that was used in the early version of the Belmadur™ process operated by BASF company between 2010 and 2016. This is an example of treatment that has been used in other industrial areas; in this case, as an anti-wrinkling agent in cellulose and cellulose-blended fabrics (Schindler and Hauser, 2004). Originally, the agent was considered to be an alternative to formaldehyde-containing resins, but the emission of small amounts of formaldehyde cannot be avoided with DMDHEU-modified wood (Emmerich et al., 2019). Nevertheless, DMDHEU has some similarities to furfurylated wood (see Section 2.5), such as hardness and decay resistance and, when produced in the correct manner, it gives only minor colouring of the material. The chemical has a melting point of 161−163°C and is, thus, less volatile than other liquid modifying agents (acetic anhydride and furfuryl alcohol). The basic features of the process using DMDHEU are similar to those of other chemical modification processes, such as impregnation with reagents in vacuum/pressure followed by curing by heating. The process conditions depend on the wood species and on the wood dimensions. Products from solid wood, veneers and wood fibres have been tested and applications in decking, windows, garden furniture and plywood chairs have been used in small amounts.

The production of Belmadur™ using DMDHEU was stopped in 2016, but Archroma Management GmbH (Reinach, Switzerland) together with the University in Göttingen, Germany, have now resumed investigations to improve the technology using DMDHEU (Emmerich, 2016). Recently, another cross-linking agent (glyoxal) has been advertised by BASF in a process named Belmadur™ (BASF, 2020). Radiata pine is the preferred species due to the cooperation between TimTechChem International Ltd. in Auckland, New Zealand (Emmerich et al., 2019).

Wood modification with DMDHEU is an environmentally benign technology which enhances dimensional stability, surface hardness and resistance to both wood-destroying fungi and marine borers. Property enhancement depends on the homogeneous distribution of reacted chemical, chemical loading (WPG) and high fixation of the reagent to give long-term performance. Both weathering and coating performance were improved by the modification, and infestation by staining fungi was reduced but not prevented. Thus, DMDHEU technology is a promising technique for giving wood species a low natural durability applicable in outdoor areas, the transfer from textile to wood processing being achieved with the superheated steam curing of DMDHEU-treated wood (Emmerich et al., 2019).

Material selection and preparation

Process development to an industrial scale has been limited to Scots pine (Schaffert, 2006; Krause, 2006), the sapwood of which is fairly easily impregnated resulting in a homogeneous performance without the risk of developing strength gradients in the material. Other wood species generally show a high-level improvement in durability and dimensional stability as well as in selected mechanical properties as a result of DMDHEU modification. Permeable wood species such as rubberwood (Krause, 2006), slash pine (Militz et al., 2011; Militz and Norton, 2013), radiata pine (Borges et al., 2005; Derham et al., 2017), albizzia wood (Yusuf et al., 1995), ponderosa pine (Weaver et al., 1960; Nicholas and Williams, 1987), sweetgum (Ashaari et al., 1990), maritime pine (Lopes, 2013) and balsam poplar (Yuan et al., 2013) have been tested. Although many properties have been improved (Rademacher et al., 2009), DMDHEU-modified European beech gave a poor yield of crack-free material, even after process optimisation (Bollmus, 2011). In the case of plywood, species such as European beech, Norway spruce, Scots pine and silver birch have been studied (Wepner, 2006; Dieste Märkl, 2009), while European beech and Scots pine have been investigated for particleboards (Bartholme, 2005).

In conclusion, while the modification of solid wood is limited to permeable wood species, small particles or thin veneers of most species may easily be impregnated (Wepner, 2006), for the production of bent European beech veneer products, for example.

Modification process

The past few decades have seen DMDHEU progress from a laboratory concept to a potentially commercial opportunity, and these developments have been reviewed by Emmerich et al. (2019).

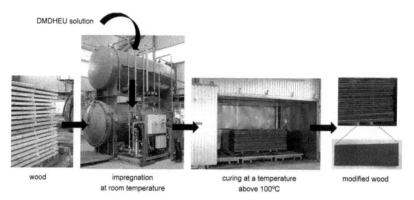

Figure 2.26 Scheme of the DMDHEU process.

An autoclave is filled with batches of dried sawn timber, separated by stickers, and then pressure-treated (1 hour of vacuum and 2 hours at a pressure of 1.2 MPa) to ensure that the chemicals (DMDHEU with or without catalysts) penetrate the timber (Figure 2.26).

By using a curing schedule for Scots pine including heating to 120°C, curing, cooling, and conditioning a homogeneous distribution of reacted DMDHEU, a good fixation (> 90% DMDHEU retention after hot-water extraction at 90°C) and low formaldehyde emissions were obtained. At the same time, good drying qualities, i.e., little formation of drying cracks and little variation in moisture content within large wood samples, could be achieved. The final moisture content at the end of the process was 6–8% (Schaffert, 2006). However, reduced drying quality with European beech made it necessary to optimise the curing processes for each wood species, and for different timber dimensions to make modified timber with a unique property profile (Schaffert et al., 2006; Breuer, 2008; Bollmus, 2011). Curing conditions were found to be important, such as the use of superheated steam (Emerich et al., 2017) and a good air circulation, so as to minimise cracking, especially for species such as European beech.

European beech has been the focus for further development of the drying and curing process (Emmerich et al., 2019). The curing is preferably done in superheated steam, as it allows rapid heat transfer and curing of the DMDHEU under wet-state conditions. Heating alone led to incomplete polymerisation and the release of formaldehyde (Krause, 2006). Curing under dry conditions is unsatisfactory. It leads to capillary movement and a heterogeneous distribution of the DMDHEU during the drying stage.

Magnesium chloride and other catalysts have been found to accelerate the curing process. However, acidic and metallic salts may be harmful during the use of the material and have been shown to reduce the mechanical strength (Yuan et al., 2013), probably by degradation of the hemicellulose (Xie et al., 2007). A load of 5% magnesium chloride seemed to lead to benign curing conditions and at the same time high dimensional stability, resistance against wood-destroying fungi and moderate hydrolysis of wood cell wall components, mainly polysaccharides (Krause, 2006).

DMDHEU-modified plywood and LVL production

Water-proof shaped wood from beech veneer has been investigated as one possible application (Emmerich et al., 2019). For the production of waterproof bent products from beech veneer (Figure 2.27), European beech trunks are sprayed with water on storage, prior to being cut to the desired lengths and debarked. The wood is then softened by steaming prior to peeling of veneers, which are then cut to the appropriate size and quality controlled. The veneers are subsequently impregnated and cured, dried on a roller conveyor and quality sorted electronically.

A scheme for the final stages in the manufacture of such a product is shown in Figure 2.28 following the preparatory stages shown in Figure 2.27. The DMDHEU-treated and sorted veneers are glued with waterproof glue and then pressed and shaped in a heated press, allowing the glue to

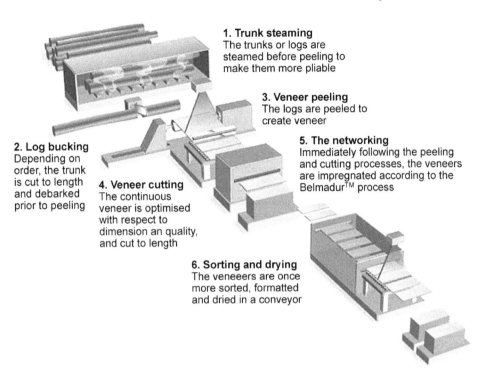

1. Trunk steaming
The trunks or logs are steamed before peeling to make them more pliable

3. Veneer peeling
The logs are peeled to create veneer

2. Log bucking
Depending on order, the trunk is cut to length and debarked prior to peeling

5. The networking
Immediately following the peeling and cutting processes, the veneers are impregnated according to the Belmadur™ process

4. Veneer cutting
The continuous veneer is optimised with respect to dimension an quality, and cut to length

6. Sorting and drying
The veneeers are once more sorted, formatted and dried in a conveyor

Figure 2.27 Preparation of DMDHEU-treated beech veneer intermediate product.

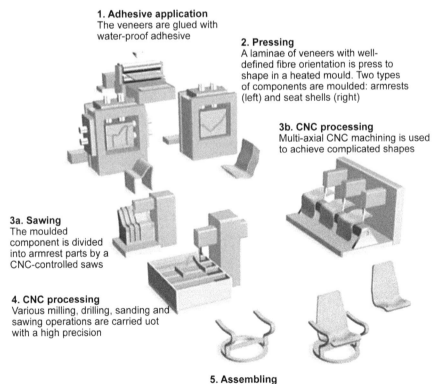

1. Adhesive application
The veneers are glued with water-proof adhesive

2. Pressing
A laminae of veneers with well-defined fibre orientation is press to shape in a heated mould. Two types of components are moulded: armrests (left) and seat shells (right)

3b. CNC processing
Multi-axial CNC machining is used to achieve complicated shapes

3a. Sawing
The moulded component is divided into armrest parts by a CNC-controlled saws

4. CNC processing
Various milling, drilling, sanding and sawing operations are carried uot with a high precision

5. Assembling
The different parts are assembled to the final products. Finishing may be done before assembling

Figure 2.28 Formation of waterproof bent wood products from European beech veneer.

harden. Computer Numerical Control (CNC) machines then finish the material produced either by sawing out profiles or by finishing the products further.

The influence of micro and chemical structure

A permanently swollen and hard structure was obtained in the early Belmadur™ process using DMDHEU, the same being expected for any commercially produced materials from TimTech company. This could be due to the diffusion of DMDHEU molecules into the cell wall during the impregnation step. The chemicals may not only migrate into the cell wall but also fill up the lumen, especially with a high loading. The pore size distribution, determined by differential scanning calorimetry, indicated that DMDHEU reduced the pore size of the samples by occupying the voids in the cell wall (Dieste et al., 2009c).

Under the agent is thought to bond to cellulose upon heating under suitable conditions or preferentially to hemicellulose and possibly by cross-links, as it has at least two reactive methylol groups (see Figure 1.44). This process probably starts with a reaction with one of these methylol groups. The existence of cross-linking is indicated by comparing wood treated at various moisture contents, as reswelling is hindered by cross-links (Krause, 2006). Figure 2.29 shows that the cross-linking effect of DMDHEU was lower than the bulking of the cell wall during the treatment.

Subsequent trials (Wepner, 2006; Bollmus, 2011; Emmerich, 2016) could not however confirm this 'cross-linking-effect'. FTIR was used to identify such bonds, but a detailed cross-linked structure has not been presented.

DMDHEU is not stable and formaldehyde can be released and the adduct can react with the methylol group in another molecule forming a condensed product together with water (Figure 2.30). Polycondensation of DMDHEU and mDMDHEU molecules was found to occur by reaction of the pure resin with the formation of solid, brittle polymers (Krause, 2006) but filling of the lumen is rare, and the compound does not seem to polymerise (condense) with itself to any significant extent. It is, therefore, suggested that it mainly penetrates the cell wall reacting with the wood polymers.

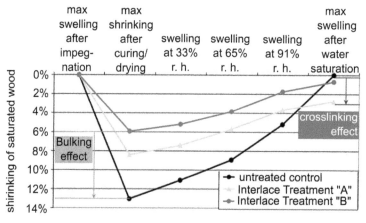

Figure 2.29 Reduction of swollen structure by a cross-linking reaction after treatment with DMDHEU, r. h. - relative humidity.

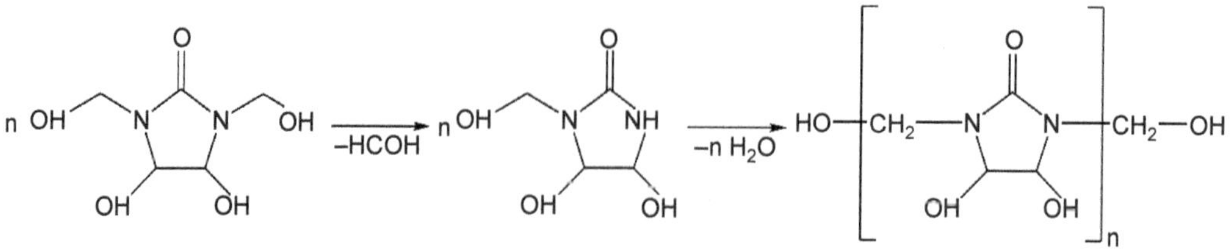

Figure 2.30 Self-condensation of DMDHEU.

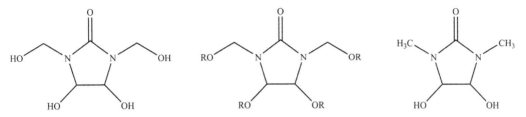

Figure 2.31 Structural formula of modified cyclic N-methylol compound, from the left: DMDHEU, methylated DMDHEU (R=H or methyl group), and DMeDHEU.

Formaldehyde emission may be lowered by the addition of a methylated product, mDMDHEU (Figure 2.31). The formaldehyde-free substrate DMeDHEU entered more slowly into the wood or the wood fibre, but it seemed to work in a real process (Krause, 2006). DMeDHEU caused higher bulking than the formaldehyde-containing reagents and the dimensional stability was greater in the short-term, but it decreased noticeably with long-term exposure due to minor changes in fixation and leaching.

The modified product

Since its development, the use of DMDHEU in wood modification has been shown not to be a biocide, fungicide or an insecticide. The process converts non-durable wood into "modified" wood with tropical hardwood properties, where there is a permanent swelling of cell walls, bulking the wood and improving its hardness and density.

Physical and chemical changes

DMDHEU can be obtained as a pale and yellow solution at 40%. This means that, especially in an unreacted state, it can coordinate with water molecules. The absorption energy of moisture at a low EMC corresponding to a monolayer was higher for DMDHEU-modified wood than for untreated wood (Dieste et al., 2008b). An increase in EMC at low relative humidity and a decrease at high relative humidity was found for modified (1.3 M DMDHEU) European beech wood (Bollmus, 2011). In contrast, as the reaction was incomplete due to wet curing conditions, the modified wood was more hygroscopic, due to the hygroscopic character of the non-reacted DMDHEU monomer (Krause, 2006). This conclusion was based on calculations of the maximum swelling (Krause, 2006), and subsequent findings showed that modified wood is not able to accommodate as many water molecules as untreated wood (Dieste et al., 2009c), and the fibre saturation point (FSP) decreased with increasing WPG (Wepner, 2006). Furthermore, the stability on cyclic climate exposure was found to be increased (Figure 2.32).

The absolute amount of water absorbed was reduced by the modification, as well as the instant speed of water uptake during water submersion. The reduced water uptake was assumed to be

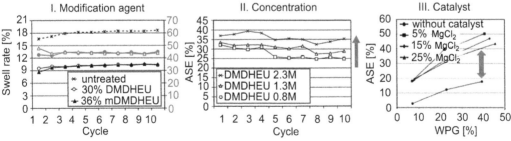

Figure 2.32 Dimensional stability resulting from DMDHEU treatment: (I) reduction in swelling due to increased modification, (II) long-term dimensional stability with DMDHEU treatment, and (III) increased stability due to increased catalyst.

affected by the space occupied by DMDHEU molecules within the cell wall and the blocking of cell wall pores, hindering the entrance of water molecules (Krause, 2006).

The reduced water uptake influences the swelling of the DMDHEU-modified material. At a WPG of 30% the swelling of European beech was reduced from 17% to below 12% and at a WPG of 60% the swelling dropped to around 6%. Industrial-scale production using superheated steam with a proper concentration (30% DMDHEU, catalyst $MgCl_2$) led to an anti-shrinking efficiency (ASE) of 45–50% for Scots pine (Schaffert, 2006) and of 30–35% for European beech (Bollmus, 2011). Depending on the wood species, chemical reagent, applied concentration (WPG), catalyst and curing temperature, a permanent ASE of up to 70% could be achieved (Militz, 1993; Krause, 2006; Bollmus, 2011). Magnesium chloride was found to be the most suitable catalyst for wood applications so far, since it gave high dimensional stability (high ASE) accompanied by high fixation, so that the long-term material performance was guaranteed at a concentration of $MgCl_2$ > 5% (Krause, 2006).

A light brownish colour was obtained after treatment of Scots pine and radiata pine with DMDHEU (Figure 2.33).

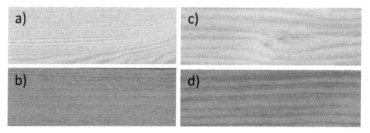

Figure 2.33 Colour of Scots pine (SP) and radiata pine (RP) after treatment with DMDHEU: (a) untreated SP, (b) modified SP, (c) untreated RP, and (d) modified RP (Photos courtesy of Lukas Emmerich, University of Göttingen, Germany).

The discolouration and greying of modified wood surfaces, caused by UV degradation of cell wall components and the subsequent colonisation and growth of blue stain and moulds, was less than that of untreated wood, but it was not prevented (Krause, 2006; Wepner, 2006; Xie, 2006). It was found that latewood was more coloured compared to earlywood, which was grey. A similar result was noted for weather-induced surface erosion (roughness, waviness). Deformation and cracking were reduced in the long term, but not initially.

Curing in a superheated steam atmosphere gave formaldehyde emissions which fulfilled legal requirements (≤ 0.1 ppm; E1) for wood-based products (ChemVerbotsV, 2019) for both European beech and Scots pine (Schaffert, 2006; Bollmus, 2011). Although formaldehyde emission increased slightly with rising WPG (Krause, 2006; Bollmus, 2011), methylated DMDHEU derivatives (Figure 2.30) were able to reduce formaldehyde emission by the final product when both solid wood and plywood were used (Krause, 2006; Wepner, 2006). Curing under wet conditions led to a high amount of unreacted DMDHEU monomer, and this led to formaldehyde emissions above the allowed limit (Krause, 2006; Schaffert, 2006).

Mechanical properties

DMDHEU-treated poplar was harder and had a higher compression strength perpendicular to grain, but the MOR and impact strength decreased as the WPG increased (Jiang et al., 2014). The work to maximum load (WMLB) under bending was lower in the modified wood (Dieste et al., 2008a). Dynamic mechanical properties such as impact bending strength and structural integrity, detected by a high-energy multiple impact test, decreased significantly as a result of the modification, indicating a greater embrittlement (Wepner, 2006; Dieste et al., 2008a; Bollmus, 2011).

For parquet flooring, at least 50% of DMDHEU seems to be required in order to obtain a two-fold increase in hardness (Figure 2.34). Higher contents of DMDHEU increase the density

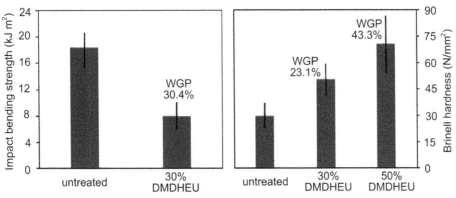

Figure 2.34 Impact bending strength and Brinell hardness of DMDHEU-treated rubber wood veneer glued on a plywood core (Emmerich, 2016).

and hardness further. The cell wall porosity is believed to be reduced, especially at higher WPG of DMDHEU, when the cell wall becomes saturated with chemicals.

Biological properties

The durability of the treated materials was studied by determining the mass loss (ML) on exposure to decay fungi. The majority of studies found ML < 5%, corresponding to Durability Class (DC) 1–2 ('very durable to durable'). Other studies reported a ML for DMDHEU-modified European beech wood corresponding to DC 4 'slightly durable', where tests were conducted according to EN 113 (CEN, 1996) and DC assigned on the basis of EN 350 (CEN, 1994) (Bollmus et al., 2018). At similar WPG levels, DMDHEU-modified Scots pine had a lower ML caused by fungal decay than the modified European beech wood (Verma et al., 2009). Results from the grave yard test ENV 807 (Figure 2.35) showed that a treatment with DMDHEU corresponding to a WPG of 6% was sufficient to give a durability class 3 while a WPG above 15% gave Class 1.

DMDHEU-modified wood was exposed above ground in Australian test fields located in sub-tropical and wet-tropical climate areas (Use Class 3.1 according to EN 335 (CEN, 2013)) and in ground contact (Use Class 4 according to EN 335). After 5.5 years, Scots pine and slash pine treated with high DMDHEU concentrations (2.1 M DMDHEU) showed a significantly improved resistance against attack by wood-destroying basidiomycetes. Much of the protective effect remained after 9 years of exposure, although the tough conditions in South Johnstone, Australia, also affected the modified Scots pine (Emmerich et al., 2020). The performance of European beech wood was worse than of that of Scots pine under aggressive wet-tropical climate conditions (Militz and Norton, 2013).

The high resistance of DMDHEU modification to wood-destroying fungi was assumed to be based on the explanation given by Hill (2006) and Ringman et al. (2014) of the improved resistance

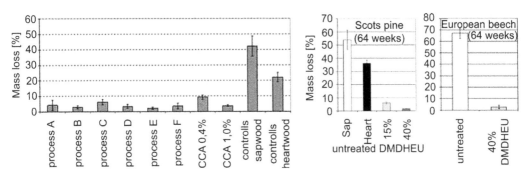

Figure 2.35 Grave yard (ENV 807) tests: European beech treated with DMDHEU and CCA (left), and Scots pine and European beech treated with DMDHEU (right).

of modified material against fungal decay, namely: (1) a decrease in FSP, (2) a decrease in pore size and (3) changes in polymer structure (Dieste et al., 2009c).

Damage by termites was inhibited by the modification to a great extent; 20–35% lower ML than that of control specimens using albizzia wood and 5% DMDHEU (Yusuf et al., 1995); 85–95% lower ML than that of control specimens using Scots pine and 1.3 M and 2.1 M DMDHEU (Militz et al., 2011). Dry-cured samples showed 'slight attack' by termites after 30 months in ground contact when 'severe attack' was already detected in wet-cured samples (Schaffert et al., 2006).

After 3-years exposure in marine environments according to EN 275 (CEN, 1992) in the North Sea (Germany) and Baltic Sea (Denmark), Scots pine treated with 0.8 M, 1.3 M and 2.1 M DMDHEU was almost not infested by the shipworm *Teredo navalis*, apart from a single animal found within the material treated with 1.3 M DMDHEU and exposed in the North Sea (Klüppel et al., 2012). Untreated wood was totally degraded within one year, but the modified wood was almost completely intact after 9 years of exposure in the Baltic sea (Emmerich et al., 2020).

Technological aspects

DMDHEU-treated conifer woods are similar to broad-leaved woods, but an increasing content of catalyst increases the wear on metallic tools.

PUR was found to be the most appropriate adhesive to meet the requirements of EN 301 (CEN, 2017), but all the adhesives tested apart from PVAc led to sufficient bonding in moist conditions, i.e., Class D4 (Schmid, 2006). DMDHEU-modified Scots pine was licensed for glued products by the German Association of Windows and Facades (VFF). The setting and drying times of adhesives may increase, due to the lower moisture absorption by the DMDHEU-modified wood compared to untreated wood. Real-time curing behaviour, with respect to process optimisation and final adhesion quality of adhesives on DMDHEU-modified wood surfaces, has not been tested nor monitored to date.

The shear strength, the cohesive wood failure and the delamination were determined in plywood made with DMDHEU-modified veneers of European beech, silver birch and Scots pine using phenolic resins. The samples constructed with unmodified veneers had a higher shear strength and higher wood failure than the samples constructed with modified veneers, but all the shear strength values met the European requirements for plywood designed for exterior conditions (Dieste et al., 2009a).

Coating with acrylic-based and alkyd-based systems was not affected by pre-treatment with DMDHEU or mDMDHEU with respect to blocking, drying rate, or pull-off strength (tested according to standard ASTM D 4541 (ASTM, 2002); nor was the interface between the wood surface and the coating films. The wet adhesion of some water-borne and solvent-borne systems appeared to be improved by previous modification (Wepner, 2006; Xie, 2006). Petrič et al. (2007) reported that the wettability was improved, with lower contact angles of water-borne coating systems on modified wood surfaces than on untreated wood. The colour may change slightly after a coating is applied (Wepner, 2006; Xie, 2006), and the service life may be extended (Xie et al., 2008).

Environmental aspects

The process uses non-toxic chemicals to make wood material durable, and this is a great benefit. No particular conditions are required during treatment, except for the use of superheated steam for less permeable wood like European beech. Formaldehyde emission may occur, but production at low levels appear to be possible, below the E1 level (down to 2 mg extracted formaldehyde in 100 g dry wood).

Industrial use and application

Formaldehyde is an efficient agent for modifying wood, and good dimensional stability can be reached at low WPG, probably cross-links are formed with wood component which hinder the movement of the wood matrix on exposure to moisture. However, it is toxic and, in 2004, it was classified by the International Agency for Research on Cancer (IARC) as a "known human carcinogen", an upgrade from the previous "probable human carcinogen". The formation of N-methylol groups in melamine-formaldehyde (MF) resins is shown in Figure 1.49. In this case, the formation of chemical bonds to wood is less likely, and a higher WPG and stable bulking of the cell wall is required to achieve adequate stabilisation of the wood. The cyclic N-methylol compound DMDHEU has been used in other industrial areas; for example, as an anti-wrinkling agent in cellulose and cellulose-blended fabrics (Schindler and Hauser, 2004). Already in the late 1950s, wood was treated with low-molecular-weight N-methylol compounds of ethylene urea. Weaver et al. (1960) found that DMEU improved the dimensional stability of ponderosa pine. Since 1990, work has focused on the treatment of Scots pine and European beech wood with 1,3-dimethylol-4,5-dihydroxyethyleneurea (DMDHEU), and in the early 2000s, a process using DMDHEU was developed for Scots pine (Belmadur™ Technology, BASF). Market penetration was not however reached, but investigations were resumed in 2016.

Upscaling aspects

An advantage of the technology is that water can be used as a solvent (impregnation solution includes DMDHEU, catalyst and tap water). This simplifies the impregnation process and makes this technology of interest for smaller and medium-sized companies. The material has so far only been launched to a limited level in New Zealand, under the tradename HartHolz™. This seemed to be more an issue of established and firm structures in the wood working industry, than worse material performance, since this is a principle challenge of innovative wood modification technologies (Mai, 2010).

Three parties are involved in such an implementation process, mainly:

- Chemical manufacturer: global player, who supports the modification companies, but does not have alone the structure necessary to build production capacity.

- Wood working industry: requires the material but does not have the technical know-how to implement the process.

- Impregnating plant for wood preservatives: suitable for the impregnation but serving markets other than those served by the manufacturers of modified wood.

   Successful implementation of new technologies for chemical wood modification (e.g., DMDHEU technology) requires the formation of new networks within existing structures, but the creation of new companies specialising in the modification process is essential (Mai, 2010).

Further developments and research

In the future, in addition to DMDHEU, the transfer to wood processing of further "textile technologies", especially water-based systems (e.g., fire protection, water-repellent agents) may be possible. Combined treatments with DMDHEU might also be applicable.

   Cross-linking resins from paper applications may be promising since high reactivity is obtained at moderate temperatures (lower than 100°C). Non-formaldehyde cross-linkers such as polycarboxylic acid (e.g., butyl tetracarboxylic acid, BTCA) have been tested on a small scale, but they have so far not been tried in larger plants.

The following research needs have been identified (Emmerich et al., 2019):

- Assessment and evaluation of durability studies in Germany, Austria and Sweden and field tests in marine environments in Germany and Denmark, in order to predict the long-term durability and practical feasibility of DMDHEU-modified wood in outdoor applications.

- Investigations of real-time curing of adhesives and coating systems with respect to process optimisation and the final adhesive strength on modified wood surfaces.

- Studies of the general applicability of DMDHEU modification technology to permeable, fast-growing wood species.

Applications

Products based on solid wood, veneers and wood fibres have been developed in high-end wooden windows, doors and related joinery, quality decking, posts for organic vineyard (where conventionally treated wooden posts are not permitted) and for both indoor and outdoor furniture. Treatment with DMDHEU also adds strength and stability to plywood chairs and other engineered wood products (Figure 2.36).

Whilst there have been a wide range of products manufactured using DMDHEU under the brand Balemadur™, the continued expansion in this form of modification will incorporate the use of HartHolz™, which is reflected in the summary in Table 2.13.

Figure 2.36 Applications of DMDHEU-modified wood (Rademacher et al., 2009) (Photos courtesy of professor Peter Rademacher, Germany).

Table 2.13 Applications of DMDHEU modified wood divided into Use Classes, see Table 1.7.

	Interior		Exterior		
Product type/Use Class	**1**	**2**	**3**	**4**	**5**
Indoor furniture	(x)	(x)			
Floor and non-structural interior uses	(x)	(x)			
Exterior joinery			(x)		
Cladding			x		
Decking			x		
Fencing			(x)		
Outdoor furniture			(x)		
Construction elements					
In-ground timber					
Products exposed to water					

where: x = products have been produced by companies using the modified wood
(x) = products may be produced, based on pre-commercial trials, research, etc.

2.7 Silicates and silanes

The use of soluble silicate, i.e., water glass, as a way to improve the resistance of wood to fire has been known since at least 1825, and many mineralising surface treatments are currently in use, although impregnation processes are also used. The latter use mostly aqueous solutions of silicates, in either their sodium or potassium salt form. These can be fixated or sealed creating a silver-grey wood product processing fire stability, and fungal and water resistance. Decking, facades and garden furniture are typical examples of current applications.

Water glass is an alkaline, colourless, viscous aqueous solution of sodium silicate formed by the reaction of silica (SiO_2) with alkaline sodium oxide (Na_2O) in water. Other counter ions than sodium, such as potassium, are also used commercially. Recently, solid wood products have been produced using treatment with water glass (TimberSIL™). The process is described as a vacuum-pressure impregnation with water glass, followed, according to a patent, by heat-treatment up to 200°C (Slimak et al., 2000), and Stora-Enso company developed a cladding material called Q-treat™ by the thermal curing of a water-glass-treated material, but neither of these materials has the properties expected and they are no longer being produced. A number of surface methods exist on the market, such as Everwood™, based on an aqueous water glass solution with a special inorganic catalyst used for a penetrating surface wood treatment (Everwood Ecobeton, 2020), which is said to reduce water absorption and increase the resistance to insects and fire stability. Nitor™ wood protection uses a mixture of sodium and potassium silicate in aqueous solution to protect wood from discolouring fungi and algae (Alfort and Cronholm, 2019). Silicates can be fixated to the wood surface by reaction with CO_2 in air to create a silver-grey colour. The Finnish company Aurekoski produces a material (Kivipuu™) that is understood to imitate the natural silication of wood and give good water repellancy and stability (Aureskoski, 2020).

Silicates are, however, sensitive to moisture and a hydrophobation of the wood surface can be achieved using organic silicon compounds (silanes, siloxanes, silicones, etc.) (Mai et al., 2003; Ritschkoff et al., 2003). Their potential has been evaluated within the European project *Hydrophob* (full name "Improvement of wood product properties by increased hydrophobicity obtained by the use of silicon compounds"), which ran from 2003 to 2006 (Hydrophob, 2002). Sol gel films have also been studied (Böttcher et al., 1999). The commercial application of gels based on tetraethoxysilane (TEOS) for the treatment of wood has been described in the patent literature (Böttcher et al., 2000). The Swedish company Prebona treats wood with modified silicic acid colloids under mild alkali-neutral conditions, in order to create a stabilised surface on drying. Nano-skin™ from Belgium is also a product having hydrophobic and antiseptic wood surface properties.

Material selection and preparation

It is possible to impregnate the sapwood of Scots pine using water glass, and silicate-impregnated products can also be manufactured from species such as Norway spruce, although it is unclear how deep the penetration is into sapwood. Q-treat™ from StoraEnso was based on Scots pine, and TimberSil™ used Southern yellow pine during their production period. The impregnation of wood is usually best at a moisture content of ca. 20%. A higher moisture content will give less penetration and hence a lower WPG.

The modification process

Although patents have been filed for impregnation with aqueous solutions of alkali silicates, the details seldom indicate how the process is actually performed. Here, we will focus on pressure impregnation processes of the alkaline silicate in which the sapwood is modified by the treatment. Dried Scots pine boards are impregnated with a water glass solution. In earlier industrial attempts, drying of the alkaline silicate-impregnated wood caused a silver-grey material to develop, assisted by a reaction with CO_2. However, such products were not stable to outdoor exposure and further treatment with an organic silane emulsion is said to fixate the silicate-treated wood, giving a more hydrophobic surface. Such treatments have been described in a series of patents using hydrophobic silanes and water glass and they are thought to be the basis for the impregnation of solid wood products such as Organowood™ (Figure 2.37) (Organowood, 2019). The production of Organowood™ in

Figure 2.37 Scheme of the Organowood™ process.

Sweden in 2018 was estimated to be 8,000 m³ (Jones et al., 2019). Norway spruce boards have also been treated, but the depth of impregnation with the water glass is lower. Based on accelerated decay tests and outdoor decking tests, the Organowood™ producers claim that a product with high fire stability as well as high durability is produced. Upon outdoor exposure, the silicates will suffer some degree of wood fiber loss, probably assisted by the alkaline or silane treatment.

In the SIOO:X™ process, potassium silicate solution is used for the surface impregnation of softwood boards followed by an organic silane emulsion (SIOO:X, 2019).

The influence of the micro- and chemical structure of wood

Water glass at 25% is rather viscous, and this may hamper its penetration into wood, and an increase in concentration of sodium silicate ($Na_2O.nSiO_2$, n = 3.22) from 12.5% to 25% resulted in only a small change in WPG after pressure impregnation of Scots pine sapwood (Scharf et al., 2019). The viscosity is influenced by the proportions of the two components (n-value) as well as by the concentration in the aqueous solution. Adequate fire retardancy of wood was achieved by treatment with a dilute solution followed by treatment with a higher concentration of water glass to increase its uptake. Treatment of wood with water glass is said not to have a bulking effect, although it gives rise to less shrinkage/swelling (ASE). Electron probe X-ray microanalysis (EPMA) showed that various silicates adducts were located mainly in the cell lumen (Furuno et al., 1992), particularly after extended periods of weathering. Heat treatment of water-glass impregnated wood has been used to fixate the water glass in the wood (Slimak et al., 2000), and single-stage treatments with silicates ($Na_2O \cdot nSiO_2$, n = 2.06–2.31) have also been reported (Matthes et al., 2002). Because of the hydrophilic nature of silicate, the moisture exclusion effect (MEE) significantly decreased with increasing silicate content. Drying of a pine sapwood impregnated with sodium silicate at 103°C was not sufficient to fixate the silicate and the silicate could be removed by leaching with water (Scharf et al., 2019). During exposure of water-glass-impregnated wood, carbon dioxide protonates the silicate, and this may give a more stable silicate, probably enhanced by heating as outlined in Figure 2.38.

The slightly acidic character of wood and its buffering capacity is not sufficient to stabilise the treated wood and the first stage treatment needs to be complemented with a second stage to stabilise the product, aiming at a pH reduction and/or exchange of ions. Treatments with metal salts and acids (aluminium sulfate ($Al_2(SO_4)_3$), calcium chloride ($CaCl_2$), barium chloride ($BaCl_2 \cdot 2H_2O$), and with acids like boric acid (H_3BO_3), borax ($Na_2B_4O_7 \cdot 10H_2O$), potassium borate ($K_2B_4O_7 \cdot 4H_2O$), and ammonium borate ((NH_4)$_2O \cdot 5B_2O_3 \cdot 8H_2O$) have been studied (Furuno, 1992; Furuno et al., 1992; Furuno et al., 1993). A two-step treatment with sodium silicate followed by aluminium sulfate together with a common fire retardant showed the importance of forming a water-stable sealing in order to obtain a leaching-resistant product (Scharf, 2019). Treatment with water glass can be combined with esterification by acetylation or propionylation (Li et al., 2000; Li et al., 2001). The esterification and the treatment with water glass were performed in two separate steps, but the order varied: wood was either first treated with water glass (and infiltrated with acetic acid to precipitate silicate) and then dried and acetylated or propionated (Li et al., 2000), or first subjected to esterification and then treated with water glass (Li et al., 2001). The ASE of the silicate-esterified material was slightly less than that of the esterified material in proportion to the silicate content. A white sol-gel product was formed when sodium silicate was mixed with $Al_2(SO_4)_3$ but it was not stable in water and was not able to penetrate deeply into the wood, even when using small specimens and vacuum treatment. A

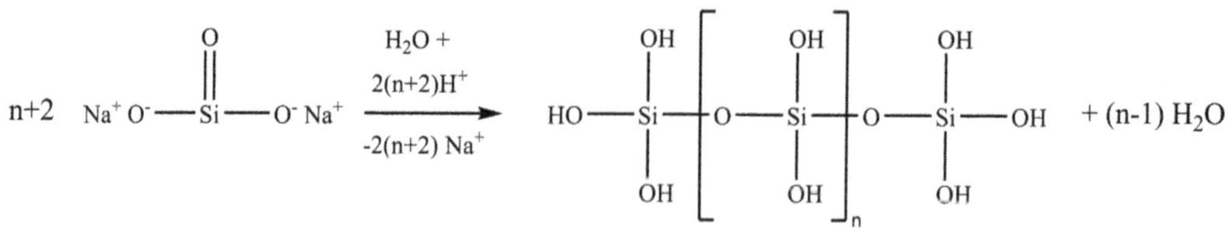

Figure 2.38 Water glass fixation by the addition of acid.

solid, rubbery product can be formed by simply mixing ethanol and water glass, but the bonds are not water-resistant and the material dissolves in water. This indicates that interactions with alcohol groups in wood are possible but that the products are unlikely to be stable when exposed to water.

When tetraethoxy silane (tetraethyl orthosilicic acid; TEOS) alone was applied to hinoki, X-ray mapping (SEM-EDX) showed that most of the silicon in the TEOS-treated specimen was located in the cell wall of the wood, but that the silicon was deposited in the cell lumina in specimens that were saturated with water before incubation (Saka et al., 1992; Saka et al., 2001). In the case of organic silanes, such as tetramethoxysilane (TMOS)/methanol, tetraethoxysilane (TEOS)/ethanol and tetrapropoxysilane (TPOS)/ n-propanol, hydrolysis led to the formation of the corresponding silic acid before heat-assisted coupling reactions occurred (see Figure 1.45) (Mai and Militz, 2004). Bulking of the cell wall also occurred, leading to less swelling in the wood and a greater durability. It has been suggested that silane chemicals in the lumen may evaporate during the curing phase and thus not contribute to the WPG, and that the lumen may not be filled in such a process. Under dry conditions, such bonds should, however, be fairly stable on exposure to water and moisture, although the reaction should be reversible so that an improvement in properties of the material will not be permanent.

The modified product

The Organowood™ process focuses on the impregnation of Scots pine for decking, water bridges, poles and construction details and of Norwegian spruce for cladding (Organowood, 2019). Product properties are limited but testing according to EN 113 (CEN, 1996) with leaching in water according to EN 84 (CEN, 1997) showed a Class 1 durability against brown-rot. Long-term outdoor tests have not yet been reported. The material achieved a B rating by the Swedish organisation "Sunda hus" (a company specialising in the health and environmental assessment of building materials) and they meet the European Parliament and Council Regulation (EC) No. 1272/2008, and the Swedish Chemicals Agency Priority Guide PRIO. The resistance to fire has been tested using EN 13501-1 (CEN, 2018) and the material achieved Bf1-1 classification. A 10-year warranty was given, as long as both treatment solutions are used for cladding, no additional treatments are performed and newly cross-cut ends are duly treated with both solutions. A loosening of fibres may occur during end-use, probably by a degradation of lignin, the process with possible being accelerated by the alkaline treatment. Resistance to mould is poorly documented, but in a report from RISE (Sweden), the surface properties of impregnated Organowood™ appeared to be similar to those of other wood products used as decking (Jermer et al., 2016).

Physical and chemical properties

Enhanced mechanical and physical properties of silicate-treated wood have been reported (Lahtela and Kärki, 2006). The anti-shrink efficiency (ASE) achieved by treating with silicates in combination with $Al_2(SO_4)_3$ (between 3–69%) varied a great deal, although the cell-wall bulking at a high ASE was rather small (Furuno et al., 1992). All the specimens treated using the two-step process displayed a high fire resistance, except for those treated with barium chloride in the second step (Furuno et al., 1991; Furuno et al., 1992; Furuno et al., 1993).

Little or no ASE was observed when sol-gel silicon compounds were used to modify wood, but when the silicon chemicals were able to penetrate into cell wall the ASE increased to 42% with increasing WPG (Saka et al., 1991; Saka et al., 2001; Mai et al., 2004). The WPG due to incorporation of silicon into the cell wall increased further when ultrasonic radiation was used after impregnation with tetraethyl orthosilicate (TEOS) (Ogiso and Saka, 1993).

Fibre loosening may occur, and these fibres may be removed mechanically. The greyish colour that is typical after outdoor exposure is expected to be relatively stable. Using SiOO:X™ in a two-step treatment, including potassium silicate followed by a silane emulsion, a fairly high resistance against mould colonisation was observed (Myronycheva et al., 2019), but the protective effect is expected to decrease with increasing outdoor exposure. According to the producer of Organowood™, surface treatment is not recommended after application of a sealant, whereas water-glass-based treatment (Everwood™) is advertised as being suitable for subsequent overpainting of the treated surface (Everwood Ecobeton, 2020).

The oxygen index was determined (Saka et al., 1992) and thermo-gravimetric analysis (TGA) was used (Ogiso and Saka, 1993) to test the flammability of sol-gel treated wood. The flammability was significantly reduced by all treatments, but the effect was more pronounced when silicon was incorporated in the cell wall than when it was deposited in the lumen. Some silicon systems alone were reported to improve the fire resistance, but they were more successful in combination with other compounds, such as water glass and boron compounds (Furuno et al., 1991; Furuno et al., 1992; Furuno et al., 1993), P_2O_5, B_2O_3, or Na_2O in SiO_2-gel systems (Miyafuji and Saka, 1996; Miyafuji et al., 1998; Saka et al., 2001). Water glass treatment has also been applied to acetylated or propionylated wood in order to increase its fire resistance (Li et al., 2000; Li et al., 2001).

Nearly all the specimens treated via the two-step process displayed a high fire resistance, except for those treated with barium chloride in the second step (Furuno et al., 1991; Furuno et al., 1992; Furuno et al., 1993).

Mechanical properties

Treatment with water glass significantly reduced the bending strength, but the dynamic and static moduli of elasticity (MOE) were only slightly changed (Furuno et al., 1992). The strength properties were found to be dependent on the curing temperature after impregnation. With air drying at 20°C, the strength of the treated wood was more or less unchanged, but high temperature drying (103°C) led to a significant loss of strength.

The bending strength was unchanged, and the Young modulus slightly reduced by treatment with tetraethyl orthosilicate (TEOS) alone, but a mixture of TEOS (sol-gel), silicic acid monomer and colloidal silicic acid slightly increased the strength and dimensional stability (Mai and Militz, 2004).

Biological properties

Wood treated with water glass alone (without precipitation) exhibited a high decay resistance (EN 113), both with and without leaching (EN 84) prior to testing (Matthes et al., 2002). The authors deduced that the resistance was achieved not only by the water-soluble alkali metal oxide but also by the insoluble silicate in the cell lumen. The highest resistance against the brown rot fungus *Tyromyces palustris* and the white rot fungus *Coriolus versicolor* was given by a combination of water glass and boron salts. Treatment with either boron salts or with water glass alone gave lower durability (Furuno et al., 1991; Furuno et al., 1992; Furuno et al., 1993; Furuno and Imamura, 1998; Chen, 2009). The moisture uptake and release kinetics and the damage by termites and decay fungi on mineralised wood depended on the wood species (Kutnik and Reynaud, 2015).

In general, the durability after treatment with water glass, silicic acid, or tetraalkoxysilanes was not satisfactory. Decay by the brown rot fungus *Poria placenta* according to EN 113 (CEN, 1996) resulted in a weight loss of 12–16% in TEOS-treated specimens compared to about 40% in untreated specimens (Cai and Militz, 2014).

In single treated samples, as well as in samples subjected to a combined treatment with boron trioxide, aluminium sulfate, calcium chloride and barium chloride, the mortality of termites was lower than in untreated wood (Furuno and Imamura, 1998). The termite resistance of leached specimens was particularly enhanced in samples treated with boric acid, borax, or potassium borate combined with water glass. The specimens displayed a weight loss of less than 2.5% (26% in untreated wood). Wood treated solely with these boron compounds (without water glass) showed a 5–10 times greater weight loss. Termite mortality on leached specimens was very high (80–100%) when boric acid, borax, potassium borate, or ammonium borate were combined with water glass.

Specimens treated with tetraethyl orthosilicate (TEOS) showed a high resistance against termite attack (*Reticulitermes speratus*), especially when the silicon was deposited in the cell wall (Ogiso and Saka, 1993). Stable sols has also been prepared from TEOS prior to impregnation, hydrolysis and condensation being started outside the wood (Bücker et al., 2001; Reinsch et al., 2002), but it is more difficult to prepare an impregnation solution that is more stable over a long time and only reacts within the wood than the treatment technique applied by Saka (1992; 2001).

In a test of the decay resistance against larvae of *Hylotrupes bajulus* according to EN 46, the larvae failed to attack TEOS-treated wood (Reinsch et al., 2002).

While treatment of wood with water glass was not able to increase the resistance to marine borers (Edmondson, 1953; Roe et al., 1957; Serpa, 1980), TEOS (partly combined with CCA) provided effective protection against the marine boring *teredinidae* genus. All tested timber species were, however, attacked by the crustacean genera *Limnoria* and *Sphaeroma*. Radiata pine sapwood and spotted gum natural rounds were protected against *teredinidae*, but the resistance of alpine ash heartwood was not enhanced (Scown et al., 2001).

Technological aspects

Silicates are inorganic materials and they have a wearing effect on machine tools, especially at high WPG. The poor bonding properties of silicone-modified wood were improved by using hydroxymethylated resorcinol as a coupling agent (Kurt et al., 2008). With Organowood™-treated materials, stainless steel (A2 or A4 quality), or surface-treated (C4) screws are recommended. Alkaline conditions may not be suitable with aluminium profiles.

Environmental aspects

During the impregnation and fixation processes, the temperature is low and for example the Organowood™ process is certified with the Nordic Swan™.

Sodium silicate is produced by fusing sodium carbonate with sand, and CO_2 is released in the process, but at least a part of it is fixated in the product. Otherwise, the Organowood™ material can be treated as normal wood after use. The silicates are rather alkaline and may be a skin irritant, but they have a low volatility, which makes the impregnation treatment easier to handle than processes producing more toxic fumes.

Industrial use and application

Treatment with water glass has a historical origin, but only in recent years have developments allowed the commercial exploitation of a silicon-based treatment. Fuchs reported in 1825 that water glass could be used to make wood "incombustible". Since then, treatments have been tested to stabilise the silicate, such as hydrochloric acid followed by oil, ferrous sulfate, volatile acids, boric acid or borax and calcium chloride. Experience from the early silicate impregnation process showed that treatment may be difficult to upscale.

It is difficult to find out how many commercially available wood preservatives contain water glass or other silicates, since several formulations available on the market contain these compounds as additives. Some of them were mentioned in the introduction to this section, but new products are continually appearing on the market. As an example, a crucial contribution of water glass in a wood preservative formulation has been described in the patent literature (Eck, 2002), where the role of water glass in the formulation is assumed to be the silication of wood, which seals the pores and prevents recognition of the wood substrate by fungi or insects.

Practical applications

Treatments including soluble silicates and sealing surface treatments give the products desirable properties, such as light grey wooden facades (Figure 2.39). In a fast-evolving economy, it is difficult to launch a new durable wood product that can with certainty withstand the long-term conditions expected for such a product. The company behind TimberSIL™ claimed that the product had superior properties without being transparent about their data and gave a 40-year guarantee against rot for their products, but problems with product failure, distribution, lawsuits and other legal actions made it difficult to continue with the production.

Table 2.14 summarises where products have been made using silicates or silanes.

Figure 2.39 Application of silicate-based treated wood, Organowood™.

Table 2.14 Applications of silicate or silane treated wood divided into Use Classes, see Table 1.7.

	Interior		Exterior		
Product type/Use Class	**1**	**2**	**3**	**4**	**5**
Indoor furniture					
Floor and non-structural interior uses	x	x			
Exterior joinery			x		
Cladding			x		
Decking			x		
Fencing			(x)		
Outdoor furniture			x		
Construction elements			x		
In-ground timber					
Products exposed to water					

where: x = products have been produced by companies using the modified wood
(x) = products may be produced, based on pre-commercial trials, research, etc.

2.8 Chitosan

Chitosan is polydisperse and can be produced by the alkaline treatment of chitin, a polymer found in shells of shrimp and other sea crustaceans. The chemical structures of the two polymers are shown in Figure 1.48. Chitosan is in many respects a promising substance with which to modify wood, but it has not yet been tried on a large scale (Eikenes et al., 2005a,b). The total annual chitin bioproduction has been estimated to be more than 10^9 tonnes (Tracey, 1957), but more recent figures (Dhillon et al., 2013) suggest a global production level of 10^{12}–10^{14} tonnes. The potential uses of chitin and chitosan are expected to expand globally by 4–5% per year, up to 2024 (Ravi Kumar, 2000). Key uses for chitin and chitosan include water treatment and cosmetics; a significant amount of chitin being used for the production of glucosamine.

In contrast to chitin, which is completely insoluble in water, chitosans are generally water-soluble especially under acidic conditions. The amine is then protonated to form a salt. Chitosans with a fraction of N-acetylated residues (F_A) of ca. 0.5 are also soluble under alkaline conditions (Vårum et al., 1991; Vårum et al., 1994).

Material selection and preparation

So far, dried and conditioned samples of Scots pine and European beech have been treated on a small scale (Alfredsen et al., 2004; Larnøy, 2006a).

The modification process

The suggested process involves impregnation and fixation steps, including drying to a suitable moisture content (Figure 2.40). To be able to reach the inner parts of the wood, chitosan must

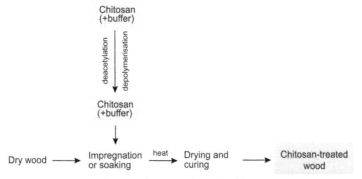

Figure 2.40 Suggested process scheme for chitosan treatment.

be soluble, which means that the molecular weight profile and the degree of deacetylation of chitin are important (Eikenes et al., 2005a). To be able to reach the desired decay resistance, a sufficiently concentrated solution is necessary but, at the same time, the viscosity must be controlled to guarantee a facile migration into the wood (Larnøy, 2006a). Selective degradation conditions to control such parameters are important and may involve acid degradation or treatment with a specific enzyme. Fixation of a chitosan product to wood was found to be favoured by a pH of 5.1–5.9 using acetic acid to regulate the pH (Larnøy et al., 2006a). By exposing the samples to 80°C in an open container, a chitosan retention ratio of 90% was reached after 4 hours, but the resulting crack formation indicated that a lower drying temperature was necessary.

Influence of the micro- and chemical structure of wood

Chlorine-labelled chitosan was used to study the penetration of chitosan into Scots pine wood using energy-dispersive X-ray spectroscopy with scanning electron microscopy (Figure 2.41). High molecular weight chitosan interacted more with the cell wall structure than low molecular chitosan (Larnøy et al., 2011). Mehrtens (1999) reported that the penetration of chitosan into Scots pine was limited to the outermost tracheids, probably due to the use of very high molecular weight material.

Adding polyethylene glycol during the impregnation with chitosan is said to increase the bulking of the cell wall, and to reduce the water uptake and subsequent swelling of the wood (Nowrouzi et al., 2016).

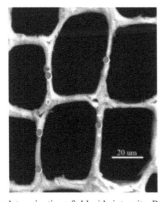

Figure 2.41 Example of EDS spots for the determination of chloride intensity. Red dots are taken in the earlywood cell wall. SEM photographs of Scots pine wood treated with Chitosan D with an average molecular weight 14.5 kDa.

The modified product

Larnøy et al. (2006b) studied wood properties after chitosan impregnation. Chitosan is biocompatible and biodegradable and has antifungal and antibacterial properties, and it can increase the durability of wood and, if a relatively low molecular weight profile is chosen, it can penetrate the wood cell wall and contribute to a better resistance to swelling and shrinking. The protection of wood from fungi by means of chitosan has been studied by many groups in the past few decades (Lee et al., 1992; Lee et al., 1993; Kobayashi and Furukawa, 1995a,b; Laflamme et al., 1999; Mehrtens, 1999; Frederiksen, 2001; Chittenden et al., 2003; Eikenes and Alfredsen, 2003; Alfredsen et al., 2004; Eikenes et al., 2005b). Chitosan-treated wood showed changes in sorption properties, antifungal properties, fire-retardant properties and mechanical properties (Larnøy, 2006b). The colours of wood modified by chitosan was similar to that of untreated wood after accelerated weathering tests (Termiz et al., 2007).

Industrial use and application

Chitosan is a biopolymer with antibacterial and fungal properties and it is used in agriculture, medicine and as a bioplastic. So far, chitosan-impregnated wood has not been produced commercially, showing the difficulty in introducing new environmentally friendly material into the wood sector.

Table 2.15 summarises where products have been made using chitosan.

Table 2.15　Applications of chitosan treated wood divided into Use Classes, see Table 1.7.

	Interior		Exterior		
Product type/Use Class	1	2	3	4	5
Indoor furniture					
Floor and non-structural interior uses					
Exterior joinery					
Cladding			(x)		
Decking			(x)		
Fencing			(x)		
Outdoor furniture			(x)		
Construction elements					
In-ground timber					
Products exposed to water					

where:　x = products have been produced by companies using the modified wood
　　　　(x) = products may be produced, based on pre-commercial trials, research, etc.

2.9　Indurite™ and Lignia™

The Indurite™ technology was started indirectly via Scion's Indurite™ development from 1985 to 1988, when a new strategy for wood modification was devised. Patents were granted for the process (Franich and Anderson, 1998), and the Indurite™ technology was scaled-up by the Engineered Wood Solutions company in New Zealand, after which it was obtained by the Osmose company (Franich, 2007). A more traditional resin is now used and the material is produced under a new product brand, Lignia™, in the United Kingdom.

Material selection and preparation

The abundancy of radiata pine in New Zealand and its excellent impregnation properties was the basis for the material. Radiata pine sapwood was dried to 12% moisture content in an industrial drying process before the modification was started.

The modifying process

The Indurite™ process is shown in Figure 2.42. A major advantage is that it requires no significant investments other than a drying kiln, an impregnation vessel and a curing kiln. The dried radiata pine

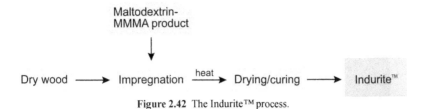

Figure 2.42 The Indurite™ process.

is placed in a pressure vessel together with the Indurite™ formulation, achieved by the condensation polymerisation of maltodextrin with methylol melamine. The pressure is lowered to an absolute pressure of 0.015 MPa for 10 minutes, followed by the introduction of the Indurite™ formulation which is kept at ambient temperature (20°C) while the pressure is brought back to atmospheric conditions. The pressure is then increased to 1.4 MPa and held for 1 hour. The impregnated material is held in a covered area for a few hours, and the curing then takes place in a temperature-controlled conventional kiln (70°C).

Product properties

The process was found to increase the stiffness of radiata pine by ca. 12% in addition to wood hardening at a weight percentage gain (WPG) of approx. 40%. An estimated 5–10% of this WPG was deposited in the cell wall. It was claimed that the modified wood could be used in exterior applications such as cladding and decking. In contrast to the traditionally phenol formaldehyde resin treatment, Indurite™-processed veneers showed a significantly improved glueability (Franich and Anderson, 1998), probably due to the increase in hydroxyl groups, and therefore hydrogen bond density, at the glued surface.

The use of chitosan to replace starch in the Indurite™ process has been studied, as β-1→4 linked polysaccharides, in both chitin (poly-N-acetylglucosamine) and chitosan (deacetylated chitin) have a stiffness (41 GPa and 65 GPa, respectively, Nishino et al. (1999)) greater than that of starch. Chitin and chitosan polymers can be converted to low molecular weight oligomers using enzymatic or acid-catalysed hydrolysis (Blumberg et al., 1982; Yalpani and Pantaleone, 1994) or by nitrous acid deaminative depolymerisation, a process specifically for chitosan (Allan and Peyron, 1995). Chitin and chitosan oligosaccharides, with degrees of polymerisation ranging from one to six sugar units, can be produced by acid-catalysed hydrolysis and nitrous acid deaminative depolymerisation respectively. Microwave treatment can partly depolymerise and deacetylate chitosan (Sahoo and Nayak, 2011). Hexamethyl methylol melamine (HMMM) was successfully used to co-polymerise with chitosan oligomers but was less effective with chitin (Torr et al., 2006). The yield of co-polymer of chitosan oligosaccharides and HMMM within the lignocellulosic material on drying was found to be critical for improving the stiffness of treated veneers. A threshold of > 30% co-polymer yield was required before any stiffness improvement was observed. Microscopy was used to investigate the penetration of resin into the porous wood structure (Figure 2.43), and the results suggested that the distribution of chitosan or chitin hexamethyl methylol melamine (HMMM) co-polymers within the wood cell was a factor contributing to the stiffness of the treated veneers (Torr et al., 2006).

Industrial use and application

In 2004, the technology was passed on to Fibre7 who then developed a technology similar to but independent of the original Indurite™ formulation (currently owned by Osmose UK). Fibre7 have production facilities in Tauranga, New Zealand, but currently global sales are still small. Lignia™, a recent commercial venture in the United Kingdom, uses resin monomers as the basis of a polymerisation modification which gives products with an increased hardness in a range of colours for interior applications, such as kitchen bench tops, furniture and stairs. Recently, an exterior version, LigniaXD™, has been developed for use in above-ground applications. Another product is

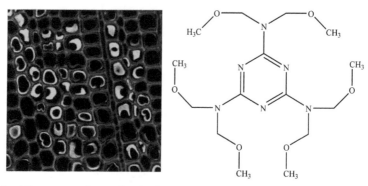

Figure 2.43 Confocal fluorescence micrographs of radiata pine (left) modified with chitin oligomer hexa(methoxymethyl) melamine (HMMM) co-polymer (right) (Torr et al., 2006).

LigniaYacht™, a substitute for tropical wood (Lignia, 2019). In this case the wood resource is defect-free, available in clear, long lengths and in dimensions which may not be available for premium hardwoods. This high-quality wood supply is currently obtained from New Zealand's pruned radiata pine source, which is also available in limited quantities in Australia (particularly Tasmania) and Chile. Lignia™ intends to export products to Europe and North America. An increase in hardness (by 50–60%), a higher density (650 kg/m³) and a small improvement in stability (15–25%) can be achieved and the products are estimated to have a service life up to 50 years above ground. Although a phenol-urea-formaldehyde (PUF) resin is used, the formaldehyde emission from Lignia™ is said to meet the lowest classification (JISA 1460) and not to give any corrosion on fasteners as the product is pH neutral. The resin can also be modified to increase the fire stability of the wood. At present, cladding, decking, joinery, boat decking and flooring are produced (Figure 2.44) (Lignia, 2019). Products that have been used for boat decking survive exposure significantly better than untreated wood.

While Lignia™ currently uses only radiata pine, it has been suggested that this modification is suitable for any wood species capable of being pressure-impregnated (Mater, 1999), which suggests that there is a potential for species such as hoop pine, maritime pine and slash pine all of which have treatable sapwood. Broad-leaved woods which produce sufficient treatable sapwood may also be suitable.

Table 2.16 summarises where products have been made using the Indurite™ or Lignia™ treated wood.

Figure 2.44 Lignia™ products: flooring (left) and boat decking (right).

2.10 Oil and wax

The wood modification techniques reported so far typically involve impregnation and heating to achieve the required results. The greater understanding of these processes, combined with the

Table 2.16 Applications of Indurite™ and Lignia™ treated wood divided into Use Classes, see Table 1.7.

Product type/Use Class	Interior		Exterior		
	1	2	3	4	5
Indoor furniture					
Floor and non-structural interior uses		x			
Exterior joinery			(x)		
Cladding			x		
Decking			x		
Fencing			x		
Outdoor furniture			x		
Construction elements			(x)		
In-ground timber				(x)	
Products exposed to water				x	(x)

where: x = products have been produced by companies using the modified wood
(x) = products may be produced, based on pre-commercial trials, research, etc.

availability of equipment for operating on a small to medium commercial scale, has opened up opportunities for looking at other systems. The application of oils and waxes to wood surfaces is well established historically, but the potential of applying wood modification techniques to these treatments is now enabling the development of new modification processes.

Pitch and tar have been used since ancient times to increase the resistance of wood to water and decay. The need to develop durable sleepers and telephone poles during the industrial revolution led to treatment with the more potent creosote oil using pressurised autoclave techniques, patented by Moll in 1836 and by John Bethell in 1838 (Freeman et al., 2003). Apart from being hydrophobic, creosote oil has a strong biocidal effect and contains compounds that may be carcinogenic, but it is still used as a wood preservative in certain water and ground contact applications. Due to a greater awareness of the negative effect on human health and the environment of creosote oil and other preservatives like copper-chrome arsenic (CCA) and pentachlorophenol (PCP), there has been the search for more environmentally friendly materials, like vegetable oils and waxes.

Material selection and preparation

Under laboratory conditions, various wood species, such as Norway spruce and Scots pine, have been tried (Ulvcrona, 2006). In the case of spruce, the moisture content before impregnation was important, drying to low moisture content tended to close the bordered pits, whereas at a high moisture content only a small amount of oil could penetrate into the wood. Boards of such wood species have been used for impregnation with linseed oil in the Linax™ process. Wax treatment has been undertaken on species such as European beech (Lesar and Humar, 2011) and Norway spruce (Brischke and Melcher, 2015). The slow migration of wax in the transverse direction could hamper the use of long boards (Scholz et al., 2010a). In the Dauerholz™ process, Scots pine has been used in the manufacture of treated wood products (Dauerholz, 2020).

Modification process

In order to achieve a suitable result with oils and waxes, it is necessary to go beyond the conventional brush application of materials on the wood surface, and methods for the impregnation of wood with vegetable oils such as linseed oil, hemp oil and tall oil have recently been developed (Sailer et al., 2000). Most systems aim to hinder the uptake of liquid water, but the establishment of a true equilibrium means that the moisture uptake and swelling of the cell wall are close to what is achieved with untreated wood. The assessment of the anti-swell-efficiency (ASE) in the laboratory revealed low dimensional stability of wood treated with oils, whereas in the field, oil-treated lap joints (CEN/TS, 2003) changed their dimensions to only a very small extent and only a few cracks were detected. A two-step oil-heated process has been developed at the French Agricultural Research and International Cooperation Organisation (CIRAD) (Grenier et al., 2003) which includes an initial hot treatment in groundnut oil, followed by soaking in linseed oil. The resulting reduced pressure inside the wood sucks the colder linseed oil into the wood. An uptake of 30–50% linseed oil by the sapwood of Norway spruce could be achieved by pressure impregnation under laboratory conditions (Ulvcrona, 2006). A moderate increase in ASE was found, but repeated exposure needs to be studied. The treatment conditions developed by the Linotech AB company in Sweden to produce Nordic softwood impregnated with linseed oil are shown in Figure 2.45. Acclimatisation of the sawn timber in the preheated oil both before and after a pressure step allowed the product to be more homogeneously modified. The heated oil lowers the viscosity without letting it dry, favouring a deeper penetration into the sawn timber. A final vacuum treatment helps to remove excess of oil from the surface of the product.

Most vegetable oils are, however, easily colonised by bacteria, which can lead to dark discolouration on wood surfaces (Rapp et al., 2005) and is unacceptable for above-ground outdoor applications without the addition of a biocide. The linseed oil derivative Linogard™ is manufactured from cold-pressed linseed oil in several steps including, for example, heating, the addition of inorganic acid and alkali, and the separation of precipitated materials (Selder, 2003). Linogard™ essentially consists of linoleic, linolenic and oleic acids, mainly in the form of triglycerides, its content of free tocoferol (vitamin E) being less than about 100 ppm. Linogard™ also used a quaternary ammonium salt to increase the resistance to microorganisms.

The hot oil impregnation of wood has been explored (Spear et al., 2006). Samples of Corsican pine and Norway spruce were treated in hot linseed oil, rapeseed oil and a proprietary resin developed by Foreco Dalfsen (The Netherlands) derived from linseed oil, under reduced pressure at temperatures of 180°C and 200°C. Very high uptakes of the oils or resin were recorded for Scots pine, but the weight percentage gain by Norway spruce was less than 20%. The resin-treated blocks had a lower weight loss at the end of a fungal decay test than blocks from the two oil treatments, probably because polymerisation of the resin immediately after treatment reduced the accessibility of the timber to fungal decay. A wider range of temperatures was investigated with linseed oil on black poplar (Bazyar et al., 2010), and a higher temperature showed a reduction in moisture uptake, as well as reductions in radial, tangential and volumetric shrinkage.

Impregnation of solid wood with wax can improve wood quality in a manner similar to that with vegetable oils. Waxes are widely used as water repellents for wood surfaces and paper materials (Taman et al., 1990; Huang et al., 2012), in wood conservation (Unger et al., 2001) and for improving the properties of wood-based panels (Müller, 1962; Amthor, 1972). Pressure impregnation of Norway spruce and Scots pine sawn timber using the Rüping (empty cell) process with three synthetic waxes heated to a temperature 20°C higher than their dropping point gave an uptake of roughly 150 kg/m³ (Brischke and Melcher, 2015). Although the decay and moisture uptake were lower than that of untreated sawn timber, the effect of the treatment decreased with longer outdoor exposure time and the sawn timber could not be recommended for practical use. Dipping impregnation (DipI) as well as vacuum pressure-impregnation of Norway spruce with a suspension of a natural

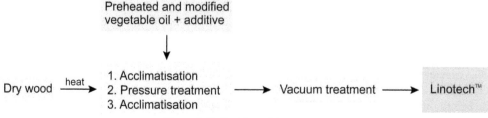

Figure 2.45 The Linotech™ process.

wax and subsequent thermal modification have been studied to reduce water uptake (Humar et al., 2017). The wax emulsion was pressure-impregnated into European beech and Norway spruce and left to dry in air. The uptake and retention of the emulsion was higher by European beech than Norway spruce and decreased with higher contents of emulsified particles (Lesar and Humar, 2011). Decay was reduced but there was no protection against fungal staining, under laboratory conditions.

Water repellents such as vegetable oils and waxes are considered to be suitable for wooden components in above-ground applications (Use Class 3, EN 335 (CEN, 2013)) in temperate climates, where they are not exposed to permanent wetting, but not for exposure in ground contact or under tropical conditions with heavy rainfall and high moisture loads (Brischke and Melcher, 2015).

The introduction of hot-melt wax (melting point 80°C) is said to give good dimensional stability and durability as well as strength. According to the patented Dauerholz™ process, the wood is impregnated with a liquid wax inside an autoclave, followed by a defined post-conditioning process to achieve an equilibrium moisture content and consistent wax distribution inside the wood. The treated wood can then be passed through the usual processing steps, such as sawing, planing and profiling.

Influence of the micro- and chemical structure of wood

Even though linseed oil dries relatively rapidly (as the degree of unsaturation of carbon-carbon double bonds is high) the oxygen supply and additional factors, such as the presence of antioxidants and the density of the wood, influence the immobilisation of the oil (Salehi, 2012). This can lead to a loss of oil by exudation and result in a patchy appearance. The use of an iron catalyst with an emulsion of raw tall oil gave an accelerated oxidation and polymerisation (Koski, 2008). A two-step process with epoxidised linseed oil catalysed by acetic acid was shown to give a high ASE (40–57%) with Scots pine sapwood (Fernández-Cano, 2013). To ensure resistance to the tested fungi (improved up to Durability Class 2), a copolymer of vinyl acetate and epoxidised linseed oil at a WPG of 8% has been used on a laboratory scale, and this has been proposed for above-ground applications (Shengzhen, 2016). Enhancing the UV-protection of clear coated wood, utilising a reactive UV-absorber and epoxy functionalised soybean oil, has also been studied (Olsson, 2014). At the SHR Timber Research unit (The Netherlands), systems have been developed using modified linseed oil as part of an EU-funded project (Van Acker et al., 1999; Epmeier et al., 2004; Tjeerdsma et al., 2005). Linseed oil was altered by an ene-reaction followed by a Diels-Alder-reaction to provide the molecule with a maleic anhydride group which may be chemically bonded to hydroxyl groups in wood constituents. This led to high durability, high ASE and no loss of strength under laboratory conditions. The use of this chemical for wood modification has been patented by DSM Resins (Dekker, 2001).

Attempts have been made to modify and improve the properties of wood by impregnation by wax including the effects of wax modification processes on water repellence (Colak and Peker, 2007; Scholz et al., 2010a; Lesar et al., 2011a). It has been reported that treating wood with various paraffins reduces the moisture sorption and water uptake, improving the dimensional stability of European beech and Scots pine sapwood (Scholz et al., 2010a). This study also noted that the viscosity and polarity of the wax melts and the size of the cell cavities significantly affected the depth of penetration into the wood. Lateral penetration was slower in European beech than in Scots pine sapwood. In another study, paraffin wax was used as a water repellent, and this decreased the hygroscopicity of European beech (Colak and Peker, 2007). The equilibrium moisture content of wood impregnated with Montan wax was reduced by up to 25%, but the addition of boric acid did not give consistent results for different compositions (Lesar et al., 2011b). It was found that wax treatment decreased the water uptake of pre-treated timber via multiple techniques, such as acetylation, thermal modification and DMDHEU modification (Scholz et al., 2012). Natural wax-like extractions from the leaves and bark of Aleppo pine exhibited hydrophobic properties in pine and beech, and they could replace 50% of the paraffin wax in water repellent formulations (Passialis and Voulgaridis, 1999).

The modified product

The improvements in mechanical properties achieved with treatment by vegetable oil or wax include an increase in density and a reduction in moisture content, since the flexible wax macromolecules mechanically reinforce the wood (Scholz et al., 2012). Such treatments thus maintain the mechanical properties of wood which are reduced by many other wood modification treatments. However, wax treatment reduces the adhesion of wood with other materials (Scholz et al., 2010b) and it does not improve subterranean resistance to termites (Buchelt et al., 2014). The wax fills the large cell lumens and retards the sorption of moisture, and it also improves the dimensional stability, weathering durability, resistance to white rot and brown rot fungi, and mechanical properties (Lesar and Humar, 2011; Lesar et al., 2011a,b; Palanti et al., 2011) as well as hardness, MOR, MOE, and impact strength, depending on the weight percentage gains, wood species, wax type, and wax properties (Kocaefe et al., 2015).

The water absorption and dimensional changes in Dauerholz™-treated wood over a period of 30 days were reduced by more than 60% compared to untreated wood, and the product obtained Durability Class 1 according to EN 350 (CEN, 2016) and even Hazard Class 4 (in ground contact and in water). A high melting point contributes to a stable and odourless product.

Industrial use and applications

Although oil treatment has been proven to improve the decay resistance of non-durable timber species, such as Norway spruce and Scots pine, the enhancement is not maintained on long-term exposure to exterior conditions, and resistance to discolouring microorganisms is poor unless a biocide is added to the oil. Vegetable oils are used in the Royal processes, which add hydrophobicity to wood subjected to a "second" oil impregnation stage. In the Royal treatment (Treu et al., 2003), the wood preservatives are cured by hot oil treatment. Apart from making the wood hydrophobic, this also has a positive effect against leaching of the preservative compounds. This technology is used for Linax™ boards, sold by Bergs timber company (Linax, 2019), where a copper-impregnated package of boards is treated in an autoclave under vacuum followed by the introduction of a preheated linseed oil product which heats and evaporates residual water under the reduced pressure at 80°C for about 7 hours, until the moisture content drops to 16%. A similar product, Royal Linoljetrall™, is produced by SCA Timber (SCA Smart Timber, 2019), where oil is used as a heating medium in the production of thermally modified timber while adding hydrophobicity to the product (see Chapter 3 about thermal modification).

Exudation may be a minor problem when waxes are used as they are solid materials over a wide temperature interval. Paraffins must be heated as well as the wood to ensure a deep penetration into the wood and they may be more difficult to manage. Aqueous emulsions do not suffer from temperature aspects directly, but a low viscosity can only be achieved at low concentrations, and the amount of wax present must be sufficient to protect the wood. Most of the impregnation methods aim to provide a superficial surface treatment.

When wax-treated Dauerholz™ wood is being used, grinding should be avoided due to the risk of excessive wear of tools, and coating is difficult, except when the company's UV-protecting oil is used. For similar reasons, only PUR (not PVAc) adhesives are regarded as suitable. Dauerholz™ is not regarded as waste according to current monitoring processes, and it can be exploited both as a material and as a source of energy.

Table 2.17 summarises where products have been made using oil- or wax-treated wood.

2.11 Polyethylene glycol (PEG)

Impregnation with polyethylene glycol (PEG) is commonly used to dimensionally stabilise wet archaeological wood due to its good anti-shrinkage properties (Morén and Centerwall, 1961; Norimoto et al., 1992). The treatment allows the material to be conserved in its initial swollen state

Table 2.17 Applications of Linotech™ treated wood divided into Use Classes, see Table 1.7.

Product type/Use Class	Interior		Exterior		
	1	2	3	4	5
Indoor furniture		(x)			
Floor and non-structural interior uses		(x)			
Exterior joinery			x		
Cladding			x		
Decking			x		
Fencing			x		
Outdoor furniture			(x)		
Construction elements			(x)		
In-ground timber					
Products exposed to water					

where: x = products have been produced by companies using the modified wood
(x) = products may be produced, based on pre-commercial trials, research, etc.

as the free water molecules are replaced by PEG molecules. Compared with the non-impregnated material, the main effects of PEG impregnation are a higher mass density, increased hygroscopicity of the dried material and material softening, since PEG acts as a plasticiser (Hoffmann et al., 2013). PEG serves as a bulking agent which penetrates the wood cell wall and lumen and replaces the water on drying (Stamm, 1959b).

Material selection and preparation

PEG is formed by polymerisation of ethylene oxide and it can be prepared in various molecular profiles, making it possible to achieve size distributions that can more efficiently enter into wood cell walls. An average molecular weight of 200 g/mol was found to be better than 1,500 g/mol during PEG-impregnation of Scots pine (Wallström et al., 1995). A molecular weight of 200 g/mol was suitable for the treatment of European oak, but the monomer was not stable when exposed to drying at 103°C (Hoffmann, 1988). A range of common Japanese softwoods was impregnated, in which the presence of extractives, as well as low permeability, was expected to hinder the penetration of PEG (Ohkoshi, 2002). Spruce was easily impregnated with PEG 1000 (molecular weight of 1,000 g/mol) by boiling for 3 hours (Norimoto et al., 2002).

The modification process

The methods used for PEG treatment are very similar to those already described for oils and waxes. The treatment has been used mostly to preserve ancient wooden ships. The Vasa ship hull in Sweden was conserved by spraying the wood (90% European oak) with aqueous solutions of PEG for 17 years starting in 1962, during which time the moisture content was carefully reduced to equilibrium conditions in the Vasa repository, before the hull was moved to the present museum in 1989 (Håfors, 2001). During the conservation of the Vasa ship, PEGs with different average molecular weights (Håfors, 2001) were used. The best control of shrinkage and wood collapse was achieved with PEG 600 followed by PEG 1450, which was found to be better than PEG 3350. Low molecular-weight PEG (typically < 1000 g/mol) gave a higher hygroscopicity in the treated wood (Stamm, 1974; Gregory et al., 2012). The improved properties were attributed to the better ability of the low molecular weight grades to bulk the cell wall. Small objects were soaked in a warm solution with increasing concentrations of PEG to avoid osmotic collapse of the wood, as well as drying at 65–70% relative humidity, and the wood surface was finally sprayed with a PEG solution for 6 months (Barkman, 1975; Grattan and Clarke, 1987). Similar treatment regimes have been employed in other conservation projects, such as the Mary Rose warship in the United Kingdom.

Influence of micro- and chemical structure of wood

As mentioned above, PEG bulks the cell wall, but it is not fully clear how this occurs, although penetration of PEG from pits into the middle lamella of the wood cell is believed to occur (Wallström, 1998). The importance of solvent and moisture content for the diffusion of PEG into the cell wall was confirmed by Raman microscopy (Dragica et al., 2007). PEG is fairly polar but has no reactive groups, and it can therefore be leached out from the wood on exposure to water, and it can also be redistributed in solid wood on exposure to such conditions. One way to circumvent such behaviour can be to increase the reactivity by attaching reactive groups (such as epoxides (e.g., epichlorohydrin)) to the polymer (Figure 2.46).

The epoxide can then react with accessible hydroxyl groups in the wood and become chemically bonded to the wood. It can however also react with itself, and this may hinder further penetration into the cell wall. Epoxides are used in this way to produce hydroxyalkylcelluloses, which have a gel structure (Klug, 1971). Hitherto, epoxides have been mostly used in wood adhesives, although only to a moderate extent, but small-scale studies on wood modifications with various epoxides have been performed. PEG hydrogels have been formed in wood by curing wood impregnated with PEG-diacrylate (Ermeydan, 2018).

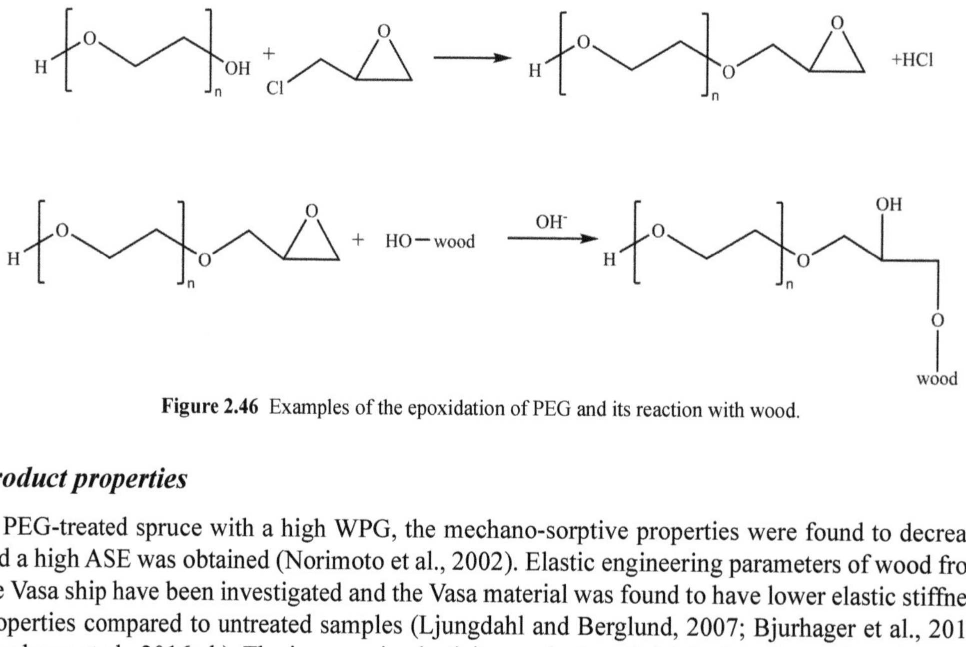

Figure 2.46 Examples of the epoxidation of PEG and its reaction with wood.

Product properties

In PEG-treated spruce with a high WPG, the mechano-sorptive properties were found to decrease and a high ASE was obtained (Norimoto et al., 2002). Elastic engineering parameters of wood from the Vasa ship have been investigated and the Vasa material was found to have lower elastic stiffness properties compared to untreated samples (Ljungdahl and Berglund, 2007; Bjurhager et al., 2012; Vorobyev et al., 2016a,b). The increase in elasticity can be beneficial for bending without breaking sawn timber but it leads to a deformation of the construction without support (Hoffmann, 2010). Colour differences were less in PEG-treated wood due to less lignin degradation, but some oxidation occurred in PEG (Ohkoshi, 2002).

The wood from ancient ships may deteriorate while being exhibited in museums, leading to strength losses. Mechanical tests have shown that the axial tensile modulus and strength were only slightly affected by PEG, whereas the radial compressive modulus and yield strength were reduced by up to 50% (Bjurhager et al., 2010). The main reasons for this appear to be the state of degradation of the material and the presence of PEG, which acts as a plasticiser, softening the wood cell wall. The cause of the degradation has been under serious discussion, but the presence/formation of acids that catalyse the hydrolysis of the cellulosic material, as well as oxidative degradation possibly catalysed by iron ions from fasteners used in the ship, have been proposed (Westermark et al., 2005; Mortensen, 2009).

Industrial use and applications

PEG has been used in the preservation of ancient sunken wooden ships, such as the Vasa warship (Figure 2.47) that is on display in a dedicated museum in Stockholm, Sweden, but it is not being used as a commercially available process.

Table 2.18 summarises where products have been made PEG treated wood.

Figure 2.47 The Vasa warship from 1628.

Table 2.18 Applications of PEG treated wood divided into Use Classes, see Table 1.7.

Product type/Use Class	Interior		Exterior		
	1	2	3	4	5
Indoor furniture	x				
Floor and non-structural interior uses	(x)				
Exterior joinery					
Cladding					
Decking					
Fencing					
Outdoor furniture					
Construction elements					
In-ground timber					
Products exposed to water					

where: x = products have been produced by companies using the modified wood
(x) = products may be produced, based on pre-commercial trials, research, etc.

2.12 Summary and outlook

Since the early work undertaken by Alfred Stamm and his co-workers in the 1930s, there has been a lot of interest in the chemical modification of wood. For several decades, countless research groups across the world looked at ways to improve the properties of locally grown timber species, but in the past 2–3 decades, in combination with a better understanding of chemical processes, chemical engineering and changing legislation and environmental awareness, the commercial opportunities for chemically modified wood have expanded dramatically.

Acetylation of solid wood focuses mainly on radiata pine and other easily impregnated wood species. Most applications of acetylated solid wood are related to exterior use, such as window frames, doors, external cladding, decking conditions and structural items such as bridges. The surface is better but not inert to photodegradation and discolouring microorganisms and it will eventually become grey. A painted surface using acrylate paint may be better than untreated wood, due to its good dimensional stability. A new plant in the United Kingdom led by Tricoya Ventures UK Limited (TVUK) for medium density fibreboards (MDF) has recently begun construction (Tricoya, 2017). They will produce acetylated fibres and use them for making fibreboards which are much more resistant to moisture and thereby have a greatly improved durability (Durability Class 1) and dimensional stability. Products for outdoor conditions like door-skins, façade panelling, trim, fascias, soffits, etc., are expected to be manufactured.

Compreg™ is an established method for achieving a wood material with good mechanical, physical, chemical and biological properties comparable to those of low specific weight steel. The use of more sustainable furfuryl alcohol resin to produce a compressed product is possible, but it has not been developed (Westin et al., 2009). Wood constituents can be removed to give even higher strength, but this involves additional steps that prolong the process and use more chemicals and more energy. Impreg™ methods exist for producing artistic furniture and handles and other modified wood solid wood products (as exemplified by Lignia™).

The brown colour of furfurylated wood makes it suitable for exterior uses, such as decking and cladding, similar to those for thermally modified timber. However, it is a more dense and hard material that withstands contact with water better the Clear™ product, whereas Character™ competes more in the same league as thermally modified timber, although heartwood is not protected. The production of the material, which has so far been quite limited compared to thermally modified timber, will increase with the opening of a new plant in Antwerp, Belgium. Furfurylated wood may be used in WPC to give greater durability than with untreated wood.

The small-scale development of modification processes using DMDHEU is continuing, particularly by TimTech in New Zealand. Surface treatment with silicates and silane emulsions gives a homogeneous silver-grey surface, but other sealing processes are also available. Although silicates can impart fire-retardant properties, leaching and loosening of fibres in the treated wood surface can be a problem in exterior conditions.

Polyethylene glycol has not been used on a commercial scale, but it has been used for the conservation of wooden ships and museum artefacts, probably due to its instability to moisture and its action as a softening agent. For large-dimension sawn timber, the Impreg™ process uses large amounts of resin to give a homogeneous impregnation, but melamine resins are expensive and give only a moderate improvement in wood properties. In the Indurite™ process, mixing melamine resin with maltodextrin make it environmentally more attractive. In 2004, the technology was transferred to Fibre7 who then independently developed a technology similar to the original Indurite formulation (currently owned by Osmose UK) and produced both indoor and outdoor products in a plant in New Zealand, although there is no commercial production, with developments focussing on using more traditional synthetic resins, as demonstrated by developments by Lignia in the UK. Chitosan formulations from the chemical treatment of chitin can impart both decay resistance and stability to wood but they have not yet been developed into a commercial biological wood protection agent. Linseed oil was used to impregnate Norway spruce and Scots pine by the Linotech™ process, but it was not effective due to difficulties in fixation to the wood and the risk of the exudation of oil. Studies to improve the drying ability of oils have been undertaken. A moderate improvement in moisture exclusion and decay resistance can be achieved, but if the oil is not modified, microorganisms may discolour the surfaces in outdoor applications. The Royal process, in which wood is pretreated with conventional copper-based preservatives followed by drying in heated modified biobased oils or mixtures under reduced pressure, is used in decking products, and such a treatment could be an alternative to creosote-impregnated poles and fences.

Table 2.19 summarises the processes covered in this chapter.

Table 2.19 Summary of chemical modification processes and typically used wood species, process parameters, properties and Technology Readiness Level (TRL). T and P are process temperature and pressure, respectively. EPD – Environmental product declaration. TRL – technology readiness level.

Process	Species used	Process parameters	Properties of the modified wood	EPD	TRL scale*
Accoya™	Radiata pine	T: < 170°C P: pressurised 2.2 MPa	Improved dimensional stability, durability, low mould resistance, corrosive to fastener	Yes	9
Compreg™	European beech (veneer)	T: 125–150°C P: 7 MPa	Improved strength (hardness), durability permeability, electric resistance, etc., high density		9
Kebony Clear™	Radiata pine	T: < 140°C P: < 1.2 MPa	Improved durability, dimensional stability, hardness, corrosion to fasteners, lower toughness		9
Kebony Character™	Scots pine	Similar conditions as Kebony Clear™	Improved sapwood durability, corrosion to fasteners		
DMDHEU	European beech Scots pine	T: > 100°C P: 1.2 MPa	Improved durability		8
Organowood™	Norway spruce Scots pine	T: 20°C 120°C P: low 1.6 MPa	Stable silver-grey surface, improved durability		9
Impreg™ (MF)	European beech Scots pine	T: 60–150°C P: 0.005–1.2 MPa	Improved durability, less swelling/shrinking, lower hardness and toughness		7
Chitosan	European beech Scots pine	T: 20–80°C P: 0.01–1.2 MPa	Improved durability		2
Indurite™/Lignia™	Radiata pine	T: 70°C. P: 0.015–1.4 MPa	Improved stability and durability	Yes	8
Linotech™	Scots pine (Norway spruce)	T: 60–140°C P: 0.8–1.4 MPa	Improved durability, oil exudation		8
PEG	European oak	T: 20–60°C P: 0.1 MPa	Lower moisture uptake and swelling, lower stability		4

References

Accoya. 2018. https://www.accoya.com/ (2020-03-23).

Adamopoulos, S., A. Bastani, P. Gascon-Garrido, H. Militz and C. Mai. 2012. Adhesive bonding of beech wood modified with phenol-formaldehyde compound. European Journal of Wood and Wood Products 70(6): 897–910.

Adebawo, F.G., H. Sadeghifar, D. Tilotta, H. Jameel, Y. Liu and L. Lucia. 2019. Spectroscopic interrogation of the acetylation selectivity of hardwood biopolymers. Starch 71(11/12): Article ID 1900086.

Akhtari, M. and M. Arefkhani. 2016. The effect of acetylation on physical properties of beech (*Fagus orientalis*) and alder (*Alnus subcordata*) wood. *In*: The Proceedings IRG Annual Meeting, Lisbon, Portugal. International Research Group on Wood Protection IRG/WP 16-40759.

Alexander, J., J. Hague, F. Bongers, Y. Imamura and M. Roberts. 2014. The resistance of Accoya® and Tricoya® to attack by wood-destroying fungi and termites. *In*: The Proceedings IRG Annual Meeting, St. George, Utah, USA. International Research Group on Wood Protection IRG/WP 14/40658.

Alfort and Cronholm. 2019. Nitor wood protection. https://www.alfort.se/Documents/Nitor_Wood_Care_folder_288137_1605.pdf (2020-03-11). (2020-01-20).

Alfredsen, G., M. Eikenes, H. Militz and H. Solheim. 2004. Screening of chitosan against wood-deteriorating fungi. Scandinavian Journal of Forest Research 19(Suppl. 5): 4–13.

Alfredsen, G., R. Ringman, A. Pilgård and C.G. Fossdal. 2015. New insight regarding mode of action of brown rot decay of modified wood based on DNA and gene expression studies: A review. International Wood Products Journal 6(1): 5–7.

Alfredsen, G., C.G. Fossdal, N.E. Nagy, J. Jellison and B. Goodell. 2016. Furfurylated wood: Impact on *Postia placenta* gene expression and oxalate crystal formation. Holzforschung 70(10): 747–962.

Allan, G.G. and M. Peyron. 1995. Molecular weight manipulation of chitosan. I: Kinetics of depolymerization by nitrous acid. Carbohydrate Research 277(2): 257–272.

Amthor, J. 1972. Paraffindispersionen zur Hydrophobierung von Spanplatten [Paraffin dispersions for the waterproofing of particle board.] Holz als Roh- und Werkstoff 30: 422–429.

Andersson, M. and A.-M. Tillman. 1989. Acetylation of jute. Effects on strength, rot resistance and hydrophobicity. Journal of Applied Polymer Science 37: 3437–3447.

Ando, D., F. Nakatsubo and H. Yano. 2017. Acetylation of ground pulp: Monitoring acetylation via HSQC-NMR spectroscopy. ACS Sustainable Chemistry & Engineering 5(2): 1755–1762.

Ang, A.F., Z. Ashaari, E.S. Bakar and N.A. Ibrahim. 2018. Possibility of enhancing the dimensional stability of jelutong (*Dyera costulata*) wood using glyoxalated alkali lignin-phenolic resin as bulking agent. European Journal of Wood and Wood Products 76: 269–282.

Ashaari, Z., H.M. Barnes, R.C. Vasishth, D.D. Nicholas and D.E. Lyon. 1990. Effect of aqueous polymer treatments on wood properties. Part I: Treatability and dimension stability. *In*: The Proceedings IRG Annual Meeting, Rotorua, New Zealand. International Research Group on Wood Protection IRG/WP/90–3610.

ASTM. 2002. D4541-02 Standard test method for pull-off strength of coatings using portable adhesion testers. American Society for Testing and Materials (ASTM International), West Conshohocken (PA), USA.

Aureskoski. 2020. http://aureskoski.fi/en/kivipuu/ (2020-03-22).

Azeh, Y., G.A. Olatunji, C. Mohammed and P.A. Mamza. 2013. Acetylation of wood flour from four wood species grown in Nigeria using vinegar and acetic anhydride. International Journal of Carbohydrate Chemistry 2013: Article ID 141034.

Baird, B.R. 1969. Dimensional stabilization of wood by vapor phase chemical treatments. Wood and Fiber Science 1: 54–63.

Bakar, E.S., J. Hao, Z. Ashaari and A.C.C. Yong. 2013. Durability of phenolic-resin-treated oil palm wood against subterranean termites a white-rot fungus. International Biodeterioration & Biodegradation 85: 126–130.

Barkman, L. 1975. Preserving the Wasa. The Forbes Prize Lecture, IIC-NKF Congress, Stockholm, June 4, 18 p.

Bartholme, M. 2005. Eigenschaften von Spanplatten aus DMDHEU-modifizierten Spänen [Properties of particleboards from DMDHEU-modified particles.] M.Sc. Thesis, University of Göttingen, Germany.

BASF. 2020. http://www.intermediates.basf.com/chemicals/glyoxal/crosslinker-in-wood-hardening (2020-03-31).

Bastani, A., S. Adamopolous, T. Koddenberg and H. Militz. 2015. Study of adhesive bondlines with fluorescence microscopy and X-ray micro-computed tomography. International Journal of Adhesion and Adhesives 68: 351–358.

Bastani, A., S. Adamopolous and H. Militz. 2015. Water uptake and wetting behaviour of furfurylated, N-methylol melamine modified and heat-treated wood. European Journal of Wood and Wood Products 73: 627–634.

Bastani, A., S. Adamopolous and H. Militz. 2017. Shear strength of furfurylated, N-methylol melamine and thermally modified wood bonded with three conventional adhesives. Wood Material Science & Engineering 12(4): 236–241.

Bazyar, B., D. Parsapajouh and H. Khademiesalam. 2010. An investigation on some physical properties of oil heat treated poplar wood. Proceedings 41st International Conference on Wood Protection, Biarritz, France. IRG/WP 10-40509.

Beck, G., E.E. Thybring, L.G. Thygesen and C.A.S. Hill. 2018. Characterization of moisture in acetylated and propionylated radiata pine using low-field nuclear magnetic resonance (LFNMR) relaxometry. Holzforschung 72(3): 225–233.

Beckers, E.P.J. and H. Militz. 1994. Acetylation of solid wood. Initial trials on lab and semi industrial scale, pp. 125–133. *In*: Steiner, P.R. [ed.]. The Second Pacific Rim Bio-Based Composites Symposium, Vancouver, Canada. University of British Columbia.

Beckers, E.P.J., M. van der Zee and F. Bongers. 2003. Acetyl content determination using different analytical techniques, pp. 341–350. *In*: Van Acker, J. and Hill, C.A.S. [eds.]. The Proceedings of the First European Conference on Wood Modification, Ghent, Belgium.

Behr, G., A. Gellerich, S. Bollmus, S. Brinker and H. Militz. 2018a. The influence of curing conditions on properties of melamine modified wood. European Journal of Wood and Wood Products 76: 1263–1272.

Behr, G., S. Bollmus, A. Gellerich and H. Militz. 2018b. The influence of curing conditions on the properties of European beech (*Fagus sylvatica*) modified with melamine resin assessed by light microscopy and SEM-EDX. International Wood Products Journal 9(1): 22–27.

Benediktsen, R., M. Eilertsen and P. Brynildsen. 2010. Apparatus and operating systems for manufacturing impregnated wood. Patent No. PCT/IB2010/000991.

Bjurhager, I., J. Ljungdahl, L. Wallström, E.K. Garmstedt and L.A. Berglund. 2010. Towards improved understanding of PEG-impregnated waterlogged archaeological wood: A model study on recent oak. Holzforschung 64(2): 243–250.

Bjurhager, I., H. Halonen, E.L. Lindfors, T. Iversen, G. Almkvist, E.L. Gamstedt and L.A. Berglund. 2012. State of degradation in archaeological oak from the 17th century Vasa ship: Substantial strength loss correlates with reduction in (holo) cellulose molecular weight. Biomacromolecules 13(8): 2521–2527.

Blumberg, K., F. Liniere, L. Pustilnik and A. Bush. 1982. Fractionation of oligosaccharides containing N-acetyl amino sugars by reverse-phase high-pressure liquid chromatography. Analytical Biochemistry 119: 407–412.

Bollmus, S. 2011. Biologische und technologische Eigenschaften von Buchenholz nach einer Modifizierung mit 1,3-dimethylol-4,5-dihydroxyethyleneurea (DMDHEU) [Biological and technological properties of beech wood after modification with 1.3-dimethylol-4.5-dihydroxyethylurea (DMDHEU).] PhD. Thesis, University of Göttingen, Germany.

Bollmus, S., F. Bongers, A. Gellerich, C. Lankveld, J. Alexander and H. Militz. 2015. Acetylation of German hardwoods, pp. 164–173. *In*: Hughes, M., Rautkari, L., Uimonen, T., Militz, H. and Junge, B. [eds.] The Proceeding of the Eighth European Conference on Wood Modification, Helsinki, Finland.

Bollmus, S., A. Gellerich, C. Brischke and H. Militz. 2018. Towards durability classification of preservative treated wood—first attempts using different European standards. *In*: The Proceedings IRG Annual Meeting, Johannesburg, South Africa. International Research Group on Wood Protection IRG/WP 18-20638.

Bongers, F. and E.P.J. Beckers. 2003. Mechanical properties of acetylated solid wood treated on pilot scale, pp. 341–350. *In*: Van Acker, J. and Hill, C.A.S. [eds.]. The Proceedings of the First European Conference on Wood Modification, Ghent, Belgium.

Bongers, F. and M. de Meijer. 2012. Coating performance on acetylated wood: A review paper, pp. 1–33. *In*: Paint Research Association Secretariat [ed.]. The 8th International Wood Coatings Congress: Science and Technology for Sustainable Design, Amsterdam, The Netherlands.

Bongers, F. and S.J. Uphill. 2019. The potential of wood acetylation, pp. 49–57. *In*: van de Kuilen, J.-W. and Gard, W. [eds.]. ISCHP 2019, the 7th International Scientific Conference on Hardwood Processing, Delft, The Netherlands.

Bongers, F., J. Alexander and J. Marcroft. 2012. Structural design with Accoya® wood, pp. 3–12. *In*: Jones, D., Militz, H., Petrič, M., Pohleven, F., Humar, M. and Pavlič, M. [eds.]. The Proceedings of the Sixth European Conference on Wood Modification, Ljubljana, Slovenia.

Bongers, F., S. Palanti, A. Gellerich, J. Morrell, J. Creemers and J. Hague. 2018. Performance of acetylated wood in aquatic applications. *In*: The Proceedings IRG Annual Meeting, Johannesburg, South Africa. International Research Group on Wood Protection IRG/WP 18-40822.

Borges, L.M., S. Cragg, M.E. van der Zee and W.J. Homan. 2005. Laboratory and field tests of the anti-marine borer potential of wood modified with dimethyloldihydroxyethyleneurea (DMDHEU) and phosphobutane tricarboxylic acid (PBTC), pp. 198–201. *In*: Millitz, H. and Hill, C. [eds.]. The Proceedings of the Second European Conference on Wood Modification: Wood Modification: Processes, Properties and Commercialisation, Göttingen, Germany.

Brelid, P.L. and M. Westin. 2007. Acetylated wood. Results from long-term field tests, pp. 71–78. *In*: Hill, C.A.S. Jones, D., Militz, H. and Ormondroyd, G.A. [eds.]. The Proceedings of the Third European Conference on Wood Modification, Bangor, UK.

Breuer, A.K. 2008. Optimierung eines Heißdampftrocknungsprozesses für Holzvernetzung mit Buche [Optimisation of a superheated steam curing process for modification of beech wood.] M.Sc. Thesis, University of Göttingen, Germany.

Brischke, C. and E. Melcher. 2015. Performance of wax-impregnated timber out of ground contact: results from long-term field testing. Wood Science and Technology 49: 189–204.

Buchelt, B., T. Dietrich and A. Wagenführ. 2014. Testing of set recovery of unmodified and furfurylated densified wood by means of water storage and alternating climate tests. Holzforschung 68(1): 23–8.

Bücker, M., W. Böcker and B. Unger. 2001. Entwicklung von umweltvertra glichen Holzverbundwerkstoffen mit verbesserter biologischer und Feuchtebesta ändigkeit [Development of environmentally compatible wood composite materials with improved biological and moisture resistance], pp. 463–467. *In*: Wielage, B. and Leonhardt, G. [eds.]. Verbundwerkstoffe und Werkstoffverbunde. Wiley-VCH Verlag, Weinheim, Germany.

Böttcher, H., C. Jagoda, J. Trepe, K.H. Kallies and H. Haufe. 1999. Sol-gel composite films with controlled release of biocides. Journal of Controlled Release 60: 57–65.

Böttcher, H., K.H. Kallies and J. Trepte. 2000. Holzschutzmittel [Wood preservative.] German patent No. DE19833479A1.

Cai, X., B. Riedl, S.Y. Zhang and H. Wan. 2007. Effects of nano fillers on water resistance and dimensional stability of solid wood modified by melamine-urea-formaldehyde resin. Wood and Fiber Science 39(2): 307–18.

Callow, H.J. 1951. Acetylation of cellulose and lignin in jute fiber. Journal of the Indian Chemical Society 43: 605.

CEN. 1992. EN 275 Wood preservatives. Determination of the protective effectiveness against marine borers. European Committee for Standardisation, Brussels, Belgium.

CEN. 1996. EN 113 Wood preservatives. Test method for determinating the protective effectiveness against wood destroying basidiomycetes. Determination of the toxic values. European Committee for Standardisation, Brussels, Belgium.

CEN. 1997. EN 84 Wood preservatives. Accelerated ageing of treated wood prior to biological testing. Leaching procedure. European Committee for Standardisation, Brussels, Belgium.

CEN. 2004. EN 13986 + A1:2015 Wood-based panels for use in construction. Characteristics, evaluation of conformity and marking. European Committee for Standardisation, Brussels, Belgium.

CEN. 2013. EN 335 Durability of wood and wood-based products—Definition of use classes—Part 1: General. European Committee for Standardisation, Brussels, Belgium.

CEN. 2016. EN 350 Durability of wood and wood-based products. Testing and classification of the durability to biological agents of wood and wood-based materials. European Committee for Standardisation, Brussels, Belgium.

CEN. 2017. EN 301 Adhesives, phenolic and aminoplastic, for load-bearing timber structures. Classification and performance requirements. European Committee for Standardisation, Brussels, Belgium.

CEN. 2018. EN 13501-1 Fire classification of construction products and building elements. Classification using data from reaction to fire tests. European Committee for Standardisation, Brussels, Belgium.

CEN/TS. 2003. CEN/TS 12037 Wood preservatives: Field test method for determining the relative protective effectiveness of a wood preservative exposed out of ground contact: Horizontal lap-joint method. European Committee for Standardisation, Brussels, Belgium.

ChemVerbotsV. 2019. Germany announces new test standard for formaldehyde emission from wood-based materials. https://www.sgs.com/en/news/2019/03/safeguards-04019-germany-announces-new-test-standard-for-formaldehyde-emission (2020-01-23).

Chen, G.C. 2009. Treatment of wood with polysilic acid derived from sodium silicate for fungal decay protection. Wood and Fiber Science 41(3): 220–228.

Chittenden, C., R. Wakeling and B. Kreber. 2003. Growth of two selected sap stain fungi and one mould on chitosan amended nutrient medium. *In*: The Proceedings IRG Annual Meeting, Brisbane, Queensland, Australia. International Research Group on Wood Protection IRG/WP/10466.

Colak, M. and H. Peker. 2007. Effects of some impregnation chemicals and water repellents on the hygroscopicity of beech wood. Wood Research 52(1): 87–98.

Dauerholz. 2020. file:///D:/wax%20dauerholz.pdf (2020-03-22).

Deckmagazine. 2020. https://www.deckmagazine.com/business/end-of-the-road-for-perennial-wood_o (2020-03-22).

Deka, M. and C.N. Saikia. 2000. Chemical modification of wood with thermosetting resin: Effect on dimensional stability and strength property. Bioresource Technology 73(2): 179–181.

Dekker, G.H. 2001. Wood preserver. European Patent application No. EP 1 174231 A1.

Delignit. 2020. https://www.delignit.de/en/about-us.html (2020-03-22).

Derham, B.R., T. Singh and H. Militz. 2017. Commercialisation of DMDHEU modified wood in Australasia. *In*: The Proceedings IRG Annual Meeting, Ghent, Belgium. International Research Group on Wood Protection IRG/WP/17–40772.

Dieste Märkl, A. 2009. Wood-water relationships in wood modified with 1,3dimethylol-4,5-dihydroxy ethylene urea (DMDHEU). PhD. Thesis, University of Göttingen, Germany.

Dieste, A., A. Krause, S. Bollmus and H. Militz. 2008a. Physical and mechanical properties of plywood produced with 1.3-dimethylol-4.5dihydroxyethyleneurea (DMDHEU)-modified veneers of *Betula* sp. and *Fagus sylvatica*. European Journal of Wood and Wood Products 66(4): 281–287.

Dieste, A., A. Krause and H. Militz. 2008b. Modification of *Fagus sylvatica* (L.) with 1,3-dimethylol-4,5-dihydroxyethylene urea (DMDHEU). Part 1: Estimation of heat adsorption by the isosteric method (Hail wood Horrobin model) and by solution calorimetry. Holzforschung 62(5): 577–583.

Dieste, A., A. Krause, S. Bollmus and H. Militz. 2009a. Gluing ability of plywood produced with DMDHEU-modified veneers of *Fagus* sp., *Betula* sp., and *Picea* sp. International Journal of Adhesion and Adhesives 29(2): 206–209.

Dieste, A., A. Krause, C. Mai and H. Militz. 2009b. The determination of EMC and its effect on the analysis of moisture sorption in wood modified with DMDHEU, pp. 85–91. *In*: Englund, F., Hill, C.A.S., Militz, H. and Segerholm, B.K. [eds.]. The Proceeding of the Fourth European Conference on Wood Modification, Stockholm, Sweden.

Dieste, A., A. Krause, C. Mai, G. Sèbe, S. Grelier and H. Militz. 2009c. Modification of *Fagus sylvatica* L. with 1,3-dimethylol-4,5-dihydroxy ethylene urea (DMDHEU). Part 2: Pore size distribution determined by differential scanning calorimetry. Holzforschung 63(1): 89–93.

DIN. 1975. DIN 53453 Testing of Plastics Impact Flexural Test, edn. May 1975. German Institute for Standardization, Germany.

Ding, W.D., A. Koubaa, A. Chaala, T. Belem and C. Krause. 2008. Relationship between wood porosity, wood density and methyl methacrylate impregnation rate. Wood Material Science & Engineering 3(1/2): 62–70.

Dong, Y., Y. Qin, K. Wang, Y. Yan, S. Zhang, J. Li and S. Zhang. 2016. Assessment of the performance of furfurylated wood and acetylated wood: Comparison among four fast-growing wood species. BioResources 11: 3679–3690.

Dragica, J., P.A. Cooper and D. Heyd. 2007. PEG bulking of wood cell walls as affected by moisture content and nature of solvent. Wood Science and Technology 41(7): 597–606.

Dreher, W.A., I.S. Goldstein and G.R. Cramer. 1964. Mechanical properties of acetylated wood. Forest Products Journal 14: 66–68.

Eck, G. 2002. Verfahren zum Schützen von Holz gegen das Eindringen und Wachsen von Schädlingen [Process for protecting wood against the penetration and growth of pests.] German patent No. DE0010063127A1.

Edmondson, C.H. 1953. Response of marine borers to chemically treated woods and other products. Bishop Museum Occasional Papers 21: 87–13.

Eikenes, M. and G. Alfredsen. 2003. Kitosan fra rekeskall til impregnering av trevirke [Citosan from shrimps shells for the impregnation of sawn timber.] Norwegian Forest Research Institute, Glimt fra Skogforskningen, No. 10 (In Norwegian).

Eikenes, M., G. Alfredsen, E. Larnøy, H. Militz, B. Kreber and C. Chittenden. 2005a. Chitosan for wood protection: State of the art. *In*: The Proceedings IRG Annual Meeting, Bangalore, India. International Research Group on Wood Protection IRG/WP/30378.

Eikenes, M., G. Alfredsen, B. Christensen, H. Militz and H. Solheim. 2005b. Comparison of chitosan with different molecular weights as possible wood preservative. Journal of Wood Science 51: 387–394.

Ermeydan, M.A. 2018. Modification of spruce wood by UV-crosslinked PEG hydrogels inside wood cell walls. Reactive and Functional Polymers 131: 100–106.

Emmerich, L. 2016. Holzmodifizierung von Kiefer (*Pinus sylvestris* L.) mit DMDHEU und modifizierten DMDHEU-Varianten im Vergleich [Comparative study on wood modification of Scots pine (*Pinus sylvestris* L.) with DMDHEU and modified DMDHEU.] M.Sc. Thesis, University of Göttingen, Germany.

Emmerich, L., S. Bollmus and H. Militz. 2019. Wood modification with DMDHEU (1.3-dimethylol-4.5-dihydroxyethyleneurea)—State of the art, recent research activities and future perspectives. Wood Material Science & Engineering 14(1): 1–16.

Emmerich, L., H. Militz and C. Brischke. 2020. Long-term performance of DMDHEU-treated wood installed in different test set-ups in ground, above ground and in the marine environment. International Wood Products Journal 11(1): 27–37.

Epmeier, H., M. Westin and A. Rapp. 2004. Differently modified wood: Comparison of some selected properties. Scandinavian Journal of Forest Research 19(5): 31–37.

Epmeier, H., M. Johansson, R. Kliger and M. Westin. 2007. Material properties and their interration in chemically modified clear wood of Scots pine. Holzforschung 61: 34–42.

Esteves, B., L. Nunes and H. Pereira. 2009. Furfurylation of *Pinus pinaster* wood, pp. 415–418. *In*: Englund, F., Hill, C.A.S., Militz, H. and Segerholm, B.K. [eds.]. The Proceeding of the Fourth European Conference on Wood Modification, Stockholm, Sweden.

Evans, P.D. 2009. Review of the weathering and photostability of modified wood. Wood Material Science & Engineering 4(1/2): 2–13.

Evans, P.D., A.F.A. Wallis and N.L. Owen. 2000. Weathering of chemically modified wood surfaces. Natural weathering of Scots pine acetylated to different weight gains. Wood Science and Technology 34(2): 151–165.

Everwood Ecobeton. 2020. https://www.ecobeton.com/prodotti/everwood (2020-03-11).

Fernández-Cano, V. 2013. Epoxidised linseed oil as hydrophobic substance for wood protection – technology of treatment and properties of modified wood. M.Sc. Thesis, Swedish University of Agricultural Sciences, Uppsala, Sweden.

Fodor, F., C. Lankveld and R. Németh. 2017. Testing common hornbeam (*Carpinus betulus* L.) acetylated with the Accoya method under industrial conditions. iForest 10(6): 948–954.

Fodor, F., R. Nemeth, C. Lankveld and T. Hofmann. 2018. Effect of acetylation on the chemical composition of hornbeam (*Carpinus betulus* L.) in relation with the physical and mechanical properties. Wood Material Science & Engineering 13(5): 271–278.

Franich, R.A. 2007. The Indurite process: A review from concept to business, pp. 23–29. *In*: Hill, C.A.S., Jones, D., Militz, H. and Ormondroyd, G.A. [eds.]. Proceedings of the Third European Conference on Wood Modification, Cardiff, UK.

Franich, R.A. and K. Anderson. 1998. Densification of lignocellulosic material. U.S. Patent No. 5,770,319.

Fredriksson, M. 2019. On wood-water interactions in the over-hygroscopic moisture range-mechanisms methods, and influence of wood modification. Forests 10(9): 779: 1–16.

Frederiksen, O. 2001. Fungicid fra rejer [Fungicides from shrimps.] (Prosjekt nr. P99088, Nordisk Industrifond Slutrapport). Teknologisk Institutt. (In Danish.)

Freeman, M.H., T.F. Shupe, R.P. Vlosky and H.M. Barnes. 2003. Past, present, and future of preservative treated wood. Forest Products Journal 53(10): 8–15.

Frihart, C.R., R. Brandon and R.E. Ibach. 2004. Selectivity of bonding for modified wood. *In*: Chaudhury, M.K. and G.L. Anderson [eds.]. Proceedings of the 27th Annual Meeting of the Adhesion Society. "From Molecules and Mechanics to Optimization and Design of Adhesive Joints", Wilmington (NC), USA. Adhesion Society 27(1): 329–331.

Furuno, T. and Y. Imamura. 1998. Combinations of wood and silicate. Part 6. Biological resistance of wood mineral composites using water glass–boron compound system. Wood Science and Technology 32: 161–170.

Furuno, T., T. Uehara and S. Jodai. 1991. Combinations of wood and silicate. 1. Impregnation by water glass and applications of aluminium sulfate and calcium chloride as reactants. Mokuzai Gakkaishi 37: 462–472.

Furuno, T., K. Shimada, T. Uehara and S. Jodai. 1992. Combinations of wood and silicate. Part 2. Wood-mineral composites using water glass and reactance of barium chloride, boric acid, and borax and their properties. Mokuzai Gakkaishi 38: 448–457.

Furuno, T., T. Uehara and S. Jodai. 1993. Combinations of wood and silicate. 3. Some properties of wood-mineral composites using the water glass-boron compound system. Mokuzai Gakkaishi 39(5): 561–570.

Furuno, T., Y. Imamura and H. Kajita. 2004. The modification of wood by treatment with low molecular weight phenol-formaldehyde resin: a properties enhancement with neutralized phenolic-resin and resin penetration into wood cell walls. Wood Science and Technology 37: 349–361.

Gabrielli, C.P. and F.A. Kamke. 2010. Phenol–formaldehyde impregnation of densified wood for improved dimensional stability. Wood Science and Technology 44: 95–104.

Gan, W., S. Xiao, L. Gao, R. Gao, J. Li and X. Zhan. 2017. Luminescent and transparent wood composites fabricated by poly(methyl methacrylate) and γ-Fe₂O₃@YVO₄:Eu³⁺ nanoparticle impregnation. ACS Sustainable Chemistry & Engineering 5(5): 3855–3862.

Gérardin, P. 2016. New alternatives for wood preservation based on thermal and chemical modification of wood—a review. Annals of Forest Science 73: 559–570.

Gindl, W. and H.S. Gupta. 2002. Cell-wall hardness and Young's modulus of melamine-modified spruce wood by nano-indentation. Composites Part A: Applied Science and Manufacturing S 33: 1141–1145.

Gindl, W., E. Dessipri and R. Wimmer. 2002. Using UV-microscopy to study diffusion of melamine-urea-formaldehyde resin in cell walls of spruce wood. Holzforschung 56(1): 103–107.

Gindl, W., F. Zargar-Yaghubi and R. Wimmer. 2003. Impregnation of softwood cell walls with melamine-formaldehyde resin. Bioresource Technology 87: 325–330.

Girotra, K. 2009. Process of wood acetylation and product thereof. Patent No. WO 2009/095687 A1.

Gobakken, L.R. and M. Westin. 2008. Surface mould growth on five modified wood substrates coated with three different coating systems when exposed outdoors. International Biodeterioration & Biodegradation 62: 397–402.

Gobakken, L.R. and P.K. Lebow. 2010. Modelling mould growth on coated modified and unmodified wood substrates exposed outdoors. Wood Science and Technology 44: 315–333.

Gobakken, L.R., O.A. Høibø and H. Solheim. 2010. Mould growth on paints with different surface structures when applied on wooden claddings exposed outdoors. International Biodeterioration & Biodegradation 64: 339–345.

Goldstein, I.S. 1959. Impregnating solutions and method of impregnation therewith. U.S. Patent No. 2 909 450.

Goldstein, I.S., E.B. Jeroski, A.E. Lund, J.F. Nielson and J.W. Weaver. 1961. Acetylation of wood in lumber thickness. Forest Products Journal 8: 363–370.

Gomez-Bueso, J., M. Westin, R. Torgilsson, P.O. Olesen and R. Simonson. 2000. Composites made from acetylated lignocellulosic fibers of different origin—Part I. Properties of dry-formed fiberboards. Holz als Roh- und Werkstoff 58(1/2): 9–14.

Grattan, D.W. and R.W. Clarke. 1987. Conservation of waterlogged wood, pp. 164–206. *In*: Pearson, C. [ed.]. Conservation of Marine Archaeological Objects. Elsevier, New York, USA.

Gregory, D., P. Jensen and K. Strætkvern. 2012. Conservation and *in situ* preservation of wooden shipwrecks from marine environments. Journal of Cultural Heritage 13(3): S139–S148.

Grenier, D., H. Baillères, J.-M. Méot, P. Langbour and J.-D. Lanvin. 2003. A study of water loss and oil absorption during oleothermic treatment of wood, pp. 23–32. *In*: Van Acker, J. and Hill, C.A.S. [eds.]. The Proceedings of the First European Conference on Wood Modification, Ghent, Belgium.

Gsöls, L., M. Rätzsch and C. Ladner. 2003. Interactions between wood and melamine resins: Effect on dimensional stability properties and fungal attack, pp. 221–225. *In*: Van Acker, J. and Hill, C.A.S. [eds.]. The Proceedings of the First European Conference on Wood Modification, Ghent, Belgium.

Hadi, Y.S., M. Westin and E. Rasyid. 2005. Resistance of furfurylated wood to termite attack. Forest Products Journal 55(1): 85–88.

Hadi, Y.S., I.S. Rahayu and S. Danu. 2013. Physical and mechanical properties of methyl methacrylate impregnated jabon wood. Journal of the Indian Academy of Wood Science 10(2): 77–80.

Hadi, Y.S., M.Y. Massijaya, D. Hermawan and A. Arinana. 2015. Feeding rate of termites in wood treated with borax, acetylation, polystyrene, and smoke. Journal of the Indian Academy of Wood Science 12(1): 74–80.

Hagstrand, P.O. 1999. Mechanical analysis of melamine-formaldehyde composites. PhD. Thesis, Chalmers University of Technology, Gothenburg, Sweden.

Hansmann, C., M. Deka, R. Wimmer and W. Gindl. 2006. Artificial weathering of wood surfaces modified by melamine formaldehyde resin. Holz als Roh- und Werkstoff 64: 198–203.

Hemmilä, V., S. Adamopoulos, O. Karlsson and A. Kumar. 2017. Development of sustainable bio-adhesives for engineered wood panels: A review. RSC Advances 7: 38604–38630.

Hellberg, M. and A. Ohm. 2016. Environmentally friendly wood treatment process. U.S. Patent No. 9,415,526 B2.

Hill, C.A.S. 2003. The kinetics of acetylation reactions, pp. 103–111. *In*: Van Acker, J. and Hill, C.A.S. [eds.]. The Proceedings of the First European Conference on Wood Modification, Ghent, Belgium.

Hill, C.A.S. 2006. Wood Modification: Chemical, Thermal and Other Processes. John Wiley & Sons Ltd., Chichester, U.K.

Hill, C.A.S. 2009. Why does acetylation protect wood from microbiological attack? Wood Material Science and Engineering 4(1–2): 37–45.

Hill, C.A.S. and D. Jones. 1996. The dimensional stabilisation of corsican pine sapwood by reaction with carboxylic acid anhydrides: The effect of chain length. Holzforschung 50: 457–462.

Hill, C.A.S. and D. Jones. 1999. Dimensional changes in Corsican pine sapwood due to chemical modification with linear chain anhydrides. Holzforschung 53: 267–271.

Hill, C.A.S. and J.G. Hillier. 1999. Kinetic studies of the reaction of carboxylic acid anhydrides with wood. Experimental determination and modelling of kinetic profiles. Physical Chemistry Chemical Physics 1: 1569–1576.

Hill, C.A.S. and G.A. Ormondroyd. 2004. Dimensional changes in Corsican pine (*Pinus nigra* Arnold) modified with acetic anhydride measured using a helium pycnometer. Holzforschung 58(5): 544–547.

Hill, C.A.S., D. Jones, G. Strickland and N.S. Cetin. 1998. Kinetic and mechanic aspects of the acetylation of wood with acetic anhydride. Holzforschung 52: 623–629.

Hoffmann, P. 1988. On the stabilization of waterlogged oakwood with polyethylene glycol (PEG) III. Testing the oligomers. Holzforschung 42(5): 289–294.

Hoffmann, P. 2010. On the long-term viscoelastic behaviour of polyethylenen glycol (PEG) impregnated archaeological oak wood. Holzforschung 64(6): 725–728.

Hoffmann, P., I. Bojesen-Koefoed, E.D. Gregory and P. Jensen. 2013. Conservation of Archaeological Ships and Boats: Personal Experiences. Archetype Publications, London, U.K.

Hon, D.N.S. and A.P. Bangi. 1996. Chemical modification of juvenile wood. Part 1. Juvenility and response of southern pine OSB flakes to acetylation. Forest Products Journal 46(7/8): 73–78.

Hoydonckx, H.E., W.M. Van Rhijn, W. van Rhijn, D. Hueting, B. Tjeerdsma, M. van der Zee and J. Van Acker. 2007. Renewable furfuryl resin technology for wood modification, pp. 81–86. *In*: Hill, C.A.S., Jones, D., Militz, H. and Ormondroyd, G.A. [eds.]. The Proceeding of the Third European Conference on Wood Modification, Cardiff, UK.

Hydrophob. 2002. Improvement of wood product properties by increased hydrophobicity obtained by the use of silicon compounds. Grant agreement ID: QLK5-CT-2002-01439.

Huang, X., D. Kocaefe, Y. Kocaefe, Y. Boluk and A. Pichette. 2012. Study of the degradation behavior of heat-treated jack pine (*Pinus banksiana*) under artificial sunlight irradiation. Polymer Degradation and Stability 97(7): 1197–1214.

Humar, M., D. Kržišnik, B. Lesar, N. Thaler, A. Ugovšek, K. Zupančič and M. Žlahtič. 2017. Thermal modification of wax-impregnated wood to enhance its physical, mechanical, and biological properties. Holzforschung 71(1): 57–64.

Håfors, B. 2001. Conservation of the Swedish warship Vasa from 1628. The Vasa Museum, Stockholm, Sweden.

Ibach, R.E. 2010. Speciality treatments, Chapter 19. *In*: Ross, R.J. [ed.]. Wood Handbook - Wood as an Engineering Material. General Technical Report FPL–GTR–190, U.S. Department of Agriculture, Forest Service, Forest Products Laboratory, Madison (WI), USA.

Inoue, M., S. Ogata, M. Nishikawa, Y. Otsuka, S. Kawai and M. Norimoto. 1993. Dimensional stability, mechanical properties, and color changes of a low molecular weight melamine-formaldehyde resin impregnated wood. Mokuzai Gakkaishi 39: 181–189.

Insulam. 2018. http://www.insulam.com/#cookie-law-more-info (2020-03-22).

Jiang, T., X. Feng, Q. Wang, Z. Xiao, F. Wang and Y. Xie. 2014. Fire performance of oak wood modified with N-methylol resin and methylolated guanylurea phosphate/boric acid-based fire retardant. Construction and Building Materials 72: 1–6.

Jebrane, M., F. Pichavant and G. Sèbe. 2011. A comparative study on the acetylation of wood by reaction with vinyl acetate and acetic anhydride. Carbohydrate Polymers 83(2): 339–345.

Jermer, J., S. Bardage, T. Anderson and N. Nilsson. 2016. Försök med olika material i bryggor vid Öresund [Testning different materials exposed in jetties at Öresund.] SP Technical Research Institute of Sweden, Report No. 2016:83.

Jermer, J., B.-L. Andersson and J. Schalnat. 2017. Corrosion of fasteners in furfurylated wood: Final report after 9 years exposure outdoors. *In*: The Proceedings IRG Annual Meeting, Ghent, Belgium. International Research Group on Wood Protection IRG/WP 17-40810.

Jeremic, D., P. Cooper and D. Heyd. 2007. PEG bulking of wood cell walls as affected by moisture content and nature of solvent. Wood Science and Technology 41: Article ID 597.

Jones, D. and C.A.S. Hill. 2007. Wood modification—A brief overview of the technology, pp. 1–9. *In*: Sernek, M. [ed.]. Proceedings of the 5th COST E34 International Workshop, Bled, Slovenia. University of Ljubljana.

Jones, D., D. Sandberg, G. Goli and L. Todaro. 2019. Wood Modification in Europe. A State-of-the-art about Processes, Products and Applications. Firenze University Press, Florence, Italy.

Kajita, H., T. Furuno and Y. Imamura. 2004. The modification of wood by treatment with low molecular weight phenol-formaldehyde resin: A properties enhancement with neutralized phenolic-resin and resin penetration into wood cell walls. Wood Science and Technology 37(5): 349–361.

Karlson, I. and K. Svalbe. 1972. Method of acetylating wood with gaseous ketene. Uchen. Zap., Latvian University Science Reports 166: 98–104.

Kebony. 2014. http://www.thenaturel.com/upload/data/files/catalogs/kebony_technical_presentation.pdf (2020-03-22).

Kebony. 2020. https://kebony.com/en (2020-03-22).

Kielmann, B.C., S. Adamopoulos, H. Militz and C. Mai. 2016. Decay resistance of ash, beech and maple wood modified with N-methylol melamine and a metal complex dye. International Biodeterioration and Biodegradation 89: 110–114.

Kim, I., O. Karlsson, O. Antzutkin, F.U. Shah, D. Jones and D. Sandberg. 2019. Wood modification with maleic anhydride and sodium hypophosphite. 4 pp. *In*: Yokoyama, T. and Matsumoto, Y. [eds.]. Proceedings of the 20th International Symposium on Wood, Fiber and Pulping Chemistry, ISWFPC20, Tokyo, Japan.

Klaassen, R., B. Tjeerdsma and R. Hillebrink. 2018. Monitoring the performance of Accoya® in different applications, pp. 623–629. *In*: Creemers, J., Houben, T., Tjeerdsma, B., Militz, H., Junge, B. and Gootjes, J. [eds.]. The Proceeding of the Ninth European Conference on Wood Modification, Arnhem, the Netherlands.

Klug, E.D. 1971. Some properties of water-soluble hydroxyalkyl celluloses and their derivatives. Journal of Polymer Science Part C: Polymer Symposia 36(1): 491–508.

Klüppel, A., H. Militz and C. Mai. 2012. Resistance of modified wood to the common shipworm (*Teredo navalis*) as assessed by marine trial, pp. 239–242. *In*: Jones, D., Militz, H., Petrič, M., Pohleven, F., Humar, M. and Pavlič, M. [eds.]. The Proceedings of the Sixth European Conference on Wood Modification, Ljubljana, Slovenia.

Kobayashi, T. and I. Furukawa. 1995a. Optimum conditions for the formation of chitosan-metal salts and their fixation in wood. Journal of Antibacterial and Antifungal Agents 23: 263−269 (In Japanese).

Kobayashi, T. and I. Furukawa. 1995b. Wood-preserving effectiveness of chitosan metal salts against wood decaying fungi. Journal of Antibacterial and Antifungal Agents 23: 343–348 (In Japanese).

Kocaefe, D., X. Huang and Y. Kocaefe. 2015. Dimensional stabilization of wood. Current Forestry Reports 1: 151–161.

Koppers' Acetylated Wood. 1961. Dimensionally stabilised wood. New Materials Technical Information No. (RDW-400) E-106.

Kollmann, F.F.P., E.W. Kuenzi and A.J. Stamm. 1975. Principles of Wood Science and Technology. Vol 2: Wood Based Materials Springer-Verlag, Berlin, Germany.

Koski, A. 2008. Applicability of crude tall oil for wood protection. PhD. Thesis, University of Oulu, Finland.

Kovač Kralj, A. 2007. Checking the kinetics of acetic acid production by measuring the conductivity. Journal of Industrial and Engineering Chemistry 13(4): 631–636.

Krause, A. 2006. Holzmodifizierung mit N-Methylolvernetzern [Wood modification with cross-linking N-methylol compounds.] PhD. Thesis, University of Göttingen, Germany.

Kumar, S. and S.C. Agarwal. 1982. Chemical modification of wood with thioacetic acid, in: graft copolymerisation of lignocellulosic fibres. *In*: Hon, D.N.S. [ed.]. ACS Symposium Series 187, Americal Chemical Society, Washington D.C., USA.

Kurt, R., C. Mai, A. Krause and H. Militz. 2008. Hydroxymethylated resorcinol (HMR) priming agent for improved bondability of silicone modified wood glued with a polyvinyl acetate adhesive. Holz als Roh- und Werkstoff 66: 305–307.

Kutnik, M. and C. Reynaud. 2015. The water glass technology: Improving wood resistance against subterranean termites and decay fungi by the mineralization process, pp. 449–547. *In*: Hughes, M., Rautkari, L., Uimonen, T., Militz, H. and Jungen, B. [eds.]. Proceedings of the Eighth European Conference on Wood Modification, Helsinki, Finland.

Kwon, J.H., C.A.S. Hill, G.A. Ormondroyd and S. Karim. 2007. Changes in the cell wall. Volume of a number of wood species due to reaction with acetic anhydride. Holzforschung 61: 138–142.

Laflamme, P., N. Benhamou, G. Bussires and M. Dessureault. 1999. Differential effect of chitosan on root rot fungal pathogens in forest nurseries. Canadian Journal of Botany 77: Article ID: 14601468.

Lande, S., M. Westin and M. Schneider. 2004. Properties of furfurylated wood. Scandinavian Journal of Forest Research 19(5): 22–30.

Lande, S., M. Eikenes, M. Westin and M. Schneider. 2008. Furfurylation of wood: chemistry, properties and commercialization. *In*: Schultz, T.P., Militz, H., Freeman, M.H. and Nicholas, D.D. (eds.). Development of Commercial Wood Preservatives. ACS Symposium Series 982: 337–355.

Lande, S., M. Westin and M. Schneider. 2010. Development of modified wood products based on furan chemistry. Molecular Crystals and Liquid Crystals 484(1): 1(367)–12(378).

Larnøy, E., M. Eikenes and H. Militz. 2006a. Evaluation of factors that have an influence on the fixation of chitosan in wood. Wood Material Science & Engineering 1(3/4): 135–148.

Larnøy, E., S. Dantz, M. Eikenes and H. Militz. 2006b. Screening of properties of modified chitosan-treated wood. Wood Material Science & Engineering 1(2): 59–68.

Larnøy, E., M. Eikenes and H. Militz. 2011. Detection of chlorine-labelled chitosan in Scots pine by energy-dispersive X-ray spectroscopy. Wood Science and Technology 45: 103–110.

Larnøy, E., A. Karaca, L. Ross Gobakken and C.A.S. Hill. 2018. Polyesterification of wood using sorbitol and citric acid under aqueous conditions. International Wood Products Journal 9(2): 66–73.

Larsson, P. and R. Simonson. 1994. A study of strength, hardness and deformation of acetylated Scandinavian softwoods. Holz als Roh- und Werkstoff 52(2): 83–86.

Larsson-Brelid, P. 2013. Benchmarking and state-of-the-art report for modified wood. SP Report no. 54, SP Technical Research Institute of Sweden, Stockholm, Sweden, pp. 1–31.

Larsson-Brelid, P. and R. Simonson. 1999a. Acetylation of solid wood using microwave heating Part 1. Studies of dielectric properties. Holz als Roh- und Werkstoff 57(4): 259–263.

Larsson-Brelid, P. and R. Simonson. 1999b. Acetylation of solid wood using microwave heating Part 2. Experiments in laboratory scale. Holz als Roh- und Werkstoff 57(5): 383–389.

Larsson Brelid, P. and M. Westin. 2007. Acetylated wood: Results from long-term field tests, pp. 71–78. *In*: Hill, C.A.S., Jones, D., Militz, H. and Ormondroyd, G.A. [eds.]. Proceedings of the Third European Conference on Wood Modification, Cardiff, UK.

Larsson-Brelid, P. and M. Westin. 2010. Biological degradation of acetylated wood after 18 years in ground contact and 10 years in marine water. *In*: The Proceedings IRG Annual Meeting, Biarritz, France. International Research Group on Wood Protection IRG/WP 10-40522.

Larsson-Brelid, P., R. Simonson O. Bergman and T. Nilsson. 2000. Resistance of acetylated wood to biological degradation. Holz als Roh- und Werkstoff 58(5): 331–337.

Lahtela, V. and T. Kärki. 2006. Effects of impregnation and heat treatment on the physical and mechanical properties of Scots pine (*Pinus sylvestris*) wood. Wood Material Science & Engineering 11: 217–227.

Lee, J.-S., I. Furukawa and T. Sakuno. 1992. Micro distribution of elements in wood after pre-treatment with chitosan and impregnation with chrome copper arsenic preservative. Mokuzai Gakkaishi 38: 186–192 (In Japanese).

Lee, J.-S., I. Furukawa and T. Sakuno. 1993. Preservative effectiveness against *Tyromyces palustris* in wood after pretreatment with chitosan and impregnation with chromated copper arsenate. Mokuzai Gakkaishi 39: 103–108 (In Japanese).

Lesar, B. and M. Humar. 2011. Use of wax emulsions for improvement of wood durability and sorption properties. European Journal of Wood and Wood Products 69: 231–238.

Lesar, B., A. Straže and M. Humar. 2011a. Sorption properties of wood impregnated with aqueous solution of boric acid and montan wax emulsion. Journal of Applied Polymer Science 120(3): 1337–1345.

Lesar, B., M. Pavlič, M. Petrič, A.S. Škapin and M. Humar. 2011b. Wax treatment of wood slows photodegradation. Polymer Degradation and Stability 96(7): 1271–1278.

Li, J.-Z., T. Furuno, S. Katoh and T. Uehara. 2000. Wood modification by anhydrides without solvents or catalysts. Journal of Wood Science 46(3): 215–221.

Li, J.-Z., T. Furuno and S. Katoh. 2001. Preparation and properties of acetylated and propionylated wood-silicate composites. Holzforschung 55: 93–96

Li, W., D. Ren, X. Zhang, H. Wang and Y. Yu. 2016. The furfurylation of wood: A nanomechanical study of modified wood cells. BioResources 11(2): 3614–3625.

Lignia. 2019. Lignia yacht, Endurance for Yacht Decks. https://www.lignia.com/ (2020-03-17).

Lin, C-F., O. Karlsson, G. Mantanis and D. Sandberg. 2020. Fire performance and leach resistance of pine wood impregnated with guanyl-urea phosphate/boric acid and a melamine resin. European Journal of Wood and Wood Products 78: 107–111.

Linax. 2019. http://www.linax-royal.se/en/ (2020-03-22).

Ljungdahl, J. and L.A. Berglund. 2007. Transverse mechanical behaviour and moisture absorption of waterlogged archaeological wood from the Vasa ship. Holzforschung 61(3): 279–284.

Lopes, D.B. 2013. Technological improvement of Portuguese pine wood by chemical modification. PhD. Thesis, University of Göttingen, Germany.

Lukowsky, D. 1999. Holzschutz mit Melaminharzen [Wood protection with melamine resin.] PhD. Thesis, University of Hamburg, Germany.

Mai, C. 2010. Review: Prozess der chemischen Holz modifizierung – Stand der industriellen Entwicklung [Review: processes of chemical wood modification – state of the industrial development.] Holztechnologie 51(5): 21–26.

Mai, C. and H. Militz. 2004. Modification of wood with silicon compounds: Inorganic silicon compounds and sol-gel systems: a review. Wood Science and Technology 37: 339–348.

Mai, C., S. Donath and H. Militz. 2003. Modification of wood with silicon compounds, pp. 239–251. In: Van Acker, J. and Hill, C.A.S. [eds.]. The Proceedings of the First European Conference on Wood Modification, Ghent, Belgium.

Månsson, P. and B. Samuelsson. 1981. Quantitative determination of O-acetyl and other O-acyl groups in cellulosic materials. Svensk Papperstidning 84: R15.

Mantanis, G. 2017. Chemical modification of wood by acetylation or furfurylation: a review of the present scaled-up technologies. BioResources 12(3): 115–122.

Mantanis, G. and C. Lykidis. 2015. Evaluation of weathering of furfurylated wood decks after a 3-year outdoor exposure in Greece. Drvna Industrja 66(2): 115–122.

Mater, C.M. 1999. Emerging technologies for sustainable forestry: A case study from "The Business of Sustainable Forestry", a Project of the sustainable forestry working group. Island Press, Washington, D.C., USA.

Matsuda, H. 1987. Preparation and utilization of esterified woods bearing carboxyl groups. Wood Science and Technology 21: 75–88.

Matsunaga, M., Y. Kataoka, H. Matsunaga and H. Matsui. 2010. A novel method of acetylation of wood using supercritical carbon dioxide. Journal of Wood Science 56(4): 293–298.

Matthes, R., H.O. Nehring and W. Dellith. 2002. Wasserglas-Holzschutz im Holzbau [Water glass wood protection in timber construction], pp. 104–108. In: Proceeding of Intergrierter Umweltschutz im Bereich der Holzwirtschaft, Göttingen, Germany.

McDonald, A.G., M. Fernandes, B. Kreber and F. Laytner. 2000. The chemical nature of kiln brown stain in radiata pine. Holzforschung 54(1): 12–22.

Mehrtens, S. 1999. Untersuchungen zur Schutzwirkung von Chitosan gegenuber Holzpilzen [Studies on the protective effect of chitosan against wood fungi.] M.Sc. Thesis, Fachbereich Biologie, University of Hamburg, Germany (In German).

Militz, H. 1991a. Die Verbesserung des Schwind- und Quellverhaltens und der Dauerhaftigkeit von Holz mittels Behandlung mit unkatalysiertem Essigs iureanhydrid [The improvement of dimensional stability and durability of wood through treatment with non-catalysed acetic-acid anhydride]. Holz als Roh- und Werkstoff 49: 147–152.

Militz, H. 1991b. Improvements of stability and durability of beech wood (*Fagus sylvatica*) by means of treatment with acetic anhydride. In: The Proceedings IRG Annual Meeting, Kyoto, Japan. International Research Group on Wood Protection IRG/WP/3645.

Militz, H. 1993. Treatment of timber with water soluble dimethylol resins to improve their dimensional stability and durability. Wood Science and Technology 27(5): 347–355.

Militz, H. and J. Norton. 2013. Performance testing of DMDHEU-modified wood in Australia. In: The Proceedings IRG Annual Meeting, Stockholm, Sweden. International Research Group on Wood Protection IRG/WP/13–30613.

Militz, H., S. Schaffert, B.C. Peters and C.J. Fitzgerald. 2011. Termite resistance of DMDHEU-treated wood. Wood Science and Technology 45(3): 547–557.

Minato, K. and Y. Ito. 2004. Analysis of the factors influencing the acetylation rate of wood. Journal of Wood Science 50: 519–523.

Minato, K., R. Takazawa and K. Ogura. 2003. Dependence of reaction kinetics and physical and mechanical properties on the reaction systems of acetylation II: Physical and mechanical properties. Journal of Wood Science 49: 519–524.

Miroy, F., P. Eymard and A. Pizzi. 1995. Wood hardening by methoxymethyl melamine. Holz als Roh- und Werkstoff 53: 276.

Miyafuji, H. and S. Saka. 1996. Wood-inorganic composites prepared by sol-gel processing. 5. Fire resisting properties of the SiO_2-P_2O_5-B_2O_3 wood–inorganic composites. Mokuzai Gakkaishi 42: 74–80.

Miyafuji, H., S. Saka and A. Yamamoto. 1998. SiO_2-P_2O_5-B_2O_3 wood-inorganic composites prepared by alkoxide oligomers and their fire-resisting properties. Holzforschung 52: 410–416.

Moghaddam, M.S., M.E.P. Wållinder, P.M. Claesson, J. Van Acker and A. Swerin. 2017. Microstructure of chemically modified wood using X-ray computed tomography in relation to wetting properties. Holzforschung 71(2): 119–128.

Mohebby, B. and H. Militz. 2010. Microbial attack of acetylated wood in field trails. International Biodeterioriation and Biodegradation 64: 41–50.

Moore, G.R., D.E. Kline and P.R. Blurlkenhorn. 1983. Impregnation of wood with a high viscosity epoxy resin. Wood and Fiber Science 15(3): 223–234.

Morén, R. and B.R. Centerwall. 1961. Use of polyglycols in the stabilizing and preservation of wood. The Historical Museum of Lunds University, Meddelande, pp. 176–196.

Mortensen, M.N. 2009. Stabilization of polyethylene glycol in archaeological wood. Kgs. Lyngby, Technical University of Denmark.

Müller, H. 1962. Erfahrungen mit Paraffin-Emulsionen als Quellschutzmittel in der Spanplattenindustrie [Experience with paraffin-wax emulsions as anti-swelling agents in chipboard industry.] Holz als Roh- und Werkstoff 20: 434–437.

Myronycheva, O., F. Poohphajai, M. Sehlstedt-Persson, T. Vikberg, O. Karlsson, H. Junge and D. Sandberg. 2019. Application of GRAS compounds for the control of mould growth on Scots pine sapwood surfaces: Multivariate modelling of mould grade. Forests 10(9): Article ID 714.

Narayanamurti, D. and B.K. Handa. 1953. Acetylated woods. Das Papier 7(5/6): 87–92.

Németh, R., G. Gohér, T. Hofmann and R. Rákosa. 2010. Physical, mechanical and colour properties of acetylated poplar and robinia wood, pp. 231. *In*: Kúdela, J. and Lagana, R. [eds.]. Proceedings of 6th IUFRO Symposium "Wood Structure and Properties 10". Podbanské, Slovakia. Arbora Publishers.

Nicholas, D.D. and A.D. Williams. 1987. Dimensional stabilization of wood with dimethylol compounds. *In*: The Proceedings IRG Annual Meeting, Honey Harbour, Ontario, Canada. International Research Group on Wood Protection IRG/WP/87–3412.

Nishino, Y. 1991. Simplified vapor phase acetylation of small specimens of hinoki (*Chamaecyparis obtusa*) wood with acetic anhydride. Mokuzai Gakkaishi 37(4): 370–374.

Nishino, T., R. Matsui and K. Nakamae. 1999. Elastic modulus of the crystalline regions of chitin and chitosan. Journal of Polymer Science Part B Polymer Physics 37(11): 1191–1196.

Nordstierna, L., S. Lande, M. Westin, O. Karlsson and I. Furo. 2008. Towards novel wood-based materials: chemical bonds between lignin-like model molecules and poly (furfuryl alcohol) studied by NMR. Holzforschung 62(6): 709–713.

Norimoto, M. and J. Gril. 1993. Structure and properties of chemically treated woods, pp. 135–154. *In*: Shiraishi, N., Kajita, H. and Norimoto, M. [eds.]. Recent Research on Wood and Wood-based Materials. Elsevier.

Norimoto, M., J. Gril and R.M. Rowell. 1992. Rheological properties of chemically modified wood: relationship between dimensional and creep stability. Wood and Fiber Science 24(1): 25–35.

Nowrouzi, Z., B. Mohebby and H. Younesi. 2016. Treatment of fir wood with chitosan and polyetylene glycol. Journal of Forestry Research 27(4): 959–966.

Obataya, E. and K. Minato. 2009. Potassium acetate-catalyzed acetylation of wood at low temperatures II: Vapor phase acetylation at room temperature. Journal of Wood Science 55: 23–26.

Ogiso, K. and S. Saka. 1993. Wood-inorganic composites prepared by sol-gel process II. Effects of ultrasonic treatments on preparation of wood-inorganic composites. Mokuzai Gakkaishi 39(3): 301–307.

Ohkoshi, M. 2002. FTIR-PAS study of light-induced changes in the surface of acetylated or polyethylene glycol-impregnated wood. Journal of Wood Science 48: 394–401.

Ohkoshi, M. and A. Kato. 1997. ^{13}C-NMR analysis of acetyl groups in acetylated wood II: Acetyl groups in lignin. Mokuzai Gakkaishi 43: 364–369.

Ohkoshi, M., A. Kato and N. Hayashi. 1997. ^{13}C-NMR analysis of acetyl groups in acetylated wood I: Acetyl groups in cellulose and hemicellulose. Mokuzai Gakkaishi 43: 327–336.

Ohmae, K., K. Minato and M. Nonmoto. 2002. The analysis of dimensional changes due to chemical treatments and water soaking for hinoki (*Chamaecyparis obtusa*) wood. Holzforschung 56: 98–102.

Olsson, S. 2014. Enhancing UV protection of clear coated exterior wood by reactive UV absorber and epoxy functional vegetable oil. PhD. Thesis, Royal Institute of Technology (KTH), Stockholm, Sweden.

Organowood. 2019. http://organowood.com/ (2020-03-11).

Ozmen, N. 2007. Dimensional stabilization of fast growing forest species by acetylation. Journal of Applied Sciences 7: 710–714.

Palanti, S., E. Feci and A.M. Torniai. 2011. Comparison based on field tests of three low-environmental-impact wood treatments. International Biodeterioration & Biodegradation 65(3): 547–552.

Pantze, A., O. Karlsson and U. Westermark. 2008. Esterification of carboxylic acids on cellulosic material: Solid state reactions. Holzforschung 62(2): 136–141.

Papadopoulos, A.N. 2010. Chemical modification of solid wood and wood raw material for composites production with linear chain carboxylic acid anhydrides: A brief review. BioResources 5: 499–506.

Papadopoulos, A.N. and C.A.S. Hill. 2002. The biological effectiveness of wood modification with linear chain carboxylic acid anhydrides against Coniophora Puteana. Holz als Roh- und Werkstoff 60: 329–332.

Passialis, C.N. and E.V. Voulgaridis. 1999. Water repellent efficiency of organic solvent extractives from Aleppo pine leaves and bark applied to wood. Holzforschung 53(2): 151–155.

Pawar, P.M.-A., S. Koutaniemi, M. Tenkanen and E.J. Mellerowicz. 2013. Acetylation of woody lignocellulose: significance and regulation. Frontiers in Plant Science 4: Article ID 118.

Peydecastaing, J. 2008. Chemical modification of wood by mixed anhydrides. PhD. Thesis, University of Toulouse, Toulouse, France.

Petrič, M., B. Knehtl, A. Krause, H. Militz, M. Pavlič, M. Pétrissans, A. Rapp, M. Tomažič, C. Welzbacher and P. Gérardin. 2007. Wettability of waterborne coatings on chemically and thermally modified pine wood. Journal of Coatings Technology and Research 4(2): 203–206.

Pilgård, A., A. Treu, A.N. Zeeland, R.J. Gosselink and M. Westin. 2010. Toxic hazard and chemical analysis of leachates from furfurylated wood. Environmental Toxicology and Chemistry 29(9): 1918–1924.

Pittman, C.U., M.G. Kim, D.D. Nicholas, L. Wang, F.R.A. Kabir, T.P. Schultz and L.L. Ingram. 1994. Wood enhancement treatments. Part I. Impregnation of southern yellow pine with melamine formaldehyde and melamine-ammeline-formaldehyde resins. Journal of Wood Chemistry and Technology 14(4): 577–603.

Popescu, C.-M., C.A.S. Hill, S.F. Curling, G.A. Ormondroyd and Y. Xie. 2014. The water vapor sorption behaviour of acetylated birch wood. How acetylation affects the sorption isotherm and accessible hydroxyl content. Journal of Material Science 49(5): 2362–2371.

Puttmann, S., A. Krause, A. Pilgård, A. Treu and H. Militz. 2009. Furfurylated wood for wooden window constructions, pp. 569–576. *In*: Englund, F., Hill, C.A.S., Militz, H. and Segerholm, B.K. [eds.]. The Proceeding of the Fourth European Conference on Wood Modification, Stockholm, Sweden.

Rabi'atol Adawiah, M.A., Z. Ashaari, F.A. Nur Izreen, E. Suhaimi Bakar, M. Hamami Sahri and P.M. Tahir. 2013. Addition of urea as formaldehyde scavenger for low molecular weight phenol formaldehyde-treated Compreg wood. Journal of Tropical Forest Science 24(3): 465–473.

Rademacher, P., S. Bollmus, S. Stumpf and A. Dieste. 2009. BMBF Verbundprojekt: Innovative, modifizierte Buchenholzprodukte: Teilvorhaben: Zusammenarbeit und Produktbeispiele mit den Industriepartnern Fahlenkamp, Variotec und Becker [BMBF joint project: Innovative, modified beech wood products: Subproject: Cooperation and product examples with the industrial partners Fahlenkamp, Variotec and Becker]. Final report, University of Göttingen, Germany.

Rafidah, K.S., C.A.S. Hill and G. A. Ormondroyd. 2006. Dimensional stabilization of rubberwood (*Hevea brasiliensis*) with acetic or hexanoic anhydride. Journal of Tropical Forest Science 18: 261–268.

Ranprex. 2020. http://www.rancan.com/rancan/eng/ranprex.html (2020-03-22).

Rapp, A.O. and R.-D. Peek. 1999. Melaminharzimprägniertes sowie mit Wetterschutzlasur oberflächenbehandeltes und unbehandeltes Vollholz während zweijähriger Freilandbewitterung [Solid wood impregnated with melamine resin and surface treated with weather protection glaze and untreated during two years of outdoor weathering.] Holz als Roh- und Werkstoff 57: 331–339.

Rapp, A.O., H. Bestgen, W. Adam and R.D. Peek. 1999. Electron loss spectroscopy (EELS) for quantification of cell-wall penetration of a melamine resin. Holzforschung 53(2): 111–117.

Rapp, A.O., C. Beringhausen, S. Bollmus, C. Brischke, T. Frick, T. Haas, M. Sailer and C.R. Welzbacher. 2005. Hydrophobierung von Holz: Erfahrungen nach 7 Jahren Freilandtest [Hydrophobation of wood: Experience after 7 years field testing], pp. 157–170. *In*: 24th Holzschutztagung der DGFH, Leipzig, Germany.

Ravi Kumar, M.N.V. 2000. A review of chitin and chitosan applications. Reactive and Functional Polymers 46(1): 1–27.

Reinsch, S., W. Böcker, M. Bücker, S. Seeger and B. Unger. 2002. Development of wood–inorganic composites with enhanced properties and environmental stability. *In*: Proceeding of the 4th International Wood and Fibre Symposium, Kassel, Germany.

Ringman, R., A. Pilgård, C. Brischke and K. Richter. 2014. Mode of action of brown rot decay resistance in modified wood: A review. Holzforschung 68(2): 239–246.

Ringman, R., A. Pilgård and K. Richter. 2020. Brown rot gene expression and regulation in acetylated and furfurylated wood: A complex picture. Holzforschung 74(4): 301–399.

Ritschkoff, A.-C., R. Mahlberg, L. Suomi-Lindberg, L. Viikari and A. Nurmi. 2003. Properties of wood treated with hydrophobisation agents. Poster presentation, pp. 267–271. *In*: Van Acker, J. and Hill, C.A.S. [eds.]. The Proceedings of the First European Conference on Wood Modification, Ghent, Belgium.

Roe, T., H. Hochman and E.R. Holden. 1957. Performance tests of heavy metal compounds as marine borer inhibitors, pp. 29–32. *In*: Markwardt, L.J. and Wakeman, C.M. [eds.]. Proceeding of the Symposium on Wood for Marine use and its Protection from Marine Organisms'. ASTM Special Technical Publication No. 200.

Rowell, R.M. 1983. Chemical modification of wood. Forest Products Abstracts 6(12): 363–382

Rowell, R.M. 1984. Penetration and reactivity of cell wall components, pp. 175–210. *In*: Rowell, R.M. [ed.]. The Chemistry of Solid Wood. American Chemical Society, Washington, DC, USA.

Rowell, R.M. 1986. Reaction conditions for acetylation of fibers, flakes, chips, thin and thick woods. Internal Progress Report, Chalmers University, Sweden.

Rowell, R.M. 1990. Chemical modification of wood: Its application to composite wood products, pp. 57–67. *In*: Proceedings of the Composite Wood Products Symposium, Rotorua. New Zealand, November 1988. Ministry of Forestry, FRI Bulletin No. 153.

Rowell, R.M. 2006. Acetylation of wood. Forest Product Journal 56: 4–12.

Rowell, R.M. 2012. Handbook of Chemistry and Wood Composites. 2nd edition, CRC Press, London, New York.

Rowell, R.M. 2014. Acetylation of wood: A review. International Journal of Lignocellulosic Products 1(1): 1–27.

Rowell, R.M. 2016. Dimensional stability and fungal durability of acetylated wood. Drewno 59(197): 139–150.

Rowell, R.M. and W.B. Banks. 1985. Water repellency and dimensional stability of wood. General Technical Report FPL-50. 24 p., US Department of Agriculture, Forest Service, Forest Products Laboratory, Madison (WI), USA.

Rowell, R.M. and M. Norimoto. 1987. Acetylation of bamboo fiber. Aspen Bibliography, Article ID 3469.

Rowell, R.M. and D.V. Plackett. 1988. Dimensional stability of flakeboards made from acetylated *Pinus radiata* heartwood or sapwood flakes. New Zealand Journal of Forestry Science 18: 124–131.

Rowell, R.M. and J.S. Rowell. 1989. Moisture Sorption of Various Types of Acetylated Lignocellulosic Fibers. *In*: Schuerch, C. [ed.]. Cellulose and Wood. John Wiley and Sons, New York, USA.

Rowell, R.M. and F.M. Keany. 1991. Fibreboard made from acetylated bagasse fiber. Wood and Fiber Science 23(1): 15–22.

Rowell, R.M. and S.E. Harrison. 1993. Property enhanced kenaf fiber composites, pp. 129–136. *In*: Bhangoo, M.S. [ed.]. Proceedings of the Fifth Annual International Kenaf Conference, California State University Press, Fresno (CA), USA.

Rowell, R.M. and F. Bongers. 1994. Review: Coating acetylated wood. Coatings 5(4): 792–801.

Rowell, R.M., A.-M. Tillman and R. Simonson. 1986a. Vapor phase of southern pine, douglas-fir and aspen wood flakes. Journal of Wood Chemistry and Technology 6(2): 293–309.

Rowell, R.M., R. Simonson and A.-M. Tillman. 1986b. A simplified procedure for the acetylation of chips for dimensionally stabilized particleboard products. Paperi ja Puu 68(10): 740–744.

Rowell, R.M., R. Simonson and A.-M. Tillman. 1990. Acetyl balance for the acetylation of wood particles by a simplified procedure. Holzforschung 44(4): 263–269.

Rowell, R.M., R. Simonson, S. Hess, D.V. Plackett, D. Cronshaw and E. Dunningham. 1991. Acetyl distribution in acetylated whole wood and reactivity of isolated wood cell wall components to acetic anhydride. Wood and Fiber Science 26: 11–18.

Rowell, R.M., R. Simonsen, S. Hess, D.V. Plackett, D. Cronshaw and E. Dunningham. 1994. Acetyl distribution in acetylated whole wood and reactivity of isolated cell wall components to acetic anhydride. Wood and Fiber Science 26(1): 11–18.

Rowell, R.M., R.E. Ibach and T. Nilsson. 2007. Influence of moisture on brown-rot fungal attack, pp. 65–69. *In*: Rikala, J. and Sipi, M. [eds.]. Proceedings 3rd Nordic Baltic Network in Wood Material Science and Engineering, Helsinki, Finland.

Rowell, R.M., B. Kattenbroek, P. Ratering, F. Bongers, F. Leicher and H. Stebbins. 2008. Production of dimensionally stable and decay resistant wood components based on acetylation (unpaginated proc.). *In*: Türkeri, A.N. and Sengül, Ö. [eds.]. Proceeding of the 11DBMC International Conference on Durability of Building Materials and Components, Istanbul, Turkey.

Ryu, J.Y., M. Takahashi, Y. Imamura and T. Sato. 1991. Biological resistance of phenol-resin treated wood. Mokuzai Gakkaishi 37(9): 852–858.

Ryu, J.Y., Y. Imamura, M. Takahashi and H. Kajita. 1993. Effects of molecular weight and some other properties of resins on the biological resistance of phenolic resin treated wood. Mokuzai Gakkaishi 39(4): 486–492.

Sahoo, D. and P.L. Nayak. 2011. Chitosan: The most valuable derivative of chitin, pp. 129–159. *In*: Kalia, S. and Avérous, L. [eds.]. Biopolymers: Biomédical and Environmental Applications. Scrivener Publishing, Salem, USA.

Sailer, M., A.O. Rapp, H. Leithoff and R.-D. Peek. 2000. Vergütung von Holz durch Anwerdung einer Öl-Hitzebehandlung [Upgrading of Wood by Application of an Oil-Heat Treatment.] Holz als Roh- und Werkstoff 58(1): 15–22.

Salehi, A.M. 2012. Chemical Interactions between Fatty acids and Wood Components during Oxidation Processes. PhD. Thesis, Royal Institute of Technology (KTH), Stockholm.

Saka, S., M. Sasaki and M. Tanahashi. 1992. Wood–inorganic composites prepared by sol-gel processing. Part 1. Wood–inorganic composites with porous structure. Mokuzai Gakkaishi 38: 1043–1049.

Saka, S., H. Miyafuji and F. Tanno. 2001. Wood-inorganic composites prepared by the sol-gel process. Journal of Sol-Gel Science and Technology 20: 213–217.

Sandberg, D., A. Kutnar and G. Mantanis. 2017. Wood modification technologies: A review. COST action FP1407. Goli, G., Kutnar, A., Jones, D. and Sandberg, D. [eds.]. Understanding Wood Modification Through an Integrated Scientific and Environmental Impact Approach. IForest Biogeosciences and Forestry 10: 895–908.

SCA Smart Trall. 2019. https://www.smarttimber.com/produkter/altan-och-utemiljo/royaltrall/ (2020-03-23).

Schaffert, S. 2006. Steuerung und Optimierung von Holzvernetzungsprozessen [Control and optimization of wood crosslinking processes.] PhD. Thesis, Georg-August-Universität Göttingen.

Schaffert, S., L. Nunes, A. Krause and H. Militz. 2006. Resistance of DMDHEU-treated pinewood against termite and fungi attack in field testing according to EN 252. Results after 30 months. *In*: The Proceedings IRG Annual Meeting, Tromsø, Norway. International Research Group on Wood Protection IRG/WP/06–40354.

Scharff, A. 2019. Improvement of leaching resistance of for retardant wood by formation of insoluble compounds, pp. 54–55. *In*: LeVan-Green, S. [ed.]. SWST 2019 International Convention, Tenaya Lodge, Yosemite National Park, USA.

Schindler, W.D. and P.J. Hauser. 2004. Chemical Finishing of Textiles. Woodhead, Cambridge, UK.

Schneider, M.H. 1995. New cell wall and cell lumen wood polymer composites. Wood Science and Technology 29: 121–127.

Schmid, J. 2006. Di-santa-Ein heimisches dimensionsstabilisiertes Holz für den Fenster- und Fassadenbau – Endbericht [Di-sta – Native wood species with improved dimensional stability for window and facade construction – Final report.] DGfH, German Society for Wood Research e.V., Munich, Germany.

Schneider, M.C. 1994. Wood polymer composites. Wood and Fiber Science 26(1): 142–151.

Scholz, G., A. Krause and H. Militz. 2010a. Exploratory study on the impregnation of Scots pine sapwood (*Pinus sylvestris* L.) and European beech (*Fagus sylvatica* L.) with different hot melting waxes. Wood Science and Technology 44(3): 379–388.

Scholz, G., E. Nothnick, G. Avramidis, A. Krause, H. Militz and W. Viöl. 2010b. Adhesion of wax impregnated solid beech wood with different glues and by plasma treatment. European Journal of Wood and Wood Products 68(3): 315–21.

Scholz, G., A. Krause and H. Militz. 2012. Full impregnation of modified wood with wax. European Journal of Wood and Wood Products 70(1/3): 91–98.

Scown, D.K., L.J. Cookson and K.J. McCarthy. 2001. Silica treatments to protect timber from marine borers. *In*: The Proceedings IRG Annual Meeting, Nara, Japan. International Research Group on Wood Protection IRG/WP 01–30270.

Sehlstedt-Persson, M. 2020. Personal communication. Luleå University of Technology, Skellefteå, Sweden.

Sejati, P.S., A. Imbert, C. Gérardin-Charbonnier, S. Dumarçay, E. Fredon, E. Masson, D. Nandika, T. Priadi and P. Gérardin. 2017. Tartaric acid catalyzed furfurylation of beech wood. Wood Science and Technology 51(2): 379–394.

Selder, M. 2003. Linseed oil and method for preparation thereof. U.S. Patent No. US10/089,285.

Serpa, F.G. 1980. Laboratory tests of wood impregnated with sodium silicate against the attack of Limnoria tripunctata Menzies. Revista Floresta 11: 42–44.

Shams, I. and H. Yano. 2011. Compressive deformation of phenol formaldehyde (PF) resin-impregnated wood related to the molecular weight of resin. Wood Science and Technology 45: 73–81.

Sheen, A.D. 1992. The preparation of acetylated wood fibre on a commercial scale. Chemical modification of lignocellulosics, pp. 14–21. *In*: Simonson, R. and Rowell, R.M. [eds.]. FRI Bull. No. 176. 1st Pacific Rim Bin-Based Composite Symposium, Rotorua, New Zealand.

Shengzhen, C. 2016. Scots pine (*Pinus sylvestris* L.) sapwood modification by vinyl acetate-epoxidized plant oil copolymer. PhD. Thesis, Swedish University of Agricultural Sciences, Uppsala, Sweden.

SHR. 2007. Dimensional stability of Accoya™ wood under different moisture content, Report code: 6.322, 2 March 2007. www.erlebe-accoya.de/files/dimensional_stability_accoya__different_moisture_conditions_.pdf.

Sid, W.W.Y. and S. Jiaozhang. 1981. A study on liquor phase acetylation of wood. Journal of Nanjing Forestry University 4: 33–41.

SIOO:X. 2019. https://sioox.com/se/traskydd-original/ (2020-03-11).

Skaar, C. 1988. Wood-Water Relations. Springer-Verlag, Berlin, Heidelberg, Germany.

Skrede, I., M.H. Solbakken, J. Hess, C.G. Fossdal, O. Hegnar and G. Alfredsen. 2019. Wood modification by furfuryl alcohol resulted in a delayed decomposition response in *Rhodonia (Postia) placenta*. Applied and Environmental Microbiology 85(14): 1–21.

Slimak, R.A., C.C. Haudenshild and K.M. Slimak. 2000. Enhancing strength, moisture resistance, and fire-resistance of wood, timber, lumber, similar plant derived construction and building materials, and other cellulosic materials. U.S. Patent No. 6,040,057 (45).

Spear, M.J., C.A.S. Hill, S.F. Curling, D. Jones and M.D. Hale. 2006. Assessment of the envelope effect of three hot oil treatments: Resistance to decay by *Coniophora puteana* and *Postia placenta*. *In*: The Proceedings IRG Annual Meeting, Tromsø, Norway. International Research Group on Wood Protection IRG/WP 06-40344.

Stamm, A.J. 1959a. The dimensional stability of wood. Forest Products Journal 9(10): 375–381.

Stamm, A.J. 1959b. Effect of polyethylene glycol on the dimensional stability of wood. Forest Products Journal 9(10): 375–381.

Stamm, A.J. 1964. Wood and Cellulose Science. Ronald Press, New York.

Stamm, A.J. 1974. Dimensional stabilization of wood with water soluble fire retardant bulking chemicals compared with polyethylene glycol-1000. Wood Science and Technology 8(4): 300–306.

Stamm, A.J. and R.M. Seborg. 1936. Minimizing wood shrinkage and swelling, treatment with synthetic resins forming materials. Industrial and Engineering Chemistry 289(10): 1164–1169.

Stamm, A.J. and R.M. Seborg. 1939. Resin-treated plywood. Industrial & Engineering Chemistry Research 31(7): 897–902.

Stamm, A.J. and R.M. Seborg. 1943. Resin treated wood (Impreg). Lab. Report No. 1380, US Department of Agriculture, Forest Service, Forest Products Laboratory, Madison (WI), USA.

Stamm, A.J. and R.M. Seborg. 1944. Resin treated laminated compressed wood (Compreg). Lab. Report No. 1381, US Department of Agriculture, Forest Service, Forest Products Laboratory, Madison (WI), USA.

Stamm, A.J. and H. Tarkow. 1947. Acetylation of lignocellulosic board materials. U.S. Patent No. 2,417,995.

Stamm, A.J. and R.M. Seborg. 1955. Resin-treated, laminated compressed wood (Compreg). Report No. 1977, US Department of Agriculture, Forest Service, Forest Products Laboratory, Madison (WI), USA.

Stamm, A.J. and R.H. Bachelor. 1960. Decay resistance and dimensional stability of five modified woods. Forest Products Journal 10: 22–26.

Stora Enso. 2015. Nature under one roof. Accessible: https://www.storaenso.com/en/newsroom/news/2015/2/nature-under-one-roof (2020-03-11).

Strømdahl, K. 2000. Water sorption in wood and plant fibres. Report Serie R, Technical University of Denmark (DTU). Institut for Baerende Konstruktioner og Materiale, Kgs. Lyngby, Denmark.

Subagiyo, L., E. Rosamah and Hesim. 2017. Modification of oil palm wood using acetylation and impregnation process. 6 pp. *In*: Fatimah, I. [ed.]. AIP Conference Proceedings 1823: 020083.

Sun, R. and X.F. Sun. 2002. Structural and thermal characterization of acetylated rice, wheat, rye, and barley straws and poplar wood fibre. Industrial Crops and Products 16(3): 225–235.

Sun, X.F. and R.C. Sun. 2002. Comparative study of acetylation of rice straw fiber with or without catalysts. Wood and Fiber Science 34(2): 306–317.

Swed handling. 2015. Kalivattenglas [Potassium silicate.] http://www.swedhandling.se/produkter/kalivattenglas/ (2020-03-11).

Swedish Wood. 2015. Design of timber structures: Structural aspects of timber construction. Volume 1. Swedish Forest Industries Federation, Stockholm, Sweden.

Takahashi, M. and Y. Imamura. 1990. Biological resistance of phenol-resin treated wood. *In*: The Proceedings IRG Annual Meeting, Rotorua, New Zealand. International Research Group on Wood Protection IRG/WP 3602.

Taman, A.R., S.Z. Mohamed and Z.R. Negieb. 1990. Effect of addition of petroleum wax on wood pulp for papermaking. Research and Industry 35(1): 52–56.

Tarkow, H., A.J. Stamm and E.C.O. Erickson. 1946. Acetylated wood. Report. 1593. US Department of Agriculture, Forest Service, Forest Products Laboratory, Madison (WI), USA.

Termiz, A., N. Terziev, M. Eikenes and J. Hafrén. 2007. Effect of accelerated weathering on surface chemistry of modified wood. Applied Surface Science 253(12): 5355–5362.

Thybring, E.E. 2013. The decay resistance of modified wood influenced by moisture exclusion and swelling reduction. International Biodeterioration & Biodegradation 82: 87–95.

Thygesen, L.G. and T. Elder. 2008. Moisture in untreated, acetylated, and furfurylated Norway spruce studied during drying using time domain NMR. Wood and Fiber Science 40(3): 309–320.

Thygesen, L.G., S. Barsberg and T.M. Venås. 2010. The fluorescence characteristics of furfurylated wood studied by fluorescence spectroscopy and confocal laser scanning microscopy. Wood Science and Technology 44: 51–65.

Tjeerdsma, B.F., P. Swager, B.J. Horstman, B.W. Holleboom and W.J. Homan. 2005. Process development of treatment of wood with modified hot oil, pp. 186–197. *In*: Militz, H. and Hill, C.A.S. [eds.]. Proceedings of the Second European Conference on Wood Modification, Göttingen, Germany.

Torr, K.M., A.P. Singh and R.A. Franich. 2006. Improving stiffness of lignocellulosics through cell wall modification with chitosan-melamine co-polymers. New Zealand Journal of Forestry Science 36(1): 87–98.

Tracey, M.V. 1957. Chitin revue. Pure and Applied Chemistry 7(1): 1–14.

Transfuran chemicals. 2020. https://www.polyfurfurylalcohol.com/ (2020-03-22).

Treu, A., J. Habicht, R. Klaucke and H. Militz. 2003. Improvement of wood properties by combined impregnation process—the Royal process, pp. 3–13. *In*: Van Acker, J. and Hill, C.A.S. [eds.]. Proceedings of the First European Conference on Wood Modification, Ghent, Belgium.

Tricoya. 2017. https://tricoya.com/wp-content/uploads/2017/11/Tricoya-Datasheet-NA-15.08.2017-FINAL.pdf (2020-03-22).

Ulvcrona, T. 2006. Impregnation of Norway spruce (*Picea abies* L. Karst.) wood with hydrophobic oil. PhD. Thesis, Swedish University of Agricultural Sciences, Umeå, Sweden.

Unger, A., A.P. Schniewind and W. Unger. 2001. Conservation of Wood Artifacts: A Handbook. Springer, Berlin.

Van Acker, J., A.J. Nurmi, S.M. Gray, H. Militz, C. Hill, H. Kokko and A.O. Rapp. 1999. Decay resistance of resin treated wood. Proceedings 30th International Research Group on Wood Preservation. Rosenheim, Germany. IRG/WP 99-30206.

van der Zee, M.E., N.L. Schipholt, B.F. Tjeerdsma, P. Brynildsen and I. Mohoric. 2007. Glueability and paintability of furfurylated wood (Kebony), pp. 231–234. *In*: Hill, C.A.S., Jones, D., Militz, H. and Ormondroyd, G.A. [eds.]. Proceedings of the Third European Conference on Wood Modification, Cardiff, UK.

Vårum, K., M. Anthonsen, H. Grasdal and O. Smidsrød. 1991. Determination of the degree of N-acetylation and the distribution of N-acetyl groups in partially N-deacetylated chitins (chitosans) by high-field n.m.r. spectroscopy. Carbohydrate Research 211(1): 17–23.

Vårum, K., M. Ottøy and O. Smidsrød. 1994. Water-solubility of partially N-acetylated chitosans as a function of pH: effect of chemical composition and depolymerization. Carbohydrate Polymer 25: 65–70.

Venås, T.M. and A.H.H. Wong. 2008. Feasibility study on three furfurylated non-durable tropical wood species evaluated for resistance to brown, white and soft rot fungi. *In*: The Proceedings IRG Annual Meeting, Istanbul, Turkey. International Research Group on Wood Protection IRG/WP 08-40395.

Verma, P., U. Junga, H. Militz and C. Mai. 2009. Protection mechanisms of DMDHEU treated wood against white and brown rot fungi. Holzforschung 63(3): 371–378.

Vick, C.B. and R.M. Rowell. 1990. Adhesive bonding of acetylated wood. International Journal of Adhesion and Adhesives 10(4): 263–272.

Vick, C.B., P.C. Larsson, R.L. Mahlberg, R. Simonson and R.M. Rowell. 1993. Structural bonding of acetylated Scandinavian softwoods for exterior lumber laminates. International Journal of Adhesion and Adhesives 13(3): 139–149.

Vladimirs, B., M. Fleckenstein, C. Mai and H. Militz. 2020. Suitability of a lignin-derived mono-phenol mimic to replace phenol in phenol-formaldehyde resin for use in wood treatment. Holzforschung 74(4): 344–350.

Vorobyev, A., O. Arnould, D. Laux, R. Longo, N.P. van Dijk and E.K. Gamstedt. 2016a. Characterisation of cubic oak specimens from the Vasa ship and recent wood by means of quasi-static loading and resonance ultrasound spectroscopy (RUS). Holzforschung 70(5): 457–465.

Vorobyev, A., I. Bjurhager, N.P. van Dijk and E.K. Gamstedt. 2016b. Effects of barrelling during axial compressive tests of cubic samples with isotropic, transversely isotropic and orthotropic elastic properties. Composites Science and Technology 137: 1–8.

Wallström, L. 1998. Cell wall bulking and distribution of different chemicals in pine, *Pinus sylvestris*. PhD. Thesis, Luleå University of Technology, Skellefteå, Sweden.

Wallström, L., H. Lindberg and I. Johansson. 1995. Wood surface stabilization. Holz als Roh- und Werkstoff 53: 87–92.

Weaver, J.W., J.F. Nielson and I.S. Goldstein. 1960. Dimensional stabilization of wood with aldehydes and related compounds. Forest Products Journal 10(6): 306–310.

Wellons, J.D. 1977. Adhesion to wood substrates, pp. 150–168. *In*: Goldstein, I.S. [ed.]. Wood Technology: Chemical Aspects. ACS Symposium Series 43, Washington DC, USA.

Wepner, F. 2006. Entwicklung eines Modifizierungsverfahrens für Buchenfurniere (*Fagus sylvatica* L.) auf Basis von zyklischen N-MethylolVerbindungen [Development of a modification process for beech veneers (*Fagus sylvatica* L.) based on cyclic N-methylol compounds]. PhD. Thesis, University of Göttingen, Germany.

Westermark, U., B. Steenberg and B. Sundqvist. 2005. Impregnation with PEG and solvolysis of wood: Reflections from analysis of the ancient warship Vasa, pp. 229–231. *In*: Proceedings the 59th Appita Annual Conference and Exhibition. Auckland, New Zealand.

Westin, M., T. Nilsson and Y.S. Hadi. 1998. Field performance of furfuryl alcohol treated wood, pp. 305–331. *In*: Haidi, Y.S. [ed.]. Proceedings of the 4th Pacific Rim Bio-Based Composites Symposium, Bogor, Indonesia.

Westin, M., A.O. Rapp and T. Nilsson. 2004. Durability of pine modified by 9 different methods. *In*: The Proceedings IRG Annual Meeting, Ljubljana, Slovenia. International Research Group on Wood Protection IRG/WP 04-40288.

Westin, M., A.O. Rapp and T. Nilsson. 2006. Field test of resistance of modified wood to marine borers. Wood Material Science & Engineering 1(1): 34–38.

Westin, M., M. Sterley, F. Rossi and J.-J. Hervé. 2009. Compreg-type products by furfurylation during hot-pressing. Wood Material Science & Engineering 4(1/2): 67–75.

Westin, M., P. Larsson-Brelid, T. Nilsson, A. Rapp, J.P. Dickerson, S. Lande and S. Cragg. 2016. Marine borer resistance of acetylated and furfurylated wood: Results from up to 16 years of field exposure. *In*: The Proceedings IRG Annual Meeting, Lisbon, Portugal. International Research Group on Wood Protection IRG/WP 16-40756.

Winandy, J.E. and R.M. Rowell. 1984. The chemistry of wood strength, pp. 211–255. *In*: Rowell, R.M. [ed.]. The Chemistry of Solid Wood. ACS Symposium Series 208, Washington DC, USA.

Wålinder, M., P.L. Brelid, K. Segerholm, C.J. Long II and J.P. Dickerson. 2013. Wettability of acetylated Southern yellow pine. International Wood Products Journal 4(3): 197–203.

Xie, Y. 2006. Surface properties of wood modified with cyclic N-methylol compounds. PhD. Thesis, University of Göttingen, Germany.

Xie, Y., A. Krause, H. Militz, H. Turkulin, K. Richter and C. Mai. 2007. Effect of treatments with 1,3-dimethylol-4,5-dihydroxyethyleneurea (DMDHEU) on tensile properties of wood. Holzforschung 61(1): 43–50.

Xie, Y., A. Krause, H. Militz and C. Mai. 2008. Weathering of uncoated and coated wood treated with methylated 1,3-dimethylol-4,5-dihydroxyethyleneurea (mDMDHEU). Holz als Roh- und Werkstoff 66(6): 455–464.

Yalpani, M. and D. Pantaleone. 1994. An examination of the unusual susceptibilities of aminoglycan to enzymatic hydrolysis. Carbohydrate Research 256: 159–175.

Yang, T., E. Ma and J. Cao. 2019. Synergistic effects of partial hemicellulose removal and furfurylation on improving the dimensional stability of poplar wood tested under dynamic conditions. Industrial Crops & Products 139: Article ID 111550.

Yano, H., K. Mori, P.J. Collins and Y. Yazaki. 2000. Effects of element size and orientation in the production of high strength resin impregnated wood based materials. Holzforschung 54: 443–447.

Yano, H., A. Hirose, P.J. Collins and Y. Yazaki. 2001a. Potential strength for resin-impregnated compressed wood. Journal of Materials Science Letters 20(12): 1127–1129.

Yano, H., A. Hirose, P.J. Collins and Y. Yazaki. 2001b. Effects of the removal of matrix substances as a pretreatment in the production of high strength resin impregnated wood based materials. Journal of Materials Science Letters 20(12): 1125–1126.

Yelle, D.J. and J. Ralph. 2016. Characterizing phenol–formaldehyde adhesive cure chemistry within the wood cell wall International. International Journal of Adhesion and Adhesives 70: 26–36.

Yuan, J., Y. Hu, L. Li and F. Cheng. 2013. The mechanical strength change of wood modified with DMDHEU. BioResources 8(1): 1076–1088.

Yusuf, S., Y. Imamura, M. Takahashi and K. Minato. 1995. Physical and biological properties of albizzia waferboard modified with cross-linking agents. *In*: The Proceedings IRG Annual Meeting, Helsingör, Denmark. International Research Group on Wood Protection IRG/WP/95–40043.

Zelinka, S.L., G.T. Kirker, A.B Bishell and S.V. Glass. 2020. Effects of wood moisture content and the level of acetylation on brown rot decay. Forests 11(299): 1–10.

Zhao, G.J., M. Norimoto, F. Tanaka, T. Yamada and R.M. Rowell. 1987. Structure and properties of acetylated wood. Part I. Changes in the degree of crystallinity and dielectric properties by acetylation (in Japanese). Mokuzai Gakkaishi 33(2): 136–142.

Chapter 3
Thermally-based Modification Processes

3.1 Introduction

Since the dawn of mankind, fire—and particularly its control—has played an important role in civilisation. Despite the destructive aspects of thermal processes on wood, it has long been known that burnt wood has an increased stability and is more resistant to rot and fungi. This was developed into some of the first wood treatment processes by civilisations such as the Vikings and their predecessors, where burning the wood for jetty piles and in-ground parts of the hall-building frame was known to increase the product longevity. Unfortunately, burnt wood was also known to be dry and brittle, hence such treatments were originally limited to the wood surface.

More recently, a deeper understanding of the components of wood and their behaviour at elevated temperatures has allowed the development of controlled treatments. In his seminal book, Hill (2006) defined thermal modification as "*the application of heat to wood in order to bring about a desired improvement in the performance of the material*". The increased understanding of wood chemistry and its potential processing in the past 200 years has enabled the development of a range of thermally-based modification (TBM) processes.

As shown in Figure 3.1, TBM processes can be split into four categories—*thermo (T)*, *thermo-hydro (TH)*, *thermo-mechanical (TM)*, and *thermo-hydro-mechanical (THM)* processes. The conventional charring of wood (Section 3.2) can be classed as a T method, whereas thermolysis and pyrolysis methods can be classed as T or TH methods, depending on the conditions. Similarly, TM methods occur in the presence or absence of moisture, although moisture is present in most cases.

Several TBM techniques of considerable importance, such as wood drying, reconstituted wood processing, Thonét wood bending, and laminated veneer processing, have a long industrial tradition,

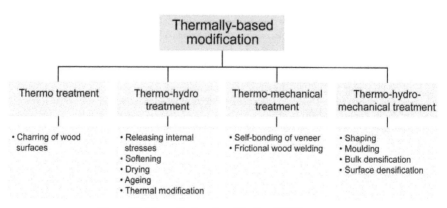

Figure 3.1 Thermally-based modification (TBM) processes.

and numerous books and reviews are dedicated to each of them. This chapter focusses on processes that have recently been successfully industrialised or which are believed to be close to industrial implementation, i.e., thermal modification, wood ageing, charring of wood surfaces, self-bonding of veneer, frictional wood welding, wood bulk densification, surface wood densification, and moulded tubes and shells. Challenges faced during the commercialisation of TH and THM processes are also discussed.

Thermal degradation of wood

The result of a thermal treatment is highly dependent on the processing conditions, such as the presence or absence of oxygen, the temperature, and the moisture content.

There are a range of different processes involving the heating of wood:

1) wood drying,
2) thermally-based modification (TBM),
3) heating in the absence of air, i.e., *pyrolysis* and *thermolysis*,
4) heating in the presence of air, i.e., *combustion*:
   a. complete combustion with full access to oxygen, and
   b. incomplete combustion when the availability of oxygen access is limited.

The processes involving heat and the typical temperature ranges in which they occur and their effects on individual wood components are shown in Figure 3.2. An elevated temperature is an important component when wood is to be modified solely with the help of water or moisture, but a temperature above 300°C is of limited practical value due to the risk of severe degradation of all the main wood constituents, but there are exceptions. The degradation starts or at least becomes identifiable at different temperatures for the different main constituents of wood, the extractives being the most sensitive to a temperature increase due to their low-molecular nature and low boiling point, followed in turn by hemicelluloses, cellulose, and lignin.

In the absence of an oxidising agent or other catalyst, the thermal treatment of wood is called pyrolysis. The wood does not combust, but thermally degrades into solid, liquid and gaseous components. The production of charcoal is one of the oldest and historically most common pyrolysis processes.

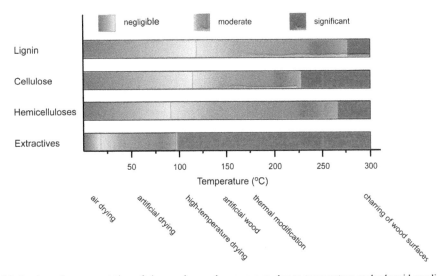

Figure 3.2 A schematic representation of changes in wood components due to temperature under humid conditions, but without regard to time (Navi and Sandberg, 2012).

When wood is heated it releases volatile, flammable gases which burn when they contact a source of ignition and the presence of oxygen. Below a temperature of ca. 40°C the thermal decomposition of wood is negligible, but above 100°C the decomposition proceeds slowly, becomes violent at about 250°C with a strongly exothermic character and ends at about 350°C where spontaneous ignition occurs.

In general, the thermal degradation of wood proceeds along one of two reaction pathways. At temperatures up to 200–300°C, carbon dioxide and traces of organic compounds are formed in addition to the release of water vapour. At this stage, the wood polymers degrade by the breaking of internal chemical bonds, resulting in the formation of free radicals, carbonyl, carboxyl, and hydroperoxide groups, carbon monoxide, carbon dioxide and reactive carbonaceous char (Rowell, 2005). The second mechanism, which takes over at temperatures above 300°C, leads to a much more rapid decomposition and the cleavage of secondary bonds. The pyrolysis gases contain 200 or more different components (Brenden, 1967). The degradation is accompanied by a reduction in weight depending on the temperature and on the duration of heating.

Wood itself does not burn; the wood material decomposes on heating and the gases emitted burn. Kollmann (1960) defined three phase points in the exothermic reactions (release of energy) in wood:

1) The flame point, 225–260°C, at which decomposed gases burn if an ignition source is present.
2) The burning point, 260–290°C, at which burning occurs with a steady flame. The decomposition is exothermic during the burning and causes a self-induced flash.
3) The flash point, 330–470°C, where spontaneous ignition occurs.

The rate of thermal degradation differs for the different constituents of wood, being highest for hemicelluloses, much lower for cellulose and lowest for lignin (Figure 3.2). The rate of degradation of wood is intermediate between the degradation rates of cellulose and lignin. Figure 3.3 shows a Differential Thermal Analysis (DTA) curve for solid wood, with a minor endothermic reaction (uptake of energy) just above 100°C, corresponding to the removal of water. In general, the thermographs for wood first show an endothermal maximum at 120–150°C, attributed to the evaporation of more strongly absorbed water. The exothermal peaks at 200–250°C and 280–320°C and those above 400°C are due to the degradation of the wood components (Fengel and Wegener, 2003).

There are a number of difficulties in describing the changes that take place when wood is heated. Several of chemical reactions which are combinations of both endothermic and exothermic

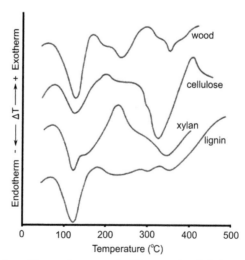

Figure 3.3 Thermal behaviour of the wood components of European beech during pyrolysis (Košík et al., 1968).

reactions take place simultaneously, making the determination of the onset temperatures for the different reactions nearly impossible. The analysis is further complicated by interactions between reactions of different constituents, so that an analysis performed on an isolated derivative of one of the components can be very different from what actually takes place inside wood, where there are not only interactions between the components inside the wood but also interactions between the wood and the treatment atmosphere. The products of completely pyrolysed wood were, however, reported to be the same as the combined products of the individual components (Browne, 1958). The chemistry of the thermal degradation of the isolated wood components is undoubtedly different from that taking place within the cell wall, where the various reactions can act synergistically with the wood material.

Temperatures below ca. 100°C

It is not possible to specify an exact temperature limit for the thermo-chemical decomposition of wood, since wood is not absolutely stable even at low temperature (about 40°C) if the duration of the heat exposure is long enough and provided that weathering effects are not considered (Sandermann and Augustin, 1963). The changes that occur in wood at temperatures below 40°C are mainly physical changes, such as the emission of water and volatile extractives such as terpenes (Manninen et al., 2002), the first weight loss being due to the loss of water, followed by the loss of a variety of degradation products and volatile gases (Shafizadeh and Chin, 1977). Mitchell et al. (1953) concluded that, in the early stages of degradation, 83% of the weight loss is water. Some minor chemical changes probably start to occur between 40 and 90°C, predominately due to certain extractives. Englund and Nussbaum (2000) found high concentrations of Volatile Organic Compounds (VOC), mainly monoterpenes, when they dried Scots pine and Norway spruce in this temperature range.

Temperatures above ca. 100°C

Browne (1958) suggested that of the pyrolysis process, in the absence of air could be divided into four regimes, or temperature ranges, all of which can occur simultaneously in wood of appreciable thickness:

- Phase A, below 200°C, in which only non-combustible gases, primarily water vapour, with traces of carbon dioxide, formic and acetic acids, and glyoxal are produced. The evaporation of sorbed water is complete.
- Phase B, from 200°C to 280°C, in which the same gases as in phase A are produced, but with much less water vapour and some carbon monoxide. The reactions are endothermic, and the products are almost entirely non-flammable.
- Phase C, from 280°C to 500°C, in which active pyrolysis takes place under exothermic conditions leading to secondary reactions among the products which are largely combustible (carbon monoxide, methane, etc.), and include highly flammable tars in the form of smoke particles. The charcoal residue catalyses secondary reactions.
- Phase D, above 500°C, in which the residue consists primarily of charcoal, which provides an extremely active site for further secondary reactions. Early combustion stages are similar to the pyrolysis stages, modified slightly by oxidation.

The course of events when wood is heated in air can be similarly divided into phases, but these include oxidation reactions and, after ignition, the combustion of pyrolysis and oxidation products. Using the same temperature divisions as in pyrolysis, combustion in the presence of air may be categorised as follows:

- Phase A, below 200°C, which, in addition to the evolution of non-combustible gases, is affected by some exothermic oxidation processes.

- Phase B, from 200°C to 280°C, in which the primary exothermic reaction takes place without ignition. The ignition point may, however, also be defined as the temperature at which the exothermic reactions begin.

- Phase C, from 280°C to 500°C, in which ignitable combustible gases are produced after secondary pyrolysis. Flaming combustion can then occur if the gases are ignited, but the combustion is restricted to the gas phase. If ignition is not induced, flaming may not occur until near the end of the pyrolysis when the evolved gases cannot insulate the charcoal layer from oxygen. Spontaneous ignition of the charcoal takes place at a temperature lower than the ignition temperature of any of the products evolved.

- Phase D, above 500°C, in which the charcoal glows and is consumed. Above 1,000°C, non-luminous flames are supported by the combustion of hydrogen and carbon monoxide.

Fengel (1966a,b,c) reported certain anatomical changes in spruce heated at 180°C and 200°C. The S-layers of latewood tissue became fractured, and the encrusting materials in the torus began to flow at these temperatures, which represents the transition between phase A and phase B defined by Browne (1958).

The results of the process depend on several variables including time and temperature, treatment atmosphere, wood species, moisture content, wood dimensions and the use of a catalyst (Stamm, 1956). Temperature and time of treatment are the most critical factors, and treatment in air leads to oxidation reactions, which are detrimental to the properties of the treated wood.

When wood is heated in the absence of air, zones develop parallel to the heat-absorbing surface, delimited by the temperatures attained. The zones are well marked in wood because of its relatively low thermal conductivity and density, and its relatively high specific heat.

The chemical changes occurring in the main components of wood due to heat treatment are summarised in Figure 3.4.

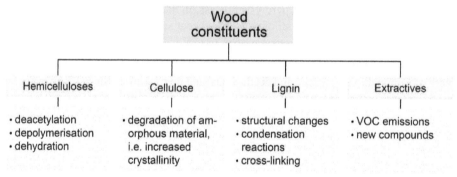

Figure 3.4 Changes in the main wood constituents during heat treatment.

3.2 Charring of wood surfaces

The surface charring of wood is a process that burns and modifies the wood surface in a controlled manner. The charring process mimics the combustion of wood, but the char layer is an efficient insulator and a poor conductor of heat and it effectively inhibits heat transfer to the active pyrolysing zone, thus retarding further combustion.

The first, or at least a very early description of thermal modification as a means of improving durability dates from the 1st Century AD in Rome when Vitruvius stated that the city walls should be reinforced by charred olive timbers. Charred olive wood is a material that is not destroyed by decay or weathering. It may lay in the ground or in water for an indefinite amount of time without decaying (Dahlgren, 1989). Charring as a type of surface-treatment has also been in use in Japan for centuries. The technique is called *yakisugi*, which is literally translated as *burnt sugi wood*, and the tradition

Figure 3.5 Exterior panelling of traditional charred Japanese cedar (sugi) with different degrees of charring (Kyoto, Japan).

speaks of an appearance and protection that can last for decades (Figure 3.5). The ancient Japanese art of charring timber can now be found in various modern processes where charred finishes and textures can be provided for interior and exterior use, from the traditional highly charred fragile looking surface (known as sumi-tsuki) to the sleek and contemporary finish (known as migaki). The yakisugi process is, however, a Japanese product defined by narrow specification parameters both for the material and for the process used. Japan has influenced western thought and design since the country opened up some 150 years ago, and yakisugi has significantly contributed to modern architecture with its contemporary black monolithic wall aesthetic. Yakisugi material is becoming more and more accepted worldwide as a sustainable and desirable aesthetic wood cladding option for both exterior and interior use. It has been interpreted as a chic, high-design building material, but on the Japanese market it is a standard, utility wood siding, affordably priced and with a greater longevity than untreated wood.

The depth of the treatment has a major influence on the performance of the product and affects certain properties, such as sorption, cracking during weathering, and thermal insulation, which can be controlled by the process conditions. With suitable combinations of time and temperature, cracking can also be avoided. Brushing can be used to finish the surfaces and even out the properties. This is especially useful after modification at high temperature where the surface may tend to flake. Brushing, however, makes the char layer thinner and may affect the final properties, and the choice of species influences, both the properties and the appearance with a colour ranging from light brown to shiny black. The ultrastructure of the char may also differ between wood species and charring method.

Material selection and preparation

In the traditional Japanese wood-charring process, the sugi or Japanese cedar was the most common species. The process starts with a careful log selection, grading for straightness and diameter, growth-ring width, wood colour, and other quality aspects such as knottiness. The logs are sawn to produce either timber with vertical growth rings (quarter-sawn timber) or purely flat-sawn timber. According to tradition, the sawn timber should be seasoned in the open air rather than kiln dried.

The thermal treatment is intense, and the wood is quenched when the charred layer has reached the desired thickness and appearance. After drying, the wood can either be used as it is or brushed to smooth the charred layer and oil applied to achieve the desired appearance.

Because Japanese cedar is indigenous only to Japan, other species such as Douglas fir, Norway spruce, oak spp., Scots pine, Siberian larch, Southern cypress, and western red cedar are nowadays used in other parts of the world. Modified wood, such as acetylated, furfurylated or thermally modified timber, can also be charred to achieve an overall more durable product for exterior use.

Depending on how the process is performed, and on the wood species used, different degrees of surface charring (texture) and colour can be achieved. There are differences in process conditions for conifers and broad-leaved woods. Conifers have a shallower char depth because of a larger flame spread than broad-leaved woods, and the resin in conifers may also lead to non-uniform thermal conductance during treatment.

Industrial charring processes

Charcoal cannot burn as long as pyrolysis gases are streaming from the interior, providing a barrier to the presence of oxygen and preventing combustion. As the wood constituents evaporate and the wood shrinks, its surface cracks, resulting in a sharp increase in surface temperature and combustion at around 370°C. A good understanding of the different phenomena taking place during the process is, thus, required in order to avoid combustion and to "steer" the cracking of the charcoal layer so that the desired appearance is reached. Pyrolysis of wood is a well-researched process (e.g., Zaror and Pyle, 1982; Nyazika et al., 2019; Sinha et al., 2000), but there are few studies of surface charring (e.g., Kymäläinen et al., 2017).

Traditionally, the surface is burned with a naked flame. While it is possible to regulate the appearance, the actual surface temperature and the evenness of the surface properties are hard to control and regulate. The surface tends to crack and zones of char layers of varying thickness are created that behave differently when exposed due to weathering, for example. A thick char layer of at least 2–3 mm must be formed in order to provide a layer durable to weathering. Many broad-leaved woods do not achieve this thickness, raising doubts about the suitability of broad-leaved woods for charred surfaces. When exposed to rain and UV radiation, the sacrificial char layer erodes slowly, maintaining its black char colour and its preservative benefits. The use of an oil to create a harder char layer may improve the durability of the layer. For indoor conditions, the thickness of the char layer is not critical.

A hot plate with a weight can be used to control the temperature during the process (e.g., Tu et al., 2008). In addition, applying simultaneous surface densification may promote favourable properties of the products making the surface harder and less porous, and giving a more even depth and physical properties of the char layer. The charring time should be kept short, but the charring temperature can be very high, although a high temperature promotes cracking. For optimal performance, a sufficient pyrolysis zone is needed, and this requires optimising both holding time and temperature.

The traditional way of preparing a charred surface involves charring the wood surface over an open flame, cooling, cleaning with a wire brush, and finishing with a clear oil. The industrialised process has the same flow but is more automated (Figure 3.6). The process speed is in most cases only a few metres per minute, the speed depending on the degree of charring to be achieved.

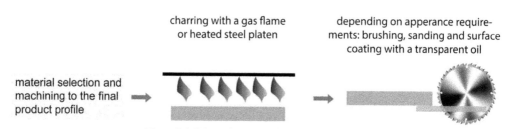

Figure 3.6 Schematic presentation of wood charring.

Properties of charred wood

The charring process not only changes the appearance but is also said to improve properties such as fire-resistance, and lower the water-uptake through the carbonisation and thus make the wood more durable. The charred surface also protects against attack by insects and prevents greying of wood as a result of weathering.

Figure 3.7 show examples of standard traditional charred surfaces: Suyaki (original charred), Gendai (brushed once), and Pika-Pika (brushed twice). The hydrophobic char layer and hardened

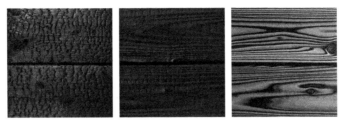

Figure 3.7 Traditional yakisugi surfaces: Suyaki (left), oiled Gendai (middle), and oiled Pika-pika (right).

surface retards weathering, making it maintenance-optional. The surface can also be stained to give the surface a specific colour or appearance.

Kymäläinen et al. (2017) studied the moisture behaviour of Norway spruce and Scots pine sapwood subjected to a series of charring processes (30–120 minutes) at a moderate temperature of 250°C and to a short process (30 seconds) at a high temperature of 400°C, using a contact-heating system with a hot plate to achieve charring. The result was an increase in moisture resistance of charred spruce sapwood but an increase in water uptake by pine sapwood. Heat conduction measurements showed that only a thin layer of the wood was thermally modified. Čermák et al. (2019) performed similar tests but with European beech at a temperature of 220°C under atmospheric pressure for 15 or 40 minutes. The surface charring gave a 20% reduction in the equilibrium moisture content as a result of a decrease in hydroxyl groups, an increase in cellulose crystallinity and a further crosslinking of lignin in the thermally modified layer. The absorption of water decreased by about 15% compared to that of the untreated wood. A significant increase in soluble carbohydrates as well as phenolic compounds was found, and the one-sided charring affected the wood properties to a depth of 2–3 mm beneath the surface.

Applications for charred wood

Yakisugi is a traditional Japanese wall and ceiling cladding made exclusively from sugi and burned intensely as a preservative thermal treatment. The Japanese charring process is never used on timber for flooring or furniture since sugi is too soft for flooring, and yakisugi timber is too thin for most furniture applications. The traditional charred timber cladding is available under a number of brands, including *Shou Sugi Ban*. The charring procedure improves siding longevity by preventing decay and insect infestation, makes the wood more dimensionally stable as the water uptake is reduced, and improves fire retardancy. Yakisugi is a maintenance-optional exterior wood siding, being either re-oiled periodically to slow down the weathering process, or simply replaced after its lifetime is ended.

Traditionally in Japan, yakisugi is combined with white stucco on exterior walls, each region having a different design aesthetic, and it is used nowadays in residential, commercial, and institutional applications as a healthy, sustainable, and beautiful alternative to inorganic, carbon-intensive materials. It is installed as exterior siding either vertically or horizontally, and is also used as exposed roof deck, soffit, and interior wall and ceiling panelling. Typical dimensions of yakisugi claddings are a thickness of 10–15 mm, and a width of 90–200 mm.

Various engineered wood products (EWPs) with charred surfaces have become popular with architects for their appearance and they are mostly used for interior walls and exterior façades, decking and fences. The degree of charring can be adapted according to the use and desired appearance. There are several producers of charred wood worldwide, who either follow the Japanese yakisugi tradition or use their own charring processes and their own trademarks.

Table 3.1 summarises the applications for charred wood.

Table 3.1 Applications of charred wood divided into Use Classes, see Table 1.7.

Product type/Use Class	Interior 1	2	Exterior 3	4	5
Indoor furniture	x				
Floor and non-structural interior uses	x	x			
Exterior joinery			x		
Cladding			x		
Decking					
Fencing			x		
Outdoor furniture			x		
Construction elements			x		
In-ground timber					
Products exposed to water			(x)		

where: x = products have been produced by companies using the modified wood
(x) = products may be produced, based on pre-commercial trials, research, etc.

3.3 Water as a modification agent for wood

From an environmental perspective, the thermally-based modification (TBM) processes shown in Figure 3.8 are extremely interesting because they are implemented to improve the properties of the wood, to produce new materials and to provide the form and functionality desired by engineers, architects, and designers without changing the eco-friendly characteristics of the material.

More recent process developments, like *frictional wood welding*, are described in Section 3.7 and the recent development of moulded tubes is considered in Section 3.9. A more thoroughly history of the TH, TM and THM treatments can be found in Navi and Sandberg (2012).

Water is a good plasticiser of wood, transforming wood to a state where the material has a much lower elastic modulus and can be formed plastically. This happens when the wood material is heated above its *glass-transition temperature* T_g (cf. Figures 1.87 to 1.89), which is strongly affected by its moisture-content, an increase in moisture content decreasing the T_g of the amorphous components of wood and vice versa (cf. Figure 1.88). There is a risk that an increase in temperature will degrade the constituents of the wood material (i.e., by thermolysis and ultimately pyrolysis), but the manner in which the degradation process develops is strongly dependent on the temperature and on the environment, i.e., access to oxygen, relative humidity, air/process pressure, and wood species. The degradation products from the wood constituents may also be involved in the degradation process. The temperature is an important component when wood is to be modified solely with the help of water or moisture, but a temperature above 300°C is of limited practical value due to the severe degradation of the wood constituents, even though there may be exceptions (see Section 3.2).

A TBM treatment has an important advantage over a chemical treatment because water is the only additive, and this is a good base for producing an environment-friendly product. However, additives may be included in the TM and THM processes, as with laminated veneer products, where an adhesive is used to lock the veneers into the desired shape, and some additives may have a negative environmental impact.

In a TH process, wood is heated in a moist atmosphere or in water. This softens the material, releases internal stresses and chemically changes some of the wood constituents. The TH treatments include many types of process:

- wet heating of wood to release internal stresses and to soften the wood before peeling veneer, for example, and this may also change the colour of the wood,
- industrial wood drying at elevated temperatures,

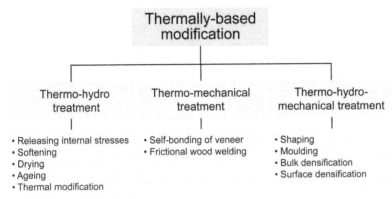

Figure 3.8 TBM processes were water act as an modification agent in the process.

- accelerated ageing of wood mostly for indoor use, to make the wood surface appear older (see Section 3.5), and

- thermal modification (see Section 3.4) to reduce the wood hygroscopicity, improve the dimensional stability, and enhance its resistance to micro-organisms.

TH treatment of raw material to achieve the desired properties of reconstituted wooden composites, such as paper, fibreboards, particleboard, plywood and wood plastic composites (WPCs), is sometimes also included in the group of TBM processes.

In a TM process, heat from an external source or generated by the process itself is combined with external forces to join wood. Moisture is involved only as a certain moisture content of the material, and no special attention is given to the moisture effect of the process. Examples of typical TM products are:

- densified and thermally modified veneer-based panels without adhesive,

- welded wood dowels in cross-laminated timber, and

- products based on welded solid-wood components.

In a THM process, moisture has an intended effect on the process result and is, therefore, more controlled than in a TH or TM process. Force may be applied to the wood in the longitudinal direction, in the transverse directions, or in a combination of both. In the longitudinal direction, the force may be tensile or compressive, but in the transverse directions, the force is usually compressive. The purpose may be either to compress the cell structure to permanently increase the bulk density or merely to increase the density of the wood surface, to shape the wood material in its cross-section or into a 3D-form. Examples of typical THM products are:

- surface-densified flooring,

- bulk-densified wood components for electrical installations or wear-resistant mechanical transmissions, and

- various types of shaped wood mainly for furniture and interior joinery.

Several TBM techniques, such as wood drying, reconstituted wood processing, wood bending, and laminated veneer processing (cf. Fig. 3.9), have a long industrial tradition and are well described in other handbooks (e.g., Navi and Sandberg, 2012) and are, therefore, not discussed further herein. This chapter focusses on processes that have recently been successfully industrialised or which are believed to be close to an industrial implementation. These include the following:

TH processes

- thermal modification

- wood ageing

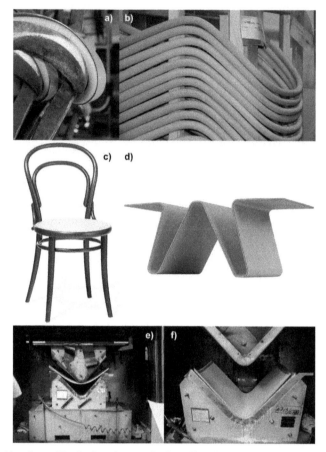

Figure 3.9 Solid-wood bending and lamination of veneer (laminated bending) are two traditional THM processes, which are common in the wood industry for the manufacture of furniture components, for example. Solid wood bending: (a) European beech under bending, (b) furniture components, and (c) Thonét chair No. 14. Laminated bending: (d) finished product (newsstand) of laminated white birch, and (e–f) moulding of veneer for a chair seat.

TM processes

- self-bonding of veneer
- frictional wood welding

THM processes

- wood bulk densification
- surface wood densification
- moulded tubes and shells

All the processes listed above, together with wood charring in Section 3.2, have in common that at least some degradation of the wood occurs during the processing.

Chemistry of TBM treatment

In the thermal treatment of wood, the chemical structure is transformed by autocatalytic reactions of the cell-wall constituents. Under moist conditions, carboxylic acids, mainly acetic acid, are initially formed as a result of cleavage of the acetyl groups, particularly of hemicelluloses (Kollmann and Fengel, 1965). Depending on the acid concentration and the temperature, the hemicelluloses are hydrolysed into oligomeric and monomeric structures (Klauditz and Stegmann, 1955; Bobleter and Binder, 1980), and the monomeric sugar units are subsequently dehydrated to aldehydes, furfural being formed from pentoses and hydroxymethylfurfural from hexose sugar units (Burtscher et al., 1987; Kaar et al., 1991; Ellis and Paszner, 1994).

As the temperature increases, cell-wall polymers start to degrade. Pyrolysis of the hemicelluloses takes place at about 270°C, followed closely by that of the cellulose. Lignin is more stable and degrades at high temperatures (Stamm, 1956).

The thermally labile acetyl groups significantly affect the thermal degradation of hemicelluloses. The degradation starts with deacetylation and the acetic acid released acts as a depolymerisation catalyst and increases the polysaccharide decomposition (Tjeerdsma et al., 1998). Acid-catalysed degradation leads to the formation of formaldehyde, furfural, and other aldehydes (Tjeerdsma et al., 1998). At the same time, hemicelluloses undergo dehydration with a loss of hydroxyl groups (Weiland and Guyonnet, 2003).

Rowell et al. (2009) undertook a sugar analysis of aspen before and after a treatment with saturated steam at 220°C for 8 minutes in a closed system, and they showed that, in the early stages of weight loss, the hemicellulose polymers broke down while the cellulose remained unchanged. Over half of the arabinans and rhamnans were lost during this initial heating (Table 3.2).

The greater resistance of cellulose than of hemicelluloses has been reported by the likes of Bourgois and Guyonnet (1988) and Yildiz et al. (2006). The amorphous cellulose degrades forming furans such as hydroxymethylfurfural and furfural (Figure 3.10), and the loss of amorphous cellulose leads to an increase in cellulose crystallinity (Bhuiyan et al., 2000, 2001). The hemicelluloses

Table 3.2 Sugar analysis of aspen before and after heat treatment with saturated steam at 220°C in a closed system for 8 minutes (Rowell et al., 2009).

	Before heat treatment	**After heat treatment**
Weight loss (%)	0	2.2
Arabinan (%)	0.56	0.20
Galactan (%)	0.68	0.58
Rhamnan (%)	0.30	0.14
Glucan (%)	42.4	42.2
Xylan (%)	16.3	14.6
Mannan (%)	1.6	1.5
Total carbohydrate (%)	61.8	59.2

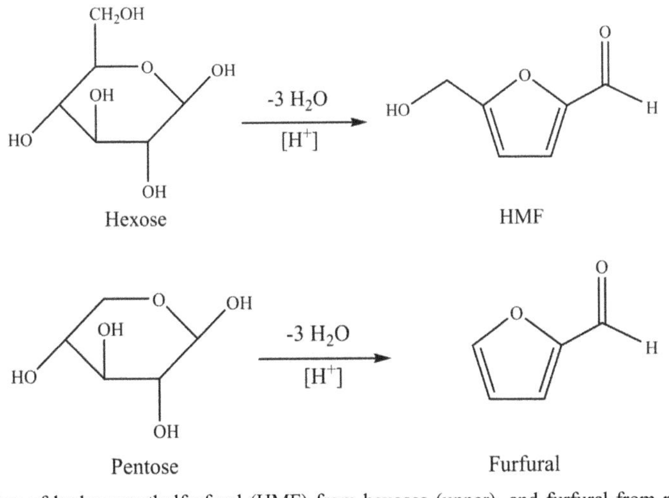

Figure 3.10 Formation of hydroxymethylfurfural (HMF) from hexoses (upper), and furfural from pentoses (lower) as a result of the thermal modification of wood.

and cellulose are also degraded to internal ethers and other rearrangement products. The maximum amount of water that can be lost is three molecules of water from two anhydroglucose units, i.e., 16.7% of the carbohydrate polymers or 12% of the wood (Stamm and Baechler, 1960).

Lignin is the least reactive wood component but, at temperatures above 200°C, bonds within the lignin complex are cleaved, resulting in a higher concentration of phenolic groups (Runkel, 1951). This increase in reactivity of the lignin leads to various condensation reactions of aldehydes and lignin and to the auto-condensation of lignin. Polycondensation reactions with other cell-wall components, resulting in further cross-linking, contribute to an apparent increase in the lignin content (Bourgois and Guyonnet, 1988; Dirol and Guyonnet, 1993). The cleavage of ether linkages, especially β-O-4 linkages, and a reduction of the methoxyl content leads to a more condensed structure (Nuopponen et al., 2004; Wikberg and Maunu, 2004).

Most of the extractives evaporate or are degraded during the heat treatment, especially the most volatile, but new compounds that can be extracted are created by the degradation of cell-wall structural components. Bourgois et al. (1989) extracted waxes, carbohydrates, tannins, resins, and small amounts of hemicelluloses from maritime pine treated at temperatures between 240°C and 290°C.

Liquid and gaseous phases are formed at temperatures between 200°C and 300°C. The liquid phase is almost exclusively water and acetic acid with small amounts of formic acid, furfural, and methanol. The acids catalyse the degradation of polysaccharides and reduce their degree of polymerisation (Militz, 2002a).

Thermal degradation and process conditions

Wood degrades faster when heated in steam or water than when heated under dry conditions (MacLean, 1951; MacLean, 1953). With increasing treatment time, the wood becomes more brittle (Yao and Taylor, 1979). In general, broad-leaved woods are less thermally stable than conifers, which is attributed to differences in the content and composition of hemicelluloses (Hill, 2006). The weight loss from broad-leaved woods is greater than that from conifers, probably due to the greater content of acetyl groups in broad-leaved woods and the release of acetic acid during heat treatment which promotes acid hydrolysis (MacLean, 1951; MacLean, 1953).

The strength loss during thermal treatment is due to the hydrolysis of hemicelluloses, which is influenced by moisture, temperature, time and access to oxygen. Heating wood in the presence of water or steam leads to the formation of organic acids, mainly acetic acid, which catalyse the hydrolysis of the hemicelluloses to soluble sugars, thus speeding up the degradation process (Hillis, 1975; McGinnis et al., 1984). This means that higher temperatures are needed to achieve the same degree of degradation in the case of dry wood versus moist wood.

Differences in degradation have been found between wood treated in a closed system and wood treated in an open system (Stamm, 1956; Stamm, 1964). Heating in a closed system results in more rapid degradation, because there is a build-up of degradation products, such as acetic acid, that can interact with the chemical reactions taking place and trigger the degradation process.

The rate of thermal degradation is also dependent on the surrounding atmosphere, especially with regard to the presence or absence of oxygen. Stamm (1956) demonstrated that the thermal degradation of wood is more rapid in the presence of oxygen than in an oxygen-free atmosphere. The presence of oxygen results in a process known as wet oxidation, where the initial reaction is the formation of acids. As these acids increase in concentration, hydrolytic reactions become favourable. The rate of hydrolysis is increased not only for hemicelluloses but also for cellulose (McGinnis et al., 1984). Thus, both hydrolysis and oxidation occur in the thermal degradation of wood. The degradation is greater in oxygen than in a vacuum, but this is also related to a lower energy transfer in a vacuum (Stamm, 1964). The presence of oxygen can be prevented by using an inert atmosphere, such as nitrogen, oil, steam or water. Using steam is an efficient and cheap way of creating an inert atmosphere, but the moisture influences the reactions that take place during treatment.

3.4 Thermal modification processes

The modification of wood by heat without chemical additives and with a limited supply of oxygen to prevent oxidative combustion, i.e., *thermal modification*, is a generally accepted and commercialised procedure for improving some characteristics of wood (Jones et al., 2019). The resulting product, *thermally modified timber (TMT)* according to CEN (2008), should be distinguish it from heat sterilisation at lower temperature ($\approx 55°C$) with the purpose of killing pests in solid wood materials and preventing their transfer between continents and regions. The idea in thermal modification is to alter the internal chemical composition of the material by exploiting the internal reactivity of the material and the removal of some of its active sites instead of adding reagents capable of interacting with the reactive sites. The changes in the wood during thermal modification are fairly-well understood, involving softening and the redistribution of lignin components, the loss of acid groups and cross-linking and repolymerisation that occur to varying degrees depending on the wood species. The process conditions play a significant role in the chemistry which takes place, hydrolysis and catalysis occurring more in closed system processes, for example.

The control of wood moisture during a process, e.g., an increased but unsaturated steam pressure, avoids the development of internal stresses and excessive brittleness in the TMT. One of the key reactions in thermal modification is the conversion of polysaccharides present within the hemicelluloses.

At temperatures between 160°C and 220°C (CEN, 2008), the main purpose is to ameliorate material properties, such as to increase the biological durability, to enhance the dimension stability, and also to control the colour changes. Thermal modification has also been applied to reduce resin bleed. The principal effects of heating wood were known already in the early 19th Century. Tredgold (1820) quoted the Encyclopaedia Britannia and states that steaming of wood improves its resistance to white rot, but he referred also to Duhamel du Monceau (1767) stating that steaming and boiling led to mass loss. Other early examples of wood being thermally modified to improve its resistance to decay are postholes from Scandinavian Bronze-age buildings, showing concentrations of charcoal indicating that the ends of the posts had been charred (Källander, 2016). Charring (see Section 3.2) is now seen as a separate process from thermal modification, and is mainly applied to wood for exterior use above ground in façades, or for interior use for aesthetic reasons.

More systematic studies of the influence of drying temperature and humidity on the strength of different species began in the early 20th Century and were related to the development of the aviation industry in the United States (Tiemann, 1915; Tiemann, 1920; Wilson, 1920; Koehler and Pillow, 1925; Pillow, 1929; Stamm and Hansen, 1937). Tiemann (1942) summarised the results of these studies, showing that wood treated at temperatures between about 60°C and 170°C in dry air, in saturated steam, or in superheated steam for various lengths of time and then re-soaked or exposed to atmospheric conditions for several months or a year had a lower strength and hygroscopicity and a darker colour, particularly after treatment at higher temperatures.

According to CEN (2008), thermally modified timber is wood in which the composition of the cell-wall material and its physical properties have been modified by exposure to a temperature higher than 160°C with limited access to oxygen. There are various processes to achieve this, mostly differing in the way they exclude air/oxygen from the system (Navi and Sandberg, 2012). A steam or nitrogen atmosphere can be used, or the wood can be immersed in hot oil.

During the 1980s, French and Japanese industries began to modify wood by heating in order to increase the resistance to microbial attack, and since then interest has increased all over the world. The underlying reason for applying thermal modification is the increasing demand for an environment-friendly highly durable construction material, where the service life has been increased without the use of toxic chemicals.

Material selection and preparation

Thermal modification processes can be applied to a wide range of wood species, but the process must be optimised for each species. Species with a low resistance to microbiological attack or poor shape stability are the most preferred, but the improvements gained are highly dependent on the process conditions.

Conifer woods were thermally modified and commercially available during the introduction of the process, but companies have recently started to look at broad-leaved woods. Thermal modification can be used simply to achieve timber with a darker and more uniform colour. Several high-value tropical species with high durability have been thermally modified (e.g., Gašparík et al., 2019; Ditommaso et al., 2020) but it is difficult to understand the reason for the modification of such species. Table 3.3 summarises the thermal treatment of various species reported in scientific articles, but other species may also have been tested.

Table 3.3 Thermal modification of various wood and plant species. P – pressure, RH – relative humidity.

Specie	Temperature (°C)	Duration (hours)	Reference
Acacia hybrid (sapwood)	210–230	2–6	Tuong and Li (2011)
Balkan beech	170, 190, 210	4	Todorović et al. (2015)
Bamboo	130, 180	2 or 5	Nguyen et al. (2012)
	130, 220	2 or 5	Bremer et al. (2013)
Bamboo	140–200	0.5–2	Manalo and Garcia (2012)
Black pine	130, 180, 230	2 or 8	Akyildiz and Ates (2008)
Black spruce	190, 200, 210		Lekounougou and Kocaefe (2014)
Calabrian pine	130, 180, 230	2 or 8	Akyildiz and Ates (2008), Ates et al. (2009)
Common aspen	195		Wikberg and Maunu (2004)
	160–170	1 or 3	Grinins et al. (2013)
	170	1	Cirule et al. (2016)
Common oak	160		Wikberg and Maunu (2004)
	160, 180, 210, 240		Barcík et al. (2015ab)
European alder	150, 180, 200	2, 6 or 10	Yildiz et al. (2011)
European ash	180, 200	3	Majka and Roszyk (2018)
	190	2.5	Cai et al. (2020)
European beech	180, 200, 220	4	Bächle et al. (2010)
	160, 190		Boruszewski et al. (2011)
	170, 180, 190, 212	2	Kol and Sefil (2011)
	125–130	6.5	Dzurenda (2013)
	170	3	Altgen et al. (2020a)
European white birch	160, 190		Boruszewski et al. (2011)
Fir	170, 180, 190, 212	2	Kol and Sefil (2011)
	160, 220		Allegretti et al. (2012)
	100, 150, 200, 220, 240, 260, 280	1, 3 or 5	Kučerová et al. (2019)
Flooded gum	180, 200, 220, 240	4 or 8	de Cademartori et al. (2013a)
Grey alder	160–170	1 or 3	Grinins et al. (2013)
Gympie messmate	180, 200, 220, 240	4	de Cademartori et al. (2013b)
Mantsurian poplar	160, 180, 200, 220, 240	4	Wang et al. (2015)
	180–220	4	Ling et al. (2016)
Maritime pine	170–200	2–24	Esteves et al. (2008a)
Meranti	160, 180, 210	about 3	Gašparík et al. (2019)

Table 3.3 Contd. ...

...Table 3.3 Contd.

Specie	Temperature (°C)	Duration (hours)	Reference
Merbau	160, 180, 210	about 3	Ditommaso et al. (2020)
Narrow-leaved ash	160, 180	2 or 4	Korkut et al. (2012)
	140, 180, 200, 220	2, 4 or 6	Yalcin and Sahin (2015)
Norway spruce	160–260	2–8	Kotilainen et al. (2000)
	195		Wikberg and Maunu (2004)
	200	2, 4, 8, 10 or 24	Bekhta and Niemz (2003)
	100, 150	24	
	200	0.08, 0.5 or 1	Follrich et al. (2006)
	180, 200, 220	4	Bächle et al. (2010)
	160, 220		Allegretti et al. (2012)
	113, 134, 158, 187, 221, 237, 253, 271	1.5	Kačíková et al. (2013)
	180	2	Cai et al. (2020)
Oil palm mesocarp fibre	190–230	1, 2 or 3	Nordin et al. (2013)
Oleaster-leafed pear	160, 180, 200	3, 5 or 7	Gunduz et al. (2009)
Oriental beech	130, 150, 180, 200	2, 6, or 10	Yildiz et al. (2005)
	150, 160, 170	1, 3, 5, or 7	Charani et al. (2007)
Paulownia	160, 180, 200	3, 5 or 7	Kaygin et al. (2009)
	150, 170	0.75	Candan et al. (2013)
Rubberwood	210–240	1–8	Srinivas and Pandey (2012)
Red-bud maple	120, 150, 180	2, 6 or 10	Korkut et al. (2008a,b), Korkut and Guller (2008)
Scots pine	160	5	Burmester (1973)
	160–260	2–8	Kotilainen et al. (2000)
	120, 150, 180	2, 6 or 10	Korkut et al. (2008a,b)
	180, 200, 240		Kekkonen et al. (2010)
	160, 180, 210, 240		Barcík et al. (2015a)
	125, 140, 155, 170	3	Altgen et al. (2020b)
	180	2	Cai et al. (2020)
	225	3	Willems et al. (2020)
Sessile oak	130, 180, 230	2 or 8	Akyildiz and Ates (2008)
Silver oak	210–240	1–8	Srinivas and Pandey (2012)
	185–230	2–3	Sikora et al. (2018)
Small-leaved lime	140	up to 504	Popescu et al. (2013a,b), Popescu and Popescu (2013)
Sweet chestnut	130, 180, 230	2 or 8	Akyildiz and Ates (2008)
	160, 180	2 or 4	Korkut et al. (2012)
Teak	160, 180, 210	about 3	Gašparík et al. (2019)
Turkish hazel	120, 150, 180	2, 6 or 10	Korkut and Hiziroglu (2009)
Warty birch	195		Wikberg and Maunu (2004)
	140, 160, 180	1	Biziks et al. (2013)
	160–170	1 or 3	Grinins et al. (2013)
	160, 180, 210, 240		Barcík et al. (2015a)
Western red cedar	220	1 or 2	Awoyemi and Jones (2011)

Several quality specifications must be met for sawn timber to be thermally modified, such as knot type, size and number, and also heartwood content.

Industrial thermal modification processes

Industrial thermal modification processes typically aim at improving the biological durability of less durable wood species and enhancing the dimensional stability of the wood or wood-based products. Stamm et al. (1946) made the first systematic attempts to increase the resistance to wood-destroying fungi by heating wood beneath the surface of molten metal, with a patent granted to Stamm (1942) that was perhaps the first thermal modification process. Stamm et al. (1946) found that heating Sitka spruce to between 140 and 320°C resulted in reduced swelling, improved the dimensional stability, and increased the resistance to microbial attack. The success of the method was, however, limited, and the work extended with a focus on different gaseous atmospheres by Thunell and Elken (1948), and with heating beneath a molten metal by Buro (1954, 1955).

The *Feuchte-Wärme-Druck (FWD) process* was introduced by Burmester in the 1970s (1970, 1973, 1975, 1981) where Scots pine at an initial moisture content of 20–30% was modified in a closed system at 160°C and 0.6 MPa pressure, for about 5 hours in steam. This was one of the first commercial wood modification units in Europe. It started in Germany around 1980 but it never reached any significant production volume (Giebler, 1983). The work by Burmester was, however, pioneering in the field and it has been the basis of several successful thermal-modification processes, but it was not until 1990, when the Finnish Research Centre VTT together with the Finnish industry developed the ThermoWood™ process, that thermal treatment was established as an industrial process for the improvement of wood properties. This process is nowadays licenced to members of the International ThermoWood Association, which was founded in 2000 and through which ThermoWood™ was officially established and the treatment classes Thermo-S and Thermo-D introduced.

In most industrialised processes, thermal modification involves temperatures between 160°C and 260°C (CEN, 2008) and is usually carried out in a vacuum, in steam or in an inert gas, such as nitrogen. Pre-heated oil can also be used, in which case the oil acts as a heat-transfer medium and excludes oxygen from the wood. The thermal treatment of wood above 300°C is of limited practical value due to the severe degradation of the wood material (see Sections 3.1 and 3.2).

Thermal modification is a complex process involving both physical processes, such as the evaporation of moisture and volatile components, the rearrangement of resins, shrinkage, and chemical changes, such as depolymerisation, re-condensation, carbonisation, and devolatilisation, that may act in the same direction or counteract each other. The complexity of the process increases as the temperature is raised in the process, and degraded products can act as catalysts for further reactions. Moisture available for both hydrolysis and catalysts is formed, continuously moving from the interior to the wood surface and evaporating (cf. Perré, 2011). Both the physical and chemical environments inside the wood change during the process, and the dimensions of the material treated influence both the heat and the mass flux. The internal temperature, moisture levels, concentration of catalysts, and removal of volatile and non-volatile products in a small wood sample differ greatly from those in sawn timber (Källander, 2016).

In an overview of the existing European thermal modification processes, Jones et al. (2019) state that the estimated annual production of thermally modified timber is about 535,000 m³, and they list several commercial processes that have become established the Finnish ThermoWood™, the Plato Wood™ and FirmoLin™ processes in The Netherlands, the German OHT™ process, and the French Retification™ and Bois Perdure™ processes, the Danish WTT™ process, and the Huber Holz™ process in Austria. To date, several different production technologies are being used on various natural wood species with a wide range of process conditions, each leading to a customised type of material, which needs to be individually characterised for production quality control and for assurance of the application-dependent product performance. Table 3.4 summarises the main commercial processes.

Thermally modified timber (TMT) is wood material that has been subjected to a thermal treatment, leading to the significant and simultaneous modification of properties, such as mass, colour, equilibrium moisture content, moisture swelling, toughness and fungal resistance. It is defined, according to CEN (2008), for a specific temperature ranges, but such a definition is meaningless without further specification of the heating process and the wood species, and the lack of a generally accepted objective measure of the thermal modification level means that this material is still poorly defined. It is, therefore, important to state and define the specifications of the product and thus the specific thermal-modification process used.

Although several thermal-modification techniques have been commercialised, all the processes have similar process flows that can be described as shown schematically in Figure 3.11.

The main differences between the methods are in the materials used (e.g., wood species, green or dried wood, moisture content, dimensions), the process conditions applied (e.g., one or two process stages, wet or dry, steaming, heating medium, or nitrogen for the protection of the wood from oxygen, heating and cooling velocity) and the equipment employed (e.g., process vessel or kiln).

The *open* and *closed systems* differ mainly in the humidity during treatment and in the treatment of the degradation components. In open systems at atmospheric pressures, volatile organic compounds (VOCs) are released from the treated wood and the modification zone. The removal of VOCs is even more pronounced in processes operating at sub-atmospheric pressure under vacuum conditions (Allegretti et al., 2012), but in closed reactor systems at elevated pressures, VOCs are retained and these accumulated degradation products act as catalysts for further reactions (Stamm, 1956).

The ThermoWood™ process (Viitanen et al., 1994) is currently the most used process, based on heating in atmospheric superheated steam. Other atmospheric processes are being used in smaller industrial plants, employing inert gas (Dirol and Guyonnet, 1993) or hot oil heating (Sailer et al., 2000). In sub-atmospheric autoclave processes, wood is heated convectively with low-pressure steam (Alegretti et al., 2012) or conductively between hot plates (Van Acker et al., 2010). The common features of all the open processes are the temperature range up to 240°C and the continuous removal of degradation products, whereas closed processes (cf. Seborg et al., 1953; Burmester, 1973; Giebeler, 1983) all adopt water vapour pressures of at least several hundred kPa and temperatures ranging between 160°C and 200°C, leading to faster kinetics than at atmospheric pressure at the same temperature.

A typical process with a gaseous oxygen-excluding medium is the Retification™ process developed by École des Mines de Saint-Étienne in France. Wood at a moisture content of approximately 12% is heated slowly in a vessel to between 210°C and 240°C in a *nitrogen atmosphere* with less than 2% oxygen present. A typical time for the process is between 8 and 24 hours.

Oil as an oxygen-excluding medium was used in the OHT™ (oil-heat treatment) process, developed by the Menz Holz company in Germany. The process normally uses crude vegetable oils, such as rapeseed, linseed or sunflower oil, at a temperature between 180°C and 220°C for a period of 2–4 hours. The typical duration of a whole treatment cycle, including the heating and cooling stages (which strongly depend on the dimensions) for timber with a cross section of 100 mm by 100 mm and a length of 4 metres is 18 hours (Rapp and Sailer, 2000). For maximum durability with minimum oil consumption, the process should be operated at 220°C. The wood takes up oil to an amount in the region of 20–60 kg/m³ timber, although this is of secondary importance when the wood properties are compared with the actual thermal modification. Before the process vessel is unloaded, the hot oil is pumped back into the stock vessel and recycled for the next batch of timber to be treated. The consistency and colour of the oil may however change during thermal treatment and, depending on the oil-type, it may become thicker because of the evaporation of volatile compounds, and because products from decomposition of the wood accumulate in the oil.

The most common procedure is to use steam under atmospheric conditions or in a closed system. There are several different technical concepts (vacuum processes, atmospheric processes,

Table 3.4 Examples of thermal-modification processes and their process conditions. Treatment temperatures for different stages of the process are separated by /. MC – moisture content, FWD – Feuchte-Wärme-Druck, OHT – oil heat treatment. X, Y and Z mean information not available.

Process	Patent[1] (year)	First ind.[2] (year)	Trademarks™	System[3] Open/closed	MC[4] (%)	Temperature[5] (°C)	Process duration[6] (hours)	Heat transfer[7]	Heating medium[8]	Atmosphere[9]	Pressure[10] (MPa)	Reactor type[11]
Bicos (RU)				Open	X/wet_dry/Z	180–240	32–54	Fluid contact	Organic oil		0.3	Autoclave
FirmoLin (NL)	2008–2009 (NL)		Firmolin	Closed	12/moist/8	150–175	up to 24/x	Convective	Steam	Pressurised	0.45–0.8	Autoclave
FWD (DE)	1979 (DE)	~ 1975, 2001	FWD-Holz, Baldur-Antikholz (CH)	Closed	8–12 (30)/ wet/Z	170–200	16–30/5–7	Convective	Steam	Pressurised	0.5–0.7	Autoclave
Le Bois Perdure (FR)		~ 1990	Perdure		green/Y/Z	200–230 (240)	12–36	Convective	Steam	Atmospheric	0.1	Autoclave
Lignius (NL)	Yes	2002	SmartHeat	Open	X/Y/Z	200–240	X/Y	Contact heating	Metal plate	Vacuum	0.1	
Stellac (FI)	1997 (FI)		StellacWood	Open	< 15/OD/5	up to 250	X/Y	Convective	Dry-steam	Atmospheric	0.1	Kiln
OHT (DE)	1979 (DE)	2000	OHT, Menzholz, pannaq	Open	6/OD/Z	180–200 (240)	18–30/2–4	Fluid contact	Vegetable oils	Atmospheric	0.1	Immersion tank
Plato (NL)	1989 (EU)	2001	PlatoWood	Hybrid	14–18/ OD/4–6	150–180/150– 190 (165–185)	70–120 up to 2 weeks/4-5/	Convective & condensing	Saturated steam	Pressurised	0.6–0.8	Auotclave/ kiln
Retification (FR)	1996 (FR)	1986 (FR)	Retibois, NOW - New Option Wood	Open	~ 12/OD/Z	210–240 (260)	8–24/Y	Convective	Nitrogen	Atmospheric	0.1	Autoclave
SilvaProduct (SI)	2004 (SI)	2012	SilvaproWood	Open	X/Y/Z		X/Y			Vacuum	0.09	Autoclave
Staybwood (US)	1942 (US)		Staybwood	Open	~ 10/0/0	~ 260–315	0.2–2/Y	Fluid contact	Molten metal, fused salts, etc.	Atmospheric	0.1	Immersion tank
Tanwood				Closed	X/wet/Z	160–180	X/Y	Condensing	Steam		0.6–1.0	Autoclave

Process	Patent[1]	First industrial plant[2]	System[3]	MC[4] X/OD/Z	Temperature[5]	Process duration[6]	Heat transfer[7]	Heating medium[8]	Atmosphere[9]	Pressure[10]	Reactor type[11]
TERMOVUOTO (IT)	2011 (IT)		Open	X/OD/Z	160–220	up to 25/Y	Convective	Steam	Vacuum	0.015–0.035	Autoclave
ThermoWood (FI)	1993 (FI)	1998–1999	Open	10(G)/OD/4–7	130/185–215/80–90*	30–70/Y	Convective	Dry-steam	Atmospheric	0.1	Kiln
Vacu3 (DE)		2008	Open	14–18/OD/Z	200–240 (175–230)	11–28/1–4	Solid contact	Metal plate	Vacuum	0.015–0.060	Kiln with press
VAP Holzsysteme (BR)			Closed	X/wet/Z	160–180	ca. 16/0.75	Condensing	Steam	Pressurised	0.3–1.0	Autoclave
WDE-Maspell (DE)				X/Y/Z		X/Y	Convective	Dry steam	Sub-athmospheric		
WTT (DK)		2005	Closed	X/Y/Z	160–210 (180)	up to 12/Y	Fluid contact	Vegetable oils	Pressurised	0.7–0.8	Autoclave
WTT 2.0 (DK)	2016 (DK)		Closed	X/wet/Z	170	up to 12/1.5–2.5	Convective	Nitrogen	Pressurised	0.7–1.4	Autoclave

Notes

[1] Patent: Priority year and country (abbreviations for country names) for the first patent application for the method

[2] First industrial plant: When an industrial production line has been built and the product starts to be available on the market

[3] System: If the thermal-modification process is in an open, closed hybrid system

[4] MC: Moisture content (MC) when the process start (X), during the thermal-modification regime (Y), and after the thermal-modification process (Z), i.e., X/Y/Z% (G – green wood; OD – oven-dry wood)

[5] Temperature: Temperature at which the thermal-modification regime operate

[6] Process duration: Process time for the whole process (X), and only for the thermal modification regime (Y), i.e., X/Y hours

[7] Heat transfer: Convective heating transfer (dry/wet steam, inertgas), fluid contact (water, condensing water, hot oil, melted metal), solid contact to a, e.g., metal plate

[8] Heating medium

[9] Atmosphere: Vacuum, sub-atmospheric, atmospheric or pressurised

[10] Pressure: Absolute pressure

[11] Reactor type: kiln, immersion tank, autoclave

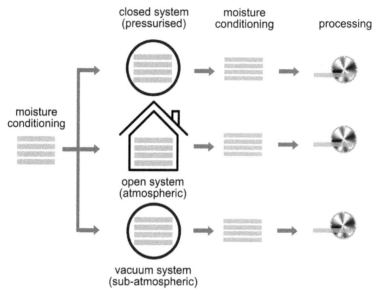

Figure 3.11 Diagram of the process for thermal modification of wood.

pressurised processes) of how to perform the treatment, and the choice has a considerable influence both on the production and on the properties of the thermally modified timber, the choice of process type being related to the company business model.

The ThermoWood™ process is an open four-stage process: (1) an initial heating stage, where the kiln temperature is raised rapidly to about 100°C using heat and steam, (2) a drying process where the temperature is raised slowly from 100°C to 130°C, (3) the modification stage for 2–3 hours at the treatment temperature of 192°C for Thermo-S (S for stability), or at 212°C for Thermo-D (D for durability), and finally (4) a cooling and moisture conditioning stage to a final moisture content of about 4%. To prevent surface and internal cracking, the process is regulated with respect to the internal temperature of the sawn timber, the difference between kiln temperature and wood temperature being dependent on the dimension of the timber. Other modification temperatures may be used, depending on the species used. The ThermoWood™ process in New Zealand treats radiata pine at 230°C, whereas European white birch and aspen are treated at temperatures of 185°C or 200°C for Thermo-S and Thermo-D, respectively.

Steam is also used as the process medium for Le Bois Perdure™, which is a two-step process developed by the French holding company BCI-MBS. Green wood is dried in the kiln and then heated to a temperature of 240°C in a steam atmosphere (steam generated only from moisture from the sawn timber). Sawn timbers processed by this method properties similar to those from the Retification™ process.

The Plato™ (Providing Lasting Advanced Timber Option) process was invented in the 1980s based on findings of Ruyter (1989) who developed the process in the Koninklijke Shell Laboratory in Amsterdam (KSLA) (Ruyter, 1989; Boonstra et al., 1998; Boonstra, 2008). This technology consists of a two-stage treatment under relatively mild conditions, i.e., temperatures below 200°C, with a steam-hydrolysis regime followed by a dry-curing regime. The abundant moisture in the cell wall during the hydro-thermolysis increases the reactivity of the cell-wall components of a relatively low temperature. The stages in this open-system process are: (1) Pre-drying to reduce the moisture content to 14–18%, (2) a hydro-thermolysis regime (stage one) in a stainless steel reactor at a temperature typically between 160°C and 190°C for 4–5 hours in an aqueous environment at a superatmospheric pressure (including saturated steam as the heating medium), (3) conventional wood drying (3–5 days) to dry the treated wood to a low moisture content (ca. 10%), (4) a curing regime (stage two) where the intermediate dry product is heated in a special stainless steel curing kiln to a temperature between 170°C and 190°C for 14–16 hours under dry and atmospheric conditions, and (5) a conditioning regime for 2–3 days to reach a final moisture content between 4 and 6%. The conditioning is carried out in the same conventional industrial wood kiln as the drying stage, and saturated steam is used to increase the moisture content of the treated timber. The total process duration depends on the wood species and on the thickness of the material.

The FirmoLin™ process (*firmo*- is Latin for strong, durable, and -*lin* is the abbreviated of – lignum, i.e., wood in Latin) is a modified and expanded version of the Burmester process (Burmester, 1970; Burmester, 1973; Burmester, 1975; Burmester, 1981) and was developed in The Netherlands (Willems, 2006; Willems, 2008). The process includes thermal treatment of kiln-dried sawn timber or round timber at a moisture content of about 12% under moisture-controlled conditions in pressurised superheated steam (control of air-flow, temperature, relative humidity, total pressure and water-vapour pressure) to avoid excessive drying. Treatment is carried out on a variety of species, but mainly ayous, frake, movingui, poplar spp., Norway spruce, radiata pine and Scots pine are used. With an accurate control strategy, the wood is kept close to a hygroscopic equilibrium with its surroundings during the entire treatment cycle. Treatment-induced internal wood stresses and associated wood degradation are thus minimised. The autoclave is completely closed during the treatment cycle and is, by definition, devoid of any emission of volatile organic substances. The reactive volatiles stay available for re-incorporation into the wood matrix, optimise both strength properties and biological durability, achieved at moderately high temperatures up to a maximum of 175°C. The process usually consists of four steps: (1) A pre-vacuum process to assist reaching the desired pressure, followed by (2) a temperature increase between 10 to 12°C per hour until a peak temperature is reached between 150 and 175°C; (3) A holding step at the peak temperature for 2 to 3 hours, is followed by (4) a finishing and cooling step lowering the temperature by between 15 and 20°C per hour until it reaches 65°C (Willems, 2009). The technique is suitable for the large-scale industrial production of high-quality thermally-modified timber. The first plant using this technology has commenced operation in The Netherlands. An advantage of the FirmoLin™ process is that the moisture content at the end of the process is about 8%, i.e., considerable higher than that achieved in other processes. This means that the risk of internal stresses, hornification, and internal cracking of the wood is much lower, especially for large-dimension timber.

A typical *vacuum process* is Termovuoto™, a patented thermal-modification technology that has been developed by the National Research Council of Italy (IVALSA) and is based on the combination of efficient vacuum drying and thermal modification. In the thermal modification stage, the atmosphere (including the oxygen) inside the vessel is evacuated to create a partial vacuum, and heating is provided by forced convection (Allegretti et al., 2012; Jebrane et al., 2018). The wood is dried initially in air at 100°C until the moisture content reaches 0%. Thereafter, the temperature is raised to 160–220°C under vacuum. Finally, the wood is cooled to 100°C. The total time is between 5 and 9 hours. The vacuum pump continuously removes all volatile compounds that would otherwise contribute to a degradation of polysaccharides in the cell wall. The Termovuoto™ process has several advantages, such as a shorter duration and lower energy consumption, easier and cheaper management of the volatile waste, and less corrosion. The lower mass loss and the odourless product are assumed to be due to the vacuum pump, in that it continuously removed volatile compounds that would otherwise interact with the degradation process (Candelier et al., 2013a,b).

SilvaPro™ is another vacuum-based thermal-modification process developed in Slovenia (Rep et al., 2004; Pohleven and Rep, 2004; Pohleven and Rep, 2008). In 2012, the process was commercialised by the company Silvaprodukt d.o.o. under the trade name SilvaproWood™. The process consists of the three main stages: (1) Wood is initially dried while the temperature is raised to the target temperature of 180°C to 220°C, while the pressure is raised to 900 mbar, (2) the wood is heated at the constant temperature for three hours at the constant pressure, and (3) the wood is cooled to 100°C. The whole process takes between 18 and 20 hours, depending on the temperature. Silvapro™ wood has a greater resistance to natural pests than natural wood, and it has a lower thermal conductivity, a lower equilibrium moisture content and greater dimensional stability, like other TMT. The process can be applied to solid wood and to veneers of conifer woods and broad-leaved woods.

The potential of thermal modification in the US timber market has led to several companies launching their own range of modified wood. One product, VikingWood™, is produced by AHC Hardwood Group, where species such as poplar, ash, red oak, white oak, soft maple, eastern white pine and Southern yellow pine are treated in a pressurised closed reactor at a temperature of 205°C. Another product, Pakari™, is produced by Sunset Moulding in California, USA. The name, meaning *maturity* or *toughness* in Maori, involved modifying radiata pine to temperatures up to 260°C, with the product sold for the decking and cladding applications.

The importance of the ThermoWood™ system for the introduction onto the market of thermal modification should not be underestimated. ThermoWood™ provided a technical solution combined with a branding organisation and a third-party certification system, and it thus created a platform for both joint marketing and joint research and development, both critical aspects in the introduction of any new kind of material.

Industrial quality control

It is important not only for quality control but also for scientific comparison of thermally modified specimens to be able to quantify the degree of modification achieved. Several markers have been proposed for this purpose since it is doubtful whether all the wood properties that are changed by heat treatment can be characterised by a single measurement.

Thermal modification in industry is certified by measuring the temperature and duration of the process, which in turn affect the colour of the wood, and measurement of the wood colour is thus an indirect measure of the treatment intensity. Brischke et al. (2007) stated that measuring colour on chipped wood (shavings, wood dust) from the surface region resulted in less colour variation than measuring the colour directly on the surface of the sawn timber. Thus, colour measurement of chipped wood was recommended for reliable (better statistical significance) quality control. An alternative colour-measuring method suggested by Brischke et al. (2007) was to measure at six locations on each surface of the sawn timber to compensate for natural colour variation. Torniainen et al. (2016) have since confirmed that the colour of thermally modified timber is measurable and predictable with a margin of error that is acceptable for a commercial application.

Research on wood modification is primarily carried out in laboratories, using clear wood specimens treated under well-defined conditions. Laboratory tests differ from industrial treatment with respect to both the size and homogeneity of the material treated and to the size of the batch and kiln used. Källander (2016) showed that both the size of the wood material treated and the size of the kiln or batch strongly influenced the process and the resulting wood properties, and that the sample size influenced different material properties in different ways. The equilibrium moisture content (EMC) was reduced less during the thermal treatment of small clear wood specimens than during the treatment of sawn timber. The mass loss, on the other hand, was larger in small specimens. The reduction in impact bending strength and mass loss, and the reduction in equilibrium moisture content of sawn timber did not seem to be correlated. The laboratory treatment of small clear wood specimens had a much greater influence on the wood properties than the industrial treatment of similar specimens.

Several quality control methods have been suggested for thermally modified timber based on the measurement of various physical or chemical properties such as:

- Colour
- Equilibrium moisture content
- Mass loss
- Porosity
- Strength (bending, hardness or impact tests)
- Surface characteristics (surface roughness or He-Ne laser reflectance)

- Total soluble carbohydrates
- Volatile release during treatment

and several detection techniques have been used:

- Electrical resistivity
- Electron spin resonance (ESR)
- Nuclear magnetic resonance (NMR)
- Near infrared (NIR) spectroscopy
- Thermal analysis (TA)
- X-ray photoelectron spectroscopy (XPS)

A excellent overview of studies incorporating these methods has been given by Willems et al. (2015).

Sandak et al. (2015) examined the use of near infrared (NIR) spectroscopy to predict decay resistance and for the optimisation of treatment procedures on an industrial scale and reported that it could be successfully used for process control. Other methods for quality control include oxygen/carbon ratio analysis and various spectroscopic analysis methods (NIR or FT-IR), etc. (Candelier et al., 2016). More recently, it has been suggested that mechanical tests on sawn timber before and after thermal modification could help to quantify the modification regime. An acoustic, non-destructive method known as Beam Identification by Non-destructive Grading (licensed under the name BING™) provides resonant frequency spectra quickly and easily (Candelier et al., 2016). This method is widely and effectively used on an industrial scale, but it requires calibration steps in order to be used correctly. Monitoring the temperature within the timber undergoing thermal modification can provide an overview of the process, and a combination of these methods can help both qualitative and quantitative process analysis (Candelier et al., 2016).

Willems et al. (2010) suggested that Electron Spin Resonance (ESR) may be used to assess the quality of thermally modified timber by the detection of thermally generated free radicals. Altgen et al. (2012) suggested that the measured ESR signal is directly proportional to the antioxidant capacity of the timber, and that the antioxidant capacity may solely determine the durability, i.e., a correlation independent of wood species is expected to be found between the free radical density and the durability, so that the free radical density could be used to assess the durability of thermally modified timber directly. In a patent application for the estimation of durability using the ratio of the ESR signal amplitudes for treated and untreated wood, Viitaniemi et al. (2001) suggested an untested hypothesis the observed free radicals possibly had on antioxidant function. A toxicological study of pine dust by Long et al. (2004) showed that thermally-treated wood does indeed have a greater antioxidant capacity than untreated wood, and the same conclusion was reached with European beech and Norway spruce by Ahajji et al. (2009). Natural as well as synthetic antioxidants have been shown to contribute to the durability of wood (Green III and Schultz, 2003), but neither of these studies investigated whether there was a direct correlation between the content of stable free radicals in thermally-treated wood and the antioxidant capacity. The effectiveness of antioxidants may be due to their strongly delaying action on the incipient phase of fungal decay by the sacrificial scavenging of reactive oxygen species. Willems et al. (2010) demonstrated that ESR spectroscopy gave data that correlated directly with the maximum median mass loss in a basidiomycete exposure test for wood durability. Separate curves for softwoods and hardwoods were found, and these could be used to estimate the durability of high-pressure-superheated-steam modified timber.

The moisture in wood greatly influences the thermal modification result and it must, therefore, be controlled during the process. During the thermal-treatment cycle, the steam pressure and moisture gradients in wet wood may lead to severe structural damage, and the usual way to reduce this problem is to carefully dry the wood to a low moisture content at a sufficiently low temperature before it is exposed to the high-temperature regime. A problem arises in most of the existing processes when the sawn timber reaches the high-temperature regime, in a very dry state ($\approx$ 0% MC), where the stresses due to shrinkage and to the structural anisotropy and inhomogeneity of the timber reach very high levels and where the risk of damage to the sawn timber is consequently very high.

The heating during the modification process can under different moisture conditions influence the wood response (Table 3.5). As stated by Hill (2006), "*steam can be injected into the reactor to act as a heat-transfer medium and can additionally act as an inert blanket to limit oxidative processes. Such steam treatment processes are referred to as hygrothermal treatments. Where the wood is heated in water, this is known as a hydrothermal process*".

The largest process-related chemical differences in thermally modified timber are expected to be between of wood heated at atmospheric and wood heated at a high steam pressure. Most of industrial thermal modification processes operate at a relatively low water-vapour pressure (0–0.1 MPa) on wood in its oven-dried state, such as the ThermoWood™ processes in steam, the OHT™ process in hot oil, the Retification™ process in nitrogen, and other vacuum heating processes. Other processes operate at a high water-vapour pressure (0.5–0.8 MPa), sufficient to retain the moisture at high temperature, as in the FWD™ processes, the Plato™ process, and the FirmoLin™ process. At a high steam pressure, organic degradation products and moisture may be retained inside the wood matrix, instead of being lost by evaporation in an open reactor. Figure 3.12 show the working regimes of three principal different thermal-modification processes as described in Table 3.5.

Table 3.5 Hygro-thermolytic wood modification.

Process	Heating environment	Moisture content (MC)	Effect on the wood
Hydro-thermolysis	Heating in hot water or saturated stem	Saturated	The cell-wall is completely swollen
			Loss of integrity of structure
			Structural damage
Hygro-thermolysis	Heating in superheated steam at a high pressure	Intermediate	Low internal stresses
			Preservation of integrity of structure
			Low degree of structural damage
Thermolysis	Heating in superheated steam at a low pressure, or in vacuum	Oven-dry conditions	The cell-wall is completely dry (max shrinkage)
			Brittle material
			High risk for structural damage

Properties of thermally modified wood

Sawn timber is thermally modified to improve its resistance to fungi and insects, to improve its shape stability, to alter the colour, and to reduce resin bleed. Furthermore, the thermal treatment reduces the hygroscopicity, which reduces shrinkage and swelling of the sawn timber under conditions of changing relative humidity and gives improved dimensional and shape stability. The targeted properties are, however, reached at the cost of mass loss (up to 20%) during the thermal treatment, together with a loss of strength. Other property changes in colour, odour, glueability, and coating performance also occur (Table 3.6).

The property improvements gained are highly dependent on the process conditions, the treatment intensity (temperature, duration), the wood species and the dimensions of the sawn timber. Thermally-modified wood has a lower density than untreated wood, due to the thermal degradation of cell-wall components and the loss of mass during treatment. The durability generally increases with the applied temperature and the exposure period. At the same time, mechanical properties of the wood are reduced. Thus, thermal treatment always constitutes a compromise between increased resistance against fungi and decreased strength properties.

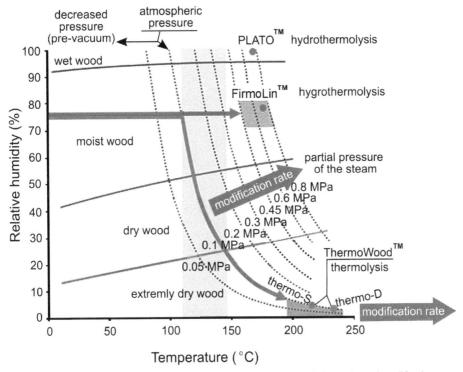

Figure 3.12 Diagram of RH versus temperature showing regions relevant for different thermal-modification processes.

Table 3.6 Main changes in properties for thermally-modified timber compared with untreated timber (Sandberg et al., 2017).

Desirable property changes	Undesirable property changes
Lower equilibrium moisture content	Decreased MOR and to some extent MOE
Greater dimensional stability	Decreased impact strength
Greater durability against decay	Increased brittleness
Lower thermal conductivity	Decreased hardness
Lower density	
Darker brown colour	
Characteristic smell	
Absorption of liquid water	
Prolonged pressing time for gluing	

Thermal modification processes can be applied to a wide range of wood species but need to be optimised for each species.

Hygroscopicity and dimensional stability

Thermal modification leads to changes in the chemical composition of the wood. During the treatment, acetic acid is released from the hemicelluloses and further catalyses carbohydrate cleavage, causing a reduction in the degree of polymerisation of the carbohydrates. Acid-catalysed degradation leads to the formation of formaldehyde, furfural and other aldehydes. In addition, although the extent of these reactions is mild, they nevertheless lead to an increase in cross-linking with a consequent decrease in hygroscopicity of the wood and an improvement in its dimensional stability (cf. Tjeerdsma et al., 1998; Militz, 2002a,b).

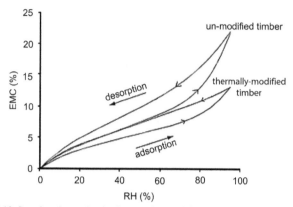

Figure 3.13 Sorption-desorption isotherms of unmodified and thermally-modified wood.

The decreased hygroscopicity of wood, i.e., its capacity for the absorption of moisture from the air, may have a partially reversible physical nature, as shown by Obataya et al. (2002) and Maejima et al. (2015). Such reversible changes have also been observed in relation to kiln-drying at moderate temperatures (Suchy et al., 2010) and in oven-drying at 103°C (Hoffmeyer et al., 2011).

The limiting moisture content achieved by a sufficiently long exposure at constant temperature and relative humidity (RH) is the equilibrium moisture content (EMC), and its dependence on humidity and temperature can be graphically represented by a diagram of EMC vs. RH for several constant temperatures (moisture sorption isotherms) or as lines of constant MC (isosteres) in a plot of RH against temperature. Since hygroscopic hemicellulosic polymers are lost during thermal modification, the equilibrium moisture content decreases, and the swelling and shrinking of thermally modified timber are decreased. On average, the equilibrium moisture content is decreased to about half the value of the untreated wood (Figure 3.13). The hygroscopicity of thermally-modified timber can vary considerably, depending on the process parameters. An excellent analysis of the hygroscopic behaviour of thermally-modified timber is given by Willems (2015).

Durability against microbiological degradation

The durability is a measure of the intrinsic resistance of a wood species to wood-degrading fungi, the most destructive organisms for wood, although the actual performance of wood in service may be affected by factors other than fungi, not only other wood-destroying organisms (e.g., termites, shipworms, carpenter bees, wood-boring beetles) but also deteriorating/enabling physical influences such as wood moisture, UV-radiation, mechanical loading and application-dependent failure criteria (see Chapter 1). All thermal-modification processes to increase the durability of naturally non-durable wood species if the treatment is sufficiently intense, as has been reported in numerous studies, using the same laboratory efficacy tests as for preservative-treated wood.

With increasing temperature, the durability of the wood against wood-degrading fungi is improved, but Ringman et al. (2019) say that thermally-modified timber does not provide permanent protection from brown rot decay, even under harsh conditions. Since brown rot fungi express the genes necessary for the oxidative degradation of modified wood, they also suggested that the effectiveness of treatment could be related either to the inhibition of chelator-mediated Fenton metabolites or to the inhibition of the Fenton process itself. According to the requirements of the EN 113 standard (CEN, 2004), the mass loss after exposure to the fungi should be less than 3% for outdoor applications. To fulfil this condition, the mass loss of conifers during modification should exceed 8% (Esteves and Pereira, 2009).

Thermally modified broad-leaved woods are however generally more susceptible to degradation, so that sufficient protection against fungi is hard to achieve even for specimens that have been modified at the highest temperatures (Hill, 2006).

The improvement in durability by thermal modification of wood up to Durability Class 2 according to the EN 350 standard (CEN, 2016) seems to be due to the inherent stability against biochemical oxidation achieved by the preferential removal of oxygen from the wood. This mechanism appears to be the same for wood species such as European ash, European beech, fir, poplar and Scots pine (Willems, 2015).

Thermal conductivity

The thermal conductivity (λ) of a material is a measure of its ability to conduct heat, i.e., the quantity of heat which flows in one second through a cube one cubic metre in size with a temperature difference of one Kelvin between the opposite sides. The unit of conduction is $Wm^{-1}K^{-1}$. Heat transfer occurs at a lower rate in materials of low thermal conductivity than in materials of high thermal conductivity. Materials with high thermal conductivity are widely used in heat-sink applications, and materials with low thermal conductivity are used for thermal insulation. The reciprocal of thermal conductivity is called the thermal resistivity.

Thermal conductivity is calculated from Fourier's Law for heat conduction:

$$q = -\lambda \, \Delta T \tag{3.1}$$

where q is the local heat flux density, λ is the thermal conductivity, and ΔT is the temperature gradient. The tensorial description is necessary only in materials which, like wood, are anisotropic.

The thermal conductivity decreases with decreasing density, and this means that thermally-modified timber has a lower thermal conductivity at a given moisture content than untreated wood of the same species.

Density

The density of thermally-modified timber is lower than that of untreated timber because of the mass loss during treatment. Seborg et al. (1953) and Burmester (1973) reported that the gaseous products of thermal modification accumulate in a closed vessel and a pressurised atmosphere is achieved, activating the kinetics of a temperature-dependent mass-loss limit. The kinetic rate towards this limit was found to depend on the initial moisture content, but the mechanism behind the rate increment has not been fully clarified, as neither the gas pressure nor the wood moisture content were recorded. Stamm (1956) suggested that the relatively high acetic acid content in thermally-modified timber in a closed system acts as a catalyst for higher mass-loss rates.

Kinetic studies of thermal modification often consider the dry mass loss to be the variable of interest, since it can be monitored in real time in laboratory scale reactors and it correlates well with the properties of the thermally-modified timber. Mass-loss rates may also be measured after completion of the treatment as a function of the duration at the highest temperature. By taking the derivative of the mass loss with respect to duration after reaching the treatment temperature, the mass-loss rate is obtained independent of mass the loss occurring during the ill-defined heating phase.

Colour

During the thermal modification process, wood becomes darker in colour, but the final colour depends on the species and on the process (Figure 3.14). Noticeable colour changes can occur with a small mass loss of only 2–4%, but the final effect depends on the treatment time and on the temperature (Bekhta and Niemz, 2005; Esteves et al., 2008b). In air, the rate of lightness reduction is greater up to a mass loss of 4%, when the thermally-modified timber becomes approximately 50% darker than the original wood.

During thermal modification, both the polysaccharides and the lignin change colour due to the overall introduction of unsaturated carbon-carbon bonds, which increase the light absorption in the blue-violet range. One of the most important thermal degradation products of polysaccharides, furfural, is commonly found in thermally-modified timber (Karlsson et al., 2012) and is known to

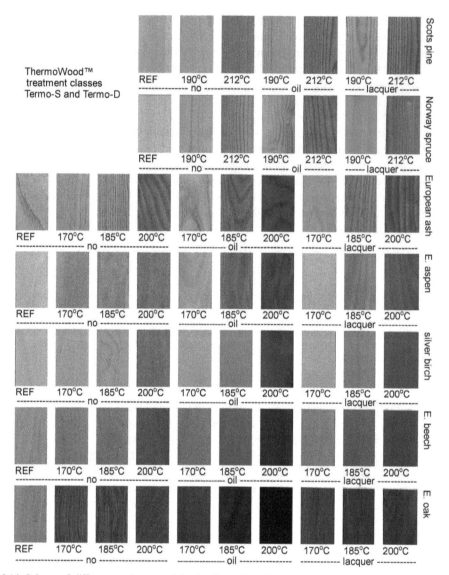

Figure 3.14 Colours of different species treated by the ThermoWood™ processes, and treated with a transparent oil or lacquer.

slowly change by polymerisation from a colourless fluid into a dark brown liquid upon exposure to oxygen at room temperature (Zeitsch, 2000). Coloured degradation products from hemicelluloses (Sundqvist, 2004) and from extractives contribute to the colour of hydrothermally treated wood (Sundqvist and Morén, 2002), and the colour change has also been related to the formation of oxidation products, such as quinines (Bekhta and Niemz, 2005). The cleavage of α- and β-ether bonds in lignin produces intermediate lignin degradation compounds, such as quinone and quinonemethide, which are also strongly coloured.

Odour

Thermally-modified timber has a smoke-like smell, which comes from compounds, mainly furfurals, that develop during the processing. At room temperature, furfural is in a liquid state and is a relatively volatile compound. It contributes to the VOCs emitted during the process and from the final product (Miller, 1998). The degree of odour may differ between thermally modified timber from various processes. The VOC emissions from thermally modified wood are discussed in more detail in Chapter 6.

Absorption of liquid water

The capacity to absorb liquid water in thermally-modified timber is only partly related to adsorption of moisture in the hygroscopic range below 95% relative humidity. Thermally-modified timber can in fact show an increase in the uptake of liquid water although its hygroscopicity is markedly reduced (Scheiding and Direske, 2014). Hakkou et al. (2005) found an increase in the contact angle of water on thermally modified European silver fir and Scots pine at modification temperatures in the range of 100°C to 160°C. This decrease in wettability influences the glueability and paintability of wood surfaces, and probably also the capillary absorption of water in wood (Sehlstedt-Persson, 2008).

The effect of thermal modification on longitudinal water absorption differs between species. Sehlstedt-Persson (2008) studied the absorption of liquid water in thermally modified European white birch, Norway spruce and Scots pine by X-ray computed tomography, and found differences between the species, and in the behaviour of the sapwood of the conifers.

The longitudinal water absorption in Scots pine sapwood increased substantially due to thermal modification at a temperature of 170°C, but in Scots pine heartwood, the absorption was low and only minor changes were observed as a result of thermal modification. Norway spruce timber showed a low water absorption in sapwood and heartwood both before and after thermal modification, the longitudinal absorption being at the same level as that of Scots pine heartwood. European white birch, which does not develop heartwood, showed a decreasing longitudinal uptake of water with increasing treatment temperature. Couceiro et al. (2017) also showed that the longitudinal water flow in thermally modified birch and aspen timber was less than that in the unmodified timber, and that the moisture gradient formed above the liquid water was also reduced.

Sehlstedt-Persson (2008) explained the difference in capillary water absorption between the sapwood and heartwood of Scots pine by differences in ray parenchyma due to the processing. During heartwood formation in the tree, the dying parenchyma cells are slowly emptied, whereas the living parenchyma cells in green sapwood are emptied much faster during kiln drying, resulting in large capillary strains on the pit membranes, which may rupture and, hence, give more effective water absorption.

Mechanical properties

Thermal modification leads to a decrease in density and to a loss of mechanical strength (Militz, 2002a,b; Mayes and Oksanen, 2003; Hill, 2006; Kocaefe et al., 2008; Kasemsiri et al., 2013), to an extent which depends on the wood species and on the process conditions. The temperature in the absence of oxygen plays a predominant role (Mitchell, 1988; Militz, 2002a,b). The modulus of elasticity (MOE) and bending strength decrease with increasing temperature and increasing time of the thermal treatment. The intensity of the thermal treatment is commonly evaluated in terms of the mass loss. The mass loss is greater at higher temperatures and longer treatment times, and a small change in mass loss can result in a large change in mechanical properties. Esteves et al. (2008a) showed that thermal modification of maritime pine at temperatures between 170°C and 200°C resulted in a mass loss of less than 4% and a decrease in MOE of 5%, while a mass loss of 6% gave a decrease in MOE of 16%. Bakar et al. (2013) compared the changes in shear strength and hardness after thermal treatment at 190°C for 8 hours, and found that eastern red cedar had a shear strength 69.4% lower than that of a control sample, red oak 56% and rubberwood 53%. The hardness was also much lower, resulting in crushing and splitting during the hardness tests.

Technological properties

In general, thermal modification leads to increased brittleness and this can influence the result of machining, for example.

The sawing of thermally-modified timber does not differ considerably from the sawing of untreated wood and knotty areas usually show tearing. The wood is practically resin-free, so less power is required for the operation of cutting and routing tool, and the service life and maintenance intervals of the tools increase significantly. A saw blade with widely spaced teeth can cause splintering the sawn timber were the saw teeth leave the timber and it is recommended that a sawblade with closely-spaced teeth be used. A high rotation cutting speed results in a cleaner and more precise saw-kerf. Milling thermally-modified timber wood is similar to the milling of high-density and brittle broad-leaved woods.

Less friction is encountered in feeding when thermally-modified timber wood is planed, and the process goes more smoothly. The planing results improve if the moisture content is slightly increased, and if the cutting-tool angle is adapted to the material. As the equilibrium moisture content is lower in thermally-modified than in untreated timber (cf. Figure 3.13), the modified sawn timber must be stored at a higher relative humidity in order to reach the same moisture content as the untreated sawn timber. ThermoWood™ Norway spruce, for example, has an equilibrium moisture content of about 5% at a temperature of 20°C and a relative humidity of 65%, compared to an equilibrium moisture content of about 12% in untreated Norway spruce.

The sanding of thermally-modified timber is easy because the timber contains little or no resin. The wood-particle size of the dust released from sawing, planing and sanding is, however, small and this must be taken into consideration when arranging dust removal.

Examples of adhesives suitable for gluing thermally modified wood are 1- and 2-component PVAc and polyurethane (PU), resorcinol-phenolic (RF) and emulsion polymer isocyanate (EPI) adhesives. The glueability is dependent on the thermal-modification process. The shear strength of the glue line decreases with increasing treatment temperature due to a loss in strength of the material (Mayes and Oksanen, 2003). The application of high-range thermal-modification intensity reduces the shear strength of the adhesive bond-line as the wood becomes brittle. The modification process also affects the wettability of the wood surface and the absorption of adhesive and water into the wood is retarded. Some PVAc adhesives can require significantly prolonged drying times because the water must penetrate the wood, since the curing of the adhesive is based on the loss of water. Adhesives usually have normal curing times, but polyurethane-based adhesives require water in order to achieve curing, the water being taken up either from the wood or from the environment. The amount of moisture required dependens on the adhesive, but if both wood and air are very dry, the gluing may be unsuccessful.

It is recommended that fastners are made of stainless steel for outdoor use and similar conditions. Splitting of the timber can be prevented by using screws with a sparse thread or by using hidden fasteners. Pneumatic nailing is a good alternative.

In general, thermally-modified timber can be surface treated in the same way as unmodified wood, and it is an advantage for surface treatment if any resin has been removed during the process. Oil-based coatings are preferred over water-based coatings as a first coating layer because the thermally modified timber has a lower water-absorption capacity than untreated wood. Good test results have been obtained with UV-hardening paints and varnishes and also with oils and waxes. When applying a finish, attention must be paid to the working conditions, temperature, moisture content and cleanliness of the wood surface.

Applications of thermally-modified timber

The market for thermally-modified timber has developed considerably over the last few decades, and this timber has now achieved a market position as an alternative for natural wood in many applications, such as in cladding, decking, flooring, garden structures, fencing, window frames and acoustic barriers. Thermal-modification processes were initially viewed as an alternative to chemical preservation processes but manufacturers have relaxed their emphasis on biological durability and are instead focussing on the colour, dimensional stability, and durability compared to that of other naturally durable wood species. The added value of the modification must, however, outweigh the costs of creating it. Thermally-modified timber has to cope with a number of difficulties, imposed by the high-quality requirements of the input timber, the competition of alternative raw materials and the high production, development and marketing costs. High-value markets, e.g., the wall-cladding market, have been found for high-quality thermally-modified timber of various wood species, which meet the needs of the growing thermal modification industry in Europe. Beneath these niche markets, there are huge volume markets, where thermally-modified timber can compete technically but not yet economically. Adding extra value by the adjacent conversion of relatively expensive thermally -modified timber into finished products would not fundamentally improve the thermal-modification business. It has been suggested that a more sound approach to open new markets for thermally-modified timber would be a process improvement requiring input material of a less stringent quality; the Firmolin™ concept is one example of that strategy (Willems, 2009).

The type of thermal-modification system can be related to the type of market segment or market advantage:

- Vacuum processes:
    - small volume, high-quality production,
    - full VOC removal, and
    - suitable for high-value indoor applications.
- Atmospheric processes:
    - high volume and "medium-quality" production, and
    - lower value, i.e., low-risk applications.
- Pressurised processes:
    - medium volume, "high-quality" production,
    - excellent performance in exterior use with a wide range of relative-humidity variation, and
    - preferable for large dimension timber, and species that are susceptible to cracking during drying.

The main characteristics of the thermally-modified timber are its improved durability and dimensional stability. Target markets are both indoors and outdoors where these material qualities are required, such as claddings, doors, flooring, garden products, windows, and specialty products (sauna, bathrooms, etc.)

The durability of thermally-modified timber is dependent on the process conditions and ranges in Durability Classes 2–4, although not comparable to that achieved with copper-chromium containing preservatives. The use of thermally-modified timber in contact with soil and water is, therefore, not usually advised.

The main drawback of thermally-modified timber treated at high temperatures is, however, its poorer mechanical properties (bending strength, impact strength). Thermally-modified timber should, therefore, not be used in load-bearing constructions or in circumstances where a high sudden impact can occur (e.g., poles). One of the technological drawbacks is in the fact that it is difficult to produce a highly durable product (where high temperatures are needed) and at the same time a strong material (where lower temperatures are needed). From this reason, some producers like the Finnish ThermoWood Association have defined quality classes, in which end-uses are linked to material quality classes (Mayes and Oksanen, 2003).

Table 3.7 shows areas were thermally modified timber are commonly used, and Figure 3.15 shows some examples of use.

3.5 Wood ageing

Wood ageing is an *accelerated ageing process* similar to thermal modification but using a mild temperature in the range of 100°C to 150°C, in some cases under controlled relative humidity and

Table 3.7 Application areas for thermally-modified timber divided into Use Classes, see Table 1.7.

	Interior		Exterior		
Product type/Use Class	**1**	**2**	**3**	**4**	**5**
Indoor furniture	x	x			
Floor and non-structural interior uses	x	x			
Exterior joinery			x		
Cladding			x		
Decking			x		
Fencing			x		
Outdoor furniture			x		
Construction elements					
In-ground timber			(x)		
Products exposed to water			(x)		

where: x = products have been produced by companies using the modified wood
(x) = products may be produced, based on pre-commercial trials, research, etc.

Figure 3.15 Some examples of the use of thermally-modified timber, from the left: indoor panelling of PlatoWood™ (Ecology Institute Wageningen, The Netherlands), a façade of ThermoWood™ (private house, Hudiksvall, Sweden), and a façade of Firmolin™ (Castellum Hoge Woered, Utrecht, The Netherlands).

pressure (Sandberg et al., 2013). In general terms, Froidevaux (2012) defined wood ageing as a *process in which wood has been chemically modified by time and slight moisture (under the fibre saturation point) and thermal variation only*, but ageing can also be understood as an irreversible change in the physical, chemical, and mechanical properties of a material during extended storage or use. In many cases, the *natural ageing* of wood can be compared with the effect of a low-temperature thermal modification, which is used to accelerate the natural ageing process of wood (Kránitz et al., 2016). The degradation of wood due either to natural or accelerated ageing should not be confused with other degradation phenomena, such as biological degradation and UV-degradation. Natural ageing occurs under indoor or under sheltered exterior conditions (cf. weathering described in Chapter 1).

The changes in wood properties during ageing are not drastic in any sense, and it has been suggested by several researchers that there are no changes in wood properties due solely to time and small variations in moisture content. The Japanese researcher Jiro Kohara tested the chemical and mechanical properties of 300 and 1,300-year-old hinoki timber-construction elements in Japan, and the results show that the longitudinal Young's modulus of aged wood increases by ca. 20% during the first 300 years and that thereafter it decreases slowly (Kohara, 1952; Kohara, 1953; Kohara, 1954a,b; Kohara, 1955a,b). The results were summarised in English by Obataya (2007, 2009). The suggested explanation of this phenomenon is that two chemical changes in the wood occur at the same time, viz. an increase in the crystallisation of cellulose and a depolymerisation of hemicelluloses. The strength also decreases with ageing time due to a degradation of the interface between the lignin matrix and the fibres. Yokoyama et al. (2009) showed that the higher rigidity of naturally aged wood observed by Kohara was an indirect effect of density, and they found that the degradation of the mechanical properties of naturally aged wood was small in the longitudinal direction but important in the radial direction, where the strength is drastically decreased by about 40%. Kránitz et al. (2016) summarise data for changes in the properties of naturally aged wood from studies of wood up to 4,400 years old, showing similar results.

Froidevaux (2012) studied the natural ageing of Norway spruce and showed that the mechanical and physical properties, such as moduli of elasticity, viscoelastic parameters, sorption of water and diffusion of water, remain more or less unchanged after several centuries. On the other hand, the colour of the wood changes (darkened) and the radial strength was strongly reduced. For further information about the effects of natural ageing on the physical, mechanical and chemical degradation of wood during weathering, see Section 1.6. The ageing phenomenon is a slow process involving only a slight change in the chemical composition and structure over time. In order to repeat such a process in a more industrial manner, it is necessary to find a way to accelerate the process.

The accelerated wood-ageing process is a further development of the thermal-modification process, and the negative effects of thermal modification on the strength and brittleness of wood are considerably reduced due to the lower temperature. The main purpose is to increase the use of thermally-modified timber in construction, enabling its use for load-bearing construction elements, or to reproduce the aesthetic features of old wood, by giving wood an antique appearance. Wood ageing is also used for restoration purposes in old buildings, for example, to harmonise the appearances of old and new wooden constructions. Obataya et al. (2000) studied the effect of artificial ageing on the mechanical properties of timber for use in the repair of ancient Japanese wooden constructions. The effect of ageing is also of interest in the renovation and new construction of classical musical instruments such as violins and grand pianos, where it is of interest to understand whether the acoustic properties of the wood are affected by time (Bonamini, 2012; Karami et al., 2013; Zeniya et al., 2016). Kránitz (2014) studied the effect of natural ageing on different wood properties and Froidevaux et al. (2012) focused their studies on the use of natural and artificial aged wood in the cultural heritage, specifically in wood panels for paintings.

Material selection and preparation

The material to be used in an artificial wood-ageing process should be selected with regard to its final use rather than to the process itself. Thus, all kinds of wood species can be used for artificial wood ageing.

Industrial wood ageing processes

Industrial processes for wood ageing are similar to or even the same as those used for thermal modification. Most aged wood production with a low-temperature thermal modification process is carried out in Switzerland and Poland, and the annual production of aged wood in Europe is small, probably less than 10,000 m³ (Jones et al., 2019). Closed systems are used in the two plants that are producing aged wood in Switzerland (FWD and WTT-type processes) (see Table 3.4), but open systems can also be used. The Balz Holz AG company is a sawmill company producing a product called Baladur-Antikholz™ from European oak or Norway spruce, providing an alternative to old wood for the construction of chalets. The Corbat AG company applies a VAPO™-treatment steaming process were the timber is exposed to saturated steam at a temperature of 110–130°C (the HPS-Wood process). This corresponds to high-pressure steaming (HPS) and ensures the perpetuation of the structural properties of timber, while giving the wood a rustic and antique appearance that can be combined with brushing. Although several types of wood-ageing processes exist, they all have a similar process flow that can be described schematically as shown in Figure 3.16.

Obataya (2007) has compared the effects of dry and wet (saturated) thermal treatments with the natural ageing of wood and has concluded that it is important to control the relative humidity

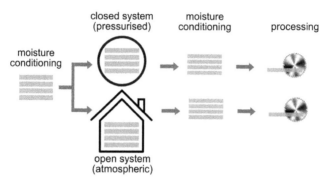

Figure 3.16 Schematic presentation of the process for artificial wood ageing in temperature between 100°C and 150°C.

level during the treatment to introduce some hydrolysis reactions. Borgin et al. (1975) showed evidence of lignin hydrolysis in their investigation, and the relative humidity during the accelerated ageing treatment should, therefore, be controlled and stabilised in order to promote and control the hydrolysis (cf. Figure 3.12).

Properties of aged wood

The treatment parameters influence the result as in thermal modification, but the effect is smaller due to the lower temperature. The transverse strength properties (in the radial direction) of thermally modified wood are always lower and are strongly dependent on the treatment conditions, and artificial wood ageing is no exception. The loss of radial strength increases with treatment time, treatment temperature, treatment relative humidity, open/closed system, and the reactor pressure. The increased brittleness of aged wood reduces the bending and tensile strength perpendicular to the fibre direction as well as the impact-bending strength and especially the plastic strain (Kránitz et al., 2016). Negligible or inconsistent trends were found in many cases for the mechanical properties parallel to the fibre direction, therefore, the influence of ageing was very small (Kránitz et al., 2016).

The effect of the treatment temperature on strength is clearly non-linear. The strength values for wood treated at 130°C were about 15% lower in all duration studies than the values at 110°C, whilst those at 150°C values were about 55% lower (Froidevaux, 2012).

In artificial ageing, the chemical reactions that occur in wood due to the raised temperature are not exactly the same as those occurring during natural ageing. In order to keep the chemical reactions close to those occurring in natural ageing, and to obtain an "acceptably short" duration for the process, a temperature between 100°C and 150°C is preferable.

In order to predict the loss of strength and the loss of colour lightness, the use of a thermo-hydro treatment to accelerate the ageing of wood was investigated by Froidevaux (2012). Two small experimental thermo-hydro reactors (for details, see Navi and Sandberg, 2012) were developed to precisely control the variables, such as time, temperature, RH and pressure. The artificially aged wood showed some similarities with naturally aged wood, i.e., only small or no changes in the elastic and viscoelastic behaviour, but a clear loss of strength in the radial direction. The artificially aged wood had a lower water sorption and moisture diffusion than naturally aged wood, indicating that the chemical changes in the hemicellulose were different. The relative radial strength and colour change of artificially aged wood can be fitted to a kinetic law of ageing dependent upon the treatment variables, and this kinetic law can be extrapolated to standard conditions (i.e., as if the treatment were performed at ambient temperature and RH) in order to predict the natural ageing (Froidevaux and Navi, 2013). A linear relation between radial strength and colour of the aged wood can then be used to predict the loss in radial strength due wood-colour changes of aged wooden panels used for antique paintings.

It is typical of both naturally and artificially aged wood that the wood darkens with increasing age or duration of the process, and the colour tends to give higher chromaticity values. Many studies have been performed regarding the colour change of thermally modified timber (e.g., Gonzalez-Pena and Hale, 2009; Matsuo et al., 2010), and the Arrhenius law has been successfully applied to predict colour changes. Matsuo et al. (2010, 2011) compared the colour change of naturally aged wood in historical buildings with that of thermally modified timber, and they extrapolated the kinetic law at ambient temperature and found that the colour change after 921 years at ambient temperature was almost equivalent to that taking place during thermal modification at a temperature of 180°C for 6–7 hours.

Applications of aged wood

The main application for aged wood is indoors as its durability and hygroscopic properties are only slightly improved. Aged wood (oak and spruce) can typically be used as an alternative to old wood for the construction and renovation of chalets, e.g., in Switzerland (Figure 3.17). Other uses include musical instruments, both the renovation of old and the manufacture of new instruments (Table 3.8).

Figure 3.17 Steam modified Norway spruce (Baladur-Antikholz™) from Balz Holz AG.

Table 3.8 Application areas for aged wood divided into Use Classes, see Table 1.7.

Product type/Use Class	Interior		Exterior		
	1	2	3	4	5
Indoor furniture	X	X			
Floor and non-structural interior uses	X	X			
Exterior joinery					
Cladding					
Decking					
Fencing					
Outdoor furniture					
Construction elements			(x)		
In-ground timber					
Products exposed to water					

where: x = products have been produced by companies using the modified wood
(x) = products may be produced, based on pre-commercial trials, research, etc.

3.6 Self-bonding of veneer

The manufacture of panels from veneers, i.e., plywood or laminated veneer lumber (LVL) need not require an adhesive or other binder. The combination of high temperature and high pressure can suffice to produce panels with excellent mechanical properties, and the veneers are then self-bonded, a term introduced by Mason (1928), i.e., having the capacity to stick together without a binder. Wood is special in this sense; it is one of the natural materials which can constitute both the piece to be bonded and the adhesive itself, due to its complex chemical structure. The self-bonding process requires only heat and mechanical compression in an open or closed system, and no other treatment of the veneer is generally needed (Cristescu, 2015). The self-bonding phenomenon is well known when the steam explosion of wood is utilised to make a binder-less "Masonite" fibreboard and particleboard (cf. Irvine and Frederick, 1946; Norton, 1947; Dunlop, 1948; Xu et al., 2003; Xu et al., 2004; Xu et al., 2006; Rowell and McSweeny, 2008). Comprehensive reviews of the processes and bonding mechanisms have been presented by Back (1987), Pintiaux et al. (2015), and Zhang et al. (2015).

Technologies for self-bonding veneers without any binder or chemical activation prior to pressing were introduced in Germany in the 1940s by Runkel and Jost (1948) and in the USA. by Boehm (1951). These processes were developed as an extension of the existing fibreboard and chipboard processes.

It has been believed that wood surfaces need a pre-treatment prior to self-bonding since they accumulate water-soluble compounds as well as fats and waxes which may hinder the self-bonding process. Besides Mason's steam injection, activation of the surface was intensively studied in the 1970s and 1980s, with oxidative pre-treatments and enzymes being proposed as promising technologies, although they have not yet been industrially applied (see Section 5.2).

During the 1970s, progress was made in non-conventional bonding technologies for small-sized and waste wood (Stofko, 1974), but there was little interest in self-bonding for joining veneers or solid wood. One reason for this low interest was the ease of handling, adjustable viscosities, good moisture durability and low price of the synthetic adhesives used on the market since the 1940s (Müller et al., 2007). The new bonding technologies included many methods of bonding through surface activation, radically different from the conventional phenol-formaldehyde and urea-formaldehyde adhesive systems. According to Zavarin (1984), the development of these methods was delayed by an insufficient knowledge of the chemical composition of wood and fibre surfaces and of the processes involved in bonding.

A breakthrough in wood self-bonding was the discovery that it was possible to weld wood by applying friction to the wood surfaces to be joined (Suthoff et al., 1996; Sandberg et al., 2013). This technique is called *frictional wood welding* and is described in Section 3.7.

Material selection and preparation

Veneer for use in self-bonding processes should have a uniform thickness and smooth surfaces, i.e., the surfaces should at least be roughly sanded, and the veneer sheets should be roughly sized before pressing.

A broad range of species have been tested with successful bonding results, but the self-bonding process is not well established as a marketed process and the choice of species for the process must be further studied before production is established.

Large knots in the veneer may reduce the bonding ability in the knot region and should be avoided.

Industrial self-bonding processes

The capacity of wood to self-bond was discovered by William H. Mason around 1925. He developed the idea of pressing fibre bundles of steam-exploded wooden chips. Steam-explosion was the key process in this technology. In his first patent, Mason (1928) reports that under proper conditions of heat, steam and pressure, lignin supplies the welding effect, particularly on the surfaces when the product is dried. Later, a similar process was applied to plywood production by the Masonite company (Boehm, 1951). Steam pre-treatment was also used in the veneer bonding method, since Mason was convinced that lignin provided a bonding material that needed to be activated by steam.

Between 1940 and 1950, several processes similar to the Masonite™ process were developed and industrialised in Europe, based not only on wood as a raw-material, but also on agricultural waste. Thereafter, the development of processes based on self-bonding has stagnated, especially for the bonding of veneers and other types of solid wood raw material.

In the beginning of the 21st Century, the Romanian-Swedish researcher Carmen Cristescu developed and patented a self-bonding process for the production of high-density and thermally modified veneer products (Cristescu et al., 2006). At the time of publication (2021), this process has still not been industrialised, but it has been well researched through Cristescu's studies described in her PhD thesis (Cristescu, 2015).

The Masonite-plywood™ process

The *Masonite-plywood™ production process* described in a patent application from 1945 by the Masonite company (Boehm, 1951) does not require a closed pressing system, but the veneers must undergo a steaming (hydrolysis) process in an autoclave prior to pressing (Figure 3.18). Boehm emphasised the strong dependency between the steaming and the pressing parameters if, for example, the veneers are heated in the autoclave with steam at a temperature of 285°C and a pressure of 7 MPa for 30 seconds, the lignin is activated to a relatively high degree and the pressing temperature and pressure should then not exceed 220°C and 5 MPa, in order to avoid excessive flow of the wood material. However, if the veneers are heated at a relatively low steam temperature and pressure, the pressing temperature and pressure need to be higher. Cooling under pressure at the end of the process was considered compulsory.

Unlike the "Masonite" hardboard made of steam-exploded chips, the plywood product was not industrialised, and no reference can be found to the mass production of plywood according to the Masonite™ method.

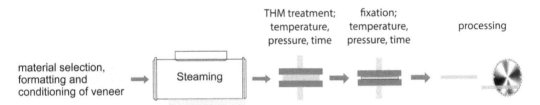

Figure 3.18 Schematic presentation of the Masonite plywood™ process.

The Thermodyn-plywood™ process

The *Thermodyn™ process* was developed by Runkel and Jost in Germany and was patented in 1948 for the production of moulded bodies based on wood waste, chips from low-quality round timber, or other vegetable raw materials (Runkel and Jost, 1948). Industrial processes for manufacturing products similar to the Thermodyn™ product were developed during the same period, such as the Collipress™ process and the Wersalit™ process. These processes have been described by Kollmann (1955) and Kollmann et al. (1975).

The patent for the Thermodyn™ process describes how the process could also be applied to veneer (Figure 3.19): nine European beech veneers, each 3 mm in thickness and with a moisture content adjusted to lie between 10 and 17%, were subjected to 15 MPa pressure at a temperature of 170°C in a gas-tight pressure mould and compressed to a laminate with a density of 1,300–1,400 kg/m³. After hot-pressing, a cooling phase to a temperature below 100°C was

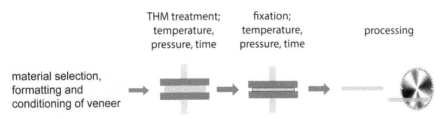

Figure 3.19 Schematic presentation of the Thermodyn plywood™ process.

necessary in order to obtain a shape-stable product. It is not known whether this process was ever commercialised.

The Cristescu process

A densified laminated board can be obtained by pressing layers of veneers under elevated temperature in a parallel or cross-wise laminated construction with no bonding additive (Cristescu, 2006). The process does not require steam pre-treatment, surface activation, a gas-tight press, friction or adhesive, but requires only heat and mechanical compression in an open system (Figure 3.20). It is possible to achieve a water-resistant bond-line with a strength comparable to that given by conventional wood adhesives for constructional purposes.

The parameters for pressing a European beech panel of five 2 mm veneers are a temperature range of 200–250°C, a pressure of 4–6 MPa and a pressing time of 4–6 minutes (Cristescu et al., 2015a). Depending on the selected combination of these process parameters, boards with different densities, water resistance, and colour can be produced. The five-ply panels studied were divided into three categories with respect to panel properties and water resistance (cf. Table 3.9):

1. panels pressed under mild pressing conditions with a weak bonding strength and tending to delaminate when soaked in water,

2. panels pressed under medium pressing conditions with a mixed character, where the outer bond-lines show a better bonding and sometimes also greater water-resistance than the inner bond-lines, and

3. panels pressed under harsh pressing conditions, i.e., at a temperature of 250°C, that are water-resistant, with a high shear strength and high bending strength.

Ruponen et al. (2014) have studied the process further, with particular attention to the influence of a post-thermal modification and the initial moisture content of silver birch veneers on the moisture resistance of an eight-layer laminate. They found that a thermal post-treatment at a target temperature of 200°C at atmospheric pressure for 4 hours using superheated steam eliminated the risk of delamination of the laminates under moist conditions. Laminates produced from veneers that were soaked in water at 20°C for 24 hours were found to have a bond-line with greater water resistance than the bond-lines in laminates produced by dry veneers.

The temperature during pressing in combination with the pressing time causes the colour of the veneers throughout the panel to darken, the final colour depending on the pressing parameter levels (Figure 3.21).

The temperature evolution within the laminate during hot-pressing is important for the chemical and physical processes that contribute to the auto-adhesion between the veneers, and thereby also to the mechanical and moisture related properties of the board (Cristescu et al., 2015a). This means that the desired properties of the board will not be reached unless the target temperature of the process is achieved in all the bond-lines of the laminate. This can be critical for central bond-lines in the laminate, especially when as short a pressing time as possible is sought both for economic reasons and to prevent thermal degradation of the wood material. The temperature evolution within the laminate depends on species, moisture content, and density of the veneers (i.e., the thermal

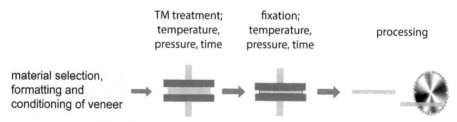

Figure 3.20 Schematic presentation of the Cristescu process.

Figure 3.21 The colour of the panels produced by the Cristescu process depends on the process conditions. From the upper left: unprocessed European beech veneer, and panels produced under mild, medium and harsh pressing conditions (cf. Table 3.9).

diffusivity of the wood material), the compression and speed of compression of the laminate (i.e., pressure and press-closing time), and the press temperature, the variation in temperature during pressing, and the duration of the compression (Cristescu et al., 2015b).

Properties of self-bonded veneer

After a short but intense thermo-mechanical treatment, the self-bonded panels are denser and darker in colour than common plywood, exhibiting features of both compressed and thermal-modified wood.

One important issue when joining wood surfaces without adhesive is the water-resistant properties of the bond-line. Apart from the influence of the pressing condition, the mechanisms behind the water-resistance of the bond-line is still not fully explained. It seems probable that the wood extractives and degradation products from the thermally modified wood play a major role.

Cristescu and Karlsson (2013) studied the chemical changes occurring in different regions of beech veneers boards pressed at 200°C, 225°C and 250°C, and their importance for water-resistance properties. It was found that the monosaccharides accumulated at the surface of the veneer were transformed during hot-pressing into hydroxymethylfurfural which, at temperatures higher than 225°C, was transformed further into other products, including furfural. It was also suggested that degraded lignin migrated towards the bond-line where a condensation reaction might occur, especially at 250°C. Hill (2006) has suggested that the possibility of cross-linking in the lignin increases during severe thermal treatment, and this can also be a factor contributing to water repellence.

In wood welding, water-resistance has been achieved using species with a high resin content, such as Scots pine, in which rosin melts and surrounds the weld line (Vaziri, 2011) or padauk wood (Ganier et al., 2013), where the extractives have a protective influence on the welded interphase due to their inherent water repellence. Applying a mixture of rosin in ethanol to beech wood surfaces and letting it dry for two days prior to welding is another way of obtaining water-resistant bonds (Pizzi et al., 2011).

One possible way to improve the water-resistance of the bond-line while hot-pressing veneers of species other than beech is via an oxidative activation, e.g., by spraying a small amount of Fenton's reagent (an aqueous solution of ferrous sulphate followed by hydrogen peroxide) on the veneers before pressing (Karlsson et al., 2015). This method was tested with good results for Scots pine and it may also yield good results for other species.

Wood powder placed as a binder between veneers prior to hot-pressing also leads to water-resistant bonding, as shown by Ando and Sato (2010), who pressed cross-laminated sugi veneers at 200°C for 20–30 minutes or at 220°C for 10 minutes. This process gave a board that met the second JAS grade (Japanese Agricultural Standard) for plywood, i.e., for use in applications where it is occasionally exposed to wet conditions. Ando and Sato (2010) determined the tensile shear strength of the bond-line under dry and wet conditions after soaking in 60°C water for 3 hours, and showed that the pressing temperature and time were important factors in the manufacture of sugi plywood bonded with sugi powder. These parameters contributed not only to compacting the powder but also to reducing the thickness recovery and water absorption of the veneers.

Ruponen et al. (2014) obtained water-resistant boards from parallel laminated 1.5 mm thick warty birch veneer. Their technique involved three steps: soaking the veneers in water at 20°C for 24 hours, pressing at 160°C and 6 MPa for 4 hours, and treating in superheated steam at a temperature of 200°C for a further 4 hours.

Table 3.9 shows some properties of five-ply self-bonded beech veneer panels manufactured according to the Cristescu process at different temperatures, i.e., the mild, medium or harsh processes. Results show that the choice of pressing parameters affected all the mechanical and physical properties tested. A statistical analysis revealed that the pressing temperature is the most influential parameter.

Panels pressed under mild conditions rapidly delaminated in water, whereas panels pressed under medium conditions delaminated only at the core layers after 48 hours and panels pressed under harsh conditions did not delaminate at all in water. Panels pressed under harsh conditions had the highest density, a higher shear and bending strength and a lower water absorption.

Table 3.9 Properties of self-bonded veneer panels manufactured according to the Cristescu process at different temperatures. Pressing time 300 seconds and 5 MPa compressive pressure. EMC − equilibrium moisture content, RH − relative humidity.

Property	Standard	200°C (Mild)	225°C (Medium)	250°C (Harsh)	Reference
Three-point bending test:					Cristescu et al. 2015a
maximum load (N)	EN 310	912 ± 52	1,897 ± 74	2,148 ± 39	
ultimate strength (MPa)	EN 310	1.9 ± 0.0	4.9 ± 1.9	19.8 ± 3.8	
type of failure		Inter-laminar shear	Inter-laminar shear	Tension	
Shear strength (MPa)	EN 314	2.0 ± 0.2	5.1 ± 0.4	4.6 ± 0.0	Cristescu et al. 2015a
Density (kg/cm³)	EN 323	670 ± 20	744 ± 39	901 ± 19	Cristescu et al. 2015a,c
Brinell hardness (Kg/mm³)	EN 1534	4.3 ± 0.0	6.4 ± 2.7	10.8 ± 0.7	Cristescu et al. 2015c
Thickness swelling (%)	EN 317	-	22.7 ± 3.2	16.0 ± 2.8	Cristescu et al. 2015a
Water absorption[1] (%)		72.2 ± 0.0	61.5 ± 1.5	40.9 ± 0.8	Cristescu et al. 2015a
pH		4.75	4.62	4.54	Cristescu et al. 2015c
EMC (%) at 20°C, 50% RH		5.1	3.7	2.4	Cristescu et al. 2015c
Mass loss (%)		0.5	1.2	4.3	Cristescu et al. 2015c
Water resistant bond-line[1]	(EN 317)	No	No	Yes	Cristescu et al. 2015a

[1] Water uptake after soaking in water at a temperature of 20°C for 48 hours.

Applications for self-bonded veneer

Self-bonded veneer products can be used for the same purposes as plywood and other panel products. The high density of the self-bonded veneer panels means that their properties are similar to those of densified plywood or high-pressure-laminated veneer. The process temperature is over 200°C, which means that the wood is thermally modified and has about the same durability and hygroscopic properties as thermally modified timber. With a process temperature of 250°C, the bond-line is also water resistant. At present, no producer of self-bonded veneer is known, and it therefore has no certification allowing its use in load-bearing applications. The product has, however, been shown to have good strength properties (Cristescu, 2015).

Table 3.10 shows potential fields of application for self-bonded veneer.

Table 3.10 Potential fields of application for self-bonded veneer divided into Use Classes, see Table 1.7.

	Interior		Exterior		
Product type/Use Class	**1**	**2**	**3**	**4**	**5**
Indoor furniture	x	x			
Floor and non-structural interior uses	x	x			
Exterior joinery			(x)		
Cladding			(x)		
Decking					
Fencing			(x)		
Outdoor furniture			(x)		
Construction elements			(x)		
In-ground timber					
Products exposed to water					

where: x = products have been produced by companies using the modified wood
(x) = products may be produced, based on pre-commercial trials, research, etc.

3.7 Frictional wood welding

Frictional wood welding is a process that can be used to join sawn timber without the use of adhesives, metal fasteners, or any material other than wood. In the welding process, frictional heat is created by a relative motion between the wooden surfaces to be joined, while the surfaces are being pressed together by an externally applied load. In order to overcome the geometrical limitations of the timber and at the same time maintain its physical and ecological properties, adhesive-free friction-welded bonds are a promising concept. Current research into development of the welding process focus on the structural behaviour of the welded joint and its durability, and on the load-bearing capacity of the welded constructional components. A challenge is to develop this technology from small specimens to elements of a structural scale. Visual evaluation has shown that the welding process developed on small specimens cannot be applied in the same way to larger bond-line surfaces. The greatest challenge in the large-scale use of welded components is the sensitivity of the welded bond-line to moisture. The relatively brittle bond-line is extremely sensitive to swelling and shrinkage deformations which may lead to cracks within the interface. In large-scale elements, the bond-line is more sensitive than in smaller specimens, since the stresses in the bond-line due to moisture variations and external loads are larger. This problem becomes particularly important when sawn timber is welded for cross-wise laminations, as in cross-laminated timber (CLT).

The welding stage takes less than a minute, and the temperature in the welded interphase then leads to a softening and flow of the lignin and hemicelluloses. The process results in the detachment of wood cells and the formation of a fibre-entanglement network immersed in a matrix of molten material, which solidifies and results in a significant adhesion in the interphase (Figure 3.22). When the mutual motion of the work pieces ceases, the compressive force is maintained so that the softened bond-line becomes densified and ultimately solidifies, forming a high-density bond-line (Pizzi et al., 2004; Ganne-Chédeville et al., 2005; Kanazawa et al., 2005; Stamm et al., 2005a). The welded bond-line has a characteristic microstructure and chemical composition resulting from the combined effects of the thermal modification and the extensive external load.

Usually, one work piece is fixed and the other is moved, which can be achieved by translational, vibrational, or rotational motion. Welded joints of wood are of good quality and comparable in strength to adhesive bond-lines (Pizzi et al., 2003; Pizzi et al., 2006; Boonstra et al., 2006; Leban et al., 2008). The time required to form such a joint is less than one minute (Stamm et al., 2005a), whereas conventional adhesive bond-lines require several minutes or even hours of compression

Figure 3.22 Welded bond-line between two pieces of European beech. Entangled fibres and degradation products from wood in the welding region may be pressed out from the bond-line during the welding process. In this example, the amount of fibres and degradation products was extensive.

to sufficiently solidified. Within 2–4 seconds, the mechanical properties of welded bond-lines are comparable to those of adhesive joints 24 hours after bonding (Leban et al., 2005), but the eventual long-term durability of the bond-line under, for example, moisture variations has not been reported.

Wood welding is a novel technology for joining sawn timber. The first work on the frictional welding of wood was documented in a German patent granted to Suthoff et al. (1996). This patent and a subsequent patent granted to Suthoff and Kutzer (1997) have reported that sawn timber can be joined through an oscillatory frictional movement. It has also suggested that it may be possible to join sawn timber with a wood dowel using *rotary frictional welding*. The latter patent includes the concept of welding wood in an inert atmosphere or under vacuum. Since 2000, the wood welding process has been intensively developed in Switzerland (cf. Gliniorz and Natterer, 2000; Gliniorz et al., 2001; Ganne-Chédeville et al., 2005), in France (cf. Pizzi et al., 2004; Kanazawa et al., 2005; Pizzi, 2006), and in Sweden (cf. Vaziri, 2011). In 2005, the research teams in France and Switzerland were awarded the Schweighofer Prize for Woodworking Innovation for their work on wood welding (Leban, 2005).

Material selection and preparation

Most wood species can be friction welded, but each species must have its own specific machine setting in order to achieve optimal bond-line properties, and the properties of the bond-line, such as its strength and water resistance, may also depend on the species. The species most frequent studied for wood welding are European beech, Norway spruce and Scots pine, but species such as eucalyptus, poplar, rubberwood, silver birch, Sitka spruce, and various tropical and rare species have also been studied.

It is important that the surfaces to be welded come into contact in order to achieve the frictional heat that makes the process successful. This means that sawn timber to be used for wood welding should not be so distorted that the process is unable to press the surfaces together. Surfaces to be welded should be fine sawn, planed or sanded.

Industrial wood-welding processes

The friction welding of wood is based mainly on technology that has already been applied to thermoplastics and metals, and the first attempts at welding wood were made with devices intended for welding such materials. Subsequently, this welding technology was transferred to woodworking, and special woodworking machines were developed with additional control of the process parameters, making possible the continuous variation of the friction displacement amplitude, frequency, pressure and vibration mode. The friction welding technology is as yet only sparingly used for industrial applications with wood.

The thermal energy required for the process is generated through a combination of mechanically induced friction and pressure, and the movement that achieves the frictional heating can be based on: (1) linear friction, (2) orbital friction, (3) circular friction, or (4) rotary friction welding (cf. Navi and Sandberg, 2012). The welding processes suggested for industrial implementation are based on either linear or rotary friction. Linear welding is used when sawn timbers are welded together in the thickness or width directions, and rotary friction is used when dowels are used to bond laminae in cross-laminated timber, for example.

The process is simple in that the process has few stages (Figure 3.23), but the optimisation of welding parameters for a successful bond-line is a complicated procedure.

It is essential to measure the temperature during wood welding in order to have control over the physical deformation in the wood cell structure and chemical changes taking place in the wood compounds. The accurate measurement of temperature and cooling rate during the welding process is, however, difficult because the heat generated is rapidly conducted deeper into the wood.

It has been suggested that the friction welding process consists of six stages, as shown in Figure 3.24 (Stamm et al., 2005a). In the first stage, the wood surfaces are brought into contact as a result of applied pressure and surface irregularities are smoothed. The greater the roughness of the workpiece, the faster the rise in temperature. Friction displacement results in the polishing of the surface and, consequently, the friction coefficient is reduced. In the second stage of the process, the coefficient of friction is constant, and the temperature increase is, therefore, almost linear. The third phase of the process begins with a sudden increase in the frictional force that causes the formation of smoke. The components on the surface begin to melt as the frictional heat causes the temperature to rise to about 320°C. Due to the thermal decomposition of the surface, the frictional force continuously increases. In the fourth stage, the maximum temperature (420°C–640°C) is

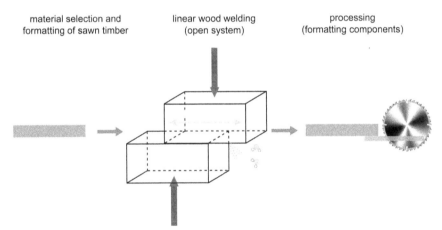

Figure 3.23 Schematic presentation of the wood-welding process.

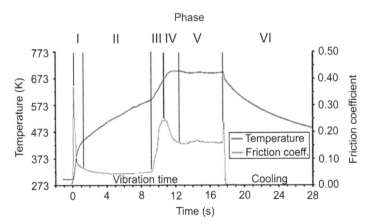

Figure 3.24 Division of the welding of Norway spruce into six different stages based on the coefficient of friction and the bond-line temperature (Stamm et al., 2005a).

reached, resulting in a balance of temperature and friction force. In the fifth phase, the friction force is maintained, and the generation of heat by the energy of friction is balanced by the "molten" wood cells and the hot smoke extracted from the boundary surface. The evaporation of volatile pyrolysis products is strongly endothermic between 300°C and 500°C. Therefore, the heat of the steam results in a cooling effect and a balance of the maximum temperature during the welding of the wood. In the sixth stage of the process, the movement of the wood is stopped, the temperature drops, the bond-line cools and the molten material in the boundary surface solidifies.

The variations in temperature and coefficient of friction shown in Figure 3.24 are typical for the welding of Norway spruce. Stamm (2005) has also studied the welding of species such as European beech, silver birch and larch, and he reported a similar behaviour as a function of welding time. The increase in temperature at the beginning of the process was much faster in beech than in the other species, probably due to a difference in surface properties. Based on the explanation given for each stage of Figure 3.24, it is possible to postulate that stages I+II, stages III+IV and stage V correspond to dry friction, transition friction and viscous friction, respectively (Navi and Sandberg, 2012).

Linear welding of wood

Linear welding is characterised by a linear oscillatory movement, in which the velocity and its corresponding frictional force (parallel to the surface) are sinusoidal. The work pieces are simultaneously exposed to a compressive force, generally constant in level, but the friction coefficient changes continuously due to the change in the direction of displacement. When the melting effect is reached, the vibration is stopped, but the work pieces are still subjected to a compressive force until the molten material in the interface between them solidifies and forms a solid joint. Linear welding of wood provides quality joints suitable for structural use.

As shown in Figure 3.25 the two pieces to be joined are brought into contact under pressure, one part being held stationary while the other part is moved along a line in an oscillating motion. When the frictional movement is stopped, the second phase of welding starts, i.e., solidification of the joint. The pressure exerted on the workpieces is called the *holding pressure* (HP) and it is applied for certain time while the workpieces are held motionless and this period is called the *holding time* (HT).

The quality of a linear friction welded joint (such as its strength and water resistance) is related to certain welding parameters which are divided into machine settings and material properties:

- Welding frequency (WF) – the frequency of the linear oscillatory movement.
- Welding amplitude – the degree of displacement (mm), i.e., the amplitude of the frictional movement.
- Welding time (WT) – the duration of the welding process until the frictional movement is stopped.
- Welding pressure (WP) – the pressure exerted on the specimen during the frictional movement.
- Holding pressure (HP) – the clamping pressure exerted on the welded specimen after termination of the frictional movement.
- Holding time (HT) – the time during which the specimen is held under the clamping pressure after termination of the frictional movement.
- Wood species and type of wood such as heartwood and sapwood.
- Moisture content – the moisture level of the welded surfaces or the equilibrium moisture content of the wood.
- Welding area (WA) – the area of the welded bond-line surfaces, i.e., length x width.

The welding frequency and the amplitude play important roles during the process, and a frequency of 100–240 Hz and an amplitude of 1–3 mm have been shown to give a good result. These parameters are defined by the machine design. The use of a higher frequency level has been shown to improve the moisture stability of the bond-line. The holding time and the holding pressure

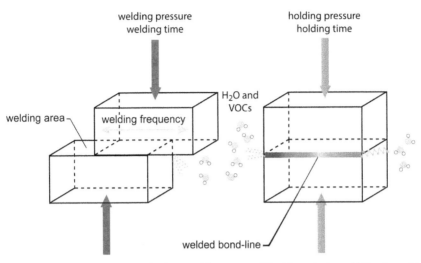

welding pressure
welding time

holding pressure
holding time

welding area

welding frequency

H_2O and VOCs

welded bond-line

Figure 3.25 Welding parameters involved in the linear-welding process. Wood flows in the weld-line due to frictional heat (left), and when the movement stops (right) the bond-line zone solidify.

Table 3.11 Some typical linear-welding parameters for different wood species.

Parameter/Species	European beech	European beech	Silver birch	Scots pine	Scots pine	Scots pine	Scots pine
Moisture content (%)	12	12	12	12	12	12	12
Welding area (mm²)	3,000	4,600	4,000	4,000	4,000	48,000	4,600
Welding frequency (Hz)	100	240	240	150	150	115	240
Welding amplitude (mm)	3	2	2	1 + 1.5 + 2 + 0	2	4	2
Welding time (s)	3	1 + 1.8	2.5 + 3	1 + 3 + 3.5	2 + 2.8	2 +10.2	2 + 3
Welding pressure (MPa)	1.3	1.6 + 1.6	1.3 + 1.8	0.5 + 0.75 + 1.25	0.75 + 1.3	1.5+1.5	1.3 + 1.7
Holding pressure (MPa)	2.0	2.5	2	2.75	1.85	1.87	2.7
Holding time (s)	5	10	10	50	70	60	10
Reference	Gfeller et al. 2003	Vaziri et al. 2020b	Zor et al. 2019	Mansouri et al. 2011	Vaziri et al. 2012	Vaziri et al. 2014	Vaziri et al. 2020a
Machine	Branson 2700	Branson M-624	Branson M-624	KLN Ultraschall LVW-2261	Mecasonic LVW-2361	Branson M-DT24L	Branson M-624

are interrelated and are strongly dependent on the wood species. A moisture content of about 12% in the sawn timber to be joined has been shown to be preferable. A higher moisture content leads to lower friction forces and consequently to a slower increase in the temperature. Too low a moisture content results in rapid thermal degradation. Typical parameter values for welding beech wood are shown in Table 3.11.

When optimal welding parameters are used, a joint strength of 10 MPa can be achieved in European beech wood (Gfeller et al., 2003; Gfeller et al., 2004a,b), and this meets the requirements of the EN 205-D1 standard (CEN, 2003). For a more detailed examination of the welding parameters, see Navi and Sandberg (2012).

Rotary friction welding

In rotary friction welding, the work pieces are joined by dowels and the dowels are welded to the work pieces to be joined. The method is usually called *dowel rotary-friction welding*. In this method, a cylindrical wood dowel is inserted into predrilled holes with a diameter smaller than that of the dowel while it is rotated around its axis at a high rotational speed (ca. 1,200 r.p.m.). A frictional force arises between the contact surfaces of the dowel and the hole as a consequence of the rotary movement of the dowel and the inward compressive force induced by the dowel because its diameter is slightly larger than the diameter of the hole. When the amorphous substances of wood are softened and melted, the rotation of the dowel is stopped momentarily and the compressive force is maintained for a few seconds (Kanazawa et al., 2005; Zoulalian and Pizzi, 2007). The dowel joins the surface of the hole to forms a solid joint (Figure 3.26). In rotary welding, the velocity and friction force are uniform if the materials are homogeneous, at all points at a given distance from the rotation axis. The bonding mechanism of rotary friction welding is the same as that of linear wood welding, i.e., the frictional heat developed causes the amorphous components of the wood to soften in the interface between the work pieces. Rotary friction welding was first developed by Pizzi et al. (2004), who showed that the method gives an effective bonding between the wooden dowel and the predrilled wood.

The parameters that affect the quality of these joints are the wood species, the relative difference in diameter between the dowel and the predrilled hole, the time of application of the compressive force after welding, and the moisture content of the dowel (Pizzi et al., 2004; Ganne-Chédeville et al., 2005). The orientation and smoothness of the dowel do not significantly affect the quality of the joint (Kanazawa et al., 2005). Rotary friction welding has been successfully used for the manufacture of laminated construction beams and flooring (Bocquet et al., 2007a,b).

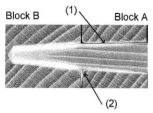

Figure 3.26 X-ray micrograph of a European beech dowel inserted and welded to two blocks of beech by rotary friction. The arrow (1) shows a section with no welding (un-sufficient bonding), and arrow (2) shows the welding with a micro-crack (Ganne-Chédeville et al., 2005).

Nailing with wooden dowels

A special case related to wood welding is a method using wooden nails, or small wooden dowels, to join wood-based materials (Figure 3.27). The nailing system (LIGNOLOC™) was developed by the Austrian company Raimund BECK KG around 2015, using a special pneumatic nail-gun to fire a wooden nail into the wood without any predrilled hole. Pre-drilled holes can be used if there is a risk that the wood will split during nailing. The nail is of densified European beech veneer treated with a resin so that it has a tensile strength comparable to that of an aluminium nail (ca. 250 MPa) and a pointed tip that enters the wood. When the nail is driven into the wood material, a large amount of heat is generated by friction, and this causes the lignin of the wooden nail to weld with the surrounding wood to form a joint, and the resin may also contribute to the bonding. The bonding process is similar to that in linear wood welding. The densified wood makes the nail stronger, and the resin-treatment hinders set-recovery of the densified wood in the nail. Any swelling and shrinkage between the nail and the surrounding wood may be a disadvantage for the bond-line strength over time. The nails have a diameter of 3.7 to 5.3 mm, and a length of 38 to 90 mm.

The use of wooden nails may have several advantages over metal nails. Pure wooden connections are preferred in ecological timber constructions, wooden nails do not create thermal bridges, and

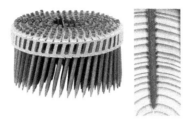

Figure 3.27 Densified wooden nails mounted for use in a nail-gun (left), and a cross-section view of a wooden nail driven into the wood to create a welded bond-line between the nail and the surrounding wood (right).

there are no traces of corrosion. Possible uses that have been mentioned by the company are sauna interiors, furniture, flooring, wood sidings (no streaking), pallets (easy recycling of the wood), boat building, and for the Jewish funeral trade where coffins cannot have metal fasteners.

Properties of the frictional welded bond-line

The specific properties of friction-welded sawn timber are related solely to the welded bond-line, which makes it relevant to discuss only bond-line properties. The energy input and, thus, the heat generated at the joint interface play a key role in the chemical/physical processes leading to the final strength of the welded joint, but the amount of lignin in the wood also influences the mechanical properties.

For the industrial application of the technology, the long-term durability of the joint has to be ensured, but to date only a few studies into construction applications from a structural perspective have been reported, in part due to the vulnerability of the weld to damage from moisture. The welded bond is highly sensitive to the swelling and shrinkage of the wood material if the climatic conditions change. These deformations may lead to cracks within the interface (Vaziri et al., 2014; Vaziri et al., 2015a).

European beech has been intensively studied in wood welding and a high bonding strength has been achieved with thin specimens having a smooth surface (Gfeller et al., 2003; Leban et al., 2004), by contrast, Norway spruce is more problematic because the cell wall tends to collapse during welding, due to the large difference in density between earlywood and latewood. Welded oak has shown a low bond-line strength due to its characteristic microstructure with large vessels. The roughness at the microscopic level affects the coefficient of friction and consequently the maximum temperature that can reach reached during welding. The cellular structure of the middle lamellae in European oak may also be a problem, since it contains a larger proportion of lignin than, for example, European beech or Norway spruce. Poor strength of welded oak joints may be due to the limited softening of the wood components which limits the degree of densification in the welding process and the density variation across the bond-line. The quality of a welded joint also depends on the orientation of the wood elements (Properzi et al., 2005; Ganne-Chédeville et al., 2006b). The strength of a welded joint between mixed tangential and radial surfaces was approximately 10% lower than that of a welded joint between radial-radial or tangential-tangential oriented sections. The strength of a welded joint of cross-laminated radial or tangential surfaces is about half that of a joint between parallel oriented surfaces.

Gases are generated during the welding process, and the higher internal gas pressure influences the bond quality. The increase in vapour pressure is believed to reduce the friction between the contact surfaces necessary to give sufficient frictional heat and, hence, viable welding. A difference has been observed between the gas pressure in the centre and that at the edge, but the internal gas pressure can be reduced significantly if gas evacuation channels are provided at the contact surface (Hahn et al., 2015). The easier transport of vapour from the interface to the outside also led to a more homogeneous distribution of the shear strength over the whole interface. By profiling the transverse surfaces to be welded, e.g., by moulding a wavy surface profile, the long-term bond-line strength and resistance to moisture was significantly improved (Hahn et al., 2015).

Moisture resistance of the bond-line

When exposed to a high moisture content or water, the welded bond-line undergoes a chemical decomposition and decreases in strength, the soluble compounds being extracted from the joint, but the residual strength locked in the strong densified wood cells tends to recover at high humidity. The combined effect of tension release and dissolution of degradation compounds leads to a rapid delamination of the welded bond-line.

Some methods for enhancing the water resistance of welded wood joints have been studied by Pizzi et al. (2011), Mansouri et al. (2011), Vaziri (2011), and Vaziri et al. (2020a-c), but such efforts are still comparatively rare, especially studies of the moisture dynamics in the weld interface. The basic understanding of the underlying mechanisms for permeability in the welded wood joints has been shown to be deficient, and this leads to a poor output on the permeability of these products.

Vaziri (2011) showed that, compared to welded European beech which cannot withstand cold water immersion for more than 30 minutes, welded Scots pine can withstand cold water immersion for more than 455 days without delamination, where the heartwood of Scots pine showed a greater water resistance than sapwood. After 210 days of cold-water immersion, welded heartwood samples of Scots pine still showed a tensile shear strength of 4.1 ± 0.5 MPa and after 4 months of outdoor exposure, they still retained half their initial tensile-shear strength. Vaziri (2011) suggested that the greater water resistance of Scots pine compared to beech could be explained by the higher content of extractives in Scots pine.

Microstructure of welded joint

Examination of the weld interface and of the adjoining areas may shed light on the structural and chemical changes in the wood material due to friction welding that are important for the mechanical and moisture-related properties of welded bond-line.

Welding involves the total destruction of the cellular structure on the welded surfaces of the wood, creating a dense amorphous mass containing portions of the cell walls. Under the influence of mechanical pressure and high temperature, the bond-line is densified and the cell walls collapse (Stamm et al., 2005a), but the densification is less pronounced in latewood.

Figure 3.28 presents a confocal microscope micrograph of a welded joint of two Norway spruce pieces achieved by circular friction. The microstructure of the weld consists of a *molten zone* and a

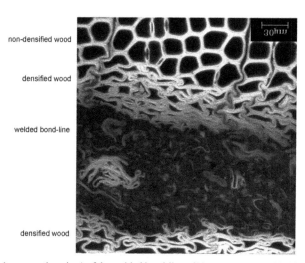

Figure 3.28 Micrograph (cross-section view) of the welded bond-line of Norway spruce welded by circular friction (Stamm et al., 2005b).

heat-affected zone that is not molten. The latter can be further divided into three sub-areas: a fully plasticised and deformed area, where the cell lumens are visible but completely closed; partially plasticised and deformed area, and an un-deformed area. Ganne-Chédeville et al. (2006b) measured the thicknesses of the different bond-line zones in welded radial surfaces, and reported that the molten zone was 155 μm thick and that the heat-affected zone was 1,076 μm thick, the fully plasticised and deformed zone was 172 μm and the partially plasticised and deformed zone 825 μm thick. The thickness of the welded bond-line depended on the welding temperature (Ganne-Chédeville et al., 2006a). The heat-affected zone was defined as the zone outside which no anatomical or density differences were noticeable.

Density profile

An effective indicator of the quality of the welded bond-line is the density. Wood is a porous material that can be compressed until the density reaches that of the cell-wall material, which has been found to range from 1,497 to 1,517 kg/m³ (Wilfong, 1966; Kellog and Wangaard, 1969). Leban et al. (2004) suggested that the main reason for the high strength of a welded joint is the higher density. The density of the welded bond-line of European beech (750 kg/m³) is ca. 1,000 kg/m³ or higher, but in rotary friction welding, the bond-line density may reach values between 1,350 kg/m³ and 1,500 kg/m³ (Pizzi et al., 2004). The welding effect is achieved only in parts where the temperature is high enough to soften the wood components.

Vaziri et al. (2015a) used nano-X-ray computed tomography (CT) for the non-invasive determination of the bond-line density profile of welded wood joints, and they showed, as expected, that welding was accompanied by a considerable increase in the bulk density, but a lower cell-wall density at the bond-line was also observed (Figure 3.29) down to ca. 1,000 kg/m³ due to thermal degradation of the cell-wall material. The heterogeneity of the wood density indicated that regions with a lower density, corresponding to earlywood, were more severely damaged than the latewood regions, particularly in the case of earlywood cells with thinner and therefore less stable cell walls.

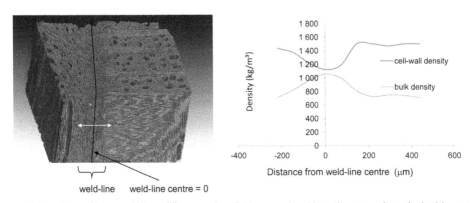

Figure 3.29 Density profile around the welding zone based (European beech) on the grey values obtained by nano-CT scanning. Nano-CT image of a weld-line and from welding unaffected wood (left), and density measurement where zero means the centre of the weld-line (right).

Chemical structure and VOC

Wood can undergo thermal degradation (Section 3.1) when exposed to an elevated temperature and wood welding, which combines temperature with mechanical friction, produces conditions conducive to the depolymerisation of hemicelluloses and lignin and to limited changes in cellulose, and the resulting conditions allow reactions to occur among the depolymerised fractions.

Studies of the effects of welding on eucalyptus (Belleville et al., 2018) using pyrolysis gas chromatography – mass spectrometry showed significant differences in the degradation of extractive compounds, fatty acid chains, and terpenoids reacting with hydroxyl groups to produce a range of esterification products which were assumed to increase the adhesive properties during the welding process. In addition, the production of citric acid as a result of the degradation of fatty acids can improve in the mechanical performance of wood welds (Amirou et al., 2017). Other studies focussing on the aqueous extracts of welded European beech and Norway spruce (Placencia-Peña et al., 2015) identified lignin, mono-oligosaccharides, acetic acid, vanillin, furfural, 5-hydroxymethylfurfural, and syringaldehyde in measureable quantities, lignin and its fragmented components being the most common, slightly higher amounts being obtained from welded European beech than from welded Norway spruce, presumably because of the reduced recondensation of syringyl lignin. Exceptionally high levels of water-soluble extractives were found within 1.5 seconds of starting the welding process, i.e., well before the time at which cross-linking and welding occur.

In addition to fibre interlacing, welding leads to various chemical reactions, particularly the cross-linking of lignin and furans (Wieland et al., 2005; Windeisen and Wegener, 2008). These chemical reactions contribute in a minor way to the mechanical strength of the joint, particularly to its modulus of elasticity, but they occur only after welding, when the workpieces are exposed to pressure, which means that the duration of application of the compressive force after welding is important for the formation of a proper joint (Gfeller et al., 2003; Gfeller et al., 2004a).

VOCs (Volatile Organic Compounds) in the smoke during the welding process are mainly decomposition products of hemicelluloses and very little from lignin (Omrani et al., 2012), and the mass balance of the welded material shows an increase in the amount of Klason lignin in the weld interphase. An analysis of welded panels of European beech and Norway spruce has shown that no harmful chemical compound is present in a concentration exceeding the allowed values for indoor applications.

Vaziri et al. (2015b) found that welded European beech emitted significant amounts of aldehydes and ketones. The main VOCs emitted from the welded wood at the end of the first day were: furfural (11,000 $\mu g/m^2 h$), formaldehyde (257 $\mu g/m^2 h$), acetone/acrolein (75 $\mu g/m^2 h$), and acetaldehyde (61 $\mu g/m^2 h$). The emission of these VOCs was lower if the moisture content of the wood was higher. Compared to the emission from wood-based panels with emission from the entire surface, the welded wood emitted formaldehyde and furfural only from its thin welded bond-line and only during the first days. After 6 days these VOC emissions had decreased to a concentration to which humans can be exposed without any adverse health effects.

These by-products relate to the chemical pathways shown by Belleville et al. (2013), who postulated that there are four mechanisms by which lignin degrades in sugar maple and yellow birch:

i) side-chain oxidation (Geib et al., 2008),

ii) free-radical thermal degradation of β-O-4-bonded structures (van der Hage et al., 1993),

iii) depolymerisation and condensation reactions (Li et al., 2007), and

iv) the formation of formaldehyde (adapted from Schäfer and Roffael (2000)).

The occurrence of these mechanisms was shown (Belleville et al., 2013) by Fourier Transform infra-red (FTIR) spectroscopy, and pyrolysis gas chromatography/mass spectrometry (py-GC/MS), whilst X-ray photoelectron spectroscopy (XPS) showed an increase in oxygen functionality for maple. This was assumed to be partly due to an increase in free phenolic groups and to a decrease in ether bonds between phenylpropane units in lignin following the welding, but similar results were not obtained with birch.

Most of pyrolysis analyses have been undertaken on linear welding, but Zhu et al. (2017) reviewed results from the rotary welding of birch dowels and they showed that the welding was successful along the length of the dowel, but not at the tip. The welding effect gave better mechanical properties, however, when the dowel was pre-immersed in copper (II) chloride.

By measuring the NMR spectra of welded bond-lines, Gfeller et al. (2003) demonstrated that physico-chemical effects and not only chemical effects occur during welding, with tracheids being interwoven in a matrix of molten polymers. The cells were not severely damaged, indicating that melting takes place mainly in the middle lamellae that are rich in lignin (Delmotte et al., 2008), and that the molten matrix consists solely of intercellular material, mainly of the amorphous polymeric material in the middle lamellae (Stamm et al., 2006). Amorphous cell-wall polymers consist mainly of lignin and a small proportion of hemicelluloses. The melting of the amorphous polymers in the middle lamella results in a partial cleavage of the cells forming a network of molten material that hardens after the welding process.

Applications of welded wood

First pioneered in 1996, the mechanical properties of the weld have been studied in the past decades across Europe and the technique been applied with some success in the furniture industry and in the bonding of wood composites (Stamm, 2005; Resch et al., 2006; Bocquet et al., 2007b; Ganne-Chédeville et al., 2007; Navi and Sandberg, 2012; Hahn et al., 2012; Hahn et al., 2014a,b). Welded wood joints can also be seen in specialised applications, such as wine barrels and sports equipment (Navi and Sandberg, 2012), but there have been few studies of construction applications from a structural perspective, partly due to the vulnerability of the welded bond-line to damage from moisture.

Wood-welding techniques have been suggested for the surface treatment of wood to create a harder surface layer in the presence of polymerisation oils, such as sunflower oil (Pizzi et al., 2005).

It can be concluded that the use of wood welding as an alternative to the use of adhesives has so far been very limited, although the possible applications may be numerous (Table 3.12).

Table 3.12 Potential fields of application for welded wood divided into Use Classes, see Table 1.7.

Product type/Use Class	Interior		Exterior		
	1	2	3	4	5
Indoor furniture	x	x			
Floor and non-structural interior uses	x	x			
Exterior joinery			(x)		
Cladding			(x)		
Decking					
Fencing			(x)		
Outdoor furniture			(x)		
Construction elements			(x)		
In-ground timber					
Products exposed to water					

where: x = products have been produced by companies using the modified wood
(x) = products may be produced, based on pre-commercial trials, research, etc.

3.8 Wood densification

Wood densification is a process whereby the density of wood is increased by compression of the cells in the transverse direction to reduce the void volume of the lumens (THM densification), by the impregnation of the cell wall or cell lumen with a synthetic resin (chemical bulking), or by a combination of THM densification and bulking (Kollmann et al., 1975). In THM densification, the volume of cell-wall material per unit volume of wood is increased, whereas in chemical bulking, new material is added to the wood through impregnation by a polymer, a natural resin, a wax, sulphur, or molten metal (Kultikova, 1999). The purpose of densification is to improve the hardness, the abrasion resistance and the strength, but compression of the cells in the transverse direction may also be used to increase the transverse bendability in moulding, for the manufacture of, e.g., shells and tubes (see Section 3.9).

Densification is in most cases carried out by compressing of wood that has first been softened or plasticised (see also Sections 1.7 and 3.3). Plasticisation acts at the molecular level and softens the gross structure of the wood material so that it becomes semi-plastic, and this generally means that less force is required to compress the wood structure, i.e., the modulus of elasticity is lowered, and the ultimate strain in both tension and compression is increased, reducing the tendency to damage under densification. The wood can be softened prior to compression: by the application of heat, steam, or chemicals (Figure 3.30). Compression can nevertheless, under certain circumstances, be successfully applied to wood without any pre-treatment or softening, an example being the radial compression of low-density coniferous wood (Nilsson et al., 2011).

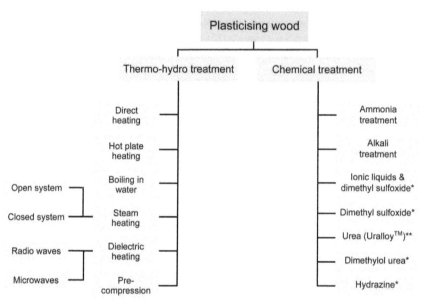

Figure 3.30 Classification of methods for making wood more flexible. * Methods that have been assessed at laboratory scale only, ** Withdrawn commercial process.

Densification can be achieved either throughout the wood (bulk densification), or in only a part of the wood, normally at the surface, i.e., surface densification (Sandberg et al., 2017). Transverse compression may be carried out in one or more directions at the same time. Multi-axial densification seems to have been fairly common in industrial production in Europe until the 1950s (see Vorreiter, 1958) but it is now considerably rarer. An example of modern multi-axial densification is the densification of dowels for the connection of the boards in cross-laminted timber (dowel CLT), that is produced in Switzerland by the Nägeli AG construction company, for example, and in Austria by the Thoma Holz GmbH company.

A compressive load may also be applied in the longitudinal direction of softened wood, so-called pre-compressed wood, but the purpose is then usually to increase the longitudinal bendability rather than to increase the density. In longitudinal compression, the bendability increases because of micro-structural changes, such as plastic deformation of the cell wall with the formation of slip planes, cell-wall buckling and, local shear-band deformation at the macro-level (Navi and Sandberg, 2012). A longitudinal densification technique was patented by Hanemann (1917, 1928), and further developed in Germany under the name *Patentbiegholz* (patent bent wood), and a similar method is nowadays applied in the industrial longitudinal compression technology for softening wood before cold bending of hardwood (Compwood™). Compwood™ was developed during the 1990s by the Danish Technological Institute in Denmark (Thomassen et al., 1991), but the equipment is now marketed by the Compwood A/S company in Denmark. The patented production equipment has the advantage that whole-wood bending can be achieved in a simple manner even for small production volumes with a reasonable investment. The raw material for compression has to meet the same quality demands as for normal furniture manufacture, i.e., it must be without large knots and other defects. Black cherry, common ash, common walnut, elm, European beech, red oak, and silver maple have been shown to be suitable for compression. The sawn timber, normally 45 × 45 × 3000 mm in size, is softened by steam before the compression stage where the timber is compressed to approximately 80% of its original length. After unloading, the timber expands and returns to approximately 85% of its original length. A typical compression cycle takes 9–10 minutes if the moisture content is 20–25%. The capacity is typically 0.5–4.5 m³ of hardwood every eight hours, depending on the wood species, moisture content, the quality of the wood and the choice of machine. After longitudinal densification, the pre-densifed timber are sealed in plastic to avoid drying, and can be bent in a cold state at a later date.

The densified materials available on the market today are produced by a lumen-filling method or by a combination of resin impregnation and transverse compression to increase the density, but thermal-hydro-mechanical (THM) densification is strongly under development.

THM densification takes place under steamed conditions, where both the softening of the wood prior to densification and the fixation in the compressed state are achieved without damage to the cell-wall structure (Navi and Sandberg, 2012). Figure 3.31 shows the morphological changes occurring in hybrid poplar as a result of THM densification. The future development of THM densification will probably lead to the use of additives in the process, but with less resin and other high-volume bulking substances, in order to achieve an effective process with low environmental impact.

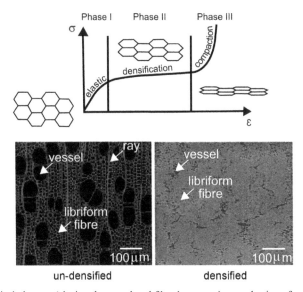

Figure 3.31 Morphological changes (closing the vessel and fibre lumens, zig-zag shaping of rays) of hybrid poplar as a result of THM densification. Densification at 170°C and 5.5 MPa; increased the density from 371 kg/m³ to 1,210 kg/m³.

An historical overview of densification

The oldest evidence of wood densification is a heat-hardened tip of a more than 100,000-year-old Lehringen spear found in 1948, buried inside the skeleton of an elephant, produced either by *Homo Heidelbergensis* or *Homo Neanderthalensis* (Adam, 1951; Källander, 2016). At the end of the 19th Century, more industrialised wood-densification techniques started to be used.

Vorreiter (1942) reported that in 1886 the idea of densifying massive wood by applying a compressive force was patented by Robert Stöckhart in Leipzig (Germany), probably one of the first patents in the field. This technique was intended for the production of shuttles, but it is uncertain whether production was ever started. In the Stöckhart method, wood was first impregnated with an oil and then densified in the longitudinal direction. Other methods followed, and many of them were patented in the United States: Sears in 1900, Walsh and Watts in 1923, Olesheimer in 1929, Brossman in 1931, Esselen in 1934, and Olson in 1934 (Vorreiter, 1958; Kollmann et al., 1975; Navi and Sandberg, 2012). The first industrial production of densified wood goes back, however, to a chance discovery by the Austrian brothers Pfleumer during the First World War (Kollmann, 1936). After many slow improvements, they developed the well-known and still existing product Lignostone™.

In the spring of 1915, Fritz and Hermann Pfleumer discovered the new material, Lignostone, in their Dresden laboratory while developing a synthetic rubber. In June 1915, they applied for a patent for a "method for compacting wood" (Pfleumer and Pfleumer, 1915), which was granted on May 17, 1916. During the First World War, they founded, together with partners, the company Holz-Veredlung GmbH in Berlin, but it never started production. According to the Treaty of Versailles, German patent rights had to be extradited on request to the Allies, so that the rights could be temporarily outsourced abroad. The Pfleumer brothers withdrew from the company, but Ludwig Roselius, a coffee trader and founder of the Bremen-based company Kaffee Hag, took over and in 1919, he financed the construction of a Lignostone™ factory in The Netherlands on a license basis. In 1920, Hermann Röchling (the Röchling Group) took over all the activities with Lignostone™, and Holzveredelung GmbH was relocated from Berlin to Haren in the Emsland region of Germany, and this is now (2020) the oldest Röchling Group location. The method is based on a simple process in which wood with a moisture content less than 13% is placed between heated platens in a hydraulic jack and compressed to 2.5 MPa in the radial direction. The temperature is raised to ca. 140°C with a processing time of two hours. Today, the Lignostone™ trademark also includes a resin-impregnated veneer-laminate.

Other trademarks for resin-impregnated densified wood are based more or less on the Pfleumer concept, include Compreg™ (see Section 2.3) which was presented by Stamm and Seborg in the 1940s. Compreg™ was produced for aircraft propellers by the Formica Insulation Company in the 1940s under the trade name of Pregwood™ and Compreg™ is still being produced on an industrial scale in, e.g., Germany, Poland, and the USA.

The main products in which densified wood is used on the market are based on resin-impregnated densified veneers, and the resin-impregnation of full-size timber is rare. Among some of the names or trade names of densified material either currently or formely in production are: BakelisiertesHolz, Compreg, Carbonwood, Dehonit, Delignit, Delignit-Feinholz, Hydulignum, Insulam, Insulcul, Jablo, Jabroc, Jicwood, Kunstharzschichtholz, Le Bois Bakélisé, Lignofol (Preßschichtholz), Lignostone (Preßvollholz), MyWood2, obo-Festholz, Panzerholz (Delignit), Permali, Permawood, Pregwood, Ranprex, Sonowood, Staypak, Surendra, Transformerwood, and VANyCARE. Typical products based on this type of densified wood are storage containers for liquid natural gas (LNG) and associated support structures, wear plates for machinery and transportation vehicles, machine-pattern moulds, tooling, jigs, bullet-proof barriers, security panels, transformer components, neutron shielding, audio component cases, and some structural building components.

The use of metals for bulking wood, *metalised wood*, dates from work in Germany in the 1930s (Kollmann et al., 1975). Through impregnation with a molten metal alloy consisting of 50% bismuth, 31% lead, and 19% tin, a highly conductive, non-burning composite with anisotropic properties considerably different from those of untreated wood was achieved, but so far, the uses of metalised wood seem to have been limited.

After the early work on wood densification in Europe, much of the research into wood modification, especially within the area of adhesive impregnation, was carried out by Alfred Stamm and co-workers at the Forest Products Laboratory in Madison (WI), USA. To overcome the problem of the recovery after compression, Stamm and Seborg (1941) impregnated thin veneers with an aqueous solution of a phenol-formaldehyde pre-polymer whose molecules were small enough to penetrate the cell wall together with the water. The pre-polymer caused the cell wall to swell up to 25% more than when swelling in water. After curing, the composite had a final volume equal to roughly that of the water-swollen wood. The veneer was dried, but the pre-polymer was not polymerised, and the desired thickness could be obtained by assembling multiple layers of veneer. Under heat and pressure sufficient to bond the veneers, the impregnant polymerised to yield a cohesive composite with an anti-shrink efficiency of 70–75%. Stamm and Seborg called this product *Impreg* (see Chapter 2.4). A similar product was patented in USA already in the 1920s by Walsh and Watts (1923).

In a similar process, the impregnated veneers were placed in a press at a temperature of about 150°C for 15 to 30 minutes per 25 mm total thickness and densified under a pressure of up to about 7 MPa. After polymerisation, a high-density (up to 1,460 kg/m³) product with very low volume swelling (< 4%) when soaked in water was obtained. This material has been given the generic name of *Compreg* (see Chapter 2.3).

Later, the process was improved to further decrease the degree of recovery, and the product was called *Staypak* (Seborg et al., 1945; Stamm et al., 1948). Staypak is heat-stabilised, compressed wood that has been heated during the pressing process under conditions such that the compression is not lost when the wood is subsequently swollen. Although it can swell appreciably, it returns to practically the original compressed thickness when dried to its original moisture content. It is thus wood that "stays compressed" (Seborg and Stamm, 1941).

In a comprehensive review article describing most of the early studies, Schneider (1994) reported improvements in hardness and dimensional stability as a result of impregnation with agents such as methyl methacrylate, styrene, phenol-, urea-, and melamine-formaldehyde, epoxy, furfuryl alcohol, or isocyanates.

A common process in which the densification of veneer is an important feature is the production of plywood. The veneers are densified to different levels depending on the properties required of the plywood, and the laminate becomes dimensionally stable through the gluing together of the veneers. In MDF and particleboard production, the surfaces of the panels are densified to some extent.

In the late 1900s, several new densification projects with approaches different from that of resin-impregnated densified wood were started. Some of the projects were initiated by university research, others by a more industrial environment, but to date (2020), none of these innovative processes have been successfully introduced on a large industrial scale (Neyses, 2019). The processes referred to by Neyses (2019) are the CaLignum process, the PrimWood concept, the VTC process, the MDF-press concept, and the moulded tube concept; all of which will be described later in this section.

The Swiss Wood Solutions company was founded in 2016 as a spin-off from ETH Zürich and EMPA in Switzerland. Their main product is impregnated and densified wood for advanced use instead of expensive tropical species in, for example, musical instruments (Sonowood™) (Jones et al., 2019).

There have also been some less successful flooring products on the market where attempts to eliminate the set-recovery with various methods of curing resin have been tried, e.g., with wax impregnation (Tarkett flooring company) or by mechanical locking in a layered construction (Kährs flooring company).

For further studies of older densification techniques, further reading is recommended in Kollman (1936, 1955), Miedler (1943), Vorreiter (1958), Stamm (1964), Kollmann et al. (1975), and Navi and Sandberg (2012). A comprehensive historical background and state-of-the-art in the field of wood densification, dealing mainly with the period after 1950, is given in the doctoral thesis by Neyses (2019).

Permanent fixation of compressive deformation

The main problem associated with densification is the need for fixation of the transverse compressive deformation, to eliminate the two forms of recovery which tend to arise after the compressive load has been removed: elastic spring-back and moisture-induced set-recovery. Besides spring-back and set-recovery, there may also be natural swelling and shrinkage of the cell-wall material due to moisture variations, but this is not considered further here (cf. Section 1.4).

The more the wood is densified, the greater is the potential for the compressive deformation to recover (Blomberg et al., 2006; Kutnar et al., 2009), a behaviour that can be attributed to a combination of the cellular structure and the properties of the cell-wall polymers (Wolcott and Shutler, 2003). Norimoto et al. (1993) considered three mechanisms to be essential to prevent the recovery:

1. the formation of cross-links between molecules of the matrix,
2. the relaxation of the stresses introduced in the microfibrils and the matrix during densification, and
3. the polymerisation of hydrophilic materials inside the cell wall to avoid the softening of hemicelluloses when the densified wood is exposed to moisture.

Compression ratio, spring-back and set-recovery

The interaction between the glass-transition temperatures (T_g) of the wood constituents (see Chapter 1.7) and the moisture content determines the conditions for plasticisation, densification and locking of the densified wood. Figure 3.32 shows how the un-densified wood is plasticised, e.g., through combining heat and moisture, and then put under a transverse load so that the cells deform. In order to reduce the immediate *elastic spring-back* when the press is opened, the material is cooled before the press is opened in order to lower the temperature to below ca. 80°C. The cooling stage will not, however, completely eliminate the spring-back, some elastic strain from the compression normally remains. If the densified wood in an "un-loaded state" is plasticised by exposure to moisture, for example, it will almost completely recover to its state before densification. Depending on the severity of the re-plasticisation, this set-recovery can take from less than an hour to several years. The set-recovery can be reduced by various pre- and post-treatments incorporated into the densification process.

The degree of densification may be described by the *compression ratio* (CR) which, in the one-dimensional case, can be calculated as the reduction in thickness due to densification divided by the initial thickness:

$$CR = \frac{B_0 - B'_c}{B_0} \tag{3.1}$$

where B_0 is the original dimension of the specimen in the densification direction before densification and B'_c is the actual dimension of the specimen after densification (after unloading). The CR is thus meaningful only with regard to bulk densification. Densifying only the wood surface may lead to a large CR close beneath the densified surface, although the total CR of the wood piece is much lower. The level of densification of surface-densified wood should instead be measured locally.

Spring-back occurs immediately when the pressure is released after the densification and can be attributed to the release of elastic strains which develop within the chemical bonds of the wood material, when the external load is applied in order to achieve densification. Depending on the compression ration, the moisture content and the temperature of the wood material, the densified wood cells recover to different extents. Densified wood that is plasticised when the compressive load is released recovers more than densified wood that is dry and below its glass-transition temperature. Complete elimination of the spring-back is almost impossible.

The elastic spring-back (SB) is calculated as:

$$SB = \frac{B'_c - B_c}{B_0 - B_c} \tag{3.2}$$

where B'_c is the actual dimension of the specimen after densification, B_c is the target dimension of the specimen after densification, and B_0 is the original dimension of the specimen in the densification

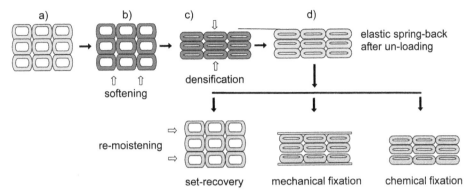

Figure 3.32 Schematic illustration of wood densification in the transverse direction at the cell level, spring-back, set-recovery and different methods of fixation of the compression set: (a) initial un-deformed state, (b) softening of the wood by, e.g., steam, (c) densification, (d) cooling and unloading of the compressive force resulting in elastic spring-back. Re-moistening of the densified wood leads to total set-recovery if the densified wood is not fixated by mechanical, chemical or THM-treatment.

direction before densification. The spring-back can thus vary between 0% and 100%, where 0% indicates no spring-back and 100% indicates total spring-back to the original dimension before densification.

The set-recovery (SR) is calculated as:

$$SR = \frac{R'_C - R_C}{R_0 - R_C} \tag{3.3}$$

where R'_c is the dimension of the densified specimen after the wet-dry cycling, R_c is the dimension of the specimen after densification, and R_0 is the oven-dry dimension of the specimen in the densification direction before densification. The set-recovery can vary between 0% and 100%, where 0% indicates that there is no set-recovery, i.e., that the compressive deformation is completely fixed, and 100% indicates that the recovery is total.

One of the major theories describing the underlying mechanisms of elastic spring-back and set-recovery was presented by Navi and Sandberg (2012) and further described by Navi and Pizzi (2014), who suggested that the set-recovery is due to the elastic recovery of the deformation of crystalline cellulose, which is 'frozen' inside the plastically deformed matrix of lignin and hemicellulose. A re-plasticisation of the matrix after it has been densified, e.g., through moisture, leads to a recovery of the elastic deformation in the crystalline cellulose.

Mechanical fixation to hinder the set-recovery

One well-established way of mechanically restraining the set-recovery is by impregnation of the wood before densification with an adhesive. A more sofisticated method to hinder the set-recovery has been presented by Nilsson et al. (2001), who studied the shape stability of a three-layered cross-laminated wood panel where one or both outermost layers were of densified wood and the core or the core and one of the outermost layers were of non-densified wood. The combined laminate mechanically restrains the set-recovery of the densified layers (see further the PrimWood densification method). A quarter sawn piece of Scots pine, 45 × 95 mm in cross section, with a moisture content of 12% was densified in the radial direction (CR = 50%) at room temperature without any softening treatment. The densified timber was then split in the longitudinal-radial section to several ca. 4 mm thick lamellae that were cross-laminated glued on a core of un-densified wood. By optimisation of the thickness ratio of the surface to the bottom layer, shape-stable products with no set-recovery were achieved (Figure 3.33).

Figure 3.33 A three-layered cross-laminated panel, with a top-layer of densified Norway spruce.

Steam treatment to reduce set-recovery

Steam treatment prior to compression can markedly increase the compressibility of wood, and significantly reduce the internal stresses built-up during the compression stage (Hsu et al., 1988; Inoue et al., 1993; Inoue et al., 1996; Dwianto et al., 1999; Esteves et al., 2007). Inoue et al. (2008) studied the influence of *pre-steaming* between 120 and 220°C for 5 to 20 minutes on the fixation of densified sugi and Japanese red pine. The set-recovery generally decreased with increasing pre-steaming temperature and time, and the level of decrease correlated closely with the weight loss of wood material during the pre-steaming process, and was explained as being due to a reduced of accessibility to moisture and a reduction of residual stresses.

Inoue et al. (1993) have shown that the use of saturated steam during the post treatment (*post-steaming*) greatly reduces the time necessary for the heat treatment to achieve a certain degree of set-recovery reduction (Figure 3.34), compared to that required when dry-heating is used (cf. Figure 3.35). They found that almost complete fixation may be achieved by steaming densified wood for 1 minute at 200°C or for 8 minutes at 180°C. There is a clear reduction in set-recovery with increasing time and temperature, as shown in Figure 3.34. Similar results were reported by Dwianto et al. (1999), who achieved a degree of permanent fixation after the compressive deformation of wood by high-temperature steaming of densified sugi. The results showed that the recovery decreased with increasing steaming time and almost reached zero after 10 minutes at 200°C. Navi and Heger (2004) reported that complete fixation of compression set can be achieved by the post-treatment of compressed wood under saturated steam conditions, such as 165°C for 30 minutes, 190°C for 8 minutes, or 200°C for 2 minutes. Reynolds (2004) also concluded that set-recovery could be significantly reduced by exposure to saturated steam at 200°C.

Kutnar and Kamke (2012) densified low-density hybrid poplar by mechanical compression under saturated steam, superheated steam, and transient conditions at temperature levels of 150°C, 160°C and 170°C, and they also compressed wood under saturated steam conditions at 170°C, followed by post heat-treatment at 200°C for 1, 2 and 3 minutes. They found that a higher temperature during

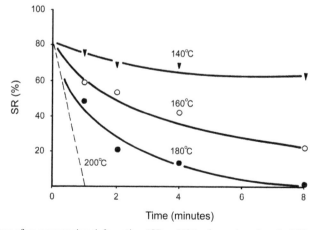

Figure 3.34 Set-recovery after compressive deformation (CR = 51%) of samples of sugi of 20 × 20 × 30 mm (LxRxT) densified under saturated vapour as a function of the temperature and time of treatment (Inoue et al., 1993).

the compression resulted in less set-recovery and that compression under saturated steam at 170°C significantly reduced the set-recovery and swelling upon exposure to water in comparison with densification under superheated or transient conditions, but that an increase in temperature to 200°C only marginally improved the dimensional stability. In specimens compressed under saturated steam at 170°C and thereafter heat-treated at 200°C for 3 minutes, the set-recovery was only 6% after five water soaking/drying cycles. This low set-recovery of wood densified under saturated steam was explained as being due to a break-down of the cross-links, coupled with a softening of the lignin and the possibility that covalent bonds were formed in the deformed position (Inoue et al., 2008).

Popescu et al. (2014) made a THM densification of small-leaved lime wood at 140°C in saturated steam and exposed the densified wood to post-treatment at 140°C, 160°C or 180°C in saturated steam, and they showed that the post-treatment at 160°C for 80 minutes or at 180°C for 10, 15 and 20 minutes gave a permanent fixation of the transversal compression deformation.

The principal phenomenon of set-recovery does not depend on whether the wood have been bulk or surface densified, as shown by Gong et al. (2010) and Laine et al. (2013), for example.

Thermal treatment

In the absence of steam, high temperature alone can permanently fixate the compressive deformation (cf. thermo-mechanical treatment). The high-temperature treatment of wood reduces its hygroscopicity, due to changes in the polar side groups on the molecular structures of cellulose, hemicelluloses, lignin and extractives (Hillis, 1984; Morsing, 2000). Fang et al. (2011, 2012) showed that the set-recovery of veneers densified at low temperatures was very high, but that the set-recovery decreased dramatically when the densification temperature exceeded 180°C and that the recovery was almost zero for veneers densified at 220°C.

The effect on set-recovery of the post-treatment temperature alone (dry heating) and time has been studied by Inoue et al. (1993) and the results are shown in Figure 3.35. Similar results were achieved by Dwianto et al. (1997). The reduction in set-recovery with increasing time and temperature is clear, and it also clear that the time needed for reduction of set-recovery is much longer than that required for post-treatment in a moist atmosphere. Li et al. (2013) also found that the dimensional stability of densified wood treated in an open system can be considerably improved by elevating the temperature to 200°C.

Welzbacher et al. (2008) showed that the set-recovery of thermo-mechanically densified Norway spruce was almost completely eliminated by OHT thermal modification treatment at a temperature

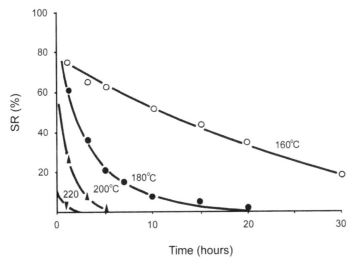

Figure 3.35 Set-recovery after compressive deformation (CR = 51%) of samples of sugi of 20 × 20 × 30 mm (LxRxT) densified as a function of the temperature and time of treatment dry air in a owen (Inoue et al., 1993).

above 200°C (cf. Table 3.4). Fang et al. (2011) also studied the influence of OHT but on densified veneer at 180°C, 200°C, or 220°C, and they found that thermal modification significantly reduced the set-recovery, and that the effect increased with increasing temperature and time.

Chemical treatment

Gabrielli and Kamke (2008) combined different types of chemical modification (phenol-formaldehyde, tung oil, and acetylation with acetic anhydride) with the viscoelastic thermal compression (VTC) process in order to study the dimensional stability. After it had been soaked for 24 hours in water at 20°C, the phenol-formaldehyde-modified and acetylated wood showed an increase in dimensional stability compared to un-impregnated VTC wood. The tung-oil-treated wood showed no improvement. Gabrielli and Kamke (2010) have also shown that impregnation with phenol-formaldehyde with a high molecular weight improves the stability.

Pfriem et al. (2012) suggested a densification process in which European beech wood was impregnated with a solution consisting of furfuryl alcohol and maleic anhydride, followed by densification and curing in a heated press. The set-recovery was clearly reduced by the *in situ* polymerisation of the furfuryl alcohol solution to a furan resin.

Recent studies by Neyses et al. (2020, 2021) showed a strong plastification effect on wood can be achieved with ionic liquids (ILs) and organic superbases, which can reduce or even eliminate the elastic and set-recovery components of deformation of surface-densified wood. The elastic spring-back was eliminated, and the set-recovery after two wet/dry cycles in water was reduced to a value as low as 10%. The superbases had an effect more or less equal to that of the ILs, but it is not yet clear whether treatment with superbases involves to the same mechanism as treatment with ILs.

Material selection and preparation

It is possible to densify any wood species by a THM treatment or other methods, and the wood can be densified in one or more directions at the same time. Neyses and Sandberg (2015) developed a structured, quantifiable and easy-to-use methodology to identify wood species suitable for a specific product, in which processes based on quality function deployment (QFD), and multivariate data analysis (MVDA) were combined in a four-step workflow, taking various criteria into consideration. The input data consisted of relevant customer needs and product requirements and a large wood species dataset, in which the wood species were represented by 22 properties, including density, hardness, texture, arrangement of vessels, availability, etc. Through its four steps, the method generated a quantitative ranking that identified the wood species which best fulfilled customer needs and product requirements, and the method was used here to find a species suitable for use in a surface densification process (Neyses and Sandberg, 2015; Neyses, 2019). The results of the study confirmed the suitability of those wood species that had been used in previous studies of wood densification, but beech was not in the top ten wood species in the ranking. More importantly, the method yielded several high-scoring alternatives to the species that had previously been used. Examples are species domestic to boreal and temperate forests, such as alder, cedar and basswood, as well as exotic species such as obeche, avodire, makore and okoume.

The degree of densification is dependent on the initial density of the species, the growth-ring structure and the orientation in relation to the applied compressive force. Densification tends to be easier on diffuse porous broad-leaved woods than on coniferous woods. The densification of conifers is easiest in the radial direction, while broad-leaved woods with large aggregated rays can most easily be compressed in the tangential direction. The stress-strain curve under compressive loading of wood in the transverse direction is explained in Section 1.7. The densification pattern and resulting density profile depend on the morphology of the wood and on the plasticisation of the material at the time of compression (Kutnar et al., 2009).

Industrial densification processes

Densification can be performed in a static, semi-static or continuous press under open or closed conditions.

The typical stages in a densification process are:

1. plasticisation of the cell-wall material,
2. transverse compression in the softened state,
3. setting under compression load by cooling and drying in the deformed state, and
4. fixation of the deformed state, i.e., the reduction or elimination of the set-recovery.

Figure 3.36 shows schematically a densification process in both an open and a closed system. In the open system, wood is compressed in a conventional heated press, whereas in the closed system, plasticisation and compression are achieved in a sealed vessel. The softening of the wood material when open densification is applied is achieved by a pre-impregnation with a chemical that softens the wood (chemical treatment, cf. Figure 3.30) or a pre-conditioning of the wood to a high moisture content. The most commonly used method of plasticisation in a closed system is by steam injection into the vessel.

Only a few wood THM densification processes have been industrialised. There are many reasons for this relatively poor transfer of research results to fully up-scaled industrial production, some of which are related to unsolved problems at the laboratory level with small-sized samples and others are related to the scaling-up process in industry, with a lack of adequate consideration of the plasticisation or stability of the products. The latter problem was solved with the development of resin-impregnated laminated densified products, which are now available on the market (Jones et al., 2019).

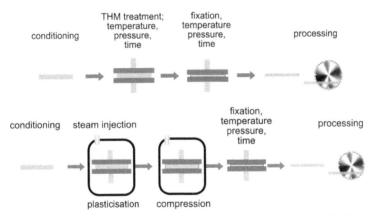

Figure 3.36 Schematic presentation of an open densification process (top), and a closed densification process (bottom).

Processes without softening before densification

Several wood densification processes have been developed where no heat, resin or other chemicals are used in the process, of which the CaLignum™ and PrimWood processes are examples (Göthe et al., 2013; Sandberg and Johansson, 2007a,b).

In the CaLignum™ process, wood is densified through semi-isostatic compression in a Quintus press (Figure 3.37), which was developed by the ABB company (today Quintus Technologies AB, Sweden) and is used for the high-pressure forming of sheet metal. A single rigid tool half is combined with a flexible rubber diaphragm as the other half of the tool. The diaphragm leads to a hydrostatic pressure on the material in the rigid tool as it is filled with oil. The pressure used is extremely high (80–140 MPa) compared to the pressure used in wood densification, i.e., a few MPa.

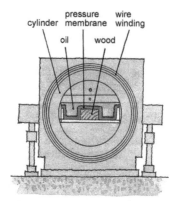

Figure 3.37 The semi-isostatic compression of wood.

The idea of how to densify wood in a Quintus press was patented by Castwall and Lindhe (1999), hence the name of the process. When wood is compressed in a Quintus press, the density is increased, and the strength properties are improved without any major macroscopic checking (Sandberg, 1998a,b). The rubber-diaphragm compression means that regions in the wood having a higher density are compressed less than softer structures, giving the compressed wood a more homogeneous density but an irregular shape, unless the main directions in the wood are almost parallel to the surfaces of the densified wood. The process takes about 3 minutes. The pressure gradually rises up to at least 80 MPa and is then immediately lowered to atmospheric pressure. No heating or other softening is needed. The moisture content of the wood is important and should be between 5 and 15% (Blomberg et al., 2005). At the beginning of the compression process, the pressure is unidirectionally perpendicular to the press plate. As the pressure increases due to the filling of the rubber diaphragm with oil, the diaphragm closes around all the wood faces except for the face placed on the rigid press table, and the pressure becomes semi-isostatic. Blomberg (2006) showed that wood compressed at 140 MPa had an almost compact structure but that the spring-back was large when the pressure was released, indicating that the application of a high pressure does not reduce the elastic strain.

Products based on the CaLignum™ process reached the market and a production was built up in Sweden and continued for several years. The technology was also acquired by the Tarkett Company (Nanterre Cedex, France), who announced that they intended to produce a densified eucalyptus flooring product in 2011. Ultimately, the product was not successful, apparently due to an unclear long-term performance in terms of set-recovery and due to high process costs, due partly to the process itself and partly to large material losses from further processing.

The PrimWood process is a simple solid-wood densification technique based on compressing clear solid pieces of coniferous wood with vertical annual rings in the radial direction by restraining the tangential expansion, e.g., with cross-lamination. The Swedish company PrimWood AB was granted a patent for the method in 2000, presenting a continuous process using an open-system band press to compress wood in the radial direction (Kifetew and Wiklund, 2000). Unsuitable knots were removed and the clear component was finger-jointed if long lengths were needed. No softening of the wood is needed before densification, and the set-recovery problem was solved by lamination, after the densified sawn timber had been split to thinner sections. Nilsson et al. (2011) developed this idea further in a three-layered cross-laminated composite product intended for flooring and tabletops, where the densified wood was used as a service layer. This approach circumvents the problem of having knots in the wood when a bulk-densification method is used. The proposed product is not however commercially available.

Densification using resin impregnation and heat pressing

All commercialised densification processes that rely on resin impregnation with a thermo-setting resin are performed on veneer or sawn timber (cf. Compreg, Section 2.4). During the curing stage, a cross-linked polymer matrix is formed within the cell walls of the wood. Phenol formaldehyde (PF) resin is often used to enhance the properties of wood and wood-composites related to dimensional stability, colour stability, exterior exposure, acoustics, and resistance to fungi, termites and other pests.

A densified laminated-veneer product has been manufactured under the trade name Lignofol™, and similar materials, Jicwood™ and Jablo™, were produced in England until the 1990s (Kultikova, 1999). Another method for stabilisation was developed in the United States under the name Staypak™ (Seborg et al., 1945).

The densification pressure depends on the density, moisture content and temperature. To reach a density of 1,300 kg/m^3, Seborg et al. (1945) found that a pressure of 10–17 MPa was needed at a temperature of 160°C for yellow-poplar veneer (Staypak™) with a moisture content of 12%. It should be noted that the temperature applied in making Staypak™ is not sufficiently high and the pressing time not sufficiently long to ensure dimensional stability of the product. Staypak™ has, however, distinctly better strength properties than both normal densified wood and Compreg™ (Seborg et al., 1945). One of the problems associated with the production of Staypak™ was that the panels must be cooled below 100°C under full pressure. Due to the thermoplastic nature of the lignin, and because the moisture content of the wood is only slightly lower after compression than prior to densification, considerable spring-back occurs if the product is removed while it is still hot (Kollmann et al., 1975). These disadvantages of Staypak™ prevented this product from being generally adopted by industry.

An early patent granted in USA described a method of impregnating wood with chemicals by pressure and, if required, under vacuum (Landau, 1914). Thermosetting resins have been used on veneers in combination with densification to produce multi-laminated materials in sheet form. Examples of commercialised products are Compreg™, Delignit™, Dehonit™, Permawood™, Permali™, RANPREX™, and products manufactured by Insulcul Services Ltd. and Surendra Composites Private Ltd. Table 3.13 provides short descriptions of these processes and the types of wood to which they are applied.

Recently, Metadynea Austria company applied for a European patent for impregnation of the micro-structure of the wood with a curing resin prior to densification (Kantner et al., 2019). The process is a development of earlier densification methods using resin impregnation for locking the set-recovery. It involves four stages (Figure 3.38) and is applied to wood with a porous structure suitable for impregnation in a dry state. The wood is vacuum impregnated with an aqueous solution of a phenol resin (Stage 1), air dried (Stage 2A), subjected to a controlled drying regime (Stage 2B), and the compressed in a heated open-system press (Stage 3A–C) and heat-treated under pressure (Stage 3D). The process is completed by controlled cooling under pressure (Stage 3E) before the press is opened and the specimens removed (Stage 3F). The material is then conditioned (Stage 4) and the final product is densified wood with no set-recovery. The degree of densification is controlled in the compression stage.

The use of a low molecular weight PF resin enables wood blocks with a thickness of up to at least 50 mm to be densified (Figure 3.39). Penetration of adhesive into the cell walls leads to plasticisation and the fixation of the compressive deformation. An increase in density of up to 300% can be achieved with a small amount of PF resin, and the cell walls are deformed without any visible cell-wall fracture Figure 3.40.

Compreg™ (Panzerholz™, Delignit™) is an extremely hard multi-laminated material in sheet form produced in Germany (see also Section 2.3) and made of European beech veneers with a synthetic resin. Under extreme heat, pressure and moisture, the wood is compressed to half its original thickness, and the product is used for security panels, tooling, jigs, moulds, transformer components, tank supports for liquefied natural gas (LNG) and liquefied petroleum gas (LPG) carriers, neutron shielding, and audio component cases.

Another product produced in Germany by the Deutsche Holzveredelung company is Dehonit™, a compressed laminated wood manufactured from high-quality rotary-cut European beech veneers

Table 3.13 Wood-densification processes including impregnation.

Product name (patent)	Short description	Type of wood
Compreg™ (EP3470189A1); A similar product is produced in Europe under the trade names Delignit™ – Panzerholz™	Green or dry veneer impregnated with 50% aqueous solution of phenol-formaldehyde resin prior to compression at 150–170°C for 15 to 30 minutes and laminated. High density (up to 1,400 kg/m³) product with very low volumetric swelling (< 4%) when soaked in water.	Applied to veneer and produces a laminated wood composite. The Delignit™-Panzerholz™ produced only from European beech veneer.
Dehonit™ – Deutsche Holzveredelung, Germany	Beech veneer impregnated with phenolic resin, assembled into a pack, and compressed under high pressure and temperature. Density of 850–1,250 kg/m³ used for high voltage power and distribution transformers.	Applied only to European beech veneer.
Permali™	Selected beech veneers impregnated under vacuum with synthetic resin and densified under heat and pressure. Water-resistant general-purpose densified wood with applications in cryogenic, electrical and general engineering.	Applied only to European beech veneer.
Permatred™	Beech veneers impregnated with phenolic resin and consolidated under high pressure and temperature.	Applied only to European beech veneer.
RANPREX™	Beech veneer impregnated with phenol resin, pressed at high temperature and pressure. Homogeneous flooring sheets of high mechanical strength.	Applied only to European beech veneer.
Insulcul Services Ltd.	Densified wood manufactured from beech veneers, impregnated with a synthetic adhesive, and densified under high pressure at a temperature of 90°C.	Applied only to European beech veneer.
Wood densification method developed by Haygreen and Daniels (1969)	Densifying and drying green sapwood, including 72 hours of impregnation of green wood, compression for 20 hours and drying to 0% while in the press for 75–125 minutes. The set-recovery is 1–2%.	Applied only to European beech veneer.
Mywood2™ (Japan, JPH11151703A)	Wood impregnated with aqueous boric acid solution and then THM treated. Woods like cedar or larch are impregnated with a proprietary boric-acid solution to provide resistance to water. The increase in density is about 50%.	Applied only to European beech veneer.
Process for densifying low-density woods (US4606388A)	Green solid wood impregnated with anhydrous ammonia to plasticise the wood pressed in a cyclic press with perforated platens, while keeping the temperature of the wood below 100°C. Up to 50% reduction in thickness, density increase up to 1,000 kg/m³.	Wood species like poplar, alder, oak, maple and birch can be densified. Set-recovery after water soaking can reach 30%.
Hartzel method of compressing wood (US2101542A)	Steam heating of wood veneer and solid wood of thickness to 25 mm at 150°C and then compressed and laminated. Set recovery prevented by coating with Bakelite, varnish or other moisture-resisting material after compression.	Primarily applied to veneer, but also to thin solid wood. Set recovery prevented by coating finished compressed wood preventing any further processing of material.
Compressed wood product and manufacture (WO2004056542A1; developed from NZ52329502A)	Two-step compression of conifer and broad-leaved woods including coating and impregnation with fatty acid at 60–120°C as an intermediate step. Temperature between 145–185°C for softwoods and up to 200°C for hardwoods. Process completed with 12 hours keeping the densified wood under pressure in a cold press. The densified wood should be formed into laminated products.	Intended to be used only for laminated products. Clear information about compression-related properties not provided

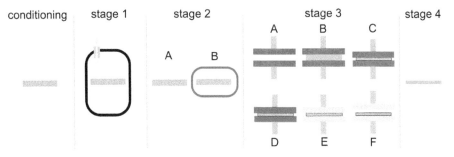

Figure 3.38 Schematic presentation of wood densification process (Kantner et al., 2019).

Figure 3.39 Untreated poplar wood with a thickness of 20 mm (light colour) and densified poplar with a thickness of 10 mm (brownish colour) after THM.

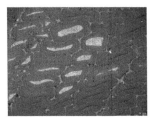

Figure 3.40 Cross section of THM-densified Norway spruce. Resin present in the cell lumens appears lighter than the wood cell wall. Lignin can also be seen as a lighter coloured material between the wood cells.

Figure 3.41 A component of Compreg™.

coated or impregnated with a special synthetic phenolic resin, and compressed under high pressure and temperature to form a high-density laminate material.

In France, Permawood™ (also known as Lignostone™) is produced. It is a laminated densified wood according to the DIN 7707 and IEC 61061 standards, and it consists of European beech veneers joined using synthetic resins cured under pressure and heat.

In the United States, densified wood is on the market under the trade name Permali™ or Insulam™. Permali™ is a phenolic laminated product made from thin veneers of European beech, impregnated with a synthetic resin under vacuum and then densified under heat. The result is a homogeneous material that combines the strength and toughness of wood fibres with the excellent stability and dielectric properties of the advanced thermosetting resins. The phenolic laminated material is furnished with cross-directional fibres and is used for electric power equipment, structural support in cryogenic environments, and electrical insulation components for rail transportation vehicles.

In Australia, Insulcul Services Ltd produces densified wood from European beech veneers, impregnated with synthetic resins and densified under extremely high pressure and temperature (Insulcul™). The veneers placed alternatively at an angle of 90° giving a material with uniform strength and stability which is used in the electric-power industry.

In Italy, Ranprex™ (Rancan Srl), is produced from laminated densified European beech. It is made with high-quality veneers, impregnated with a patented mixture of thermosetting resins and densified at a very high pressure and temperature. The product is a dense and very strong material, and the density can be adapted to suit the application. It is used in the electrical power distribution industry, e.g., for support beams, treaded rods, compression blocks, and pressure rings. It is also an excellent electrical and thermal insulator, with compression, flexion, and impact resistance, and it is also self-lubricating, extremely resistant to wear, and has an excellent resistance to both high and low temperatures.

Resin-impregnated laminated densified wood products are also produced in India. Surendra Composites Private Limited produces a resin-impregnated veneer laminate which is used in electrical power transmission equipment (Surendra™).

The Olympus company developed a three-dimensional compression-moulding process for wooden materials (Olympus™), by which the density of a piece of cypress wood can be increased from approximately 450 kg/m^3 to more than 1,000 kg/m^3. The material is thin enough to be used as a casing material for electronic products but is much harder than the acrylonitrile butadiene styrene (ABS) and polycarbonate-resin-based plastics that are normally used in these applications.

Thermal-hydro-mechanical (THM) densification

Densification by the Viscoelastic Thermal Compression (VTC) process was developed by Kamke and Sizemore (2004, 2008), and involves wood densification and post-treatment in a closed THM system, in five stages:

1. Heating and conditioning the wood to an elevated temperature and moisture content, so that the temperature of the wood substance reaches or exceeds its glass-transition temperature (T_g).

2. Rapid vapour decompression and removal of the bound water in the cell wall. This step leads to a softening of the wood, which dramatically reduces the compression modulus of the wood perpendicular to the grain and is referred to as *mechano-sorption*.

3. Compressing the wood perpendicular to the grain while the wood is in a softened state. T_g is maintained and this step increases the density of the wood.

4. Annealing the wood to relax the remaining stresses. Annealing also leads to thermal degradation of the hemicelluloses and reduces the hygroscopicity of the wood. The stresses remaining in the wood are due to the stretched polymer molecules within the cell wall. With time and with increasing molecular motion, the polymer molecules slip into a more relaxed arrangement. Increasing the temperature increases the molecular motion and assists stress relaxation.

5. Cooling the wood to below its glass-transition temperature, and increasing the moisture content, i.e., the conditioning the wood to equilibrium with the ambient temperature and humidity.

Transient heat and mass transfer in the wood lead to the development of temperature, gas pressure, and moisture content gradients in the wood during the VTC process, and this leads to a variation in compression modulus in the thickness direction. Some regions are compressed more than others, and a density profile is created. In general, the creation of a density profile can be attributed to the combined actions of time, temperature, moisture, compressive force, and stress relaxation during the densification process (Kamke and Casey, 1988; Wolcott et al., 1990; Kutnar et al., 2009).

Surface densification

Densification throughout the cross section may be a drawback in situations where, for example, it is desirable to increase the hardness and abrasion resistance of the surface layers in flooring and tabletops, while at the same time retaining the thickness to resist bending. Surface densification is usually applied only to the upper surface of the wood. One-side densification result in a density profile in the thickness direction of the wood that may cause cupping or other modes of distortion if not handled properly.

In surface densification, only the first few millimetres beneath the wood surface are compressed. Figure 3.42 demonstrates the surface densification process, which consists of plasticisation, densification, solidification, and stabilisation. The process involves softening the wood surface, where the volume to be softened depends on the level of surface densification desired. A moisture and temperature gradient allowing densification of the surface must be established, while other parts of the wood continue to resist the compressive stress applied (Wang and Cooper, 2005; Lamason and Gong, 2007). When the desired volume of wood beneath the surface has been softened, a compressive force is applied, and the process is completed by fixation of the compressive deformation.

In one surface-densification method, the process begins with dry wood (~ 12%) which is heated on one surface only, compressed in an open press, and then cooled under compression until the temperature is below 100°C (Rautkari et al., 2011a). In general, the density profile depends on the initial moisture content, fibre orientation, wood species, and press-platen temperature and holding time. In a conventional press, the density profile also depends on the closing time, i.e., the time from when the wood is placed in the heated press until the press platens reach the wood and the densification starts. With a short closing time, a density peak is created close to the surface because of heat transfer (Rautkari et al., 2011b). The higher the temperature, the greater is the degree of compression achieved (Tabarsa and Chui, 1997; Welzbacher et al., 2008).

Figure 3.43 shows a density profile in Scots pine that was compressed in the radial direction from 22 mm to 15 mm by Rautkari et al. (2013). The figure also shows the density profile of the

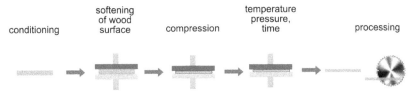

Figure 3.42 Schematic presentation of a surface densification process.

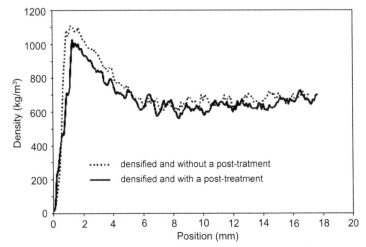

Figure 3.43 Density profile of a hydrothermally surface-densified Scots pine, with and without post-treatment (Rautakari et al., 2013).

surface-densified Scots pine specimens that were hydrothermally post-treated at 200°C after the densification. The post-treatment led to an average mass loss of 3.8%, and the density profile did not differ significantly from that of non-post-treated surface-densified wood.

The densification process is usually a batch process, and this can be a factor limiting its industrial application. In the Wood Science and Engineering division of the Luleå University of Technology in Sweden, a continuous roller pressing method of surface densification has been developed (Figure 3.44). The process enables the surface of Scots pine boards to be successfully densified at a process speed of up to 80 m/min (Neyses et al., 2016; Neyses, 2019). The process runs continuously to give plasticisation, densification, solidification, and stabilisation, and it includes both pre- and post-modification stages. The present focus is on making the process more industrially interesting by combining the roller or belt pressing technique with various pre- and post-treatments to reduce negative effects such as set-recovery, discoloration and embossment of the surface.

Sadatnezhad et al. (2017) have studied a continuous process in a conventional panel press (Siempelkamp A0361), having upper and lower heating devices with four separate adjustable heating sections, two sets of rolling elements to reduce the friction between the stationary heating plates, and movable steel belts. The steel belts transfer heat and pressure to the wood while the wood passes through the press. The total length of the press is was 18 m, with a pressing zone of 6 metres.

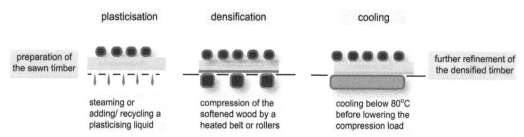

Figure 3.44 The principal set-up of the integrated continuous surface-densification concept (side view) developed at the Wood Science and Engineering division, Luleå University of Technology (Sweden).

Properties of densified wood

The stress, temperature, and steam environment during the densification process affect the properties of the densified material (Kamke and Kutnar, 2011; Kutnar and Kamke, 2012). The temperature in relation to the glass-transition of the cell wall when the compressive stress is applied create a density profile in the wood (Kutnar et al., 2009), which varies with the degree of densification.

Figure 3.45 shows density profiles in THM-treated European beech, Norway spruce, and poplar that were densified from initial thicknesses of 6 mm, 10 mm and 15 mm to thicknesses of 2 mm, 5 mm, and 7 mm, respectively. The non-densified poplar and beech wood had an almost uniform density throughout their thickness, since the difference in density between earlywood and latewood is small, but a zig-zag shape is seen in the spruce specimens due to the large difference in density between the earlywood and latewood.

In the THM-treated beech specimens, the density profile was uniform for all three thicknesses, except of a small density peak on the surface of the specimens with initial thickness of 10 mm.

The density of the THM-treated poplar with an initial thickness of 6 mm was the highest of all the tested materials, and the density was uniform throughout the thickness, but the THM-treated poplar with initial thicknesses of 10 mm and 15 mm exhibited an 'M-shaped' density profile with high surface densities and a lower core density. This kind of density profile is typical for wood-based composite panels. In the specimen with an initial thickness of 10 mm, the density slowly decreased towards the core in the first 1.5 mm from the surface and then decreased more rapidly. Similar results were found for the specimen with an initial thickness of 15 mm, but in this case, the

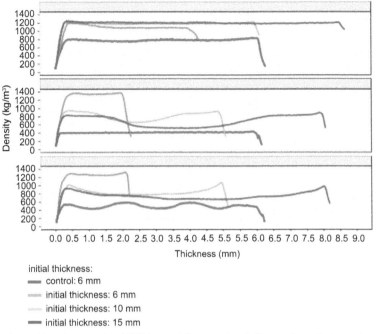

initial thickness:
- control: 6 mm
- initial thickness: 6 mm
- initial thickness: 10 mm
- initial thickness: 15 mm

Figure 3.45 Density profiles of untreated and THM-treated European beech (first row), poplar (second row), and Norway spruce (third row).

high-density surface layers had a broad plateau (approximately 2 mm wide) followed by a valley of uniform density close to 500 kg/m³ in the core with a width of approximately 2.5 mm.

The densified spruce specimens with initial thicknesses of 10 mm and 15 mm also exhibited an M-shaped density profile. The specimen with an initial thickness of 15 mm had a wider valley but the density of the valley was similar in both cases.

Since the initial thickness of the specimens varied, the moisture content and temperature distribution prior to the final compression also varied. Thinner wood specimens lose moisture more rapidly and approach a uniform distribution more rapidly than thick ones. It can be assumed that the moisture content was almost the same throughout the thickness in the 6-mm thick specimens prior to the final compression and it can be concluded that the moisture content gradient was probably non-uniform in the 10 mm and 15 mm thick specimens, so that the compression behaviour in the thickness direction was also non-uniform. The initial thickness of the specimen also influences the temperature and moisture-content profiles.

Strength properties

The deformation occurring during the densification process is largely a viscous buckling of the cell walls without any fracture, and the strength and stiffness of the wood material increase approximately in proportion to the increase in density. Kutnar et al. (2008a) studied the mechanical properties of viscoelastic thermal compressed (VTC) wood and found that the increases in the modulus of rupture (MOR) and in the modulus of elasticity (MOE) were approximately proportional to the increase in density (Figure 3.46).

Huguenin and Navi (1995) determined the impact resistance of densified European beech and reported an increase in impact strength after densification of more than 70% in the tangential direction and 50% in the radial direction, which was similar to the increase in density.

Behr et al. (2013) studied the performance of THM-densified wood under cyclic deflection using the dynamic fatigue test rig by DHM, and showed that cyclic loading to 60% of F_{max} did not lead to failure of either a control or the THM-treated wood after 50,400 cycles. The cyclic

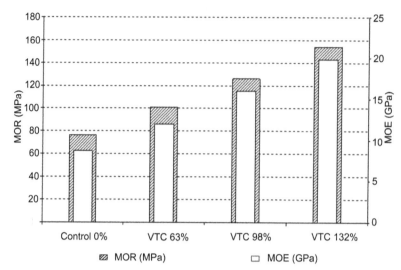

Figure 3.46 Bending test results, MOE and MOR, for control and VTC wood specimens with different degrees of densification, 63%, 98%, and 132% (Kutnar et al., 2008a).

creep rate increased gradually in both the control and the THM-treated specimens, but the absolute deformation was higher in the control specimens. Increasing the loading force to 75% of F_{max} resulted in a rapid increase in the cyclic creep in the control specimens and to failure already after 5,000 cycles, but in the THM-treated specimens, an initial rapid increase in the cyclic creep rate was followed by a gradual increase and a second rapid increase before failure after 27,700 cycles. The cyclic creep and critical deflection at failure were lower in the THM-treated specimens, but it can nevertheless be concluded that the THM densification process improves the performance of wood under cyclic loading.

Hardness

It is well known that the hardness of densified wood increasing with increased density (Pizzi et al., 2005; Rautkari et al., 2010). Rautkari et al. (2011a) studied the Brinell hardness of composites that had either one or two layers of densified wood in order to investigate the influence on the hardness test of layer thickness and found that only a thin layer of densified wood increased the hardness significantly. Boonstra and Blomberg (2007) found that the Brinell hardness of untreated radiata pine densified with a semi-isostatic process was increased by 271%. Fang et al. (2012) reported that the Brinell hardness of veneer densified using heat, steam, and pressure was two to three times that of a control for both aspen and hybrid poplar, while Rautkari et al. (2013) investigated the effect of surface compression and hydrothermal post-treatment on the density profile and on the Brinell hardness. The hydrothermal post-treatment involving heating at 140°C for 30 minutes followed by steam at 200°C for 3 hours led to an average mass loss of 3.8% regardless of the degree of compression, and the density profile of the surface densified specimens was thus not significantly affected by the hydrothermal post-treatment. Although the surface densification increased the Brinell hardness by more than 90%, the hydrothermal post-treatment at 200°C did not affect the hardness of either the control or the surface-densified specimens.

Colour

The simultaneous effect of heat, moisture, and compression leads to chemical and physical changes which can be seen as a change in colour (Tjeerdsma et al., 1998; Koch et al., 2003; Sundqvist et al., 2006; Varga and van der Zee, 2008) and which have a strong influence on the surface properties of the THM-treated wood (Jennings et al., 2006; Kutnar et al., 2008a). The heat treatment results in a darkening of the wood. Bekhta and Niemz (2003) found that the darkening accelerated when the treatment temperature exceeded 200°C and that most of the darkening occurred within the first four hours of exposure. Gonzalez-Pena and Hale (2009) suggested that the colour changes during heat treatment were linked more to changes in the acid-insoluble lignin than to changes in the carbohydrate fraction.

Diouf et al. (2011) studied the effect of densification temperature (160°C, 180°C, 200°C and 220°C) on the surface colour of veneers of trembling aspen and hybrid poplar, and reported that the colour darkened with increasing THM-densification temperature. ATR-FTIR and XPS studies confirmed that THM densification caused major chemical changes in the veneer surfaces, particularly at temperatures higher than 160°C.

Lesar et al. (2013) studied the influence of THM treatment parameters (steam environment and one minute post-heat-treatment at 200°C) on the colour of densified hybrid poplar and Douglas fir, and reported that the colour was influenced predominantly by the wood species and by the intensity of the densification process.

Figure 3.47 shows the colour of untreated hybrid poplar and densified hybrid poplar at three degrees of densification.

Figure 3.47 Untreated hybrid poplar (left) and hybrid poplar at three degrees of densification 47%, 68%, and 87%, according to equation 3.1.

Morphology

During the densification process, the wood material is softened and compressed without rupture of the wood cells. The compression takes place between 120°C and about 200°C, the heat being transferred to the interior of the material through contact with heated platens. The wood maintains its densified shape if it is cooled to below 100°C under pressure. Figure 3.47 shows a cross-section of densified Norway spruce, where the cell-wall is deformed without fracture. It is important to avoid cell-wall fracture because the increase in strength and stiffness is greater when the cell wall remains intact.

Densification is achieved under high strain by reducing the void space mainly of the cell lumen by buckling of the cell walls, but without destruction of the micro-cellular structure of the wood (Kutnar et al., 2009). The undamaged cell walls are a major feature for the improved properties of VTC wood (Wolcott, 1989; Kultikova, 1999; Navi and Girardet, 2000; Kamke and Sizemore, 2008). The morphology of THM-densified wood can vary considerably, depending on the degree of densification (Blomberg, 2006; Blomberg et al., 2006; Kutnar et al., 2009). Standfest et al. (2013) studied the anatomical structure of compressed Douglas fir and hybrid poplar using X-ray computed micro-tomography (Figure 3.49 and Figure 3.50). In both wood species the densification resulted in a significant decrease in the pore volume, and the porosity decreased to less than the half the original value for Douglas fir earlywood and to approximately one quarter for the vessels in hybrid poplar, and the mean pore size decreased to about one quarter of the original values. In contrast, the latewood in Douglas fir and libriform fibres in hybrid poplar were quite stable under compression. Douglas fir latewood retained its original shape after compression and showed no reduction in pore size.

Figure 3.51 shows a magnified cross-sectional view of untreated and surface densified Scots pine. Specimens with three different initial thicknesses (22 mm, 20 mm, and 18 mm) were compressed to a target thickness of 15 mm resulting in three different degrees of surface densification. The

Figure 3.48 Cross-section of THM-densified Norway spruce wood showing changes in the earlywood (bottom half) and latewood (upper half). Cells in the earlywood are characteristically thinner and the cell lumens are larger, which leads to a greater degree of compression and to more wavy patterns in earlywood than in latewood.

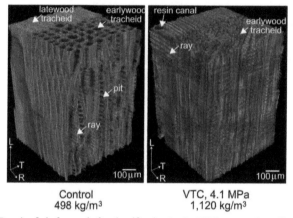

Figure 3.49 Douglas fir before and after densification by the VTC process (Standfest et al., 2013).

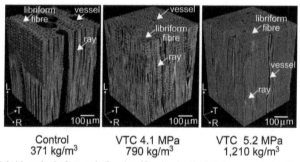

Figure 3.50 Hybrid poplar before and after densification by the VTC process (Standfest et al., 2013).

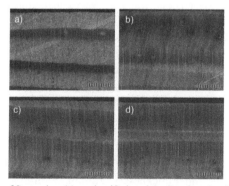

Figure 3.51 Surface densification of Scots pine: (a) un-densified, and (b–d)surface densified to a target thickness of 15 mm from an initial thickness 18 mm, 20 mm, and 22 mm, respectively. The bar is 1 mm.

temperature of compression was 150°C. Specimens were attached to the upper plate of the press, which was not heated, after which the press was closed at a speed of 10 mm/min. to the target thickness of 15 mm. When the target thickness was reached, the specimens were held under the full load for 1 minute. After this holding time, the lower (heated) platen was cooled to 80°C, while the specimens were held under compression. As shown in Figure 3.51, surface densification of specimens was achieved by the collapse of the earlywood in the surface growth rings. The number of growth rings with collapsed earlywood increased with increasing degree of densification.

Decay resistance

Densified wood that has been processes at a temperature close to 200°C is expected to have a greater resistance to microbiological attack (see Section 3.4), but the densification itself cannot ensure sufficient protection against wood degradation fungi (Kutnar et al., 2011). This is supported by Ünsal et al. (2008) who reported that wood subjected to thermal compression showed a greater mass loss after a 12-week decay-resistance test than untreated wood.

Schwarze and Spycher (2005) reported that THM-densified wood post-treated at 180°C was more resistant to colonisation and degradation by brown-rot fungi. In contrast, work by Welzbacher et al. (2008) showed that a "very durable" to "durable" THM-densified wood was produced only when the thermo-mechanical densification took place in combination with oil-heat treatment. Skyba et al. (2008) found that THM treatment increased the resistance of Norway spruce to degradation by soft-rot fungi but not that of European beech. Kutnar et al. (2011) reported that the viscoelastic thermal compression (VTC) of hybrid poplar did not increase its decay resistance to fungi such as *Pleurotus ostreatus* and *Trametes versicolor.*

Adhesive bonding

It has been shown that densified wood can be bonded using a polymeric diphenylmethane diisocyanate (MDI) adhesive, a phenol-formaldehyde film adhesive (Jennings et al., 2005) or a liquid phenol-formaldehyde (PF) adhesive (Kutnar et al., 2008a; Kutnar et al., 2008c), but the an increase in density and consequently the decrease in porosity of the densified wood will have an negative effect on the flow and penetration of the adhesive. The void volume of wood can be drastically reduced depending on the degree of densification. The depth to which and the direction in which an adhesive flows in densified wood are, therefore, very different from the depth and direction in undensified wood. Figure 3.52 shows the adhesive bond line in densified hybrid poplar and Figure 3.53 the adhesive bond line in untreated hybrid poplar. The effective penetration varies with the degree of densification (Kutnar et al., 2008c), and was the greatest in the control specimens, but decreased with increasing densification of the VTC specimens. In addition to the difference in the effective penetration, it was found that the location of the PF adhesive in the structures of the control and VTC specimens differed. In the control, the adhesive was in the vessel lumina, whereas in the VTC wood, the adhesive was also detected in the fibre lumina and ray lumina, due to the altered

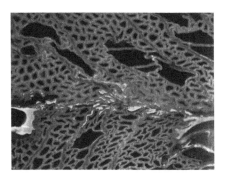

Figure 3.52 Adhesive bond-line (PF adhesive) in densified hybrid poplar (microscopic examination after soaking the adhesively bonded specimen in water).

Figure 3.53 Adhesive bond-line (PF adhesive) in untreated hybrid poplar (microscopic examination after soaking the adhesively bonded specimen in water).

porosity of the densified wood. Since the vessel lumen volume decreases with increasing degree of densification, the adhesive penetrates more into the fibre and ray lumina.

The exposure of wood to a high temperature during the densification process alters the surface properties (Kutnar et al., 2008b). The wettability of wood which has been exposed to high temperature or heat-treated decreases (Pétrissans et al., 2003; Sernek et al., 2004; Follrich et al., 2006; Gérardin et al., 2007), the wood becomes hydrophobic and less polar, and this can prevent water-borne adhesive systems from adequately wetting the surface.

Other properties

The heat, moisture and compression lead to chemical and physical changes in the wood structure which have a strong influence on the surface properties of the densified wood (Jennings et al., 2006; Kutnar et al., 2008b). Kutnar et al. (2008b) studied the changes in surface chemistry of VTC wood using Fourier Transform infra-red spectroscopy (FTIR), and compared with thermal modification, consisting of a moist step and a dry step. Polymerisation of the lignin was the major chemical change induced by the VTC process, but studies of the contact angle of water using the Wilhelmy plate method showed that the VTC wood surface was hydrophobic (Kutnar et al., 2008b). The surface free energy determined according to the Owens, Wendt, Rabel and Kaelble (OWRK) theory decreased significantly during the VTC densification, although the level of densification had little influence on the surface free energy (Kutnar et al., 2008b). Huguenin and Navi (1995) reported that the impact strength for European beech increased by more than 70% in the tangential direction and 50% in the radial direction after densification, which was similar to the increase in density.

The mechanical properties of densified wood are generally evaluated on a macro-scale, although the material characteristics that have the greatest impact on the performance of structural natural materials such as xylem occur on the nano- and micro-scales. Xylem tissue is a complex nanocomposite with excellent mechanical performance having cellular features from 10^{-6} to 10^{-4} metre in size, while the layered cell wall has important structural features from 10^{-9} to 10^{-6} metre in size. The properties must be characterised not only at the macro level, but also at the micro and nano levels in order to identify the structure-property mechanisms determining the mechanical properties.

Nano-indentation testing is a relatively new technique to measure the mechanical properties of materials. The principles are similar to micro-indentation or micro-hardness testing, the difference lying in the size of the probes and the loads, which are typically much smaller in nano-indentation producing a deformation ranging from a few micrometers only to several hundred nanometers. Nano-indentation techniques to have been successfully used investigate natural fibre composites (Lee et al., 2007) and wood (Gindl and Schoberl, 2004; Konnerth et al., 2006; Jakes et al., 2008; Konnerth et al., 2010; Vincent et al., 2014), but owing to the anisotropic nature of the wooden cell walls and the three-dimensional stress status under the indenter tip, the elastic modulus obtained is not directly comparable to the elastic modulus determined by other techniques (Konnerth et al., 2010). Nano-indentation on wood cell walls is however useful for comparative purposes. Bustos et al. (2011) have applied nano-indentation to determine the cell-wall mechanical properties of THM-densified wood at the nano and micro levels, and they evaluated the properties at three degrees of densification, including an examination of the microstructure of the densified wood, and contributed to a better understanding of its structure-property mechanisms, supporting a biomimetic approach to the development of high-performance composites from densified wood.

Applications of densified wood

Kamke (2013) presented an overview of the THM products that can be found on the market. The Calignum process is focused on flooring. The MyWood2 Corporation (Iwakura, Aichi, Japan) manufactures densified solid cedar wood products primarily for flooring in Japan and China, and their products are also sold for use in furniture. The MyWood2™ product is impregnated with a proprietary polymer to provide resistance to water, and the compression is approximately 50%.

Electric transmission support components made from THM wood are typically resin-impregnated, laminated veneer. Low molecular weight resins (typically phenol-formaldehyde) are used to impregnate the veneer, which is then partially cured in an oven before being compressed in a heated press (open system) to a density of approximately 1,300 kg/m^3. Other applications of resin-impregnated veneer include storage containers for liquid natural gas (LNG) and associated support structures, and wear plates for machinery and transportation vehicles, machine pattern moulds, bulletproof barriers, and structural building components. There are a number of products on the market, including but not limited to Insulam™ by CK-Composites (Mount Pleasant, Pennsylvania USA), Lignostone™ by Röchling (Harren, Gemany), Lignostone™ (Ter Apel, Netherlands), Dehonit™ by Deutsche Holzveredelung Schmeing GmbH & Co. KG (Kirchhundem/Würdinghausen, Germany), Ranprex™ by Rancan Srl (Vincenza, Italy), and impregnated and densified wood for advanced use in, for example, musical instruments (Sonowood™) instead of tropical species, such as ebony. Some properties for Sonowood™ are listed in Table 3.14.

It can be concluded that the use of wood densification of low-density woods as an alternative to the use of expensive high-density woods has so far been very limited, although the possible applications may be many (Table 3.15).

Table 3.14 Properties of Sonowood™ from the Swiss Wood Solutions company.

Property	Maple	Norway spruce
Density (kg/m^3)	1,200–1,400	1,300–1,400
Brinell hardness (N/mm^2)	> 80	> 100
Colour	Mocha	Caramel
Dimensional stability (Difference in swelling, % per % moisture content change)	Height ~ 0.7 Width ~ 0.3	Height ~ 0.75 Width ~ 0.33
Sound velocity (m/s)	> 4,400	> 5,500
Damping (Log. decrement)	~ 0.053	~ 0.04
Elastic modulus (GPa)	> 23	> 39

3.9 Moulded tubes

Wood in its dry state cannot be shaped to a small radius of curvature without fracture. In the case of steamed wood, heat and moisture affect the stress-strain relation to a greater extent in compression than in tension, and this makes possible to apply a high compression on the concave side, while the tensile strain (on the convex side) is protected by a steel tie because it would otherwise fail (i.e., Thonét bending method). All types of wood shaping involve local compression of the microstructure and/or release of the locally deformed microstructure, so that the internal deformations from the densification can contribute to the shaping. A curved workpiece can be achieved by local

Table 3.15 Applications of densified wood divided into Use Classes, see Table 1.7.

Product type/Use Class	Interior 1	Interior 2	Exterior 3	Exterior 4	Exterior 5
Indoor furniture	x	x			
Floor and non-structural interior uses	x	x			
Exterior joinery			x		
Cladding			(x)		
Decking			x		
Fencing			(x)		
Outdoor furniture			x		
Construction elements			x		
In-ground timber					
Products exposed to water					

where: x = products have been produced by companies using the modified wood
(x) = products may be produced, based on pre-commercial trials, research, etc.

compression on the microstructure at the inner side of the curvature, and a "stiff tie" on the tension side, or the localised release of the compressed microstructure at the outer side ("no tie"), or by a combination of these two, i.e., "soft tie" on the tension side (Kutnar et al., 2015).

The density increase and shaping are related processes, as there are local regions with a higher density in shaped wood. In the Thonét bending method, a steel band takes up tensile stresses on the convex surface so that the inner region of the bent wood piece is highly compressed, with a longitudinal compression set taking place (Exner and Lauboeck, 1922). Haller (2007) used the shape memory effect (set-recovery) of densified massive edge-glued panels to produce tubes, described below.

Material selection and preparation

Wood-shaping processes can be applied to a wide range of wood species, but the process must be optimised for each species. Ideally, straight-grained, knot-free wood material should be used, particularly if the bend is to be of a small radius, but for structural use, knot-free timber is not compulsory as their presence does not affect the formation of such large components. Cracks and other defects in the wood that lead to disturbances in the fibre structure, such as knots, ingrown bark, pitch pockets, etc. can cause losses and failure in the wood when comparatively little strain has been applied. Small knots can be tolerated to some extent on the compressed side unless the shaping radius is extremely small. Knots on the side under tension have, in general, a disastrous effect on the strength.

Examples of species that have been used for moulded tubes are abura, common beech, Norway spruce, Norway maple, small-leaved lime, and tulipwood (Haller et al., 2013b), and Knust et al. (2008) demonstrated that fast-growing native poplar is also suitable for forming.

Industrial processes for shaped wood

Haller et al. (2013a,b) suggested that profile cross sections for load-bearing and conveying applications could be produced by an open thermo-hygro-mechanical process and they described the implications for construction and the environment (Figure 3.54). They pointed out that, compared to metals and plastics, the maximum tensile strain that sawn timber can withstand is low, and that this prevents shaping. They attributed the easy workability to the low force and low energy required for material removal. Haller (2007) emphasised that a high load-bearing capacity and a great saving of both material and time for design and construction can be achieved if engineered wood products (EWPs) is used instead of sawn timber.

The manufacture of tubes has been described in Haller et al. (2002), Haller (2007), Wehsener et al. (2014a), Hartig et al. (2016, 2018), and by May et al. (2017, 2019), for example. Three different processes for moulding tubes have been developed to date, one of them is shown in Figure 3.55. In this process, boards with an initial moisture content of about 12% were densified at 120°C and cooled to 80°C in order to create edge-glued panels. The subsequent forming process utilised the set-recovery, where the edge-glued panels were pre-treated in a steam chamber before the tubes were manufactured in a specially designed plant. In this example, the tube had a diameter of 30 cm and a length of 3 metres, but tubes with other dimensions can be manufactured. Greater lengths are obtained by a finger-jointing process. Basically, this technology allows tubes to be produced with any longitudinal and transversal dimensions, provided that a minimum radius resulting from the previous degree of densification is adhered to.

Wehsener et al. (2013) describe another process where forming is achieved, not by utilising the "shape memory" but by densifying the inner surface of the tube (Figure 3.56). In terms of technology, this method corresponds to extrusion. Un-densified small-diameter round timber is used for profile manufacture and high forces and a robust plant are required, since the process is not based on the "shape memory".

A third method for the manufacture of tube-segments is under development. The idea for this technique is based on the principles for wood bending, i.e., a steel band (tie) is used on the outer

Figure 3.54 Moulded wood tubes made from (top left to right): Norway spruce, Norway maple, small-leaved lime, poplar, tulipwood, and (bottom left to right): tulipwood, abura, common beech, moulded part using beech veneer.

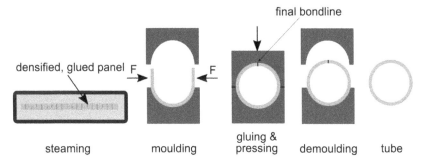

Figure 3.55 Schematic manufacture of a wooden tube.

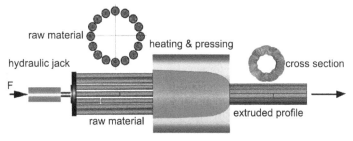

Figure 3.56 Schematic manufacture of a wooden tube by extrusion of a tube from small-diameter round timber using compression.

Figure 3.57 Prototype machine for the manufacture of moulded tube-segments with the use of a steel tie (left). Moulding of av segment of a tube is shown to the right. (Courtesy Prof. Peer Haller Technische Universität Dresden, Photo: L. Sprenger and D. Sandberg).

Figure 3.58 Tube members (length ca. 3 metres), non-reinforced (left) and reinforced with a fibre-reinforced polymer composite system (Courtesy Prof. Peer Haller Technische Universität Dresden, Photo: L. Sprenger).

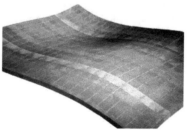

Figure 3.59 End-grain moulded shell (Courtesy Prof. Peer Haller Technische Universität Dresden, Photo: L. Sprenger).

convex surface while forming the tube in order to hinder rupture (the use of set-recovery is not considered) (Figure 3.57).

Haller (2007), Heiduschke and Haller (2009, 2010) and Heiduschke et al. (2009) reported that profiles could be optionally reinforced with technical fibres or textiles to form a compound section (Figure 3.57). Load-bearing performance was investigated by Cabrero et al. (2010), who shared that a thin fibre reinforcement of only 400 grams per metre increased the compressive strength of the tube by 100% (1,200 kN). Manthey et al. (2009) compared the environmental performance of a fibre-reinforced column of wood with a load-bearing capacity of 380 kN with that of columns made of steel and concrete, and showed that besides the lower weight, the energy consumption and the emission's of CO_2 were much lower, 0.40 kg CO_2e for wooden tube compared to 32.2 kg CO_2e for steel.

Wehsener et al. (2014b) described a similar method that makes it possible to produce double curved shells, the principle being to decrease the lumen by compression but in the case of moulded shells, an end-grain surface is produced (Figure 3.59). Haller et al. (2002) say that the panel consists of bi-axially (orthogonally) compressed square segments. This kind of densification is required to provide reserves for elongation in two directions for the double curvature. Densification can also be split non-uniformly in two directions or, in single-curved areas, it may have several orientations along a single axis.

Table 3.16 Applications of moulded wood divided into Use Classes, see Table 1.7.

Product type/Use Class	Interior		Exterior		
	1	2	3	4	5
Indoor furniture	x	x			
Floor and non-structural interior uses	x	x			
Exterior joinery			x		
Cladding					
Decking					
Fencing			x		
Outdoor furniture			x		
Construction elements			x	x	
In-ground timber					
Products exposed to water				x	

where: x = products have been produced by companies using the modified wood
   (x) = products may be produced, based on pre-commercial trials, research, etc.

Applications of moulded tubes

The high load-bearing capacity and light-weight following profiling and fibre reinforcement reveal a great potential for construction, architecture, light-weight construction, plant engineering and furniture manufacture. The tube is an elementary technical form, which can also be used to transport liquids or bulk goods, especially aggressive media.

Profiles can also be used for conveying applications, and for electric and lightning poles. Haller et al. (2013b) investigated the use of moulded tubes, fibre reinforced at the outer face, in aggressive environments, highly concentrated brine being conveyed at temperatures of up to 60°C. The Norway spruce tubes showed no noticeable erosion after 4 weeks' exposure, whereas steel tubes were considerably affected. To connect the tubes, fittings made of resin-impregnated Compreg™, specifically designed for the purpose, were used.

3.10 Summary and outlook

The awareness of the reality of climate change and its disastrous consequences are stimulating a transformation towards sustainable development, with increasing economic efficiency, the protection and restoration of ecological systems, and an improvement in human welfare. Wood as a renewable biological raw material is, therefore, gaining in importance in numerous applications, and there has been a renewed interest in developing TBM products in recent years. To ensure sustainable development, it is vital that the technical use of timber is increased and extended beyond the limits of architecture and construction to other fields. Advanced high-performance wood-based materials are well suited for architecture structures, and they will certainly play an increasing role in the future for light-weight designs in transportation, installations, masts, machines, etc. The considerable gain in performance and savings with respect to durability, strength and load-bearing capacity demonstrate that the transition from a resource-based to a knowledge-based economy will bring benefits all round: for the economy, for the environment and for mankind.

Thermally-based modification is probably the most important sector within wood modification, due to the high level of commercialisation of thermo-hydro treatment, demonstrated by products such as ThermoWood™, Firmolin™, Plato™, SilvaProWood™, VAP Holzsysteme™, etc. Many of these methods heave been developed as a result of an understanding of the processes occurring in the high-temperature drying of wood, as well as in the charring of wood. More recently, additional developments in other areas of thermally-based modifications have led to the commercialisation of wood welding and shape moulding, while new investigations have resulted in a better understanding of densification processes, with and without resin impregnation. The wide range of commercial processes and the continuing development of new methods show that the area of thermally-based modification will continue to be the largest area of wood modification in the foreseeable future.

References

Adam, K.D. 1951. Der Waldelefant von Lehringen, eine Jagdheute des diluvialen Menschen [The forest elephant of Lehringen, a hunt for the diluvial man.] Quartär 5: 79–84.

Ahajji, A., P. Diouf, F. Aloui, I. Elbakali, D. Perrin, A. Merlin and B. George. 2009. Influence of heat treatment on antioxidant properties and colour stability of beech and spruce wood and their extractives. Wood Science and Technology 43: 69–83.

Akyildiz, M.H. and S. Ates. 2008. Effect of heat treatment on equilibrium moisture content (EMC) of some wood species in Turkey. Research Journal of Agriculture and Biological Sciences 4(6): 660–665.

Altgen, M., C. Welzbacher, M. Humar, W. Willems and H. Militz. 2012. Bestimmung der Behandlungsqualität von Thermoholz mit hilfe von Schnellverfahren. Teil 1: Elektronenspin-Resonanz-Spektroskopie [Determination of the treatment quality of thermowood with the help of rapid procedures. Part 1: electron spin resonance spectroscopy.] Holztechnologie 53: 44–49.

Altgen, D., M. Altgen, S. Kyyrö, O. Paajanen, L. Rautkari and C. Mai. 2020a. Time dependent wettability changes on plasma treated surfaces of unmodified and thermally modified European beech wood. European Journal of Wood and Wood Products 78: 417–420.

Altgen, M., S. Kyyrö, O. Paajanen and L. Rautkari. 2020b. Resistance of thermally modified and pressurized hot water extracted Scots pine sapwood against decay by the brown rot fungus *Rhodonia placenta*. European Journal of Wood and Wood Products 78: 161–171.

Allegretti, O., M. Brunetti, I. Cuccui, S. Ferrari, M. Nocetti and N. Terziev. 2012. Thermovacuum modification of spruce (*Picea abies* Karst.) and fir (*Abies alba* Mill.) wood. BioResources 7(3): 3656–3669.

Amirou, S., A. Pizzi and L. Delmotte. 2017. Citric acid as waterproofing additive in butt joints linear wood welding. European Journal of Wood and Wood Products 75(4): 651–654.

Ando, M. and M. Sato. 2010. Evaluation of the self-bonding ability of sugi and application of sugi powder as a binder for plywood. Journal of Wood Science 56: 194–200.

Ates, S., M.H. Akyildiz and H. Ozdemir. 2009. Effects of heat treatment on calabrian pine (*Pinus brutia* ten.) wood. BioResources 4(3): 1032–1043.

Awoyemi, L. and I.P. Jones. 2011. Anatomical explanations for the changes in properties of western red cedar (*Thuja plicata*) wood during heat treatment. Wood Science and Technology 45: 261–267.

Back, E.L. 1987. The bonding mechanism in hardboard manufacture. Holzforschung 41(4): 247–258.

Bakar, A.F.A., S. Hiziroglu and P.M. Tahir. 2013. Properties of some thermally modified wood species. Materials and Design 43: 348–355.

Barcík, Š., M. Gašparík and E.Y. Razumov. 2015a. Effect of temperature on the color changes of wood during thermal modification. Cellulose Chemistry and Technology 49(9/10): 789–798.

Barcík, Š., M. Gašparík and E.Y. Razumov. 2015b. Effect of thermal modification on the colour changes of oak wood. Wood Research 60(3): 385–396.

Behr, G., H. Militz, F.A. Kamke and A. Kutnar. 2013. Fatigue behaviour of VTC and untreated beech wood, pp. 115–116. *In*: Popescu, C.-M. and Popescu, M.-C. [eds.]. Program and Book of Abstracts: COST Action PF0904, Iasi, Romania. Petru Poni Institute of Macromolecular Chemistry of Romanian Academy.

Bekhta, P. and P. Niemz. 2003. Effect of high temperature on the change in color, dimensional stability and mechanical properties of spruce wood. Holzforschung 57(5): 539–546.

Belleville, B., T. Stevanovic, A. Cloutier, A. Pizzi, M. Prado, S. Erakovic, P.N. Diouf and M. Royer. 2013. An investigation of thermochemical changes in Canadian hardwood species during wood welding. European Journal of Wood and Wood Products 71(2): 245–257.

Belleville, B., G. Koumba-Yoya and T. Stevanovic. 2018. Effect of wood welding process on chemical constituents of australian eucalyptus. Journal of Wood Chemistry and Technology 39(1): 43–56.

Bhuiyan, T., N. Hirai and N. Sobue. 2000. Changes of crystallinity in wood cellulose by heat treatment under dried and moist conditions. Journal of Wood Science 46(6): 431–436.

Bhuiyan, T., N. Hirai and N. Sobue. 2001. Effect of intermittent heat treatment on crystallinity in wood cellulose. Journal of Wood Science 47(5): 336–341.

Biziks, V., B. Andersons, L. Beçkova, E. Kapača and H. Militz. 2013. Changes in the microstructure of birch wood after hydrothermal treatment. Wood Science and Technology 47(4): 717–735.

Blomberg, J. 2006. Mechanical and physical properties of semi-isostatically densified wood. PhD. Thesis, Luleå University of Technology, Skellefteå, Sweden.

Blomberg, J., B. Persson and A. Blomberg. 2005. Effects of semi-isostatic densification of wood on the variation in strength properties with density. Wood Science and Technology 39(5): 339–350.

Blomberg, J., B. Persson and U. Bexell. 2006. Effects of semi-isostatic densification on anatomy and cell-shape recovery on soaking. Holzforschung 60: 322–331.

Bobleter, O. and H. Binder. 1980. Dynamischer hydrothermaler Abbau von Holz [Dynamic hydrothermal degradation of wood.] Holzforschung 34(2): 48–51.

Bocquet, J.F., A. Pizzi, A. Despres, H.R. Mansouri, L. Resch, D. Michel and F. Letort. 2007a. Wood joints and laminated wood beams assembled by mechanically-welded wood dowels. Journal of Adhesion Science and Technology 21: 301–317.

Bocquet, J.F., A. Pizzi and L. Resch. 2007b. Full-scale industrial wood floor assembly and structures by welded-through dowels. Holz als Roh- und Werkstoff 65: 149–155.

Boehm, R.B. 1951. Process of making a plywood product. U.S. Patent No. 2557071.

Bonamini, G. 2012. The assessment and functional rehabilitation of historic wooden musical instruments: The "reference voice" method and its application to the grand piano. Journal of Cultural Heritage 13S: 149–153.

Boonstra, M.J. 2008. A two-stage thermal modification of wood. PhD. Thesis in co-supervision of Ghent University, Belgium and Université Henry Poincaré, Nancy, France.

Boonstra, M.J. and J. Blomberg. 2007. Semi-isostatic densification of heat-treated radiata pine. Wood Science and Technology 41: 607–617.

Boonstra, M.J., B.F. Tjeerdsma and H.A.C. Groeneveld. 1998. Thermal modification of non-durable wood species. Part 1. The Plato technology: Thermal modification of wood. *In*: The Proceedings IRG Annual Meeting, Maastricht, The Netherlands. International Research Group on Wood Protection IRG/WP 98-40123.

Boonstra, M.J., A. Pizzi, C. Ganne-Chédeville, M. Properzi, J.M. Leban and F. Pichelin. 2006. Vibration welding of heat-treated wood. Journal of Adhesion Science and Technology 20(4): 359–369.

Borgin, K., O. Faix and W. Schweers. 1975. The effect of aging on lignins of wood. Wood Science and Technology 9: 207–211.

Boruszewski, P., P. Borysiuk, M. Mamiński and M. Grześkiewicz. 2011. Gluability of thermally modified beech (*Fagus silvatica* L.) and birch (*Betula pubescens* Ehrh.) wood. Wood Material Science & Engineering 6(4): 185–189.

Bourgois, J. and R. Guyonnet. 1988. Characterisation and analysis of torrefied wood. Wood Science and Technology 22(2): 143–155.

Bourgois, J., M. Bartholin and R. Guyonnet. 1989. Thermal treatment of wood: Analysis of the obtained products. Wood Science and Technology 23(4): 303–310.

Bremer, M., S. Fischer, T.C. Nguyen, A. Wagenführ, L.X. Phuong and V.H. Dai. 2013. Effects of thermal modification on the properties of two Vietnamese bamboo species. Part II: Effects on chemical composition. BioResources 8(1): 981–993.

Brenden, J.J. 1967. Effect of fire-retardant and other inorganic salts on pyrolysis products of Ponderosa pine at 250°C and 350°C. U.S. Forest Service Research Paper FPL 80, U.S. Department of Agriculture, Forest Service, Forest Products Laboratory, Madison (WI) USA.

Brischke, C., C.R. Welzbacher, K. Brandt and O. Rapp. 2007. Quality control of thermally modified timber: Interrelationship between heat treatment intensities and CIE L*a*b* color data on homogenized wood samples. Holzforschung 61: 19–22.

Browne, F.L. 1958. Theories of the combustion of wood and its control. Forest Service Technological Report No. 2136, U.S. Department of Agriculture, Forest Service, Forest Products Laboratory, Madison (WI), USA.

Burmester, A. 1970. Formbeständigkeit von Holz gegenüber Feuchtigkeit – Grundlagen und Vergütungsverfahren [Influnce of moisture on dimension stability of wood—theory and improvements.] BAM Berichte Nr. 4, Bundesanstalt für Materialforschung, Berlin, Germany (In German).

Burmester, A. 1973. Effect of heat-pressure treatments of semi-dry wood on its dimensional stability. Holz als Roh- und Werkstoff 31(6): 237–243.

Burmester, A. 1975. Zur Dimensionsstabilisierung von Holz [The dimensional stabilization of wood.] Holz als Roh- und Werkstoff 33(9): 333–335.

Burmester, A. 1981. Dimensational stabilisation of wood. *In*: The Proceedings IRG Annual Meeting, Sarajevo, Yugoslavia. International Research Group on Wood Protection IRG/WP/3171.

Buro, A. 1954. Die Wirkung von Hitzebehandlung auf die Pilzresistenz von Kiefern- und Buchenholz [The influence of thermal treatment on decay resistance of pine and beech wood.] Holz als Roh- und Werkstoff 12(8): 297–304.

Buro, A. 1955. Untersuchungen über die Veränderung der Pilzresistenz von Hölzern durch Hitzebehandlung in Metallschmelzen [Investigation of the change in decay resistance of wood during thermal treatment in a metal melt.] Holzforschung 9(6): 177–181.

Burtscher, E., O. Bobleter, W. Schwald, R. Concin and H. Binder. 1987. Chromatographic analysis of biomass reaction products produced by hydrothermolysis of poplar wood. Journal of Chromatography 390(2): 401–412.

Bustos, A., C. Gacitúa Escobar, W. Cloutier, A. Fang and C.H. Valenzuela Carrasco. 2011. Densification of wood veneers combined with oil-heat treatment. Part III: Cell wall mechanical properties determined by nanoindentation. BioResources 7(2): 1525–1532.

Bächle, H., B. Zimmer, E. Windeisen and G. Wegener. 2010. Evaluation of thermally modified beech and spruce wood and their properties by FT-NIR spectroscopy. Wood Science and Technology 44: 421–433.

Cabrero, J., A. Heiduschke and P. Haller. 2010. Analytical assessment of the load carrying capacity of axially loaded wooden reinforced tubes. Composite Structures 92: 2955–2965.

Cai, C., M.A. Javed, S. Komulainen, V.V. Telkki, A. Haapala and H. Heräjärvi. 2020. Effect of natural weathering on water absorption and pore size distribution in thermally modified wood determined by nuclear magnetic resonance. Cellulose 27: 4235–4247.

Candan, Z., S. Korkut and O. Ünsal. 2013. Effect of thermal modification by hot pressing on performance properties of paulownia wood boards. Industrial Crops and Products 45: 461–464.

Candelier, K., S. Dumarçay, A. Pétrissans, P. Gérardin and M. Pétrissans. 2013a. Comparison of mechanical properties of heat-treated beech wood cured under nitrogen or vacuum. Polymer Degradation & Stabilization 98: 1762–1765.

Candelier, K., S. Dumarçay, A. Pétrissans, L. Desharnais, P. Gérardin and M. Pétrissans. 2013b. Comparison of chemical composition and decay durability of heat-treated wood cured under different inert atmospheres: Nitrogen or vacuum. Polymer Degradation & Stabilization 98: 677–681.

Candelier, K., M.-F. Thevenon, A. Petrissans, S. Dumarcay, P. Gerardin and M. Petrissans. 2016. Control of wood thermal treatment and its effects on decay resistance: A review. Annals of Forest Science 73: 571–583.

Castwall, L. and C. Lindhe. 1999. Method for producing a hard wood element. U.S. Patent No. 5,904,194.

CEN. 2003. EN 205-D1: Specification for close contact structural wood joints. European Committee for Standardization (CEN), Brussels, Belgium.

CEN. 2004. EN 113 Wood preservatives – Test method for determining the protective effectiveness against wood destroying basidiomycetes – Determination of the toxic values. European Committee for Standardization, Brussels, Belgium.

CEN. 2008. Thermal modified timber – Definitions and characteristics. Technical specification no. CEN/TS 15679:2008. European Committee for Standardization, Brussels, Belgium.

CEN. 2016. EN 350. Durability of wood and wood-based products. Testing and classification of the durability to biological agents of wood and wood-based materials. European Committee for Standardization, Brussels, Belgium.

Čermák, P., A. Dejmal, Z. Paschová, M. Kymäläinen, J. Dömény, M. Brabec, D. Hess and L. Rautkari. 2019. One-sided surface charring of beech wood. Journal of Materials Science 54(13): 9497–9506.

Charani, P.R., J.M. Rovshandeh, B. Mohebby and O. Ramezani. 2007. Influence of hydrothermal treatment on the dimensional stability of beech wood. Caspian Journal of Environmental Sciences 5(2): 125–131.

Cirule, D., A. Meija-Feldmane, E. Kuka, B. Andersons, N. Kurnosova, A. Antons and H. Tuherm. 2016. Spectral sensitivity of thermally modified and unmodified wood. BioResources 11(1): 324–335.

Couceiro, J., M. Sehlstedt-Persson, L. Hansson, O. Hagman and D. Sandberg. 2017. CT scanning of capillary phenomena in bio-based materials. ProLigno 13(4): 181–187.

Cristescu, C. 2006. Bonding laminated veneers with heat and pressure only, pp. 339–348. In: Caldeira, F.J. [ed.] Proceedings of the 2nd International Conference on Environmentally-Compatible. Forest Products "Ecowood". Porto, Portugal.

Cristescu, C. 2015. Self-bonding of beech veneers. PhD. Thesis, Luleå University of Technology, Skellefteå, Sweden.

Cristescu, C. and O. Karlsson. 2013. Changes in content of furfurals and phenols in self-bonded laminated boards. BioResources 8(3): 4056–4071.

Cristescu, C., D. Johansson and Y. Chen. 2006. Method of producing a laminate comprising at least two layers of lignocellulosic material joined by heat treatment and pressing. International patent application No. PCT/SE 529 747 C2, with international publication No. WO 2007/117195A1.

Cristescu, C., D. Sandberg, M. Ekevad and O. Karlsson. 2015a. Influence of pressing parameters on mechanical and physical properties of self-bonded laminated beech boards. Wood Material Science & Engineering 10(2): 205–214.

Cristescu, C., B. Neyses, D. Sandberg and O. Söderström. 2015b. Modelling of the temperature distribution in self-bonded beech-veneer boards during hot pressing. ProLigno 11(4): 97–103.

Cristescu, C., O. Hagman, D. Sandberg and O. Karlsson. 2015c. Could colour predict hardness of hot-pressed self-laminated beech boards. ProLigno 11(4): 150–156.

Dahlgren, B. 1989. Om arkitektur [On architecture; Translation of the ten Books on Architecture "De architectura" by the Roman author, architect, civil engineer, and military engineer Marcus Vitruvius Pollio ca. 80–70 BC – after ca. 15 BC] Byggförlaget, Stockholm (In Swedish).

de Cademartori, P.H.G., E. Schneid, D.A. Gatto, D.M. Stangerlin and R. Beltrame. 2013a. Thermal modification of *Eucalyptus grandis* wood: Variation of colorimetric parameters. Maderas: Ciencia y Tecnología 15(1): 57–64.

de Cademartori, P.H.G., P.S.B. dos Santos, L. Serrano, J. Labidi and A. Gatto. 2013b. Effect of thermal treatment on physicochemical properties of *Gympie messmate* wood. Industrial Crops and Products 45: 360–366.

Delmotte, L., C. Ganne-Chédeville, J.M. Leban, A. Pizzi and F. Pichelin. 2008. CP-MAS 13C NMR and FT-IR investigation of the degradation reactions of polymer constituents in wood welding. Polymer Degradation and Stability 93: 406–412.

Diouf, P.N., T. Stevanovic, A. Cloutier, C.H. Fang, P. Blanchet, A. Koubaa and N. Mariotti. 2011. Effects of thermo-hygro-mechanical densification on the surface characteristics of trembling aspen and hybrid poplar wood veneers. Applied Surface Science 257: 3558–3564.

Dirol, D. and R. Guyonnet. 1993. The improvement of wood durability by retification process. In: The Proceedings IRG Annual Meeting, Orlando (FL), USA. International Research Group on Wood Protection IRG/WP/93-40015.

Ditommaso, G., M. Gaff, F. Kačík, A. Sikora, A. Sethy, R. Corleto, F. Razaei, L. Kaplan, J. Kubŝ, S. Das, G. Kamboj, M. Gašparík, P. Šedivka, S. Hýsek, J. Macků and M. Sedlecký. 2020. Interaction of technical and technological factors on qualitative and energy/ecological/economic indicators in the production and processing of thermally modified merbau wood. Journal of Cleaner Production 252: Article ID 119793.

Duhamel du Monceau, H.L. 1767. Du Transport, de la Conservation et de la Force des Bois [Transport, Conservation and Strength of the Woods.] L.F. Delatour, Paris, France.

Dunlop, A.P. 1948. Furfural formation and behavior. Industrial and Engineering Chemistry 40(2): 204–209.

Dwianto, W., M. Inoue and M. Norimoto. 1997. Fixation of compressive deformation of wood by heat treatment. Journal of the Japan Wood Research Society (Nippon Mokuzai Gakki) 43(4): 303–309 (in Japanese).

Dwianto, W., T. Morooka, M. Norimoto and T. Kitajima. 1999. Stress relaxation of sugi (*Cryptomeria japonica* D. Don) wood in radial compression under high temperature steam. Holzforschung 53(5): 541–546.

Dzurenda, L. 2013. Modification of wood colour of *Fagus sylvatica* L. to a brown-pink shade caused by thermal treatment. Woods Research 58(3): 475–482.

Ellis, S. and L. Paszner. 1994. Activated self-bonding of wood and agricultural residues. Holzforschung 48(1): 82–90.

Englund, F. and R. Nussbaum. 2000. Monoterpenes in Scots pine and Norway spruce and their emission during kiln drying. Holzforschung 54(5): 449–456.

Esteves, B., A. Marques, I. Domingos and H. Pereira. 2007. Influence of steam heating on the properties of pine (*Pinus pinaster*) and eucalypt (*Eucalyptus globulus*) wood. Wood Science and Technology 41(3): 193–207.

Esteves, B., I. Domingos and H. Pereira. 2008a. Pine wood modification by heat treatment in air. BioResource 3(1): 142–154.

Esteves, B., A. Marques, I. Domingos and H. Pereira. 2008b. Heat-induced colour changes of pine (*Pinus pinaster*) and eucalyptus (*Eucalyptus globulus*) wood. Wood Science and Technology 42: 369–384.

Esteves, M.B. and H. Pereira. 2009. Wood modification by heat treatment: A review. BioResources 4: 370–404.

Exner, W.F. and G. Lauboeck [eds.]. 1922. Das Biegen des Holzes. Ein für Möbelfabrikanten, Wagen- und Shiffbauer, Böttcher und anderen wichtiges Verfahren [Wood bending, an important process for furniture makers, wagon- and shipbuilder, coopers and others.] 4th edition, Verlag von Vernh. Friedrich Voigt, Leipzig, Germany (In German).

Fang, C.H., A. Cloutier, P. Blanchet, A. Koubaa and N. Mariotti. 2011. Densification of wood veneers combined with oil-heat treatment. Part I: Dimensional stability. BioResourses 6(1): 373–385.

Fang, C.H., N. Mariotti, A. Cloutier, A. Koubaa and P. Blanchet. 2012. Densification of wood veneers by compression combined with heat and steam. European Journal of Wood and Wood Products 70(1/3): 155–163.

Fengel, D. 1966a. Über die Veränderungen des Holzes und seiner Komponenten im Temperaturbereich bis 200°C. Erste Mitteilungen: Heiß- und Kaltwasserextrakte von termisch behandeltem Fichtenholz [On the changes of the wood and its components within the temperature range up to 200°C. Part I: Hot and cold water extracts of thermally treated spruce wood.] Holz als Roh- und Werkstoff 24(1): 9–14.

Fengel, D. 1966b. Über die Veränderungen des Holzes und seiner Komponenten im Temperaturbereich bis 200°C. Zweite Mitteilungen: Die Hemicellulosen in unbehandeltem und in termisch behandeltem Fichtenholz [On the changes of the wood and its components within the temperature range up to 200°C. Part II: The hemicelluloses in untreated and thermally treated spruce wood.] Holz als Roh- und Werkstoff 24(3): 98–109.

Fengel, D. 1966c. Über die Veränderungen des Holzes und seiner Komponenten im Temperaturbereich bis 200°C. Dritte Mitteilungen: Thermisch und mechanisch bedingte Strukturänderungen bei Fichtenholz [On the changes of the wood and its components within the temperature range up to 200°C. Part III: Thermally and mechanically caused structural changes in spruce wood.] Holz als Roh- und Werkstoff 24(11): 529–536.

Fengel, D. and G. Wegener. 2003. Wood: Chemistry, Ultrastructure, Reactions. Verlag Kessel, Remagen, Germany.

Follrich, J., U. Müller and W. Gindl. 2006. Effects of thermal modification on the adhesion between spruce wood (*Picea abies* Karst.) and a thermoplastic polymer. Holz als Roh- und Werkstoff 64(5): 373–376.

Froidevaux, J. 2012. Wood and paint layers aging and risk analysis of ancient panel painting. PhD. Thesis, University of Montpellier II—Sciences et Techniques du Languedoc, Montpellier, France.

Froidevaux, J. and P. Navi. 2013. Aging law of spruce wood. Wood Material Science & Engineering 8(1): 46–52.

Froidevaux, J., T. Volkmer, C. Ganne-Chédeville, J. Gril and P. Navi. 2012. Viscoelastic behaviour of aged and non-aged spruce wood in the radial direction. Wood Material Science & Engineering 7(1): 1–12.

Gabrielli, C.P. and F.A. Kamke. 2008. Treatment of chemically modified wood with VTC process to improve dimensional stability. Forest Products Journal 58(12): 82–86.

Gabrielli, C.P. and F.A. Kamke. 2010. Phenol–formaldehyde impregnation of densified wood for improved dimensional stability. Wood Science and Technology 44(1): 95–104.

Ganier, T., J. Hu and A. Pizzi. 2013. Causes of the water resistance of welded joints of paduk wood (*Pterocarpus soyauxii* Taub.). Journal of Renewable Materials 1(1): 79–82.

Ganne-Chédeville, C., A. Pizzi, A. Thomas, J.M. Leban, J.F. Bocquet, A. Despres and H. Mansouri. 2005. Parameter interactions in two-block welding and the wood nail concept in wood dowel welding. Journal of Adhesion Science and Technology 19(13/14): 1157–1174.

Ganne-Chédeville, C., J.M. Leban, M. Properzi, F. Pichelin and A. Pizzi. 2006a. Temperature and density distribution in mechanical vibration wood welding. Wood Science and Technology 40: 72–76.

Ganne-Chédeville, C., M. Properzi, J.M. Leban and F. Pichelin. 2006b. Parameters of wood welding: A study with infrared thermography. Holzforschung 60: 434–438.

Ganne-Chédeville, C., M. Properzi, A. Pizzi, J.M. Leban and F. Pichelin. 2007. Edge and face linear vibration welding of wood panels. Holz als Roh- und Werkstoff 65: 83–85.

Gašparík, M., M. Gaff, F. Kačík and A. Sikora. 2019. Color and chemical changes in teak (*Tectona grandis* L. f.) and meranti (*Shorea* spp.) wood after thermal treatment. BioResources 14(2): 2667–2683.

Geib, S.M., T.R. Filley, P.G. Hatcher, K. Hoover, J.E. Carlson, M. Jimenez Gasco, A. Nakagawa-Izumi, R.L. Sleighter and M. Tien. 2008. Lignin degradation in wood-feeding insects. Proceedings of the National Academy of Science USA 105(35): 12932–12937.

Gérardin, P., M. Petrič, M. Pétrissans, J. Lambert and J.J. Ehrhrardt. 2007. Evolution of wood surface free energy after heat treatment. Polymer Degradation and Stability 92(4): 653–657.

Gfeller, B., M. Zanetti, M. Properzi, A. Pizzi, F. Pichelin, M. Lehmann and L. Delmotte. 2003. Wood bonding by vibrational welding. Journal of Adhesion Science and Technology 17(11): 1573–1589.

Gfeller, B., M. Lehmann, M. Properzi, F. Pichelin, M. Zanetti, A. Pizzi and L. Delmotte. 2004a. Interior wood joints by mechanical fusion welding of wood surfaces. Forest Products Journal 54(7/8): 72–79.

Gfeller, B., A. Pizzi, M. Zanetti, M. Properzi, M. Lehmann and L. Delmotte. 2004b. Solid wood joints by in situ welding of structural wood constituents. Holzforschung 58: 45–52.

Giebler, E. 1983. Dimensionsstabilisierung von Holz durch eine Feuchte/Wärme/Druck-Behandlung [Dimensional stabilization of wood by moisture-heat-pressure treatment.] Holz als Roh- und Werkstoff 41(3): 87–94.

Gindl, W. and T. Schoberl. 2004. The significance of the elastic modulus of wood cell walls obtained from nanoindentation measurements. Composites Part A: Applied Science and Manufacturing 35: 1345–1349.

Gliniorz, K.U. and J. Natterer. 2000. Holzschweißen – Innovative Verbindungstechnologien im Holzbau [Wood welding - innovative joining technologies in wood construction.], pp. 9–18. *In*: Proceeding from the Symposium of the Ligna Plus World Fair for the Forestry and Timber Industry in Hanover, Germany.

Gliniorz, K.U., S. Mohr, J. Natterer and P. Navi. 2001. Wood welding, pp. 571–574. *In*: Navi, P. [ed.]. Proceedings of the First International Conference of the European Society for Wood Mechanics, Lausanne, Switzerland.

Gong, M., C. Lamason and L. Li. 2010. Interactive effect of surface densification and post-treatment on aspen wood. Journal of Materials Processing Technology 210: 293–296.

Gonzalez-Pena, M.M. and M.D.C. Hale. 2009. Colour in thermally modified wood of beech, Norway spruce and Scots pine. Part 1: Colour evolution and colour changes. Holzforschung 63: 385–393.

Green, III F. and T. Schultz. 2003. New environmentally-benign concepts in wood protection, pp. 378–389. *In*: Goodell, B., Nicholas, D.D. and Schultz, T.P. [eds.]. Wood Deterioration and Preservation: Advances in Our Changing World. ACS Symposium Series 845, American Chemical Society, Washington D.C., USA.

Grinins, J., B. Andersons, V. Biziks, I. Andersone and G. Dobele. 2013. Analytical pyrolysis as an instrument to study the chemical transformations of hydrothermally modified wood. Journal of Analytical and Applied Pyrolysis 103: 36–41.

Gunduz, G., D. Aydemir and G. Karakas. 2009. The effects of thermal treatment on the mechanical properties of wild pear (*Pyrus elaeagnifolia* Pall.) wood and changes in physical properties. Materials & Design 30: 4391–4395.

Göthe, S., O. Lindström, K. Lough-Grimsgaard and E. Sjöberg. 2013. Composition and method for treating wood. U.S. Patent No. 8372519.

Hahn, B., T. Vallée, B. Stamm and Y. Weinand. 2012. Experimental investigations and probabilistic strength prediction of linear welded double lap joints composed of timber. International Journal of Adhesion and Adhesives 39: 42–48.

Hahn, B., B. Stamm and Y. Weinand. 2014a. Linear friction welding of spruce boards: Experimental investigations on scale effects due to humidity evaporation. Wood Science and Technology 48: 855–871.

Hahn, B., B. Stamm and Y. Weinand. 2014b. Moment resisting connections composed of friction-welded spruce boards: Experimental investigations and numerical strength prediction. European Journal of Wood and Wood Products 72: 229–241.

Hahn, B., B. Stamm and Y. Weinand. 2015. Influence of surface shapes on the mechanical behaviour of friction welded wood bonds. European Journal of Wood and Wood Products 73: 29–34.

Hakkou, M., M. Pétrissans, I. El Bakali, P. Gérardin and A. Zoulalian. 2005. Wettability changes and mass loss during heat treatment of wood. Holzforschung 59: 35–37.

Haller, P. 2007. Concepts for textile reinforcements for timber structures. Materials and Structures 40: 107–118.

Haller, P., J. Wehsener and S. Ziegler. 2002. Formteil aus Holz und Verfahren zu seiner Herstellung [Wood profile and method for the production of the same.] German Patent No. DE 10 2006 009 161 B4 2008.02.21, with international publication No. WO 02/096608 A1.

Haller, P., J. Wehsener, T.E. Werner and J. Hartig. 2013a. Recent advancements for the application of moulded wooden tubes as structural elements, pp. 99–108. *In*: Aicher, S., Reinhard, H.W. and Garrecht, H. [eds.]. Material and Joints in Timber Structures. Springer, Heidelberg, Germany.

Haller, P., R. Putzger, J. Wehsener and J. Hartig. 2013b. Formholzrohre – Stand der Forschung und Anwendungen [Molded wood pipes – State of research and applications.] Bautechnik 90: 34–41.

Hartig, J.U., J. Wehsener and P. Haller. 2016. Experimental and theoretical investigations on moulded wooden tubes made of beech (*Fagus sylvatica* L.). Construction and Building Materials 126: 527–536.

Hartig, J.U., S. Facchini and P. Haller. 2018. Investigations on lateral vehicle impact on moulded wooden tubes made of beech (*Fagus sylvatica* L.). Construction and Building Materials 174: 547–558.

Haygreen, J.G. and D.H. Daniels. 1969. The simultaneous drying and densification of sapwood. Wood and Fiber Science 1(1): 38–53.

Heiduschke, A. and P. Haller. 2009. Zum Tragverhalten gewickelter Formholzrohre unter axialem Druck [On the structural behaviour of moulded wood tubes under axial compression.] Der Bauingenieur 84(6): 262–269.

Heiduschke, A. and P. Haller. 2010. Fiber-reinforced plastic-confined wood profiles under axial compression. Structural Engineering International 20(3): 246–253.

Heiduschke, A., B. Kasal and P. Haller. 2009. Shake table tests of small- and full-scale laminated timber frames with moment connections. Bulletin of Earthquake Engineering 7(1): 323–339.

Hill, C.A.S. 2006. Wood Modification: Chemical, Thermal and other Processes. John Wiley & Sons, Chichester, UK.

Hillis, W.E. 1975. The role of wood characteristics in high temperature drying. Journal of the Institute of Wood Science 7(2): 60–67.

Hillis, W.E. 1984. High temperature and chemical effects on wood stability. Part 1: General considerations. Wood Science and Technology 18(4): 281–293.

Hoffmeyer, P., L.G. Thygesen and E. Thybringen Engelund. 2011. Equilibrium moisture content in Norway spruce during the first and second desorptions. Holzforschung 65: 875–882.

Hsu, W.E., W. Schwald, J. Schwald and J.A. Shields. 1988. Chemical and physical changes required for producing dimensionally stable wood-based composites. Part I: Steam pretreatment. Wood Science and Technology 22(3): 281–289.

Huguenin, P. and P. Navi. 1995. Bois densifié sans résine synthétique [Wood densification without use of synthetic resin.] Ingénieurs et Architectes Suisses 13: 262–268 (In French).

Inoue, M., M. Norimoto, M. Tanahashi and R. Rowell. 1993. Steam or heat fixation of compressed wood. Wood and Fiber Science 25(3): 224–235.

Inoue, M., N. Sekino, T. Morooka and M. Norimoto. 1996. Dimensional stabilization of wood composites by steaming I. Fixation of compressed wood by pre-steaming, pp. 240–248. *In*: Proceedings of the Third Pacific Rim BioBased Composites Conference, Kyoto, Japan.

Inoue, M., N. Sekino, T. Morooka, R.M. Rowell and M. Norimoto. 2008. Fixation of compressive deformation in wood by pre-steaming. Journal of Tropical Forest Science 20(4): 273–281.

Irvine, F.A. and E.J. Fredrick. 1946. Moulded product and method of making. U.S. Patent No. 2402554.

Jakes, J.E., C.R. Frihart, J.F. Beecher, R.J. Moon and D.S. Stone. 2008. Experimental method to account for structural compliance in nanoindentation measurements. Journal of Materials Research 23: 1113–1127.

Jebrane, M., I. Cuccui, O. Allegretti, E. Jr. Uetimane and N. Terziev. 2018. Thermowood® vs Termovuoto process: Comparison of thermally modified timber in industrial conditions, pp. 533–538. *In*: Creemers, J., Houben, T., Tjeerdsma, B., Militz, H., Junge, B. and Gootjes, J. [eds.]. The Proceeding of the 9th European Conference on Wood Modification, Arnhem, the Netherlands.

Jennings, J.E., A. Zink-Sharp, F.A. Kamke and C.E. Frazier. 2005. Properties of compression densified wood. Part 1: Bond performance. Journal of Adhesion Science and Technology 19(13/14): 1249–1261.

Jennings, J.E., A. Zink-Sharp, C.E. Frazier and F.A. Kamke. 2006. Properties of compression densified wood. Part 2: Surface energy. Journal of Adhesion Science and Technology 20(4): 335–344.

Jones, D., D. Sandberg, G. Goli and L. Todaro. 2019. Wood Modification in Europe: A State-of-the-art about Processes, Products, Applications. Firenze University Press, Florence, Italy.

Kaar, W.E., L.G. Cool, M.M. Merriman and D.L. Brink. 1991. The complete analysis of wood polysaccharides using HPLC. Journal of Wood Chemistry and Technology 11(4): 447–463.

Kačíková, D., F. Kačík, I. Čabalová and J. Ďurkovič. 2013. Effects of thermal treatment on chemical, mechanical and colour traits in Norway spruce wood. BioResource Technology 144: 669–674.

Källander, B. 2016. Drying and thermal modification of wood: Studies on influence of sample size, batch size, and climate on wood response. PhD. Thesis, Luleå University of Technology, Skellefteå, Sweden.

Kamke, F.A. 2013. THM—A technology platform or novelty product? pp. 8–15. *In*: Medved, S. and Kutnar, A. [eds.]. Characterization of Modified Wood in Relation to Wood Bonding and Coating Performance. Proceedings of the COST FP0904 and FP1003 International Workshop. Rogla, Slovenia.

Kamke, F.A. and L.J. Casey. 1988. Fundamentals of flakeboard manufacture: Internal-mat conditions. Forest Products Journal 38(6): 38–44.

Kamke, F.A. and H. Sizemore. 2004. Viscoelastic thermal compression of wood. U.S. Patent No. 20050006004 A1.

Kamke, F.A. and H. Sizemore. 2008. Viscoelastic thermal compression of wood. U.S. Patent No. 7,404,422 B2.

Kamke, F.A. and A. Kutnar. 2011. Influence of stress level on compression deformation of wood in 170°C transient steam conditions. Wood Material Science & Engineering 6(3): 105–111.

Kanazawa, F., A. Pizzi, M. Properzi, L. Delmotte and F. Pichelin. 2005. Parameters influencing wood-dowel welding by high-speed rotation. Journal of Adhesion Science and Technology 19(12): 1025–1038.

Kantner, W., T. Zich, M. Schwarzkopf, M.D. Burnard, M. Mikuljan and A. Kutnar. 2019. Method for preparation of densified wood. European Patent EP19204677.9.

Karami, E., M. Matsuo, I. Brémaud, S. Bardet, J. Froidevaux and J. Gril. 2013. Modification of wood acoustic, hygroscopic and colorimetric properties due to thermally accelerated ageing, pp. 238–245. *In*: Medved, S. and Kutnar, A. [eds.]. Characterization of Modified Wood in Relation to Wood Bonding and Coating Performance. Proceedings of the COST FP0904 and FP1003 International Workshop. Rogla, Slovenia.

Karlsson, O., P. Torniainen, O. Dagbro, K. Granlund and T. Morén. 2012. Presence of water-soluble compounds in thermally modified wood: Carbohydrates and furfurals. BioResources 7: 3679–3689.

Karlsson, O., C, Cristescu and D. Sandberg. 2015. Autoadhesion of laminated boards from Scots pine veneers: Effect of oxidative pretreatment. ProLigno 11(4): 110–115.

Kasemsiri, P., S. Hiziroglu and S. Rimdusit. 2012. Characterization of heat treated Eastern redcedar (*Juniperus virginiana* L.). Journal of Materials Processing Technology 212: 1324–1330.

Kaygin, B., G. Gunduz and D. Aydemir. 2009. Some physical properties of heat-treated paulownia (*Paulownia elongata*) wood. Drying Technology 27(1): 89–93.

Kekkonen, P.M., V.-V. Telkki and J. Jokisaari. 2010. Effect of thermal modification on wood cell structures observed by pulsed-field-gradient stimulated-echo NMR. The Journal of Physical Chemistry C 114(43): 18693−18697.

Kellogg, R.M. and F.F. Wangaard. 1969. Variation in the cell-wall density of wood. Wood and Fiber Science 1: 180−204.

Kifetew, G. and M. Wiklund. 2000. Hårdpress (Press for densification). Swedish Patent Application No. 9901796-4.

Klauditz, W. and G. Stegmann. 1955. Beiträge zur Kenntnis des Ablaufes und der Wirkung thermischer Reaktionen bei der Bildung von Holzwerkstoffen [Contributions to the knowledge of the sequence and the effect of thermal reactions in the formation of wood materials.] Holz als Roh- und Werkstoff 13(11): 434–440.

Knust, C., P. Haller, D. Krug and S. Tobisch. 2008 Einsatzmöglichkeiten von Plantagenholz [Potential of plantation wood.] Schweizerische Zeitschrift Forstwesen 159: 146–151.

Kocaefe, D., J.L. Shi, D.Q. Yang and M. Bouazara. 2008. Mechanical properties, dimensional stability, and mold resistance of heat-treated jack pine and aspen. Forest Products Journal 58: 88–93.

Koch, G., J. Puls and J. Bauch. 2003. Topochemical characterisation of phenolic extractives in discoloured beech wood (*Fagus sylvatica* L.). Holzforschung 57: 339−345.

Koehler, A. and M.Y. Pillow. 1925. Effect of high temperatures on the mode of fracture of a softwood. Southern Lumberman 121(1576): 219–221.

Kohara, J. 1952. Studies on the durability of wood. I. Mechanical properties of old timbers. Bulletin of Kyoto Prefectural University 2: 116−131 (In Japanese).

Kohara, J. 1953. Studies on the permanence of wood. V. Shrinkage and swelling of old timbers about 300–1300 years ago. Bulletin of Kyoto Prefectural University 5: 81–88 (In Japanese).

Kohara, J. 1954a. Studies on the permanence of wood. VI. The changes of mechanical properties of old timbers. Bulletin of Kyoto Prefectural University 6: 164–174 (In Japanese).

Kohara, J. 1954b. Studies on the permanence of wood. VII. The influence of age on the components of wood (*Chamaecyparis obtusa* Endlicher). Bulletin of Kyoto Prefectural University 6: 175–182 (In Japanese).

Kohara, J. 1955a. Studies on the permanence of wood. XV. The influence of age on the components of wood (*Zelkowa serrata* Makino). Mokuzai Gakkaishi 1: 21–24 (In Japanese).

Kohara, J. 1955b. On permanence of wood. II. Differences between the ageing processes of cypress wood and zelkova wood. Wood Industry 10: 395–399 (In Japanese).

Kol, H.Ş. and Y. Sefil. 2011. The thermal conductivity of fir and beech wood heat treated at 170, 180, 190, 200, and 212°C. Journal of Applied Polymer Science 121(4): 2473–2480.

Kollmann, F. 1936. Technologies des Holzes [Wood Technology.] Verlag von Julius Springer, Berlin, Germany (In German).

Kollmann, F.F.P. 1955. Technologie des Holzes und der Holzwerkstoffe [Wood Technology and Wood-based materials.] (2 volumes) Springer-Verlag, Berlin, Göttingen, Germany (In German).

Kollmann, F. 1960. Zur Frage des Auftretens exothermer Reaktionen bei Holz [Occurence of exotermic reaction in wood.] Holz als Roh- und Werkstoff 18(6): 193–200.

Kollmann, F. and D. Fengel. 1965. Änderungen der chemischen Zusammensetzung von Holz durch thermische Behandlung [Changes in the chemical composition of wood by thermal treatment.] Holz als Roh- und Werkstoff 23(12): 461–468.

Kollmann, F.P., E.W. Kuenzi and A.J. Stamm. 1975. Principles of Wood Science and Technology. Vol. II: Wood Based Materials. Springer-Verlag, Berlin, Heidelberg, New York.

Konnerth, J., A. Jager, J. Eberhardsteiner, U. Müller and W. Gindl. 2006. Elastic properties of adhesive polymers. II. Polymer films and bond lines by means of nanoindentation. Journal of Applied Polymer Science 102: 1234–1239.

Konnerth, J., M. Eiser, A. Jager, T.K. Bader, K. Hofstetter, J. Follrich, T. Ters, C. Hansmann and R. Wimmer. 2010. Macro- and micro-mechanical properties of red oak wood (*Quercus rubra* L.) treated with hemicelluloses. Holzforschung 64(4): 447–453.

Korkut, D.S. and B. Guller. 2008. The effects of heat treatment on physical properties and surface roughness of red-bud maple (*Acer trautvetteri* Medw.) wood. BioResource Technology 99: 2846–2851.

Korkut, S. and S. Hiziroglu. 2009. Effect of heat treatment on mechanical properties of hazelnut wood (*Corylus colurna* L.). Materials & Design 30: 1853–1858.

Korkut, S., M.S. Kök, D.S. Korkut and T. Gürleyen. 2008a. The effects of heat treatment on technological properties in red-bud maple (*Acer trautvetteri* Medw.) wood. BioResource Technology 99: 1538–1543.

Korkut, S., M. Akgüla and T. Dündar. 2008b. The effects of heat treatment on some technological properties of Scots pine (*Pinus sylvestris* L.) wood. BioResource Technology 99: 1861–1868.

Korkut, S., D.S. Korkut, D. Kocaefe, D. Elustondo, A.C. Bajraktari and N. Cakicier. 2012. Effect of thermal modification on the properties of narrow-leaved ash and chestnut. Industrial Crops and Products 35(1): 287–294.

Košík, M., L. Gerátová, F. Rendoš and R. Domanský. 1968. Pyrolysis of beech wood and its components at low temperatures. II. Thermography of the beech wood and its components. Holzforschung und Holzverwertung 20(1): 15–19.

Kotilainen, R.A., T.-J. Toivanen and R.J. Alén. 2000. FTIR monitoring of chemical changes in softwood during heating. Journal of Wood Chemistry and Technology 20(3): 307–320.

Kránitz, K. 2014. Effect of natural aging on wood. PhD. Thesis, Swiss Federal Institute of Technology in Zurich (ETH), Zürich, Switzerland.

Kránitz, K., W. Sonderegger, C.-T. Bues and P. Niemz. 2016. Effects of aging on wood: A literature review. Wood Science and Technology 50(1): 7–22.

Kučerová, V., R. Lagaňa and T. Hýrošová. 2019. Changes in chemical and optical properties of silver fir (*Abies alba* L.) wood due to thermal treatment. Journal of Wood Science 65: 21–31.

Kultikova, E.V. 1999. Structure and properties relationships of densified wood. M.Sc. Thesis, Virginia Tech, Blacksburg (VA), USA.

Kutnar, A. and F. Kamke. 2012. Influence of temperature and steam environment on set recovery of compressive deformation of wood. Wood Science and Technology 46(5): 953–964.

Kutnar, A., F.A. Kamke and M. Sernek. 2008a. The mechanical properties of densified VTC wood relevant for structural composites. Holz als Roh- und Werkstoff 66(6): 439–446.

Kutnar, A., F.A. Kamke, M. Petrič and M. Sernek. 2008b. The influence of viscoelastic thermal compression on the chemistry and surface energetics of wood. Colloids and Surfaces A: Physicochemical and Engineering Aspects 329: 82–86.

Kutnar, A., F.A. Kamke, J.A. Nairn and M. Sernek. 2008c. Mode II fracture behavior of bonded viscoelastic thermal compressed wood. Wood and Fiber Science 40(3): 362–373.

Kutnar, A., F.A. Kamke and M. Sernek. 2009. Density profile and morphology of viscoelastic thermal compressed wood. Wood Science and Technology 43(1): 57–68.

Kutnar, A., M. Humar, F.A. Kamke and M. Šernek. 2011. Fungal decay of viscoelastic thermal compressed (VTC) wood. Holz als Roh- und Werkstoff 69(2): 325–328.

Kutnar, A., D. Sandberg and P. Haller. 2015. Compressed and moulded wood from processing to products. Holzforschung 69(7): 885–897.

Kymäläinen, M., S. Hautamäki, K. Lillqvist, K. Segerholm and L. Rautkari. 2017. Surface modification of solid wood by charring. Journal of Materials Science 52(10): 6111–6119.

Laine, K., L. Rautkari, M. Hughes and A. Kutnar. 2013. Reducing the set-recovery of surface densified solid Scots pine wood by hydrothermal post-treatment. Holz als Roh- und Werkstoff 71(1): 17–23.

Lamason, C. and M. Gong. 2007. Optimization of pressing parameters for mechanically surface-densified aspen. Forest Products Journal 57(10): 64–68.

Landau, M. 1914. Impregnated wood and process of making the same. U.S. Patent No. US1198040A.

Leban, J.M. 2005. Wood welding—An award-winning discovery. Scandinavian Journal of Forest Research 4: 370–371.

Leban, J.M., A. Pizzi, S. Wieland, M. Zanetti, M. Properzi and F. Pichelin. 2004. X-ray microdensitometry analysis of vibration-welded wood. Journal of Adhesion Science and Technology 18(6): 673–685.

Leban, J.M., A. Pizzi, M. Properzi, F. Pichelin, P. Gelhaye and C. Rose. 2005. Wood welding: A challenging alternative to conventional wood gluing. Scandinavian Journal of Forest Research 20: 534–538.

Leban, J.M., H.R. Mansouri, P. Omrani and A. Pizzi. 2008. Dependence of dowel welding on rotation rate. Holz als Roh- und Werkstoff 66: 241–242.

Lee, S.H., S. Wang, G.M. Pharr and H. Xu. 2007. Evaluations of interphase properties in a cellulose fiber-reinforced polypropylene composite by nanoindentation and finite element analysis. Composites Part A: Applied Science and Manufacturing 38(6): 1517–1524.

Lekounougou, S. and D. Kocaefe. 2014. Effect of thermal modification temperature on the mechanical properties, dimensional stability, and biological durability of black spruce (*Picea mariana*). Wood Material Science & Engineering 9(2): 59–66.

Lesar, B., M. Humar, F.A. Kamke and A. Kutnar. 2013. Influence of the thermo-hydro-mechanical treatments of wood on the performance against wood-degrading fungi. Wood Science and Technology 47(5): 977–992.

Li, J., G. Henriksson and G. Gellerstedt. 2007. Lignin depolymerization/repolymerization and its critical role for delignification of aspen wood by steam explosion. BioResource Technology 98(16): 3061–3068.

Li, T., J. Cai and D. Zhou. 2013. Optimization of the combined modification process of thermo-mechanical densification and heat treatment on Chinese Fir wood. BioResources 8(4): 5279–5288.

Ling, Z., Z. Ji, D. Ding, J. Cao and F. Xu. 2016. Microstructural and topochemical characterization of thermally modified poplar (*Populus cathayaha*) cell wall. BioResources 11(1): 786–799.

Long, H., T. Shi, P.J. Borm, J. Määttä, K. Husgafvel-Pursiainen, K. Savolainen and F. Krombach. 2004. ROS-mediated TNF-alpha and MIP-2 gene expression in alveolar macrophages exposed to pine dust. Particle and Fibre Toxicology 1: Article ID 3.

MacLean, J.D. 1951. Rate of disintegration of wood under different heating conditions. American Wood Preservers' Association Proceedings 47: 155–168.

MacLean, J.D. 1953. Effect of steaming on the strength of wood. American Wood Preservers' Association Proceedings 49: 88–112.

Maejima, H., K. Endo and E. Obataya. 2015. Effects of moistening treatment on the hygroscopicity and the vibrational properties of aged wood, pp. 247. *In*: Proceedings of the International Association of Wood Products Societies (IAWPS) – International Symposium on Wood Science and Technology, Tokyo, Japan.

Majka, J. and E. Roszyk. 2018. Swelling restraint of thermally modified ash wood perpendicular to the grain. European Journal of Wood and Wood Products 76: 1129–1136.

Manalo, R.D. and C.M. Garcia. 2012. Termite resistance of thermally-modified *Dendrocalamus asper* (Schultes f.) Backer ex Heyne. Insects 3: 390–395.

Manninen, A.-M., P. Pasanen and J.K. Holopainen. 2002. Comparing the VOC emissions between air-dried and heat-treated Scots pine wood. Atmospheric Environment 36(11): 1763–1768.

Mansouri, H.R., A. Pizzi, J.M. Leban, L. Delmotte, O. Lindgren and M. Vaziri. 2011. Causes for the improved water resistance in pine wood linear welded joints. Journal of Adhesion Science and Technology 25: 1987–1995.

Manthey, C., E. Günther, A. Heiduschke, P. Haller, T. Heistermann, M. Veljkovic and P. Hájek. 2009. Structural, economic and environmental performance of fibre reinforced wood profiles vs. solutions made of steel and concrete, pp. 275–289. *In*: Bragança, L., Koukkari, H., Blok, R., Gervásio, H., Veljkovic, M., Plewako, Z., Landolfo, R., Ungureanu, V. and da Silva, L.S. [eds.]. Proceedings of COST C25: Sustainable Constructions—Integrated Approach to Life-time Structural Engineering. Timisoara, Romania.

Mason, W.H. 1928. Press-dried structural insulating board and process of making same. U.S. Patent No. 1663504.

Matsuo, M., M. Yokoyama, K. Umemura, J. Gril, K. Yano and S. Kawai. 2010. Color changes in wood during heating: Kinetic analysis by applying a time-temperature superposition method. Applied Physic A 99: 47–52.

Matsuo, M., M. Yokoyama, K. Umemura, J. Sugiyama, S. Kawai, J. Gril, S. Kubodera, T. Mitsutani, H. Ozaki, M. Sakamoto and M. Imamura. 2011. Aging of wood: Analysis of color changes during natural aging and heat treatment. Holzforschung 65: 361–368.

May, N., E. Guenther and P. Haller. 2017. Environmental indicators for the evaluation of wood products in consideration of site-dependent aspects: A review and integrated approach. Sustainability 9(10): Article ID 1897.

May, N., E. Guenther and P. Haller. 2019. The sustainable use of wood as a regional resource—An ecological assessment of common and new processing technologies for wood poles. Sustainability Management Forum 27: 177–201.

Mayes, D. and O. Oksanen. 2003. ThermoWood Handbook. Finnish Thermowood Association, Helsinki, Finland.

McGinnis, G.D., W.W. Wilsonand and C.J. Bierman. 1984. Biomass conversion into chemicals using wet oxidation, pp. 89–109. *In*: Wise, D.L. [ed.]. Bioconversion Systems. CRC Press, Boca Raton (FL), USA.

Miedler, K. 1943. Die Verdichtung von Holz als neuartiges Verfahren zur wirtschaftlichen Nutzung abnorm leichter Faserhölzer [The compression of wood as a novel process for the economical use of abnormally low-weight wood.], 86 p. *In*: Heske, F. [ed.]. Sonderdruck aus Kolonialforstliche Mitteilungen, Band VI, Heft ½, J. Neumann-Neudamm, Berlin, Germany (In German).

Militz, H. 2002a. Thermal treatment of wood: European processes and their background. *In*: The Proceedings IRG Annual Meeting, Cardiff, UK. International Research Group on Wood Protection IRG/WP 02-40241.

Militz, H. 2002b. Heat treatment technologies in Europe: Scientific background and technological state-of-art, pp. 239–249. *In*: Proceedings of Conference on Enhancing the Durability of Lumber and Engineered Wood Products, Kissimmee, Orlando (FL). Forest Products Society, Madison (WI), USA.

Miller, D.D. 1998. Food Chemistry: A Laboratory Manual. John Wiley and Sons, New York, Chichester, Brisbane, Singapore, Toronto.

Mitchell, P.H. 1988. Irreversible property changes of small loblolly pine specimens heated in air, nitrogen, or oxygen. Wood and Fiber Science 20(3): 320–355.

Mitchell, R.L., R.M. Seborg and M.A. Millett. 1953. Effect of heat on the properties and chemical composition of Douglas-fir wood and its major components. Journal of the Forest Products Research Society 3(4): 38–42.

Morsing, N. 2000. Densification of wood: The influence of hygrothermal treatment on compression of beech perpendicular to the grain. PhD. Thesis, Technical University of Denmark.

Müller, C., U. Kües, C. Schöpper and A. Kharazipour. 2007. Natural binders, pp. 347–381. *In*: Kües, U. [ed.]. Wood Production, Wood Technology, and Biotechnological Impacts. Universitätsverlag, Göttingen, Germany.

Navi, P. and F. Girardet. 2000. Effects of thermo-hydro-mechanical treatment on the structure and properties of wood. Holzforschung 54(3): 287–293.

Navi, P. and F. Heger. 2004. Combined densification and thermo-hydro-mechanical processing of wood. Materials Research Society, Bulletin May: 332–336.

Navi, P. and D. Sandberg. 2012. Thermo-hydro-mechanical Processing of Wood. EPFL Press, Lausanne, Switzerland.

Navi, P. and A. Pizzi. 2014. Property changes in thermo-hydro-mechanical processing. Holzforschung 69(7): 863–873.

Neyses, B. 2019. Surface densified of solid wood: Paving the way towards industrial implementation. PhD. Thesis, Luleå University of Technology, Skellefteå, Sweden.

Neyses, B. and D. Sandberg. 2015. A new methodology to select hardwood species for wooden products. Wood Material Science & Engineering 10(4): 344–352.

Neyses, B. and D. Sandberg. 2016. A new method to select wood species suitable for surface densification, p. 96. *In*: Proceedings of BIOCOMP 2016, the 13th Pacific Rim Bio-Based Composites Symposium – Bio-based Composites for a Sustainable Future, University of Concepción, Concepción, Chile.

Neyses, B., O. Hagman, D. Sandberg and A. Nilsson. 2016. Development of a continuous wood surface densification process—The roller pressing technique, pp. 17–24. *In*: LeVan-Green, S. [ed.]. Proceedings of the 59th International Convention of Society of Wood Science and Technology. Forest Resource and Products: Moving Toward a Sustainable Future, Curitiba, Brazil.

Neyses, B., O. Karlsson and D. Sandberg. 2020. The effect of ionic liquid and superbase pre-treatment on the spring-back, set-recovery and Brinell hardness of surface-densified Scots pine. Holzforschung 74(3): 303–312.

Neyses, B., D. Buck, K. Peeters, L. Rautkari and D. Sandberg. 2021. *In situ* penetration of ionic liquids during surface densification of Scots pine. Holzforschung https://doi.org/10.1515/hf-2020-0146.

Nilsson, J., J. Johansson, G. Kifetew and D. Sandberg. 2011. Shape stability of modified engineering wood product (EWP) subjected to moisture variation. Wood Material Science & Engineering 6(3): 42–49.

Nguyen, C.T., A. Wagenführ, L.X. Phuong, V.H. Dai, M. Bremer and S. Fischer. 2012. The effects of thermal modification on the properties of two Vietnamese bamboo species. Part I: Effects on physical properties. BioResources 7(4): 5355–5366.

Nordin, N.I.A.A., H. Ariffin, Y. Andou, M.A. Hassan, Y. Shirai, H. Nishida, W.M.Z.W. Yunus, S. Karuppuchamy and N.A. Ibrahim. 2013. Modification of oil palm mesocarp fiber characteristics using superheated steam treatment. Molecules 18: 9132–9146.

Norimoto, M., C. Ota, H. Akitsu and T. Yamada. 1993. Permanent fixation of bending deformation in wood by heat treatment. Wood Research 79: 23–33.

Norton, A.J. 1947. Furan resins. Industrial and Engineering Chemistry 40(2): 236–238.

Nuopponen, M., T. Vuorinen, S. Jamsä and P. Viitaniemi. 2004. Thermal modification in softwood studied by FT-IR and UV resonance Raman spectroscopies. Journal of Wood Chemistry and Technology 24(1): 13–26.

Nyazika, T., M. Jimenez, F. Samyn and S. Bourbigot. 2019. Pyrolysis modeling, sensitivity analysis, and optimization techniques for combustible materials: A review. Journal of Fire Sciences 37(4/6): 377–433.

Obataya, E. 2007. Caractéristiques du bois ancien et technique traditionnelle japonaise de revêtement pour la protection du bois [Characteristics of old wood and traditional Japanese coating technique for wood protection.], pp. 26–43. *In*: Vaiedelich, S. and Le Conte, S. [eds.]. Proceedings Conservatione Today: The "Aging" of Wood - Cité de la Musique, Paris, France (In French).

Obataya, E. 2009. Effects of ageing and heating on the mechanical properties of wood, pp. 16–23. *In*: Uzielli, L. [ed.]. Wood Science for Conservation of Cultural Heritage: Proceedings of the International Conference held by COST Action IE0601, Florence, Italy.

Obataya, E., M. Norimoto and B. Tomita. 2000. Moisture dependence of vibrational properties of heat-treated wood. Journal of the Japan Wood Research Society 46: 88–94.

Obataya, E., T. Higashihara and B. Tomita. 2002. Hygroscopicity of heat-treated wood III. Effects of steaming on the hygroscopicity of wood. Mokuzai Gakkaishi 48: 348–355.

Omrani, P., E. Masson, A. Pizzi and H.R. Mansouri. 2012. Emission gases in linear vibration welding of wood. Journal of Adhesion Science and Technology 23(1): 85–94.

Perré, P. 2011. On the importance of the temperature level on coupled heat and mass transfer in wood and the ligno-cellulosic biomass: Fundamental aspects, formulation and modelling, pp. 7. *In*: Proceedings of the European Drying Conference – EuroDrying 2011, Palma, Balearic Island, Spain.

Pétrissans, M., P. Gérardin, I. Elbakali and M. Serraj. 2003. Wettability of heat-treated wood. Holzforschung 57(3): 301–307.

Pfleumer, F. and H. Pfleumer. 1915. Lignostone. German Patent No. DE291945.

Pfriem, A., T. Dietrich and B. Buchelt. 2012. Furfuryl alcohol impregnation for improved plasticization and fixation during the densification of wood. Holzforschung 66: 215–218.

Pillow, M.Y. 1929. Effect of high temperatures on the mode of fracture and other properties of a hardwood. Southern Lumberman 137(1766): 58–60.

Pintiaux, T., D. Viet, V. Vandenbossche, L. Rigal and A. Rouilly. 2015. Binderless materials obtained by thermo-compressive processing of lignocellulosic fibers: A comprehensive review. BioResources 10(1): 1915–1963.

Pizzi, A. 2006. Recent developments in eco-efficient bio-based adhesives for wood bonding: Opportunities and issues. Journal of Adhesion Science and Technology 20(8): 829–846.

Pizzi, A., M. Properzi, J.M. Leban, M. Zanetti and F. Pichelin. 2003. Mechanically-induced wood welding. Maderas. Ciencia y tecnología 5(2): 101–106.

Pizzi, A., J.M. Leban, F. Kanazawa, M. Properzi and F. Pichelin. 2004. Wood dowel bonding by high-speed rotation welding. Journal of Adhesion Science and Technology 18(11): 1263–1278.

Pizzi, A., J.M. Leban, M. Zanetti, F. Pichelin, S. Wieland and M. Properzi. 2005. Surface finishes by mechanically induced wood surface fusion. Holz als Roh- und Werkstoff 63: 251–255.

Pizzi, A., A. Despres, H.R. Mansouri, J.M. Leban and S. Rigolet. 2006. Wood joints by through-dowel rotation welding: Microstructure, 13C-NMR and water resistance. Journal of Adhesion Science and Technology 20(5): 427–436.

Pizzi, A., H.R. Mansouri, J.M. Leban, L. Delmotte and F. Pichelin. 2011. Enhancing the exterior performance of wood joined by linear and rotational welding. Journal of Adhesion Science and Technology 25(19): 2717–2730.

Placencia-Peña, M.I., A.L. Deutschle, B. Saake, A. Pizzi and F. Pichelin. 2015. Study of the solubility and composition of welded wood material at progressive welding times. European Journal of Wood and Wood Products 74: 191–201.

Pohleven, F. and G. Rep. 2004. The process of thermal modification of wood in vacuum. Slovenian Patent No. P-200400064.

Pohleven, F. and G. Rep. 2008. Postopek toplotne obdelave lesa in napravn za izvedbo postopka [The process of heat treatment of wood and devices for performing the process.] Slovenian Patent No. SI 22506A.

Popescu, C.-M. and M.-C. Popescu. 2013. A near infrared spectroscopic study of the structural modifications of lime (*Tilia cordata* Mill.) wood during hydro-thermal treatment. Spectrochimica Acta Part A: Molecular and Biomolecular Spectroscopy 115: 227–233.

Popescu, M.-C., J. Froidevaux, P. Navi and C.-M. Popescu. 2013a. Structural modifications of *Tilia cordata* wood during heat treatment investigated by FT-IR and 2D IR correlation spectroscopy. Journal of Molecular Structure 1033: 176–186.

Popescu, M.-C., D.E. Demco and M. Möller. 2013b. Solid state 13C CP/MAS NMR spectroscopy assessment of historic lime wood. Polymer Degradation and Stability 98(12): 2730–2734.

Popescu, M.C., G. Lisa, J. Froidevaux, P. Navi and C.M. Popescu. 2014. Evaluation of the thermal stability and set recovery of thermo-hydro-mechanically treated lime (*Tilia cordata*) wood. Wood Science and Technology 48(1): 85–97.

Properzi, M., J.M. Leban, A. Pizzi, S. Wieland, F. Pichelin and M. Lehmann. 2005. Influence of grain direction in vibrational wood welding. Holzforschung 59: 23–27.

Rapp, A.O. and M. Sailer. 2000. Heat treatment of wood in Germany—State of the art, 15 p. *In*: Proceedings of the Seminar on Production of Heat Treated Wood in Europe. Helsinki, Stockholm, Oslo.

Rautkari, L., M. Properzi, F. Pichelin and M. Hughes. 2010. Properties and set-recovery of surface densified Norway spruce and European beech. Wood Science and Technology 44: 679–691.

Rautkari, L., F.A. Kamke and M. Hughes. 2011a. Density profile relation to hardness of viscoelastic thermal compressed (VTC) wood composite. Wood Science and Technology 45: 693–705.

Rautkari, L., K. Laine, N. Laflin and M. Hughes. 2011b. Surface modification of Scots pine: The effect of process parameters on the through thickness density profile. Journal of Materials Science 46: 4780–4786.

Rautkari, L., K. Laine, A. Kutnar, S. Medved and M. Hughes. 2013. Hardness and density profile of surface densified and thermally modified Scots pine in relation to degree of densification. Journal of Materials Science 48(6): 2370–2375.

Rep, G., F. Pohleven and B. Bučar. 2004. Characteristics of thermally modified wood in vacuum. *In*: The Proceedings IRG Annual Meeting, Ljubljana, Slovenia. International Research Group on Wood Protection IRG/WP 04-40287.

Resch, L., A. Despres, A. Pizzi, J.F. Fang and J.M. Leban. 2006. Welding-through doweling of wood panels. Holz als Roh- und Werkstoff 64: 423–425.

Reynolds, M.S. 2004. Hydro-thermal stabilization of wood-based materials. M.Sc. Thesis, Virginia Tech, Blacksburg (VA), USA.

Ringman, R., G. Beck and A. Pilgård. 2019. The importance of moisture for brown rot degradation of modified wood: A critical discussion. Forests 10(6): Article ID 522.

Rowell, R.M. 2005. Handbook of Wood Chemistry and Wood Composites. Taylor and Francis, Boca Raton (FL), USA.

Rowell, R.M. and J.D. McSweeny. 2008. Heat treatments of wood fibers for self-bonding and stabilized fiberboards. Molecular Crystals and Liquid Crystals 483: 307–325.

Rowell, R.M., R.E. Ibach, J. McSweeny and T. Nilsson. 2009. Understanding decay resistance, dimensional stability and strength changes in heat treated and acetylated wood. Wood Material Science and Engineering 4(1/2): 14–22.

Runkel, R.O.H. 1951. Zur Kenntnis des thermoplastischen Verhaltens von Holz [Knowledge of the thermoplastic behaviour of wood.] Holz als Roh- und Werkstoff 9: 41–53.

Runkel, R. and J. Jost. 1948. Verfahren und Vorrichtung zur Herstellung von Formungen aus Holz, Holzabfällen oder verholzten Pflanzenteilen unter Druck, bei höheren Temperaturen [Method and apparatus for the production of mouldings from wood, wood waste or vegetable origin under fibres under pressure at elevated temperatures.] German Patent No. DE841055.

Ruponen, J., L. Rautkari, T. Belt and M. Hughes. 2014. Factors influencing properties of parallel laminated binderless bonded plywood manufactured from rotary cut birch (*Betula pendula* L.). International Wood Products Journal 5: 11–17.

Ruyter, H.P. 1989. Thermally modified wood. European Patent Office, Patent No. EP89-2031709.

Sadatnezhad, S.H., A. Khazaeian, D. Sandberg and T. Tabarsa. 2017. Continuous surface densification of wood: A new concept for large-scale industrial processing. BioResources 12(2): 3122–3132.

Sailer, M., A.O. Rapp, H. Leithoff and R.D. Peek. 2000. Upgrading of wood by application of an oil-heat treatment. Holz als Roh- und Werkstoff 58: 15–22.

Sandak, A., J. Sandak and O. Allegrtti. 2015. Quality control of vacuum thermally modified wood with near infrared spectroscopy. Vacuum 114: 44–48.

Sandberg, D. 1998a. Inverkan av isostatisk komprimering på cellstrukturen [The influence of isostatic compression on the cell-wall structure of wood.] Report No. TRITA-TRÄ R-98-35, Royal Institute of Technology (KTH), Wood Technology and Processing, Stockholm, Sweden (In Swedish).

Sandberg, D. 1998b. Value Activation with vertical annual rings—Material, production, products. PhD. Thesis, Royal Institute of Technology (KTH), Wood Technology and Processing, Stockholm, Sweden.

Sandberg, D. and J. Johansson. 2007a. Die PrimWood-Methode Teil 1: Eigenschaften und Herstellung von Holz mit stehenden Jahrringen. Holztechnologie 48(4): 5–9.

Sandberg, D. and J. Johansson. 2007b. Die PrimWood-Methode Teil 2: Das neue Produktionskonzept für die Herstellung von zweigfreien und formstabilen Holzkomponenten mit stehenden Jahresringen. Holztechnologie 48(5): 11–15.

Sandberg, D., P. Haller and P. Navi. 2013. Thermo-hydro and thermo-hydro-mechanical wood processing: An opportunity for future environmentally friendly wood products. Wood Material Science & Engineering 8: 64–88.

Sandberg, D., A. Kutnar and G. Mantanis. 2017. Wood modification technologies—A review. iForest 10: 895–908.

Sandermann, W. and H. Augustin. 1963. Chemische Untersuchungen über die thermische Zersetzung von Holz. Erste Mitteilung: Stand der Forschung [Chemical investigations on the thermal decomposition of wood. Part I: State-of-the-art.] Holz als Roh- und Werkstoff 21(7): 256–265.

Scheiding, W. and M. Direske. 2014. Comparison of reaction to water and moisture of sapwood and heartwood of *Pinus sylvestris* L., thermally modified with two treatment intensities, pp. 29–30 abstract. *In*: Nunes, L., Jones, D., Hill, C. and Militz, H. [eds.]. Proceedings of the 7th European Conference on Wood Modification. Lisbon, Portugal.

Schneider, M.H. 1994. Wood polymer composites. Wood and Fiber Science 26(1): 142–151.

Schwarze, F.W.M.R. and M. Spycher. 2005. Resistance of thermo-hygro-mechanically densified wood to colonisation and degradation by brown-rot fungi. Holzforschung 59: 358–363.

Schäfer, M. and E. Roffael. 2000. On the formaldehyde release from wood. Holz als Roh- und Werkstoff 58: 259–264.

Seborg, R.M., M. Millet and A.J. Stamm. 1945. Heat-stabilized compressed wood. Staypak. Mechanical Engineering 67(1): 25–31.

Seborg, R.M., H. Tarkow and A.J. Stamm. 1953. Effect of heat upon the dimensional stabilisation of wood. Journal of Forest Products Research Society 3(9): 59–67.

Sehlstedt-Person, M. 2008. Impact of drying and heat treatment on physical properties and durability of solid wood. PhD. Thesis, Luleå University of Technology, Skellefteå, Sweden.

Sernek, M., F.A. Kamke and W.G. Glasser. 2004. Comparative analysis of inactivated wood surface. Holzforschung 58(1): 22–31.

Sikora, A., F. Kač, M. Gaff, V. Vondrov, T. Buben and I. Kubovský. 2018. Impact of thermal modification on color and chemical changes of spruce and oak wood. Journal of Wood Science 64: 406–416.

Sinha, S., A. Jhalani, M. Ravi and A. Ray. 2000. Modelling of pyrolysis in wood—A review. Journal of the Solar Energy Society of India 10: 1–17.

Shafizadeh, F. and P.P.S. Chin. 1977. Thermal Deterioration of Wood, pp. 57–81. *In*: Goldstein, I.S. [ed.]. Wood Technology: Chemical Aspects. ACS Symposium Series 43, American Chemical Society, Washington D.C., USA.

Skyba, O., P. Niemz and F.W.M.R. Schwarze. 2008. Degradation of thermo-hygro-mechanically (THM) densified wood by soft-rot fungi. Holzforschung 62(3): 277–283.

Srinivas, K. and K.K. Pandey. 2012. Effect of heat treatment on color changes, dimensional stability, and mechanical properties of wood. Journal of Wood Chemistry and Technology 32(4): 304–316.

Stamm, A.J. 1942. Antishrink treatment for wood. U.S. Patent No. 2,296,316.

Stamm, A.J. 1956. Thermal degradation of wood and cellulose. Industrial and Engineering Chemistry 48(3): 413–417.

Stamm, A.J. 1964. Wood and Cellulose Science. Ronald Press Co., New York, USA.

Stamm, A.J. and L.A. Hansen. 1937. Minimizing wood shrinkage and swelling. Effect of heating in various gases. Industrial and Engineering Chemistry 29(7): 831–833.

Stamm, A.J. and R.M. Seborg. 1941. Resin-treated, laminated, compressed wood. Transaction of the American Institute of Chemical Engineers 37: 385–398.

Stamm, A.J. and R.H. Baechler. 1960. Decay resistance and dimensional stability of five modified woods. Forest Products Journal 10(1): 22–26.

Stamm, A.J., H.K. Burr and A.A. Kline. 1946. Staybwood. Heat stabilized wood. Industrial and Engineering Chemistry 38(6): 630–634.

Stamm, A.J., R.M. Seborg and M.A. Millet. 1948. Method of forming compressed wood structures. U.S. Patent No. 2 453 679.

Stamm, B. 2005. Development of friction welding of wood—Physical, mechanical and chemical studies. PhD. Thesis, Swiss Federal Institute of Technology in Lausanne (EPFL), Switzerland.

Stamm, B., J. Natterer and P. Navi. 2005a. Joining wood by friction welding. Holz als Roh- und Werkstoff 63: 313–320.

Stamm, B., J. Natterer and P. Navi. 2005b. Joining of wood layers by friction welding. Journal of Adhesion Science and Technology 19(13/14): 1129–1139.

Stamm, B., E. Windeisen, J. Natterer and G. Wegener. 2006. Chemical investigations on the thermal behaviour of wood during friction welding. Wood Science and Technology 40: 615–627.

Standfest, G., A. Kutnar, B. Plank, A. Petutschnigg, F.A. Kamkeand and M. Dunky. 2013. Microstructure of viscoelastic thermal compressed (VTC) wood using computed microtomography. Wood Science and Technology 47(1): 121–139.

Stofko, J. 1974. The auto-adhesion of wood. PhD. Thesis, University of California, USA.

Suchy, M., J. Virtanen, E. Kontturi and T. Vuorinen. 2010. Impact of drying on wood ultrastructure observed by deuterium exchange and photoacoustic FT-IR spectroscopy. Biomacromolecules 11: 515–520.

Sundqvist, B. 2004. Colour changes and acid formation in wood during heating. PhD. Thesis, Luleå University of Technology, Skellefteå, Sweden.

Sundqvist, B. and T. Morén. 2002. The influence of wood polymers and extractives on wood colour induced by hydrothermal treatment. Holz als Roh- und Werkstoff 60: 375–376.

Sundqvist, B., O. Karlsson and U. Westermark. 2006. Determination of formic-acid and acetic acid concentrations formed during hydrothermal treatment of birch wood and its relation to colour, strength and hardness. Wood Science and Technology 40: 549–561.

Suthoff, B. and H.-J. Kutzer. 1997. Verfahren zum reibschweißartigen Verbinden von Holz [Method for joining wood.] German Patent No. DE 19746 782 A1.

Suthoff, B., A. Schaaf, H. Hentschel and U. Franz. 1996. Verfahren zum reibschweißartigen Fügen von Holz [Method for friction welding of wood.] German Patent No. DE 196 20 273 A1.

Tabarsa, T. and Y.H. Chui. 1997. Effects of hot-pressing on properties of white spruce. Forest Product Journal 47: 71–76.

Thomassen, T., J. Ljorring and O. Hansen. 1991. Method and apparatus for compressing a wood sample. U.S. Patent No. US 5,190, 088.

Thunell, B. and E. Elken. 1948. Värmebehandling av trä för minskning av svällning och krympning [Thermal treatment of wood for decreased swelling and shrinkage.] Report No. 18, The Swedish Wood Technology Research Institute, Stockholm, Sweden (In Swedish).

Tiemann, H.D. 1915. The effect of different methods of drying on the strength of wood. Lumber World Review 28(7): 19–20.

Tiemann, H.D. 1920. The kiln drying of woods for airplanes. Report No. 65, National Advisory Committee for Aeronautics, Washington D.C., USA.

Tiemann, H.D. 1942. Wood Technology: Constitution, Properties and Uses. Pitman Publishing Corporation, New York, Chicago, USA.

Tjeerdsma, B.F., M. Boonstra, A. Pizzi, P. Tekely and H. Militz. 1998. Characterisation of thermally modified wood: Molecular reasons for wood performance improvement. Holz als Roh- und Werkstoff 56: 149–153.

Todorović, N., Z. Popović and G. Milić. 2015. Estimation of quality of thermally modified beech wood with red heartwood by FT-NIR spectroscopy. Wood Science and Technology 49(3): 527–549.

Torniainen, P., D. Elustondo and O. Dagbro. 2016. Industrial validation of the relationship between color parameters in thermally modified spruce and pine. BioResources 11(1): 1369–1381.

Tredgold, T. 1820. Elementary Principles of Carpentry. J. Taylor, High Holburn, UK.

Tu, D., Z. Gao, Y. Sun, L. Guan and L. Xia. 2008. Timber wood hot pressing charing intensification method. Chinese Patent No. CN 101214675A.

Tuong, V.M. and J. Li. 2011. Changes caused by heat treatment in chemical composition and some physical properties of acacia hybrid sapwood. Holzforschung 65(1): 67–72.

Ünsal, O., S.N. Kartal, Z. Candan, R. Arango, C.A. Clausen and F. Green. 2008. Preliminary investigation of biological resistance, water absorption and swelling of thermally compressed pine wood panels. In: The Proceedings IRG Annual Meeting, Stockholm. Sweden, Istanbul, Turkey. International Research Group on Wood Protection IRG/WP 08-40396.

Van Acker, J., S. Michon, L. De Boever, I. De Windt, J. Van den Bulcke, B. Van Swaay and M. Stevens. 2010. High quality thermal treatment using vacuum based technology to come to more homogeneous durability, pp. 107–118. In: Hill, C.A.S., Militz, H. and Andersons, B. [eds.]. Proceedings of the 5th European Conference on Wood Modification, Riga, Latvia.

van der Hage, E., M. Mulder and J. Boon. 1993. Structural characterization of lignin polymers by temperature-resolved in-source pyrolysis–mass spectrometry and Curie-point pyrolysis–gas chromatography/mass spectrometry. Journal of Analytical and Applied Pyrolysis 25: 149–183.

Varga, D. and M.E. van der Zee. 2008. Influence of steaming on selected wood properties of four hardwood species. Holz als Roh- und Werkstoff 66: 11–18.

Vaziri, M. 2011. Water resistance of Scots pine joints produced by linear friction welding. PhD. Thesis, Luleå University of Technology, Skellefteå, Sweden.

Vaziri, M., O. Lindgren and A. Pizzi. 2012. Optimization of tensile-shear strength for linear welded Scots pine. Journal of Adhesion Science and Technology 26: 109–119.

Vaziri, M., S. Berg, D. Sandberg and I. Tavakoli Gheinani. 2014. Three-dimensional finite element modelling of heat transfer for linear friction welding of Scots pine. Wood Material Science & Engineering 9(2): 102–109.

Vaziri, M., A. du Plessis, D. Sandberg and S. Berg. 2015a. Nano X-ray tomography analysis of the cell-wall density of welded beech joints. Wood Material Science & Engineering 10(4): 368–372.

Vaziri, M., C. Rogaume, E. Masson, A. Pizzi and D. Sandberg. 2015b. VOC emissions from linear vibration, pp. 26–27. In: Kutnar, A., Burnard, M., Schwarzkopf, M. and Simmons, A. [eds.]. Proceedings of the 1st COST Action FP1407 Conference: Life Cycle Assessment, EPDs and Modified Wood, Koper, Slovenia.

Vaziri, M., L. Abrahamsson, O. Hagman and D. Sandberg. 2020a. Welding wood in the presence of wollastonite. BioResources 15(1): 1617–1628.

Vaziri, M., O. Karlsson, L. Abrahamsson, C.-F. Li and D. Sandberg. 2020b. Wettability of welded wood-joints investigated by the Wilhelmy method: Part 1. Determination of apparent contact angles, swelling and water sorption. Accepted Holzforschung.

Vaziri, M., O. Karlsson, L. Abrahamsson, M. Maziar Sedighi and D. Sandberg. 2020c. Wettability of welded wood-joints investigated by the Wilhelmy method: Part 2. Effect of wollastonite additive. Holzforschung https://doi.org/10.1515/hf-2019-0308.

Vincent, M., Q. Tong, N. Terziev, G. Daniel, C. Bustos, W. Gacitúa Escobar and I. Duchesne. 2014. A comparison of nanoindentation cell wall hardness and Brinell wood hardness in jack pine (*Pinus banksiana* Lamb.). Wood Science and Technology 48(1): 7–22.

Viitanen, H.A., S. Jämsä, L.M. Paajanen, A.J. Nurmi and P. Viitaniemi. 1994. The effect of heat treatment on the properties of spruce. *In*: The Proceedings IRG Annual Meeting, Nusa Dua, Bali, Indonesoa. International Research Group on Wood Protection IRG/WP 94-40032.

Viitaniemi, P., S. Jämsä and F. Sundholm. 2001. Method of determining the degree of modification of a heat modified wood product. International patent application No. WO01/53812 (A1).

Vorreiter, L. 1942. Gehärtete und mit Metall oder Öl getränkte Hölzer [Hardened woods soaked with metal or oil.] Holz als Roh- und Werkstoff 5: 59–69.

Vorreiter, L. 1958. Holztechnologisches Handbuch, Band II: System Holz-Wasser-Wärme. Holztrocknung. Dämpfen und Kochen. Spanlose Holzverformung [Wood Technology Handbook, Volume II: Wood-water-heat System. Wood Drying. Steaming and Cooking. Chipless Wood Machining.] Verlag Georg Fromme & Co., Wien und München, Germany.

Walsh, F.J. and R.L. Watts. 1923. Composite lumber. U.S. Patent No. 1 465 383.

Wang, J.Y. and P.A. Cooper. 2005. Effect of grain orientation and surface wetting on vertical density profiles of thermally compressed fir and spruce. Holz als Roh- und Werkstoff 63(6): 397–402.

Wang, W., Y. Zhu, J. Cao and W. Sun. 2015. Correlation between dynamic wetting behavior and chemical components of thermally modified wood. Applied Surface Science 324(1): 332–338.

Wehsener, J., P. Haller, J. Hartig and T-E. Werner. 2013. Continuous wood densification process of circular profiles, pp. 97–98. *In*: Popescu, C.-M. and Popescu, M.-C. [eds.]. COST Action FP0904 3rd Action Annual Conference, Book of Abstracts: Evaluation, Processing and Predicting of THM Treated Wood Behaviour by Experimental and Numerical Methods. Iasi, Romania.

Wehsener, J., T.E. Werner, J. Hartig and P. Haller. 2014a. Advancements for the structural application of fiber-reinforced moulded wooden tubes, pp. 99–108. *In*: Aicher, S., Reinhardt, H.-W. and Garrecht, H. [eds.]. Materials and Joints in Timber Structures. RILEM Bookseries, Vol. 9, Springer, Dordrecht, The Netherlands.

Wehsener, J., T. Weser, P. Haller, O. Diestel and C. Cherif. 2014b. Textile reinforcement of multidimensional formable wood. European Journal of Wood and Wood Products 72: 463–475.

Welzbacher, C.R., J. Wehsener, A.O. Rapp and P. Haller. 2008. Thermo-mechanical densification combined with thermal modification of Norway spruce (*Picea abies* Karst.) in industrial scale—Dimensional stability and durability aspects. Holz als Roh- und Werkstoff 66: 39–49.

Weiland, J.J. and R. Guyonnet. 2003. Study of chemical modifications and fungi degradation of thermally modified wood using DRIFT spectroscopy. Holz als Roh- und Werkstoff 61(3): 216–220.

Wieland, S., B. Shi, A. Pizzi, M. Properzi, M. Stampanoni, R. Abela, X. Lu and F. Pichelin. 2005. Vibration welding of wood: X-ray tomography, additives, radical concentration. Forest Products Journal 55(1): 84–87.

Wikberg, H. and S. Maunu. 2004. Characterisation of thermally modified hard- and softwoods by 13C CPMAS NMR. Carbohydrate Polymers 58(4): 461–466.

Wilfong, J.G. 1966. Specific gravity of wood substance. Forest Products Journal 16(1): 55–61.

Willems, W. 2006. Method and apparatus for preserving wood, and wood product. The Netherlands Patent No. 2000405.

Willems, W.P.M. 2008. Method and apparatus for preserving wood, and wood product. International patent application No. WO 2008/079000 A1.

Willems, W. 2009. A novel economic large-scale production technology for high-quality thermally modified wood, pp. 31–35. *In*: Englund, F., Hill, C.A.S., Militz, H. and Segerholm, B.K. [eds.]. Proceedings of the 4th European Conference on Wood Modification, Stockholm, Sweden.

Willems, W.P.M. 2015. Physical modelling of moisture content and fungal resistance properties of thermally modified timber. PhD. Thesis, George-August-University Göttingen, Germany.

Willems, W., A. Tausch and H. Militz. 2010. Direct estimation of the durability of high-pressure steam modified wood by ESR-spectroscopy. *In*: The Proceedings IRG Annual Meeting, Biarritz, France. International Research Group on Wood Protection IRG/WP 10-40508.

Willems, W., C. Lykidis, M. Altgen and L. Clauder. 2015. Quality control methods for thermally modified wood. COST Action FP0904 2010–2014: Thermo-hydro-mechanical wood behaviour and processing. Holzforschung 69(7): 875–884.

Willems, W., M. Altgen and L. Rautkari. 2020. A molecular model for reversible and irreversible hygroscopicity changes by thermal wood modification. Holzforschung 74(4): 420–425.

Wilson, T.R.C. 1920. The effect of kiln drying on the strength of airplane woods. Report No. 68, National Advisory Committee for Aeronautics, Washington D.C., USA.

Windeisen, E. and G. Wegener. 2008. Behaviour of lignin during thermal treatments of wood. Industrial Crops and Products 27: 157–162.

Wolcott, M.P. 1989. Modelling viscoelastic cellular materials for the pressing of wood composites. PhD. Thesis, Faculty of the Virginia Polytechnic Institute and State University, USA.

Wolcott, M.P. and E.L. Shutler. 2003. Temperature and moisture influence on compression—Recovery behavior of wood. Wood and Fiber Science 35(4): 540–551.

Wolcott, M.P., F.A. Kamke and D.A. Dillard. 1990. Fundamentals of flakeboard manufacture: Viscoelastic behavior of the wood component. Wood and Fiber Science 22(4): 345–361.

Xu, J., G. Han, E.D. Wong and S. Kawai. 2003. Development of binderless particleboard from kenaf core using steam-injection pressing. Journal of Wood Science 49: 327–332.

Xu, J., R. Sugawara, R. Widyorini, G. Han and S. Kawai. 2004. Manufacture and properties of low-density binderless particleboard from kenaf core. Journal of Wood Science 50: 62–67.

Xu, J., R. Widyrini, H. Yamauchi and S. Kawai. 2006. Development of binderless fiberboard from kenaf core. Journal of Wood Science 52: 1–8.

Yalcin, M. and H.I. Sahin. 2015. Changes in the chemical structure and decay resistance of heat-treated narrow-leaved ash wood. Maderas: Ciencia y Tecnologia 17(2): 435–446.

Yao, J. and F. Taylor. 1979. Effect of high-temperature drying on the strength of southern pine dimension lumber. Forest Products Journal 29(8): 49–51.

Yildiz, U.C., S. Yildiz and E.D. Gezer. 2005. Mechanical and chemical behavior of beech wood modified by heat. Wood and Fiber Science 37(3): 456–461.

Yildiz, S., E.D. Gezer and U.C. Yildiz. 2006. Mechanical and chemical behavior of spruce wood modified by heat. Building and Environment 41(12): 1762–1766.

Yildiz, S., U.C. Yildiz and E.D. Tomak. 2011. The effects of natural weathering on the properties of heat-treated alder wood. BioResources 6(3): 2504–2521.

Yokoyama, M., J. Gril, M. Matsuo, M. Atsuo, H. Yano, J. Sugiyama, B. Clair, S. Kubodera, T. Mistutani, M. Sakamoto, H. Ozaki, M. Imamura and S. Kawai. 2009. Mechanical characteristics of aged hinoki wood from Japanese historical buildings. Comptes Rendus Physique 10: 601–611.

Zaror, C.A. and D.L. Pyle. 1982. The pyrolysis of biomass: A general review. Proceedings of the Indian Academy of Sciences (Engineering Sciences) 5: 269–285.

Zavarin, E. 1984. Activation of wood surface and nonconventional bonding, pp. 349–400. *In*: Rowell, R. [ed.]. Chemistry of Solid Wood. American Chemical Society, Washington, D.C., USA.

Zeitsch, K.J. 2000. The Chemistry and Technology of Furfural and its many Byproducts. Sugar Series 13, Elsevier, Amsterdam, The Netherlands.

Zeniya, N., E. Obataya and M. Matsuo. 2016. Hygroscoicity and vibrational properties of aged and heat-treated wood. Mokuzai Gakkaishi 62(6): 250–258 (In Japanese).

Zhang, D., A. Zhang and L. Xue. 2015. A review of preparation of binderless fiberboards and its self-bonding mechanism. Wood Science and Technology 49: 661–679.

Zhu, X., Y. Gao, S. Yi, C. Ni, J. Zhang and X. Luo. 2017. Mechanics and pyrolysis analyses of rotation welding with pretreated wood dowels. Journal of Wood Science 63(3): 216–224.

Zor, M., M. Vaziri and D. Sandberg. 2019. Shear strength of welded birch wood produced by linear friction, pp. 109–112. *In*: Dindaroğlu, T. [ed.]. 3th International Mediterranean Forest and Environment Symposium (IMFES 2019) − Future of Mediterranean Forests: Sustainable Society and Environment, Kahramanmaraş, Turkey.

Zoulalian, A. and A. Pizzi. 2007. Wood-dowel rotation welding—A heat-transfer model. Journal of Adhesion Science and Technology 21(2): 97–108.

Chapter 4

The Use of Microwaves, Plasma and Laser Light for Wood Modification

4.1 Introduction

During the last 50 years, unconventional technologies have gradually found a place in wood processing in a bid to meet the increasing demands for quality, machining accuracy and efficiency. All processes that involve the interaction of atoms are chemical on a fundamental level. The only processes that are not chemical in nature are gravitational processes and nuclear/subatomic-particle processes. In this book, however, we make a distinction between chemical modification, thermally-based modification and modification processes that use electromagnetic radiation (EMR), plasma or laser (Light Amplification by Stimulated Emission of Radiation) light for the modification. The reason is that, on a practical level, these latter processes are very different both in the equipment used and in the purpose of modification. Almost all wavelengths in the EMR spectra influence wood as a material, but in this section, we focus on microwaves as this is radiation that gives a true modification (Figure 4.1).

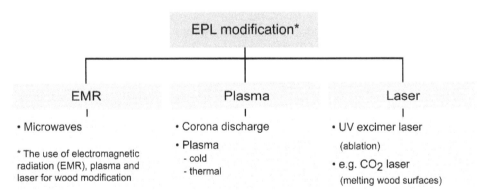

Figure 4.1 Processes that uses electromagnetic radiation (EMR), plasma or laser for the modification of wood, i.e., EPL modification processes.

Electromagnetic radiation

Electromagnetic radiation (EMR) is a form of energy that propagates as a wave in time and space. Visible light is EMR but it is only a small portion of the total electromagnetic spectrum which covers a broad range of wavelengths, generally divided into seven regions (Figure 4.2): gamma rays, X-rays, ultraviolet (UV) radiation, visible light, infrared (IR) radiation, microwaves, and radio waves.

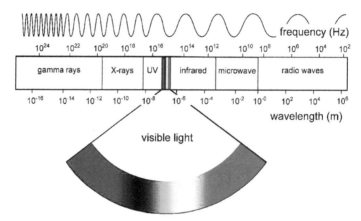

Figure 4.2 The electromagnetic spectrum is generally divided into seven regions from gamma rays to radio waves.

Lower-energy radiation, such as radio waves, is usually expressed as frequency, but microwaves, infrared, visible and UV light are usually expressed as wavelength; and higher-energy radiation, such as X-rays and gamma rays, are expressed in terms of energy per photon.

Gamma rays have frequencies greater than about 1,018 Hz and wavelengths less than 100 picometres (10^{-12} m). They cause damage to living tissue, which makes them useful for killing cancer cells when applied in carefully measured doses to small regions. Gamma rays are used for disinfestation and sterilisation of archaeological and ancient wood, for the non-destructive analysis of wood, and as a catalyst for the polymerisation of monomer-impregnated wood as well as for the chemical modification of wood to create wood-plastic composites. Struszczyk et al. (2004) mentioned three possible uses of gamma radiation: (1) as a pre-treatment in the chemical modification of cellulose, (2) as the initiator of the catalytic polymerisation of monomers in the cellulose chain and (3) as a pre-treatment for further chemical processing of cellulose in order to improve its solubility.

X-rays can be generated in a vacuum tube that uses a high voltage to accelerate the electrons released by a hot cathode to a high velocity. The high velocity electrons collide with a metal target, the anode, creating the X-rays which interact with matter in three main ways, through photo-absorption, Compton scattering, and Rayleigh scattering. The strength of these interactions depends on the energy of the X-rays and on the elemental composition of the material, but not on its chemical properties, since the X-ray photon energy is much higher than chemical binding energies. X-rays are used for non-destructive testing and for studies of the internal wood structure both in research and in industry.

UV radiation is the region of the EM spectrum between visible light and X-rays. UV radiation is a component of sunlight and is an important cause of the degradation of the wood surface due to weathering, see Section 1.6, but it is also used in the wood industry, mainly for curing coatings.

Visible light is found in the middle of the EM spectrum, between IR and UV, with frequencies from about 400 THz to 800 THz and wavelengths of about 740 to 380 nanometres (10^{-9} m). Visible light has a very low effect and is not used for the treatment of wood.

IR radiation has frequencies from about 30 THz up to about 400 THz and wavelengths of about 100 micrometres (10^{-6} m) to 740 nanometres, and is used in various processes in the wood industry, such as surface heating, drying of thin layers of wood (veneer) and wood surfaces, drying/curing of adhesive and coating systems, but not for wood modification.

Microwaves have frequencies from about 3 GHz up to about 30 THz, and wavelengths of about 10 mm to 100 micrometres. Microwaves are used for drying and modification of wood in industrial applications and for the modification of the wood structure (cf. Section 4.2).

Radio waves are at the lowest end of the EM spectrum, with frequencies of up to about 30 GHz, and wavelengths greater than about 10 millimetres. Radio waves are used primarily for communications including voice, data transfer and entertainment media.

The propagation of radiation is described by Maxwell's equations and consists of an electric and magnetic field that oscillate at right angles to each other and to the direction of movement. Electromagnetic radiation is created when an atomic particle, such as an electron, is accelerated by an electric field, causing it to move. The movement produces oscillating electric and magnetic fields, which travel at right angles to each other in a bundle of light energy called a photon (Figure 4.3). Photons travel in harmonic waves at the fastest speed possible in the universe: 299,792,458 metres per second in a vacuum, also known as the speed of light (c). The waves have certain characteristics, given as frequency, wavelength or energy. A wavelength is the distance between two consecutive peaks of a wave and is given in metres (m) or fractions thereof. Frequency is the number of waves that form in a given length of time. It is usually given as hertz, the number of wave cycles per second (Hz).

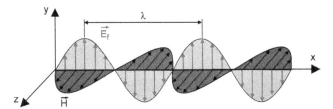

Figure 4.3 Representation of the spread of electromagnetic radiation. Electromagnetic waves are formed when an electric field (E_f) couples with a magnetic field (H). Magnetic and electric fields of an electromagnetic wave are perpendicular to each other and to the direction of propagation of the wave.

Plasma

When a gas is heated sufficiently, the electrons become separated from the atomic nuclei and a plasma is formed, i.e., a gas of charged particles, ions and electrons. Plasma lacks the properties of a gas and instead forms a magnetic field and emits electromagnetic radiation. For the gas to become a plasma, its next state of aggregation, energy is required (Figure 4.4). Plasma is used in many areas where it is desired to combine different materials, to change their surfaces, to reduce the contact angle, to increase the adhesion, etc.

There are two types of plasma: low pressure plasma and atmospheric plasma. Low pressure plasma is a small amount of gas in a vacuum chamber that is activated by a radio frequency. Energy-

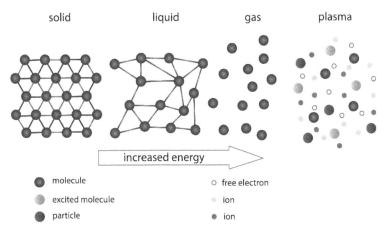

Figure 4.4 Plasma is the fourth state of aggregation. Ions are formed when the electrons separate from their nuclei and the substance passes from gas to plasma.

rich ions and electrons are created together with other reactive particles that make up the plasma which can have be used in three ways: in micro sand blasting using ion bombardment, in chemical reactions, where ionised gas reacts chemically with the surface, and in UV radiation that breaks down long, complex carbon chain compounds. In atmospheric plasma technology, a gas (air) flows through a nozzle at atmospheric pressure and is affected by a high voltage so that a plasma ignites. The gas turns on as plasma flows out of the nozzle. The atmospheric plasma has two different effects: activation and precision cleaning, which takes place through the reactive particles in the plasma, any loosely adherent particles being removed from the surface to be washed/activated by means of the compressed gas, which gives an active gas jet.

Laser light

A laser is an electric-optical device that produces and amplifies coherent radiation, i.e., a narrow, intense beam of coherent light, due to the special properties of the laser beam tool, e.g., precise, locally limited energy input, good geometric and temporal controllability of the laser-material interaction process using different wavelengths, power densities and interaction times, and easy handling of the beam by optical fibres or mirrors.

There are about 600 different types of lasers commercially available. The laser medium may consist of, e.g., a solid body, a gas, a liquid or a semiconductor. Figure 4.5 shows a classification of different types of laser depending on the laser medium. Of the different laser types, only a few are useful for material processing.

As a wear-free tool, laser cutting is one of the most widely used thermal-energy based contact-free advanced machining processes, which can be applied on a large range of materials, and is already in use in many branches of material processing. Bryan (1963) showed that wood can be cut with a continuous ruby laser beam of sufficiently high energy. The cutting kerf, i.e., the width of material removed by the laser beam when cutting wood, is only a few tenths of a millimetre, far less than the kerf when using conventional sawing tools (Martínez-Conde et al., 2017). The reduction in kerf loss is important in wood-machining processes. For further reading about wood cutting by laser, see Szymani and Dickinson (1975).

Laser processing is also used in other wood-working operations, such as engraving (McMillin and Harry, 1964; Kudapa et al., 1991; Hattori, 1995; Chitu et al., 2003; Martínez-Conde et al., 2017), for the contactless perforation of solid wood to improve penetration of preservatives, for example (Hattori et al., 1991; Kitayama et al., 1997; Grad and Mozina, 1998; Nath et al., 2020), for removing the outer fibre layer on a wood surface and cleaning wood surfaces from externally added particles (Seltman, 1995; Lenk et al., 1997; Henneberg, 1998; Panzner et al., 1998; Naderi et al., 1998), and in the field of restoration and monument conservation (Beyer et al., 1999; Wiedemann et al., 2001). In addition to the typical pyrolytic degradation or ablation effects when wood is

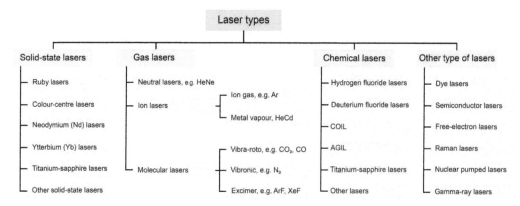

Figure 4.5 Classification of laser types.

subjected to laser radiation, melting is also a secondary conversion process (Arai et al., 1976; Necesany, 1979a; Klobetzkova, 1980; Necesany and Kleskenova, 1986).

Surface processing and especially cutting by laser technology have gained in importance in wood technology for certain special tasks such as cutting inlays. Most studies have been a practical nature, and there have been few basic investigations into the processes taking place when using laser technology.

Wust (2005) examined the structural, chemical and physical changes that result from the processing of wood with different laser configurations on European beech, Norway spruce, and sapele with lasers of varying power and pulse durations. The wetting behaviour of the wood surfaces changed as a result of laser irradiation, but choice of species was important, the wetting of European beech and Norway spruce was clearly influenced, but there was hardly any change in the wetting of sapele.

In this chapter, the presentation of the laser technique is limited to the surface modification of the wood material, i.e., laser ablation and surface melting. Cutting, cleaning and other similar laser processes are beyond the scope of this chapter.

4.2 Wood modification with microwaves

If the moisture content is high, wood is capable of absorbing a large amount of electromagnetic energy, the amount of energy required to raise the temperature being determined by the specific heat capacity of the material. A low value requires less electromagnetic energy to increase the temperature. The specific heat capacity of wood is influenced by its moisture content, its dry density and the temperature.

High-power microwave sources use specialised vacuum tubes to generate microwaves, where the ballistic motion of the electrons in a vacuum is under the influence of controlling electric or magnetic fields. The most common example of such a tube is the household microwave oven. These devices use a density-modulated mode, where groups of electrons travel together, as opposed to a continuous stream of electrons. Low-power sources use solid-state to generate the microwaves. A *maser* is an instrument similar to a laser, amplifying microwaves in a manner similar to how a laser amplifies light waves.

Material selection and preparation

All wood and wood-based materials can be processed by microwaves. The electrical parameter of a non-ferromagnetic material such as wood that determines its degree of interaction with an electromagnetic field is the complex dielectric constant (ε) which consists of a real part (ε'), the dielectric constant, and an imaginary part (ε''), the loss factor:

$$\varepsilon = \varepsilon' - i\varepsilon'' \qquad (4.1)$$

The manner in which the complex dielectric constant depends on the properties of wood and on wood-based parameters is described by Torgovnikov (1993).

Wood modification with microwaves: processes, properties, applications

The application of microwaves to wood is based on the excitation of compounds, particularly water, in the wood material to improve its drying or to accelerate chemical reactions.

Microwave drying of wood

Whenever wood is used as a construction material, there is a need to dry the material, and many studies have been undertaken to improve the drying procedure and the resulting timber. The concept of accelerated drying has received considerable attention in recent years, focusing especially on high-temperature drying, although processes such as freeze-drying and microwave drying have also been assessed. The concept of microwave drying has its origin in the early commercialisation of microwave processing in the 1960s, due to the realisation that microwave energy excites the dipole within water (Wang and Shi, 1988), increasing its internal energy to a point above its boiling point. Leonelli and Mason (2010) reported that the use of microwaves for drying has several advantages:

- rapid energy transfer,
- volumetric and selective heating,
- uniformity of heating,
- faster throughput,
- rapid control of delivery (switching on and off),
- compact equipment,
- clean environment at the point of use,
- high power densities developed in the processing zone, and
- superior moisture levelling.

One of the first applications was by the Varian Corporation in California, USA (Varian, 1969), who developed a microwave drying process in order to overcome the serious degradation, such as honeycombing and cell collapse, suffered by tanoak during normal drying. The wood, which was previously of little value, was found to be of sufficient quality after microwave drying for use in baseball bats. To achieve this, the green blanks were first placed for 4 hours in a microwave applicator where the humidity was kept at saturation and then immediately transferred to a warm-air kiln where drying was completed in 4 days. This first application was thus a combination of microwave and conventional drying.

The development of microwave technologies continued in the United States and in Canada on timber species previously considered to have a relatively low value, and with inherent drying problems. Among the species studied during the 1970's was ponderosa pine, cross-sectional discs of which were dried using various methods. McAlister and Resch (1971) found that the application of microwaves considerably increased the rate of drying, although care was required to prevent the formation of interior checks with discs having a thickness of ca. 2.5 centimetres, with a drying time of 3 hours being considered as a practical possibility. This work was elaborated upon with a study into larger samples (Illingworth and Klein Jr., 1977), where it was shown that microwave drying was applicable to moderately thick discs of species with uniseriate rays and a relative density less than 400 kg/m³, for the production of herbarium specimens, etc., free from radial splits.

By the mid-1970s, developments had led to continuous microwave systems (Barnes et al., 1976), and a prototype sawn-timber-drying system consisting of a 25 kW microwave-generating and waveguide-applicator system was developed and placed at the centre of a 40-metre long reciprocating conveyor. The whole system was maintained at the temperature and humidity required to minimise degradation in each species and to ensure the optimum utilisation of the microwave energy to dry the wood. Tests on large western hemlock and Douglas fir sawn timber (50 × 200 × 3,000 mm) showed that the microwave system could reduce the drying time from the conventional 9 days to between 5 and 10 hours, with a low degree of degradation and a uniform moisture profile in the boards. Microwave drying was expected to be most likely to be economical for species of wood having a relatively low initial moisture content, a high level of degradation in conventional kiln-drying, or a high commercial value (e.g., high-quality broad-leaved woods for the furniture industry).

The microwave drying process has continued to be developed. A comprehensive overview of the process (Antti, 1992) considered the effects of microwave treatment on the pressure, temperature and weight reduction in a range of broad-leaved species, including European ash, European beech and European oak. Continuous measurements were made of the weight, internal vapour pressure and temperature of sawn timber with maximum dimensions 50 × 50 × 500 mm. The size and quantity of vessels in the wood were measured using a digital image processor, and the permeability was calculated. Ash and beech were found to be suitable for microwave drying but oak was more difficult. The increase in temperature was similar in all cases. The speed of heating varied between 0.2 and 3°C per second, depending on the specimen dimensions. The internal vapour pressure curves were similar in beech and ash, but the maximum value was considerably higher in beech, where the pressure could reach 8 kPa. The increase in pressure in oak appeared later in the process and continued until the process was interrupted. The pressure was independent of specimen dimensions in ash and oak but increased with increasing length in beech. The moisture flux varied between 0.05 and 0.32 g/s but was independent of specimen dimensions and lower in oak than in the other species. Two different methods of determining the permeability constant give almost the same value and there was no significant difference between species.

Antti (1995) also considered the application of microwaves for drying Norway spruce and Scots pine, and this work was continued by Zielonka and Dolowy (1998) who treated Norway spruce using 350 W microwaves generated at 2.45 GHz. Sized samples were treated in order to determine the moisture content as a function of heating time, the temperature distribution, and the heat-energy distribution. It is necessary to control the microwave process to prevent a 'runaway effect' in the final stages of drying. If this energy is absorbed within the surface of the timber it can result in charring of the material, and this may be partly avoided using a 'horn' system to focus the microwaves at a point below the surface. The surface is partly cooled by heat transmission to the surrounding air. Zielonka and Dolowy (1988) found that for spruce, the constant drying rate period may be extended beyond the critical moisture content since the energy is more efficiently transferred to the remaining water molecules.

Work on western red cedar considered the potential benefit that may be gained by avoiding cell collapse during drying (Kobayashi, 1985; Kobayashi, 1986). Short pieces were cut in the green condition and dried by hot-air or microwave methods, and the anatomic structure of the collapsed wood was studied by SEM. Crushing of tracheids and distortion of latewood occurred with both drying methods. Crushed tracheids formed a layer perpendicular to the growth rings, the crushed layer being near the surface of wood dried by the hot-air method and in the centre of wood dried by the microwave method. It is suggested that the earlywood tracheids crushed first and developed into a distorted layer that caused buckling of the latewood zone. Ray parenchyma cells were not crushed but buckled following the deformation of the adjacent tracheids. It was concluded that the western red cedar wood collapsed as a result of drying stresses caused by the moisture gradient during the drying process.

The application of microwaves has been carried out in vacuum on Japanese beech (Hamano and Nishio, 1988). The use of microwaves under atmospheric conditions may not be suitable for this timber species, given the level of honeycombing, and the surface- and end-checks occurring, as well as the presence of a partially carbonised zone. These problems with sapwood were reduced in vacuum, but they remained within the heartwood. It was suggested that end-checks in the heartwood were due to the poor permeability of the material, combined with the rapid increase in wood temperature. It was also reported that the moisture content was unevenly distributed across the specimens, which was assumed to be due to the uneven application of microwave energy across the material.

Wang and Lin (1986) evaluated a range of timber species (concentrating on local species in S.E. Asia) in terms of the modulus of elasticity (MOE) and toughness, and showed that irradiation for 2–4 minutes gave the best results. With this irradiation time, the deformation of the wood was more than twice as great, the toughness was more than six times as great, and the MOE was only 20–30% that of air-dried wood. The maximum toughness of irradiated wood was found to increase linearly with increasing value of the inverse of the MOE. The effects of microwave irradiation in increasing the plasticity were species-dependent, with conifers being improved more than native broad-leaved species, which in turn were improved more than broad-leaved species imported from southeast Asia.

More recent studies have suggested that varying the drying temperature between 60 and 110°C had little effect on the hardness (Hansson and Antti, 2006). Higher-energy microwave treatment was found to reduce the mechanical properties, as shown by a 60% reduction in tensile strength for Caribbean pine (Oloyede and Groombridge, 2000) and an average reduction of 15% of both MOE and MOR on radiata pine (Torgovnikov and Vinden, 2009). Microwave drying has been reported for European beech (Rajewska et al., 2019), Norway spruce (Hansson and Antti, 2006), red stringybark (Balboni et al., 2017), rubberwood (Ratanawilai et al., 2015), and tuart (Habouria et al., 2018).

The application of a vacuum during microwave drying was considered by Leiker and Adamska (2004), following work by Seyfarth et al. (2003) and Cividini and Travan (2003). It is well established that the application of vacuum can reduce the drying time, although there can be a difference in the final quality of the sawn timber. Heat transfer has proven to be more difficult and flow distribution problems can be more severe. Seyfarth et al. (2003) and Cividini and Travan (2003) suggested that vacuum and microwaves be combined, so that wood could be dried at a temperature between 30 and 40°C over a very short period of time. This helped to avoid thermal degradation and most of the reactions that cause wood discolouration, and they showed that the process could be tailored for individual boards, suited to a continuous sawmill process. A pilot-scale dryer was developed (Leiker and Adamska, 2004) using a vacuum microwave drier as used in fruit drying, as shown in Figure 4.6, based on a stainless steel vessel 8 metres long and 0.7 metres in diameter. This chamber had three distinct processing regions: the first and third sections being used for material handling and cooling of the material after drying, respectively. The middle section (approximately 1 metre in length) contained the microwave unit, in this case two magnetrons with a maximum power of 2 kW each operating at a frequency of 2,450 MHz, with the field distributed by two horn radiators. The system operated at a pressure as low as 40 kPa, suitable for achieving a boiling temperature of water as low as 29°C, and was suitable for European beech, maple and Norway spruce.

Microwave drying is now playing an important role in the preparation of wood packaging for international shipment. ISPM15 is an international standard for material that has undergone sufficient treatment to eradicate insects and larvae. Three methods have been certified as conforming to this standard; heat treating the core material to 56°C for a minimum of 30 minutes, chemical fumigation with methyl bromide and, more recently, the use of dielectric heating using microwaves or radio frequency (RF) radiation.

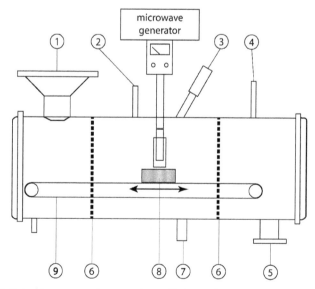

Figure 4.6 Diagram of pilot-scale vacuum microwave dryer: (1) input of wood (chips) for drying, (2) pressure sensor, (3) infra-red sensor, (4) valve, (5) output of wood, (6) microwave seal, (7) connection to vacuum pump, (8) wood, (9) conveyor belt (Based on a drawing in Leika and Adamska, 2004).

Microwave induced pyrolysis of wood

It is well known that excessive heating can lead to the thermal decomposition and pyrolysis of natural materials, and the same applies to the excessive use of microwaves. Robinson et al. (2010) showed that wood pellets can be successfully pyrolysed by the addition of activated carbon or char which absorbs the microwave energy, and Miura et al. (2004) showed that large wood blocks can be pyrolysed with less electric power consumption per unit weight than small samples.

Modification of wood with microwaves

Since microwaves are able to provide a heating source for various materials, it is logical that research has focussed on the use of microwave technology for treating wood beyond its accepted use for wood drying. Advances in these other uses have been made by Peter Vinden and Grigory Torgovnikov at CRC Wood Innovations, University of Melbourne, Australia, who developed commercial applications – Vintorg™ and Torgvin™ processes – which will be described later. Their efforts in building semi-commercial systems (Figure 4.7), in cooperation with workers at several other locations, led to the application of microwaves to increase the permeability of wood, advanced curing processes and direct application in order to accelerate other wood modification processes.

Work has been carried out on the use of microwaves a means of softening sawn timber prior to processing (e.g., for furniture). The wood is usually softened by immersion in water followed by heating (see e.g., Navi and Sandberg, 2012). The softened wood can then be shaped as required. High-temperature steam and ammonia can also bring about the softening of wood, and similar processing is possible using microwaves (Norimoto and Gril, 1989), where it was shown that the use of a frequency of 2.45 GHz with an output power of 600 to 2,400 W can raise the surface temperature to 90–110°C within 3 minutes, with higher temperatures in the core of the wood. These are the maximum temperatures as long as moisture remains within the wood. If the moisture content in the wood becomes too low, there is a risk of a 'runaway' heating, resulting in charring of the wood. Similarly, timber species that exhibit low vapour diffusion may also experience higher temperatures, due to cavity obstruction by the tylose present. The use of aqueous phenol-formaldehyde resin has also been recommended as a means of ensuring a permanent drying set (i.e., preventing some degree of shape recovery). The use of such an aqueous system would allow drying, shaping and curing of the resin at the same time.

The creep of the microwave treated material has been seen as a key factor in implementing the process within areas such as furniture design. Creep and moisture content were recorded during the microwave irradiation and hot-air drying of 13 species (5 conifers, 4 diffuse-porous and 4 ring-porous broad-leaved species). The average drying rate was found to be more than five times faster during microwave irradiation than during hot-air drying. Creep deflection during microwave drying increased rapidly from the start of the process. The ratio of the creep deflection from green to 30% moisture content to the maximum creep deflection differed between species, but was constant within species, and was not related to the stress.

The use of microwaves has been shown to increase the pore width and volume in several species. Significant increases in pore width were observed in Japanese beech once a temperature of

Figure 4.7 A semi-commercial 60 kW microwave system at CRC Wood Innovations, University of Melbourne, Australia.

190°C was reached (Magara et al., 1988), especially in the 35–110 Å range, which was attributed to the partial degradation of cellulose and lignin. The accompanying increase in surface area led to an enhancement of the enzymatic hydrolysis of lignocellulosic material, even in the presence of lignin. The increase in pore width depends on the timber species (Magara and Koshijima, 1990) and the concept of degradation of the cellulose is apparently confirmed. Microwave radiation caused lignin condensation in conifer species that inhibited the increase in surface area available for enzymatic hydrolysis. Higher yields of sugars seem to occur at a temperature of about 220°C, suggesting that the decrease in sugar yield at higher temperatures was probably due to decomposition of the monosaccharides (Nakayama and Okamura, 1989).

A number of wood species, particularly broad-leaved species, have low permeability, which can cause problems with the drying time, the material loss after drying, and the cost of the drying process, and the impregnation of low permeability timber with preservatives and resins causes problems and premature failure of the product. Ways to increase the permeability of wood have therefore been sought in order to extend the lifetime of timbers exposed to harsh conditions (e.g., in-ground contact), and this has focussed on mechanical incising. More recently, biological incising (see Section 5.2) has been considered, but since the excitation of water molecules with microwaves has been found to be effective, it was a logical progression to use microwaves to increase the permeability.

One species that has attracted particular attention for microwave irradiation is Siberian larch, since the bordered pits in the heartwood affect the migration of the moisture during drying. Liu et al. (2005) showed with Olga Bay larch that the pit membranes and parenchyma broke within the wood, forming new channels for liquid and gas transfer and thus increasing the permeability. They also suggested that with careful control of the radiation process, the required increase in permeability could be achieved while retaining most of the mechanical properties.

Terziev et al. (2020) studied changes in the structure of Norway spruce and radiata pine after microwave irradiation at 0.922 and 2.45 GHz. High intensity microwave application to moist wood, where the average microwave power to the interaction zone was 22–25 W/cm^3 and the microwave energy absorbed by the wood was 79–102 kWh/m^3, caused severe damage to the cell-wall structure and resulted in a significant increase in the permeability to liquids and gases of the wood.

Xu et al. (2014) subjected poplar wood to a high-intensity microwave pre-treatment and showed that the transverse permeability was significantly increased by the microwave pre-treatment. The permeability increased at first and then decreased with increasing initial wood moisture content, and with increasing microwave radiation power and radiation time. The optimum parameters giving the highest water absorption were reported to be for the initial moisture content, radiation power and radiation time 25–65%, 10–20 kW and 60–90 seconds, respectively. The increase in permeability was assumed to be due to the generation by the microwave pre-treatment of the high internal steam pressure that ruptured the cell pore membranes and ray cells.

The Torgvin™ process

Having established the potential of microwaves to increase the permeability of wood, work was undertaken at the University of Melbourne in Australia to improve the process with very intensive microwaves, which led to the product, Torgvin™, which has a multitude of longitudinally oriented cavities (Figure 4.8). Voids form from ruptured rays and then propagate in the tangential, radial and longitudinal directions, the number of voids depending on the timber species and on the number of rays present in a given wood volume. The greater the percentage ray tissue the greater is the number of cavities formed.

Materials with modified and unmodified zones may be produced by radiating selected areas of the wood, or by intermittent or pulsed radiation. Torgvin™ has a very high permeability, greater flexibility, different shrinkage and mechanical properties, and a lower density than unmodified wood. Torgvin™ has been successfully produced from a number of different wood species, including Douglas fir, English oak, jarrah, manna gum, messmate and mountain ash and radiata pine.

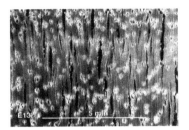

Figure 4.8 Voids produced in wood as a result of Torgvin™ processing.

As a result of the large number of voids in Torgvin-processed wood, there is a reduction in density of typically 10%, depending on the species. Torgovnikov et al. (2015) showed using blue gum an average density reduction from 697 kg/m³ to 637 kg/m³, with a similar reduction in mechanical performance, the MOR value relative to that of the untreated material being in the radial direction approximately 44% and 34% in the tangential direction. The MOE was reduced by 38% and 48% in the radial and tangential directions, respectively, and the corresponding hardness values by approximately 36% and 43%.

Microwave-induced curing

As described in the sections on Compreg™ (Section 2.3) and Impreg™ (Section 2.4), the use of resins is a recognised way to modify wood. Their effectiveness depends on the degree of impregnation possible, which in turn is related to the quality of the timber (e.g., the amounts of heartwood and sapwood, defects, etc.) and to the permeability of the species, and microwave irradiation can increase the permeability by its destruction of the wood microstructure or by the formation of microcracks (Mekhtiev and Torgovnikov, 2004; Torgovnikov and Vinden, 2009; Li et al., 2010).

A range of patents have been granted relating to the microwave curing of resins in general, including some relating specifically to resins in wood. Pike and Barnes (1977) showed that microwave energy could be used to cure the resin applied to plywood in a much shorter time than that used in a conventional hot-press process, and did not suffer the arcing and tracking problems associated with radio frequency dielectric heating. In order to focus the microwaves on the interior bonding regions, Harris et al. (1998) developed a computer-controlled system for the delivery of circular-mode magnetic-microwave energy to reduce the reflection of radiation and optimise the use of microwave energy to heat the wood.

Xu et al. (2015) suggested that microwave pre-treatment of poplar before impregnation with low molecular-weight PF resin ruptured the cell pore membranes and ray cells, increasing the permeability in the radial and longitudinal directions with an increase of almost 50% in density. The modified material was considered suitable for both interior and exterior use, particularly in the manufacture of high value-added furniture.

The use of microwaves can help the polymerisation of resins in other lignocellulosic materials, such as bamboo with phenolic resins (Zheng et al., 2014). The use of microwaves led to rapid curing, requiring only half the time necessary with a conventional heating system. Treatment at 100°C for 10 minutes resulted in optimum mechanical performance, but a slightly higher temperature resulted in carbonisation and weakening of the bamboo. Microscopic analysis showed that the rapid curing by microwave irradiation caused the resin to expand so that it became embedded in the pores of the bamboo, increasing the bonding strength and reducing in substrate-resin interface defects.

The Vintorg™ process

Having learned to increase the permeability of wood using high intensity microwaves in the Torgvin™ process, researchers at the University of Melbourne focussed their efforts on introducing isocyanate or melamine urea formaldehyde (MUF) resin systems, and named the result Vintorg™ (Przewloka et al., 2006; Torgovnikov et al., 2015). The process for making Vintorg™ is shown in Figure 4.9.

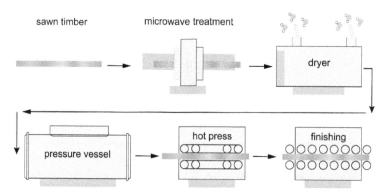

Figure 4.9 Diagrammatic overview of the Vintorg™ process.

Przewloka et al. (2006) impregnated wood with various phenolic resins and reported that, if the resin viscosity was too low, there was a risk of migration leading to poor adhesion and low product performance whereas, if the viscosity was too high, the resin penetrated the timber too slowly. The higher molecular-weight materials then remain on the surface and was incapable of penetrating the ruptures and excess resin had to be removed from the surfaces.

The increase in permeability has been considered in different Vintorg™ processes, and the incorporation of metallic alloys could offer interesting properties such as high electro-conductivity, high thermo-conductivity and very high density. A bismuth/lead/tin/cadmium alloy pressure impregnated into Torgvin™-treated wood (Torgovnikov et al., 2015) was shown clearly microscopically to fill the voids created in the wood by the increase in average density of the blue gum tested. The microwave-treated wood had a density of 637 kg/m³, while the Vintorg™ alloy-impregnated wood had an average density of 3,275 kg/m³ (the density of the pure alloy was 7,400 kg/m³). This technique could provide new products where conductivity is required.

Use of microwaves in the modification of wood

The chemical modification of wood, as described in Chapter 2, is an established method of wood protection. All the processes require some degree of heating to initiate and maintain the chemical reaction involved. In some cases, the heat energy helps to drive the reaction through the removal of by-products such as water and, since microwaves can be used for heating, attempts have been made in recent years to see whether microwaves can improve the reaction processes.

Acetylation: As described in Section 2.2, the acetylation of wood has progressed to a commercial product sold as Accoya™. The acetylation process is exothermic (i.e., it gives off heat as it proceeds), but it is nevertheless necessary to heat the material to drive off excess acetic acid released as a by-product. The heat provided for this purpose must pass from the heating element, through the reaction medium (in this case acetic anhydride) and into the wood and, since wood has a poor heat conductivity, a long reaction time is often required, particularly for large dimension samples. If a sufficient core temperature is not reached, the acetylation at the core may be incomplete, and this may lead to product failure in the future. Larsson Brelid et al. (1999) showed that using microwaves, the heating of acetic anhydride and acetic acid could be achieved to depths of around 10 centimetres, and Larsson Brelid and Simonson (1999) subsequently showed that microwaves could be used to heat impregnated wood to a temperature of 123°C, and that if the microwave generator was then switched off, the temperature continued to increase to 130°C, which was assumed to be due to the exothermic acetylation reaction. By pulsing the microwave on and off, it was possible to maintain the reaction temperature at 130°C for the desired duration. The use of microwaves was also shown to be effective in removing residual anhydride and any acetic acid provided during vacuum drying. Acetylated Norway spruce and Scots pine could undergo a vacuum clean-up step for two hours at 120°C, such that the level of residual chemicals was about 3%. This was particularly important, considering the difficulties previously noted in removing acetic acid from treated wood. The microwave-assisted acetylation of wood was also studied by, e.g., Rowell et al. (1987), Nilsson et al. (1988) and Militz (1991).

Dömény et al. (2015) took samples that had previously been vacuum impregnated with acetic anhydride and compared the effects of conventional heating methods with those achieved with microwaves. They found that the physical properties of the acetylated beech were similar, indicating that the microwaves had little detrimental effect on the wood ultrastructure and instead that the energy was absorbed by the polar acetic anhydride. The rate of acetylation increased with increasing microwave intensity, but the treatment time had little or no effect on the degree of acetylation.

The acetylation of cellulose with acetic anhydride under microwave heating has been studied by Li et al. (2009) using iodine as a catalyst in a solvent-free process. The microwave radiation power was varied from 300 W to 800 W. The reaction time and temperature had an active influence on the extent of acetylation, the optimum conditions being 30 minutes at 130°C. Given that the microwave-assisted acetylation of wood and of cellulose has been demonstrated, it should be only a matter of time before its application is shown for wood fibres. Small-scale production of microwave-assisted acetylation of fibres has been reported by the Danish company A-Cell and subsequently DanAcell (Jones et al., 2009), though insufficient financial backing prevented commercial production.

Furfurylation: The furfurylation process commercialised by Kebony™ (see Section 2.4) involves impregnation with furfuryl alcohol and its subsequent polymerisation within the wood cell wall. Normally, the polymerisation process is achieved by heating to a temperature above 120°C, in order to remove water produced as a by-product and to increase the extent of the reaction. Since microwaves can increase the permeability and also provide a heating source, the application of microwaves in the furfurylation process seems desirable. This has been proven in provisional studies (Treu et al., 2007) and in the subsequent patent sought by Kebony™ (Treu and Militz, 2008) covering the polymerisation of furan-based systems including furfural, furfuryl alcohol, bishydroxymethylfuran and combinations thereof, the curing being undertaken with microwaves at temperatures between 70°C and 140°C.

Reaction with DMDHEU: Timber treatment with dihydroxydimethylolethylene urea (DMDHEU) is an example of a process that was developed in another industry (the textile industry) and has been applied to wood science (see Section 2.5), with studies showing it can improve dimensional stability and protect against biological degradation. Katović et al. (2004) reacted European beech and fir with DMDHEU, using conventional heating and microwave irradiation, and they reported that microwaves were less reactive than conventional heating, but further studies are warranted.

Other chemical modification methods: The reaction of wood with various linear anhydrides has been demonstrated by Hill and Jones (1999), and Chang and Chang (2003) assessed the use of microwave irradiation for 3–6 minutes to achieve butyrylation after vacuum impregnation of samples with butyric anhydride. The results indicated that the esterification level was higher in the central part of the sample than in the surface layer when microwaves were used.

Katović et al. (2004) studied the reaction of wood with citric acid comparing the activation of the reaction of citric acid and a catalyst SHP (sodium hypophosphite) using microwaves and using conventional heating. Both types of heating yielded successful levels of reaction.

The use of citric acid with 1,2,3,4-butanetetracarboxylic acid was reported as a possible wood modification process by Vukusic et al. (2006). In order for these compounds to react, it is necessary to use a phosphono-based catalyst, such as sodium hypophosphite. Reasonable reaction conditions could be achieved using conventional heating, but the use of microwaves intensified the reaction, leading to greater cross-linking between the wood and the reagents and as a result there was a retention of tensile strength.

The use of microwave radiation to facilitate the reaction of a wood pulp with a polymer containing carboxylic acid has been considered (Goetz et al., 2011) using poly(methyl vinyl ether *co*

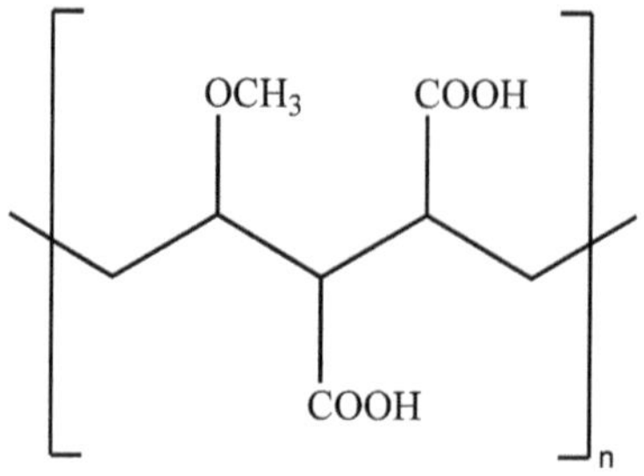

Figure 4.10 Structure of with poly(methyl vinyl ether co maleic acid) (PMVEMA).

maleic acid) (PMVEMA, Figure 4.10) in conjunction with polyethylene glycol (PEG) in reactions with kraft pulp. The results were PMVEMA-PEG cross-linked cellulose-based hydrogels, achieved after a reaction time of only 105 seconds, in contrast to conventional thermal cross-linking which required 6.5 minutes.

4.3 Wood modification with plasma

Since wood is susceptible to weathering (Chapter 1.6), some sort of surface protection is necessary if the wood is intended for outdoor use, but the effectiveness of the coating is related to the substrate onto which it has been applied, particularly its cleanliness, moisture content and interaction with the applied coating. Extractives, such as hydrophobic resins, esters of fatty acids, waxes, etc., interfere with the bonding of wood to other materials if they are present on the surface. They form a low energy structure on the wood surface, which affects the reactivity of the surface. In order to achieve an active surface, some form of treatment is necessary, such as a chemical treatment with compound such as glycidyl methacrylate, which may undergo grafted polymerisation with methyl methacrylate on the surface (Rozman et al., 1994). Reactions of glycidyl methacrylate activated with a peroxide initiator have also been demonstrated after wood has been modified with a cyclic anhydride (Matsuda et al., 1988), while Hill and Cetin (2000) modified the surface with crotonic or methacrylic anhydride. The fact that these processes were solvent-based processes made them unsuitable however for commercial application.

Corona and plasma treatments: processes properties, applications

In addition to this "direct" chemical activation of the wood surface, two "indirect" activation methods have emerged: the use of a corona discharge and of plasma modification. A corona discharge is a process whereby current passes from an electrode with a high potential into a neutral fluid, usually air, and causes the fluid (air) to ionise, generating a plasma around the electrode. The ions generated pass to nearby areas of lower potential (such as a wooden surface), pass the charge to nearby areas of low potential or recombine to form neutral gas molecules. More recently, plasma treatment has come to replace corona treatment, mainly because of the low intensity often associated with a corona discharge, which can have only a limited impact on the surface. It is technically possible to increase the energy of the corona discharge, but this would increase the temperature of the wood being treated and this might have an undesirable effect.

Plasma is often referred to as the fourth state of matter, generated by a discharge induced in a partial vacuum. It is an excited gas that consists of atoms, ions, molecules, free radicals, electrons and metastable species (Boenig, 1982; Inagaki, 1996), which react with the substrate surface (in this case wood) in a variety of chemical and physical processes. It is possible to treat the surfaces in a flat, linear, selective or three dimensions (Tendero et al., 2006). There are various ways of producing technical plasmas, ranging from low-pressure discharges excited by microwaves to plasma-jet systems, and these yield a variety of surface properties depending on the nature of the gas used. A typical plasma system for treating wood is shown in Figure 4.11.

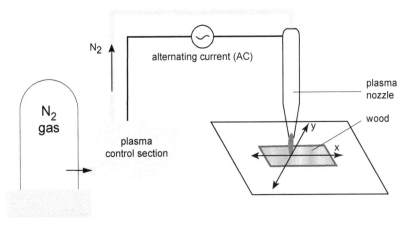

Figure 4.11 Diagram of a basic atmospheric plasma system.

There are two forms of plasma, thermal and non-thermal (cold) plasmas, the difference being in the thermodynamic equilibrium between the electrons and the ions. In a thermal plasma, everything is in thermal equilibrium, whereas in a non-thermal plasma, the electron temperature is much hotter than the temperature of the heavier ions and neutral species present. As only electrons are thermalised, their Maxwell-Boltzmann velocity distribution differs from the velocity distribution of the ions. When velocity of one of the species does not follow a Maxwell-Boltzmann distribution, the plasma is said to be non-Maxwellian. A cold plasma arises when a low-pressure gas at room temperature is subjected to an electric discharge, e.g., a radio frequency or a microwave field. The difference between a thermal and a non-thermal plasma is shown in Table 4.1 (Tendero et al., 2006).

Tendero et al. (2006) outline the various plasma sources, including a range of atmospheric systems that use direct current, radio frequency or microwaves, while a literature review by Žigon et al. (2018) considers the role of dielectric barrier discharge (DBD) as an effective treatment.

As a whole, the plasma is neutral, consisting mainly of neutral species with small fractions of free electrons, ions, radicals, excited molecules, and photons. The activated species interact with the surface in different ways, and the result depends on the gas used, the treatment time and parameters associated with the equipment, such as gas flow, energy input and geometry.

Modification with plasma treatment appears to be a more environmentally friendly way of treating a surface. Although the consumption of electricity is high, the treatment avoids the use of solvents or excessive heating, and the only by-product is usually ozone (Aydin and Demirkir, 2010; Rowell, 2013). This has led to an expansion into commercial operations, and several companies produce equipment suited to the surface treatment of wood. Most of these devices operate at low pressure (Žigon et al., 2018), and are used in batch treatments. When the treatment is carried out at close to atmospheric pressure, it is possible to achieve a dielectric barrier discharge, where the

Table 4.1 Main characteristics of thermal and non-thermal plasmas, where T_e is the electron temperature and T_h is the heavy particle temperature.

	Thermal plasma	Non-thermal (cold) plasma
Properties	$T_e = T_h$ High electron density: 10^{21}–10^{26} m^{-3} Inelastic collisions between electrons and heavy particles create the plasma reactive species whereas elastic collisions heat the heavy particles (the electron energy is thus consumed)	$T_e \ll T_h$ Lower electron density: $< 10^{19}$ m^{-3} Inelastic collisions between electrons and heavy particles induce the plasma chemistry. Heavy particles are slightly heated by a few elastic collisions (that is why the electron energy remains very high)
Examples	Arc plasma (core) $T_e = T_h \approx 10{,}000$ K	Glow discharges T_e 10,000–100,000 K $T_h \approx 300$–1,000 K

electrons produced can break up chemical bonds on the surface. A plasma treatment can thus increase surface wetting due to the formation of polar groups on the surface (e.g., C=O, O-C-OH) by a reaction between the substrate surface and the plasma-generated oxygen species (Klarhöfer, 2010). This means that the general cleansing of the wood surface is often accompanied by a smoothing effect, and these freshly generated surfaces and active chemical groups increase the surface energy and can increase both liquid adsorption and coating application integrity. These factors are summarised in Figure 4.12 (Žigon et al., 2018). The activation of wood has been shown by Lütkemeier et al. (2016) to be limited to the surface layers, and it has been reported that the is no loss of strength, hardness or density (Potočňáková et al., 2013).

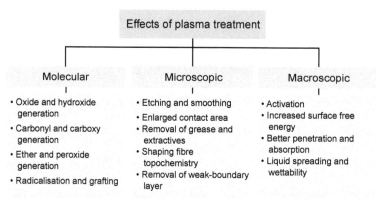

Figure 4.12 The effects of plasma treatment on the wood substrate (Žigon et al., 2018).

Potential of plasma treatment as a commercial process

So far, most treatments have been carried out on laboratory-scale equipment, but several industrial companies are considered larger scale application where, for example, a simple plasma treatment is applied to a wood surface, to increase the wettability of the surface to increase coating and resin adhesion. This seems to be particularly applicable to veneer treatment, where treatment by conventional methods such as sanding would leave materials too thin for use. Plasma treatment can be seen as a way to improve curing and drying times, particularly of veneers.

Increasing the wettability of wood

The intimate contact of a liquid adhesive to a solid substrate is necessary for durable bonding, and the bond quality between a paint and a solid surface, for example, is thus dependent on the wettability, a factor that has become especially important with the more from oil-based to water-based coating systems, since the surface may become deactivated with time. The traditional method of measuring wood wettability is to determine the contact angle using the two liquids phase method (Podgorski et al., 2000), where the wood is first dipped in octane and the contact angle of water is recorded along the grain. Later work has shown the effect on a range of timber species, including black spruce (Busnel et al., 2010), common walnut (Topala and Dumitrascu, 2007), European beech (Avramidis et al., 2010; Altgen et al., 2020), Norway spruce (Avramidis et al., 2010), pedunculate oak (Odrášková et al., 2008) and sugar maple (Busnel et al., 2010). It has also been shown that plasma is more effective than conventional sanding for reactivation of the surface of aged timber (Wolkenhauer et al., 2009), and the reasons for the increased wettability have been reviewed by Wascher et al. (2018)

One of the possible causes of surface deactivation is the migration of extractive substances to the surface, resulting in a weak boundary layer that inhibits the penetration of coatings or adhesives (Hancock, 1963; Hse and Kuo, 1988). Wolkenhauer (2008) has suggested that plasma treatment can increase the surface roughness and increase the wettability, having an effect similar to that achieved with UV-laser ablation (see Section 4.4) of wood (Mertens et al., 2006). Wettability of a modified surface may be altered, as has been shown for thermally-modified timber (Nguyen et al., 2017; Altgen et al., 2020) so that the hydrophobic properties are eliminated and the uptake of water-borne modifying reagents is increased, a fact that is being explored with impregnated plywood from thermally-modified timber veneers for outdoor use. The use of plasma pre-treatment can also increase the uptake of modification solutions, as has been shown with the increased uptake of DMDHEU solution by plasma-treated European beech veneers (Wascher et al., 2015).

Improving the hydrophobicity of wood

Most of plasma treatments have focussed on increasing the hydrophilicity/wettability of a wood surface, but the technique can also be used to increase the hydrophobicity of the surface. Increased wettability is a result of surface activation, whereas increased hydrophobicity is due to deactivation where another material, typically a hydrophobic coating, is deposited on the wood surface. The idea of depositing materials onto a wood surface was developed from similar work on metals, glass and plastics (Inagaki, 1996; Hippler et al., 2001). The deposition of a hydrophobic (or superhydrophobic) coating is a means of applying a factory-finished treatment for wood, using a compound such as hexamethyldisiloxane (HMDSO), as shown in Figure 4.13. There has been considerable interest in using HMDSO to date (Mahlberg et al., 1998; Denes et al., 1999; Odrášková et al., 2007; Avramidis et al., 2009), and Zanini et al. (2007) used HMDSO in conjunction with sulphur hexafluoride (SF_6). The treatment of wood with HMDSO is a silicon-based modification process (see Chapter 2.7), and plasma treatment increase polymerisation and reaction with the wood surface. Mai and Militz (2004) reported that a surface is created that has a contact angle for water greater than 120° (almost 0° on untreated, fresh wood) and that the uptake of water in an immersion test was significantly reduced. Spectroscopic analysis has confirmed the presence of Si-O-C bonds, indicating chemical bonding with the wood surface.

The use of SF_6 to increase the hydrophobicity has been considered as a way to improve the interaction of wood fibres with a polymer matrix in the manufacture of wood plastic composites (WPCs), Cordeiro et al. (2018), showed that WPCs manufactured with wood fibres treated with SF_6 plasma in a polypropylene matrix had a higher modulus of elasticity, where scanning electron microscopy (SEM) studies showed stronger fibre-matrix interactions. The SF_6 plasma treatment was more effective than oxygen and methane plasma systems. The use of SF_6 plasma has been shown to achieve superhydrophobic lignin-based coatings (Souza et al., 2019), having a higher modulus of elasticity (MOE). Extending the duration of the plasma treatment resulted in a reduction in the MOE, but it was still better than that achieved with a conventionally applied coating.

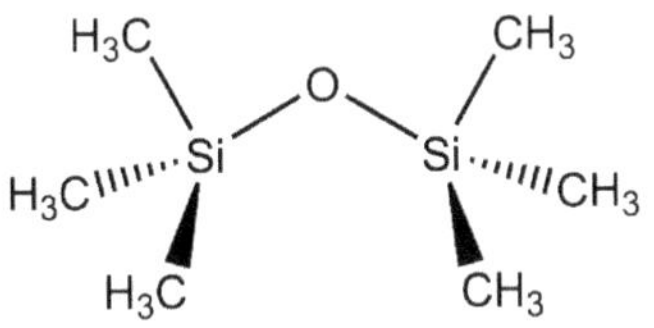

Figure 4.13 Structure of hexamethyldisiloxane (HMDSO).

Treatment of wood veneers

One of the advantages of plywood is that many of the direction-dependent properties of solid wood, such as swelling and shrinkage are reduced or even eliminated, but further improvements can be achieved if the surface properties of the veneers can be improved and this opens the way for plasma treatment. The effects on veneers of plasma treatment have already been reviewed by Wascher et al. (2018).

The bonding of veneers requires the presence of moisture otherwise the adhesion properties are poor. Huang et al. (2011) assessed the potential of atmospheric cold plasma treatment on over-dried poplar veneers, and they showed that atmospheric cold plasma was effective in treating over-dried poplar veneers since a low contact angle was achieved, leading to a high adhesive-bond shear strength when using as urea formaldehyde (UF) resin. Although the over-drying of veneers can cause gluing problems, an excess of moisture can also lead to difficulties with the emerging water-based coatings and adhesive systems unless the excess water can be removed during the polymerisation process. Avrimadis et al. (2011) have shown the potential of plasma treatment on veneers from a range of species (European beech, oak, sycamore maple, and teak) with a polyvinyl acetate (PVAc) adhesive. Shear bond strength measurements showed that the plasma treatment significantly increased the adhesion of the samples.

Wascher et al. (2018) reported that the adhesive properties of modified veneers can be altered through the use of plasma, and Wascher et al. (2017) showed that a plasma pre-treatment can reverse the undesirable hydrophobic effects of thermal modification, the water uptake of thermally-modified European beech being greater than that of untreated beech. Furthermore, the uptake of melamine resin increased and as well as the resultant plywood has not only a stronger adhesion but also a greater dimensional stability.

4.4 Wood modification with laser light

In the wood industry, laser has, since its initial development about 60 years ago, been the most widely used contact-free technique to cut wood and wood-based materials, especially when a thin "saw kerf" is desirable to reduce the waste of an expensive species or to saw in an advanced pattern where a conventional sawblade or milling tool is not suitable. Laser wood-cutting is primarily a rapid high-temperature vaporisation/burning process combined with the evaporation and pyrolysis of volatile constituent material. It is estimated that laser plasma may reach a temperature of several thousand degrees. The principle of laser machining of a material is to focus the laser beam on the surface of the material. Part of the radiation energy is absorbed and converted to heat, and if sufficient energy is absorbed this leads to a destruction of the material, i.e., melting and subsequent evaporation. The advantage is that the laser beam does not destroy the reminder of the material and that it can be focused to a diameter of only a few micrometres, achieving a high irradiance (10^6–10^8 W·m^{-2}) using a small amount of total energy. The quantity of compounds removed (evaporated) is directly proportional to the energy supply to the laser (Kubovský et al., 2012). Laser light is also used for engraving wood, and this is one of the most promising technologies for use in wood carver operations (Leone et al., 2009). Such applications are however wood machining rather than wood modification.

Laser light is used to change the properties of the wood surface in two ways:

- by ablation, or
- by melting the outermost layer of the wood.

Joachim Seltman of the Wood Technology and Processing department at the Royal Institute of Technology (KTH) in Sweden was the first to publish results of ablation experiments on a wood surface by using a UV excimer laser (Seltman, 1995). The aim of those investigations was to improve the adhesion of adhesive and protective coatings by ablation of the thin layer of wood damaged by the mechanical processing. The thickness of this layer was typically 60 μm, depending on the quality of the tool edge and on its pressure on the surface during machining. The surface structure obtained by ablation was similar to that achieved with a microtome cut or sanding (Wu and Seltman, 1998). An UV excimer laser has since been in use at KTH in Stockholm for surface preparation.

The phenomena that arise at the micro-level during the friction welding of wood have an interesting relation to the laser treatment of wood (cf. Section 3.7). Depending on the laser-radiation parameters, laser treatment may be a thermal treatment concentrated in space and time, leading to a molten surface or removal of material from the wood surface with a high laser flux, for example. A molten surface was observed by Sandberg (1999) when handling weathered samples of pine and spruce with the help of UV excimer-laser ablation. Haller et al. (2004) and Wust (2005) have investigated the effect of laser irradiation on wood with regard to changes in chemical and physical properties, and they have identified the parameters which guarantee the melting of wood without pyrolysis. It has been suggested that this improves the mechanical and water-related properties of the surface, but the technique is not well developed and further research is required before the technical and commercial potentials can be fully evaluated.

Radaition with laser light may lead to other effects of laser radiation may also occur. Vidholdová et al. (2017) used a CO_2 laser to increase the resistance to mould growth of wood surfaces. A radiation dose of more than 25 J/cm^2 gave a high resistance to *Aspergillus niger*, but the resistance to *Penicillium brevicompactum* increased only slightly. Radiation of the wood surface with laser light may also induce change in the colour (e.g., Kubovský and Babiak, 2009), or in the chemical constituents, such as polysaccharides (Kačík et al., 2010; Kačík and Kubovský, 2011) and lignin (Barcikowski et al., 2006). Changes at the anatomical and chemical level due to laser light irradiation are most intense at the surface directly exposed to the laser beam, and the effects decrease as the beam penetrates into the wood.

Material selection and preparation

There are no specifications regarding how sawn-timber should be selected or prepared for treatment with laser light. For both ablation and surface melting, however, the surface should not be too rough as this increases the time required to achieve the desired effect. Structural differences in different wood species, or in a single species, in the interaction with laser light and to significant differences in the irradiated wood surface. The laser beam interacts with the wood at a chemical level, so the chemical composition of wood influences the result of the laser-light treatment.

The density of the substrate is an important parameter in laser cutting, having a great influence on the cutting speed. Low-density species can be cut at a higher speed than high-density species, but the speed is also influenced by the moisture content (Gajtanská et al., 2004), which affects the physical properties and the thermal behaviour of the wood by softening the material and also influences the pyrolysis process.

The capacity of the wood to absorb moisture depends on the porosity, and the rate of absorption depends on the density, the initial moisture content, and the temperature of the material. The absorbency and the permeability of the sapwood are much greater than those of heartwood, and the absorptivity in the fibre direction is about 10–20 times greater than in the radial or tangential directions (see Section 1.4).

The moisture content affects the heating and thermal conductivity of wood and, therefore, also the temperature profile; an increase in the moisture content increases the thermal conductivity but an increasing part of the laser-radiation energy is consumed in heating and, above 100°C, for the evaporation of moisture, so that the heating of the wood is reduced (Seiferth, 1982).

Laser modification: processes, properties, applications

When laser-light irradiation is used, the interaction with the material may lead to a purely physical process or to the activation of chemical reactions. These processes can have both a thermal and a non-thermal character. In practice, both processes occur together, but the ratio between them depends on the wavelength, since the interaction is determined by the photon energy of the laser light. The relationship between the photon energy E_{photon} and the wavelength λ in vacuum is given by:

$$E_{photon} = \frac{h \cdot c}{\lambda} \tag{4.2}$$

where E_{photon} is the photon energy (eV), h is the Planck constant h = 6.626 10^{-34} Js, c is the speed of light, and λ is the wavelength of the laser light (m).

The importance of the binding energy for material processing with laser light is shown in Figure 4.14. If the photon energy of the laser is less than 3 eV, a thermal coupling occurs by vibrational excitation of the molecules, but if the photon energy is higher than 3 eV, molecular bonds can be broken directly, with little or no heat being induced. The result can thus be influenced directly by selecting a suitable wavelength of the laser light.

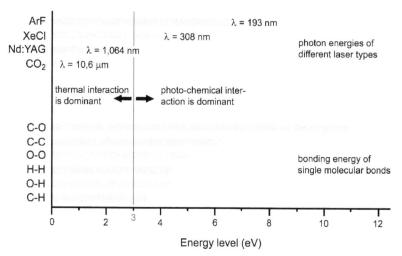

Figure 4.14 Binding energies of important molecular building blocks in relation to the photon energy of laser radiation (after Wust, 2005).

Although laser radiation is mainly absorbed directly on the surface of the material, absorption by deeper layers must be taken into account, due to the difference in absorption of different wavelengths and the porous structure of the wood. Fengel and Wegener (1984) say that the optical penetration depth for IR radiation, regardless of the type of wood, is 1 mm to 1.5 mm, in contrast to that of visible light which reaches a depth of about 200 μm, while UV radiation does not penetrate to a depth of more than 75 μm (Hon and Shiraishi, 1991). The optical penetration depth at which approximately 63% of the irradiated intensity is absorbed is given by the equation (Hartwig et al., 1996):

$$d_{opt} = \frac{1}{\alpha(\lambda)} \qquad (4.3)$$

where d_{opt} is the depth of penetration (m), α is the absorption coefficient (m^{-1}), which is dependent of the wavelength of the light (λ).

The thermal effect of electromagnetic radiation is the result of absorption of the radiation by the cellulose, hemicelluloses and lignin, and by the moisture in the wood. The structure, the direction of the cut in relation to the main direction in the wood, and the texture, gloss and colour also play important roles.

In addition to the optical penetration depth, the absorption area available for absorption is important (Necesany et al., 1979a,b). Depending on the type of wood, only 30% to 50% of the surface is available when the radiation is perpendicular to the cross-section but, in contrast, 80% to 90% of the transverse section is available for absorption (Wust, 2005). For this reason, the cross section of the laser radiation can penetrate much deeper into the wood in the transverse direction, the penetration depth being limited by the size of the lumens and the length of the cells. The length of the tracheids in conifer woods is typically no more than 3 millimetres, but the vessels of broad-leaved woods reach lengths ranging from a few centimetres to several metres (see Section 1.2). Due to the high proportion of reflection, the radiation is scattered in the cavity of the cell and only a fraction of the radiation introduced is absorbed per surface element and per unit time. Lignin-rich regions of the cell wall are more sensitive to laser radiation than other parts of the cell wall. The

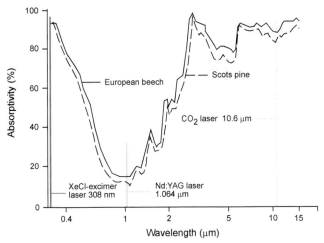

Figure 4.15 Absorption of light of different wavelengths by European beech and Scots pine, and the wavelengths of CO_2 laser (10.6 µm), Nd:YAG laser (1.064 µm), and XeCl-excimer laser (0.308 µm) indicated (Orech and Kleskenová, 1975).

absorption depends on the colour of the wood, and Hon and Shiraishi (1991) describe the absorption by wood in the UV-region between 200 nm and 460 nm as being a combination of the absorption curves of lignin and of cellulose.

Laser-based techniques permit a precise control of the energy input to the wood by the choice of laser type (e.g., between UV excimer, CO_2 and Nd:YAG lasers), and by the intensity, duration and frequency of the laser pulse, so that cell-wall material can be modified either by opening up the cell structure or by sealing the surface by melting and solidification.

Figure 4.15 shows that the absorption of light by European beech and Scots pine has a minimum at a wavelength of about 1 µm. Outside the wavelength range of 0.4 to 3 µm, more than 75% of the incoming light is absorbed (Orech and Kleskenová, 1975), which means that a Nd:YAG laser ($\lambda = 1.064$ µm) is of little interest for ablation (lowest ablation per pulse) compared to a UV excimer laser ($\lambda = 0.308$ µm; XeCl-excimer laser), and for cutting and melting compared to a CO_2 laser ($\lambda = 10.6$ µm). The low absorptivity at wavelengths of about 1 µm in wood, however, makes Nd:YAG lasers suitable for the removal of layers of non-wood particles (e.g., dirt, soil, etc.) from wood surfaces without damage to the wood beneath (Haller et al., 2001).

The pulsed-gas laser-induced ablation process using the excimer laser, may take place without any change in the overall chemical composition of the material and the process is adiabatic (Stafast, 1993; Bäuerle, 2011), and in contrast to laser chemical processing, foremost by YAG-lasers, where there is a change in the chemical composition or the activation of a chemical reaction, in which case the surface melts.

Laser ablation

Laser ablation is usually the removal of material with a pulsed laser, but it is possible to ablate material with a continuous laser beam if the intensity is sufficiently high. Ablation to remove the outermost machined layer of the wood surface has mainly two purposes: (1) to open up the wood structure for microscope or similar studies, or (2) to remove a weak-boundary layer to improve the adhesion between the wood and the adhesive or coating, or to improve penetration of liquids for a different purpose. Stehr (1999a) accomplished extensive studies in both these areas.

Laser-ablation as a preparation for microscopic studies has the following advantages compared to microtome preparation, for example:

- the specimen need not be moistened for softening or dried if wet wood is studied,
- the result is much less sensitive to how hard, soft or fragile the material is, and
- the material is not affected by any mechanical force other than that of the specimen holder.

These advantages reduce the risk for artefacts in the preparation of specimens, and the ablation technique is, therefore, especially useful for fragile archaeological and weathered wood and for very dense and hard wood (cf. e.g., Sandberg, 1998a,b; Sandberg, 1999 for the study of densified and weathered wood).

The laser beam can be directed either parallel to or perpendicular to the wood surface to be ablated, giving a difference in surface typography. A laser beam perpendicular to the surface removes material in proportion to the density profile given by the annual rings, and the surface becomes wavy on the microscopic level (Figure 4.16), whereas a beam parallel to the surface gives a very smooth cut (Figure 4.17), although small grooves may sometimes be present after the ablation, see Stehr et al. (1998).

Figure 4.16 Norway spruce ablated with a laser beam perpendicular to a radial surface (scanning electron micrograph, 25x magnification). A wavy ablated surface due to the difference in density between earlywood and latewood, and a crushed fibre layer in the surface in the upper part of the micrograph caused by machining. UV excimer laser QUESTEWK 2520 vβ, wavelength 248 nm, energy 500 mJ·cm^{-2}, frequency 5 Hz.

Figure 4.17 Weathered Norway spruce ablated with a laser beam directed parallel to the surface photomicrograph, 50x magnification). The outermost section of the weathered surface (top) contains fragile and cracked wood and is not damaged by the laser treatment. UV excimer laser QUESTEWK 2520 vβ, wavelength 248 nm, energy 500 mJ·cm^{-2}, frequency 5 Hz.

Stehr (1999b) and Stehr et al. (1999) studied laser ablation at five different wavelengths, using three different lasers (excimer, Nd:YAG and TEA lasers) on cross-section surfaces of Norway spruce and Scots pine, and the effect on subsequent gluing. The weakly bound layers were removed in all cases but, despite the removed of this layer, the bond strength did not improve. They used conventional adhesives, and if the adhesive recipe is not adapted to surface chemistry after the laser treatment, the effect may be lost. Pöpel (1997) maintains that a stronger adhesion is achieved after laser ablation of the wood surface due to greater penetration if a specially adapted adhesive or coating is used.

Surface melting

Wust (2005) has made a thorough study of the effect of laser irradiation on wood (Figure 4.18), and the main findings are that, in addition to the dependence on wavelength, the absorption of the laser radiation varied essentially with the structure of the wood.

Different distributions of cellulose, hemicelluloses and lignin in the cell wall led to different threshold values of laser-beam intensity and interaction time for changes to occur, and the changes were more pronounced in the cross-section because of the greater optical penetration depth through the open cells and the larger surface area available for absorption (the cross-sectional cell surfaces and the inner surface of the open cells are significantly greater than in transverse sections).

Microscopic examinations have shown that the laser radiation is absorbed mainly in the S_2-layer in the secondary wall (see Section 1.2) as this layer constitutes the geometrically largest part of the cell wall. The heating of the cell wall starts in the S_2-layer, but due to the different softening temperatures of the main wood constituents, this leads first to a softening and melting of the lignin-rich middle lamella (cf. Figures 1.26 and 1.88). Because of their high cellulose content, the S_2- and S_3-layers in the secondary wall are more thermally stable, which was particularly evident during irradiation of the transverse sections, where the S_3-layer including the warts layer was mainly exposed to the radiation.

Especially in the transverse section, it was clear that the thickness of the cell wall has an important influence on the energy absorbed. The cell-wall layers are very thin compared to the depth of penetration of the laser radiation, and to achieve absorption by the transverse cell-wall section comparable to that of the cross section of the cell wall, a longer time or a higher intensity was required. This increases the erosion and pyrolysis or burns the cell walls due to the low thermal conductivity of the structure, and this can cause local overheating and subsequent removal of material or burning.

Wust (2005) showed that with a CO_2 laser beam the heat-penetration depth with an irradiation time of about 5 ms exceeds the optical-penetration depth. When a Nd:YAG laser is used, the threshold value is ten times greater with an irradiation time of about 50 ms. This superposition of the optical and heat penetration depths may lead to an increase in the temperature gradient below the irradiated surface and thus to a greater removal of wood material.

From the heat-penetration depth and the optical-penetration depth, the development of the heat front in the wood was determined as a function of the interaction time. An approximate comparison between the mathematical expression of the heat front and the removal of material showed good agreement with the experimental data first, but with increasing interaction time, the erosion increased more than was indicated by the movement of the heat front. The difference can be due to the wood structure and the material characteristics that change with temperature and moisture content.

$$d_{heat,total}\ (t) = d_{heat}\ (t) + d_{opt} \qquad (4.4)$$

where $d_{heat,\ total}$ is the distance between the heat front and the laser-irradiated surface (m), d_{heat} is the thickness of the heated wood (m), d_{opt} is the depth of penetration of light (m), and t is the time (hours).

The effect of laser radiation of a wooden surface can be described in general terms as follows:

- The laser radiation is absorbed by the wood and converted into heat, and loose cell fragments or parts of cells crushed by the mechanical processing are removed from the surface (ablation).
- The energy absorbed by the undamaged wood structure leads to heating and melting of cell-wall material, and the spread of the melt into the lumens causes a further volume loss.

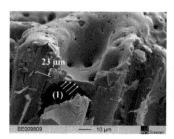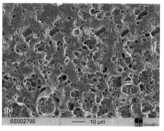

Figure 4.18 SEM micrographs of CO_2 laser irradiated and melted surfaces: a cross-section of European beech, showing (1) direction of the laser beam (left), and a transverse latewood section of Norway spruce (right) (Courtesy of Prof. Peer Haller, Dresden University of Technology, Germany).

- Above a certain threshold for the laser-energy input, the heat transport is no longer sufficient to take the added heat further into the wood. Overheating and erosion occur by evaporation, and the removal increases with increasing energy input. Charring of the surface begins and leads to the shielding of the layers beneath from further removal of cell-wall material.

The example shown in Figure 4.19 for the radiation with a CO_2 laser at an interaction time of 10 ms clarifies this, and also shows that there is a range of radiation parameters where the thickness of the melted layer does not increase the removal of material and no pyrolysis is observed.

The formation of a melted layer on the wooden surface can be clearly recognised by its glassy appearance. The surface appears smooth and colourless, but also milky or brown when the decomposition products have solidified.

The changes depend on the parameter combination and on the species, and a lower threshold for processing with a CO_2 laser was specified (Figure 4.20), i.e., a threshold for the formation of a melted surface. Above this threshold, removal of the wood substance, discolouration of the surface, and pyrolysis may occur (Figure 4.20).

When a Nd:YAG laser is used with an interaction time of 50 ms, the intensity required for a given degree of removal is eight times greater than when a CO_2 laser is used.

Microscopic examination after laser radiation showed that the melting began in the central lamella of the cell wall, and that this led to the expansion of the cell wall parallel to and perpendicular to the cell-wall plane with the formation of pores on the surface. The widening was concentrated in

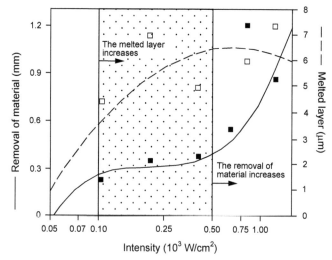

Figure 4.19 Influence of the radiation intensity on the removal and thickness of the melted layer when the material is irradiated with CO_2 laser; cross-section of Norway spruce and pulse duration (τ_p) = 10 ms (Wust, 2005).

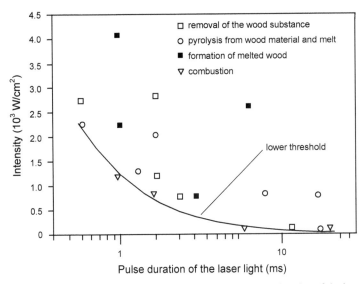

Figure 4.20 The threshold for a change in the wood surface with a CO_2 laser as a function of the intensity (E) and pulse duration (τ_p) of the laser beam.

the middle lamella, but was also found in the secondary wall. The observed widening of the softened cell wall resulted from the evaporation of water bound in the cell wall and the sudden expansion of trapped air.

The middle lamella appeared to be empty beneath the melted layer, and this led to the conclusion that the melt was predominantly lignin, and spectroscopic studies showed that the lignin melt had accumulated on the radiated surface. Since, in addition to lignin, hemicelluloses predominate in the middle lamella, the pyrolysis phenomenon was attributed to the thermal decomposition of hemicelluloses, due to the superposition of the softening and decomposition temperatures of the hemicelluloses. It has been suggested that the temperatures that were briefly reached in the melted layer were between 100°C and 160°C (Hatakeyama et al., 1969) and certainly not higher than about 300°C (Pecina, 1982; Wang and Low, 1990), so that the cellulose does not suffer any chemical change owing to the thermal effect of the laser radiation.

Both the wetting behaviour and the absorption of water are changed by the laser radiation, the degree of change being dependent on the species, a contact angle of 80° being measured for all types of wood, regardless of the laser parameters, this means an increase of 130% compared to an un-treated wood surface for Norway spruce and about 60% for European beech. This meant that the wetting of the wooden surface was incomplete, regardless of the type of wood and laser parameters. A microscopic examination showed a relationship between the melted layer and incomplete wetting, that the main reason for the change in wetting behaviour was the formation of melt on the cell-wall surface and not the fusing together of pores.

A clear temporal influence on the water absorption by the laser irradiation was shown with the water absorption coefficient was determined for different laser-parameter combinations. A reduction in water absorption by about 50% was be measured for European beech, Norway spruce and sapelli wood, but a swelling of the surface may increase the absorption if cracking occurs in the melted layer.

The methods used make possible the reproducible production of melted layers on wood, depending on the laser, wavelengths, interaction time and intensity of the laser radiation.

4.5 Conclusions on microwaves, plasma and laser-light modification

Studies have shown that there are considerable benefits to be gained by using microwave technologies in wood modification. Provisional data suggest that reactions can be accelerated with less energy than is required with conventional methods.

It appears that the commercialisation of plasma treatment for improving the surface properties of wood is of considerable interest. Companies are now producing semi-commercial equipment, indicating that the sector is approaching the transition to the next stage, i.e., large-scale production. The fact that this technique has been shown to improve the surface of veneer suggests that it will first be used in plywood manufacture, where the individual veneers are passed through a plasma stream in order to activate their surfaces and increase their gluability. If the adhesive properties of veneers have already been improved by thermal modification, for example, there is a potential for producing plywood of high dimensional stability and improved adhesion suitable for exterior use. Alternatively, the use of plasma systems for the application of hydrophobic and superhydrophobic films and coatings could open up new opportunities for factory-finished products.

Wood modification with laser light is one of the emerging methods for treating the surface to achieve new applications for wood. The industrial laser systems available for the processing of wood offer far more options than the separation methods (cutting) that have so far been used almost exclusively. A suitable choice of laser parameters make possible the selective removal of layers on wood (cleaning), the removal of fibres damaged by machining, or the melting of surfaces to change the surface properties.

It is clear that further investigation of basic laser processes, such as smoothing, sealing and melting with the inclusion of foreign materials and the sterilisation of wood, will open new fields for wood processing beyond the previously known laser applications.

References

Altgen, D., M. Altgen, S. Kyyrö, L. Rautkari and C. Mai. 2020. Time-dependent wettability changes on plasma-treated surfaces of unmodified and thermally modified European beech wood. European Journal of Wood and Wood Products 78: 417–420.

Antti, A.L. 1992. Microwave drying of hardwood: Simultaneous measurements of pressure, temperature, and weight reduction. Forest Products Journal 42(6): 49–54.

Arai, T., S. Shimakawa and D. Hayashi. 1976. Study on laser machining on wood. Mokuzai Gakkaishi 22(12): 655–660.

Avramidis, G., E. Hauswald, A. Lyapin, H. Militz, W. Viöl and A. Wolkenhauer. 2009. Plasma treatment of wood and wood-based materials to generate hydrophilic or hydrophobic surface characteristics. Wood Material Science & Engineering 4(1/2): 52–60.

Avramidis, G., B. Tebbe, E. Nothnick, H. Militz, W. Viöl and A. Wolkenhauer. 2010. Wood veneer modification by atmospheric pressure plasma treatment for improved absorption characteristics, pp. 365–372. In: Hill, C.A.S. and Andersons, B. [eds.]. The Fifth European Conference on Wood Modification (ECWM5), Riga, Latvia.

Avramidis, G., E. Nothnick, H. Militz, W. Viöl and A. Wolkenhauer. 2011. Accelerated curing of PVAc adhesive on plasma-treated wood veneers. European Journal of Wood and Wood Products 69(2): 329–332.

Aydin, I. and C. Demirkir. 2010. Activation of spruce wood surfaces by plasma treatment after long terms of natural surface inactivation. Plasma Chemistry and Plasma Processing 30(5): 697–706.

Balboni, B.M., B. Ozarska, J.N. Garcia and G. Torgovnikov. 2017. Microwave treatment of *Eucalyptus macrorhyncha* timber for reducing drying defects and its impact on physical and mechanical wood properties. European Journal of Wood and Wood Products 76(3): 861–870.

Barcikowski, S., G. Koch and J. Odermatt. 2006. Characterisation and modification of heat affected zone during laser material processing of wood and wood composites. Holz als Roh- und Werkstoff 64: 94–103.

Barnes, D., L. Admiraal, R.L. Pike and V.N.P. Mathur. 1976. Continuous system for the drying of lumber with microwave energy. Forest Products Journal 26(5): 31–42.

Beyer, E., L. Morgenthal, H. Wust, G. Wiedemann, M. Panzner, R. Fischer and P. Haller. 1999. Laserinduzierte Modifikationen an Holzoberflächen [Laser-induced modifications on wooden surfaces.] Wissenschaftliche Zeitschrift der Teschniche Universität Dresden 48(2): 66–72.

Boenig, H.V. 1982. Plasma Science and Technology. Cornell University Press, Ithaca (NY), USA.

Bryan, E.L. 1963. Machining wood by light. Forest Products Journal 13(1): 14.

Busnel, F., V. Blanchard, J. Pregent, L. Stafford, B. Riedl, P. Blanchet and A. Sarkissian. 2010. Modification of sugar maple (*Acer saccharum*) and black spruce (*Picea mariana*) wood surfaces in a dielectric barrier discharge (DBD) at atmospheric pressure. Journal of Adhesion Science and Technology 24(8/10): 1401–1413.

Bäuerle, D. 2011. Laser Processing and Chemistry. 4th edition, Springer-Verlag Berlin, Heidelberg, Germany.

Chang, H.-T. and S.-T. Chang. 2003. Improvements in dimensional stability and lightfastness of wood by butyrylation using microwave heating. Journal of Wood Science 49: 455–460.

Chitu, L., R. Cernat, I. Bucatica, A. Puiu and D.C. Dumitras. 2003. Improved technologies for marking of different materials. Laser Physics 13: 1108–1111.

Cividini, R. and I. Travan. 2003. Microwave heating in vacuum-press drying of timber: Practical investigation, pp. 150–155. *In*: Ispas, M., Campean, M., Cismar, I., Marinescu, I. and Budau, G. [eds.]. Proceedings of 8th International IUFRO Wood Drying Conference, Brasov, Romania.

Cordeiro, R.C.P., L. Villela, S. Schierl, H. Víana and R.A. Simão. 2018. Effects of different plasma treatments of short fibers on the mechanical properties of polypropylene-wood composites. Polymer Composites 39: 1468–1479.

Denes, A., M. Tshabalala, R.M. Rowell, F. Denes and R. Young. 1999. Hexamethyldisiloxane-plasma coating of wood surfaces for creating water repellent characteristics. Holzforschung 53: 318–326.

Dömény, J., P. Čermák, P. Pařil, F.P. Fodor, A. Dejmal and P. Rademacher. 2015. Application of microwave heating for acetylation of beech (*Fagus sylvatica* L.) and poplar (*Populus* hybrids) wood. BioResources 10(4): 8181–8193.

Fengel, D. and G. Wegener. 1984. Wood: Chemistry, Ultrastructure, Reaction. Walter de Gruyter, Berlin, New York.

Gajtanská, M., I. Christov and R. Igaz. 2004. Lasers and their exploration in industry. Report, Technical University in Zvolen (In Slovak).

Goetz, L.A., J.R. Sladky and A.J. Ragauskas. 2011. Preparation of microwave-assisted polymer-grafted softwood kraft pulp fibers. Enhanced water absorbency. Journal of Applied Polymer Science 119: 387–395.

Grad, L. and J. Mozina. 1998. Optodynamic studies of ER:YAG laser interaction with wood. Applied Surface Science 127/129: 973–976.

Habouria, M., S. Ouertani, S. Azzouz, W. Jomaa, M.T. Elaib and M.A. Elcafci. 2018. Influence of intermittent and continuous microwave heating on drying kinetics and wood behavior of *Eucalyptus Gomphocephala*, pp. 1519–1526. *In*: Cárcel, J.A., Polo, G.C., García-Pérez, J.V., Mulet, A. and Rosselló, C. [eds.]. Proceedings of IDS 2018 21st International Drying Symposium, Valencia, Spain.

Haller, P., E. Beyer, G.J. Wiedemann, M.J. Panzner and H. Wust. 2001. Experimental study of the effect of a laser beam on the morphology of wood surfaces, pp. 345–354. *In*: Navi, P. [ed.]. First International Conference of the European Society for Wood Mechanics, Lausanne, Switzerland.

Haller, P., J. Wehsener and S. Ziegler. 2004. Wood profile and method for the production of the same. U.S. Patent No. 10/479439.

Hamano, Y. and S. Nishio. 1988. Vacuum drying of wood with microwave heating. I. New drying method combining microwave heating and a vacuum. Mokuzai Gakkaishi 34(6): 485–490.

Hancock, W.V. 1963. Effect of heat treatment on the surface of Douglas-fir veneer. Forest Products Journal 40: 81–88.

Hansson, L. and A.L. Antti. 2006. The effect of drying method and temperature level on the hardness of wood. Journal of Materials Processing Technology 171(3): 467–470.

Hartwig, A., H. Schäfer, G. Vitr, K. Wissenbach and C. Dietz. 1996. Laserforschung. Präzisionsbearbeitung mit CO_2-Hochleistungslaser (Abtragen). Teilvorhaben: Abtragendes Vorbehandeln von faserverstärkten Kunststoffen mit CO_2-Laserstrahlung [Laser research. Precision machining with CO_2 high-power laser (ablation). Subproject: Removal pre-treatment of fibre-reinforced plastics with CO_2 laser radiation.] Report No. FKZ 13N6042, Federal Ministry of Education and Research (BMBF), Bonn, Berlin, Germany (In German).

Hatakeyama, H., J. Nakano, M. Hatano and N. Migita. 1969. Variation of infrared spectra with temperature for lignin and lignin model compounds. Tappi 52(9): 1724–1728.

Hattori, N. 1995. Laser processing of wood. Mokuzai Gakkaishi 37(8): 703–709.

Hattori, N., A. Ida, S. Kitayama and M. Noguchi. 1991. Incising of wood with a 500 watt carbon-dioxide laser. Mokuzai Gakkaishi 37(8): 766–768.

Henneberg, K. 1998. Untersuchungen zur Oberflächenbearbeitung von Massivholz mittels Laserstrahlung [Studies on the surface processing of solid wood using laser radiation.] M.Sc. Thesis, Technical University of Dresden, Germany (In German).

Hill, C.A.S. and D. Jones. 1999. Dimensional changes in Corsican pine due to chemical modification with linear chain anhydrides. Holzforschung 53: 267–271.

Hill, C.A.S. and N.S. Cetin. 2000. Surface activation of wood for graft polymerisation. International Journal of Adhesion and Adhesives 20: 71–76.

Hippler, R., S. Pfau, M. Schmidt and K.H. Schoenbach [eds.]. 2001. Low Temperature Plasma Physics. Wiley-VCH Verlag, Berlin, Germany.

Hon, D.N.-S. and N. Shiraishi. 1991. Wood and Cellulosic Chemistry: Photochemistry of Wood. Dekker, New York, USA.

Hse, C.-Y. and M.-L. Kuo. 1988. Influence of extractives on wood gluing and finishing—A review. Forest Products Journal 38(1): 52–56.

Huang, H., B.J. Wang, L. Dong and M. Zhao. 2011. Wettability of hybrid poplar veneers with cold plasma treatments in relation to drying conditions. Drying Technology 29(3): 323–330.

Illingworth, P. and H. Klein Jr. 1977. Microwave drying of ponderosa pine cross-sectional disks. Forest Products Journal 27(2): 36–37.

Inagaki, N. 1996. Plasma Surface Modification and Plasma Polymerization. CRS Press, Boca Raton (FL), USA.

Jones, D., M. Lawther, R. Torgilsson and R. Simonson. 2009. Acetylated wood fibres—next stop: Commercialisation, pp. 505–513. *In*: Englund, F., Hill, C.A.S., Militz, H. and Segerholm, B.K. [eds.]. Proceedings of the 4th European Conference on Wood Modification, Stockholm, Sweden.

Kačík, F. and I. Kubovský. 2011. Chemical changes of beech wood due to CO_2 laser irradiation. Journal of Photochemistry and Photobiology A: Chemistry 222(1): 105–110.

Kačík, F., I. Kubovský, I. Jamnický and J. Sivák. 2010. Changes of saccharides due to CO_2 laser irradiation of maple wood. Acta Facultatis Xylologiae 51(1): 33–40.

Katović, D., J. Trajković, V.S. Bischof and B. Šefc. 2004. Alternative agents and methods for chemical modification of wood. Drvna Industrija 55(4): 175–180.

Kitayama, S., K. Ando and N. Hattori. 1997. Application of laser incising to microwave drying of Sugi (*Cryptomeria japonica*) square lumber with black-heart. Forest Resources and Environment 35: 53–60.

Klarhöfer, L., W. Viol and W. Maus-Friedrichs. 2010. Electron spectroscopy on plasma treated lignin and cellulose. Holzforschung 64: 331–336.

Klobetzkova, T. 1980. Einfluss der Laserstrahlung auf die physikalischen und mechanischen Eigenschaften von Holz und Holzwerkstoffen [Influence of laser radiation on the physical and mechanical properties of wood and wood-based materials.] Drevna Vyskum (Drevo) 25(4): 13–28.

Kobayashi, Y. 1985. Anatomical characteristics of collapsed western red-cedar wood I. Mokuzai Gakkaishi 31(8): 633–639.

Kobayashi, Y. 1986. Anatomical characteristics of collapsed western red-cedar wood II. Mokuzai Gakkaishi 32(1): 12–18.

Kubovský, I. and M. Babiak. 2009. Colour changes induced by CO_2 laser irradiation of wood surface. Wood Research 54(3): 61–66.

Kubovský, I., M. Babiak and S. Cipka. 2012. A determination of specific wood mass removal energy in machining by CO_2 laser. Acta Facultatis Xylologiae Zvolen 54(2): 31–37.

Khan, A.A., M. Cherif, S. Kudapa, V. Barnekov and K. Mukherjee. 1991. High speed, high energy automated machining of hardwoods by using a carbon dioxide laser: ALPS, pp. 238–246. *In*: The Proceedings of SPIE, the International Society for optical Engineering. Paper presented at ICALEO.

Larsson Brelid, P. and R. Simonson. 1999. Acetylation of solid wood using microwave heating. Part 2. Experiments in laboratory scale. Holz als Roh- und Werkstoff 57: 383–389.

Larsson Brelid, P., R. Simonson and P.O. Risman. 1999. Acetylation of solid wood using microwave heating. Part 1. Studies of dielectric properties. Holz als Roh- und Werkstoff 57: 259–263.

Leiker, M. and M.A. Adamska. 2004. Energy efficiency and drying rates during vacuum microwave drying of wood. Holz als Roh- und Werkstoff 62: 203–208.

Lenk, A. M. Panzner and G. Wiedemann. 1997. Verfahren zur Modifizierung von Holzoberflächen [Process for modifying wooden surfaces.] Deutsche Patent No. DE19718287.

Leone, C., V. Lopresto and I. de Iorio. 2009. Wood engraving by Q-switched diode-pumped frequency-doubled Nd:YAG green laser. Optics and Lasers in Engineering 47(1): 161–168.

Li, J., L.-P. Zhang, F. Peng, J. Bian, T.-Q. Yuan, F. Xu and R.-C. Sun. 2009. Microwave-assisted solvent-free acetylation of cellulose with acetic anhydride in the presence of iodine as a catalyst. Molecules 14: 3551–3566.

Li, X.J., Y.D. Zhou, Y.L. Yan, Z.Y. Cai and F. Fu. 2010. A single cell model for pretreatment of wood by microwave explosion. Holzforschung 64(5): 633–637.

Liu, H.-H., Q.-W. Wang, L. Yang, T. Jiang and Y.-C. Cai. 2005. Modification of larch wood by intensive microwave irradiation. Journal of Forestry Research 16(3): 237–240.

Lütkemeier, B., J. Konnerth and H. Militz. 2016. Bonding performance of modified wood. Distinctive influence of plasma pretreatments on bonding strength, pp. 518–527. *In*: World Conference on Timber Engineering e-book.

Magara, K. and T. Koshijima. 1990. Low level of enzymatic susceptibility of microwave-pretreated softwood. Mokuzai Gakkaishi 36(2): 159–164.

Magara, K., M. Tsubouchi and T. Koshijima. 1988. Change of pore-size distribution of lignocellulose by microwave irradiation. Mokuzai Gakkaishi 34(10): 858–862.

Mahlberg, R., H.E.M. Niemi, F. Denes and R.M. Rowell. 1998. Effect of oxygen and hexamethyldisiloxane plasma on morphology, wettability and adhesion properties of polypropylene and lignocellulosics. International Journal of Adhesion and Adhesives 18: 283–297.

Mai, C. and H. Militz. 2004. Modification of wood with silicon compounds. Treatment systems based on organic silicon compounds: A review. Wood Science and Technology 37(6): 453–461.

Martínez-Conde, A., T. Krenke, S. Frybort and U. Müller. 2017. Review: Comparative analysis of CO_2 laser and conventional sawing for cutting of lumber and wood-based materials. Wood Science and Technology 51: 943–966.

Matsuda, H., M. Ueda and H. Mori. 1988. Preparation and crosslinking of oligoesterified woods based on phthalic anhydride and glycidyl methacrylate. Wood Science and Technology 22: 335–344.

McAlister, W.R. and H. Resch. 1971. Drying 1-inch ponderosa pine lumber with a combination of microwave power and hot air. Forest Products Journal 21(3): 26–34.

McMillin, J. and H.E. Harry. 1964. Laser machining. Forest Products Journal 10: 34–37.

Mekhtiev, M.A. and G.I. Torgovnikov. 2004. Method of crack analysis of microwave-modified wood. Wood Science and Technology 38(7): 507–519.

Mertens, N., A. Wolkenhauer, M. Leck and W. Viöl. 2006. UV laser ablation and plasma treatment of wooden surfaces—A comparing investigation. Laser Physics Letters 3(8): 380–384.

Militz, H. 1991. The improvement of dimensional stability and durability of wood through treatment with non-catalysed acetic acid anhydride. Holz als Roh- und Werkstoff 49(4): 147–152.

Miura, M., H. Kaga, A. Sakurai, T. Kakuchi and K. Takahashi. 2004. Rapid pyrolysis of wood block by microwave heating. Journal of Analytical and Applied Pyrolysis 71(1): 187–199.

Naderi, N., S. Legacey and S.L. Chin. 1998. Preliminary investigations of ultrafast intense laser wood processing. Forest Products Journal 49(6): 72–76.

Nakayama, E. and K. Okamura. 1989. Influence of a steam explosion and microwave irradiation on the enzymatic hydrolysis of a coniferous wood. Mokuzai Gakkaishi 35(3): 251–260.

Nath, S., D. Waugh, G. Ormondroyd, M.J. Spear, A.J. Pitman, S. Sahoo, S.F. Curling and P. Mason. 2020. CO_2 laser interactions with wood tissues during single pulse laser-incision. Optics & Laser Technology 126: Article ID: 106069.

Navi, P. and D. Sandberg. 2012. Thermo-hydro-mechanical Processing of Wood. Presses Polytechniques et Universitaires Romandes, Lausanne, Switzerland.

Necesany, V. and M. Kleskenova. 1986. Chemical substance of the glassy amorphous material effused from beech wood during the cutting by laser radiation. Drevna Vyskum (Drevo) 110–115.

Necesany, V., M. Kleskenova and T. Orech. 1979a. Zmeny struktury dreva sposobene laserom. I. Vplyv mnozstva energie [Modification of the wood structure by laser radiation. Part 1: Influence of the amount of energy.] Drevna Vyskum (Drevo) 24(3): 19–27.

Necesany, V., M. Kleskenova and T. Orech. 1979b. Zmeny struktury dreva sposobene laserom. II. Vplyv głębokości cięcia [Modification of the wood structure by laser radiation. Part 2: Influence of the depth of cut.] Drevna Vyskum (Drevo) 24(3): 29–42.

Nguyen, T.T., X. Ji, T.H. Van Nguyen and M. Guo. 2017. Wettability modification of heat-treated wood (HTW) via cold atmospheric-pressure nitrogen plasma jet (APPJ). Holzforschung 72(1): 37–44.

Nilsson, T., R.M. Rowell, R. Simonson and A.M. Tillman. 1988. Fungal resistance of pine particle boards made from various types of acetylated chips. Holzforschung 42(2): 123–126.

Norimoto, M. and J. Gril. 1989. Wood bending using microwave heating. Journal of Microwave Power and Electromagnetic Energy 24(4): 203–212.

Odrášková, M., Z. Szalay, J. Ráhel', A. Zahoranová and M. Černák. 2007. Diffuse coplanar surface barrier discharge assisted deposition of water repellent films from N2/HMDSO mixtures on wood surface, pp. 803–806. In: Schmidt, J., Šimek, M., Pekárek, S. and Prukner, V. [eds.]. Proceedings of the 28th International Conference on Phenomena in Ionized Gases, Prague, Czech Republic.

Odrášková, M., J. Ráhel', A. Zahoranová, R. Tiňo and M. Černák. 2008. Plasma activation of wood surface by diffuse coplanar surface barrier discharge. Plasma Chemistry and Plasma Processing 28: 203–211.

Oloyede, A. and P. Groombridge. 2000. The influence of microwave heating on the mechanical properties of wood. Journal of Materials Processing Technology 100(1/3): 67–73.

Orech, T. and M. Kleskenová. 1975. Untersuchungen über die Holzbearbeitung mit Laserstrahlen [Studies on woodworking with laser.] Drevna Vyskum (Drevo) 30: 324.

Panzner, M., G. Wiedemann, K. Henneberg, R. Fischer, T. Wittke and R. Dietsch. 1998. Experimental investigation of the laser ablation process on wood surfaces. Applied Surface Science 127/129: 787–792.

Pecina, H. 1982. Zur Aussagefähigkeit von Infrarot-Spektrogrammen über chemische Strukturveränderungen des Holzes mit dem Beispiel thermischer Behandlung [The informative value of infrared spectrograms on chemical structural changes in wood using the example of thermal treatment.] Holztechnologie 23(2): 78–84.

Potočňáková, L., J. Hnilica and V. Kudrle. 2013. Increase of wettability of soft- and hardwoods using microwave plasma. International Journal of Adhesion and Adhesives 45: 125–131.

Pike, R.L. and D. Barnes. 1977. Microwave curing of alkaline phenolic resins in wood-resin compositions. U.S. Patent No. 4,018,642.

Przewloka, S.R., J.A. Hann and P. Vinden. 2006. Assessment of commercial low viscosity resins as binders in the wood composite material *Vintorg*. Holz als Roh- und Werkstoff 65: 209–214.

Pöpel, L.V. 1997. Untersuchen der Eigenschaften laserbehandelter Holzoberflächen bezüglich Verkleb- und Imprägnierbarkeit [Investigation of the properties of laser-treated wooden surfaces with regard to the ability to be bonded and impregnated.] Dresden University of Technology, Germany (In German).

Rajewska, K., A. Smoczkiewicz-Wojciechowska and J. Majka. 2019. Intensification of beech wood drying process using microwaves. Chemical and Process Engineering 40(2): 179–187.

Ratanawilai, T., C. Nuntadusit and N. Promtong. 2015. Drying characteristics of rubberwood by impinging hot-air and microwaves. Wood Research 60(1): 59–70.

Robinson, J.P., S.W. Kingman, R. Barranco, C.E. Snape and H. Al-Sayegh. 2010. Microwave pyrolysis of wood pellets. Industrial & Engineering Chemistry Research 49(2): 459–463.

Rowell, R.M. 2013. Handbook of Wood Chemistry and Wood Composites. CRC Press, Boca Raton, USA.

Rowell, R.M., G.R. Esenther, D.D. Nicholas and T. Nilsson. 1987. Biological resistance of southern pine and aspen flakeboards made from acetylated flakes. Journal of Wood Chemistry and Technology 7(3): 427–440.

Rozman, H.D., W.B. Banks and J.M. Lawther. 1994. FTIR characterization of chemically modified fibreboard. International Journal of Polymeric Materials 26: 19–24.

Sandberg, D. 1998a. Inverkan av isostatisk komprimering på cellstrukturen [The influence of isostatic compression on the cell wall structure of wood.] Report No. TRITA-TRÄ R-98-35, Royal Institute of Technology (KTH), Wood Technology and Processing, Stockholm, Sweden (In Swedish).

Sandberg, D. 1998b. Value Activation with vertical annual rings—material, production, products. PhD. Thesis, Royal Institute of Technology (KTH), Wood Technology and Processing, Stockholm, Sweden.

Sandberg, D. 1999. Weathering of radial and tangential wood surfaces of pine and spruce. Holzforschung 53(4): 355–364.

Seiferth, C. 1982. Aus Wissenschaft und Technik: Laser-Technik [From science and technology: Laser technology.] Holztechnologie 23(2): 119–120.

Seltman, J. 1995. Freilegen der Holzstruktur durch UV-Bestrahlung [Exposing the wood structure by UV radiation.] Holz ald Roh- und Werkstoff 53: 225–228.

Seyfarth, R., M. Leiker and N. Mollekopf. 2003. Continuous drying of lumber in a microwave vacuum kiln, pp. 159–163. *In*: Ispas, M., Campean, M., Cismar, I., Marinescu, I. and Budau, G. [eds.]. Proceedings of 8th International IUFRO Wood Drying Conference, Brasov, Romania.

Souza, J.R., J.R. Araujo, B.S. Archanjo and R.A. Simão. 2019. Cross-linked lignin coatings produced by UV light and SF_6 plasma treatments. Progress in Organic Coatings 128: 82–89.

Stafast, H. 1993. Angewandte Laserchemie—Verfahren und Anwendungen [Applied laser chemistry—processes and applications.] Springer-Verlag Berlin, Heidelberg, Germany (In German).

Stehr, M. 1999a. Adhesion to machined and laser ablated wood surfaces. PhD. Thesis, Royal Institute of Technology (KTH), Wood Technology and Processing, Stockholm, Sweden.

Stehr, M. 1999b. Laser ablation of machined wood surfaces. 2. Effect on end-grain gluing of pine (*Pinus silvestris* L.). Holzforschung 53(6): 655–661.

Stehr, M., J. Seltman and I. Johansson. 1998. UV laser ablation – an improved method of sample preparation for microscopy. Holzforschung 52(1): 1–6.

Stehr, M., J. Seltman and I. Johansson. 1999. Laser ablation of machined wood surfaces. 1. Effect on end-grain gluing of pine (*Pinus silvestris* L.) and spruce (*Picea abies* Karst.). Holzforschung 53(1): 93–103.

Struszczyk, H., D. Ciechańska, D. Wawro, A. Niekraszewicz and G. Strobin. 2004. Review of alternative methods applying to cellulose and chitosan structure modification. Radiation processing of polysaccharides, International Atomic Energy Agency (IAEA), pp. 55–65.

Szymani, R. and F.E. Dickinson. 1975. Recent developments in wood machining processes: Novel cutting techniques. Wood Science and Technology 9(2): 113–128.

Tendero, C., C. Tixier, P. Tristant, J. Desmaison and P. Leprince. 2006. Atmospheric pressure plasmas. A review. Spectrochimica Acta Part B. 61: 2–30.

Terziev, N., G. Daniel, G. Torgovnikov and P. Vinden. 2020. Effect of microwave treatment on the wood structure of Norway spruce and radiata pine. BioResources 15(3): 5616–5626.

Topala, I. and N. Dumitrascu. 2007. Dynamics of the wetting process on dielectric barrier discharge (DBD)-treated wood surfaces. Journal of Adhesion Science and Technology 21(11): 1089–1096.

Torgovnikov, G.I. 1993. Dielectric Properties of Wood and Wood-based Materials. Springer-Verlag, Berlin, Heidelberg, Germany.

Torgovnikov, G. and P. Vinden. 2009. High-intensity microwave wood modification for increasing permeability. Forest Products Journal 59(4): 84–92.

Torgovnikov, G., P. Vinden and B. Balboni. 2015. High intensity microwave modification of blue gum wood and impregnation with a metal alloy, 6p. *In*: 15th International Conference on Microwave and High Frequency Heating (AMPERE 2015), Krakow, Poland.

Treu, A. and H. Militz. 2008. Microwave curing of impregnated wood. International Patent No. WO2008/140324.

Treu, A., E. Larnøy and H. Militz. 2007. Microwave curing of furfuryl alcohol modified wood. *In*: The Proceedings IRG Annual Meeting, Jackson Hole, USA. International Research Group on Wood Protection IRG/WP 07-40371.

Vidholdová, Z., L. Reinprecht and I. Ratislav. 2017. The impact of laser surface modification of beech wood on it color and occurance of molds. BioResources 12(2): 4177–4186.

Vukusic, S.B., D. Katovic, C. Schramm, J. Trajkovic and B. Sefc. 2006. Polycarboxylic acids as non-formaldehyde anti-swelling agents for wood. Holzforschung 60(4): 439–444.

Wang, S.Y. and J.L. Lin. 1986. Studies on the use of microwave irradiation to improve the plasticity of wood. II. The effects of microwave irradiation on the modulus of elasticity and toughness of wood. Journal of Forest Products and Industries 5(3): 31–44.

Wang, T.K. and W.C. Shi. 1988. The polarization theory of microwave drying of timbers. Journal of Northeast Forestry University 16(3): 41–49.

Wang, N. and M.J.D. Low. 1990. Spectroscopic studies of carbons. XV. The pyrolysis of a lignin. Materials Chemistry and Physics 26(1): 67–80.

Wascher, R., N. Leike, G. Avramidis, A. Wolkenhauer, H. Militz and W. Viol. 2015. Improved DMDHEU uptake of beech veneers after plasma treatment at atmospheric pressure. European Journal of Wood and Wood Products 73: 433–437.

Wascher, R., C. Kühn, G. Avramidis, S. Bicke, H. Militz, G. Ohms and W. Viöl. 2017. Plywood made from plasma-treated veneers: Melamine uptake, dimensional stability, and mechanical properties. Journal of Wood Science 63(4): 338–349.

Wascher, R., G. Avramidis, H. Militz and W. Viöl. 2018. Plasma treatment of wood veneers: A review, pp. 216–223. *In*: Jos Creemers, J., Houben, T., Tjeerdsma, B., Militz, H., Junge, B. and Gootjes, J. [eds.]. Proceedings of 9th European Conference on Wood Modification, Arnhem, The Netherlands.

Wiedemann, M., J. Hauptmann, T. Heinze, A. Kempe, H.-G. Kusch, M. Panzner and H. Wust. 2001. Laserabtragen dünner Schichten – eine alternative Reinigungsmethode für die Reastaurierung und Denmalpflege – Möglichkeiten und Grenzen [Laser ablation of thin layers – an alternative cleaning method for restoration and monument preservation - possibilities and limits.] Arbeitsblätter für Reastauratoren 2: 69–102.

Wolkenhauer, A., G. Avramidis, E. Hauswald, H. Militz and W. Viol. 2008. Plasma treatment of wood–plastic composites to enhance their adhesion properties. Journal of Adhesion Science and Technology 22(16): 2025–2037.

Wolkenhauer, A., G. Avramidis, E. Hauswald, H. Militz and W. Viöl. 2009. Sanding vs. plasma treatment of aged wood: A comparison with respect to surface energy. International Journal of Adhesion and Adhesives 29(1): 18–22.

Wu, R. and J. Seltman. 1998. Microstructural investigation of UV-laser irradiated pine (*Pinus silvestris* L.). Wood Science and Technology 32: 183–195.

Wust, H. 2005. Die Wirkung von Laserstrahlung auf strukturelle, chemische und physikalische Eigenschaften von Holz. PhD. Thesis, Technical University of Dresden, Germany.

Xu, K., J. Lü, X. Li, Y. Wu and Y. Liu. 2014. Process of wood high-intensity microwave pretreatment based on response surface methodology. Scientia Silvae Sinicae 50(11): 109–114.

Xu, K., Y. Wang, J. Lv, X. Li and Y. Wu. 2015. The effect of microwave pretreatment on the impregnation of poplar wood. BioResources 10(1): 282–289.

Zanini, S., C. Riccardi, M. Orlandi, V. Fornara, M.P. Colombini, D.I. Donato, S. Legnaioli and V. Palleschi. 2007. Wood coated with plasma-polymer for water repellence. Wood Science and Technology 42(2): 149–160.

Zheng, Y., Z. Jiang, Z. Sun and H. Ren. 2014. Effect of microwave-assisted curing on bamboo glue strength: Bonded by thermosetting phenolic resin. Construction and Building Materials 68: 320–325.

Zielonka, P. and K. Dolowy. 1998. Microwave drying of spruce: Moisture content, temperature and heat energy distribution. Forest Products Journal 48(6): 77–80.

Chapter 5
Other Modification Processes

5.1 Introduction

So far, the aim of this book has been to provide an overview of the advances in wood modification in the past 20 years, particularly in the case of commercial processes. Each of these processes (acetylation, furfurylation, resin impregnation/polymerisation, thermally-based treatments, etc.) has become commercialised only after considerable research leading to a multitude of scientific publications and patents, and it has been necessary for the skills in application to match the needs of the science, such as an understanding of the thermodynamics of the process (to prevent overheating and the risk of fire or explosion) and the design of equipment to achieve safe reactions (such as vacuum systems or high-pressure cylinders).

In most cases, the process from proof of concept to commercial production for any wood modification method has taken 20+ years. The knowledge base gained with these processes in terms of equipment and processing may provide a way to reduce the development time for future ideas, but new modification systems still need to be proven with regard to both the science and the performance of the resulting products.

This chapter aims to provide an oversight into emerging methods. Some of these have already been shown on a laboratory scale or in prototype products, others are based on scientific concepts from other sectors and are listed herein only to demonstrate what way be possible. It is hoped that this chapter may provide readers with "food for thought" into how the future of wood modification may look in another 10–20 years.

The potential modification systems can be categorised under the common group "Other processes" having a biological theme or an inorganic theme, or being treatments enhanced by the reaction media used. Examples of treatments considered in this chapter are shown in Figure 5.1.

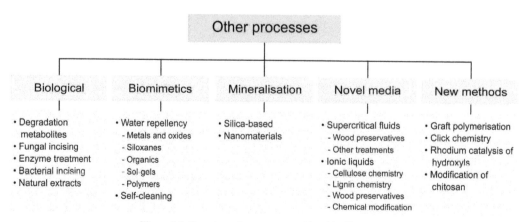

Figure 5.1 Overview of processes considered in Chapter 5.

5.2 Biological treatment of wood

Given that wood is a natural organic material, it is not surprisingly that it is susceptible to decay and degradation, the rate at which this occurs depending upon the species (and its inherent natural durability), the conditions to which the wood is exposed (its environmental surroundings) and the treatment that may have been applied to prolong its service life. Many of these factors are covered in Sections 1.4 to 1.6. However, the factors that lead to the deterioration of wood and its properties may, if controlled correctly, provide opportunities for developing better treatments. This section considers two such areas: fungal metabolites as a potential wood treatment and improving the permeability of wood by controlling its decay by fungal species.

Metabolites from wood-destroying organisms to protect wood

The increasing demand for wood-based products in recent years has led to a better understanding of environmental and societal issues. Many of the concepts developed within these fields have helped the development of wood modification as a possible option for the commercial protection of wooden products, alongside a greater awareness of the biocidal activity of the treatments used to limit biological attack. There has been a growing understanding of how certain mould and fungal species and their respective metabolites can limit or eradicate decay due to other, more aggressive species known to have significant impacts on crops. Many of these concepts were developed in order to limit the decay of food crops. Gindrat et al. (1977) successfully learned how to control *Phomopsis sclerotioides* Van Kesteren, a fungus known to cause black root rot in mature cucumber plants, by introducing soil treatment with inoculants containing *Gliocladium roseum* Bainier or *Trichoderma* spp. under a range of conditions.

At the same time, work was in progress to identify fungal metabolites capable of acting as antagonists to wood decay. Based on initial reports by Denis and Webster (1971), the effectiveness of *Trichoderma* spp. against *Neolentinus lepideus* was demonstrated by Bruce et al. (1984). Further agents (Bruce and Highley, 1991, and references therein), along with Penicillium and Aspergillus, were tested against a wide range of white and brown rot fungi, particulary *Trametes versicolor* and *Neolentinus lepideus*, by agar interaction tests and by measuring the toxicity of culture filtrates. This method of inoculation on agar plates has been shown to provide fast, effective screening of the efficacy of reagents under examination.

Bruce and Highley (1991) considered the potential of *Trichoderma* spp. based on other studies in the scientific literature, and they suggested various modes of action, including the production of fungistatic and fungicidal volatile and non-volatile metabolites, the achievement of a high inoculum potential by rapid colonisation and removal of available nutrients, and mycoparasitism by hyphal coiling associated with the production of a range of enzymes capable of disrupting the cell-wall membranes of other fungi. Of the three species tested, Aspergillus was found to have the greatest level of inhibition, being particularly effective against white rot Basidiomycetes. The effectiveness of metabolites from *Trichoderma harzianum* on a range of decay-causing basidiomycetes was evaluated by Schoeman et al. (1996) who assessed isolates of basidiomycetes known to decay pine wood, viz. *Coniophora puteana, Heterobasisdion annosum, Ischnoderma benzoinum, Peniophora gigantea* and *Stereum sanguinolentum*, using an *in vitro* bilayer system, which allowed the effects of the diffusible metabolites of *T. harzianum* to be studied. The temperature was, as expected, found to have an effect on some of the tested resembling the diurnal and seasonal temperature fluctuations occurring in actual decay conditions in nature. It was found by controlling the temperature variation, the results could be varied, i.e., the equilibrium between fungal species being altered, being possible an overgrowth of a specific species. Analysis of the VOCs produced during the growth of various *Trichoderma* isolates (Wheatley et al., 1997) suggested that five compounds, 2-propanone, 2-methyl-1 butanol, heptanal, octanal and decanal, were produced in significantly larger proportions in the malt medium and it was postulated that they played some role in inhibition process. Further studies (Humphris et al., 2001) looked at the effectiveness of acetone, 2-methyl-1-butanol, heptanal and octanal, respectively against *Neolentinus lepideus, Postia placenta, Gloeophyllum trabeum* and *Trametes versicolor*. The effects of testing against biomass growth and respiration of fungi were studied over a range of concentrations, and varying degrees of efficacy of compounds in relation to specific fungi were found, as well as the effect of different exposure concentrations. For example, 2-methyl-1-butanol inhibited all four fungi at the highest concentration tested (2,500 mg ml^{-1}), while octanal at the same concentration was effective against three of the four fungi, but not against *G. trabeum*. Heptanal was interesting, in that it inhibited the growth of *T. versicolor* and *G. trabeum* at concentrations of 2.5 and 25 mg ml^{-1}, but stimulated the growth at higher concentrations (250 and 2,500 mg ml^{-1}). Similarly, at the highest concentration, 2-methyl-1-butanol had a significant impact on the respiration rate of all four fungi, although a lower concentration stimulated *P. placenta* respiration.

Biological degradation ultimately represents the end of the service life of a wood-based product, but the presence of sapstain is more of an aesthetic issue, which if left to develop further could lead to the onset of a decay process. Despite the lack of any effect on, say, mechanical properties with sapstain, customers do not appreciate its presence and this means that there is a need to limit its development. Sapstain is caused by initial colonising fungi, such as *Ophiostoma, Ceratocystis, Leptographium* or *Sphaeropsis,* a key factor being their ability to utilise simple carbohydrates, fatty acids, triglycerides and other components of the sapwood, leaving a resultant dark stain due to melanin-based compounds within the fungal hyphae (Zink and Fengel, 1988; Zimmerman et al., 1993). The normal method of prevention is either through thorough drying before the onset of any staining and/or treatment with preservatives. As environmentally acceptable protocols have increased in popularity and necessity, the option of using a fungal treatment to limit and prevent sapstain has become more established. Much of this has been based on the use of albino strains of sapstain fungi using, for example, colourless strains of *Ophiostoma* (e.g., Behrendt et al., 1995a,b; White-McDougall et al., 1998). Much of the recent expansion in wood modification has been based on the use of uniformly grown sustainable conifer woods, one of the more popular species being radiata pine. However, this species, as with all pine species, is prone to sapstain discolouration. Held et al. (2003) successfully demonstrated the potential of using albino strains of *Ophiostoma* to achieve a preferential, non-staining colonisation of pine. Another species that has attracted interest is *Bacillus subtilis* (Kreber and Morrell, 1993), which is known to produce antifungal compounds, such as bacitracin, iturin and subtilin (Figure 5.2) (Zuber et al., 1993), which can inhibit the activity of species such as *Aspergillus* and *Penicillium* (Munimbazi and Bullerman, 1998). The effectiveness of *Bacillus subtilis* was found to be enhanced when it was combined with a natural oil, such as myrtlewood oil, orange oil, lime oil or cypress needle oil (Wang et al., 2012).

Susi et al. (2011) have presented a thorough review of antagonistic fungi and the effectiveness of the VOCs that they release, that provides insight into the use of antagonistic bacteria and effective ways of introducing these antagonists so that the bacteria do not adversely change the appearance of the wood. Among species reported as proving beneficial are the gram-negative Pseudomonas family (such as *P. aeruginosa, P. fluorescens, P. putida, P. aureofaciens* and *P. syringae*) and several Streptomyces species (including *S. chrestomycetius, S. rimosus, S. cinnamoneum, Pseudomonas cepacian* and *Xenorhabdus luminescens*). However, some Streptomyces species can colour and degrade wood. Similarly, bacteria of the Bacillus family are known to produce a range of compounds that act as antibiotics as well as a range of anti-fungal enzymes capable of degrading fungal cell walls, acting as inhibitors and in some cases producing better results than chemical fungicides (Ali and Reddy, 2000; Aktuganov et al., 2008).

Susi et al. (2011) have also summarised antibiotics affecting RNA and protein synthesis in decay fungi, non-volatile antibiotics, lytic peptides (that cause the destruction of the cell wall and its membrane) and siderophores (capable of transferring iron via chelation mechanisms).

These metabolites have the capability of being produced by a range of biological systems, often during the simultaneous attack by decay fungi, and they may act as antagonists specific for preventing wood degradation. They can also act as factories, producing more complex antimicrobial

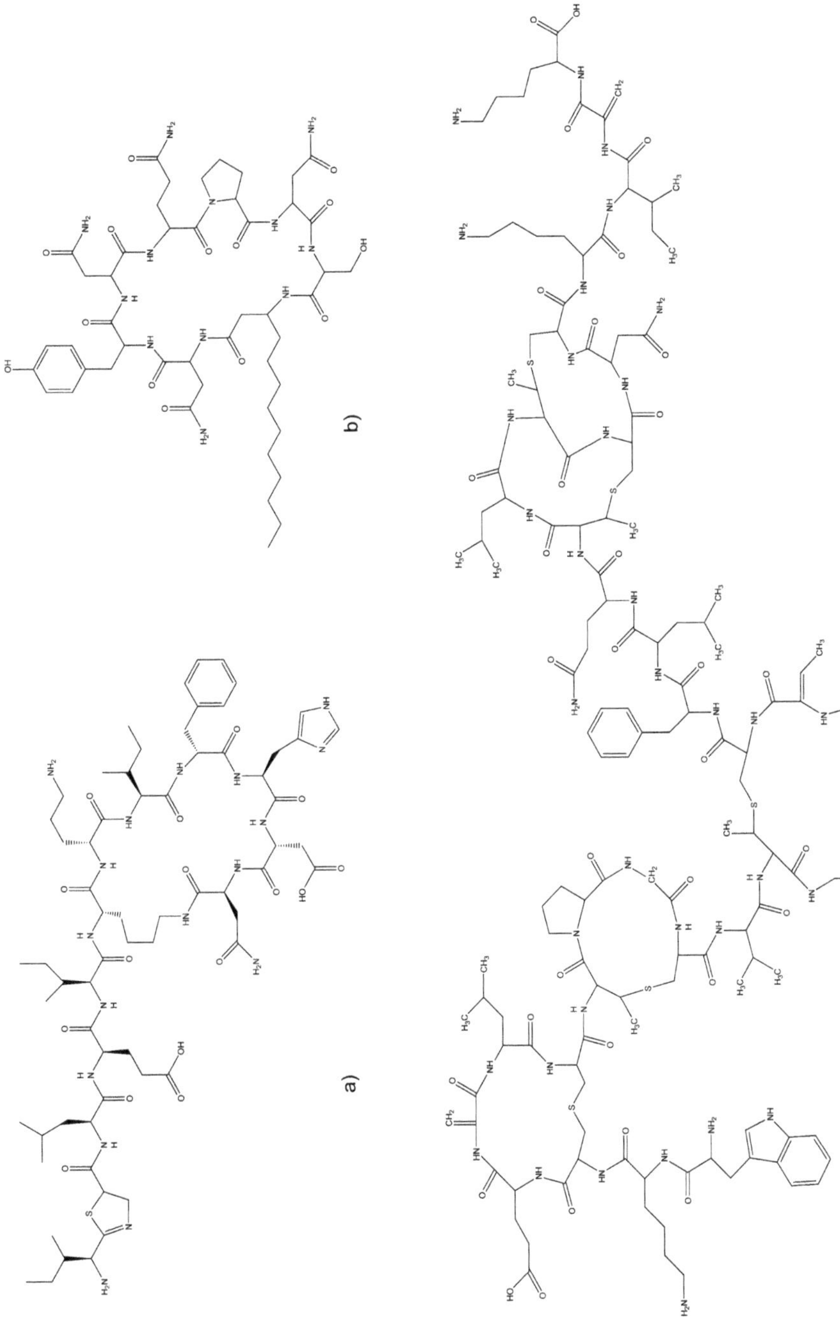

Figure 5.2 Chemical structures of (a) batricidin, (b) iturin and, (c) subtilin.

compounds. Researchers have been able to define their biosynthesis and extraction, and this may allow novel treatments incorporating these compounds directly into wood as a protective treatment to be developed.

Fungal incising

The permeability of many of the currently used wood species, e.g., Douglas fir, fir, Norway spruce, and Sitka spruce, which are referred to as "refractory" species, can be reduced to 1–5% of that of green timber when dried, so that chemical solutions can penetrate only a few millimetres in the radial direction. Although wood preservatives have been applied to timber products for several decades, the uptake of such reagents by refractory species has always been relatively low, at best resulting in only envelope treatments. This normally means that refractory species can be treated so that the outer layers of the wood can be protected, which should guarantee the performance if they remain intact. However, wood preservation has also been applied to timbers exposed to harsh conditions, where decay is expected over time, as in in-ground contact or burial, and wood preservatives have played an important role in products such as fence posts, telegraph poles, etc. These products are, however, usually forcibly driven into the ground, and this can damage the outer protective layer, through contact with rocks in the ground splitting the wood. Such damage increases the risk that moisture and decay organisms may bypass the treated regions and directly attack the untreated core of the product, ultimately leading to failure.

In attempts to overcome this, mechanical incising has been used to improve preservative penetration, but it does not result in through-treated wood, it reduces the wood's mechanical properties, and it alters the appearance (Morris et al., 1994; Evans, 2016). Early methods of incision, as reported by Evans (2016), were adopted as far back as the mid-9th Century, by manually hammering holes into timber. In the early 20th Century, equipment was patented for the incising of railway sleepers. Although incision is not popular, due to the unsightly holes in the timber surface, the method is still occasionally used. Laser incision has been developed as an alternative to mechanically incised holes (Ruddick, 1991).

Another alternative is the use of bioincising, which uses biological agents to increase the permeability of timber to subsequent treatments. As described in Section 1.5, wood can be opened up by wood fungi and bacteria, with different genera (i.e., white rot, brown rot, soft rot) and species within each genus having different modes of operation and levels of reactivity.

Early work on fungal treatment

Biodegradation of wood by fungi has been known since mankind started to use wood, but it was only during the 20th Century that more systematic studies allowed scientists to expand their understanding of the process and its potential. As far back as 1943, there were projects, led by the German scientist Walter Luthardt, aimed at producing fungi for human consumption, focussing mainly on *Kuehneromyces mutabilis* (Schaeffer ex Fr.) Sing and Smith (commonly known as the sheathed woodtuft, an edible mushroom that grows in clumps on tree stumps or other dead wood). Interest in fungi-derived food diminished after World War Two, but Luthardt noticed that wood samples that had been treated with *K. mutabilis* had a low density and exceptional permeability and were easily processed. As a result, treated wood was marketed under the name "Mykoholz" and it was sold between 1949 and 1964 for the manufacture of pencils, rulers and drawing boards. In addition, work during this period was extended to the use of *Pleurotus ostreatus* (pearl oyster mushroom or tree oyster mushroom), which was originally considered as a food mushroom during World War One and is today grown for that purpose globally. During the 1960s, *Trametes versicolor* L. was used to pre-treat beech as part of the Mykoholz brand (Schwarze and Schubert, 2017), with an emphasis on the ability of *T. versicolor* to break down wood components as part of a pulping process (Messner, 1998) where, on Norway spruce chips, it significantly reduces the levels of triglycerides and stearyl esters (Van Beek et al., 2007).

Development of bioincising

Having established the potential of bioprocessing with *T. versicolor* (Messner, 1998), combined with earlier studies into treating wood chips with *Ophiostoma piliferum* (Blanchette et al., 1992), the Lignocell Holz-Biotechnologie GmbH company developed the bioincising treatment technique using fungi such as *Trichoderma viride*, *Trichoderma aureoviride*, *Trichoderma harzianum*, *Hypocrea piluliferum*, and *Gliocladium roseum*, as well as methods using fungi known for their weakly wood-degrading characteristics, such as *Phanerochaete chrysosporium* and *Dichomitus squalens* (Messner et al., 2000). Typically, the treatment began with decontamination of the wood surface, preferably with steam at 100–120°C for 10 seconds to 30 minutes, depending on the degree of contamination, followed by a cooling phase. The growth-promoting medium may be applied separately or jointly with the fungal inoculum with an additional feed liquor, the incubation and growth period being maintained at or slightly above room temperature for up to 4 weeks, depending on the timber species being treated and the fungus that had been inoculated. The long periods of time necessary for the treatment were, however, perceived to be commercially unfeasible, although the concept of bioincising still remains of scientific interest.

Ongoing research into bioincising

At the same time as Lignocell Holz-Biotechnologie GmbH, additional research was being undertaken by other groups. Schwarze and Landmesser (2000) investigated the basidiomycete *Physisporinus vitreus* on Douglas fir and Norway spruce, and they showed that in naturally infected Norway spruce and artificially inoculated Douglas fir and Norway spruce, a selective delignification occurred, and that the fungus selectively degraded the membranes of the bordered pits and half-bordered pits. One of the advantages of using *P. vitreus* was that, with a treated wood (Norway spruce and silver fir), high permeability could be obtained, with little loss of impact bending strength (Schwarze et al., 2006), and in 2008 the term "bioincising" was proposed (Schwarze, 2008). Similar improvements in permeability without any reduction in compression stiffness were noted using *Dichomitus squalens*, and full preservative penetration was reached in spruce samples (Dale et al., 2019). The brown rot fungus *Antrodia vaillantii*, the white rot fungus *Hypoxylon fragiforme*, a blue stain fungus *Sclerophoma pithyophila* (Thaler et al., 2012) and the soft rot fungus *Xylaria longipes* (Emaminasab et al., 2016) have also been studied. The delignification capacities of *Phlebia brevispora*, *Phlebia radiata*, *Phlebia tremellosa* and *Oxyporus latemarginatus* were also assessed and these have been proposed as bioincising fungi (Fackler et al., 2006).

Bioincising with wood modification

So far, most bioincising studies have been focussed on ways to increase the permeability of wood to subsequent preservative treatment, but the same concepts can be applied to refractory species undergoing wood modification, where the introduction of a chemical is limited by the properties of the wood. Thus, species such as spruce and Douglas fir are not suitable for initial impregnation as part of a wood modification process, particularly when large dimension timbers are undergoing treatment (Homan and Jorissen, 2004). Bioincising with *Dichomitus squalens*, followed by acetylation using the semi-commercial process developed by SHR Timber Research, Wageningen, The Netherlands (Messner et al., 2003) led to a significant increase in the heartwood acetylation of Norway spruce (around 18% acetyl content compared to 8% in non-bioincised samples). Similar levels of acetylation were noted in sapwood without bioincising. Given these levels of uptake by heartwood, it was concluded that levels of acetylation could be achieved in large dimension timber sufficient to give adequate protection against biological decay.

Modification of wood with PF resins without the need for compression, as in the case of Compreg™-type products, is increasing in popularity as a method of treating wood (Sections 2.3 and 2.4). Again, issues may exist to the degree of uptake of phenolic solution prior to its polymerisation with *Ophiostoma piceae* (wood staining fungus), *Gliocladium roseum* (mould fungus), *Trametes versicolor*, or *Irpex lacteus* (white rot fungi) for durations up to 8 weeks, which led to an increase uptake of phenol-formaldehyde resin, aided by the resin flowing through pit pairs of neighbouring cells, a fact confirmed microscopic examination of by hyphal growth in aspen when under.

In this doctoral studies, Christian Lehringer (2011) considered the bioincision of Norway spruce with *Physisporinus vitreus*, and they reported the following:

- organofunctional silanes – after a bioincision period of 9 weeks, the penetration depth of the silane treatment increased from 80 μm to around 250 μm;

- methylated melamine-formaldehyde resin – the weight percentage gain (WPG) increased from 3% (control samples) to 8% in the incised samples, and it was suggested that embedding in the cell-wall layers contributed to the hardness improvement noted;

- 1,3-dimethylol-4,5-dihydroxyethyleneurea (DMDHEU) – impregnation/polymerisation with DMDHEU resulted in a slightly lower WPG (around 13% compared to 15% for control samples), DMDHEU cross-links with wood components and self-polycondensation within the cell wall, though cell-wall effects led to similar hardness effects to melamine resins; and

- Montan wax – the WPG for bioincised samples was ca. 30% (compared to 20% for control samples). The waxes filled the cell lumina without swelling. The increased hardness was attributed to the greater weight uptake.

It would appear that there are opportunities for further advances in bioincising as a means of improving wood modification.

Enzymatic treatment of wood

Although the bioincision of wood often involves the effect of enzymes on wood components, the process acts by partly damaging or destroying the structural integrity of the wood in a mild and controlled degradation process. It is necessary to consider whether similar enzymatic processing, or alternative enzyme systems, can perhaps have an even milder effect on wood and its components. Such milder processing conditions would be applicable to the more reactive components of wood, particularly lignin, and this has been the aim of studies to the enzymatic treatment of wood with laccase.

Laccase is a globular glycoprotein consisting of 10–30% of carbohydrates, typically with a molecular mass between 50 and 130 kDa (kiloDaltons, where 1 Dalton is equal to 1/12 the mass of an unbound neutral atom of carbon-12 in its nuclear and electronic ground state and at rest). Laccase has four copper atoms located at the catalytic centre and belongs to the group known as multicopper oxidases.

Laccase has been shown to occur in a wide range of organisms with bacterial, insect, plant and fungal origins (Arregui et al., 2019). They are typical components of white rot fungi and the related group of litter-decomposing fungi which cause lignin degradation. The fungal sources identified include *Trametes versicolor*, *Trametes pubsecens* and *Pleurotus ostreatus*, each recognised for its wood degradation ability. At the time of publication, Novozymes had a commercially available laccase (marketed as Novozym™ 51003), derived from *Aspergillus oryzea* (a filamentous fungus used in East Asia to ferment soybeans to make soy sauce and fermented bean paste, and also to saccharify rice, other grains, and potatoes to make alcoholic beverages such as sake and shōchū). Harris (2017) published a thorough overview of the isolation and uses of laccase.

Laccase in wood treatment

Laccase is currently used in a variety of bioprocesses (Harris 2017), and particularly for bioremediation, biosensors, dye removal, food and beverage processing and pulp and paper applications. In the pulp and paper sector, the use of laccase has mainly focussed on the delignification of feedstocks necessary for paper-based products. Lignin is normally removed in chemical pulping using toxic chlorine-based chemicals, but this does not achieve total removal of all the lignin components. Total removal of lignin requires initiating the degradation of polysaccharides, which

Figure 5.3 The oxidation cycle of a laccase-mediator system.

Figure 5.4 Direct laccase oxidation of fibres in composite production.

can reduce the product quality, but the addition of laccase facilitates the lignin removal (Camarero et al., 2007), and the process can be enhanced through the use of mediators such as acetosyringone, syringaldehyde or *p*-coumaric acid. The role of the mediators in the process is shown in Figure 5.3.

An understanding of how laccase treatment removes lignin led researchers to realise that a more controlled lignin activation could be an advantage in self-binding technologies, and studies of the use of laccase in composite formation, initially with fungi-degraded lignin as a binder (Jin et al., 1990) showed how laccase can be used to activate the lignin. Kharazipour et al. (1997) showed that it was possible to reactivate the lignin on the surface of the wood fibres, the activation achieved after 12 hours incubation being sufficient to enable binding within wood composites when the fibres were compressed. This work, along with that of Felby et al. (1997, 2002, 2004) confirmed the potential to achieve self-bonded composites. The work of Felby et al. (1997) suggested the direct oxidation cycle shown in Figure 5.4.

The free radicals resulting from the oxidised lignin components released by the laccase oxidation (either direct or mediator-assisted) can undergo polymerisation, resulting in a new network by methods reminiscent of thermosetting resins (Kunamneni et al., 2008; Spulber et al., 2014). It is thus possible to use surface coating and modification of solid wood via lignin activation and to achieve new networks with, for example, resin systems.

Other enzymes for treating wood

While laccase is the enzyme that has attracted the most research in recent years, the development of bio-refining as part of green chemistry has increased interest in using enzymes to produce chemicals from low-value feedstock. Treating celluloses and hemicelluloses with enzymes has been considered (Cheng and Gu, 2012) by ester formation, amidation, oxidation, glycosylation and hydrolysis. Typically, the media used have been polar aprotic solvents, water, or mixed solvents. Applying these reactions requires that the reagent used be soluble in a chosen solvent, and low molecular-weight by-products, which can further enhance reactivity by secondary reactions (e.g., through the release and reaction of aldehydes or acids) or via catalytic activity may be produced.

Bacterial incising

Wood degradation may also occur through bacterial decay. Such decay usually occurs in an oxygen-depleted anoxic environment where conventional decay fungi cannot function, as with erosion bacteria in waterlogged samples under water. As far back as the early 1970's, studies were undertaken to better understand how bacteria affect wood and Greaves (1971) classified bacteria causing wood degradation into four categories:

1) those that affect permeability but cause no loss of strength,
2) those that attack the wood structure,

3) those that work synergistically with other bacteria to break down wood, and

4) passive colonisers that may be antagonists to other bacterial populations.

Thorough overviews of bacterial decay, including how bacterial decay affects the wood permeability, have been published, e.g., Rossell et al. (1973), Clausen (1996) and Johnston et al. (2016). Some bacterial decay can be very slow but bacterial incising of wood can work in ways similar to fungal incising, with total penetration of wood samples after 4–6 weeks exposure. Liese and Bauch (1967) and Greaves (1969) showed that bacterial pectinases attack the membrane and the bordered pit, resulting in complete degradation of the pit membrane, as well as erosion of the secondary wall layers of fibres and tracheids, but longer exposure times are necessary for the degradation of refractory softwoods with lignified parenchyma (e.g., Norway spruce) than for species such as Scots pine (Daniel, 2014) and this needs to be taken into account when considering new treatment protocols.

Pánek and Reinprecht (2011) reported that the bacterium *Bacillus subtilis* has attracted interest for several reasons:

- the bacterium is common in soil, water and also in humans,
- it is non-toxic to humans and also to aquatic organisms, which means that it can be regarded as environmentally-friendly,
- it is highly resistant, capable of surviving unfavourable conditions, and
- it increases the durability of wood towards other wood-destroying agents.

Refractory species has been incised with *Bacillus subtilis* (Pánek and Reinprecht, 2008), *Bacillus licheniformis* (Yildiz et al., 2012), and *Bacillus polymyxa* (Knuth and McCoy, 1962). The use of further genera has been reported by Rossell et al. (1973) and Schmidt and Dietrichs (1976), including Pseudomonas, Flavobacterium and Serratia, while Kurowski and Dunleavy (1976) identified *Cytophaga johnsonii* and Macken and Pickaver (1979) suggested *Enterobacter cloacae* as potential species for improving permeability. While log-pond storage ("ponding") has long been a means of storage, it has also been found to promote degradation by bacteria such as *Pseudomonas* sp. and *Staphylococcus* sp. (Kobayashi et al., 1998).

The mechanism of bacterial incising is now fairly-well understood, but the method has not yet been applied as a pre-treatment prior to wood modification. The only uses of bacteria for wood protection appear to be in an increased uptake of wood preservatives or as an antagonist treatment to prevent subsequent fungal decay.

Treatment with natural extracts

The various biosynthetic pathways adopted by nature have led to a vast range of compounds, many of which provide some degree of protection for the species in question. Natural oils form one group of chemicals, consisting of many thousands of molecular types of varying size and complexity. Some of these oils have been found to have physiological or therapeutic activities, either on their own or as part of a synergistic system, and they are, therefore, used in the pharmaceutical, agronomic, food, sanitary, and cosmetic industries, with some plants having been in use as medicines by humans for around 60,000 years, and it is estimated that 65% of the world's population currently relies on plants for their primary health care (Cowan, 1999). The most common types of natural oils are alkaloids, flavonoids, tannins, and phenolic compounds. Some extracted compounds that have been structurally characterised are shown in Figure 5.5. These have been isolated from the heartwood of the tropical species Angelique (Anouhc et al., 2018), and they contribute to the natural durability of the species, but the extraction of these compounds as a subsequent wood treatment has often been unsuccessful, probably due to synergistic effects of the chemicals to the wood structure.

Xavier-Junior et al. (2016) considered the roles of these compounds, particularly in their application as aqueous microemulsions for non-wood end uses. Mohareb et al. (2013) demonstrated

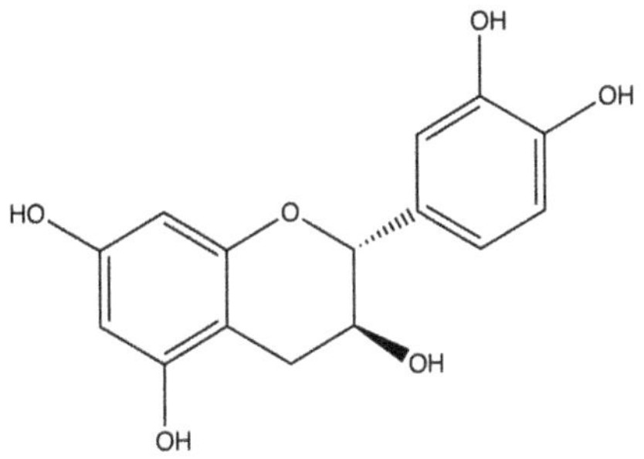

Figure 5.5 Some extracted compounds contributing to the natural durability of Angelique (Anouhe et al., 2018). (1) is (+)-catechin, (2) is (-)-epicatechin, (3) is neoastilbin, (4a) is astilbin and (4b) is isoastilbin.

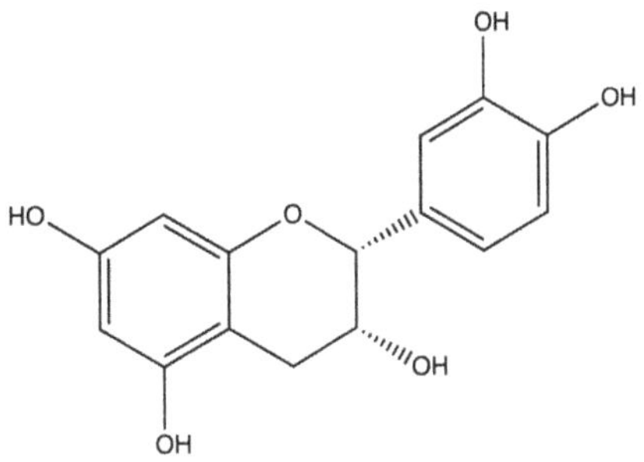

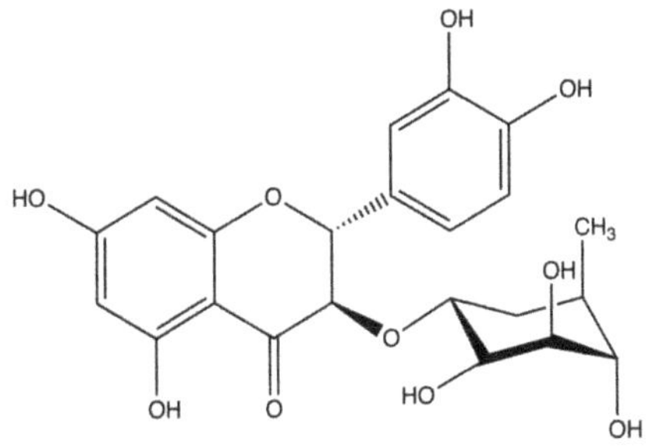

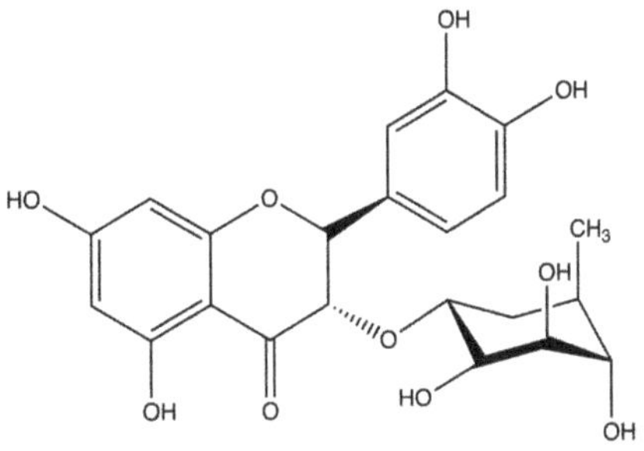

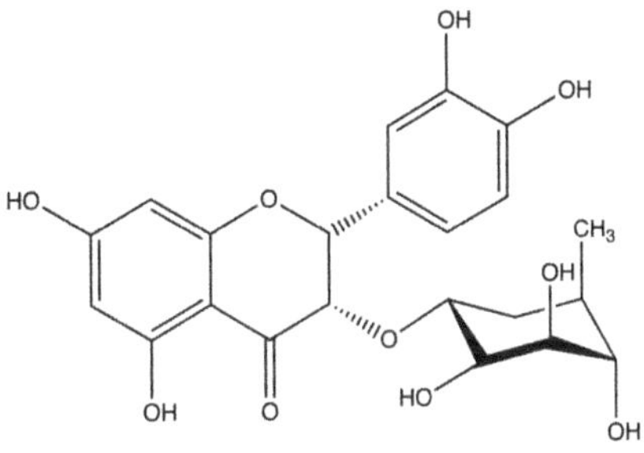

the *in vitro* and *in vivo* antifungal activity of essential oils against wood decay fungi and the potential use particularly of oils from the leaves or fruit of the American pepper, citrus tree, eastern white cedar, Italian cypress, sweet scented geranium (*Pelargonium graveolens* L'Hér.) and wormwood as preservatives to inhibit wood decay caused by *Hexagonia apiaria* and *Ganoderma lucidum*. However, if essential oils are to be used as alternatives for synthetic wood preservatives, further studies are required to evaluate their toxicity and the long-term effectiveness of treatment on wood.

Chittenden and Singh (2011) evaluated natural extracts against a range of commonly occurring rot fungi and moulds, and they showed that geranium oil, eugenol and cinnamaldehyde extracts had beneficial effects in preventing decay, but when specimens were subjected to leaching (as prescribed in standard methods such as EN84) the high levels of mass loss indicated that such treatments were unsuitable for outdoor use (such as cladding or decking) unless some additional fixation or sealing was undertaken. A similarly comprehensive overview of various natural oils (Table 5.1) was presented by Pánek et al. (2014), who found the oils to be effective against *Coniophora puteana*, suggesting that they would be effective for interior use. The need to fixate the oils was also suggested, together with encapsulation of the treated wood with a surface coating.

Table 5.1 Various natural oils and their effective components (Pánek et al., 2014).

Common name	Major effective components
Birch	Methyl salicylate (99%)
Clove	Eugenol (82%), caryophyllene (16.5%)
Lavender	Linalyl acetate (37.1%), linalool (33.6%), terpinen-4-ol (2.6%)
Oregano	Carvacrol (71.8%), thymol (5%), γ-terpinene (4.5%)
Sweet flag	*Cis*-isoasarol trimethylether (78%)
Savory	γ-terpinene (41.3%), carvacrol (31.6%), *p*-cymol (13.8%)
Sage	α-thujone (26.7%), camphor (20.2%), 1-8-cineole (9.6%)
Tea-tree	Terpinen-4-ol (42.2%), γ-terpinene (20.8%), α-terpinene (9.8%), 1,8-cineole (3.6%)
Thyme	Thymol (41.3%), *p*-cymol (22.6%), γ-terpinene (7.7%), carvacrol (2.9%)
Oil mixture (1:1:1:1:1 by mass) of sage, thyme, eucalyptus, lavender and lemon	α-thujone (5.3%), thymol (8.2%), 1-8-cineole (18.3%), linalool (7.8%), linalyl acetate (7.4%), limonene (14.2%), *p*-cymol (4.5%)

Another way of using plant extracts was proposed by Shiny et al. (2019), who suggested that leaf extracts of neem, pongamia, lantana and the extract of orange peel mixed with copper sulphate solution gave a nano-copper oxide preservative system that was a stable and environmentally benign wood preservative.

Another natural compound that has attracted attention in recent years is propolis or "bee glue" which consists of wax and resin, but has a variable composition and colour depending on bee species, on the plants from which the material is collected, and on the local environment and time of year when it is collected. It has been studied for use as a wood-finishing product (Budija et al., 2008), based on its favourable colour. The colour depends on its age, since it becomes darker the longer it is present in the hive. Propolis is usually found around the entrance to the hive (where the greatest accumulation is found) and around the frames. It acts as a disinfectant, providing bio-protection for the hive, which is important due to the high operating temperature and humidity of the hive environment. The key components of propolis (Woźniak et al., 2020) include pinocembrin, galangin, chrysin, kaempferol, apigenin and *p*-coumaric acid (Figure 5.6).

Early studies into the use of propolis showed that treatment of Scots pine with propolis was capable of achieving very high durability against *Coniophora puteana* and *Poria placenta* when no leaching cycle, as required by EN 84, was applied (Jones et al., 2011), but leaching according to EN 84 lead to a loss of durability. Similarly, Budija et al. (2008) demonstrated that propolis extract derived effective resistance against *Trametes versicolor*, *Antrodia vaillantii*, and *Gloeophyllum trabeum*, and Woźniak et al. (2020) have also reported its effectiveness against *C. puteana*, although there is some uncertainty as to whether their samples underwent EN 84 extraction prior to fungal decay testing.

A wide range of fungal species are known to produce coloured metabolites, where most research has focussed on food chemistry, and in particular, replacements for conventional carotenoid colourants. Mapari et al. (2005) reported that different fungal species produce a variety of compounds specific to the needs of the fungus, whether it be in preventing lethal photo-oxidation (typically through the production of carotenoids), limiting environmental stress (through the production of melanins) or producing compounds to assist in their enzymatic process (flavins). Mapari et al. (2005) received food colouring from environmentally-friendly sources, and Duran et al. (2002) showed that anthraquinone compounds, such as catenarin, chrysophanol, cynodontin, helminthosporin, tritisporin and erythroglaucin (Figure 5.7), can be obtained from fungal species such as *Eurotium* spp., *Fusarium* spp., *Curvularia lunata* and *Drechslera* spp.

Some of the metabolites extracted from different fungi are listed in Table 5.2 (Mapari et al., 2005). Of these, the compounds from *Monascus* spp., and in particular those of *Monascus purpureus*,

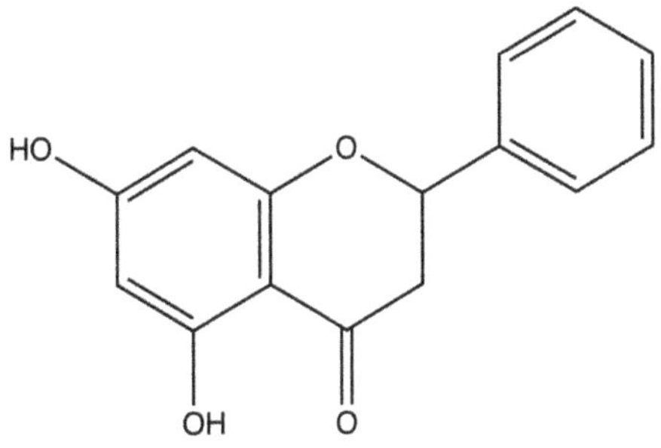

Pinocembrin

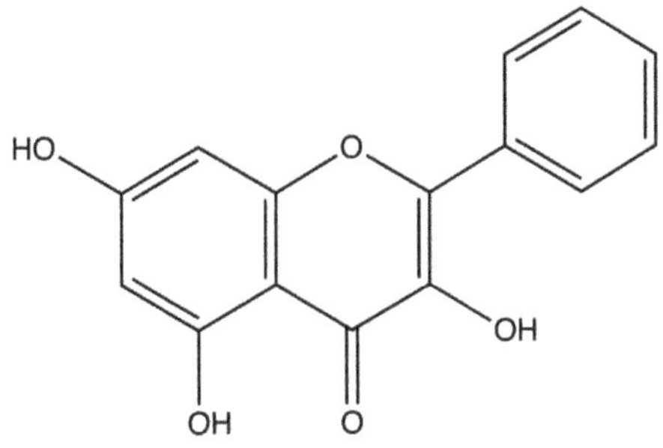

Galangin

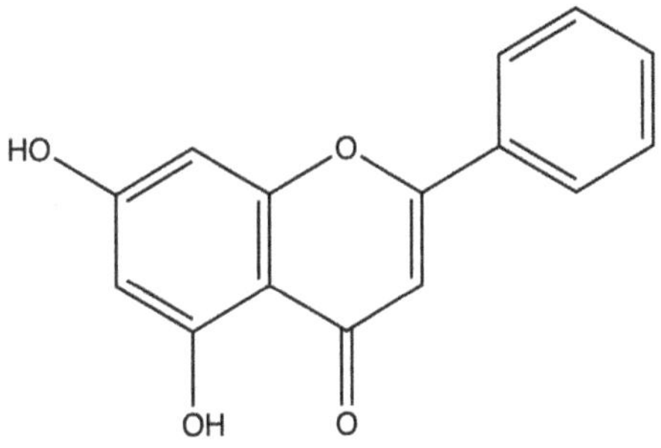

Chrysin

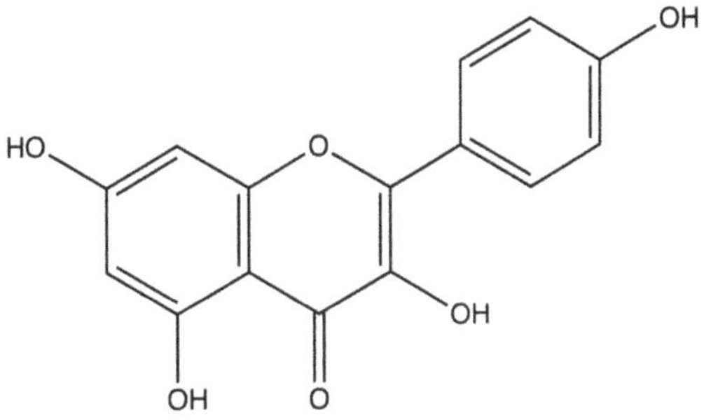

Kaempferol

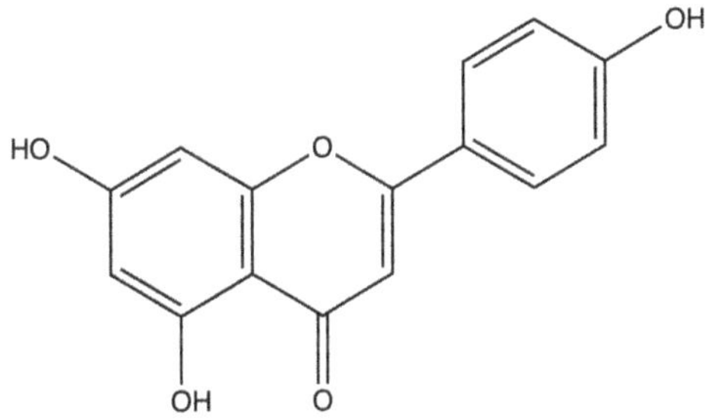

Apigenin

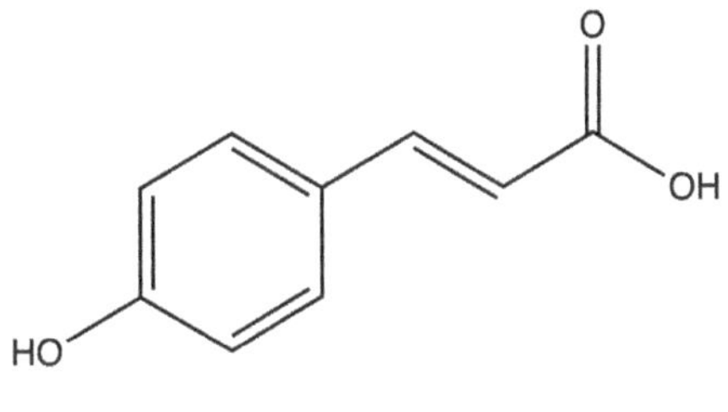

p-Coumaric acid

Figure 5.6 Major components extractable from propolis (Woźniak et al., 2020).

have become well-established in the food industry, since many of the coloured compounds have a high reactivity to primary amines, resulting in deep red-coloured compounds.

The application of coloured metabolites to materials has gained interest in other fields, such as the textile industry. Dramada is an orange-red pigment derived from *Scytalidium cuboideum* (Sacc. & Ellis) Sigler & Kang that has been assessed for textiles (Weber et al., 2014) and paints (Robinson et al., 2018), and similar assessments have been made with xylindein, a green dimeric naphthoquinone pigment produced by the *Chlorociboria* fungi. The highly conjugated nature of the latter pigment has meant that it has also attracted interest as a possible semiconductor. Xylindein occurs naturally in the colouration produced in wood spalting and this topic, more commonly associated with arts and crafts, is gaining interest as alternative ways of achieving wood modification are being explored. The fungus *Scytalidium ganodermophthorum* Kang, Sigler, Y.W. Lee & S.H. Yun is known to leave a yellow colouration on spalted timber and Van Court et al. (2020) recently showed that the colour depends on the exposure time and pH level, with the long-term exposure of *S. ganodermophthorum*

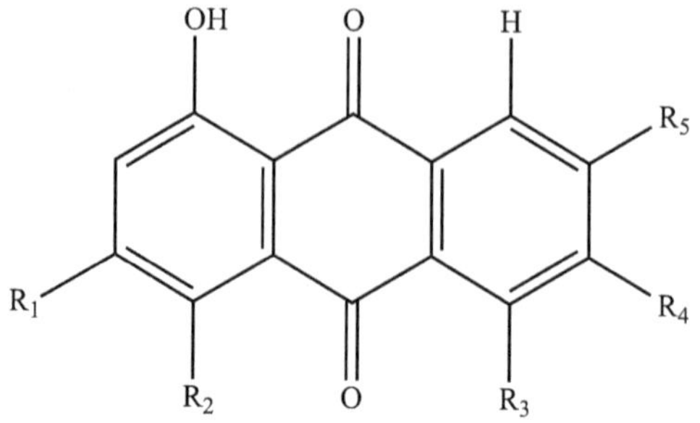

Hydroxyanthraquinones

Name	R_1	R_2	R_3	R_4	R_5	Colour
Catenarin	OH	H	OH	CH$_3$	H	Red
Chrysophanol	H	H	H	CH$_3$	H	Red
Cynodontin	H	OH	OH	H	CH$_3$	Bronze
Helminthosporin	H	OH	H	CH$_3$	H	Maroon
Tritisporin	OH	H	OH	CH$_2$OH	H	Red-brown
Erythroglaucin	OCH$_3$	H	OH	CH$_3$	H	Red

Figure 5.7 Anthroquinone compounds derived from fungal species such as *Eurotium* spp., *Fusarium* spp., *Curvularia lunata* and *Drechslera* spp. (Mapari et al., 2005).

leading to a purple colouration. The modification of wood in terms aesthetics, conductivity and optical-electric properties is a rapidly expanding area of research.

Conclusions regarding biological treatment

Biological treatments and pre-treatments have been applied to wood for some time, and the potential to alter the properties of wood through biological treatment has meant that new products and processes have been developed, particularly in conjunction with wood preservation. Work continues to further improve these methods and assess their applicability either directly to modify wood or as a part of a combined wood modification process. It is evident that the combined use of biological treatment and wood modification is entering a new period of interest and application.

5.3 Biomimetics

Humanity is constantly striving towards better ways of manufacturing and constructing our built environment. Over the past centuries, styles and materials of choice have varied considerably, but in recent times, architects and designers have focused on trying to copy what we see every day in the designs of nature. Originally, the focus was on structural components, but the emphasis is now on applying specific natural traits of materials, some of which are directly related to wood modification. This section briefly summarises the development of biomimetics and how wood modification can play a role in delivering high-performance materials.

Table 5.2 Overview of coloured metabolites from various fungal species (Mapari et al., 2005).

Fungal source	Pigment	Colour	Comments
Ascomycetes			
Monascus spp.	Monascorubrin	Orange	Well known in the Orient. Heat and pH-stable, give water-soluble red pigments on reacting with amino acids.
	Rubopunctatin	Orange	
	Monascin	Yellow	
	Ankaflavin	Yellow	
	Monascusones	Yellow	
Anamorphic Ascomycetes			
Epicoccum nigrum	Flavipin	Yellow	Water-soluble, antioxidant properties, high degree of colouring
	Orevactaene	Orange	
	Unknown	Yellow	
Paecilomyces sinclairii	Unknown	Red at pH 3–4, violet at pH 5–9 and pink at pH 10–12	Light-stable, production via submerged cultivation. A known insect pathogen.
Penicillium herquei	Atrovenetin	Yellow	Antioxidant
Roesleria hypogea and *Penicillium atrovenetum*	Herqueinone	Red	
	Norherqueinone	Red	
	Unknown	Bluish green	
Penicillium oxalicum var. *armeniaca*	Arpink Red™	Dark red	Commercial product, pH- and heat-stable.
Penicillium purpurogenum	Purpurogenone	Orange-yellow	Typically dark pink pigments
	Mitorubrin	Yellow	
	Mitorubrinol	Orange-red	
Penicillium persicinum	Unknown	Reddish pink	Still under investigation
Penicillium fagi	Unknown	Greenish blue	Difficult to extract from mycelium

What is biomimetics?

Biomimetics or biomimicry is the imitation of the models, systems, and elements of nature in order to solve a specific human problem. The terms *biomimetics* and *biomimicry* derive from Ancient Greek: βίος (bios), life, and μίμησις (mīmēsis), imitation, but although the term biomimetics literally means life-imitation, the breadth and scope of this term has become vast.

Living organisms have evolved well-adapted structures and materials over geological time through natural selection. Biomimetics has given rise to new technologies inspired by the way nature has solved engineering problems, such as self-healing, tolerance and resistance to environmental exposure, hydrophobicity, self-assembly, and the harnessing of solar energy.

Biomimetics in architecture

Since historical times, architecture has drawn inspiration from nature for constructions, resulting in the architectural style referred to as biomorphism. Early examples incorporating the styles and strengths of naturally occurring shapes and elements can be seen in the work of the ancient Greeks and Romans, where natural motifs such as tree-inspired columns were incorporated into building structures. Trees and their expansion into the crowns have been copied ever since. One example of architectural design based on but not using trees and timber is the Sagrada Família church in Barcelona, designed by Antoni Gaudi, where branching canopies of trees provided the inspiration for solving the problem of supporting the main vault in the cathedral. Another tree-inspired supporting structure can be found in Stuttgart airport, where the main hall has branched supporting columns resembling trees, but the best example of tree-inspired architecture is perhaps the vertical garden structures in the Marina Bay area in Singapore, where 18 giant tree-like structures provide the framework for integrating over 226,000 plants consisting of over 200 species with a host of other functions, such as solar power generation, rainwater collection and acting as ventilation towers for the horticultural conservatories below. Sometimes, smaller inspirations can lead to constructional units such as the FAZ Pavilion in Frankfurt, which is a structure inspired by the microarchitecture of a conifer cone.

Biomimetics for wood treatment

Durai Prabhakaran et al. (2019) recently reviewed the importance of biomimetics and outlined a range of characteristics and mechanisms that are providing bio-derived solutions to existing problems. Among these are methods directly related to wood treatment and particularly wood modification to achieve water repellence and self-cleaning.

Biomimetics and water repellency

The interaction of wood with moisture in a structural concept has long been a cause for concern (see Section 1.4), and reducing the moisture sensitivity is one of the key tasks of wood modification, but when the biomimicry of a biological system for water repellence is considered it is superhydrophobicity that is commonly referred to. The basis for this is the water repellence of lotus (*Nelumbo* spp.) leaves, which is due to a combination of papillae with a dense coating of wax tubules grouped together (Ensikat et al., 2011). High levels of wax are known to result in water repellence, and this has led to the development of modification methods incorporating waxes and natural oils.

In order to achieve a level of superhydrophobicity similar to that exhibited by the lotus leaf (with contact angles of water in excess of 150°), the wood surface must be modified to give a permanent change in properties using methods such as those briefly described below:

Deposition of metals and metal oxides

The idea of the depositing a metal onto a surface is well established for the protection particularly of other metal surfaces, often via electrodeposition (Losey et al., 2017), and the deposition of metal and metal oxide layers onto wood has gained interest in recent years. Gao et al. (2015) investigated the chemical deposition of silver nanoparticles onto Ussuri poplar by treatment with $AgNO_3$ followed by a reduction with glucose, and they obtained a rough nanometallic surface which exhibited not only electrical conductivity but also sterilising properties. Superhydrophobisation was established through a secondary treatment with (heptadecafluoro-1,1,2,2-tetradecyl)trimethoxysilane $(CF_3(CF_2)_7CH_2CH_2Si(OCH_3)_3)$. The deposition of nano-silver onto wood was also studied by Moya et al. (2017), where silver nitrate was reduced using ethylene glycol and polyvinylpyrrolidone was used to prevent agglomeration of the resulting nanoparticles. The presence of silver nanoparticles on the surface of several tropical hardwood species was found to prevent white rot decay by *Trametes versicolor*, although it was less effective against the brown rot fungus *Lenzites acuta*.

Wang et al. (2010) used zinc oxide to grow zinc nanorods on the wood surface presumably as a result of an initial reaction between zinc and guaiacol groups in the wood lignin, as shown in Figure 5.8. Zinc-guaiacol bonds are stronger than wood-water interactions and they are, thus, relatively stable. Wang et al. (2010) used zinc nitrate hexahydrate $(Zn(NO_3)_2.6H_2O)$, ammonium chloride (NH_4Cl), urea $((NH_2)_2CO)$, ammonia hydroxide (NH_4OH), sodium hydroxide $(NaOH)$, and stearic acid $(C_{17}H_{35}COOH)$, with the use of cyclic vacuum and pressure cycles to accelerate the nanorod growth.

In addition to providing a microstructure on the wood surface, zinc also enhances bacterial, fungal and termite resistance (Clausen et al., 2009; Kartal et al., 2009; Bak et al., 2012), as well as UV-resistance (Blanchard and Blanchett, 2011), leaching resistance (Clausen et al., 2010) and water repellence and dimensional stability (Soltani et al., 2013).

Similar interactions between metals and guaiacol groups have been shown for lead (II), lead (IV), tin (II), chromium (VI) (Kubel and Pizzi, 1981). Whereas lead and zinc were found to form

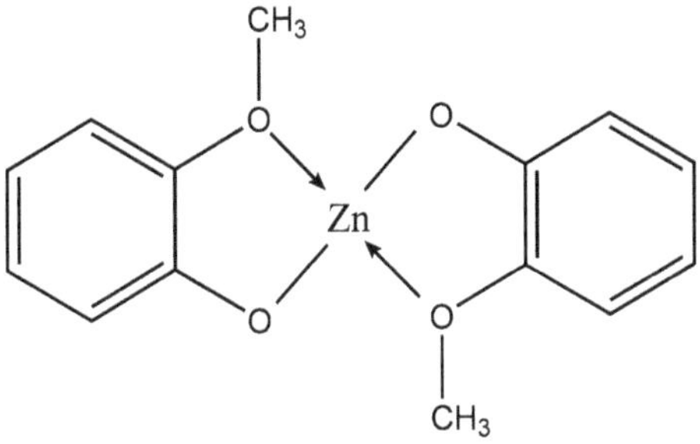

Figure 5.8 Proposed interaction between zinc and guaiacol groups (Wang et al., 2010).

dimeric links to guaiacol units, IR spectroscopy has shown that tin (II) and especially chromium (VI) were capable of forming polymeric links to guaiacol. It is this ability of chromium (VI), usually in the form of chromium trioxide with lignin groups, that is responsible for the UV-stability of chromium-treated wood samples (Evans et al., 1992).

The use of concentrated electrolytic solutions has been reported to be an efficient way of introducing metal salts into polymeric systems (Merk et al., 2017), and this method has been used to deposit barium sulfate into the cell lumen and secondary walls. The location and structure of the salt deposit were determined using a combination of scanning electron microscopy, Raman mapping and scanning micro-focused wide-angle X-ray scattering. They growth appeared to progress from the mineralised cell walls towards the lumen centre via dendritic crystals. This method could lead to templated crystal engineering and the design of new bio-inspired materials.

Some bacterial species, such as *Aquaspirillum magnetotacticum*, which are found in marine sediments, have a built-in degree of magnetism, due to their ability to produce chains of intracellular magnetite crystals. Similar magnetic properties can be built into other naturally occurring polymeric systems, including wood and lignocellulosic materials, through the introduction of maghemite (γ-Fe_2O_3) or ferrite (Fe_3O_4) using thermo-mechanical pulp (TMP) (Raymond et al., 1994), cellulosic fibres (Marchessault et al., 1992a) or paper (Marchessault et al., 1992b). A cationic polyelectrolyte, such as polyethyleneimine (PEI), has been used as an aid to improve filler retention, and its use in papermaking improves properties such as drainage and wet strength (Zakaria, 2005). Marchessault et al. (1992a) suggested that magnetic properties could also be incorporated into cross-linked sulfate-containing polysaccharides gels, oxidised starch and chitosan.

Most of the applications where magnetic properties have been introduced into lignocellulosic systems have been at the fibrous level, where the hierarchal structure has been mechanically or chemically removed. The use of the hierarchal structure of wood within biomimetics has been reviewed by Berglund and Burgert (2018). Trey et al. (2014) showed that Southern yellow pine veneers could be pressure impregnated with Fe_3O_4, $MnFe_2O_4$ or $CoFe_2O_4$, and that uptakes of up to 20% by weight could be achieved. Scanning electron microscopy combined with energy-dispersive X-ray spectroscopy (SEM-EDX) showed that the magnetic material was dispersed in the lumen, as well as in the cell walls and middle lamella. The uptake was higher in treated early wood. Crystal structure analysis showed that the magnetic deposition resulted in faceted shapes and flakes, depending on the wood cell structure, in contrast to the conventional spheres and cubes when allowed to form freely.

Treatment with organic compounds

The idea behind biomimicry of naturally occurring items, such as lotus leaves, is inspired by the presence of waxes on the leaf surface, leading to treatment with oils and waxes, as reported in Section 2.10. Similarly, treatment of wood with silane compounds can impart hydrophobicity, depending on the character of the side-chain groups present (see Section 2.7). However, to achieve superhydrophobicity, longer chain groups are required, as shown by Wang et al. (2013), who studied

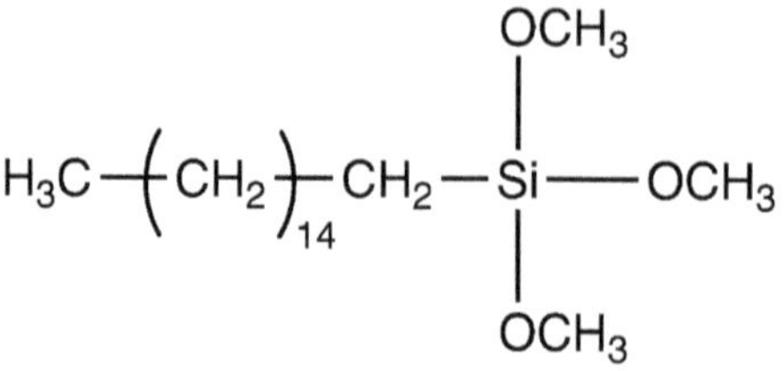

$$H_3C-(CH_2)_{14}-CH_2-\underset{\underset{OCH_3}{|}}{\overset{\overset{OCH_3}{|}}{Si}}-OCH_3$$

Figure 5.9 Structure of hexadecyltrimethyoxysilane.

the effect of treating wood with hexadecyltrimethoxysilane (Figure 5.9), the hexadecyl group often being called a cetyl group.

It is possible to increase the hydrophobicity of siloxanes by incorporating long-chain alkyl groups, and this concept has already been applied within the textile sector to create water-repellent finishes, often using waterborne polyurethanes. In their traditional form, these waterborne polyurethanes are soluble and wash out of materials, so longer side chains are incorporated to increase their hydrophobicity, opening the door to the use of waterborne polyurethanes as wood surface treatments. Liu et al. (2019) used glyceryl monostearates for alter the properties of the polyurethane, resulting in glyceryl monostearate-modified waterborne polyurethanes through self-emulsification. More complex polyurethane structures were also produced using branched alcohols, such as trimethylolpropane (a trihydric alcohol). They reported that the glyceryl monostearate-modified waterborne polyurethanes provided an effective surface coating comprising siloxane moieties linked together by groups having three stearyl groups protruding from the material surface, forming hydrophobic "hairs" that water molecules were unable to bind to or penetrate.

A recent development by Janssen in Belgium (Mookerjee et al. 2017) has focused on the development of complex formulations for the hydrophobisation of various surfaces, including wood. The treatment is claimed to consist of (i) a metal C_{3-8} alkyloxide, such as tetrabutyl orthotitanate (TBOT) or aluminum isopropoxide (AlIP), and (ii) an alkyl ketene dimer (AKD), in association with (iii) a combined UV-absorber/radical scavenger UV protection system. This is still at the prototype scale, with the company seeking collaborative activities with other parties.

Sol-gel techniques

As mentioned in Section 2.7, wood modification treatments involving silicon compounds are often referred to as sol-gel techniques, where solid materials are produced from small molecules by the conversion of a monomer into a colloidal solution (sol) that acts as the precursor for an integrated network (or gel) of either discrete particles or network polymers. This applies not only to silicon, but also to nanoparticulate treatments.

Some of the key alkoxysilanes that have been used to modify wood are tetraethoxysilane (TEOS), methyl triethoxysilane (MTEOS), propyl triethoxysilane (PTEO), and methyltrimethoxysilane (MTMOS). In a recent review of the hydrophobisation of wood, Wang and Piao (2011) described the preparation and deposition using these components according to the following steps:

1) solution stage – silanol formation from the hydrolysis of alkoxysilanes, leading to a combination of alkoxysilanes with mono- and oligosilanols,

2) gelation stage – linking of liquid and solid elements in a 3-dimensional gel-type lattice, stabilised by hydrogen bonding between the components, and

3) drying stage – where the cross-linked, highly condensed gels become covalently bonded to the wood substance.

These three stages are shown in Figure 5.10, as proposed by Tshabalala et al. (2003).

Table 5.3 lists some of the alkoxysilanes used in the sol-gel treatment of wood. There are countless examples of the use of alkoxysilanes in non-wood applications, e.g., disubstituted dialkoxysilanes for lipase immobilisation (Bolagh-Weiser et al., 2012).

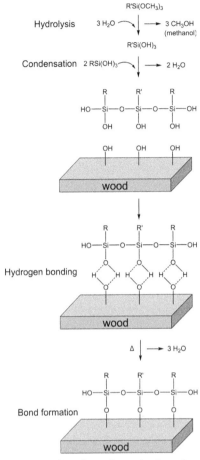

Figure 5.10 Diagram of the alkoxysilane sol-gel reaction with wood.

Table 5.3 Examples of alkoxysilanes used in sol-gel processes.

Chemical name	Reference
Tetraethoxysilane (TEOS)	Donath et al., 2004
Tetra-l-propoxysilane (TPOS)	Bernards et al., 1991
Methyltrimethoxysilane (MTMOS)	Saka and Ueno, 1997
Methyl triethoxysilane (MTES)	Donath et al., 2004
Propyl triethoxysilane (PTEO)	Donath et al., 2004
Hexadecyltrimethoxysilane (HDTMOS)	Tshabalala et al., 2009
Phenyltrimethoxysilane (PTMOS)	Jermouni et al., 1995
Diphenyldimethoxysilane (DPDMOS)	Jermouni et al., 1995
Phenyltriethoxysilane (PTEOS)	Lee and Hsu, 2007
Silica/1H,1H, 2H,2H-perfluoroalkyltriethoxysilane (POTS)	Wang et al., 2011

The hydrophobicity of alkoxysilane-treated wood can be greatly increased by adding water-repellent agents, such as decyltrimethoxysilane, trifluoroacetic acid, and 2-hepta-decafluorooctylethyltri-methoxysilane (HFOETMOS), to the sol-gel system (Saka et al., 1992; Tanno et al., 1998; Tshabalala et al., 2003a).

The sol-gel process has also been used to improve the durability and fire retardancy of wood using alkoxysilane compounds, and it can also be used for the application of metallic salts such as titanium oxide (Hübert and Mahr, 2017).

Treatment with polymers

One of the easiest ways to protect the surface of wood (and hence its interior) is by applying a coating to the surface, and Sakhno et al. (2016) have recently identified polymer systems according to the following classifications:

1) coatings based on carboxyl-containing water-soluble polymers which are easily cross-linked by inorganic salts or OH-containing compounds, e.g., polyacrylic and polymethacrylic acids,

2) pH-sensitive coatings, e.g., by the copolymerisation of compounds such as vinyl acetate with maleic anhydride, maleic acid monoesters or crotonic acid, and

3) polymer multi-layer structures established through multiple hydrogen bonding between the layers based on the functionalities in each layer, e.g., poly(vinylpyrrolidone), poly(vinyl alcohol), poly(acrylamide) and poly(ethylene oxide).

A polymer such as poly(vinyl alcohol) is not suitable for direct use as a coating system to protect wood because of its poor mechanical properties, inorganic compounds such as silica must be used to create a composite film with appropriate properties, after which superhydrophobicity is achieved through the addition of octadecyltrichlorosiloxane (Liu et al., 2013).

Poly(vinyl alcohol) has been shown to provide good polymeric film capabilities in association with tetraethoxysiloxane (Guo et al., 2006), γ-mercaptopropyltriethoxysilane (Guo et al., 2007) and γ-aminopropyltriethoxysilane (Zhang et al., 2007), but Wang et al. (2014) suggested that polystyrene be used instead of poly(vinyl alcohol).

Treatment with plasma

It is important to achieve a clean surface before a coating is applied to wood. One of the best ways of achieving this is through a plasma treatment, as described in Section 4.3, which yields a hydrophobic surface, especially when combined with a secondary chemical treatment with, e.g., fluorinated monomer such as carbon tetrafluoride (Poaty et al., 2012) or sulfur hexafluoride (Zanini et al., 2008). The use of fluorinated compounds has gained interest in recent years. Pentafluoroethane, for example, has been used in an oxygen plasma (Xie et al., 2015), resulting in a thin, fluorocarbon layer with an atomic concentration of fluorine close to 50% and a highly hydrophobic wood surface.

Biomimetics and self-cleaning

Biomimicry has a particular potential benefit for wood treatment and coating is the area of self-cleaning. Studies of the lotus leaf show that hydrophobicity is linked to the potential of self-cleaning, because the repelled water droplets are associated with dirt particles on the surface, leading to their removal. Thus, all the reactions with siloxanes, polymers and plasma which give hydrophobic coatings can all be applied to some degree to the self-cleaning of wood, provided the water droplets are sufficient in size for their easy movement on the surface (Bhushan et al., 2009). An example of this overlapping of properties can be seen in the anti-stain, self-cleaning effects of a hydrophobic coating produced by the reaction of titanium dioxide nanoparticles and perfluorooctyltriethoxysilane (Pandit et al., 2019). Similarly, alkoxysilanes and metal oxides have a potential as self-cleaning surfaces, such as the dip coating method devised for alumina and polydiemethylsiloxane (Shah et al., 2017).

In recent years, nanocellulose has been shown to have hydrophobic properties suitable for use in coatings provided the costs are not prohibitive. Huang et al. (2018) recently treated cellulose nanocrystals (CNC) with 1H,1H,2H,2H-perfluorooctyltrichlorosilane, which was added in multiple stages.

Other potential biomimetic wood modifications

There are many areas where biomimicry can be applied in wood coating and modification technologies, as outlined in a comprehensive table of properties and potential applications by Durai Prabhakaran et al. (2019).

The method that has the greatest potential in modern society is self-healing coatings and treatments. Having a polymer capable of repairing cracks or other damage by a process of fluidisation of components in the coating is a desirable property making the material maintenance-free. A review by Mauldin and Kessler (2010) suggested several ways in which self-healing could be achieved, including crack filling, diffusion, bond reformation and mechanophoric strengthening where a mechanophore undergoes a mechanochemical transformation under external applied force. With bond reformation, particularly when initiated by UV radiation, it seems to be possible to achieve self-healing with wood coatings.

5.4 Mineralisation of wood

The natural mineralisation of wood is well known, in the fossil remains of trees found in predominantly sedimentary rock formations. Mineral salts dissolved in water permeate the wood tissue in a low oxygen environment which inhibits decay and the organic content of the wood is replaced by minerals, but the original cellular structure is retained. One of the most famous petrified forests is Ormachea, in Argentina, where the surface of the land is littered with petrified tree trunks that grew approximately 65 million years ago. These fossilised remains were washed from alongside rivers in the area, to be deposited in a sandy estuary where they were covered with sediment. Ultimately, with time, dissolved silica replaced the organic material of the tree and increasing temperature and pressure turned the trees and encasing sand to stone. Later, geological movement and upheaval of the surrounding sandstone rocks led to their proximity to the surface, continued exposure to weathering eroded the surrounding rocks, and the fossilised trunks were exposed.

Technically, Ormachea is not a petrified forest, but rather a geological "dumping ground". Another site in Argentina, Cerro Cuadrado, is a spectacular and famous Middle Jurassic fossil site where colossal trees have remained in their original position. Huge tree trunks and ancient monkey-puzzle trees can be found close to where they originally grew, their felling being a result of volcanic eruptions during the Jurassic period.

In addition to these sites in Argentina, other sites include the petrified forest in Arizona, USA (from the late Triassic epoch, approximately 225 million years ago). Even older is the petrified forest of Phoraxis, Namibia, which dates from approximately 280 million years ago. In fact, it has been suggested that these fossilised trees were not native to the region that is now Namibia but that they were washed to their final resting place by rivers in the old Godwanaland supercontinent.

The Sigri, Plaka and Nissiopi petrified forests on the Greek island of Lesbos represent more recent geological petrification, dating from 18–20 million years ago, with several modern-day species (e.g., pine, laurel, cinnamon plants, cottonwood, plane trees and palms) being fossilised as a result of local volcanic activity.

The petrification process includes a range of crystalline structures, including silica, calcite, dolomite, pyrite, goethite and apatite (Nowak et al., 2005), and various crystalline structures have been deposited at cell-wall interfaces, such as calcite-goethite, pyrite-calcite and goethite-silica. The deposition of silicic acid during the mineralisation can result in the formation of crystal (chalcedony) and opal (wood opal) over the millions of years of the process.

Since minerals have replaced organic material in petrified wood samples, the concept of replacing the cellular structures within wood with minerals by deposition is a subject that has been explored as a means of modifying the properties of wood.

Mineralisation with silica compounds

Since the natural mineralisation of wood involves silicon-based deposition, silicon was an obvious starting point for research into the modification of wood by partial mineralisation. Götze et al. (2008) used a colloidal solution of silicon dioxide to deposit siliceous glass on the surface of cell walls, significantly increasing the Brinell hardness and resulting in 40% less water absorption than untreated samples.

Doubek et al. (2018) investigated the reaction of European beech and silver fir with 0%, 1%, 5% and 10% colloidal solutions of SiO_2, impregnated at a pressure of 0.8 MPa for 1 hour at 20°C, but no mould resistance against *Aspergillus niger* and *Penicillium purpurogenum* according to EN 15457 (CEN, 2014) was observed, in contrast to earlier studies into alkoxysilanes such as methyl-tripotassium silanol (Reinprecht et al., 2013), or methyltrimethoxysilane (MTMS), vinyltrimethoxysilane (VTMS), propyltrimethoxysilane (PTMS), and 3-aminopropyltrimethoxysilane (APTMS) as described by Reinprecht and Grznárik (2015).

A key area of wood protection in recent years has been the incorporation of nano-silica. Bak et al. (2019) considered the deposition of silica nanoparticles alone or after a polydimethylsiloxane (PDMS) pre-treatment in both European beech and Scots pine. PDMS was used to improve the bonding of the silica nanoparticles to the wood structure. The shrinkage and swelling were reduced and the water uptake and equilibrium moisture content (EMC) were significantly decreased, particularly in combination with the PDMS pre-treatment.

In recent years, nano-silica has, been used as a filler and binder in new coating systems for wood, giving greater abrasion resistance and scratch resistance (Vu and Laferte, 2006). It has a similar filling effect when mixed with wood flour in the manufacture of wood plastic composites (WPCs) (Ma et al., 2020), using tetraethyl orthosilicate (TEOS) as the precursor. The subsequent inclusion of 3.8% nano-silica within a polypropylene-based WPC was found to significantly improve the thermal stability of the WPC, and also to improve the oxygen-aging resistance of the composite.

Clay is sometimes added to wood, primarily to act as a fire retardant. Wang et al. (2014) impregnated Cathay poplar with montmorillonite clay to improve its thermal stability. Montmorillonite is a naturally occurring aluminosilicate clay classed as a 2:1 phyllosilicate, where two tetrahedral silica layers sandwich an octahedral alumina layer, each layer being 1 nm thick. Montmorillonite is able to undergo metal cation exchange and encapsulation, providing an inert frame which permits regioselective reactions within the inter-layer spacings. The naturally occurring sodium cations can be replaced by quaternary ammonium groups such as didecyldimethylammonium chloride (Fang et al., 2012) and cetyltrimethylammonium bromide (Lin et al., 2011). SEM-EDX analysis of wood impregnated with organomontmorillonites showed the intercalation of the silicate layers in the cell walls (Wang et al., 2014).

With most wood-clay systems, the wood is delignified prior to impregnation with the clay layers. Fu et al. (2017) delignified balsa wood in order to provide a nanoporous scaffold essentially consisting of cellulose. This delignification necessary since untreated balsa was only able to take up a small amount of clay, ca. 4%. The delignified sample had a higher uptake of ca. 17%. The treatment led to a coherent organic/inorganic charred residue being formed in combustion tests, which strongly reduced both the heat release rate peak and smoke generation.

Clays such as montmorillonite have also been used as additives in adhesive systems. Lü et al. (2006) showed that the clay could be mixed with a water-soluble phenol formaldehyde (PF) resin to bond Chinese fir, and FTIR spectroscopy indicated that there was some form of bonding between the montmorillonite and the wood. Montmorillonite has also been used with melamine-urea formaldehyde (MUF) resin (Cai et al., 2010), urea-formaldehyde (UF) resin (Moya et al., 2015), polyvinylacetate (PVAc) resin (Moya et al., 2015) and protein resin (Bacigalupe et al., 2020).

Mineralisation with nanomaterials

Although nano-silica is used in wood modification, either through surface modification or as a coating, nanometals are used more for wood protection, due to their ability to alter the physicomechanical properties and durability of wood against biodegradation. It is generally agreed that nanosized metals may interact with bacterial elements causing cell death (Civardi et al., 2015b) and enzyme functions (Goffedo et al., 2017). Nano-copper is particularly important within the wood preservation industry (Freeman and McIntyre, 2008), and nanosized zinc and silver are also effective for wood protection (Akhtari et al., 2013).

Popadopoulos (2019) has reviewed key areas where nanometallic compounds may provide benefits in wood treatments:

- hydrophobisation—through a reduction of the pore size and space available within the cell wall,
- UV-stability—stability to UV radiation enhances the photoresistant properties of the wood,
- fire performance—nanoparticles alone or in combination with other fire-retardant chemicals reduce the ignitability of wood and the leaching of fire-retardant additives,
- antimicrobial properties—providing some degree of bioresistance in addition to its hydrophobic character reducing moisture uptake,
- mechanical properties—an increase in hardness, for example, because the nanomaterials fill cavities in the wood surface.

Nano-titania (nanosized titanium dioxide) has been shown to have a combined antimicrobial and cleaning effect against algal species (Polo et al., 2011), and similar effects are obtained when textile materials are treated with titanium dioxide in the presence of butane tetracarboxylic acid (BTCA) (Montazer and Seifollahzadeh, 2011). A more detailed description of self-cleaning properties has been given by Tung and Daoud (2011).

Mineralisation with carbonates

One of the most common minerals associated with the mineralisation of ancient biological samples is calcium carbonate. Merk et al. (2016) reported a simple strategy involving *in situ* mineral formation based on a solution-exchange process using alternating cycles with $CaCl_2$ in ethanol and $NaHCO_3$ in water, achieving mass gains of ca. 30% and 35% for European beech and Norway spruce, respectively. These levels of carbonate within the wood provide effective fire protection. Tsioptsias and Panayiotou (2011) proposed the use of supercritical carbon dioxide to convert calcium hydroxide, produced by reacting impregnated calcium chloride with sodium hydroxide, to calcium carbonate. This provided sufficient fire retardancy for spruce and beech samples that had a degree of hydrophobicity as a result of treatment with a commercial silane-siloxane solution.

Calcium carbonate can also be deposit in wood via a biomineralisation process attributed to by-products from metabolic pathways of various microbes (Dhami et al., 2013) such as:

1) photosynthetic organisms – cyanobacteria and algae,
2) sulphate reducing bacteria – responsible for dissimilatory reduction of sulphates,
3) organisms utilising organic acids, and
4) organisms that are involved in the nitrogen cycle – ammonification of amino acids/nitrate reduction/hydrolysis of urea.

Dhami et al. (2013) considered microbially induced calcium-carbonate precipitation (MICCP) via urea hydrolysis to be the simplest way to precipitate carbonates but, although this method has been used to introduce carbonates into rubber and plastic, it does not appear to have been applied to date in wood products.

5.5 Supercritical fluid treatments

Reagents are typically introduced into a material in liquid or gaseous form, but during recent decades, the use of supercritical fluids has gained popularity.

A supercritical fluid is a substance at a temperature and pressure above its critical point, where neither a distinct liquid nor a distinct gas phase exists, but which behaves as a gas and a liquid, effusing through solids like a gas, and dissolving materials like a liquid. As can be seen in Figure 5.11, a supercritical fluid exists at a critical pressure and temperature point where the properties of gases and liquids merge, where there is a convergence of the critical temperature (the highest temperature at which a gas can be converted into a liquid by an increase in pressure) and the critical pressure (the highest pressure at which a liquid can be converted into a gas by an increase in the temperature).

Almost all gases can be transformed into supercritical fluids above their specific critical pressure and temperature values, although very high temperatures and pressures are sometimes required. The critical pressure and temperature values increase with increasing molecular weight, intermolecular hydrogen bonding, or polarity, so most compounds that have been considered as supercritical fluids have a fairly low molecular weight (typically under 100 g/mol, although there are some exceptions, such as sulfur hexafluoride). Some examples of supercritical fluids are given in Table 5.4.

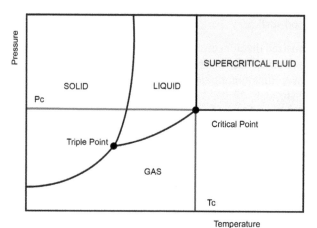

Figure 5.11 Schematic interpretation of a supercritical fluid in relation to other phases. P_c is the critical pressure and T_c is the critical temperature.

Table 5.4 Properties of some commonly used supercritical fluids.

Supercritical fluid	Chemical formula	Molecular weight (g/mol)	Critical temperature (°C)	Critical pressure (MPa)
Carbon dioxide	CO_2	44.01	31.2	7.4
Methane	CH_4	16.04	-82.7	4.6
Trifluoromethane	CHF_3	70.01	25.9	4.7
Ethane	C_2H_6	30.07	32.2	4.9
Propane	C_3H_8	44.09	96.7	4.3
Ethylene	C_2H_4	28.05	9.1	5.1
Propylene	C_3H_6	42.08	36.5	4.6
Methanol	CH_3OH	32.04	240	8.1
Ethanol	C_2H_5OH	46.07	241	6.1
Acetone	$(CH_3)_2O$	58.08	235	4.7
Nitrous oxide	N_2O	44.01	36.5	4.1
Water	H_2O	18.02	374	22
Sulfur hexafluoride	SF_6	146.06	45.5	3.8
Xenon	Xe	54.0	16.6	5.9

Carbon dioxide (CO_2) is currently the most accepted supercritical fluid in practical applications. As a result of the increasingly stringent environmental regulations, supercritical CO_2 (SC-CO_2) has become a popular alternative to toxic solvents, being non-toxic, non-combustible, recyclable, abundantly available, eco-friendly, and cost-efficient. This has led to its use in a variety of technologies such as chromatography, extraction, dry-cleaning, impregnation and decomposition processes. The non-toxicity carbon dioxide makes it commercially viable, particularly within the food and pharmaceutical industries, often for purification or extraction purposes, such as the decaffeination of coffee and the production of resin-free cork for wine bottles.

The main advantages of processes based on SC-CO_2 are:

- mild processing temperatures, generally below 50°C,
- inert atmosphere, suitable for processing unstable compounds,
- absence or reduced use of organic solvents and, in the latter case, residual levels below legal limits, and
- high purity products, avoiding post-processing steps, i.e., filtration and drying as in conventional crystallisation/precipitation processes.

Since SC-CO_2 is a non-polar solvent, it has a very poor ability to dissolve highly polar water molecules. This can be resolved by modifying SC-CO_2 with a polar compound such as methanol or ethanol (as they have similar molar masses and critical temperatures to carbon dioxide) to improve its affinity with polar compounds, although other compounds can be used to modify the properties of the supercritical fluid for specific applications.

Supercritical fluid extraction and liquefaction processes for wood

Cellulosic material has been converted with supercritical water at its high critical temperature and pressure (e.g., Adschiri et al., 1990; Saka and Ueno, 1999), but under such harsh conditions complete degradation of additional volatiles occurs. Processes using alcohols gave a gentler extraction process, with much of the wood structure remaining (Yamazaki et al., 2006), although the critical temperatures are only slightly lower, but increasing homologues of alcohols were less effective in extraction.

Demirbaş (2001) indicated in studies that included oriental beech and oriental spruce that acetone, methanol or ethanol resulted in similar percentages of extractives, despite their critical temperatures being more than 100°C lower. Fatty acids predominated over resin acids with supercritical acetone (Demirbaş, 1991) and it was suggested that the reduction in resin acids was due to compounds such as levopimaric, palustric and neoabietic acids being isomerised to abietic acid and then dehydrogenated to dehydroabietic acid (Joye and Lawrence, 1961; Hafızoğlu, 1979). Fractionation of the hemicelluloses can be influenced by supercritical fluids, particularly when the SC-CO_2 has an acidic additive, such as acetic acid (Bogolitsyn et al., 2017).

The desire to convert naturally occurring sugars in hemicellulose, for example, into chemicals normally derived from petrochemicals has led to a great increase in biochemical refining. A key reaction is the conversion of sugars into furfural (see Section 2.5), which is widely used in the manufacture of inks, plastics, antacids, adhesives, nematicides, fungicides, fertilisers, and flavouring compounds. It is also used as a solvent and can be converted into a range of compounds, including furfuryl alcohol, tetrahydrofuran (THF) and levulinic acid. Levulinic acid can also be derived from 5-hydroxymethyl furfural (HMF) (Antonetti et al., 2016). Gairola and Smirnova (2012) have shown that D-xylose and hemicelluloses can be converted to furfural in catalyst-free SC-CO_2.

Supercritical fluids may also be used commercially to obtain extractives and volatiles from wood and lignocellulosic materials, including monoterpenes (Wong et al., 2001), flavours and fragrances (Capuzzo et al., 2013), and oils extracted from three different cedar species (Du et al., 2009), which were found to be effective to different extent against a brown rot fungus (*Gloeophyllum trabeum*) and a white rot fungus (*Trametes versicolor*).

Although the supercritical fluid extraction of wood is based on the production of high-value chemicals, it may be possible to limit the extraction in order to activate the wood structure for subsequent modification reactions and processes.

Use of supercritical fluids in wood preservation

Wood preservation has been a key concern of the wood technology for the past 100+ years, where materials of known bioactivity are introduced into the wood cellular structure. This topic has been thoroughly reviewed (e.g., Richardson, 1993), and some of the recent developments in the field of wood protection (including wood modification) have also been considered (Civardi et al., 2015a; Gerardin, 2016; Borges et al., 2018). The introduction of these preservatives normally requires vacuum and pressurised impregnation. With the onset of supercritical fluid technology, it was logical to apply supercritical fluids to preservation technology.

As far back as 1991, Sunol (1991) proposed the use of supercritical fluids to: (1) solubilise a monomer, monomer mixture or polymer which may or may not include additives, (2) introduce the supercritical solvent mixture that has been created into the wood matrix, (3) remove extractives from the wood, (4) precipitate the monomer or polymer within the wood, and (5) polymerise the monomer *in situ* in the wood. Supercritical CO_2 was used to solubilise fatty acids prior to the impregnation of chromated copper arsenate (CCA), but Kumar and Morrell (1993) suggested that the supercritical fluid treatment improved preservative uptake not only by removing fatty acids but also by removing encrustations on the pit surfaces and opening aspirated pits. Some examples of other preservatives that have been used in combination with supercritical fluids are given in Table 5.5.

Most early work focussed on small-scale laboratory equipment, and first commercial plant for treating wood was reported in 2002 in Hampen, Denmark (Figure 5.12) with the formation of the Superwood company.

Based on developments on a pilot scale since 1996, it was possible to scale up production, as indicated in Table 5.6. The developments prior to the start-up of the commercial plant and some of the findings of larger-scale processing have been reported in an overview by Kjellow and Henriksen (2009b).

Supercritical fluids can be used not only to impregnate wood with bioactive compounds but also to extract harmful compounds, for example at the end of the service life of a product. The extraction of heavy metal residues from treatments such as CCA can be improved using organic chelating agents with supercritical fluids (Yin et al., 1995), and Abd El-Fatah et al. (2004) showed that bis(2,4,4-trimethylpentyl) monothiophosphinic acid (Cyanex™ 302), 2,4-Pentanedione (acetyl acetone, AA), thenoyltrifluoroacetone (TTA), trioctylphosphine oxide (TOPO), and tri-n-octylmethyl ammonium

Table 5.5 Preservatives impregnated into wood using supercritical fluids.

Preservative	Reference
Creosote	Legay et al., 1998
Cyproconazole	Kang and Morrell, 2003
3-Iodo-2-propynyl butylcarbamate (IPBC)	Muin and Tsunoda, 2003
Pentachlorophenol (PCP)	Legay et al., 1998
Permethrin	Qader et al., 2005
Propiconazole	Kjellow and Henriksen, 2009a
Silafluofen [(4-Ethoxyphenyl)(3,4-(4-fluoro-3-phenoxyphenyl) propyldimethyl silane)]*	Muin and Tsunodo, 2004
Tebuconazole	Acda et al., 2001
Thiocyanomethylthiobenzothiazole (TCMTB)	Kim et al., 1997

* a termiticide

Figure 5.12 Commercial facilities at Superwood™.

Table 5.6 Pilot-scale and commercial-scale supercritical fluid treatment facilities.

	Pilot plant	Commercial plant
Start-up date	November 1996	March 2002
Vessel size (litres)	1×30	$3 \times 8,000$
Maximum wood dimensions (mm)	$150 \times 75 \times 75$	$6,600 \times 1,100 \times 1,100$
CO_2 recovery (%)	Not determined	$> 96\%$
Cycle time (hours)	1.5–5.0	2.0–5.0
Annual capacity (m³)	Not determined	40,000–60,000

chloride as chelating agents, led to high levels of extraction of copper, but to considerably less for chromium and arsenic. Subsequent complementary processes did not increase the level of extraction.

Knowing that aspirated pits within the wood structure can be opened using supercritical fluids, Smith et al. (1993) studied the effect of supercritical CO_2 on white spruce heartwood where conventional wood preservation techniques caused cell-wall collapse and a reduction in the moduli of rupture and elasticity. They found that supercritical treatment had no impact on the wood structure and that the mechanical properties were retained, although the process was detrimental to Douglas fir, yellow poplar, western red cedar, and Engelmann spruce (Anderson et al., 2000).

Among other compounds that have been successfully extracted from wood samples are the pesticide DDT (1,1,1-trichloro-2, 2-bis (*p*-chlorophenyl)ethane) (Kang et al., 2013), and agricultural pesticides (e.g., *o,o*-diethyl *o*-(2-isopropyl-6-4-pyrimidinyl) phosphorothioate, Diazinon™) can also be successfully removed (Zimmt et al., 2007).

Other uses of supercritical fluids

The acetylation of wood (Section 2.2) is well established and often involves extended reaction times (depending on the level of acetylation required). Using supercritical technology, Matsunaga et al. (2010) showed that the acetylation of sugi progressed rapidly, using considerably less acetic anhydride than is needed in a conventional modification treatment and they suggested that acetylation in supercritical CO_2 had a higher bulking effect than the equivalent liquid-phase and vapour-phase acetylation reactions to achieve a WPG of 15% or higher.

As mentioned in Section 2.7, silicon-containing chemicals can help impart fire resistance to wood, and supercritical fluids have been used to treat aspen samples with siloxanes such as polymethylhydrosilane, 1,3,5,7-tetravinylcyclotetrasiloxane and 1,3,5,7-tetramethylcyclo-tetrasiloxane, the reaction being aided by Karstedt's catalyst (a disiloxane organoplatinum complex) (Eastman et al., 2009). As a result of *in situ* crosslinking reactions, a continuous network of aspen and silicone was created, resulting in improvements in both the fire resistance and the post-degradation properties of aspen.

The idea of thermal activation of wood cell walls was considered by Bogolitsyn et al. (2017), using supercritical CO_2 for the selective treatment of the weak hydrogen bonds within the ligno-carbohydrate matrix in common juniper, to obtain a new understanding of the structure and composition of the wood substance and its components. It appeared that supercritical CO_2 could be used as a means of activating certain components within the cell wall and might provide a means of increasing the reactivity of individual compounds, so offering new routes to modify wood.

Overview of supercritical fluids

Although, supercritical fluids have been used for more than 30 years, their commercial application has been limited to activities by Superwood™ in Denmark. Recent experiments have nevertheless shown that supercritical fluids can affect the cellular structure of wood and increase the permeability of certain refractory species. Supercritical fluids have also been used to replace conventional solvents for both wood protection and wood modification, and have also been shown to be useful in removing compounds from timber in end-of-life situations. It is possible that there will be more developments in the use of supercritical fluids in the near future.

5.6 Ionic liquids in wood modification

Many of the methods of wood modification mentioned by Alfred Stamm and his co-workers at the Forest Products Laboratory in the United States have been studied and revised with the ultimate aim of achieving a commercial process, normally focussing on how reaction improvements may be achieved, including choice of solvents, reaction temperatures and catalysts. Studies often focus on whether to use an organic polar or non-polar liquid, an aqueous solvent or a solvent-less solid phase or gaseous system. The use of supercritical fluids (see Section 5.5) has recently emerged as an interesting possibility, but another topic that has attracted considerable attention is the use of ionic liquids (ILs).

What is an ionic liquid?

An ionic liquid is normally defined as a compound completely composed of ions with a melting point below 100°C and these compounds have been known for more than 100 years. Ethanolammonium nitrate (m.p. 52–55°C) was reported in 1888, but one of the earliest truly room-temperature ionic liquids was ethylammonium nitrate (m.p. 12°C), reported in 1914.

There have been a number of publications dealing with ILs in recent years (e.g., Wasserscheid and Welton, 2002; Kokorin, 2011; Shiflett, 2020), but the main focus with regard to ILs and PILs (macromolecular forms of polymerisable ILs) has been on nitrogen-based salts, such as imidazolium (Zheng et al., 2014), ammonium systems (Tolesa et al., 2017), pyridinium (Javed et al., 2018), and 1,2,3-triazolium (Brehm et al., 2019). Quaternary phosphonium-based ILs and their polymeric systems (Chen et al., 2019) have received less attention although they are more thermally stable and have a greater ion conductivity than the nitrogen-based ILs.

The description of ILs has increased in complexity, so that they are often classed as "non-volatile, non-flammable, and air- and water-stable" in some cases, and the direct opposite, i.e., distinctly volatile, flammable, and unstable, in others due to the vast array of possible anion and cation combinations that have been proposed, so that one can develop an IL almost for any desirable situation. This ability to tailor properties to meet individual cases has made it possible not only to focus on the basic physical properties of ILs (i.e., volatility, stability, density, flammability and solubility) but also to devise ways of introducing antimicrobial activity (Hough et al., 2007), where the biological activity is structure dependent, such as the length and composition of the cation side chain as well as of the anion moiety (Costa et al., 2017).

One of the advantages of ILs has been their potential to replace traditional organic solvents, but Costa et al. (2017) have shown that the preparation, use and disposal of ILs also have an environmental impact. A range of method specific IL classifications (Lei et al., 2017), such as room-temperature ILs (RTILs), task-specific ILs (TSILs), polyionic liquids (PILs) and supported IL membranes (SILMs), have been reported, but Ghandhi (2014) had used the abbreviation PIL to refer to protic ionic liquids, where there is a proton transfer from a Brønsted acid to a Brønsted base, as opposed to an aprotic ionic liquid (APIL). Recent studies have also reported the synthesis of solvate ionic liquids (SILs), where a cation (typically lithium, a Lewis acid) is chelated to a Lewis base, resulting in a complex cation, which can be countered by a range of anions (Eyckens and Henderson, 2019).

Ionic liquids and wood components

In recent years, the development of commercial biorefining has led to opportunities to replace petrochemically-derived chemicals, by converting lignocellulosic components into industrially important and financially valuable resource streams. To avoid the harsh conventional processing, such as liquefaction, used to break the covalent links between the cellulose, hemicellulose and lignin, better systems have been sought for extracting components, while limiting the level of degradation via the use of ILs has been suggested.

Dissolution of cellulose

One of the benefits of cellulose is its high level of crystallinity, but this means that cellulose is poorly soluble in conventional organic solvents, and that more aggressive systems, such as DMA/LiCl, have to be used to dissolve cellulose. The usual way of dissolving cellulose on a commercial scale is to use sodium hydroxide with conversion to a xanthate using carbon disulfide (CS_2) and subsequent regeneration of the cellulose via acid treatment. The dissolution of cellulose with ILs has been known for several decades, with Graenacher (1934) showing that N-ethylpyridinium chloride in the presence of a nitrogen-containing base can dissolve cellulose. To avoid the environmental problems with the xanthate process commonly used in textile processing to produce Rayon, the use of N-methylmorpholine-N-oxide monohydrate has been commercialised in the Lyocell process (Rosenau et al., 2001).

The first comprehensive study into the use of ILs to dissolve cellulose was published by Swatloski et al. (2002), who used the 1-butyl-3-methyl imidazolium cation with different anions as solvents for cellulose. The chloride anion, known to be a small hydrogen bond acceptor, was found to be the most effective anion. Zhu et al. (2006) reported that imidazolium-based ILs are suitable for dissolving cellulose and Vitz et al. (2010) showed the potential of using 1-butyl-3-methylimidazolium chloride ([BMIM]Cl) (Figure 5.13 left) or 1-allyl-3-methylimidazolium chloride ([AllylMIM]Cl) (Figure 5.13 right) for a range of reactions. The dissolution can be accelerated through the application of microwaves (Zhu et al., 2006). The use of these and other ILs has been shown together with acetylation (Wu et al., 2004; Barthel and Heinze, 2006), esterification (Heinze et al., 2005), etherification (Myllymaeki and Aksela, 2005; Moellmann et al., 2009), carbanilation (Barthel and Heinze, 2006), and trimethylsilylation (Köhler et al., 2008). These and several other reactions with cellulose are shown in Figure 5.14 (Isik et al., 2014).

A wide range of solvents has been used to dissolve cellulose, including ILs such as 3-methyl-N-butylpyridinium chloride and benzyldimethyl(tetradecyl)ammonium chloride (Heinze et al., 2005), tetradecyltrihexylphosphonium bis(trifluoromethylsulfonyl)imide for functionalising with various anhydrides (Tome et al., 2011), and 1-butylpyridinium chloride, 1-octyl pyridinium chloride (Saher et al., 2018). The preparation of various 1,2,3-triazolium-based and 1,2,4-triazolium-based ILs (Brehm et al., 2019) offers a new group of potential ILs for dissolving cellulose, the degree of solubility increasing with increasing anion basicity; the cation appears to have little or no effect on the solubility level.

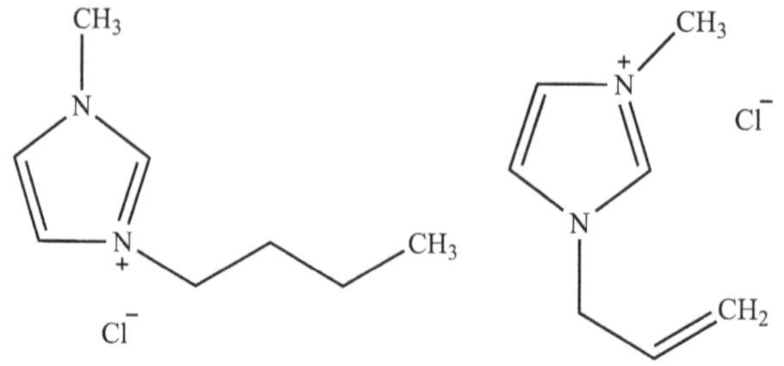

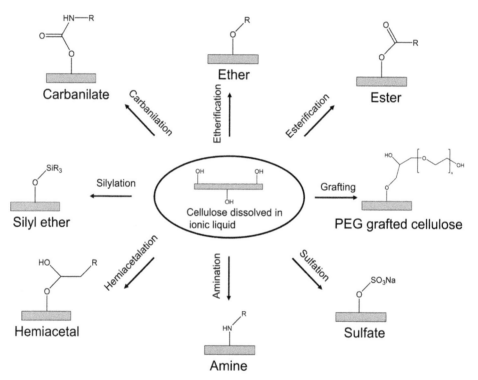

Figure 5.13 Structure of 1-butyl-3-methylimidazolium chloride ([BMIM]Cl) (left) and 1-allyl-3-methylimidazolium chloride ([AllylMIM]Cl) (right).

Figure 5.14 Examples of generic reactions of dissolved cellulose with ILs (Isik et al., 2014).

Lignin

As indicated in Section 1.3, all forms of lignin are extensively aromatic, and they also have extensive ether, aryl–ether and aryl–aryl linkages. The lignin structure varies from species to species, and particularly between broad-leaved trees, conifer trees, and grasses, with regard to its composition of H-type (*p*-hydroxyphenylpropane), G-type (guaiacylpropane) and S-type (syringylpropane) units (Figure 1.38). During extraction, fragmentation tends to occur in the following bonds within the lignin: β-O-4 (45–62%), 5–5' (3–27%), β-5 (3–12%), 4-O-5' (4–9%), β-1 (1–9%), and dibenzodioxocin (< 1–7%) (Zakzeski et al., 2010). Since the 5-position is occupied by S-units, such bonds are fewer in lignin than in broad-leaved woods, which is one reason why lignin from broad-leaved woods is less cross-linked and more easily delignified.

When Kraft lignin from conifer woods is dissolved in an IL based on imidazolium cations, the solubility varies with the anion in the following order: $(CF_3SO_3)^- \approx (MeSO_4)^{2-} >> (OAc)^- > (HCOO)^- >> Cl^- \approx Br^- >> (BF_4)^- >> (PF_6)^-$ (Pu et al., 2007). In some cases, due to the high cost of ILs and their high viscosities, a polar organic solvent, such as dimethylsulfoxide (DMSO) or N,N-dimethylformamide (DMF), has been used to dissolve lignin (Mai et al., 2014; Pinkert et al., 2011).

Other ILs that have been used include 1-butyl-4-methylpyridinium hexafluorophosphate (Pu et al., 2007) and a range of protic pyridinium ILs, such as pyridinium formate, pyridinium acetate and pyridinium propionate (Rashid et al., 2016).

Recently, most studies of lignin have focussed on organic feedstocks and bioenergy, and aggressive fragmentation processes, such as Lewis acids, have been used, to yield phenols in low yields at temperatures up to 300°C. The dealkylation of fragmented portions of lignin provides routes to the synthesis of many important compounds, e.g., in the conversion of eugenol to guaiacol (Binder et al., 2009). Yinghuai et al. (2013) focussed on oxidation, dehydration and esterification, where esterification was often accompanied by neutralisation with triethylamine or pyridine.

Ionic liquids as wood preservatives

ILs have been reported to have biocidal properties, while having low toxicity towards animals (Thuy Pham et al., 2010; Oliveira et al., 2016). To replace arsenic and pentachlorophenol, a wide range of preservative treatments have been developed, including water-soluble quaternary ammonium compounds (QACs) with interesting antifungal properties (Oertel, 1965). The synthesis and testing of alkyl ammonium compounds (AACs) has been reported by, e.g., Preston and Nicholas (1982).

The potential of ILs to assist in the wood protection industry has been demonstrated by Pernak et al. (1998) with 1-alkyl-3-benzyloxymethylimidazolium, 3-alkoxymethyl-1–benzylimidazolium, and 1-alkyl-3-(3-phenylpropoxymethyl)imidazolium chlorides, all of which showed antifungal activity against *Coniophora puteana* (Schum.: Fr.) Karst., *Trametes versicolor* (L.: Fr.) Pilát and *Chaetomium globosum* (Kunze: Fr.). Later work by the same group (Pernak et al., 2004) showed that 3-alkoxymethyl-1-methylimidazolium tetraborate and hexafluorophosphate had antifungal activities similar to those of benzalkonium chloride and didecylmethylammonium chloride (DDAC).

Stasiewicz et al. (2008) have shown that pyridinium ILs, such as 1-alkoxymethyl-3-dimethylaminopyridinium and 1-alkoxymethyl-4-dimethylaminopyridinium chlorides, where the alkoxy groups vary in length from C_3 to C_{18} are also as effective wood preservatives. The chloride anion can be replaced with an anion derived from the sweetener acesulfamate (Figure 5.15), which is marketed under the trade names Sunett™ and Sweet One™, labelled as E950. In addition to its anti-fungal properties, the C_{10} alkoxy IL significantly reduced the hygroscopicity and water absorption capacity of the treated wood, since the ILs modifying the tracheid cell walls and possibly filled the free cell space. Replacing the chloride anion with the acesulfamate anion was found to increase the hydrophobicity.

The polymerisation of imidazolium-based ILs has attracted a lot of interest since their development in the late 1990s (Ohno and Ito, 1998), the logical step being to assess whether they could be polymerised within the wood structure to provide protection against degradation. Sakagami et al. (2018) synthesised polymeric 1-butyl-3-vinylimidazolium iodide and found it to be effective against the brown rot fungus *Formitopsis palustris* (FFPRI 0507) and the polymerisation process also imparted a resistance to leaching.

Zabielska-Matejuk et al. (2017) showed that a range of ILs could be produced from naturally occurring compounds, such as (-)-menthol, known for its bioactivity against pathogenic bacteria and fungi (Figure 5.16), and a range of 3-alkyl-1-[(1R,2S,5R)-(−)-menthoxymethyl]-imidazolium chlorides with various alkyl substituents (from C_1 to C_{12}) and one symmetric 1,3-bis[(1R,2S,5R)-

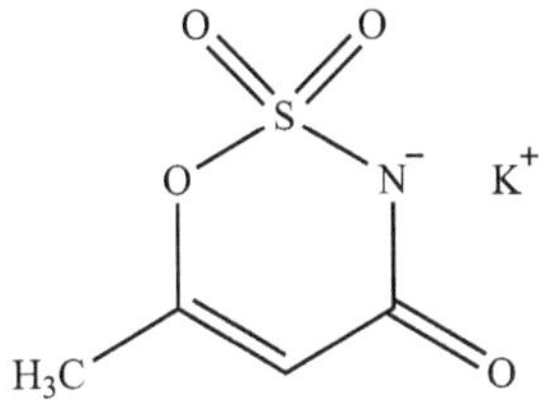

Figure 5.15 Chemical structure of potassium acesulfamate.

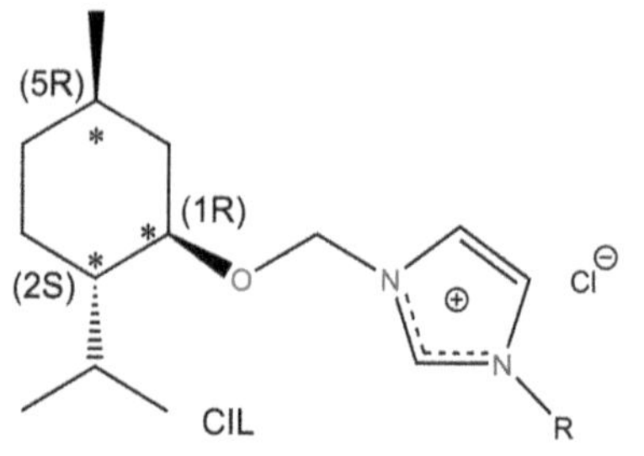

R= $CH_3, C_4H_9, C_5H_{11}, C_6H_{13}$,   Abbreviation: $[C_n\text{-Im-Men}][Cl]$,

    $C_8H_{17}, C_9H_{19}, C_{12}H_{25}$;   n=1, 4, 5, 6, 8, 9, 12

R= (1R, 2S, 5R)-(—)-menthol;   Abbreviation: [Men-Im-Men][Cl]

Figure 5.16 Structures of chiral ionic liquids incorporating (–)-menthol (Zabielska-Matejuk et al., 2017).

(–)-menthoxymethyl]imidazolium chloride containing two (1R,2S,5R)-(–)-menthol substituents were tested against several fungi using the agar dilution method (Ważny and Thornton, 1986).

Langmuir and Freundlich adsorption isotherms confirmed the multilayer sorption of the synthesised salts onto Scots pine wood, while ATR-IR spectral analysis suggested an ion exchange mechanism, leading to intermolecular H-bond interactions between the IL and the wood.

Chemical modification of wood with ionic liquids

Kilpeläinen et al. (2007) showed that ILs, such as 1-butyl-3-methylimidazoliumchloride and 1-allyl-3-methylimidazoliumchloride, were effective in achieving the total dissolution of wood, and the latter was used (Wu et al., 2004) prior to the acetylation of wood using acetic anhydride in the absence of any catalyst.

Xie et al. (2007) showed the potential of wood modification aided by ILs with the proposed reactions shown in Figure 5.17.

In their work, acylation was undertaken with benzoyl chloride and carbanilation was performed with phenyl isocyanate, both at 70°C, with the product being isolated after precipitation with methanol and water (Xie et al., 2007). Shen et al. (2017) were pre-treated wood fibres with 1-butyl-3-methylimidazonium chloride at 125°C, which significantly reduced the crystallinity of the fibres and extracted some of the lignin (up to 34%), prior to the reaction with acetic anhydride in the presence of toluene and pyridine (the latter to counteract acidic by-products). An increase in wood content in the IL solution was found to reduce the effectiveness of the reductions in crystallinity and lignin levels, but the higher wood levels led to higher acetylation levels as well as a lower moisture sorptivity.

The acetylation of dissolved cellulose has been undertaken at room temperature in various imidazolium-based ILs in the presence of acetyl chloride or acetic anhydride (Abe et al., 2016) and the use of microwaves to aid the dissolution and to heat the esterification process has been demonstrated by Possidinio et al. (2010), where the esterification was carried out with acetic, propanoic, butanoic, pentanoic, and hexanoic anhydride, achieving functionalisation easily and rapidly without the need for a base catalyst. The degree of substitution decreased, but then increased upon reaching the reaction with pentanoic and hexanoic anhydrides, and this was concluded to be due to "hydrophobic interactions between the voluminous acyl anhydride and the hydrophobic chains of the partially esterified cellulose".

Once the components of wood have been separated, they may be modified with ILs (Kakko, 2019). Isolated cellulose has been acetylated, as shown in Figure 5.18 with vinyl acetate

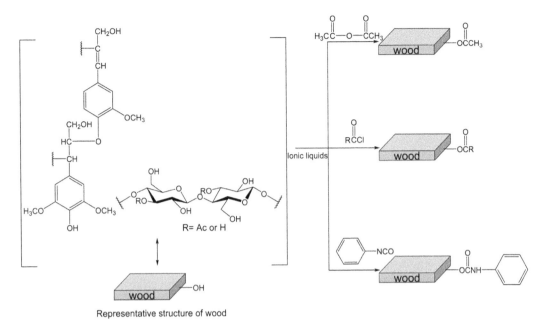

Figure 5.17 Examples of functionalisation reactions carried out in Ionic Liquids (Xie et al., 2007).

A.

B.

C.

Figure 5.18 Acylation of cellulose in the presence of 1,5-diazabicyclo[4.3.0]non-5-ene acetate (Kakko et al., 2017).

(route A), isopropenyl carboxylate (route B) or acetic anhydride (route C) in the presence of 1,5-diazabicyclo[4.3.0]non-5-ene acetate (Kakko et al., 2017).

Ren et al. (2007) reported the acetylation of hemicelluloses with 1-butyl-3-methylimidazolium chloride, iodine as a catalyst between 85 and 110°C for up to 60 minutes (Figure 5.19). More recent studies (Stepan et al., 2013) have shown that both 1-ethylmethylimidazolium and 1,5-diazabicyclo[4.3.0]non-5ene (DBN)-based ILs can achieve full acetylation without any co-solvent.

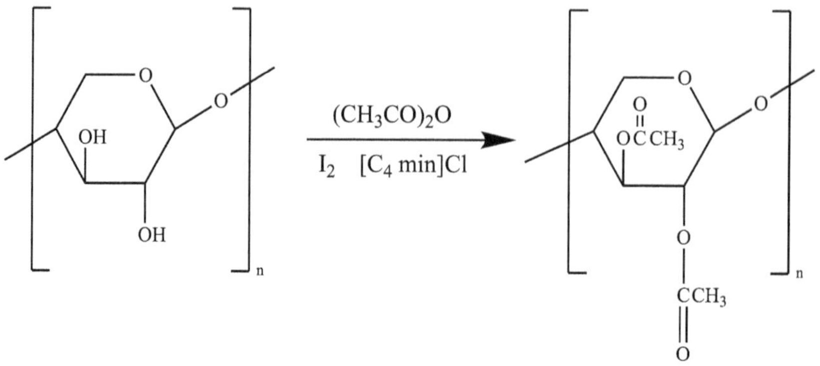

Figure 5.19 Acetylation of hemicelluloses in the presence of 1-butyl-3-methylimidazolium chloride (Ren et al., 2007).

Another method of modifying wood has been through thermal compression (see Section 3.8) and certain ILs can act as plasticisers, where they affect the hydrogen bonds within the wood structure (Kilpeläinen et al., 2007), and soften the fibre structure (Lucas et al., 2011; Miyafuji and Suzuki, 2012). Ou et al. (2014) impregnated discs of hybrid poplar with a series of imidazolium-based ILs, dissolved in ethanol and, after the evaporative removal of ethanol, the samples were subjected to thermal compression, during which the temperature was raised to a maximum of 200°C. It was concluded that the ILs had a high plasticisation effect with a viscous buckling of the cell walls and no cell-wall fracture. The introduction of a permanent strain in the wood helped to eliminate the set-recovery.

A further investigation into the role of 1-ethyl-3-methylimidazolium chloride as part of a compreg-style treatment of Scots pine involving methyl methacrylate resin (Neyses et al., 2017; 2019; 2020) confirmed that the IL reduced the set-recovery by almost 30%, increased the hardness, and had a strong plasticising effect, although the depth of penetration was inadequate with the application method adopted (cf. Section 3.8).

Conclusions regarding ionic liquids

ILs are becoming increasingly important in wood science in many bio-refining processes, dissolving the wood or its components. These dissolved components can undergo chemical modification in ways not possible within the solid wood matrix, and ILs can also partially break down the crystalline structure, allowing densification through a high degree of plasticisation.

In addition to wood modification, ILs have been applied as wood preservatives, either in their monomeric form or through polymerisation within the wood cell walls. These polymerised systems also resist leaching and increase the hydrophobicity.

The next step in using of ILs could combine the properties of polymerised ILs with their wood preservative qualities, modifying the components either chemically or physically. The next steps in wood modification will be wholly or partially based on ILs.

5.7 Opportunities for future wood modification

So far, this chapter has dealt with concepts that have been applied to wood on a small scale, thereby helping prove the feasibility of an idea. Some of the following ideas in this section have had limited applications or build on ideas from other areas of materials research and general chemistry. As such, these areas of research could form part of the future of wood modification. The aim of this Section is to develop new ideas that are, in ways that wood acetylation and thermal modification were "new" ideas in the 1990s, demonstrable in the laboratory but have yet to make commercial in-roads. Yet, with greater understanding, not only of the science but also of the chemical engineering, these and other methods have become mainstream, and some of the following ideas may provide an inroad to future developments.

Grafting of components to enable polymerisation

Wood is in itself a complex polymeric system, but the reactivity of its cellulose, hemicelluloses and lignin means that chemical groups capable of undergoing polymeric grafting can be incorporated. This differs from the conventional impregnation/polymerisation of wood with phenol formaldehyde (PF) resin, for example (see Section 2.4), where a low molecular weight oligomer is absorbed into the lumen and cell walls prior to the formation of a polymeric network, which may include cross-linking to the wood components.

Until recently, the cross-linking of a polymer with wood was limited to wood fibres and its disintegrated components, such as nanocellulose (reference needed). The linking of polymers with wood fibres has led to the development of wood-plastic composites (WPCs) and a wide range of commercialised products. In most cases, the wood fibres act only as a filler, reducing the weight and cost of the product, although the oligomers sometimes penetrate and fill the cell walls and lumen without undergoing chemical bonding to the wood components.

Minoura et al. (1969) showed that maleic anhydride could react with polypropylene, for example, via a radical mechanism initiated by benzoyl peroxide, leading to a permanent linking of maleic anhydride groups onto the polymer chain. Since maleic anhydride reacts with wood (Matsuda et al., 1984a,b), the synthesis of a maleic anhydride – polypropylene (MAPP) system offered a means of achieving direct bonding with wood. The structure of MAPP is shown in Figure 5.20, although the frequency of the maleic anhydride moiety and the termination of the polypropylene chain are unclear (Harper, 2003). The maleic anhydride group can react with one or two hydroxyl groups, as shown in Figure 5.21 (Bledzki et al., 1996), and it has been shown to react with hydroxyl groups in lignin (Kazayawoko et al., 1997), although these is some uncertainty regarding the level of reactivity when using MAPP due to steric effects.

Bledzki et al. (2005) have shown the potential of using MAPP in preparing both broad-leaved-based and conifer-based fibre composites. MAPP has been used in WPCs with styrene–ethylenebutylene–styrene (SEBS) (Tjong et al., 2002), linear low-density polyethylene (LLDPE) (Dikobe and Luyt, 2010a), ethyl vinyl acetate (Dikobe and Luyt, 2010b), and high-density polyethylene (HDPE) (Dikobe and Luyt, 2017).

Recent work (Cebane et al., 2014) has focussed on keeping wood as a natural framework and introducing a new functionality to the wood components while retaining as many as possible of its inherent properties (e.g., Aldrus and Ulbricht, 2012). In order to achieve grafting, Cebrane et al. (2014) initially impregnated and reacted wood samples with 4,4'-azobis(4-cyanopentanoyl chloride) (ACPC), after which styrene and two pH-responsive monomers (2-(dimethylamino) ethyl methacrylate (DMAEMA) and methacrylic acid (MAA)) were polymerised in wood at a temperature of ca. 75°C. The styrene was introduced in order to provide hydrophobicity. The modes of reaction are shown in Figure 5.22.

The concepts developed by Cebrane et al. (2014) have been adopted by others, including hydrophobisation with nano-silica and polydimethylsiloxane (Chang et al., 2015), and the development of transparent wood (Li et al., 2016; Gan et al., 2017).

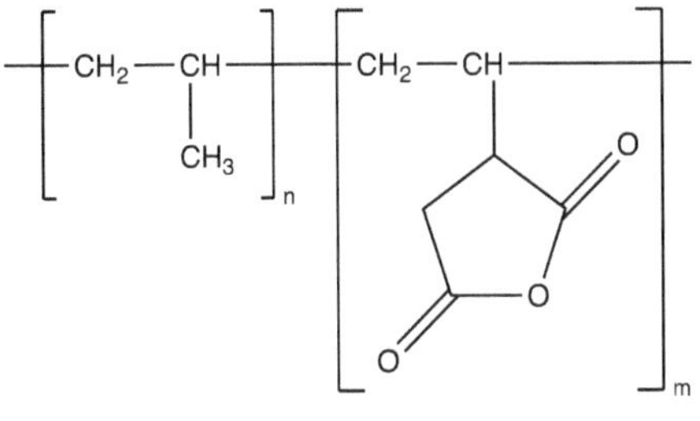

Figure 5.20 Structure of maleic anhydride polypropylene (Harper, 2003).

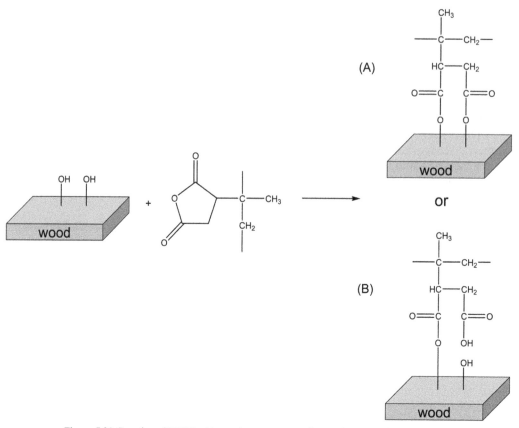

Figure 5.21 Reaction of MAPP with wood at one or two adjacent sites (Bledzki et al., 1996).

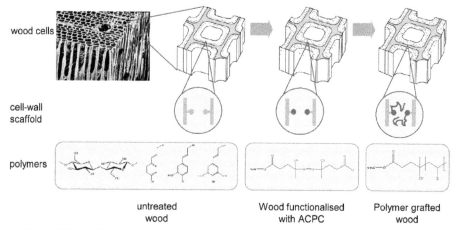

Figure 5.22 Grafting of polymers onto ACPC-initiated wood samples (after Cebrane et al., 2014).

Click chemistry

The activity of a compound is related to the functional units present and to the reagents introduced. Chemical reactions proceed at different rates depending on the temperature, accessibility, catalysts used, etc. If a bifunctional molecule is used, one end can react while the other functional group can undergo further reactions. This concept has provided the basis for *click chemistry*, biocompatible small molecule reactions commonly used in bioconjugation, allowing substrates to be joined with specific biomolecules.

Click chemistry is a way of generating products that follow examples in nature by joining small modular units. The concept of "click chemistry" was first coined by Sharpless and his co-workers (Kolb et al., 2001) and now encompasses a wide range of biological, pharmacological and biomimetic subjects, but not wood modification.

The copper-catalysed Huisgen reaction has been reported to be a typical example of click chemistry that can be applied to polysaccharide cellulose (Liebert et al., 2006), where a triazole functional group can be added as a result of the insertion and reaction of a tosyl (*p*-toluene sulfonyl) group and its substitution by an azide compound. This azide group can then undergo a cyclic reaction with an alkyne to yield the triazole (Figure 5.23). The potential of introducing azido groups into cellulose was shown by Zhang et al. (2008), with further reactions of the azide group with polysaccharide compounds (Elchinger et al., 2011).

Another example of click chemistry is the thiol-ene reaction, with the radical addition of thiols to double bonds in pentanoate groups introduced by a reaction with pentenoic anhydride. Hoyle and Bowman (2010), reported that there is a wide range of opportunities for using thiol-ene click chemistry to create and functionalise polymers and surfaces in a wide range of high-performance materials. The main issue when applying click chemistry to wood modification is the accessibility of the wood components.

The hydroxyl groups within lignin can also be replaced with other functional groups using click chemistry. Han et al. (2016) used elevated temperatures to allow the lignin-lignin polymerisation reaction to proceed and suggested a range of subsequent reactions based on the alkyne or azide moiety (Figure 5.24). Another example was shown by Yuan et al. (2019), where alkyne-modified lignin underwent a cycloaddition reaction with azide-modified soybean oil to provide a thermoset elastomer.

So far these click chemistry reactions have been carried out on extracted material not on bulk wood it is now necessary to determine the degree of activity possible on solid wood and its long-term stability.

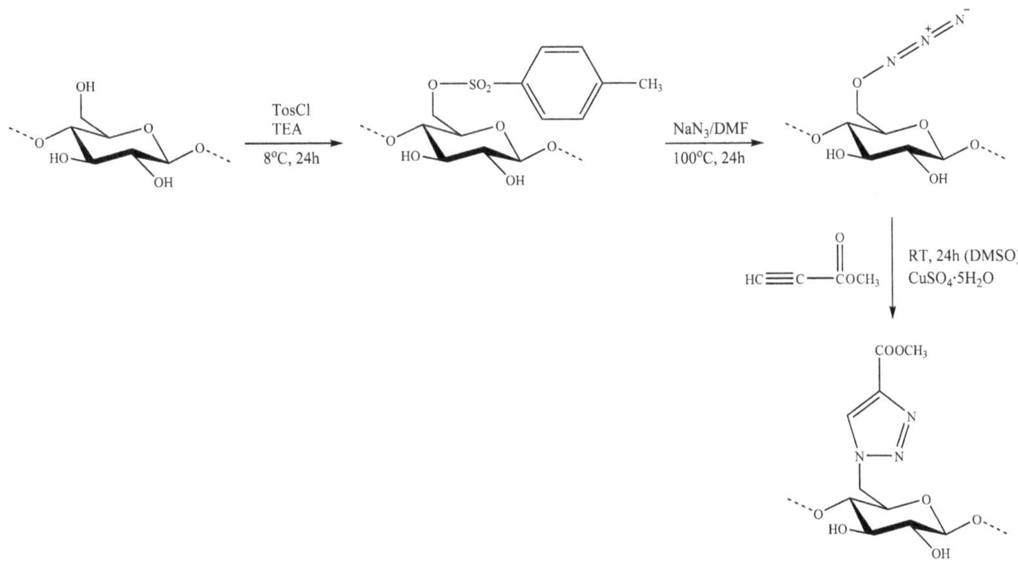

Figure 5.23 Huisgen reaction for the introduction of triazole into cellulose via click chemistry (Liebert et al., 2006).

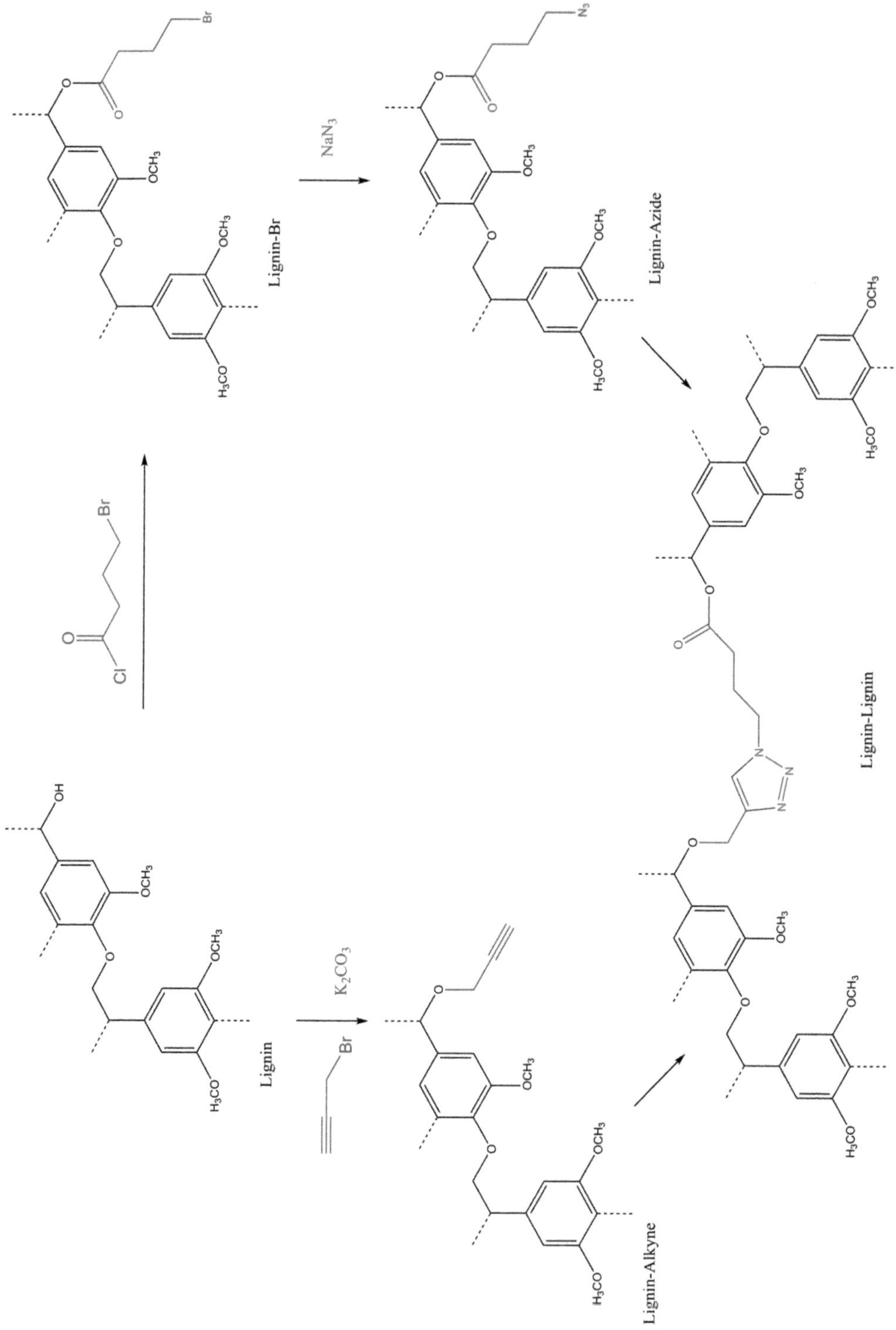

Figure 5.24 Synthesis of lignin-lignin polymers via a copper-free click reaction of an alkyne-modified lignin with an azide-modified lignin (Han et al., 2016).

Rhodium-catalysed reactions of hydroxyl groups

Wood components have a range of accessible hydroxyl groups, which can be modified by, for example, esterification with acetylation (see Section 2.2), but many modification processes involve the use of highly acidic or basic conditions or lead to by-products, so there is a need to develop treatments as close to pH-neutral as possible. In the early 1970s, Teyssié and Hubert considered the use of rhodium (II) acetate, while Paulissen et al. (1973) reported that a carbenoid group readily undergoes O-H insertion reactions with alcohols and water to yield alkoxyacetates in high yields (Figure 5.25).

This appears to be far from wood modification, but the reverse scenario, the addition of an α-diazo ester to a hydroxyl-containing biological compound, has been proposed (Trader and Carlson, 2012), based on reactions where metal-catalysed insertion reactions of α-diazo esters with alcohols (Figure 5.26) reported by Peddibhotla et al. (2007). The concept of using diazo ester compounds with added functionality rather than an enzyme group makes it possible to use a range of modifications that introduce groups capable of undergoing subsequent reaction.

Figure 5.25 Rhodium-catalysed reaction of an α-diazo ester to form an alkoxyacetates (Paulissen et al., 1973).

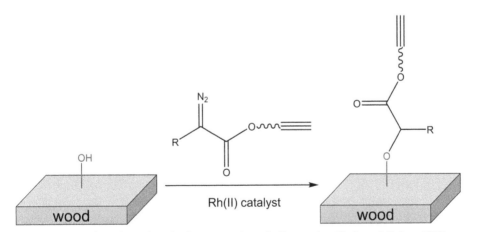

Figure 5.26 Schematic reaction of α-diazo ester using a rhodium catalyst (Trader and Carlson, 2012).

Modification of chitosan

Chitosan (Figure 5.27) is a linear polysaccharide composed of randomly distributed β-(1→4)-linked deacetylated D-glucosamine and acetylated N-acetyl-D-glucosamine made by treating the chitin shells of shrimps and other crustaceans with a strong alkali. Chitosan resembles cellulose, and recent developments in chitosan chemistry may be applicable to cellulose and/or hemicellulose and lignin, including graft polymerisation. Bratskaya et al. (2019) considered the use of poly(ethylene glycol) diglycidyl ether (PEGDGE) and ethylene glycol diglycidyl ether (EGDGE), with a reaction on the C6 position of the glucosamine unit.

Chitosan has been considered with atom transfer radical polymerisation (ATRP) (El Tahlawy and Hudson, 2003; Zohuriaan-Mehr, 2005; Munro et al., 2007), and (Munro et al., 2009) demonstrated the use of ATRP for the grafting of poly(oligoethylene glycol methacrylate) or poly(OEGMA).

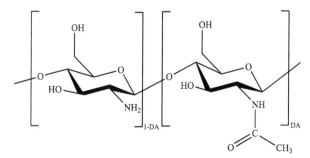

Figure 5.27 Chemical structure of chitosan (where DA is the degree of acetylation).

Any reaction that can occur at the C6 position on the glucosamine unit of chitosan can in principle be applied to a cellulosic structure, although it may be necessary to increase the accessibility with an ionic liquid or with supercritical carbon dioxide.

5.8 Conclusions on other methods

The modification of wood has achieved a long way in the last 30 years, with several methods moving towards commercial reality. At the same time, researchers are constantly striving to find new and improved methods for existing and innovative modification treatments.

The aim of this chapter has been to present some of the methods that may provide innovative routes to new products. Some of the ideas are more advanced than others and there are no doubt many ideas that have not been included. There are a wide range of affiliated technologies, based on molecules such as chitosan, cotton, natural and synthetic polyphenolic compounds, food chemistry, and textile technologies. At the same time, a better understanding of biological systems may lead to ways to develop superhydrophobicity, which with the use of supercritical fluids and ionic liquids may offer many new opportunities.

The subject of wood modification has grown considerably in recent years, and it is probable that a range of methods and technologies for protecting wood will emerge in the near future.

References

Abd El-Fatah, S., M. Goto, A. Kodama and T. Hirose. 2004. Supercritical fluid extraction of hazardous metals from CCA wood. The Journal of Supercritical Fluids 28(1): 21–27.

Abe, M., K. Sugimura and Y. Nishio. 2016. Regioselectivity in acetylation of cellulose in ionic liquids. Chemistry Select 1(10): 2474–2478.

Acda, M.N., J.J. Morrell and K.L. Levien. 2001. Supercritical fluid impregnation of selected wood species with tebuconazole. Wood Science and Technology 35(1/2): 127–136.

Adrus, N. and M. Ulbricht. 2012. Novel hydrogel pore-filled composite membranes with tunable and temperature-responsive size-selectivity. Journal of Materials Chemistry 22(7): 3088–3098.

Adschiri, T., S. Hirose, R. Malaluan and K. Arai 1993. Noncatalytic conversion of cellulose in supercritical and subcritical water. Journal of Chemical Engineering of Japan 26: 676–680.

Akhtari, M., H.R. Taghiyari and M.G. Kokandeh. 2013. Effect of some metal nanoparticles on the spectroscopy analysis of paulownia wood exposed to white-rot fungus. European Journal of Wood and Wood Products 71(2): 283–285.

Aktuganov, G., A. Melentjev, N. Galimzianova, E. Khalikova, T. Korpelia and P. Susi. 2008. Wide-range antifungal antagonism of *Paenibacillus ehimensis* IB-X-b and its dependence on chitinase and beta-1,3-glucanase production. Canadian Journal of Microbiology 54(7): 577–587.

Ali, G.S. and A.S. Reddy. 2000. Inhibition of fungal and bacterial plant pathogens by synthetic peptides: *In vitro* growth inhibition, interaction between peptides and inhibition of disease progression. Molecular Plant-Microbe Interactions 13(8); 847–859.

Anderson, M.E., R.J. Leicht and J.J. Morrell. 2000. The effects of supercritical CO_2 on the bending properties of four refractory wood species. Forest Products Journal 50(11/12): 85–94.

Anouhe, J.S., F.B. Niamké, M. Faustin, D. Virieux, J.-L. Pirat, A.A. Adima, S. Kati-Coulibaly and N. Amusant. 2018. The role of extractives in the natural durability of the heartwood of *Dicorynia guianensis* Amsh: New insights in antioxidant and antifungal properties. Annals of Forest Science 75(1): Article ID 15.

Antonetti, C., D. Licursi, S. Fulignati, G. Valentini and A.M.R. Galletti. 2016. New frontiers in the catalytic synthesis of levulinic acid: From sugars to raw and waste biomass as starting feedstock. Catalysts 6(12): Article ID 196.

Arregui, L., M. Ayala, X. Gómez-Gil, G. Gutiérrez-Soto, C.E. Hernández-Luna, M.H. de los Santos, L. Levin, A. Rojo-Domínguez, D. Romero-Martínez, M.C.N. Saparrat, M.A. Trujillo-Roldán and N.A. Valdez-Cruz. 2019. Laccases: structure, function, and potential application in water bioremediation. Microbial Cell Factories 18(1): Article ID 200.

Bacigalupe, A., M. Fernández, P. Eisenberg and M.M. Escobar. 2020. Greener adhesives based on UF/soy protein reinforced with montmorillonite clay for wood particleboard. Journal of Applied Polymer Science 137(37): Article ID 49086.

Bak, M., B.M. Yimmou, K. Csupor, R. Németh and L. Csóka. 2012. Enhancing the durability of wood against wood-destroying fungi using nano-zinc, pp. 1–6. *In*: Neményi, M., Heil, B., Kovács, J. and Facskó, F. [eds.]. Proceedings of the International Scientific Conference on Sustainable Development and Ecological Footprint, Sopron, Hungary.

Bak, M., F. Molnár and R. Németh. 2019. Improvement of dimensional stability of wood by silica nanoparticles. Wood Material Science & Engineering 14(1): 1–11.

Barthel, S. and T. Heinze. 2006. Acylation and carbanilation of cellulose in ionic liquids. Green Chemistry 8(3): 301–306.

Behrendt, C.J., R.A. Blanchette and R.L. Farrell. 1995a. An integrated approach, using biological and chemical control, to prevent blue stain in pine logs. Canadian Journal of Botany 73: 613–619.

Behrendt, C.J., R.A. Blanchette and R.L. Farrell. 1995b. Biological control of blue-stain fungi in wood. Phytopathology 85: 92–97.

Berglund, L.A. and I. Burgert. 2018. Bioinspired wood nanotechnology for functional materials. Advanced Material 30: Article ID 1704285.

Bernards, T.N.M., M.J. van Bommel and A.H. Boonstra. 1991. Hydrolysis-condensation processes of the tetra-alkoxysilanes TPOS, TEOS and TMOS in some alcoholic solvents. Journal of Non-Crystalline Solids 134(1/2): 1–13.

Bhushan, B., Y.C. Jung and K. Koch. 2009. Self-cleaning efficiency of artificial superhydrophobic surfaces. Langmuir 25(5): 3240–3248.

Binder, J.B., M.J. Gray, J.F. White, Z.C. Zhang and J.E. Holladay. 2009. Reactions of lignin model compounds in ionic liquids. Biomass and Bioenergy 33(9): 1122–1130.

Blanchard, V. and P. Blanchett 2011. Color stability for wood products during use: Effects of inorganic nanoparticles. BioResources 6: 1219–1229.

Bledzki, A.K., S. Reihmane and J. Gassan. 1996. Properties and modification methods for vegetable fibers for natural fiber composites. Journal of Applied Polymer Science 59(8): 1329–1336.

Bledzki, A.K., M. Letman, A. Viksne and L. Rence. 2005. A comparison of compounding processes and wood type for wood fibre-PP composites. Composites Part A: Applied Science and Manufacturing 36(6): 789–797.

Bolagh-Weiser, D., Z. Boros, G. Hornyánsky, A. Toth and L. Poppe. 2012. Disubstituted dialkoxysilane precursors in binary and ternary sol-gel systems for lipid-immobilisation. Process Biochemistry 47(3): 428–434.

Bratskaya, S., Y. Privar, D. Nesterov, E. Modin, M.I. Kodess, A. Slobodyuk, D. Marinin and A.V. Pestov. 2019. Chitosan gels and cryogels cross-linked with diglycidyl ethers of ethylene glycol and polyethylene glycol in acidic media. Biomacromolecules 20(4): 1635–1643.

Brehm, M., M. Pulst, J. Kressler and D. Sebastiani. 2019. Triazolium-based ionic liquids – A novel class of cellulose solvents. The Journal of Physical Chemistry B 123: 3994–4003.

Bogolitsyn, K.G., M.A. Gusakova, A.A. Krasikova, A.D. Ivakhnov, S.S. Khviuzov, D.G. Chukhchin and I.N. Zubov. 2017. Supercritical fluid extraction as a method of thermochemical activation of wood cell walls. Russian Journal of Physical Chemistry B 11(7): 1089–1094.

Borges, C.C., G.H.D. Tonoli, T.M. Cruz, P.J. Duarte and T.A. Junqueira. 2018. Nanoparticles-based wood preservatives: The next generation of wood protection? CERNE 24(4): 397–407.

Bruce, A. and T.L. Highley. 1991. Control of growth of wood decay Basidiomycetes by *Trichoderma* spp. and other potentially antagonistic fungi. Forest Products Journal 41(2): 63–67.

Bruce, A., W.J. Austin and G. King. 1984. Control of growth of *Lentinus lepideus* by volatiles from *Trichoderma* spp. Transactions of the British Mycological Society 82(3): 423–428.

Budija, F., M. Humar, B. Kricej and M. Petric. 2008. Propolis for wood finishing. *In*: The Proceedings IRG Annual Meeting, Istanbul, Turkey. International Research Group on Wood Protection IRG/WP 0830464.

Cabane, E., T. Keplinger, V. Merk, P. Hass and I. Burgert. 2014. Renewable and functional wood materials by grafting polymerization within cell walls. ChemSusChem 7(4): 1020–1025.

Cai, X., B. Riedl, H. Wan, S.Y. Zhang and X.-M. Wang. 2010. A study on the curing and viscoelastic characteristics of melamine-urea-formaldehyde resin in the presence of aluminium silicate nanoclays. Composites Part A: Applied Science and Manufacturing 41: 604–611.

Camarero, S., D. Ibarra, Á.T. Martínez, J. Romero, A. Gutiérrez and J.C. del Río. 2007. Paper pulp delignification using laccase and natural mediators. Enzyme and Microbial Technology 40(5): 1264–1271.

Cheng, H.N. and Q.-M. Gu. 2012. Enzyme-catalyzed modifications of polysaccharides and poly(ethylene glycol). Polymers 4(2): 1311–1330.

Capuzzo, A., M. Maffei and A. Occhipinti. 2013. Supercritical fluid extraction of plant flavors and fragrances. Molecules 18(6): 7194–7238.

CEN. 2014. EN 15457:2014. Paints and varnishes: Laboratory method for testing the efficacy of film preservatives in a coating against fungi. European Committee for Standardization, Brussels, Belgium.

Chang, H., K. Tu, X. Wang and J. Liu. 2015. Fabrication of mechanically durable superhydrophobic wood surfaces using polydimethylsiloxane and silica nanoparticles. RSC Advances 5(39): 30647–30653.

Chen, M., B.T. White, C.R. Kasprzak and T.E. Long. 2018. Advances in phosphonium-based ionic liquids and poly(ionic liquid)s as conductive materials. European Polymer Journal 108: 28–37.

Civardi, C., M. Schubert, A. Fey, P. Wick and F.W.M.R. Schwarze. 2015a. Micronized copper wood preservatives: Efficacy of ion, nano, and bulk copper against the brown rot fungus *Rhodonia placenta*. PLOS ONE 10(11): Article ID e0142578.

Civardi, C., F. Schwarze and P. Wick. 2015b. Micronized copper wood protection: An efficiency and potential health and risk assessment for copper based nanoparticles. Environmental Pollution 200: 20–32.

Clausen, C.A. 1996. Bacterial associations with decaying wood: A review. International Biodeterioration & Biodegradation 37: 101–107.

Clausen, C.A., V.W. Yang, R.A. Arang and F. Green. 2009. Feasibility of nanozinc oxide as a wood preservative. American Wood Protection Association – Proceeding 105: 255–260.

Clausen, C.A., F. Green and S.N. Kartal. 2010. Weatherability and leach resistance of wood impregnated with nano-zinc oxide. Nanoscale Research Letters 1464–1467.

Costa, S.P.F., A.M.O. Azevedo, P.C.A.G. Pinto and M.L.M.F.S. Saraiva. 2017. Environmental impact of ionic liquids: Recent advances in (eco)toxicology and (bio)degradability. ChemSusChem 10(11): 2321–2347.

Cowan, M.M. 1999. Plant products as antimicrobial agents. Clinical Microbiology Reviews 12(4): 564–582.

Daniel, G. 2014. Fungal and bacterial biodegradation: White rots, brown rots, soft rots, and bacteria, pp. 23–58. *In*: Schultz, T.P., Goodell, B. and Nichols, D.D. [eds.]. Deterioration and Protection of Sustainable Biomaterials, ACS Symposium Series 1158, American Chemical Society, Washington, DC, USA.

Demirbas, A. 1991. Fatty and resin acids recovered from spruce wood by supercritical acetone extraction. Holzforschung 45: 337–339.

Demirbaş, A. 2001. Supercritical fluid extraction and chemicals from biomass with supercritical fluids. Energy Conversion and Management 42(3): 279–294.

Denis, C. and J. Webster. 1971. Antagonistic properties of species groups of *Trichoderma*. II. Production of volatile antibiotics. Transactions of the British Mycological Society 57: 41–48.

Dhami, N.K., M.S. Reddy and A. Mukherjee. 2013. Biomineralization of calcium carbonates and their engineered applications: A review. Frontiers in Microbiology 4: Article ID 314.

Dikobe, D.G. and A.S. Luyt. 2010a. Comparative study of the morphology and properties of PP/LLDPE/wood powder and MAPP/LLDPE/wood powder polymer blend composites. Express Polymer Letters 4(11): 729–741.

Dikobe, D.G. and A.S. Luyt. 2010b. Morphology and thermal properties of maleic anhydride grafted polypropylene/ethylene-vinyl acetate copolymer/wood powder blend composites. Journal of Applied Polymer Science 116(6): 3193–3201.

Dikobe, D.G. and A.S. Luyt. 2017. Thermal and mechanical properties of PP/HDPE/wood powder and MAPP/HDPE/wood powder polymer blend composites. Thermochimica Acta 654: 40–50.

Donath, S., H. Militz and C. Mai. 2004. Wood modification with alkoxysilanes. Wood Science and Technology 38: 555–566.

Doubek, S., V. Borůvka, A. Zeidler and L. Reinprecht. 2018. Effect of the passive chemical modification of wood with silicon dioxide (silica) on its properties and inhibition of moulds. Wood Research 6(4): 599–618.

Du, T., T.F. Shupe and C.Y. Hse. 2009. Antifungal activities of three supercritical fluid extracted cedar oils. *In*: The Proceedings IRG Annual Meeting, Beijing, China. International Research Group on Wood Protection IRG/WP 09-30501.

Duran, N., M.F.S. Tixeira, R. de Conti and E. Esposito. 2002. Ecological-friendly pigments from fungi. Critical Reviews in Food Science and Nutrition 42: 53–66.

Eastman, S.A., A.J. Lesser and T.J. McCarthy. 2009. Supercritical CO_2-assisted, silicone-modified wood for enhanced fire resistance. Journal of Materials Science 44(5): 1275–1282.

Elchinger, P.-H., P.-A. Faugeras, B. Boëns, F. Brouillette, D. Montplaisir, R. Zerrouki and R. Lucas. 2011. Polysaccharides: The "click" chemistry impact. Polymers 3(4): 1607–1651.

El Tahlawy, K. and S.M. Hudson. 2003. Synthesis of a well-defined chitosan graft poly(methoxy polyethyleneglycol) methacrylate) by atom transfer radical polymerization. Journal of Applied Polymer Science 89: 901–912.

Emaminasab, M., A. Tarmian, K. Pourtahmasi and S. Avramidis. 2016. Improving the permeability of Douglas-fir (*Pseudotsuga menziesii*) containing compression wood by *Physisporinus vitreus* and *Xylaria longipes*. International Wood Products Journal 7(3): 110–115.

Ensikat, H.J., P. Ditsche-Kuru, C. Neinhuis and W. Bartholtt. 2011. Superhydrophobicity in perfection: The outstanding properties of the lotus leaf. Beilstein Journal of Nanotechnology 2: 152–161.

Evans, P.D. 2016. The effects of incising on the checking of wood: A review. International Wood Products Journal 7(1): 12–25.

Evans, P.D., A.J. Michell and K.J. Schmalzl. 1992. Studies of the degradation and protection of wood surfaces. Wood Science and Technology 26(2): 151–163.

Eyckens, D.J. and L.C. Henderson. 2019. A review of solvate ionic liquids: Physical parameters and synthetic applications. Frontiers in Chemistry 7: Article ID 263.

Fackler, K., C. Gradinger, B. Hinterstoisser, K. Messner and M. Schwanninger. 2006. Lignin degradation by white rot fungi on spruce wood shavings during short-time solid-state fermentations monitored by near infrared spectroscopy. Enzyme and Microbial Technology 39(7): 1476–1483.

Fang, C., R. Yu, Y. Zhang, J. Hu, M. Zhang and X. Mi. 2012. Combined modification of asphalt with polyethylene packaging waste and organophilic montmorillonite. Polymer Testing 31: 276–281.

Felby, C., B.R. Nielsen and P.O. Olesen. 1997. Identification and quantification of radical reaction intermediates by electron spin resonance spectrometry of laccase-catalyzed oxidation of wood fibers from beech (*Fagus sylvatica*). Applied Microbiology and Biotechnology 48(4): 459–464.

Felby, C., J. Hassingboe and M. Lund. 2002. Pilot-scale production of fiberboards made by laccase oxidized wood fibers: Board properties and evidence for cross-linking of lignin. Enzyme and Microbial Technology 31(6): 736–741.

Felby, C., L.G. Thyggesen, A. Sanadi and S. Barsberg. 2004. Native lignin for bonding of fiber boards: Evaluation of bonding mechanisms in boards made from laccase-treated fibers of beech (*Fagus sylvatica*). Industrial Crops and Products 20(2): 181–189.

Freeman, M.H. and C.R. Mcintyre. 2008. A comprehensive review of copper-based wood preservatives with a focused on new micronized or dispersed copper systems. Forest Products Journal 58(11): 6–27.

Fu, Q., L. Medina, Y. Li, F. Carosio, A. Hajian and L.A. Berglund. 2017. Nanostructured wood hybrids for fire-retardancy prepared by clay impregnation into the cell wall. ACS Applied Materials & Interfaces 9(41): 36154–36163.

Gairola, K. and I. Smirnova. 2012. Hydrothermal pentose to furfural conversion and simultaneous extraction with SC-CO_2-kinetics and application to biomass hydrolysates. Bioresource Technology 123: 592–598.

Gan, W., S. Xiao, L. Gao, R. Gao, J. Li and X. Zhan. 2017. Luminescent and transparent wood composites fabricated by poly(methyl methacrylate) and γ-Fe_2O_3@YVO_4:Eu^{3+} nanoparticle impregnation. ACS Sustainable Chemistry and Engineering 5(5): 3855–3862.

Gao, L., Y. Lu, J. Li and Q. Sun. 2016. Superhydrophobic conductive wood with oil repellency obtained by coating with silver nanoparticles modified by fluoroalkyl silane. Holzforschung 70(1): 63–68.

Gérardin, P. 2015. New alternatives for wood preservation based on thermal and chemical modification of wood: A review. Annals of Forest Science 73(3): 559–570.

Ghandi, K. 2014. A Review of ionic liquids, their limits and applications. Green and Sustainable Chemistry 4(1): 44–53.

Gindrat, D., E. Hoeven and A.R. Moody. 1977. Control of *Phomopsis sclerotioides* with *Gliocladium roseum* or *Trichoderma*. Netherlands Journal of Plant Pathology 83(S1): 429–438.

Goffredo, G.B., S. Accoroni, T. Totti, T. Romagnoli, L. Valentini and P. Munafò. 2017. Titanium dioxide based nanotreatments to inhibit microalgal fouling on building stone surfaces. Building and Environment 112: 209–222.

Graenacher, C. 1934. Cellulose solutions. U.S. Patent No. 1943176.

Greaves, H. 1969. Micromorphology of bacterial attack in wood. Wood Science and Technology 3: 150–166.

Greaves, H. 1971. The bacterial factor in wood decay. Wood Science and Technology 5: 6–16.

Guo, R., C. Hu, F. Pan, H. Wu and Z. Jiang. 2006. PVA-GPTMS/TEOS hybrid pervaporation membrane for dehydration of ethylene glycol aqueous solution. Journal of Membrane Science 281: 454–462.

Guo, R., X. Ma, C. Hu and Z. Jiang. 2007. Novel PVA-silica nanocomposite membrane for pervaporative dehydration of ethylene glycol aqueous solution. Polymer 48: 2939–2945.

Götze, J., R. Möckel, N. Langhof, M. Hengst and M. Klinger. 2008. Silicification of wood in the laboratory. Ceramics-Silikáty 52(4): 267–277.

Hafizoğlu, H. 1979. Investigations on Turkish tall oils. PhD. Thesis, Research Institute of the Åbo Akademi Foundation, Finland.

Han, Y., L. Yuan, G. Li, L. Huang, T. Qin, F. Chu and C. Tang. 2016. Renewable polymers from lignin via copper-free thermal click chemistry. Polymer 83: 92–100.

Harper, D.P. 2003. A thermodynamic, spectroscopic, and mechanical characterization of the wood-polypropylene interphase. PhD. Thesis, University of Washington, USA.

Harris, A. 2017. Laccase: Applications, Investigations and Insights. Biochemistry Research Trends. Nova Science Publishers, New York, USA.

Heinze, T., K. Schwikal and S. Barthel. 2005. Ionic liquids as reaction medium in cellulose functionalization. Macromolecular Bioscience 5: 520–525.

Held, B.W., J.M. Thwaites, R.L. Farrell and R.A. Blanchette. 2003. Albino strains of *Ophiostoma* species for biological control of sapstaining fungi. Holzforschung 57(3): 237–242.

Homan, W.J. and A.J.M. Jorissen. 2004. Wood modification developments. Heron 49(4): 361–385.

Hough, W.L., M. Smiglak, H. Rodriguez, R.P. Swatloski, S.K. Spear, D.T. Daly, J. Pernak, J.E. Grisel, R.D. Carliss, M.D. Soutullo, J.H. Davis and R.D. Rogers. 2007. The third evolution of ionic liquids: Active pharmaceutical ingredients. New Journal of Chemistry 31(8): 1429–1436.

Hoyle, C.E. and C.N. Bowman. 2010. Thiol-ene click chemistry. Angewandte Chemie International Edition 49(9): 1540–1573.

Huang, J., S. Wang, S. Lyu and F. Fu. 2018. Preparation of a robust cellulose nanocrystal superhydrophobic coating for self-cleaning and oil-water separation only by spraying. Industrial Crops and Products 122: 438–447.

Humphris, S.N., R.E. Wheatley and A. Bruce. 2001. The effects of specific volatile organic compounds produced by *Trichoderma* spp. on the growth of wood decay basidiomycetes. Holzforschung 55(3): 233–237.

Hübert, T. and M.S. Mahr. 2017. Sol-gel wood preservation, pp. 2795–2841. *In*: Klein, L., Aparicio, M. and Jitianu, A. [eds.]. Handbook of Sol-gel Science and Technology. Part IV. Applications: Preservation, Organic–Inorganic Hybrids, and Bio-related Materials. Springer International Publishing AG, Cham, Switzerland.

Isik, M., H. Sardon and D. Mecerreyes. 2014. Ionic liquids and cellulose: Dissolution, chemical modification and preparation of new cellulosic materials. International Journal of Molecular Sciences 15: 11922–11940.

Javed, M.N., S. Muhammad, I.A. Hashmi, A. Bari, S.G. Musharraf and F.I. Ali. 2018. Newly designed pyridine and piperidine based ionic liquids: aggregation behavior in ESI-MS and catalytic activity in C-C bond formation reactions. Journal of Molecular Liquids 272(15): 84–91.

Jermouni, T., M. Smaihi and N. Hovnanian. 1995. Hydrolysis and initial polycondensation of phenyltrimethoxysilane and diphenyldimethoxysilane. Journal of Materials Chemistry 5: 1203–1208.

Jin, L., T. Sellers, T.P. Schultz and D.D. Nicholas. 1990. Utilization of lignin modified by brown-rot fungi. Holzforschung 44: 207–210.

Jones, D., N. Howard and E. Suttie. 2011. The potential of propolis and other naturally occurring products for preventing biological decay. *In*: The Proceedings IRG Annual Meeting, Queenstown, New Zealand. International Research Group on Wood Protection IRG/WP 11-30575.

Joye, N.M. and R.V. Lawrence. 1961. The thermal isomerization of palustric acid. Journal of Organic Chemistry 26: 1024–1026.

Kakko, T.-A. 2019. Modification and characterisation of wood components. PhD. Thesis, University of Helsinki, Finland.

Kang, S.-M. and J.J. Morrell. 2003. Supercritical fluid impregnation of Douglas-fir heartwood with cyproconazole using temperature induced deposition. *In*: The Proceedings IRG Annual Meeting, Brisbane, Australia. International Research Group on Wood Protection IRG/WP 03-40259.

Kang, S.M., A. Unger and J.J. Morrell. 2004. The effect of supercritical carbon dioxide extraction on color retention and pesticide reduction of wooden artifacts. Journal of the American Institute for Conservation 43(2): 151–160.

Kartal, S.N., F. Green and C.A. Clausen. 2009. Do the unique properties of nanomaterials affect leachability or efficacy against fungi and termites? International Biodeterioration and Biodegradation 63: 497–514.

Kazayawoko, M., J.J. Balantinecz and R.T. Woodhams. 1997. Diffuse reflectance Fourier transform infrared spectra of wood fibers treated with maleated polypropylenes. Journal of Applied Polymer Science 66: 1163–1173.

Kilpeläinen, I., H. Xie, A. King, M. Granstrom, S. Heikkinen and D.S. Argyropoulos. 2007. Dissolution of wood in ionic liquids. Journal of Agricultural and Food Chemistry 55(22): 9142–9148.

Kim, G.-H., S. Kumar, E.S. Demessie, K.L. Levien and J.J. Morrell. 1997. Bending properties of TCMTB-treated Southern pine sapwood using supercritical carbon dioxide impregnation process. *In*: The Proceedings IRG Annual Meeting, Whistler, Canada. International Research Group on Wood Protection IRG/WP 97-40080.

Kjellow, A.W. and O. Henriksen. 2009a. Interactions between wood and propiconazole in supercritical carbon dioxide. *In*: The Proceedings IRG Annual Meeting, Beijing, China. International Research Group on Wood Protection IRG/WP 09-40461.

Kjellow, A.W. and O. Henriksen. 2009b. Supercritical wood impregnation. The Journal of Supercritical Fluids 50(3): 297–304.

Kolb, H.C., M.G. Finn and K.B. Sharpless. 2001. Click chemistry: Diverse chemical function from a few good reactions. Angewandte Chemie International Edition 40: 2004–2021.

Knuth, D.T. and E. McCoy. 1962. Bacterial deterioration of pine logs in pond storage. Forest Products Journal 12: 437–442.

Kobayashi, Y., I. Iida, Y. Imamura and U. Watanabe. 1998. Drying and anatomical characteristics of sugi wood attacked by bacteria during pond storage. Journal of Wood Science 44: 432–437.

Kokorin, A. [ed.]. 2011. Ionic Liquids: Applications and Perspectives. InTech Publications, Rijeke, Croatia.

Kreber, B. and J.J. Morrell. 1993. Ability of selected bacterial and fungal bioprotectants to limit fungal stain in ponderosa pine sapwood. Journal of Wood and Fiber Science 25(1): 23–34.

Kubel, H. and A. Pizzi. 1981. Protection of wood surfaces with metallic oxides. Journal of Wood Chemistry and Technology 1(1): 75–92.

Kumar, S. and J.J. Morrell. 1993. Effect of fatty acid removal on treatability of Douglas fir. *In*: The Proceedings IRG Annual Meeting, Orlando (FL), USA. International Research Group on Wood Protection IRG/WP 93-40008.

Kunamneni, A., S. Camerero, C. García-Burgos, F.J. Plou, A. Ballesteros and M. Alcade. 2008. Engineering and applications of fungal laccases for organic synthesis. Microbial Cell Factories 7(1): Article ID 32.

Kurowski, W.M. and J.A. Dunleavy. 1976. Pectinase production by bacteria associated with improved preservative permeability in Sitka spruce. Synthesis and secretion of polygalacturonate lyase by *Cytophaga johnsonii*. Journal of Applied Bacteriology 41(1): 119–128.

Köhler, S., T. Liebert and T. Heinze. 2008. Interactions of ionic liquids with polysaccharides. VI. Pure cellulose nanoparticles from trimethylsilyl cellulose synthesized in ionic liquids. Journal of Polymer Science Part A: Polymer Chemistry 46(12): 4070–4080.

Lee, P.-I. and S.L.-C. Hsu. 2007. Preparation and properties of polybenzoxazole–silica nanocomposites via sol–gel process. European Polymer Journal 43(2): 294–299.

Legay, S., P. Marchal and G. Labat. 1998. Alternative technologies for wood wastes recycling. Part B: Biotreatment of PCP- and creosote-treated wood. *In*: The Proceedings IRG Annual Meeting, Maastricht, The Netherlands. International Research Group on Wood Protection IRG/WP 98-50101-18 b.

Li, Y., Q. Fu, S. Yu, M. Yan and L. Berglund. 2016. Optically transparent wood from a nanoporous cellulosic template: Combining functional and structural performance. Biomacromolecules 17(4): 1358–1364.

Liebert, T., C. Hänsch and T. Heinze. 2006. Click chemistry with polysaccharides. Macromolecular Rapid Communications 27(3): 208–213.

Liese, W. and J. Bauch. 1967. On the closure of bordered pits in conifers. Wood Science and Technology 1: 1–13.

Lin, K., U. Jeng and K. Lin. 2011. Adsorption and intercalation processes of ionic surfactants on montmorillonite associated with their ionic charge. Materials Chemistry and Physics 131: 120–126.

Lin, Y., N.G. Smart and C.M. Wai. 1995. Supercritical fluid extraction and chromatography of metal chelates and organometallic compounds. Trends in Analytical Chemistry 14: 123–133.

Liu, F., S. Wang, M. Zhang, M. Ma, C. Wang and J. Li. 2013. Improvement of mechanical robustness of the superhydrophobic wood surface by coating PVA/SiO$_2$ composite polymer. Applied Surface Science 280: 686–692.

Liu, X., X. Zou, Z. Ge, W. Zhang and Y. Luo. 2019. Novel waterborne polyurethanes containing long-chain alkanes: Their synthesis and application to water repellency. RSC Advances 9(54): 31357–31369.

Losey, M.W., J.J. Kelly, N.D. Badgayan, S.K. Sahu and P.S. Rama Sreekanth. 2017. Electrodeposition, pp. 1–20. *In*: Hashmi, S. [ed.]. Volume 13: Reference Module in Materials Science and Materials Engineering. Elsevier, Oxford, UK.

Lucas, M., G.L. Wagner, Y. Nishiyama, L. Hanson, I.P. Samayam, C.A. Schall, P. Langan and K.D. Rector. 2011. Reversible swelling of the cell wall of poplar biomass by ionic liquid at room temperature. Bioresource Technology 102: 4518–4523.

Lü, W., G. Zhao and Z. Xue. 2006. Preparation and characterization of wood/montmorillonite nanocomposites. Forestry Studies in China 8(1): 35–40.

Ma, Y., H. He, B. Huang, H. Jing and Z. Zhao. 2019. *In situ* fabrication of wood flour/nano silica hybrid and its application in polypropylene-based wood-plastic composites. Polymer Composites 41(2): 573–584.

Macken, J. and A.H. Pickaver. 1979. Synthesis of polygalacturonate transeliminase and polygalacturonase by a strain of *Enterobacter cloacae* isolated from ponded Sitka spruce. Journal of Applied Bacteriology 46: 75–86.

Mai, N.L., S.H. Ha and Y.-M. Koo. 2014. Efficient pretreatment in ionic liquids/co-solvent for enzymatic hydrolysis enhancement into fermentable sugars. Process Biochemistry 49: 1144–1151.

Mapari, S.A., K.F. Nielsen, T.O. Larsen, J.C. Frisvad, A.S. Meyer and U. Thrane. 2005. Exploring fungal biodiversity for the production of water-soluble pigments as potential natural food colorants. Current Opinion in Biotechnology 16(2): 231–238.

Marchessault, R.H., S. Ricard and P. Rioux. 1992a. *In situ* synthesis of ferrites in lignocellulosics. Carbohydrate Research 224: 133–139.

Marchessault, R.H., P. Rioux and L. Raymond. 1992b. Magnetic cellulose fibres and paper: Preparation, processing and properties. Polymer 33(19): 4024–4028.

Matsuda, H., M. Ueda and M. Hara. 1984a. Preparation and utilization of esterified wood bearing carboxyl groups (I). Esterification of wood with dicarboxylic acid anhydrides in presence of a solvent. Mokuzai Gakkaishi 30: 735–741.

Matsuda, H., M. Ueda and K. Murakami. 1984b. Preparation and utilization of esterified wood bearing carboxyl groups (II). Esterification of wood with dicarboxylic acid anhydrides in the absence of a solvent. Mokuzai Gakkaishi 30: 1003–1010.

Matsunaga, M., Y. Kataoka, H. Matsunaga and H. Matsui. 2010. A novel method of acetylation of wood using supercritical carbon dioxide. Journal of Wood Science 56(4): 293–298.

Mauldin, T.C. and M.R. Kessler. 2010. Self-healing polymers and composites. International Materials Reviews 55(6): 317–346.

Merk, V., M. Chanana, S. Gaan and Ingo Burgert. 2016. Mineralization of wood by calcium carbonate insertion for improved flame retardancy. Holzforschung 70(9): 867–876.

Merk, V., J.K. Berg, C. Krywka and I. Burgert. 2017. Oriented crystallization of barium sulfate confined in hierarchical cellular structures. Crystal Growth & Design 17(2): 677–684.

Messner, K. 1998. Biopulping, pp. 63–82. *In*: Bruce, A. and Palfreyman, J.W. [eds.]. Forest Products Biotechnology. Taylor & Francis, London, UK.

Messner, K., V. Fleck, A. Bruce and B. Rosner. 2000. Processing for improving the impregnability of wood by pretreatment with fungi. U.S. Patent No. US6475566B1.

Messner, K., A. Bruce and H.P.M. Bongers. 2003. Treatability of refractory wood species after fungal pre-treatment, pp. 389–401. *In*: Van Acker, J. and Hill, C. [eds.]. Proceedings European Conference on Wood Modification, Ghent, Belgium.

Minoura, Y., M. Ueda, S. Mizunuma and M. Oba. 1969. The reaction of polypropylene with maleic anhydride. Journal of Applied Polymer Science 13(8): 1625–1640.

Miyafuji, H. and N. Suzuki. 2012. Morphological changes in sugi (*Cryptomeria japonica*) wood after treatment with the ionic liquid, 1-ethyl-3-methylimidazolium chloride. Journal of Wood Science 58: 222–230.

Moellmann, E., T. Heinze, T. Liebert and S. Koehler. 2009. Homogeneous synthesis of cellulose ethers in ionic liquids. U.S. Patent No. US8541571B2.

Montazer, M. and S. Seifollahzadeh. 2011. Enhanced self-cleaning, antibacterial and UV protection properties of nano TiO$_2$ treated textile through enzymatic pretreatment. Photochemistry and Photobiology 87(4): 877–883.

Mookerjee, P.K., V. Govindegowda and S.V. Damarla. 2017. Water repellent combinations. World patent WO2017/042120.

Morris, P.I., J.J. Morrell and J.N.R. Ruddick. 1994. A review of incising as a means of improving treatment of sawn wood. *In*: The Proceedings IRG Annual Meeting, Nusa Dua, Bali, Indonesia. International Research Group on Wood Protection IRG/WP/9440019.

Moya, R., A. Rodríguez-Zúñiga, J. Vega-Baudrit and V. Álvarez. 2015. Effects of adding nano-clay (montmorillonite) on performance of polyvinyl acetate (PVAc) and urea-formaldehyde (UF) adhesives in *Carapa guianensis*, a tropical species. International Journal of Adhesion and Adhesives 59: 62–70.

Moya, R., A. Rodriguez-Zuñiga, A. Berrocal and J. Vega-Baudrit. 2017. Effect of silver nanoparticles synthesized with NPs Ag-ethylene glycol ($C_2H_6O_2$) on brown decay and white decay fungi of nine tropical woods. Journal of Nanoscience and Nanotechnology 17(8): 5233–5240.

Muin, M. and K. Tsunoda. 2003. Preservative treatment of wood-based composites with 3-iodo-2-propynyl butylcarbamate using supercritical carbon dioxide impregnation. Journal of Wood Science 49: 430–436.

Muin, M. and K. Tsunoda. 2004. Retention of silafluofen in wood-based composites after supercritical carbon dioxide impregnation. Forest Products Journal 54(12): 168–171.

Munawar, R.F., S. Zakaria. S. Radiman, C.-C. Hua, M. Abdullah and T. Yamauchi. 2010. Properties of magnetic paper prepared via *in situ* synthesis method. Sains Malaysiana 39(4): 593–598.

Munimbazi, C. and L.B. Bullerman. 1998. Isolation and partial characterization of antifungal metabolites of Bacillus pumilus. Journal of Applied Microbiology 84: 959–968.

Munro, N.H., L.R. Hanton, S.C. Moratti and B.H. Robinson. 2007. Synthesis and characterisation of chitosan combs by ATRP. Advances in Chitin Science 10: 91–95.

Munro, N.H., L.R. Hanton, S.C. Moratti and B.H. Robinson. 2009. Synthesis and characterisation of chitosan-graft-poly(OEGMA) copolymers prepared by ATRP. Carbohydrate Polymers 77(3): 496–505.

Myllymaeki, V. and R. Aksela. 2005. A method for preparing a cellulose ether. International Patent No. WO 2005054298.

Neyses, B., L. Rautkari, A. Yamamoto and D. Sandberg. 2017. Pre-treatment with sodium silicate, sodium hydroxide, ionic liquids or methacrylate resin to reduce the set-recovery and increase the hardness of surface-densified Scots pine. iForest 10: 857–864.

Neyses, B., O. Karlsson and D. Sandberg. 2019. The effect of ionic liquid and superbase pre-treatment on the spring-back, set-recovery and Brinell hardness of surface-densified Scots pine. Holzforschung 74(3): 303–312.

Neyses, B., D. Buck, K. Peeters, L. Rautkari and D. Sandberg. 2020. *In-situ* penetration of ionic liquids during surface densification of Scots pine. Holzforschung. https://doi.org/10.1515/hf-2020-0146.

Nowak, J., M. Florek, W. Kwiatek, J. Lekki, P. Chevallier, E. Zięba, N. Mestres, E.M. Dutkiewicz and A. Kuczumov. 2005. Composite structure of wood cells in petrified wood. Material Science and Engineering C 25(2): 119–130.

Oertel, J. 1965. Novel wood preservatives of good leaching resistance based on water soluble organic compounds and their potential uses. Holztechnologie 6(4): 243–247.

Oliveira, M.V.S., B.T. Vidal, C.M. Melo, R. De C.M. de Miranda, C.M.F. Soares, J.A.P. Coutinho, S.P.M. Ventura and Á.S. Lima. 2016. (Eco)toxicity and biodegradability of protic ionic liquids. Chemosphere 147: 460–466.

Pandit, S.K., B.K. Tudu, I.M. Mishra and A. Kumar. 2019. Development of stain resistant, superhydrophobic and self-cleaning coating on wood surface. Progress in Organic Coatings 139: Article ID 105453.

Paulissen, R., H. Reimlinger, E. Hayez, A.J. Hubert and C.P. Teyssié. 1973. Transition metal catalysed reactions of diazocompounds – II insertion in the hydroxylic bond. Tetrahedron Letters 14(24): 2233–2236.

Pánek, M. and L. Reinprecht. 2008. Bio-treatment of spruce wood for improving of its permeability and soaking, part 1: Direct treatment with the bacterium *Bactillus subtilis*. Wood Research 53(2): 1–12

Pánek, M. and L. Reinprecht. 2011. *Bacillus subtilis* for improving spruce wood impregnability. BioResources 6(3): 2912–2931.

Pánek, M., L. Reinprecht and M. Hulla. 2014. Ten essential oils for beech wood protection – Efficacy against wood-destroying fungi and moulds, and effect on wood discoloration. BioResources 9(3): 5588–5603.

Peddibhotla, S., Y. Dang, J.O. Liu and D. Romo. 2007. Simultaneous arming and structure/activity studies of natural products employing O–H insertions: An expedient and versatile strategy for natural products-based chemical genetics. Journal of the American Chemical Society 129(40): 12222–12231.

Pernak, J., J. Zabielska-Matejuk and E. Urbanik. 1998. New quaternary ammonium chlorides—Wood preservatives. Holzforschung 52(3): 249–254.

Pernak, J., J. Zabielska-Matejuk, A. Kropacz and J. Foksowicz-Flaczyk. 2004. Ionic liquids in wood preservation. Holzforschung 58(3): 286–291.

Pinkert, A., D.F. Goeke, K.N. Marsh and S. Pang. 2011. Extracting wood lignin without dissolving or degrading cellulose: Investigations on the use of food additive-derived ionic liquids. Green Chemistry 13: 3124–3136.

Poaty, B., B. Riedl, P. Blanchet, V. Blanchard and L. Stafford. 2012. Improved water repellency of black spruce wood surfaces after treatment in carbon tetrafluoride plasmas. Wood Science and Technology 47(2): 411–422.

Polo, A., M.V. Diamanti, T. Bjarnsholt, N. Høiby, F. Villa, M.P. Pedeferri and F. Cappitelli. 2011. Effects of photoactivated titanium dioxide nanopowders and coating on plank-tonic and biofilm growth of Pseudomonas aeruginosa. Photochemistry and Photobiology 87: 1387–1394.

Possidonio, S., L.C. Fidale and O.A. El Seoud. 2010. Microwave-assisted derivatization of cellulose in an ionic liquid: An efficient, expedient synthesis of simple and mixed carboxylic esters. Journal of Polymer Science Part A: Polymer Chemistry 48(1): 134–143.

Prabhakaran, R.T.D., M.J. Spear, S. Curling, P. Wootton-Beard, P. Jones, I. Donnison and G.A. Ormondroyd. 2019. Plants and architecture: The role of biology and biomimetics in materials development for buildings. Intelligent Buildings International 11(3/4): 178–211.

Preston, A.F. and D.D. Nicholas. 1982. Efficacy of a series of alkylammonium compounds against wood decay fungi and termites. Wood and Fiber Science 14(11): 37–42.

Pu, Y.Q., N. Jiang and A.J. Ragauskas. 2007. Ionic liquid as a green solvent for lignin. Journal of Wood Chemistry and Technology 27(1): 23–33.

Qader, A., L.J. Cookson, J.W. Creffield and D. Scown. 2005. Termite field tests of various timber species treated with permethrin using supercritical carbon dioxide. *In*: The Proceedings IRG Annual Meeting, Bangalore, India. International Research Group on Wood Protection IRG/WP 05-10560.

Rashid, T., C.F. Kait, I. Regupathi and T. Murugesan. 2016. Dissolution of kraft lignin using Protic Ionic liquids and characterization. Industrial Crops and Products 84: 284–293.

Raymond, L., J.-F. Revol, D.H. Ryan and R.H. Marchessault. 1994. *In situ* synthesis of ferrites in cellulosics. Chemistry of Materials 6(2): 249–255.

Reinprecht, L. and T. Grznárik. 2015. Biological durability of Scots pine (*Pinus sylvestris* L.) sapwood modified with selected organo-silanes. Wood Research 60(5): 687–696.

Reinprecht, L., M. Pánek, J. Daňková, T. Murínová, P. Mec and Z. Plevová. 2013. Performance of methyl-tripotasiumsilanol treated wood against swelling in water, decay fungi and moulds. Wood Research 58(4): 511–520.

Ren, J.L., R.C. Sun, C.F. Liu, Z.N. Cao and W. Luo. 2007. Acetylation of wheat straw hemicelluloses in ionic liquid using iodine as a catalyst. Carbohydrate Polymers 70(4): 406–414.

Richardson, B.A. 1993. Wood Preservation (2nd edn.). E & FN Spoon, London, UK.

Robinson, S.C., S.M. Vega Gutierrez, R.A. Cespedes Garcia, N. Iroume, N.R. Vorland, C. Andersen, I.D. de Oliveira Xaxa, O.E. Kramer and M.E. Huber. 2018. Potential for fungal dyes as colorants in oil and acrylic paints. Journal of Coatings Technology and Research 15(4): 845–849.

Rosenau, T., A. Potthast, H. Sixta and P. Kosma. 2001. The chemistry of side reactions and byproduct formation in the system NMMO/cellulose (Lyocell process). Progress in Polymer Science 26: 1763–1837.

Rossell, S.E., E.G.M. Abbot and J.F. Levy. 1973. A review of the literature relating to the presence, action and interaction in wood. Journal of the Institute of Wood Science 6: 28–35.

Ruddick, J.N.R. 1991. Laser incising of Canadian softwood to improve treatability. Forest Products Journal 41(4): 53–57.

Saher, S., H. Saleem, A.M. Asim, M. Uroos and N. Muhammad. 2018. Pyridinium based ionic liquid: A pretreatment solvent and reaction medium for catalytic conversion of cellulose to total reducing sugars (TRS). Journal of Molecular Liquids 272: 330–336.

Saka, S. and T. Ueno. 1997. Several SiO_2 wood-inorganic composites and their fire-resisting properties. Wood Science and Technology 31: 457–466.

Saka, S. and T. Ueno. 1999. Chemical conversion of various celluloses to glucose and its derivatives in supercritical water. Cellulose 6: 177–191.

Saka, S., M. Sasaki and M. Tanahashi. 1992. Wood–inorganic composites prepared by sol-gel processing: 1. Wood—inorganic composites with porous structure. Mokuzai Gakkaishi 38: 1043–1049.

Sakagami, H., S. Higurashi, T. Tsuda, S. Seino and S. Kuwabata. 2018. Decay resistance of polymerized ionic liquid-modified woods. BioResources 13(3): 5702–5710.

Sakhno, T.V., N.N. Barashkov, I.S. Irgibaeva, S.V. Pustovit and Y.E. Sakhno. 2016. Polymer coatings for protection of wood and wood-based materials. Advances in Chemical Engineering and Science 6: 93–110.

Schoeman, M.W., J.F. Webber and D.J. Dickinson. 1996. The effect of diffusible metabolites of *Trichoderma harzianum* on *in vitro* interactions between basidiomycete isolates at two different temperature regimes. Mycological Research 100(12): 1454–1458.

Schmidt, O. and H.H. Dietrichs. 1976. Zur aktivitat von Bakterien gegenuber [About the activity of bacteria.] Holzkomponenten Material und Organismen, Supplement 3: 91–102.

Schwarze, F.W.M.R. 2008. Procedure and composition for the improvement of the uptake and distribution of soaking compositions in woods. EMPA Report No. EP1681145, Swiss Federal Laboratories for Materials Science and Technology, Zürich, Switzerland.

Schwarze, F.W.M.R. and H. Landmesser. 2000. Preferential degradation of pit membranes within tracheids by the basidiomycete *Physisporinus vitreus*. Holzforschung 54: 461–462.

Schwarze, F.W.M.R. and M. Schubert. 2017. Bioengineering of value-added wood using the white rot fungus *Physisporinus vitreus*, pp. 435–459. *In*: Mérillon, J.M. and Ramawat, K. [eds.]. Fungal Metabolites. Reference Series in Phytochemistry. Springer, Cham, Switzerland.

Schwarze, F.W.M.R., H. Landmesser, B. Zgraggen and M. Heeb. 2006. Permeability changes in heartwood of *Picea abies* and *Abies alba* induced by incubation with *Physisporinus vitreus*. Holzforschung 60: 450−454.

Shah, S.M., U. Zulfiqar, S.Z. Hussain, I. Ahmad, I. Hussain and T. Subhani. 2017. A durable superhydrophobic coating for the protection of wood materials. Materials Letters 203: 17–20.

Shen, X., Y. Xie and Q. Wang. 2016. Improved acetylation efficacy of wood fibers by ionic liquid pretreatment. BioResources 12(1): 684−695.

Shiflett, M.B. 2020. Commercial Applications of Ionic Liquids. Green chemistry and sustainable technology Series, Springer, Cham, Switzerland.

Shiny, K.S., R. Sundararaj, N. Mamatha and B. Lingappa. 2019. A new approach to wood protection: Preliminary study of biologically synthesized copper oxide nanoparticle formulation as an environmental friendly wood protectant against decay fungi and termites. Maderas. Ciencia y tecnología 21(3): 347–356.

Smith, S.M., J.J. Morrell, E. Sahle-Demessie and K.L. Levien. 1993. Supercritical fluid treatment: Effects on bending strength of white spruce heartwood. *In*: The Proceedings IRG Annual Meeting, Orlando, Florida, USA. International Research Group on Wood Protection IRG/WP 93-20008.

Soltani, M., A. Najafi, S. Yousefian, H.R. Naji and E.S. Bakar. 2013. Water repellent effect and dimension stability of beech wood impregnated with nano-zinc oxide. BioResources 8(4): 6280–6287.

Sunol, A.K. 1991. Supercritical fluid-aided treatment of porous materials. U.S. Patent No. US4992308A.

Susi, P., G. Aktuganov, J. Himanen and T. Korpela. 2011. Biological control of wood decay against fungal infection. Journal of Environmental Management 92(7): 1681–1689.

Swatloski, R.P., S.K. Spear, J.D. Holbrey and R.D. Rogers. 2002. Dissolution cellulose with ionic liquids. Journal of the American Chemical Society 124: 4974–4975.

Tanno, F., S. Saka, A. Yamamoto and K. Takabe. 1998. Antimicrobial TMSAH-added wood-inorganic composites prepared by the sol-gel process. Holzforschung 52: 365–370.

Thaler, N., B. Lesar, M. Kariz and M. Humar. 2012. Bioincising of Norway spruce wood using wood inhabiting fungi. International Biodeterioration & Biodegradation 68: 51–55.

Thuy Pham, T.P., C.-W. Cho and Y.-S. Yun. 2010. Environmental fate and toxicity of ionic liquids: A review. Water Research 44(2): 352–372.

Tjong, S.C., S.-A. Xu and Y.-W. Mai. 2002. Impact-specific essential work of fracture of maleic anhydride-compatibilized polypropylene/elastomer blends and their composites. Journal of Polymer Science Part B: Polymer Physics 40(17): 1881–1892.

Tolesa, L.D., B.S. Gupta and M.-J. Lee. 2017. The chemistry of ammonium-based ionic liquids in depolymerization process of lignin. Journal of Molecular Liquids 248: 227–234.

Tome, L.C., M.G. Freire, L.P.N. Rebelo, A.J.D. Silvestre, J.P. Neto, I.M. Marrucho and C.S.R. Freire. 2011. Surface hydrophobization of bacterial and vegetable cellulose fibers using ionic liquids as solvent media and catalysts. Green Chemistry 13: 2464–2470.

Trader, D.J. and E.E. Carlson. 2012. Chemoselective hydroxyl group transformation: An elusive target. Molecular BioSystems 8(10): 2484–2493.

Trey, S., R.T. Olsson, V. Ström, L. Berglund and M. Johansson. 2014. Controlled deposition of magnetic particles within the 3-D template of wood: Making use of the natural hierarchical structure of wood. RSC Advances 4(67): 35678–35685.

Tshabalala, M.A., P. Kinshott, M.R. VanLandingham and D. Plackett. 2003. Surface chemistry and moisture sorption properties of wood coated with multifunctional alkoxysilanes by sol-gel process. Journal of Applied Polymer Science 88: 2828–2841.

Tshabalala, M.A., R. Libert and N.R. Sutherland. 2009. Outdoor weathering of sol-gel-treated wood, 12 pp. *In*: Secretariat National Paint and Coatings Association [ed.]. Third International Coating Wood and Wood Composites Conference: Durable and Sustainable—Today and Beyond, Charlotte (NC), USA.

Tsioptsias, C. and C. Panayiotou. 2011. Thermal stability and hydrophobicity enhancement of wood through impregnation with aqueous solutions and supercritical carbon dioxide. Journal of Materials Science 46(16): 5406–5411.

Tung, W.S. and W.A. Daoud. 2011. Self-cleaning fibers via nanotechnology: A virtual reality. Journal of Materials Chemistry 21: 7858–7869.

Van Beek, T.A., B. Kuster, F.W. Claassen, T. Tienvieri, F. Bertaud, G. Lenon, M. Petit-Concil and R. Sierra-Alvarez. 2007. Fungal bio-treatment of spruce wood with *Trametes versicolor* for pitch control: Influence on extractive contents, pulping process parameters, paper quality and effluent toxicity. Bioresource Technology 98(2): 302–311.

Van Court, R.C., P. Vega Gutierrez and S.C. Robinson. 2020. Pigment production by the spalting fungus *Scytalidium ganodermophthorum* and its industry potential. *In*: IRG Webinar 2020. International Research Group on Wood Protection IRG/WP 20-10957.

Vitz, J., T. Erdmenger and U.S. Schubert. 2010. Imidazolium based ionic liquids as solvents for cellulose chemistry. ACS Symposium Series 1033: 299–317.

Vu, C. and O. Laferte. 2006. Silica nanoparticles in the optimisation of scratch and abrasion resistance of high performance UV multi-layer coatings. European Coatings Journal 6: 48–61.

Wan, H., D.-Q. Yang and C. Zhang. 2006. Impact of biological incising to improve phenolic resin retention and hardness of various wood species. Forest Products Journal 56(4): 61–67.

Wang, C., C. Piao and C. Lucas. 2010. Synthesis and characterization of superhydrophobic wood surfaces. Journal of Applied Polymer Science 119(3): 1667–1672.

Wang, C. and C. Piao. 2011. From hydrophilicity to hydrophobicity: A critical review – Part II: Hydrophobic conversion. Wood and Fiber Science 43(1): 41–56.

Wang, C., M. Zhang, Y. Xu, S. Wang, F. Liu, M. Ma, D. Zang and Z. Gao. 2014. One-step synthesis of unique silica particles for the fabrication of bionic and stably superhydrophobic coatings on wood surface. Advanced Powder Technology 25(2): 530–535.

Wang, W., Y. Zhu and J. Cao. 2014. Morphological, thermal and dynamic mechanical properties of cathay poplar/organoclay composites prepared by *in situ* process. Materials & Design 59: 233–240.

Wang, Y., J. Chang, J.J. Morrell, C.M. Freitag and J.J. Karchesy. 2012. An integrated approach using *Bacillus subtilis* B26 and essential oils to limit fungal discoloration of wood. BioResources 7(3): 3132–3141.

Wasserscheid, P. and T. Welton. 2002. Ionic Liquids in Synthesis. Wiley-VCH Verlag GmbH & Co. KGaA, Weinheim, Germany.

Ważny, J. and I.D. Thornton. 1986. Comparative testing of strains of the dry rot fungus *Serpula lacrymans* (Schum. ex Fr.) S.F. Gray II. The action of some wood preservatives in agar media. Holzforschung 40: 383–388.

Weber, G., H.-L. Chen, E. Hinsch, S. Freitas and S.C. Robinson. 2014. Pigments extracted from the wood-staining fungi *Chlorociboria aeruginosa*, *Scytalidium cuboideum*, and *S. ganodermophthorum* show potential for use as textile dyes. Coloration Technology 130(6): Aricle ID 445452.

Wheatley, R., C. Hackett, A. Bruce and A. Kundzewicz. 1997. Effect of substrate composition on production of volatile organic compounds from *Trichoderma* spp. Inhibitory to wood decay fungi. International Biodeterioration & Biodegradation 39(2/3): 199–205.

White-McDougall, W.J., R.A. Blanchette and R.L. Farrell. 1998. Biological control of blue stain fungi on *Populus tremuloides* using selected *Ophiostoma* isolates. Holzforschung 52: 234–240.

Wong, V., S. Wyllie, C. Cornwell and D. Tronson. 2001. Supercritical fluid extraction (SFE) of monoterpenes from the leaves of *Melaleuca alternifolia* (tea tree). Molecules 6(12): 92–103.

Woźniak, M., P. Kwaśniewska-Sip, A. Waśkiewicz, G. Cofta and I. Ratajczak. 2020. The possibility of propolis extract application in wood protection. Forests 11(4): Article ID 465.

Wu, J., J. Zhang, H. Zhang, J. He, Q. Ren and M. Guo. 2004. Homogeneous acetylation of cellulose in a new ionic liquid. Biomacromolecules 5(2): 266–268.

Xavier-Junior, F.H., C. Vauthier, A.R.V. Morais, E.N. Alencar and E.S.T. Egito. 2016. Microemulsion systems containing bioactive natural oils: An overview on the state of the art. Drug Development and Industrial Pharmacy 43(5): 700–714.

Xie, L., Z. Tang, L. Jiang, V. Breedveld and D.W. Hess. 2015. Creation of superhydrophobic wood surfaces by plasma etching and thin-film deposition. Surface and Coatings Technology 281: 125–132.

Yamazaki, J., E. Minami and S. Saka. 2006. Liquefaction of beech wood in various supercritical alcohols. Journal of Wood Science 52(6): 527–532.

Yildiz, C., S. Canakci, U.C. Yildiz, O. Ozgenc and E.D. Tomak. 2012. Improving the impregnability of refractory spruce wood by *Bacillus licheniformis* pretreatment. Bioresources 7(1): 565–577.

Yinghuai, Z., K.T. Yuanting and N.S. Hosmane. 2013. Applications of ionic liquids in lignin chemistry, Chapter 13. *In*: Kadokawa, J.-i. [ed.]. Ionic Liquids: New Aspects for the Future. IntechOpen Ltd, London, UK.

Yuan, L., Y. Zhang, Z. Wang, Y. Han and C. Tang. 2019. Plant oil and lignin-derived elastomers via thermal azide-alkyne cycloaddition click chemistry. ACS Sustainable Chemistry & Engineering 7(2): 2593–2601.

Zabielska-Matejuk, J., J. Feder-Kubis, A. Stangierska and P. Przybylski. 2017. Chiral ionic liquids with a (−)-menthol component as wood preservatives. Holzforschung 71(9): 751–757.

Zakaria, S., B.H. Ong, S.H. Ahmad, M. Abdullah and T. Yamauchi. 2005. Preparation of lumen-loaded kenaf pulp with magnetite (Fe$_3$O$_4$). Materials Chemistry and Physics 89: 216–220.

Zakzeski, J., P.C.A. Bruijnincx, A.L. Jongerius and B.M. Weckhuysen. 2010. The catalytic valorization of lignin for the production of renewable chemicals. Chemical Reviews 110(6): 3552–3599.

Zanini, S., C. Riccardi, M. Orlandi, F. Fornara, M.P. Colombini, D.I. Donato, S. Legnaioli and V. Palleschi. 2008. Wood coated with plasma-polymer for water repellence. Wood Science and Technology 42(2): 149–160.

Zhang, F., B. Bernet, V. Bonnet, O. Dangles, F. Sarabia and A. Vasella. 2008. 2-Azido-2-deoxycellulose: Synthesis and 1,3-dipolar cycloaddition. Helvetica Chimica Acta 91: 608–617.

Zhang, Q.G., Q.I. Liu, Z.Y. Jiang and Y. Chen. 2007. Anti-trade-off in dehydration of ethanol by novel PVA/APTEOS hybrid membranes. Journal of Membrane Science 287: 237–245.

Zheng, D., L. Dong, W. Huang, X. Wu and N. Nie. 2014. A review of imidazolium ionic liquids research and development towards working pair of absorption cycle. Renewable and Sustainable Energy Reviews 37: 47–68.

Zhu, S., Y. Wu, Q. Chen, Z. Yu, C. Wang, S. Jin, Y. Ding and G. Wu. 2006. Dissolution of cellulose with ionic liquids and its application: A mini-review. Green Chemistry 8(4): 325–327.

Zimmerman, W.C., R.A. Blanchette, T.A. Burnes and R.L. Farrell. 1993. Melanin and perithecial development in *Ophiostoma piliferum*. Mycologia 87: 857–863.

Zimmt, W.S., N. Odegaard, T.K. Moreno, R.A. Turner, M.R. Riley, B. Xie and A.J. Muscat. 2007. Pesticide extraction studies using supercritical carbon dioxide, pp. 51–57. *In*: Charola, A.E. and R.J. Koestler [eds.]. Proceedings from the MCI Workshop Series. Pesticide Mitigation in Museum Collections: Science in Conservation, Smithsonian Museum Conservation Institute Workshop on Pesticide Mitigation. Washington DC, USA.

Zink, P. and D. Fengel. 1988. Studies on the colouring matter of blue-stain fungi. Part I. General characterization and the associated compounds. Holzforschung 42: 217–220.

Zohuriaan-Mehr, M.J. 2005. Advances in chitin and chitosan modification through graft polymerization: A comprehensive review. Iranian Polymer Journal 14: 235–265.

Zuber, P., M.M. Nakano and M.A. Marahiel. 1993. Peptide antibiotics, pp. 897–916. *In*: Sonenshein, A.L., Hoch, J.A. and Losick, R. [eds.]. *Bacillus subtilis* and Other Gram-Positive Bacteria: Biochemistry, Physiology and Molecular Genetics. American Society for Microbiology, Washington DC, USA.

Chapter 6
Modified Wood Beyond Sustainability

6.1 Introduction

The forest sector and wood-based industries are being challenged by the change in resources, energy scarcity and climate change. There is a part of the discussion between economics, ecology, and social welfare that can be summed up as sustainability. Wood is a natural, renewable, reusable, and recyclable raw material that can play a major role in reducing the negative effects on the climate and environment when it is taken from sustainably managed forests. There is no question about the value of the forest for mankind and the environment, as well as the value of the multitude of products made of wood. During the last 50 years, wood, especially sawn timber, has to a large extent disappeared from technological applications (Radkau, 2007), and its contribution to sustainability thus fails to appear in the one area in which it would be most significant: as a substitute for energy-intensive materials. New methods of wood modification seek to reintroduce wood into technological applications without changing the eco-friendly characteristics of the material.

Wood is, in volume, the most important renewable material resource (Rowell, 2002). In all aspects of human existence, the utilisation of wood appears to be the most effective way to optimise resources and to decrease the environmental impact associated with mankind's activities. This is not an easy thing to achieve, however, because timber possesses good but not outstanding properties, and it becomes noticeably more difficult when consideration is given to some of the new materials emerging. The only properties wood have that reign supreme are ecological fitness and, possibly, low cost.

In the European Union (EU), measures are being discussed in economics and science to improve the sustainability of resource utilisation. European policy is affecting and, indeed, directing current research, development, and marketing in the EU. The main policies having a direct impact on the forest-based sector are the EU Sustainable Development Strategy (SDS) (European Commission, 2009), which was published in 2006 and revised in 2009, the EU Roadmap 2050 (European Commission, 2011a), and the Recycling Society Policy Directive 2008/98/EC (European Parliament Council, 2008), Bioeconomy Strategy (European Commission, 2012), and Circular Economy (European Commission, 2015). The innovation in raw material value chains, including the forest products value chain, has been under direct impact of goals defined in the Roadmap for a Resource-Efficient Europe (European Commission, 2011a), the Roadmap for a competitive low-carbon economy by 2050 (European Commission, 2011b), and a renewed EU Industrial Policy Strategy (European Commission, 2017).

Within the framework of the project *Vision and roadmap for European raw materials* funded under the European Union's Horizon 2020 research and innovation programme (grant agreement No. 690388), an Innovation Roadmap 2050 – A Sustainable and Competitive Future for European Raw Materials was prepared. The main objectives of this Roadmap are to secure a sustainable and competitive supply of raw materials, to boost the sector's jobs and competitiveness, and to contribute to addressing global challenges as well as the needs of the civil society. Among the priority areas are addressing the supply of raw materials, the production of raw materials, and the recycling and substitution of critical raw materials. The research and innovation needs are grouped into the following areas:

- Fostering a sustainable supply of raw materials to feed new and existing value chains
- Resource-efficient processing for raw materials
- Raw materials in new products and applications
- Closing material loops by maximising the recycling of products, buildings and infrastructure

In order to address the defined research and innovation needs, the forest products sector should focus on innovating in the harvesting technologies for a sustainable supply, mobilising an increased supply of raw materials, developing resource-efficient processing, refining and converting technologies, as well as developing the valorisation of production residues, and the development of recycling technologies, including sorting, separation and detection with the inclusion of a cost-benefit analysis should also be addressed. The key areas where wood modification can provide benefits are in the substitution of critical materials by enhancing the properties of wood, developing new materials and incorporating wood into hybrid and composite materials and applications.

The forest-based sector can contribute significantly to the European Commission's ambitious targets defined in the listed strategies, with innovative production technologies, reduced energy consumption, increased wood products recycling, and the reuse and refining of side-streams.

Europe's Bioeconomy Strategy addresses the production of renewable biological resources and their conversion into vital products and bioenergy, whilst the Circular Economy Strategy proposes actions that will contribute to "closing the loop" of product life cycles through greater recycling and re-use, with benefits for both the environment and the economy. One of the important elements of the strategy is the stimulation of industrial symbiosis in which by-products of one industry become another industry's raw material.

Wood products contribute to climate change mitigation throughout their entire life cycle. While in the forest, trees naturally withdraw CO_2 from the atmosphere. During their service life, wood products store the same CO_2 in products and components of the built environment. With extended service lives, the amount of carbon stored in these wood products exceeds the energy required to harvest and produce them. When substituted for fossil fuels at the end of their service life, wood products release their stored carbon back to the atmosphere and provide significant energy returns. The amount of carbon released during conversion to energy, however, was already incorporated in the biomass of the forest during the extended service life of the timber products used for energy recovery.

The efficient use of resources is the core concept of cascading, which is a sequential use of a certain resource for different purposes. This means that the same unit of a resource can be used for multiple high-grade material applications (and therefore sequesters carbon for a longer duration) followed by its final use for energy generation and returning the stored carbon to the atmosphere. Intelligent concepts for the reuse and recycling of valuable materials at the end of a single product life will reduce the amount of waste to be landfilled. For example, the stages of a hypothetical wood cascade might be: (1) collecting, remanufacturing, and reusing large sawn timber or engineered timbers in large structures as many times as possible; (2) when the structural value of the recovered timbers is no longer useful, using the timber for flooring, in solid wood furniture, in window frames, or moulding; (3) chipping, stranding or otherwise breaking the material down for use in composites such as OSB, LSL, or particleboard; or (4) using the wood material in suitable chemical processes, and, finally, (5) burning it for energy (Figure 6.1).

As a consequence of the increased competition from traditional and new industries based on renewable resources, forest resources must be considered limited. There are forecasts showing that, already in 2020, the European consumption of wood may be as large as the total European forest growth increment (Jonsson et al., 2011). According to the Communication "Innovating for

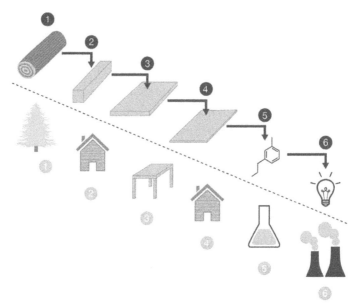

Figure 6.1 Cascade utilisation of wood in different stages (lower numbering) in the forest value chain: (1) roundwood, (2) large-dimension sawn or engineered timber assortments, (3) strand- or particle-based composites, (4) fibre-based composites, (5) chemicals, and (6) energy. This includes the following material cycles (upper numbering): (1) resource extraction, (2) 1st life cycle, (3–4) 2nd life cycle, (5) chemicals processing, (6) energy generation (adapted after Sandak et al., 2019).

Sustainable Growth: A Bio-economy for Europe", Europe needs to radically change its production, consumption, processing, storage, recycling, and disposal of resources (European Commission, 2012). Thus, bio-economy is considered one of the key elements for smart and green growth in Europe. The "Strategic Research and Innovation Agenda for 2030 of the Forest-based Sector and the Horizons – Vision 2030" sees like forest-based sector as a key actor of the bio-based society.

It is vital that wood can be used effectively throughout the whole value chain, from forest management and multiple uses of forest resources through new wood and fibre-based materials and processing technologies to new end-use concepts. Fossil fuel consumption, potential contributions to the greenhouse effect and the quantities of solid waste produced tend to be smaller for wood products than for competing products (Werner and Richter, 2007). Preservative-impregnated wood products tend to be more critical than comparative products with respect to toxicological effects and/or photo-generated smog, depending on the type of preservative used. Unfortunately, the number of life cycle assessment (LCA) studies of wood-based composites and modified wood is relatively limited, and they are geographically specific and use of a variety of databases and impact assessment protocols. More studies will have to be performed, which are further pressured by the European Green Deal (European Commission, 2019). It is a strategy that aims to transform the European Union into a fair and prosperous society, with a modern, resource-efficient and competitive economy where there are no net emissions of greenhouse gases in 2050 and where economic growth is decoupled from resource use.

Forest products have a great opportunity to become the main factors driving the European Green Deal. Such environmental impact benefits have been outlined in a range of publications in recent years (e.g., Hill, 2011; Kutnar and Muthu, 2016). Timber is a high-performance material for structures, playing an essential role in construction and light-weight design. However, several of the species used industrially have deficiencies related to poor resistance to biological degradation and low shape stability, which could previously be reduced by preservation with substances exhibiting some degree of toxicity which are now forbidden in many countries and regions. Consequently, there has been a renewed interest in developing new modification technologies in recent years.

6.2 Environmental impact of wood modification processes

Wood modification technologies are being implemented to improve the intrinsic properties of wood and to achieve the form and functionality desired by architects, designers, and engineers. Enhanced performance at low weight and low price creates a considerable market potential for modified wood products that can replace energy-intensive materials and methods of construction and these products have a considerable potential in construction, architecture, light-weight construction, and furniture manufacture. Different modification processes and parameters yield modified wood with different properties suitable for a variety of product lines. However, these processes also have different environmental impacts, which are consequently transferred into the materials and final products. An interactive assessment of process parameters, product properties, and environmental impacts should be adopted to aid the development of innovative modification processes and manufacturing technologies. Recycling, up-cycling, the cradle-to-cradle (C2C) paradigm, and end-of-life disposal options need to be integrated into a fully developed industrial ecology for modified wood processes. New advances in wood-based material processing should support and promote efficient product reuse, recycling and end-of-life use, and a low-carbon economy.

Many aspects of wood modification treatments are known, but the fundamental influence of these treatments on product performance, the environment, and end-of-life scenarios remain unknown. To contribute to the low-carbon economy and sustainable development, it is essential to integrate interactive assessments of process parameters, of product properties and of environmental impacts. To perform an objective environmental impact assessment of a commercial modification process and incorporate an environmental impact assessment into a wood modification process and product development, including recycling and upgrading at the end of its service life, the Life Cycle Assessment (LCA) method should be applied.

The common LCA methodology is defined in ISO 14040 (ISO, 2006a) and ISO 14044 (ISO, 2006b). The main steps of an LCA analysis are presented in Figure 6.2. The analysis consists of four steps: goal definition and scoping, inventory analysis, impact assessment, and interpretation. In the first step, the problem and objectives of the assessment are defined. The system is described, and functional units are defined, and the system boundaries (Figure 6.3) are set. This includes information about the part of the production line which will be studied. In the second step, all the emissions to air, water and soil, and the extraction of all resources are quantified. When the data are collected, the third step is performed by evaluating of the environmental impacts of inventoried inputs and outputs. The LCA is completed by the interpretation of the results and uncertainties, as well as by comparison and a critical analysis.

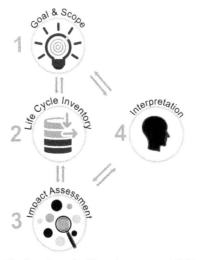

Figure 6.2 The four steps of a life cycle assessment (LCA) analysis.

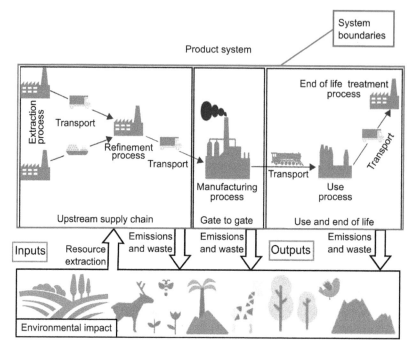

Figure 6.3 Inputs, outputs, and system boundaries life cycle assessment (LCA).

Although the first LCA studies date back to the 1960s, LCA is still regarded as an evolving subject (Hill, 2011). The aim of performing an LCA is two-fold; to determine the environmental impacts associated with a process and to identify 'hot-spots' where improvements can be made. These days, an LCA is often viewed as an essential tool for the marketing of a product and it plays a significant role in the development and use of environmental product declarations (EPDs). Since the 1980s, when LCA analysis started to become more popular, numerous methodologies have been developed to classify, characterise, and normalise environmental effects. The most common are focused on the following environmental impact indicators: acidification, eutrophication, thinning of the ozone layer, various types of eco-toxicity, air contaminants, resource usage, and green-house gas emission.

LCA is a comprehensive approach that quantifies ecological and human health impacts of a product or system over its complete life cycle or a part of its life cycle. When only the production of a product is being evaluated, a so-called cradle-to-gate LCA is performed. In this type of LCA, raw material preparation, transport of raw materials, production and waste processing are analysed. If the additional assembly and use of a product is of interest, a so-called cradle-to-grave LCA is performed, and the performance (including maintenance and repair) as well as the end of life are analysed. If phases beyond the end-of-life are considered, including reuse and recycling, a cradle-to-cradle LCA is performed.

The number of LCA studies in the wood sector is relatively limited, geographically distributed, using a variety of databases and impact assessment protocols (Kutnar and Hill, 2014). Kutnar and Hill (2014) used a cradle-to-gate analysis to present the carbon footprint of 14 primary wood products. The largest source of emissions of all sawn timber products stem from the removal of the timber from the forest, and for kiln-dried sawn timber, the drying process follows closely in second place. Kutnar and Hill (2016) discussed the merits of using wood as a building material in relation to the environmental benefits. Carbon footprints, including sequestered carbon, of wood products with different 'end-of-life' scenarios and different susceptibilities to degradation were compared. They concluded that the interactive assessment of process parameters, developed product properties, and the environmental impact including recycling and disposal options at the end of the service life, or up-cycling after the service life based on the cradle-to-cradle concept, are essential factors that must be further investigated.

Werner and Richter (2007) compared the results of international research on the environmental impact of the life cycle of wood products used in the building sector with these of functionally equivalent products of other materials. They concluded that fossil fuel consumption, potential contributions to the greenhouse effect, and quantities of solid waste tend to be less for wood products than for competing products, and also that impregnated wood products tend to be more critical than comparative products with regard to toxicological effects and/or photo-generated smog, depending on the type of preservative. Bolin and Smith (2011a) compared the environmental impact of borate-treated sawn timber, with that of galvanised steel framing and concluded that the cradle-to-grave life cycle impact of borate-treated lumber framing was approximately four times less for fossil fuel use, 1.8 times less for GHGs, 83 times less for water use, 3.5 times less for acidification, 2.5 times less for ecological impact, 2.8 times less for smog formation, and 3.3 times less for eutrophication. The results of the cradle-to-grave life cycle assessment showed the impact of that alkaline-copper-quaternary (ACQ)-treated timber was 14 times less for fossil fuel use, almost three times less for GHG emissions, potential smog emissions, and water use, four times less for acidification, and almost half for ecological toxicity than those of a wood-plastic composite (WPC) decking (Bolin and Smith, 2011b).

Van der Lugt and Vogtländer (2014) calculated the carbon footprint of acetylated timber with cradle-to-grave system boundaries and compared the result with those for steel, concrete, and unsustainably sourced azobé. The functional unit was the bearing structure of a pedestrian bridge, 16×3 metres in size. The results showed that acetylated wood had a much lower carbon footprint than steel, concrete, and unsustainably sourced azobé, and a slightly lower carbon footprint than sustainably sourced azobé. Since the calculation included carbon sequestration, and since the emissions during production and bio-energy production during the end-of-life phase were small, all the sustainably sourced wood alternatives, including acetylated wood, showed CO_2-negative LCA results over the full life cycle.

Hill and Norton (2014) discussed the environmental impact of the wood modification process in relation to the life extension of the material. By determining carbon neutrality, they identified the point at which the benefits of life extension compensated for the increased environmental impact associated with the modification. The effect of the longer maintenance intervals for modified wood products could be a powerful argument in favour of their use.

Manufacturers of modified wood products have, to some extent, considered the environmental impacts of their products, and some companies have obtained environmental products declarations (EPDs). EPDs for modified wood (thermally modified, acetylated and furfurylated) are also available (Tellnes et al., 2020), and Table 6.1 gives some examples of EPDs of commercially available modified woods.

In Europe, most EPDs follow the EN 15804 (CEN, 2013) standard, which provides core product category rules for all construction products and services in order to ensure that the EPDs are elaborated, verified and presented in a harmonised way. This standard is organised in modules (A to D) and distinguishes four stages within the life cycle of a building product: the product stage, the construction process stage, the use stage and the end of life stage (Figure 6.4). For wood and wood-based products, an additional standard has been developed, EN 16485 (CEN, 2014a), which complements and is used in conjunction with EN 15804 (CEN, 2013). Using EN 16485, aspects relevant to the specific product category (wood) are taken into account, such as the renewability of wood and its potential carbon neutrality, carbon storage, energy and water content. Furthermore, the EN 16449 standard (CEN, 2014b) is being used in order to harmonise the quantification of the potential benefits associated with carbon storage in wood and wood-based products.

The EPD Schemes/Programmes in Europe that offer EN 15804 EPDs are BRE in UK, IBU in Germany, EPD EnvironDec in Sweden, INIES in France, and EPD Norge in Norway. Although

Table 6.1 Some environmental product declarations (EPDs) for modified wood.

Trademark	EPD Ref. No.	Description
LunaWood™	RTS EPD nro: RTS_44_19	ThermoWood™ processing of Norway spruce, radiata pine and Scots pine
Woodify Natur™	NEPD-1865-805	ThermoWood™ D processing of Norway spruce and Scots pine for cladding, roof and decking
Woodify Brannpanel Natur™	NEPD-1866-805	ThermoWood™ D processing of Scots pine for cladding, roof and decking, treated with a fire retardant
Woodify Optimum™	NEPD-1867-805	ThermoWood™ D processing for Norway spruce and Scots pine treated with Jotun™ surface coating
Woodify Brannpanel Optimum™	NEPD-1868-805	ThermoWood™ D processing for Norway spruce and Scots pine treated with a fire retardant and Jotun surface coating
Moelven Termotre™	NEPD-1829-781	Thermally modified Norway spruce and Scots pine for cladding, roof and decking
Moelven Termoask™	NEPD-1830-781	Thermally modified European ash for use in cladding, roof and decking
Brimstone™ cladding and decking boards	S-P-01718	Thermally modified ash, poplar and sycamore for cladding and decking
Royal™-impregnated timber	NEPD-1818-767	Treatment of Scots pine with a copper-based preservative, followed by hot oil treatment
Royal™-impregnated timber: Talgø Møretre AS	NEPD-1808-766	Treatment of Scots pine with a copper-based preservative, followed by hot oil treatment, for use in decking, cladding and roofing
Accoya™ Wood	NEPD-376-262	Acetylation of wood by Accsys Technologies to achieve durability class 1 according to EN350-1, for a range of applications such as decking, cladding and planed timber for joinery applications
Kebony Clear™	NEPD-407-287	Furfurylation of radiata pine for a range of uses
Kebony Character Cladding™	NEPD-409-288	Furfurylation of Scots pine for cladding uses
Kebony Character Roofing™	NEPD-411-288	Furfurylation of Scots pine for roofing applications

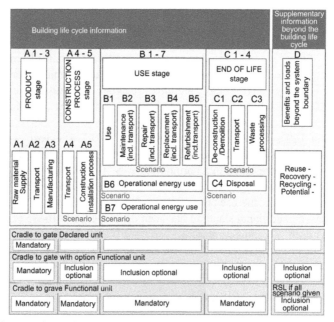

Figure 6.4 Three main types of EPD: Cradle to gate, cradle-to-gate with options, and cradle-to-grave defined in EN 15804 (CEN, 2013).

EN 15804 provides a more harmonised approach to developing EPD for construction products, it has not yet received full recognition among the scheme operators. In 2011, the EPD programmes from Sweden, Spain, Portugal, Poland, Norway, the Netherlands, Italy, Great Britain, Germany, France and Finland therefore established an International Non-Profit Association known as the ECO Platform, a group of program operators, LCA practitioners, industrial associations and other stakeholders with the primary objective of developing a common European EPD framework based on ISO 14025 (ISO, 2009) and EN 15804 (CEN, 2013). The ECO Platform EPD should be applicable across Europe. Covering over 80 product categories, more than 350 products have been certified since 2012.

The EPD environmental label is a Type III environmental label developed under ISO 14020 (ISO, 2000) which sets out the guiding principles for the development of environmental labels and declarations. The other two classes are Type I and Type II (Figure 6.5). Different labels adopt different assessment approaches, but the common goal is to present verifiable and accurate information and to promote products and services that have potentially less impact on the environment by aiding buyers to make better informed choices. Type I labels are based on a pass-fail multi-criteria approach devised to indicate the overall environmental performance of a product. If one of the criteria is not met, the product will not be awarded a label. Commonly referred to as 'ecolabels', Type I environmental labels are provided by programmes set up and operated in line with the requirements of ISO 14024 (ISO, 2018). Ecolabels are, therefore, third-party verified. They are typically simple documents useful for conveying basic relevant environmental information. Type II environmental labels are defined as 'self-declared' environmental claims made by manufacturers and businesses. Guided by ISO 14021 (ISO, 2016), the claimant is able to declare the environmental quality of his product, without set criteria, benchmarks or quality checks. However, this declaration should be verifiable and must not to be misleading. Other restrictions include the avoidance of vague or ambiguous claims such as 'environmentally friendly' or 'sustainable'. Verifiable terms such as "made from x% recycled material" are permitted.

A detailed consideration reveals that the global environmental impact of timber modification and further uses of the modified wood products are not yet included in the development of processes and products (Kutnar and Hill, 2016). Moreover, their environmental impacts are, to a considerable extent, still unknown, and this must be changed to meet the demands of increasingly conscientious business and consumer markets desiring to make environmentally responsible decisions regarding the goods and services they decide to patronise. The development of any wood modification technology should include an environmental impact assessment. The environmental load of technologies should be identified and quantified, by determining energy use, emissions released during and after the process, when the product in use, and the waste released.

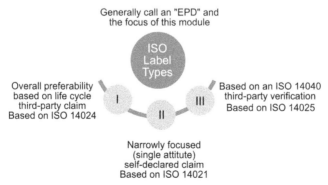

Figure 6.5 Environmental labels developed under the ISO 14020 series.

6.3 Modified wood in a circular economy

Consumer awareness and environmental legislation have led to the need for a safe return of products from the field, as well as more environmentally friendly products. An entirely new spectrum of goods has emerged at what was formerly considered to be the end of the supply chain. The transition from waste management to resource and recycling management, together with increasing prices and a scarcity of resource has led to a need for improved quality and efficiency in logistics systems. This applies to commercial and municipal waste management, as well as industry, trade and service enterprises with in-house waste disposal tasks. The reverse supply chain includes the activities required to retrieve a used product from a customer and either dispose of it or reuse it. Efficient transport chains must be designed, and complex logistics networks must be optimised, as must also waste collection, waste transport and waste handling, in order to achieve the recycling of goods. Successful reverse supply chains also require careful facilities and business planning to achieve cost efficiency and environmentally sound processing. These business concepts require innovative reverse logistics, operational transport and material flow planning to optimise their plant logistics, especially in the field of renewable bio-based resources.

The use of modified wood products includes both the forward and return flows of products, parts, sub-assemblies, scrap and packaging. After use, the modified wood products should move from the consumer back to the producer or a recycling enterprise for reuse, recycling, remanufacture, energy production or disposal. The processes through which the value of returned materials is regained should be developed, and this will increase the efficiency of utilisation of renewable bio-based resources. The preferred option is to extend the overall life cycle of a material where this is possible, by using it in multiple product lines beyond its first use. Intelligent concepts for the reuse and recycling of valuable materials at the end of the product life will reduce the amount of waste destined for landfills. The reuse of the components of large structures made with engineered solid wood products after their first life cycle is a valuable source of already graded and dried wood to be reprocessed for further use. At the end of their first product life, most wood-based products retain material qualities and quantities that permit further use in solid or disintegrated form (as strands, particles or fibres), yet recovered wood is currently mainly burned in waste incineration plants, or—with higher power efficiency—in special wood combustion facilities, ignoring the preferred option of keeping these bio-based, carbon-storing materials at their maximum quality level by reusing them in their solid form and recycling the reclaimed wood in as many steps of a material cascade as possible. The potential for efficient material cascading of engineered solid wood products is still largely underdeveloped. However, recent and ongoing projects are beginning to develop much needed solutions and technologies that will make possible the more efficient reuse and recycling of reclaimed wood. To the best of our knowledge, no specific solution for the reuse of modified wood has yet been developed. At the end of their service life, used modified wood products, should be treated and recycled to produce "raw" materials, which will compete with freshly harvested wood and forest products. This presents an opportunity for new and existing businesses to provide products, services and materials to forest-products-related companies. Logistics companies and material processors will also have to cooperate to solve challenging and increasingly complex logistic problems and to become efficient and profitable. This is especially relevant with modified wood products of which quantities may be relatively small. These challenges, together with high material costs, have led to enhanced quality and efficiency requirements for logistics systems. In addition, legal frameworks, the market and the client requirements are changing permanently. Efficient and economically sound logistics offer companies competitive advantages, and can make recycling a profitable resource trade. Reverse logistics networks are, however, complex and require the application of suitable methods of (mathematical) optimisation, each modelling the specific requirements of the value creation chain (Burnard and Kutnar, 2015). This includes the independent and comprehensive analysis, planning and optimisation of material and information flows, as well as waste disposal processes (e.g., container locations, emptying cycles, accumulation sites, decontamination sites, processing plants).

Although the cascade use of wood has been shown to be the superior option in wood material flow, several factors and restrictions need to be considered to optimise the cascade and prevent undesired, potentially negative, impacts on human health and the environment. To prevent its decay, or to enhance or achieve properties that are not inherent to solid wood, the wood may be impregnated or surface-coated with an inorganic or organic preservatives and/or coatings. Alternatively, wood modification can be used to enhance certain properties.

Many nations have established specific rules related to wood product recycling, but identifying and sorting the highly useable and desirable materials from less desirable and contaminated material remains difficult. Many of the complications with wood recycling are due to contaminants in the recovered material. These contaminants range from chemicals and adhesives to foreign objects such as nails and screws (Table 6.2), but the recovered wood products are a valuable source of raw wood material when effectively utilised (Bejune, 2001; McKeever and Falk, 2004; Höglmeier et al., 2013).

Table 6.2 Common contaminants in recovered wood (adapted from DEMOWOOD, 2013).

Contamination type	Common examples	Sources in recovered waste wood
Chemical	Halogens (e.g., chlorine, bromine)	Preservative-treated timber, coated wood (i.e., with polyvinyl chloride (PVC))
	Heavy metals (e.g., cadmium, mercury)	Painted or preservative-treated timber
	Volatile Organic Compounds (VOCs) (e.g., formaldehyde, naphthalene)	Wood-based composites using formaldehyde-based adhesives, creosote-treated timber
Physical	Metals (iron, brass, steel, aluminium)	Fastened wood (e.g., with nails, screws, or plates)
	Glass	Windows
	Plastics	Windows, fastened wood, framing lumber
	Plasters, insulation materials	Framing sawn timber, indoor wood (e.g., moulding, cabinetry)

According to European projects examining the recovery of wood products (e.g., DEMOWOOD, CaReWood, COST Action E31, COST Action FP1407), there is a great potential to expand wood recovery for uses beyond energy and particleboard production, which are currently the two most common uses. Several automatic contaminant-detection methods and the sorting and cleaning of the contaminated materials have been proposed (DEMOWOOD, 2013; Hasan et al., 2011). In addition to visual inspection and sorting, these solutions utilise a conglomerate of technologies. To detect and separate metals and other solid materials magnets, gravity sorting, rollers and sieves may be utilised (DEMOWOOD, 2012). X-ray fluorescence systems (XRF), near infrared spectrometry (NIR), laser-induced breakdown spectroscopy (LIBS), ion-mobility spectrometry (IMS), and spectrally resolved thermography can be used to study chemically treated wood waste (DEMOWOOD, 2012). When these technologies are implemented in a sorting facility, wood waste containing chemical compounds that are limited by law can be effectively identified and removed. Chemically contaminated wood products of sufficient size may be re-sawn or planed to a smaller size, removing the contaminated or otherwise damaged surfaces if the chemical penetration is not too deep. To re-enter the market, the newly produced timbers must be graded to certify their fitness for use. Removing physical contaminants such as nails or screws may require manual intervention, or sawing to remove heavily damaged or contaminated cross-sections (e.g., where large fasteners such as bolts, have left large holes). Figure 6.6 presents the closed loop of forest products. The renewable materials can close both biological and technical cycles. When wood modification technologies apply fossil-based chemicals this loop is not as evident.

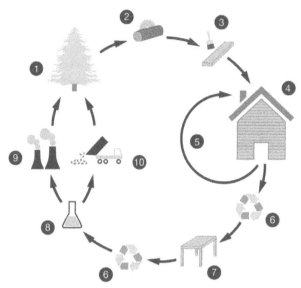

Figure 6.6 Life cycle of forest products: (1) harvesting, (2) primary processing, (3) secondary processing, (4) use phase, (5) re-use, (6) recycling, (7) second use phase, (8) cascading to tertiary use, (9) energy generation, (10) landfilling, closing the biological and technical metabolism (Adapted after Sandak et al., 2019).

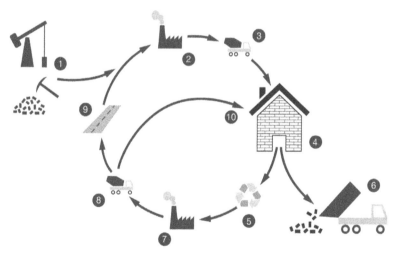

Figure 6.7 Life cycle of non-renewable materials: (1) extraction of raw material, (2) manufacturing, (3) processing, (4) use phase, (5) recycling, (6) landfilling/waste production, (7) secondary manufacturing, (8) secondary processing for re-use, (9) second use phase, (10) second re-use phase (adapted after Sandak et al., 2019).

Figure 6.7 presents the life cycle of non-renewable materials. The main difference from the renewable materials is that landfilling generates waste and a biological loop is not possible. Heräjärvi et al. (2020) discussed the challenges of modified wood in the circular economy. The longer lifetime of modified wood brings advantages provided the modification process does not introduce environmentally harmful or health-risk chemicals. The modification processes add significant environmental impacts during manufacture compared to unmodified wood products (Tellnes et al., 2020), and the service life and maintenance intervals are crucial in an environmental performance comparison.

6.4 The use of modified wood in a healthy living environment

The use of wood in many indoor environments has been shown to make beneficial contributions to a healthy living environment (Rice et al., 2006; Fell, 2010; Nyrud et al., 2010), but the benefits of using modified wood is still a matter of research. The following sections give an overview of the current state of the art.

Environmental assessment of buildings

In 2012, CEN/TC 350 published a new European Standard for the assessment of the sustainability of buildings: EN 15978 – Sustainability of construction works – Assessment of environmental performance of buildings – Calculation method (CEN, 2011). This standard provides guidance on the calculation, based on LCA, to assess the environmental credentials of a building. EN 15978 (CEN, 2011) defines the object of the assessment, the system boundary that applies at the building level, the procedure to be used for the inventory analysis, the list of procedures for the calculation of these indicators, and the requirements for the data necessary for the calculation. It takes a similar approach to EN15804 (CEN, 2013) in covering all the stages of the building life cycle and the list of indicators is the same. EN 15978 is based on the data obtained from EPD, and it provides the requirements and means to report and communicate the outcomes of the assessment. Suttie et al. (2017) published an overview of the environmental assessment of building materials, modules of life cycle assessment and the labels and certifications of environmental impacts used in the sector, and they also discussed the carbon accounting in bio-based building materials. The environmental benefits of using timber as a substitute for high-energy construction materials, including the advantages of using timber have been studied in the past (Buchanan and Levine, 1999; Börjesson and Gustavsson, 2000; Gustavsson and Sathre, 2006; Nässén et al., 2012; Pilli et al., 2015). The use of wood and other bio-based materials in the built environment provides environmental benefits due to the storage of sequestered atmospheric carbon. However, the effect of storing atmospheric carbon dioxide is dependent upon the length of time for which the carbon is removed from the atmosphere (Cacho et al., 2003; Levasseur et al., 2013), i.e., the benefits depend on the retention time. Therefore, modification technologies that extend the lifespan of a wood product through superior durability are of great importance, although the modification should at the same time increase the level of recycling. The benefits of atmospheric carbon storage in a bio-derived product can be taken into account only if the material is derived from a sustainable source. This means that the forest must be regenerated after felling to produce the timber. If the felling is followed by a change in land use (such as conversion to agriculture), the benefits of atmospheric carbon storage in the harvested wood products are no longer present and, according to the European Commission's *International reference life cycle data* (ILCD) guidelines, this biogenic carbon should be treated as if it were fossil carbon.

   The building sector can contribute significantly towards reducing emissions by the appropriate construction of new sustainable buildings and retrofitting of existing buildings. One strategy is widely known by the term *green building*, which can be characterised as integrated building practices that aim to significantly reduce the environmental footprint of a building compared with traditional practices. Descriptions of green building generally focus factors such as siting, energy, water, materials, waste, and health. One of the most important features of green building is the integration of aspects of sustainable building. Although individual elements can be addressed separately, the green building approach is more comprehensive, focusing on the environmental footprint of a building over its life cycle from initial design and construction to operations during the building's useful life and through to end-of-life strategies. The desire to integrate the various elements of green building has led to the development of rating and certification systems to assess how well a building project meets a specified set of sustainability criteria. Attributes of sustainable buildings can be divided into three categories: environmental, social, and economic (Gorse et al., 2016). The environmental attributes include energy and natural resources, water conservation, material use, durability and waste, land use, transport and accessibility and pollution. The social attributes include usability and function, indoor environment conditions, health and well-being, architectural considerations, cultural and aesthetic aspects and innovation and design. The economic attributes include flexibility and adaptability, economic performance and affordability, building manageability and whole life function and value.

Whole building assessment methodologies include rating schemes that consider the above sustainability attributes in their assessment categories. There are many green building rating systems such as the Building Research Establishment Environmental Assessment Methodology (BREEAM) from the UK, Deutsche Gesellschaft für Nachhaltiges Bauen (DGNB) from Germany, Haute Qualité Environnementale (HQE) from France, and Green Star from Australia. In the United States the most popular system is the Leadership in Energy and Environmental Design (LEED). In Japan, the Comprehensive Assessment System for Build Environment Efficiency (CASBEE) is used. While each system has certain unique features, there are significant overlaps among them. Both Jones (2009) and Sinha and Knowles (2014) compared the assessment categories of four major international green building rating systems, LEED, Green Star, DGNB, and CASBEE, and they concluded that these systems have significant commonalities in their various assessment categories and that the differences are largely terminological. However, it is important to take into account the region-specific developments which contribute variability to the rating systems.

Materials consumption and energy use during operation make up most of the environmental impact of the building. The influence of the wood modification process in relation to the extended service life of a product may result in less environmental impact of the building. To the best of our knowledge these comparisons have hitherto not been made.

Modified wood as an element of restorative environmental design

The development of new modification technologies should consider human well-being and should go beyond achieving the lowest possible environmental impact. The sustainable design principles that emphasise decreasing the environmental impact of a building construction, location, and utilisation do so by their choice of material, choice of site, and energy use through all phases of the building's lifetime. These principles should be combined with the Restorative Environmental Design (RED) paradigm, which brings together the ideas of sustainable design and biophilic design (Kellert, 2008; Derr and Kellert, 2013). RED attempts to promote a stronger connection between building occupants and nature. Derr and Kellert (2013) believe that RED is the next evolution of "green" design, and that it offers an opportunity for increased wood use. Wood that is harvested from healthy, well-managed forests is a renewable material that provides carbon storage and satisfies both the general tenets of the RED paradigm, sustainability and a connection to nature, making it an ideal material for RED. It is also possible to emphasise the aspects of wood that people recognise as natural, such as grain patterns and colour, providing the occupants of the building with a connection to nature (Nyrud et al., 2010). Any modifications to wood should minimise changes that decrease its apparent naturalness (Burnard and Kutnar, 2015). To successfully integrate modified wood into RED practices, it must have a low environmental impact (or positively affect the environment) and be a recognisable element of nature. The development should indeed go beyond RED and meet the requirements of Restorative Environmental and Ergonomic Design (REED), developed by InnoRenew CoE (Burnard, 2017), which creates ergonomic, accessible, adaptable, and sustainable buildings. It has a positive impact on human health and well-being, and on the restoration of nature and the coherent coexistence of people with the environment and the society.

Wood is an ideal material for RED because it satisfies both the general tenets of the design paradigm; sustainability and a connection to nature. Wood from a healthy, well-managed forest is a renewable material, and provides carbon storage (Hashimoto et al., 2002). It is not surprising that such a product, when used in appearance applications, also provides a connection to nature (Masuda, 2004; Rice et al., 2006; Nyrud et al., 2010).

Wood has an excellent strength-to-weight ratio and it can be used in a variety of forms (e.g., in log form, lumber form, in fibre form, and in combination with other materials), which make it an excellent building material (Kretschmann, 2010; Stark et al., 2010). In the United States, more than 90% of residential buildings are wood-framed and Japan is not far behind (Sinha et al., 2013). However, wood is predominately used in housing as a concealed structural component, so that occupant interaction with it is limited. Wood is considerably less common in non-residential constructions, than in residential constructions (O'Connor et al., 2004). Although exposed wood is present to some degree in many indoor environments, there are opportunities for greater utilisation which may contribute positively to occupant health (Rice et al., 2006; Fell, 2010; Nyrud et al., 2010). Furthermore, wood is known to sequester carbon throughout its lifetime (Hashimoto et al., 2002; Tonn and Marland, 2007; Salazar and Meil, 2009). In many industrialised countries, carbon storage in wood is greater than carbon released by harvest, disposal and all steps in between (Hashimoto et al., 2002). Therefore, the effective use of wood products can reduce the amount of carbon released to the atmosphere, while well-managed forests provide a continuous supply of sustainable material for potential use in the built environment.

Wood evokes feelings of warmth, comfort and relaxation, and is reminiscent of nature (Rice et al., 2006; Nyrud et al., 2010). Aspects of wood connecting humans to nature include its recognition as a natural product, its pattern, and its colour (Masuda, 2004; Rice et al., 2006; Fell, 2010; Nyrud et al., 2010). Although wood is often available in a variety of natural colours and patterns, the yellow-red hue with a relatively low contrast is common, and provides a positive, agreeable and pleasant image (Masuda, 2004). Colour contrast in wood is due to naturally occurring differences between earlywood and latewood, knots, and other natural features, and these features also give pattern to the viewer, contributing to the positive and agreeable image of wood and fitting well with the fascination of a restorative environment (Masuda, 2004). The presence of knots in wood products, however, demonstrates cultural differences into what humans perceive as a pleasing material. In Japan the presence of knots is considered to diminish its purity, while in North America knots are considered to be natural and rustic (Rice et al., 2006).

Wood can address each of the six biophilic design tenets (Kellert et al., 2008). Wood provides a direct link to nature, as a recognisable natural element (environmental features), it can be used in its natural form and wood grain is naturally developed (natural shapes and forms), while grain patterns, colour spectrum and the presence of knots evoke natural patterns and processes. Wood naturally has colour diversity and can be stained in a variety of colours without losing its appeal as a natural product, and it can easily be deployed in products of various sizes to fulfill space concerns (light and space). The use of locally sourced wood products can evoke a regional connection to nature; historical and regional building methods which utilise wood may also be imitated (place-based relationships), and trees and wood have long been used as a source of shelter, tools, transportation, and art (evolving human relationships with nature).

Wood modification can result in considerable changes in wood properties and thus in its restorative character. Depending on the type of modification and its extent, wood may no longer evoke feelings of warmth, comfort and relaxation reminiscent of nature. Figure 6.8 shows thermally modified spruce and beech timber after treatment at 185°C and 200°C. The temperature has a significant impact on the colour of the wood, and when thermo-hydro-mechanical treatment is used, the change goes beyond colour (Figure 6.9). The response of people to the modified wood in comparison with unmodified wood has not yet been studied. It is important, in addition to the superior properties of modified wood, that its natural characteristics and positive appeal to people are not diminished. Further developments should include interdisciplinary studies of the physio-physical responses of people exposed to modified wood products.

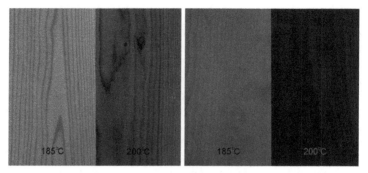

Figure 6.8 Colour of thermally-modified Norway spruce (left) and European white birch (right) modified at 185°C and 200°C.

Figure 6.9 Change of appearance as a result of thermo-hydro-mechanical treatment of poplar (left – before densification, right – after densification).

Volatile organic emissions

Many wood modification technologies utilise heat treatment which cause the degradation of wood constituents. Chemical changes occur, which result in altered physical and biological properties (Hill, 2006). The chemical changes also lead to the emission of volatile organic compounds (VOC) (Manninen et al., 2002; Mayes and Oksanen, 2003; Peters et al., 2008; Hyttinen et al., 2010; Elaieb et al., 2015; Xue et al., 2016; Čech, 2018). Pohleven et al. (2019) summarised the scientific literature on VOCs emitted of untreated and thermally modified conifer and broad-leaved species, indicating the main groups of wood VOCs and their emission properties and listing factors that influence these emissions.

The heat-induced changes depend on the wood species, as well as on the different conditions and steps of the treatment process employed in the thermal modification technique, such as temperature, duration of the treatment, the initial moisture content of the wood, oxygen level, the heat transferring medium, pressure regime, etc. (Hill, 2006; Militz and Altgen, 2014). During a thermal modification process operated in an open reactor system at atmospheric pressure, volatile compounds are released from the treated wood and reactor (Mayes and Oksanen, 2003; Militz and Altgen, 2014; Wentzel et al., 2018). The removal of VOCs is even more pronounced in processes at sub-atmospheric pressures (Allegretti et al., 2012; Hofmann et al., 2013), whereas in thermal modification processes at elevated pressure in closed reactor systems, VOCs are retained and accumulated (Stamm, 1956; Poncsak et al., 2009).

Heat treatment causes a variety changes in VOC emissions. The quantity and quality is different from that in untreated wood, and new VOCs are formed. Table 6.3 presents the VOCs emitted from different species of untreated solid wood and thermally modified wood. In general, the total VOC emission decreases from thermally treated conifer woods (Manninen et al., 2002; Mayes and Oksanen, 2003; Peters et al., 2008; Hyttinen et al., 2010; Elaieb et al., 2015), but increases from thermally treated broad-leaved woods compared to that from the untreated wood (Peters et al., 2008;

Table 6.3 VOCs emitted from different species of untreated solid wood and thermally modified wood (adopted after Pohleven et al., 2019).

Wood species	Untreated wood	Thermally modified timber
European ash	acetaldehyde, methanol, propanal, butanal, hexanal, 2-pentylfuran, acetic acid, furfural, terpenes (Risholm-Sundman et al., 1998; Larsen et al., 2000; Jensen et al., 2001; Peters et al., 2008)	acetic acid, furfural, 5-methylfurfural (Peters et al., 2008)
European ash	acetaldehyde, methanol, propanal, butanal, hexanal, 2-pentylfuran, acetic acid, furfural, terpenes (Risholm-Sundman et al., 1998; Larsen et al., 2000; Jensen et al., 2001; Peters et al., 2008)	acetic acid, furfural, 5-methylfurfural (Peters et al., 2008)
European beech	hexanal, ethanol, acetaldehyde, 2-pentylfuran, methanol, acetone, hexanoic acid, acetic acid, propanal, butanal, pentanal, furfural, formaldehyde (Meyer and Boehme, 1997; Risholm-Sundman et al., 1998; Englund, 1999; Larsen et al., 2000; Jensen et al., 2001; Peters et al., 2008; Böhm et al., 2012)	acetic acid, furfural, 5-methylfurfural (Peters et al., 2008)
Sycamore	acetic acid, hexanal, pentanal, furfural (Peters et al., 2008)	acetic acid, furfural, 5-methylfurfural (Peters et al., 2008)
European aspen	hexanal, acetic acid, pentanal, 1-pentanol, 1-penten-3-ol, 1-hexanol (Hyttinen et al., 2010)	acetic acid, furfural (Hyttinen et al., 2010)
Chinese white poplar (sapwood)	oxalic acid, methylnaphthalene, capraldehyde, decanal (capraldehyde), 2-nonenal, nonanal (Xue et al., 2016)	2-nonenal, phenol, furfural (furfuraldehyde), decanal, methylnaphthalene, methyl benzoate (Xue et al., 2016)
Scots pine	α-pinene, 3-carene, D-limonene, β-pinene, β-phellandrene, terpinolene, isoterpinolene, camphene; acetone, hexanal, nonanal, pentanal, propanal, butanal, acetic acid, hexanoic acid, furfural, ketone (6-methyl-5-hepten-2-one), formaldehyde (Meyer and Boehme, 1997; Risholm-Sundman et al., 1998; Englund, 1999; Englund and Nussbaum, 2000; Larsen et al., 2000; Jensen et al., 2001; Manninen et al., 2002; Mayes and Oksanen, 2003; Hyttinen et al., 2010; Bohm et al., 2012; Wang et al., 2018)	furfural, acetic acid, acetone (2-propanone), methyl ester of acetic acid, 1-hydroxy-2-propanone, D-limonene, ethanol α-pinene, camphene, hexanal (Manninen et al., 2002; Mayes and Oksanen, 2003; Wang et al., 2018)
Aleppo pine Radiata pine Maritime pine	hexanal, β-pinene, camphene, nonanal, isobornyl acetate, β-caryophyllene, humulene (α-caryophyllene), β-caryophyllene oxide, formaldehyde (Elaieb et al., 2015; Tasooji et al., 2017)	acetic acid, vanillin, guaiacylacetone, furfural, β-pinene, terpinyl acetate, hexanoic acid (caproic acid) (Elaieb et al., 2015)
Norway spruce	α-pinene, D-limonene, β-pinene, 3-carene, α-terpineol, sylvestrene, β-caryophyllene, γ-cadinene, δ-cadinene; hexanal, pentanal, furfural, acetone, acetaldehyde, acetic acid, hexanoic acid, nonanal, toluene, butanol, formaldehyde (Meyer and Boehme, 1997; Risholm-Sundman et al., 1998; Englund, 1999; Englund et al., 2000; Larsen et al., 2000; Jensen et al., 2001; Peters et al., 2008; Hyttinen et al., 2010; Steckel et al., 2010; 2011; Böhm et al., 2012; Czajka and Fabisiak, 2013)	acetic acid, furfural, 5-methylfurfural, α-pinene, D-limonene, hexanal (Peters et al., 2008; Hyttinen et al., 2010)

Xue et al., 2016; Čech, 2018). The difference between thermally treated conifers and broad-leaved woods is due to the high concentration of volatile terpenes in conifers. These are initially present in untreated conifers and are released as primary emissions, facilitated by high temperatures during heat treatment, resulting in lower emissions from the heat-treated conifers. On the other hand, broad-leaved woods generally contain no volatile terpenes but emit secondary VOCs formed in the wood degradation process, which is accelerated at elevated temperature. They are increasingly produced during the heat treatment and released afterwards (Pohleven et al., 2019).

Thermo-chemical reactions occurring during the heat treatment of wood, including oxidation, dehydration, decarboxylation, transglycosylation, cross-linking, depolymerisation of hemicelluloses by hydrolysis and ramification of lignin, lead to the thermal degradation of cell wall compounds and extractives, which changes their chemical composition (Kocaefe et al., 2008; Esteves and Pereira, 2009; Poncsak et al., 2009). Temperatures above 150°C permanently alter the physical and chemical properties of wood (Akgül et al., 2007), leading to new products and by-products, including VOCs that can be emitted from wood after the treatment. Most of the new (by-)products resulting from the degradation of wood polymers appear only above 200°C and are formed at temperatures of 220°C and 230°C (Esteves and Pereira, 2009; Poncsak et al., 2009; Wang et al., 2018). The decomposition temperatures of hemicelluloses and cellulose are 200–260°C and 240–350°C, respectively (Mayes and Oksanen, 2003). The heat treatment also causes the evaporation of moisture as well as VOCs, including volatile terpenes and other low-molecular weight compounds, from the wood (Manninen et al., 2002; Poncsak et al., 2009). At temperatures above 200°C, the volatiles are removed, but they start to migrate from the wood at low temperatures (under 130°C) (Poncsak et al., 2009).

In thermally modified wood, there is generally an increase in the emission of carboxylic acids and their esters, aldehydes (mainly furfural, as well as 5-methylfurfural), ketones (acetone), alcohols, aliphatic and aromatic hydrocarbons, some of which are new products formed during heat treatment, whereas volatile terpenes (broad-leaved woods), and the aldehydes hexanal and pentanal significantly decrease after the heat treatment compared to the untreated wood (Manninen et al., 2002; Mayes and Oksanen, 2003; Peters et al., 2008; Hyttinen et al., 2010; Elaieb et al., 2015; Xue et al., 2016; Čech, 2018). Formaldehyde emission from wood increases after heat treatment at higher temperatures (Schäfer and Roffael, 2000).

In thermally modified conifer woods, volatile terpenes and hexanal decrease after the heat treatment, while acetic acid and aldehyde furfural increase, and in thermally treated broad-leaved woods, the emission of the aldehydes hexanal and pentanal decreases to almost 0%, while that of acetic acid and furfural increases (Pohleven et al., 2019).

Thermal degradation of wood components (hemicelluloses, cellulose, lignin and extractives) during heat treatment leads to the formation of new VOCs that can be emitted from wood after the treatment (Esteves and Pereira, 2009; Poncsak et al., 2009; Wang et al., 2018). Thus, the amount of VOCs including acids, aldehydes, aromatics, alkanes, and some trace compounds (e.g., furans, ketones, phenols and esters) increase with increasing in heat-treatment temperature, while those of alcohols and alkenes decrease. This has been clearly demonstrated in a study on thermally treated southern yellow pine (*Pinus* spp.), where the number of VOCs increased with heat-treatment temperature, although the total VOC quantity emitted decreased. A total of 86 VOCs was identified in untreated specimens, while there were 93 VOCs in specimens treated at 140°C and 131 VOCs in specimens treated at 220°C (Wang et al., 2018).

Pohleven et al. (2019) summarised the factors influencing VOC emissions, and stated that the emission of individual wood VOCs depends on endogenous factors, including genetic and biochemical factors (e.g., wood species and type); and on exogenous (biotic and abiotic) factors, such as growth conditions, wood treatment, etc. (Englund, 1999; Roffael, 2006; Wolpert, 2012). Drying and thermal treatment lead to a decrease (conifer woods) or an increase (broad-leaved woods) in VOC emissions. Generally, surface treatment drastically reduces wood VOC emissions; but, lacquers and paints may contribute with their own VOCs from solvents and other agents, and thus can increase VOC emission rates; oils, waxes, and waterborne lacquers contain solvents, but they also allow VOCs to be emitted from the wood.

Pohleven et al. (2019) concluded that conifers emit the highest concentrations of wood VOCs because of the large (70–90%) emissions of volatile terpenes (monoterpenes and sesquiterpenes) that gradually decrease over time, and of hexanal and acetic acid. They concluded that VOC emissions from broad-leaved woods are considerably (roughly 50 times) lower than those from conifers, since they contain non-volatile terpenes, but instead emit low concentrations of hexanal and pentanal, as well as acetic acid and others, which are formed during the wood degradation processes.

It should be noted that the test chamber conditions influence the measurement of the VOCs, including factors are temperature, wood moisture content and relative humidity during measurement, and the presence of oxidising agents (Pohleven et al., 2019).

6.5 Industry 4.0 in wood supply chain

In recent years, digitalisation has greatly influenced all sectors of industry. The term *Industry 4.0* has been used since 2011, when it was first used in Germany as a vision towards a fourth industrial revolution. The evolution from *Industry 1.0* to *Industry 4.0* goes from the Age of Steam through the Age of Electricity and The Information Age to The Age of Cyber Physical Systems, which was officially presented in 2013 (GTAI, 2014). Müller et al. (2019) summarised the various definitions of Industry 4.0 as there is no single definition in use. The Industrial Internet Consortium (Lu, 2017) for example states that *Industry 4.0 is the integration of complex physical machinery and devices with networked sensors and software, used to predict, control and plan for better business and societal outcomes.*

Industry 4.0 is mainly presented in cyber physical systems (CPS), Internet of Things (IoT), cloud computing, block-chain, as well as smart devices and business process management (Xu et al., 2018). It focusses on end-to-end digitalisation and the integration of digital industrial ecosystems. Since the IoT has been successfully implemented in the existing manufacturing systems, it is considered to be a key enabler for the next generation of advance manufacturing.

Digitalisation has also had an impact on the forest sector. The changes are, however, being implemented at a slower rate. Müller et al. (2019) reviewed past studies related to the digitalisation of wood supply chains and discussed how Industry 4.0 will change the forest value chain. There is clearly a gap in research, which is fundamental in the development of modern information and communication technology, including data acquisition and processing, knowledge discovery, and digital twin applications in the field of renewable materials in general, not only in the wood sector. Using modern techniques of data acquisition for monitoring, analysing, and optimising products, processes, and building information engineering techniques can improve business productivity, design, health, and sustainability. The results of these studies can be integrated into the next generation of complex information processing frameworks for the design, production, and life-cycle management of renewable materials as well as sustainable buildings. Moreover, the massive and dynamically changing data streams acquired with modern technological tools in highly constrained and complex environments, such as those found in the forest sector, need computationally intensive solutions.

Research topics related to information management and software engineering are being intensively explored for the production of large datasets, but specific intelligent solutions with respect to renewable materials are not widely available. Sporadic results are available, when certain aspects of the field are considered, but a unified approach dedicated to renewable materials is currently a scientific impasse. A unified conceptual framework covering the whole range of forestry scenarios is still missing. Computational materials science also uses state-of-the-art methods from machine learning (Liu et al., 2017), but it is generally restricted to the use of a specific method for a single material. A unified framework in this kind of problem solving with an adaptation to renewable materials could be a significant added value to current research lines, and the integration of analytical computational models and machine learning methods must be exploited to develop new materials from "small data" (Balachandran et al., 2017). Finally, new smart technologies and advanced manufacturing approaches pose future challenges for process optimisation, especially in the emerging evolution of digital twin and additive manufacturing. Research into these future technological developments is still limited in the production of renewable materials (Behandish et al., 2018).

The technical challenges in advancing Industry 4.0 identified by Xu et al. (2018) are also relevant for wood modification technologies and processes. Existing ICT infrastructures are not ready to support the digital transformation to Industry 4.0, which should provide horizontal integration, vertical integration and end-to-end integration. This means that intra-organisational and inter-organisational integrations need to be developed. In the wood supply chain, this means the integration of data and services of forest owners, forest management companies, harvesting companies, transport companies, primary wood processing companies, secondary wood processing companies, and the final users of the products (Figure 6.10).

The digitalisation of the wood supply chain starts in the forests, where opportunities for innovation and modernisation range from high resolution scanning for forest inventory to optimised efficient harvesting and timber logistics (Figure 6.11). At the sawmills, the integration of Industry 4.0 would lead to an optimised material flow and use through enhanced grading and sorting by scanners. In the secondary wood processing industry, the opportunities are in computational design,

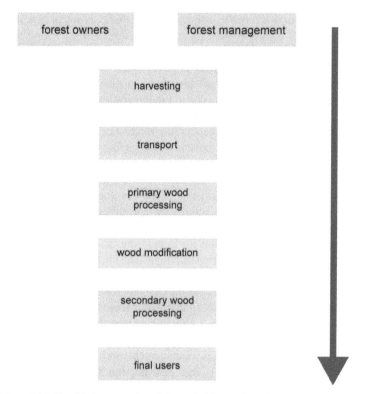

Figure 6.10 Simplified presentation of the vertical integration of the wood supply chain.

Figure 6.11 Schematic presentation of high resolution scanning for forest inventory.

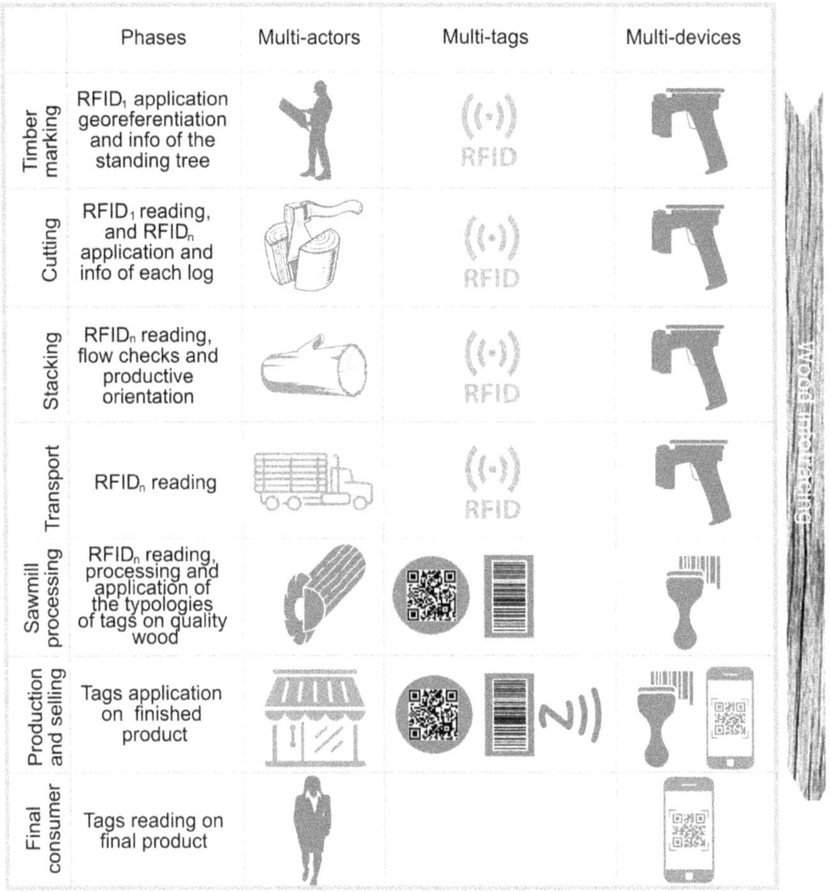

	Phases	Multi-actors	Multi-tags	Multi-devices
Timber marking	$RFID_1$ application georeferentiation and info of the standing tree		RFID	
Cutting	$RFID_1$ reading, and $RFID_n$ application and info of each log		RFID	
Stacking	$RFID_n$ reading, flow checks and productive orientation		RFID	
Transport	$RFID_n$ reading		RFID	
Sawmill processing	$RFID_n$ reading, processing and application of the typologies of tags on quality wood			
Production and selling	Tags application on finished product			
Final consumer	Tags reading on final product			

Figure 6.12 Schematic presentation of the infotracing phases in the wood supply chain (adopted from Figorilli et al., 2018).

rapid prototyping, robotics, etc., while in the final product assembly, Industry 4.0 could lead to optimisation of highly diverse and complex production chains, including virtual/augmented reality. In wood modification processes, Industry 4.0 could play the same role as in the primary production processing, and the digitalisation of quality control combined with the traceability of timber could open new horizons for wood modification processes and products.

One of the emerging field of research in the sector is distributed ledger (also called block-chain) technology (DLT), which enables the wood to be traced electronically as it travels from the forest to the final product, using an info-tracing system based on open source solutions and combined with IoT solutions relying on technologies such as Radio Frequency Identification (RFID) that stores wood data in a secure, decentralised way (Figorilli et al., 2018). Figure 6.12 shows the electronic traceability of wood along the whole supply chain. The technology is of great interest as its full implementation would enable all wood to be legally sourced. At this stage, it is a matter of speculation, but the forest products industry might, after intense research and development in the field, be able to fully implement such technology. After all, the World Economic Forum (2015) has predicted that by 2027 10% of the global GDP will be stored on DLT.

6.6 Conclusions

Modified wood processing has been gaining in importance as the world faces environmental changes and societal challenges. At the time when this book is being finalised, the world is fighting the COVID-19 pandemic. People are not allowed to spend time in public areas, travelling more or less impossible, and people are requested to stay at home. They are thus experiencing the built environment in a new perspective. The importance of restorative environmental and ergonomic design and their impact on human health and well-being has never before been so evident, while the integration of digital technologies into daily lives and the built environment has reached new dimensions. The situation the world is facing will without doubt lead to new developments and innovations. Wood modification will further enhance the importance of sustainable buildings. Ergonomic, accessible, adaptable, and sustainable buildings created by REED principles will become a new standard. Changes are expected, especially in the urban environment. The positive affect on the environment that these design principles are targeting will only be possible with new technologies and a holistic approach to the creation of the built environment. Wood modification capable of controlling the performance of the material could become the first choice. However, research and development activities in the sector have to be intensified, only in Industry 4.0, but also in Industry 5.0, where the synergy between humans and autonomous machines is expected to lead to new developments. How this is achieved, to what extent and when are questions that need to be answered. The authors do not have the answers, but hope that this book will support current research and development and inspire future holistic, interdisciplinary research and development activities, where wood scientists will work with civil engineers, computer scientists, medical doctors, psychologists, environmental scientists, etc., to deliver new knowledge and innovations in the field of wood modification.

References

Akgül, M., E. Gümüşkaya and S. Korkut. 2007. Crystalline structure of heat-treated Scots pine (*Pinus sylvestris* L.) and Uludağ fir (*Abies nordmanniana* (Stev.) subsp. *bornmuelleriana* (Mattf.)) wood. Wood Science and Technology 41(3): 281–289.

Allegretti, O., M. Brunetti, I. Cuccui, S. Ferrari, M. Nocetti and N. Terziev. 2012. Thermo-vacuum modification of spruce (*Picea abies* Karst.) and fir (*Abies alba* Mill.) wood. BioResources 7(3): 3656–3669.

Balachandran, P.V., J. Young, T. Lookman and J.M. Rondinelli. 2017. Learning from data to design functional materials without inversion symmetry. Nature Communications 8: Article ID 14282.

Behandish, M., S. Nelaturi and J. de Kleer. 2018. Automated process planning for hybrid manufacturing. Computer-Aided Design 102: 115–127.

Bejune, J.J. 2001. Wood use trends in the pallet and container industry: 1992–1999. PhD. Thesis, Virginia Polytechnic Institute and State University, USA.

Bolin, C.A. and S.T. Smith. 2011a. Life cycle assessment of borate-treated lumber with comparison to galvanized steel framing. Journal of Cleaner Production 19: 630–639.

Bolin, C.A. and S.T. Smith. 2011b. Life cycle assessment of ACQ-treated lumber with comparison to wood plastic composite decking. Journal of Cleaner Production 19: 620–629.

Buchanan, A. and S. Levine. 1999. Wood-based building materials and atmospheric carbon emissions. Environmental Science and Policy 2: 427–437.

Burnard, M. 2017. Bio-based materials and human well-being in the built environment, pp. 365–372. *In*: Jones, D. and Brischke, C. [eds.]. Performance of Bio-based Materials. Woodhead Publishing, Duxford, UK.

Burnard, M. and A. Kutnar. 2015. Wood and human stress in the built indoor environment: A review. Wood Science and Technology 49(5): 969–986.

Böhm, M., M.Z.M. Salem and J. Srba. 2012. Formaldehyde emission monitoring from a variety of solid wood, plywood, blockboard and flooring products manufactured for building and furnishing materials. Journal of Hazardous Materials 221/222: 68–79.

Börjesson, P. and L. Gustavsson. 2000. Greenhouse gas balances in building construction: Wood versus concrete from life-cycle and forest land-use perspectives. Energy Policy 28: 575–588.

Cacho, O., R. Hean and R. Wise. 2003. Carbon-accounting methods and reforestation incentives. The Australian Journal of Agricultural and Resource Economics 47: 153–179.

Čech, P. 2018. Comparison of VOC emissions from natural wood and heat treated wood. Drvna Industrija 69(4): 297–309.

CEN. 2011. EN 15978 Sustainability of construction works – Assessment of environmental performance of buildings – Calculation method. European Committee for Standardization, Brussels, Belgium.

CEN. 2013. EN 15804 Sustainability of construction works. Environmental product declarations. Core rules for the product category of construction products, German version EN 15804:2012+A12013. European Committee for Standardization, Brussels, Belgium.

CEN. 2014a. EN 16485 Round and sawn timber. Environmental product declarations. Product category rules for wood and wood-based products for use in construction. European Committee for Standardization, Brussels, Belgium.

CEN. 2014b. EN 16449 Wood and wood-based products – Calculation of the biogenic carbon content of wood and conversion to carbon dioxide. European Committee for Standardization, Brussels, Belgium.

Czajka, M. and E. Fabisiak. 2013. Emission of volatile organic compounds from cross section of pine wood (*Pinus sylvestris* L.). Forestry and Wood Technology 82: 149–154.

DEMOWOOD. 2012. Optimisation of material recycling and energy recovery from waste and demolition wood in different value chains NWP2-ER-2009-235066, Deliverable for DL – WP2.1. http://www.wwnet-demowood.eu/fileadmin/PTS/Demowood/Dokumente/DL_WP2.1 _Sorting%20Techniques_pts_120607.pdf (2020-03-17).

DEMOWOOD. 2013. Optimisation of material recycling and energy recovery from waste and demolition wood in different value chains NWP2-ER-2009-235066, Deliverable for DL – WP2.2. http://www.wwnet-demowood.eu/fileadmin/PTS/Demowood/Dokumente/DL_WP2.2_ Quality%20Assessment%20of%20Waste%20Wood.pdf (2020-03-17).

Derr, V. and S.R. Kellert. 2013. Making children's environments "R.E.D": Restorative environmental design and its relationship to sustainable design. *In*: Pavlides, E. and Wells, J. [eds.]. Proceedings of the 44th Annual Conference of the Environmental Design Research Association. The Environmental Design Research Association, McLean (VA), USA.

Elaieb, M., K. Candelier, A. Pétrissans, S. Dumarçay, P. Gérardin and M. Pétrissans. 2015. Heat treatment of Tunisian soft wood species: Effect on the durability, chemical modifications and mechanical properties. Maderas. Ciencia y Tecnología 17(4): 699–710.

Englund, F. 1999. Emissions of volatile organic compounds (VOC) from wood. Report I9901001, Swedish Institute for Wood Technology Research (Trätek), Stockholm, Sweden.

Englund, F. and R.M. Nussbaum. 2000. Monoterpenes in Scots pine and Norway spruce and their emission during kiln drying. Holzforschung 54(5): 449–456.

Esteves, B.M. and H.M. Pereira. 2009. Wood modification by heat treatment: A review. BioResources 4(1): 370–404.

European Commission. 2009. Mainstreaming sustainable development into EU policies: 2009 review of the European Union strategy for sustainable development. Commission of the European Communities, Brussels, Belgium.

European Commission. 2011a. Roadmap to a resource efficient Europe (COM2011). The European Commission.

European Commission. 2011b. Roadmap for moving to a competitive low carbon economy in 2050 (COM2011). The European Commission.

European Commission. 2012. Communication from the commission to the European parliament, the Council, the European economics and social committee and the committee of the regions. Innvating for sustainable growth: A bioeconomy for Europe. The European Commission, Brussels, Belgium.

European Commission. 2015. Communication from the commission to the European Parliament, the Council, the European economics and social committee and the committee of the regions. Closing the loop: An EU action plan for the Circular Economy, Brussels, Belgium.

European Commission. 2017. Investing in a smart, innovative and sustainable industry. A renewed EU industrial policy strategy (COM2017). The European Commission.

European Commission. 2019. Communication from the commission to the European Parliament, the Council, the European economics and social committee and the committee of the regions. The European Green Deal (COM2019). The European Commission.

European Parliament Council. 2008. Directive 2008/98/EC of the European Parliament and of the Council of 19 November 2008 on waste and repealing certain directives. The European Parliament, Brussels, Belgium.

Fell, D. 2010. Wood in the human environment: restorative properties of wood in the built indoor environment. PhD. Thesis, University of British Columbia, Vancouver (BC), Canada.

Figorilli, S., F. Antonucci, C. Costa, F. Pallottino, L. Raso, M. Castiglione, E. Pinci, D. Del Vecchio, G. Colle, A.R. Proto, G. Sperandio and P. Menesatti. 2018. A blockchain implementation prototype for the electronic open source traceability of wood along the whole supply chain. Sensors 18: Article ID 3133.

Gorse, C., F. Thomas, D. Glew and D. Miles Shenton. 2016. Achieving sustainability in new build and retrofit: Building performance and life cycle analysis, Chapter 8. *In*: Dastbaz, M., Strange, M. and Selkowitz, S. [eds.]. Building Sustainable Futures. Springer International Publishing, Switzerland.

GTAI (Germany Trade & Invest). 2014. Industries 4.0-Smart Manufacturing for the Future. Berlin, Germany.

Gustavsson, L. and R. Sathre. 2006. Variability in energy and carbon dioxide balances of wood and concrete building materials. Building and Environment 41: 940–951.

Hasan, A.R., J. Schindler, H.M. Solo-Gabriele and T.G. Townsend. 2011. Online sorting of recovered wood waste by automated XRF-technology. Part I: Detection of preservative-treated wood waste. Waste Manage 31(4): 688–694.

Hashimoto, S., M. Nose, T. Obara and Y. Moriguchi. 2002. Wood products: Potential carbon sequestration impact on net carbon emissions in industrialized countries. Environmental Science & Policy 5(2): 183–193.

Heräjärvi, H., J. Kunttu, E. Hurmekoski and T. Hujala. 2020. Outlook for modified wood use and regulations in circular economy. Holzforschung 74(4): 334–343.

Hill, C.A.S. 2006. Wood Modification: Chemical, Thermal and other Processes. John Wiley & Sons, Chichester, UK.

Hill, C.A.S. 2011. An Introduction to Sustainable Resource Use. Taylor and Francis, London, UK.

Hill, C. and A. Norton. 2014. The environmental impacts associated with wood modification balanced by the benefits of life extension, p. 83. *In*: Nunes, L., Jones, D., Hill, C. and Militz, H. [eds.]. Proceedings of the ECWM7 – European

Wood Conference on Wood Modification. Lizboa, Portugal. Laboratório Nacional de Engenhara Civil (LNEC), Lisbon, Portugal.

Hofmann, T., M. Wetzig, T. Rétfalvi, T. Sieverts, H. Bergemann and P. Niemz. 2013. Heat-treatment with the vacuum-press dewatering method: Chemical properties of the manufactured wood and the condensation water. European Journal of Wood and Wood Products 71(1): 121–127.

Höglmeier, K., G. Weber-Blaschke and K. Richter. 2013. Potentials for cascading of recovered wood from building deconstruction: A case study for south-east Germany. Resources. Conservation & Recycling 78: 81–91.

Hyttinen, M., M. Masalin-Weijo, P. Kalliokoski and P. Pasanen. 2010. Comparison of VOC emissions between air-dried and heat-treated Norway spruce (*Picea abies*), Scots pine (*Pinus sylvesteris*) and European aspen (*Populus tremula*) wood. Atmospheric Environment 44(38): 5028–5033.

ISO. 2000. ISO 14020 Environmental labels and declarations—General principles. International Organization for Standardization, Geneva, Switzerland.

ISO. 2006a. ISO 14040 Environmental management—Life cycle assessment—Principles and framework. International Organization for Standardization, Geneva, Switzerland.

ISO. 2006b. ISO 14044 Environmental management—Life cycle assessment—Requirements and guidelines. International Organization for Standardization, Geneva, Switzerland.

ISO. 2009. ISO 14025 Environmental Labels and Declarations—Type III environmental declarations—Principles and procedures. International Organization for Standardization, Geneva, Switzerland.

ISO. 2016. ISO 14021 Environmental labels and declarations—Self-declared environmental claims (Type II environmental labelling). International Organization for Standardization, Geneva, Switzerland.

ISO. 2018. ISO 14024 Environmental labels and declarations—Type I environmental labelling—Principles and procedures. International Organization for Standardization, Geneva, Switzerland.

Jensen, L.K., A. Larsen, L. Mølhave, M.K. Hansen and B. Knudsen. 2001. Health evaluation of volatile organic compound (VOC) emissions from wood and wood-based materials. Archives of Environmental & Occupational Health 56(5): 419–432.

Jones, D. 2009. Sustainability tools used in the U.K. for construction materials and products, pp. 35–44. *In*: Spear, M.J. [ed.]. Proceedings of the 2009 International Panel Product Symposium, Nantes, France. The BioComposites Centre, Bangor University, UK.

Jonsson, R., G. Egnell and A. Baudin. 2011. Swedish forest sector outlook study. United Nations, Geneva, Switzerland. http://www.unece.org/fileadmin/DAM/timber/publications/DP-58_hi_res.pdf (2020-03-12).

Kellert, S.R. 2008. Dimensions, elements and attributes of biophilic design, pp. 3–19. *In*: Kellert, R.S., Heerwagen, J.H. and Mador, M.L. [eds.]. Biophilic Design: The Theory, Science and Practice of Bringing Buildings to Life. John Wiley & Sons, Hoboken (NJ), USA.

Kocaefe, D., S. Poncsak and Y. Boluk. 2008. Effect of thermal treatment on the chemical composition and mechanical properties of birch and aspen. BioResources 3(2): 517–537.

Kretschmann, D.E. 2010. Commercial lumber, round timbers, and ties, pp. 6.1–6.25. *In*: Ross, R.J. [ed.]. Wood Handbook: Wood as an Engineering Material. General Technical Report FPL GTR-190. U.S. Department of Agriculture, Forest Service, Forest Products Laboratory, Madison (WI), USA.

Kutnar, A. and C. Hill. 2014. Assessment of carbon footprinting in the wood industry, pp. 135–172. *In*: Muthu, S.S. [ed.]. Assessment of Carbon Footprint in Different Industrial Sectors. Volume 2: EcoProduction. Springer, Singapore.

Kutnar, A. and C. Hill. 2016. End of life scenarios and the carbon footprint of wood cladding, pp. 85–100. *In*: Muthu, S.S. [ed.]. The Carbon Footprint Handbook. CRC Press, Boca Raton, USA.

Kutnar, A. and S.S. Muthu. 2016. Environmental Impacts of Traditional and Innovative Forest-based Bioproducts. Springer Science+Business Media, Singapore.

Larsen, A., L. Frost and L. Winther Funch. 2000. Emission of volatile organic compounds from wood and wood-based materials. Working Report No. 15, Miljøstyrelsen, Danish Environmental Protection Agency, Denmark.

Levasseur, A., P. Lesage, M. Margni and R. Samson. 2013. Biogenic carbon and temporary storage addressed with dynamic life cycle assessment. Journal of Industrial Ecology 17: 117–128.

Liu, Y., T. Zhao, W. Ju and S. Shi. 2017. Materials discovery and design using machine learning. Journal of Materiomics 3(3): 159–177.

Lu, Y. 2017. Industry 4.0: A survey on technologies, applications and open research issues. Journal of Industrial Information Integration 6: 1–10.

Manninen, A.-M., P. Pasanen and J.K. Holopainen. 2002. Comparing the VOC emissions between air-dried and heat-treated Scots pine wood. Atmospheric Environment 36(11): 1763–1768.

Masuda, M. 2004. Why wood is excellent for interior design? From vision physical point of view. pp. 101–106. *In*: Proceedings of the 8th World Conference on Timber Engineering: WCTE 2004, Lahti, Finland, June 14–17, 2004. Finnish Association of Civil Engineers RIL.

Mayes, D. and O. Oksanen. 2003. ThermoWood® Handbook. International ThermoWood Association, Helsinki, Finland.

McKeever, D.B. and R.H. Falk. 2004. Woody residues and solid waste wood available for recovery in the United States, 2002, pp. 307–316. *In*: Gallis, C. [ed.]. European COST E31 Conference: Management of Recovered Wood Recycling Bioenergy and Other Options, Thessaloniki, Greece.

Meyer, B. and C. Boehme. 1997. Formaldehyde emission from solid wood. Forest Products Journal 47: 45–48.

Militz, H. and M. Altgen. 2014. Processes and properties of thermally modified wood manufactured in Europe, pp. 269–285. *In*: Schultz, T.P., Goodell, B. and Nicholas, D.D. [eds.]. Deterioration and Protection of Sustainable Biomaterials. ACS Symposium Series, American Chemical Society, Washington, USA.

Müller, F., D. Haeger and M. Hanewinkel. 2019. Digitization in wood supply: A review on how Industry 4.0 will change the forest value chain. Computers and Electronics in Agriculture 162: 206–218.

Nyrud, A., K. Bysheim and T. Bringslimark. 2010. Health benefits from wood interior in a hospital room. *In*: Proceedings of the International Convention of Society of Wood Science and Technology (SWST) and United Nations Economic Commission for Europe, Geneva, Switzerland.

Nässén, J., F. Hedenus, S. Karlsson and J. Holmberg. 2012. Concrete vs. wood in buildings: An energy system approach. Building and Environment 51: 361–369.

O'Connor, J., R. Kozak, C. Gaston and D. Fell. 2004. Wood in nonresidential buildings: opportunities and barriers. Forest Products Journal 54(3): 19–28.

Peters, J., K. Fischer and S. Fischer. 2008. Characterization of emissions from thermally modified wood and their reduction by chemical treatment. BioResources 3(2): 491–502.

Pilli, R., G. Fiorese and G. Grassi. 2015. EU mitigation potential of harvested wood products. Carbon Balance and Management 10: Article ID 6.

Pohleven, J., M.D. Burnard and A. Kutnar. 2019. Volatile organic compounds emitted from untreated and thermally modified wood: A review. Wood and Fiber Science 51(3): 1–24.

Poncsak, S., D. Kocaefe, F. Simard and A. Pichette. 2009. Evolution of extractive composition during thermal treatment of jack pine. Journal of Wood Chemistry and Technology 29(3): 251–264.

Radkau, J. 2007. Holz – Wie ein Naturstoff Geschichte schreibt [Wood-like a natural product makes history.] Oekom Verlag, München, Germany (In German).

Rice, J., R.A. Kozak, M.J. Meitner and D.H. Cohen. 2006. Appearance wood products and psychological well-being. Wood and Fiber Science 38(4): 644–659.

Risholm-Sundman, M., M. Lundgren, E. Vestin and P. Herder. 1998. Emissions of acetic acid and other volatile organic compounds from different species of solid wood. Holz als Roh- und Werkstoff 56(2): 125–129.

Roffael, E. 2006. Volatile organic compounds and formaldehyde in nature, wood and wood based panels. Holz als Roh- und Werkstoff 64(2): 144–149.

Rowell, R.M. 2002. Sustainable composites from natural resources, pp. 183–192. *In*: Brebbia, C.A. and de Wilde, W.P. [eds.]. High Performance Structures and Composites. WIT Press, Boston (MA), USA.

Salazar, J. and J. Meil. 2009. Prospects for carbon-neutral housing: the influence of greater wood use on the carbon footprint of a single-family residence. Journal of Cleaner Production 17(17): 1563–1571.

Sandak, A.M., J.M. Sandak, M. Brezezicki and A. Kutnar. 2019. Bio-based Building Skin. Springer Open, Singapore.

Schäfer M. and E. Roffael. 2000. On the formaldehyde release of wood particles. Holz als Roh- und Werkstoff 58(4): 259–264.

Sinha, A. and C. Knowles. 2014. Green building and the global forest sector, pp. 261–280. *In*: Hansen, E., Panwar, R. and Vlosky, R. [eds.]. The Global Forest Sector: Changes, Practices, and Prospects. CRC Press, Boca Raton, London, New York.

Sinha, A., R. Gupta and A. Kutnar. 2013. Sustainable development and green buildings. Drvna Industrija 64(1): 45–53.

Stamm, A.J. 1956. Thermal degradation of wood and cellulose. Industrial & Engineering Chemistry 48(3): 413–417.

Stark, N.M., Z. Cai and C. Carll. 2010. Wood-based composite materials: Panel products, glued-laminated timbers, structural composite lumber, and wood-nonwood composite materials, Chapter 11. *In*: Ross, R.J. [ed.]. Wood Handbook: Wood as an Engineering Material. General Report GTR-190. U.S. Dept. of Agriculture, Forest Service, Forest Products Laboratory, Madison (WI), USA.

Steckel, V., J. Welling and M. Ohlmeyer. 2010. Emissions of volatile organic compounds from convection dried Norway spruce timber, 9 p. *In*: Ridley-Ellis, D.J. and Moore, J.R. [eds.]. Proceedings of the Final Conference of COST Action E53: Quality Control for Wood & Wood Products, Edinburgh, UK.

Steckel, V., J. Welling and M. Ohlmeyer. 2011. Product emissions of volatile organic compounds from convection dried Norway spruce (*Picea abies* (L.) Karst.) timber. International Wood Products Journal 2(2): 75–80.

Suttie. E., C.A.S. Hill, G. Sandin, A. Kutnar, C. Ganne-Chedeville, F. Lowres and A.C. Dias. 2017. Environmental assessment of bio-based building materials, pp. 546–591. *In*: Brischke, C. and Jones, D. [eds.]. Performance of Bio-based Building Materials. Elsevier, Woodhead Publishing, Duxford, UK.

Tasooji, M., G. Wan, G. Lewis, H. Wise and C.E. Frazier. 2017. Biogenic formaldehyde: Content and heat generation in the wood of three tree species. ACS Sustainable Chemistry & Engineering 5(5): 4243–4248.

Tellnes, L.G.F., G. Alfredsen, P.O. Flæte and L.R. Gobakken. 2020. Effect of service life aspects on carbon footprint: A comparison of wood decking products. Holzforschung 74(4): 426–433.

Tonn, B. and G. Marland. 2007. Carbon sequestration in wood products: a method for attribution to multiple parties. Environmental Science & Policy 10(2): 162–168.

Van der Lugt, P. and J.G. Vogtländer. 2014. Wood acetylation: A potential route towards climate change mitigation. WIT Transactions on Ecology on the Built Environment, Eco-Architecture 142: 241–252.

Wang, C., Z. Wang, Y. Qin, X. Yin and A. Huang. 2018. Released volatile organic compounds in southern yellow pine before and after heat treatment. International Journal of Environmental Research and Public Health 15(11): Article ID E2579.

Wentzel, M., M. Altgen and H. Militz. 2018. Analyzing reversible changes in hygroscopicity of thermally modified eucalypt wood from open and closed reactor systems. Wood Science and Technology 52(4): 889–907.

Werner, F. and K. Richter. 2007. Wood building products in comparative LCA. A literature review. The International Journal of Life Cycle Assessment 12(7): 470–479.

Wolpert, B.S.J. 2012. Emission and abundance of biogenic volatile organic compounds in wind-throw areas of upland spruce forests in Bavaria. PhD. Thesis, Technical University of Munich, Germany.

World Economic Forum. 2015. Deep Shift Technology Tipping Points and Societal Impact. Davos-Klosters, Switzerland.

Xu, L.D., E.L. Xu and L. Li. 2018. Industry 4.0: State of the art and future trends. International Journal of Production Research 56(8): 2941–2962.

Xue, L., Z. Zhao, Y. Zhang, D. Chu and J. Mu. 2016. Analysis of gas chromatography-mass spectrometry coupled with dynamic headspace sampling on volatile organic compounds of heat-treated poplar at high temperatures. BioResources 11(2): 3550–3560.

Appendix

Common and binomial names of tree species

Sorted by common name

Common/vernacular name	Binomial name
abachi	*Triplochiton scleroxylon* K.Schum.
abura	*Mitragyna ciliata* Aubrév. & Pellegr.
acacia	*Acacia* spp.
acacia hybrid	*Acacia mangium* × *auriculiformis*
afara	*Terminalia superba* Engl. & Diels
African baobab	*Adansonia digitata* L.
African coralwood	*Pterocarpus soyauxii* Taub.
African limba wood	*Terminalia superba* Engl. & Diels
African locust bean	*Parkia biglobosa* (Jacq.) R.Br. ex G.Don
African oil palm (monocot tree)	*Elaeis guineensis* Jacq.
African padauk	*Pterocarpus soyauxii* Taub.
African whitewood	*Triplochiton scleroxylon* K.Schum.
Alaska cedar	*Cupressus nootkatensis* D.Don
Alaska yellow cedar	*Cupressus nootkatensis* D.Don
albizzia	A genus of more than 160 species
albizzia	*Paraserienthes falcata* Becker
alder	*Alnus* spp.
Aleppo pine	*Pinus halepensis* Mill.
alligatorwood	*Liquidambar styraciflua* L.
alpine ash	*Eucalyptus delegatensis* R.T.Baker
American ash	*Fraxinus americana* L.
American aspen	*Populus tremuloides* Michx.
American basswood	*Tilia americana* L.
American beech	*Fagus grandifolia* Ehrh.
American chestnut	*Castanea dentata* (Marsh.) Borkh.
American elm	*Ulmus americana* L.
American hackberry	*Celtis occidentalis* L.
American larch	*Larix laricina* (Du Roi) K. Koch
American linden	*Tilia americana* L.

American pepper	*Schinus molle* L.
American planetree	*Platanus occidentalis* L.
American storax	*Liquidambar styraciflua* L.
American sweetgum	*Liquidambar styraciflua* L.
American sycamore	*Platanus occidentalis* L.
American tulip tree	*Liriodendron tulipifera* L.
American white birch	*Betula papyrifera* Marshall
anacahuita	*Schinus molle* L.
Andaman padauk	*Pterocarpus dalbergioides* DC.
Andaman redwood	*Pterocarpus dalbergioides* DC.
Angelique	*Dicorynia guianensis* Amshoff
Angelique batard	*Dicorynia guianensis* Amshoff
Angelique gris	*Dicorynia guianensis* Amshoff
apple	*Malus* spp.
apple	*Malus domestica* Borkh.
Arolla pine	*Pinus cembra* L.
aromatic cedar	*Juniperus virginiana* L.
ash	*Fraxinus* spp.
Asian white birch	*Betula platyphylla* Sukaczev
aspen	*Populus tremula* L.
Australian silver oak	*Grevillea robusta* A.Cunn. ex R.Br.
Austrian pine	*Pinus nigra* Arnold.
Austrian stone pine	*Pinus cembra* L.
Ayan	*Distemonanthus benthamianus* Baill.
ayous	*Triplochiton scleroxylon* K.Schum.
azobé	*Lophira alata* Banks ex Gaertn
bahia	*Mitragyna ciliata* Aubrév. & Pellegr.
balau	*Shorea* spp.
bald cypress	*Taxodium distichum* (L.) Rich.
baldcypress	*Taxodium distichum* (L.) Rich.
Balkan beech	*Fagus moesiaca* C.
balsam fir	*Abies balsamea* (L.) Mill.
balsam poplar	*Populus balsamifera* L.
Baltic pine	*Pinus sylvestris* L.
bam	*Populus balsamifera* L.
Bamboo (monocot tree)	*Dendrocalamus asper* (Schult.) Backer
Bamboo (monocot tree)	*Dendrocalamus* spp.
bamtree	*Populus balsamifera* L.
bangkirai	*Shorea* spp.
Barakaroeballi	*Dicorynia guianensis* Amshoff
Basralokus	*Dicorynia guianensis* Amshoff

Baton Rouge	*Juniperus virginiana* L.
bead-tree	*Melia azedarach* L.
beaverwood	*Celtis occidentalis* L.
beechwood	*Gmelina arborea* Roxb.
bilsted	*Liquidambar styraciflua* L.
birch	*Betula* spp.
bitter pecan	*Carya aquatica* (F.Michx.) Nutt.
bitternut hickory	*Carya cordiformis* (Wangenh.) K.Koch
black alder	*Alnus glutinosa* L.
black ash	*Fraxinus nigra* Marshall
black birch	*Betula lenta* L.
black cherry	*Prunus serotina* Ehrh.
black gum	*Nyssa sylvatica* Marshall
black larch	*Larix laricina* (Du Roi) K. Koch
black locust	*Robinia pseudoacacia* L.
black poplar	*Populus nigra var. pyramidalis* L.
black spruce	*Picea mariana* (Mill.) Britton, Sterns & Poggenburg
black tupelo	*Nyssa sylvatica* Marshall
black walnut	*Juglans nigra* L.
black wattle	*Acacia mangium* Willd.
blackjack pine	*Pinus ponderosa* Douglas ex C.Lawson
blue gum	*Eucalyptus globulus* Labill.
boabab	*Adansonia digitata* L.
broom hickory	*Carya glabra* Miller
brown top	*Eucalyptus obliqua* L'Hér.
brown top stringbark	*Eucalyptus obliqua* L'Hér.
brutia pine	*Pinus brutia* Ten.
bull pine	*Pinus ponderosa* Douglas ex C.Lawson
bullnut	*Carya tomentosa* Sarg.
buna	*Fagus crenata* Blume
bur-flower tree	*Anthocephalus chinensis* (Lamk) A. Rich. ex Walp. and *Anthocephalus macrophyllus* (Roxb.) Havil.
Burmese padauk	*Pterocarpus macrocarpus* Kurz.
Burmese teak	*Tectona grandis* L. f.
buttonwood	*Platanus occidentalis* L.
cadamba	*Anthocephalus chinensis* (Lamk) A. Rich. ex Walp. and *Anthocephalus macrophyllus* (Roxb.) Havil.
Calabrian pine	*Pinus brutia* Ten.
California black oak	*Quercus kelloggii* Newberry
California incense-cedar	*Calocedrus decurrens* (Torr.) Florin
California mountain pine	*Pinus monticola* Douglas ex D. Don

California pepper tree	*Schinus molle* L.
California redwood	*Sequoia sempervirens* (D.Don) Endl.
Canadian hemlock	*Tsuga canadensis* (L.) Carrière
canoe birch	*Betula papyrifera* Marshall
Cape lilac	*Melia azedarach* L.
Caribbean pine	*Pinus caribaea* Morelet
Carolina cedar	*Juniperus virginiana* L.
Carpathian walnut	*Juglans regia* L.
Cathay poplar	*Populus cathayana* Rehder
cativo	*Prioria copaifera* Griseb.
Caucasian alder	*Alnus subcordata* C.A. Mey.
cedar	*Pinaceae* spp.
cedar elm	*Ulmus crassifolia* Nutt.
Central Province teak (CP teak)	*Tectona grandis* L. f.
cheesewood	*Endospermum malaccense* L.S.Sm.
cherry birch	*Betula lenta* L.
chinaberry tree	*Melia azedarach* L.
China-fir	*Cunninghamia konishii* Hayata
Chinese fir	*Cunninghamia konishii* Hayata
Chinese white poplar	*Populus tomentosa* Carr.
Christmas tree	*Abies procera* Rehder
cluster pine	*Pinus pinaster* Aiton
coast Douglas-fir	*Pseudotsuga menziesii* var. *menziesii*
coast pignut hickory	*Carya glabra* Miller
coast redwood	*Sequoia sempervirens* (D.Don) Endl.
coast spruce	*Picea sitchensis* (Bong.) Carr.
coastal redwood	*Sequoia sempervirens* (D.Don) Endl.
colonial pine	*Araucaria cunninghamii* Mudie
Columbian pine	*Pseudotsuga menziesii* (Mirbel) Franco
common alder	*Alnus glutinosa* L.
common ash	*Fraxinus excelsior* L.
common aspen	*Populus tremula* L.
common beech	*Fagus sylvatica* L.
common bur-flower tree	*Anthocephalus chinensis* (Lamk) A. Rich. ex Walp. and *Anthocephalus macrophyllus* (Roxb.) Havil.
common hackberry	*Celtis occidentalis* L.
common hornbeam	*Carpinus betuls* L.
common juniper	*Juniperus communis* L.
common oak	*Quercus robur* L.
common walnut	*Juglans regia* L.
contorta pine	*Pinus contorta* Douglas

cork elm	*Ulmus thomasii* Sarg.
Cornish oak	*Quercus petraea* (Matt.) Lieb.
Corsican pine	*Pinus nigra* var. *maritima*
cottongum	*Nyssa aquatica* L.
cottonwood	*Populus nigra* L. (section *Aigeiros*)
cream of tartar tree	*Adansonia digitata* L.
creek maple	*Acer saccharinum* L.
Cunninghamia	*Cunninghamia konishii* Hayata
cypress	*Cupressus* spp.
dark-bark spruce	*Picea jezoensis* (Siebold & Zucc.) Carr.
dead finish	*Eucalyptus cloeziana* F.Muell.
djarraly	*Eucalyptus marginata* Donn ex Sm.
dodongba	*Parkia biglobosa* (Jacq.) R.Br. ex G.Don
Dorrigo pine	*Araucaria cunninghamii* Mudie
Douglas fir	*Pseudotsuga menziesii* (Mirbel) Franco
Douglas-fir	*Pseudotsuga menziesii* (Mirbel) Franco
downy birch	*Betula pubescens* Ehrh.
durmast oak	*Quercus petraea* (Matt.) Lieb.
East Asian white birch	*Betula pendula* Roth.
East Indian mahogany	*Pterocarpus dalbergioides* DC.
East Mediterranean pine	*Pinus brutia* Ten.
eastern American black walnut	*Juglans nigra* L.
eastern arborvitae	*Thuja occidentalis* L.
eastern balsam-poplar	*Populus balsamifera* L.
eastern hemlock	*Tsuga canadensis* (L.) Carrière
eastern hemlock-spruce	*Tsuga canadensis* (L.) Carrière
eastern juniper	*Juniperus virginiana* L.
eastern larch	*Larix laricina* (Du Roi) K. Koch
eastern red cedar	*Juniperus virginiana* L.
eastern redcedar	*Juniperus virginiana* L.
eastern white cedar	*Thuja occidentalis* L.
eastern white pine	*Pinus strobus* L.
ekki	*Lophira alata* Banks ex Gaertn.
elm	*Ulmus* sp.
Engelmann spruce	*Picea engelmannii* Parry ex Engelm.
English oak	*Quercus robur* L.
English walnut	*Juglans regia* L.
escobilla	*Schinus molle* L.
eucalyptus	*Eucalyptus* sp.
Eurasian aspen	*Populus tremula* L.

European alder	*Alnus glutinosa* L.
European ash	*Fraxinus excelsior* L.
European aspen	*Populus tremula* L.
European beech	*Fagus sylvatica* L.
European hornbeam	*Carpinus betuls* L.
European oak	*Quercus robur* L.
European silver fir	*Abies alba* Mill.
European spruce	*Picea abies* (L.) Karst.
European white birch	*Betula pubescens* Ehrh.
ezo spruce	*Picea jezoensis* (Siebold & Zucc.) Carr.
ezomatsu	*Picea jezoensis* (Siebold & Zucc.) Carr.
false acacia	*Robinia pseudoacacia* L.
false pepper	*Schinus molle* L.
fiddletree	*Liriodendron tulipifera* L.
filipinus pine	*Pinus ponderosa* Douglas ex C.Lawson
fir	*Abies alba* Mill.
flooded gum	*Eucalyptus grandis* W. Hill ex Maiden
forest mangrove	*Acacia mangium* Willd.
frake	*Terminalia superba* Engl. & Diels
giant arborvitae	*Thuja plicata* Donn ex D.Don
giant bamboo (monocot tree)	*Dendrocalamus barbatus*
giant cedar	*Thuja plicata* Donn ex D.Don
giant fir	*Abies grandis* (Douglas ex D. Don) Lindley
giant sequoia	*Sequoia sempervirens* (D.Don) Endl.
gmelina	*Gmelina arborea* Roxb.
golden aspen	*Populus tremuloides* Michx.
golden birch	*Betula alleghaniensis* Britt.
goomar teak	*Gmelina arborea* Roxb.
grand fir	*Abies grandis* (Douglas ex D. Don) Lindley
great silver fir	*Abies grandis* (Douglas ex D. Don) Lindley
green ash	*Fraxinus pennsylvanica* Marshall
grey alder	*Alnus incana* (L.) Moench
gulf cypress	*Taxodium distichum* (L.) Rich.
Gympie messmate	*Eucalyptus cloeziana* F.Muell.
hackberry	*Celtis occidentalis* L.
hackmatack	*Larix laricina* (Du Roi) K. Koch
hackmatack	*Populus balsamifera* L.
hairy birch	*Betula pubescens* Ehrh.
hazel pine	*Liquidambar styraciflua* L.
hazelnut	*Corylus* spp.

hickory wattle	*Acacia mangium* Willd.
hinoki	*Chamaecyparis obtuse* (Siebold & Zucc.) Endl.
hinoki cypress	*Chamaecyparis obtuse* (Siebold & Zucc.) Endl.
hognut	*Carya tomentosa* Sarg.
hoop pine	*Araucaria cunninghamii* Mudie
hybrid poplar	*Populus* spp.
incense cedar	*Calocedrus decurrens* (Torr.) Florin
Indian lilac	*Melia azedarach* L.
insignis pine	*Pinus radiata* D.Don
ipil	*Intsia* spp. (*I. bijuga, I. palembanica*)
iru	*Parkia biglobosa* (Jacq.) R.Br. ex G.Don
Italian cypress	*Cupressus sempervirens* L.
Japanese beech	*Fagus crenata* Blume
Japanese cedar	*Cryptomeria japonica* (L.f.) D.Don
Japanese cypress	*Chamaecyparis obtuse* (Siebold & Zucc.) Endl.
Japanese pine	*Pinus densiflora* Siebold & Zucc.
Japanese red pine	*Pinus densiflora* Siebold & Zucc.
Japanese redwood	*Cryptomeria japonica* (L.f.) D.Don
Japanese sugi	*Cryptomeria japonica* (L.f.) D.Don
Japanese white birch	*Betula platyphylla* Sukaczev
jarrah	*Eucalyptus marginata* Donn ex Sm.
jezo spruce	*Picea jezoensis* (Siebold & Zucc.) Carr.
Johnstone river teak	*Intsia bijuga* (Colebr.) Kuntze
kadam	*Anthocephalus chinensis* (Lamk) A. Rich. ex Walp. and *Anthocephalus macrophyllus* (Roxb.) Havil.
Kashmir tree	*Gmelina arborea* Roxb.
kelempayan	*Anthocephalus chinensis* (Lamk) A. Rich. ex Walp. and *Anthocephalus macrophyllus* (Roxb.) Havil.
Kellogg oak	*Quercus kelloggii* Newberry
Korean red pine	*Pinus densiflora* Siebold & Zucc.
korina	*Terminalia superba* Engl. & Diels
Kwila	*Intsia* spp. (*I. bijuga, I. palembanica*)
laran	*Anthocephalus chinensis* (Lamk) A. Rich. ex Walp. and *Anthocephalus macrophyllus* (Roxb.) Havil.
large maple	*Acer saccharinum* L.
large tupelo	*Nyssa aquatica* L.
lauan	*Shorea* spp.
lawaan	*Shorea* spp.
Leichhardt pine	*Anthocephalus chinensis* (Lamk) A. Rich. ex Walp. and *Anthocephalus macrophyllus* (Roxb.) Havil.
lemon tree	*Citrus limon* (L.) Osbeck
limba	*Terminalia superba* Engl. & Diels

linden	*Tilia* spp.
littleleaf linden	*Tilia cordata* Mill.
loblolly pine	*Pinus taeda* L.
lodgepole pine	*Pinus contorta* Douglas
longleaf pine	*Pinus palustris* Mill.
lowland white fir	*Abies grandis* (Douglas ex D. Don) Lindley
luan	*Shorea* spp.
macaw-fat (monocot tree)	*Elaeis guineensis* Jacq.
Madeira walnut	*Juglans regia* L.
magnolia	*Magnolia* spp.
mahogany birch	*Betula lenta* L.
Malay beechwood	*Gmelina arborea* Roxb.
mangium	*Acacia mangium* Willd.
manna gum	*Eucalyptus viminalis* Labill.
Mantsurian poplar	*Populus cathayana* Rehder
maple	*Acer* spp.
maritime pine	*Pinus pinaster* Aiton
Masson's pine	*Pinus massoniana* Lamb.
M'Boy	*Mitragyna ciliata* Aubrév. & Pellegr.
Mediterranean cypress	*Cupressus sempervirens* L.
meranti	*Shorea* spp.
merbau	*Intsia* spp. (*I. bijuga, I. palembanica*)
messmate	*Eucalyptus obliqua* L'Hér.
messmate stringybark	*Eucalyptus obliqua* L'Hér.
Mexican Douglas fir	*Pseudotsuga menziesii* var. Lindleyana (Roezl) Carrière
mindi	*Melia azedarach* L.
mockernut	*Carya tomentosa* Sarg.
mockernut hickory	*Carya tomentosa* Sarg.
molle del Peru	*Schinus molle* L.
monkey-bread tree	*Adansonia digitata* L.
Monterey pine	*Pinus radiata* D.Don
moor birch	*Betula pubescens* Ehrh.
Moreton bay pine	*Araucaria cunninghamii* Mudie
mountain ash	*Sorbus aucuparia* L.
mountain aspen	*Populus tremuloides* Michx.
mountain spruce	*Picea engelmannii* Parry ex Engelm.
movingui	*Distemonanthus benthamianus* Baill.
Nagpur teak	*Tectona grandis* L. f.
narrow-leaved ash	*Fraxinus angustifolia* Vahl.
néré	*Parkia biglobosa* (Jacq.) R.Br. ex G.Don

netetou	*Parkia biglobosa* (Jacq.) R.Br. ex G.Don
nettletree	*Celtis occidentalis* L.
Nigerian Satinwood	*Distemonanthus benthamianus* Baill.
noble fir	*Abies procera* Rehder
Nootka cedar	*Cupressus nootkatensis* D.Don
North American beech	*Fagus grandifolia* Ehrh.
northern hackberry	*Celtis occidentalis* L.
northern red oak	*Quercus rubra* L.
northern white pine	*Pinus strobus* L.
northern white-cedar	*Thuja occidentalis* L.
Norway maple	*Acer platanoides* L.
Norway pine	*Pinus resinosa* Sol. ex Aiton
Norway spruce	*Picea abies* (L.) Karst.
oak	*Quercus* spp.
obeche	*Triplochiton scleroxylon* K.Schum.
occidental plane	*Platanus occidentalis* L.
oil palm (monocot tree)	*Elaeis guineensis* Jacq.
oleaster-leafed pear	*Pyrus elaeagnifolia* Pall.
Olga bay larch	*Larix olgensis* A.Henry
Olgan larch	*Larix olgensis* A.Henry
Oregon fir	*Abies grandis* (Douglas ex D. Don) Lindley
Oregon pine	*Pseudotsuga menziesii* (Mirbel) Franco
Oriental beech	*Fagus orientalis Lipsky*
osiers	*Salix* spp.
Pacific red cedar	*Thuja plicata* Donn ex D.Don
Pacific silver fir	*Abies amabilis* Douglas ex J.Forbes
Pacific teak	*Intsia bijuga* (Colebr.) Kuntze
padauk	*Pterocarpus* spp.
paper birch	*Betula papyrifera* Marshall
Pará rubber tree	*Hevea brasiliensis* Müll. Arg.
paulownia	*Paulownia elongata* S.Y. Hu
pedunculate oak	*Quercus robur* L.
pencil cedar	*Juniperus virginiana* L.
pencil pine	*Cupressus sempervirens* L.
pepper tree	*Schinus molle* L.
peppercorn tree	*Schinus molle* L.
pepperina	*Schinus molle* L.
Persian cypress	*Cupressus sempervirens* L.
Persian lilac	*Melia azedarach* L.
Persian walnut	*Juglans regia* L.

Peruvian pepper	*Schinus molle* L.
Peruvian peppertree	*Schinus molle* L.
Philippine mahogany	*Shorea* spp.
pignut	*Carya glabra* Miller
pignut hickory	*Carya glabra* Miller
pine	*Pinus* spp.
pirul Peruvian mastic	*Schinus molle* L.
pitchpine	*Pinus palustris* Mill.
Pondcypress	*Taxodium distichum* (L.) Rich.
ponderosa pine	*Pinus ponderosa* Douglas ex C.Lawson
poplar	*Populus* spp.
Port Orford-cedar	*Chamaecyparis lawsoniana* (A. Murray) Parl.
Pride of India	*Melia azedarach* L.
pruche du Canada	*Tsuga canadensis* (L.) Carrière
quaking aspen	*Populus tremula* L.
quaking aspen	*Populus tremuloides* Michx.
Queensland pine	*Araucaria cunninghamii* Mudie
radiata pine	*Pinus radiata* D.Don
red alder	*Alnus rubra* Bong.
red ash	*Fraxinus pennsylvanica* Marshall
red cedar	*Juniperus virginiana* L.
red cypress	*Taxodium distichum* (L.) Rich.
red fir	*Abies procera* Rehder
red grandis	*Eucalyptus grandis* W. Hill ex Maiden
red hickory	*Carya ovalis* (Wangenh.) Sarg.
red ironwood tree	*Lophira alata* Banks ex Gaertn
red juniper	*Juniperus virginiana* L.
red larch	*Larix laricina* (Du Roi) K. Koch
red oak	*Quercus rubra* L.
red pine	*Pinus resinosa* Sol. ex Aiton
red savin	*Juniperus virginiana* L.
red stringybark	*Eucalyptus macrorhyncha* F.Muell. ex Benth.
red-bud maple	*Acer trautvetteri* Medw.
redgum	*Liquidambar styraciflua* L.
redwood	*Sequoia sempervirens* (D.Don) Endl.
ribbon gum	*Eucalyptus viminalis* Labill.
Richmond river pine	*Araucaria cunninghamii* Mudie
Riga pine	*Pinus sylvestris* L.
river red gum	*Eucalyptus camaldulensis* Dehnh.
rock elm	*Ulmus thomasii* Sarg.

rock maple	*Acer saccharum* Marshall
Rocky Mountain Douglas-fir	*Pseudotsuga menziesii* var. Glauca (Mayr) Franco
rose gum	*Eucalyptus grandis* W. Hill ex Maiden
rowan	*Sorbus aucuparia* L.
rubberwood	*Hevea brasiliensis* Müll. Arg.
Russian larch	*Larix sibirica* Ledeb.
sallows	*Salix* spp.
sambawawa	*Triplochiton scleroxylon* K.Schum.
sand hickory	*Carya pallida* (Ashe) Engelm. & Graebn.
sapele	*Entandrophragma cylindricum* Harms
sapelli	*Entandrophragma cylindricum* Harms
satin-walnut	*Liquidambar styraciflua* L.
Scots pine	*Pinus sylvestris* L.
scrub mahogany	*Intsia bijuga* (Colebr.) Kuntze
seraya	*Shorea* spp.
seringueira	*Hevea brasiliensis* Müll. Arg.
sesendok	*Endospermum malaccense* L.S.Sm.
sessile oak	*Quercus petraea* (Matt.) Lieb.
sharinga tree	*Hevea brasiliensis* Müll. Arg.
shinglewood	*Thuja plicata* Donn ex D.Don
shore pine	*Pinus contorta* Douglas
shortleaf pine (Southern yellow pine)	*Pinus echinata* Mill.
Siberian larch	*Larix sibirica* Ledeb.
Siberian silver birch	*Betula platyphylla* Sukaczev
Siebold's beech	*Fagus crenata* Blume
silk oak	*Grevillea robusta* A.Cunn. ex R.Br.
silky oak	*Grevillea robusta* A.Cunn. ex R.Br.
silver birch	*Betula pendula* Roth.
silver fir	*Abies alba* Mill.
silver maple	*Acer saccharinum* L.
silver oak	*Grevillea robusta* A.Cunn. ex R.Br.
silver pine	*Pinus monticola* Douglas ex D. Don
silver spruce	*Picea engelmannii* Parry ex Engelm.
silverleaf maple	*Acer saccharinum* L.
Sitka spruce	*Picea sitchensis* (Bong.) Carr.
slash pine	*Pinus elliottii* Engelm.
small-leaved lime	*Tilia cordata* Mill.
small-leaved linden	*Tilia cordata* Mill.
smoothbark hickory	*Carya glabra* Miller
soft maple	*Acer saccharinum* L.
soft pine	*Pinus strobus* L.

sour gum	*Nyssa sylvatica* Marshall
southern blue gum	*Eucalyptus globulus* Labill.
Southern cypress	*Taxodium distichum* (L.) Rich.
southern red oak	*Quercus rubra* L.
Southern silky oak	*Grevillea robusta* A.Cunn. ex R.Br.
Southern yellow pine	A number of conifer species which tend to grow in similar plant communities in USA and yield similar strong wood.
Spanish oak	*Quercus falcata* Michx.
speckled alder	*Alnus incana* (L.) Moench
spice birch	*Betula lenta* L.
spotted gum	*Corymbia maculata* (Hook.) K.D. Hill & L.A.S. Johnson
spruce	Picea spp.
star-leaved gum	*Liquidambar styraciflua* L.
stone pine	*Pinus cembra* L.
stringybark	*Eucalyptus obliqua* L'Hér.
sugar cone pine	*Pinus lambertiana* Douglas
sugar maple	*Acer saccharum* Marshall
sugar pine	*Pinus lambertiana* Douglas
sugarberry	*Celtis occidentalis* L.
sugi	*Cryptomeria japonica* (L.f.) D.Don
sumbala	*Parkia biglobosa* (Jacq.) R.Br. ex G.Don
swamp black-gum	*Nyssa biflora* Walter
swamp cypress	*Taxodium distichum* (L.) Rich.
swamp hickory	*Carya glabra* Miller
swamp mahogany	*Eucalyptus robusta* Sm.
swamp maple	*Acer saccharinum* L.
swamp messmate	*Eucalyptus robusta* Sm.
swamp tupelo	*Nyssa biflora* Walter
swan river mahogany	*Eucalyptus marginata* Donn ex Sm.
sweet birch	*Betula lenta* L.
sweet chestnut	*Castanea sativa* Mill.
sweet pignut	*Carya glabra* Miller
sweet pignut hickory	*Carya ovalis* (Wangenh.) Sarg.
sweetgum	*Liquidambar styraciflua* L.
Swiss pine	*Pinus cembra* L.
Swiss stone pine	*Pinus cembra* L.
sycamore	*Acer pseudoplatanus* L.
sycamore maple	*Acer pseudoplatanus* L.
syringa berrytree	*Melia azedarach* L.

tacamahac poplar	*Populus balsamifera* L.
tacamahaca	*Populus balsamifera* L.
tamarack	*Larix laricina* (Du Roi) K. Koch
tanbark-oak	*Notholithocarpus densiflorus* (Hook. & Arn.) Manos, Cannon & S.H.Oh
tanoak	*Notholithocarpus densiflorus* (Hook. & Arn.) Manos, Cannon & S.H.Oh
Tasmanian oak	*Eucalyptus obliqua* L'Hér.
teak	*Tectona grandis* L. f.
Texas cedar elm	*Ulmus crassifolia* Nutt.
tidewater red cypress	*Taxodium distichum* (L.) Rich.
tidewater spruce	*Picea sitchensis* (Bong.) Carr.
trembling aspen	*Populus tremuloides* Michx.
trembling poplar	*Populus tremuloides* Michx.
tuart	*Eucalyptus gomphocephala* DC.
tulip poplar	*Liriodendron tulipifera* L.
tulip tree	*Liriodendron tulipifera* L.
tulipwood	*Liriodendron tulipifera* L.
tupelo	*Nyssa* spp.
tupelo-gum	*Nyssa aquatica* L.
Turkish filbert	*Corylus colurna* L.
Turkish hazel	*Corylus colurna* L.
Turkish pine	*Pinus brutia* Ten.
Tuscan cypress	*Cupressus sempervirens* L.
twisted pine	*Pinus contorta* Douglas
upside-down tree	*Adansonia digitata* L.
Ussuri poplar	*Populus ussuriensis* Komarov
walnut	*Juglans* spp.
Vancouver fir	*Abies grandis* (Douglas ex D. Don) Lindley
warty birch	*Betula pendula* Roth.
water beech	*Platanus occidentalis* L.
water elm	*Ulmus americana* L.
water hickory	*Carya aquatica* (F.Michx.) Nutt.
water maple	*Acer saccharinum* L.
water oak	*Quercus nigra* L.
water tupelo	*Nyssa aquatica* L.
water-gum	*Nyssa aquatica* L.
wawa	*Triplochiton scleroxylon* K.Schum.
western arborvitae	*Thuja plicata* Donn ex D.Don
western hemlock	*Tsuga heterophylla* (Raf.) Sarg.
western hemlock-spruce	*Tsuga heterophylla* (Raf.) Sarg.

western larch	*Larix occidentalis* Nutt.
western plane	*Platanus occidentalis* L.
western red cedar	*Thuja plicata* Donn ex D.Don
western white fir	*Abies grandis* (Douglas ex D. Don) Lindley
Western white pine	*Pinus monticola* Douglas ex D. Don
western yellow-pine	*Pinus ponderosa* Douglas ex C.Lawson
Weymouth pine	*Pinus strobus* L.
white ash	*Fraxinus americana* L.
white birch	*Betula pubescens* Ehrh.
white cedar	*Melia azedarach* L.
white cypress	*Taxodium distichum* (L.) Rich.
white elm	*Ulmus americana* L.
white fir	*Abies concolor* (Gordon) Lindley ex Hildebrand
white gum	*Eucalyptus viminalis* Labill.
white hickory	*Carya tomentosa* Sarg.
white maple	*Acer saccharinum* L.
white milkwood	*Endospermum malaccense* L.S.Sm.
white oak	*Quercus alba* L.
white pine	*Pinus strobus* L.
white poplar	*Populus tremuloides* Michx.
white spruce	*Picea engelmannii* Parry ex Engelm.
white teak	*Gmelina arborea* Roxb.
white willow	*Salix alba* L.
whiteheart hickory	*Carya tomentosa* Sarg.
whitewood	*Endospermum malaccense* L.S.Sm.
whitewood	*Liriodendron tulipifera* L.
wild olive	*Nyssa aquatica* L.
wild pear	*Pyrus* spp.
willow oak	*Quercus phellos* L.
willows	*Salix* sp.
Virginian juniper	*Juniperus virginiana* L.
wormwood	*Artemisia monosperma* L.
yellow birch	*Betula alleghaniensis* Britt.
yellow cedar	*Cupressus nootkatensis* D.Don
yellow cypress	*Taxodium distichum* (L.) Rich.
yellow pine	A number of conifer species which tend to grow in similar plant communities in USA and yield similar strong wood.
yellow-poplar	*Liriodendron tulipifera* L.
yemane	*Gmelina arborea* Roxb.
yezo spruce	*Picea jezoensis* (Siebold & Zucc.) Carr.

Sorted by binomial name

Binomial name	Common/vernacular name
Abies alba Mill.	European silver fir, fir, silver fir
Abies amabilis Douglas ex J.Forbes	Pacific silver fir
Abies balsamea (L.) Mill.	balsam fir
Abies concolor (Gordon) Lindley ex Hildebrand	white fir
Abies grandis (Douglas ex D. Don) Lindley	giant fir, grand fir, great silver fir, lowland white fir, Oregon fir, Vancouver fir, western white fir
Abies procera Rehder	Christmas tree, noble fir, red fir
Acacia mangium Willd.	black wattle, forest mangrove, hickory wattle, mangium
Acacia mangium × *auriculiformis*	acacia hybrid
Acer platanoides L.	Norway maple
Acer pseudoplatanus L.	sycamore, sycamore maple
Acer saccharinum L.	creek maple, large maple, silver maple, silverleaf maple, soft maple, swamp maple, water maple, white maple
Acer saccharum Marshall	rock maple, sugar maple
Acer trautvetteri Medw.	red-bud maple
Adansonia digitata L.	African baobab, boabab, cream of tartar tree, monkey-bread tree, upside-down tree
Alnus glutinosa L.	European alder, common alder, black alder
Alnus incana (L.) Moench	grey alder, speckled alder
Alnus rubra Bong.	red alder
Alnus subcordata C.A. Mey.	Caucasian alder
Anthocephalus chinensis (Lamk) A. Rich. ex Walp. and *Anthocephalus macrophyllus* (Roxb.) Havil.	bur-flower tree, cadamba, common bur-flower tree, kadam, kelempayan, laran, Leichhardt pine
Araucaria cunninghamii Mudie	colonial pine, Dorrigo pine, hoop pine, Moreton bay pine, Queensland pine, Richmond river pine
Artemisia monosperma L.	wormwood
Betula alleghaniensis Britt.	golden birch, yellow birch
Betula lenta L.	black birch, cherry birch, mahogany birch, spice birch, sweet birch
Betula papyrifera Marshall	American white birch, canoe birch, paper birch
Betula pendula Roth.	East Asian white birch, silver birch, warty birch
Betula platyphylla Sukaczev	Asian white birch, Japanese white birch, Siberian silver birch
Betula pubescens Ehrh.	downy birch, European white birch, hairy birch, moor birch, white birch
Calocedrus decurrens (Torr.) Florin	California incense-cedar, incense cedar
Carpinus betuls L.	common hornbeam, European hornbeam

Carya aquatica (F.Michx.) Nutt.	bitter pecan, water hickory
Carya cordiformis (Wangenh.) K.Koch	bitternut hickory
Carya glabra Miller	broom hickory, coast pignut hickory, pignut, pignut hickory, smoothbark hickory, swamp hickory, sweet pignut
Carya ovalis (Wangenh.) Sarg.	red hickory, sweet pignut hickory
Carya pallida (Ashe) Engelm. & Graebn.	sand hickory
Carya tomentosa Sarg.	bullnut, hognut, mockernut, mockernut hickory, white hickory, whiteheart hickory
Castanea dentata (Marsh.) Borkh.	American chestnut
Castanea sativa Mill.	sweet chestnut
Celtis occidentalis L.	American hackberry,beaverwood, common hackberry, hackberry, nettletree, northern hackberry, sugarberry
Chamaecyparis lawsoniana (A. Murray) Parl.	Port Orford-cedar
Chamaecyparis obtuse (Siebold & Zucc.) Endl.	hinoki, hinoki cypress, Japanese cypress
Citrus limon (L.) Osbeck	lemon tree
Corylus colurna L.	Turkish filbert, Turkish hazel
Corymbia maculata (Hook.) K.D. Hill & L.A.S.Johnson	spotted gum
Cryptomeria japonica (L.f.) D.Don	Japanese cedar, Japanese redwood, Japanese sugi, sugi
Cunninghamia konishii Hayata	China-fir, Chinese fir, Cunninghamia
Cupressus nootkatensis D.Don	Alaska cedar, Alaska yellow cedar, Nootka cedar, yellow cedar
Cupressus sempervirens L.	Italian cypress, Mediterranean cypress, pencil pine, Persian cypress, Tuscan cypress
Dendrocalamus asper (Schult.) Backer	bamboo (monocot tree)
Dendrocalamus barbatus	giant bamboo (monocot tree)
Dendrocalamus spp.	bamboo (monocot tree)
Dicorynia guianensis Amshoff	Angelique, Angelique batard, Angelique gris, Barakaroeballi, Basralokus
Distemonanthus benthamianus Baill.	Ayan, movingui, Nigerian Satinwood
Elaeis guineensis Jacq. (monocot tree)	African oil palm, macaw-fat, oil palm
Endospermum malaccense L.S.Sm.	cheesewood, sesendok, white milkwood, whitewood
Entandrophragma cylindricum Harms	sapele, sapelli
Eucalyptus camaldulensis Dehnh.	river red gum
Eucalyptus cloeziana F.Muell.	dead finish, Gympie messmate
Eucalyptus delegatensis R.T.Baker	alpine ash
Eucalyptus globulus Labill.	blue gum, southern blue gum
Eucalyptus gomphocephala DC.	tuart
Eucalyptus grandis W. Hill ex Maiden	flooded gum, red grandis, rose gum

Eucalyptus macrorhyncha F.Muell. ex Benth.	red stringybark
Eucalyptus marginata Donn ex Sm.	djarraly, jarrah, swan river mahogany
Eucalyptus obliqua L'Hér.	brown top, brown top stringbark, messmate, messmate stringybark, Tasmanian oak
Eucalyptus robusta Sm.	swamp mahogany, swamp messmate
Eucalyptus viminalis Labill.	manna gum, ribbon gum, white gum
Fagus crenata Blume	buna, Japanese beech, Siebold's beech
Fagus grandifolia Ehrh.	American beech, North American beech
Fagus moesiaca C.	Balkan beech
Fagus orientalis Lipsky	Oriental beech
Fagus sylvatica L.	common beech, European beech
Fraxinus americana L.	American ash, white ash
Fraxinus angustifolia Vahl.	narrow-leaved ash
Fraxinus excelsior L.	common ash, European ash
Fraxinus nigra Marshall	black ash
Fraxinus pennsylvanica Marshall	green ash, red ash
Gmelina arborea Roxb.	beechwood, gmelina, goomar teak, Kashmir tree, Malay beechwood, white teak, yemane
Grevillea robusta A.Cunn. ex R.Br.	Australian silver oak, silk oak, silky oak, silver oak, Southern silky oak
Hevea brasiliensis Müll. Arg.	Pará rubber tree, rubberwood, seringueira, sharinga tree
Intsia bijuga (Colebr.) Kuntze	Johnstone river teak, Pacific teak, scrub mahogany
Intsia spp. (*I. bijuga, I. palembanica*)	Ipil, Kwila, merbau
Juglans nigra L.	black walnut, eastern American black walnut
Juglans regia L.	Carpathian walnut, common walnut, English walnut, Madeira walnut, Persian walnut
Juniperus communis L.	common juniper
Juniperus virginiana L.	aromatic cedar, Baton Rouge, Carolina cedar, eastern juniper, eastern red cedar, eastern redcedar, pencil cedar, red cedar, red juniper, red savin, Virginian juniper
Larix laricina (Du Roi) K. Koch	American larch, black larch, eastern larch, hackmatack, red larch, tamarack
Larix occidentalis Nutt.	western larch
Larix olgensis A.Henry	Olga bay larch, Olgan larch
Larix sibirica Ledeb.	Russian larch, Siberian larch
Liquidambar styraciflua L.	alligatorwood, American storax, American sweetgum, bilsted, hazel pine, redgum, satin-walnut, star-leaved gum, sweetgum
Liriodendron tulipifera L.	American tulip tree, fiddletree, fiddletree, tulip poplar, tulip tree, tulipwood, whitewood, yellow-poplar

Lophira alata Banks ex Gaertn	azobé, ekki, red ironwood tree,
Magnolia spp.	magnolia
Malus domestica Borkh.	apple
Melia azedarach L.	bead-tree, Cape lilac, chinaberry tree, Indian lilac, mindi, Persian lilac, Pride of India, syringa berrytree, white cedar
Mitragyna ciliata Aubrév. & Pellegr.	abura, bahia, M'Boy
Notholithocarpus densiflorus (Hook. & Arn.) Manos, Cannon & S.H.Oh	tanbark-oak, tanoak
Nyssa aquatica L.	cottongum, large tupelo, tupelo-gum, water tupelo, water-gum, wild olive
Nyssa biflora Walter	swamp black-gum, swamp tupelo
Nyssa sylvatica Marshall	black gum, black tupelo, sour gum
Paraserienthes falcata Becker	albizzia
Parkia biglobosa (Jacq.) R.Br. ex G.Don	African locust bean, dodongba, iru, néré, netetou, sumbala
Paulownia elongata S.Y. Hu	paulownia
Picea abies (L.) Karst.	European spruce, Norway spruce
Picea engelmannii Parry ex Engelm.	Engelmann spruce, mountain spruce, silver spruce, white spruce
Picea jezoensis (Siebold & Zucc.) Carr.	dark-bark spruce, ezo spruce, Ezomatsu, jezo spruce, yezo spruce
Picea mariana (Mill.) Britton, Sterns & Poggenburg	black spruce
Picea sitchensis (Bong.) Carr.	coast spruce, Sitka spruce, tidewater spruce
Pinaceae spp.	cedar
Pinus brutia Ten.	brutia pine, Calabrian pine, East Mediterranean pine, Turkish pine
Pinus caribaea Morelet	Caribbean pine
Pinus cembra L.	Arolla pine, Austrian stone pine, stone pine, Swiss pine, Swiss stone pine
Pinus contorta Douglas	contorta pine, lodgepole pine, shore pine, twisted pine
Pinus densiflora Siebold & Zucc.	Japanese pine, Japanese red pine, Korean red pine
Pinus echinata Mill.	shortleaf pine (Southern yellow pine)
Pinus elliottii Engelm.	slash pine
Pinus halepensis Mill.	Aleppo pine
Pinus lambertiana Douglas	sugar cone pine, sugar pine
Pinus massoniana Lamb.	Masson's pine
Pinus monticola Douglas ex D. Don	California mountain pine, silver pine, Western white pine
Pinus nigra Arnold.	Austrian pine
Pinus nigra var. maritima	Corsican pine

Pinus palustris Mill.	longleaf pine, pitchpine
Pinus pinaster Aiton	cluster pine, maritime pine
Pinus ponderosa Douglas ex C.Lawson	blackjack pine, bull pine, filipinus pine, ponderosa pine, western yellow-pine
Pinus radiata D.Don	insignis pine, Monterey pine, radiata pine
Pinus resinosa Sol. ex Aiton	Norway pine, red pine
Pinus strobus L.	eastern white pine, northern white pine, soft pine, Weymouth pine, white pine
Pinus sylvestris L.	Baltic pine, Riga pine, Scots pine
Pinus taeda L.	loblolly pine
Platanus occidentalis L.	American planetree, American sycamore, buttonwood, occidental plane, water beech, western plane
Populus balsamifera L.	balsam poplar, bam, bamtree, eastern balsam-poplar, hackmatack, tacamahac poplar, tacamahaca
Populus cathayana Rehder	Cathay poplar, Mantsurian poplar
Populus nigra L. (section *Aigeiros*)	cottonwood
Populus nigra var. *pyramidalis* L.	black poplar
Populus ssp.	hybrid poplar
Populus tomentosa Carr.	Chinese white poplar
Populus tremula L.	aspen, common aspen, Eurasian aspen, European aspen, quaking aspen
Populus tremuloides Michx.	American aspen, golden aspen, mountain aspen, quaking aspen, trembling aspen, trembling poplar, white poplar
Populus ussuriensis Komarov	Ussuri poplar
Prioria copaifera Griseb.	cativo
Prunus serotina Ehrh.	black cherry
Pseudotsuga menziesii (Mirbel) Franco	Columbian pine, Douglas fir, Douglas-fir, Oregon pine
Pseudotsuga menziesii var. Glauca (Mayr) Franco	Rocky Mountain Douglas-fir
Pseudotsuga menziesii var. Lindleyana (Roezl) Carrière	Mexican Douglas fir
Pseudotsuga menziesii var. *menziesii*	coast Douglas-fir
Pterocarpus dalbergioides DC.	Andaman padauk, Andaman redwood, East Indian mahogany
Pterocarpus macrocarpus Kurz.	Burmese padauk
Pterocarpus soyauxii Taub.	African coralwood, African padauk
Pterocarpus spp.	padauk
Pyrus spp.	wild pear
Pyrus elaeagnifolia Pall.	oleaster-leafed pear
Quercus alba L.	white oak

Quercus falcata Michx.	Spanish oak
Quercus kelloggii Newberry	California black oak, Kellogg oak
Quercus nigra L.	water oak
Quercus petraea (Matt.) Lieb.	Cornish oak, durmast oak, sessile oak
Quercus phellos L.	willow oak
Quercus robur L.	common oak, English oak, European oak, pedunculate oak
Quercus rubra L.	northern red oak, red oak, southern red oak
Robinia pseudoacacia L.	black locust, false acacia
Salix alba L.	white willow
Salix spp.	osiers, sallows, willows
Schinus molle L.	American pepper, anacahuita, California pepper tree, escobilla, false pepper, molle del Peru, pepper tree, peppercorn tree, pepperina, Peruvian pepper, Peruvian peppertree, pirul Peruvian mastic
Sequoia sempervirens (D.Don) Endl.	California redwood, coast redwood, coastal redwood, redwood
Shorea spp.	balau, bangkirai, lauan, lawaan, luan, meranti, Philippine mahogany, seraya
Sorbus aucuparia L.	mountain ash, rowan
Taxodium distichum (L.) Rich.	bald cypress, baldcypress, gulf cypress, Pondcypress, red cypress, Southern cypress, swamp cypress, tidewater red cypress, white cypress, yellow cypress
Tectona grandis L. f.	Burmese teak, Central Province teak (CP teak), Nagpur teak, teak
Terminalia superba Engl. & Diels	afara , African limba wood, frake, korina, limba
Thuja occidentalis L.	eastern arborvitae, eastern white cedar, northern white-cedar
Thuja plicata Donn ex D.Don	giant arborvitae, giant cedar, Pacific red cedar, shinglewood, western arborvitae, western red cedar
Tilia americana L.	American basswood, American linden
Tilia cordata Mill.	littleleaf linden, small-leaved lime, small-leaved linden
Triplochiton scleroxylon K.Schum.	abachi, African whitewood, ayous, obeche, sambawama, wawa
Tsuga canadensis (L.) Carrière	Canadian hemlock, eastern hemlock, eastern hemlock-spruce, pruche du Canada
Tsuga heterophylla (Raf.) Sarg.	western hemlock, western hemlock-spruce
Ulmus americana L.	American elm, water elm, white elm
Ulmus crassifolia Nutt.	cedar elm, Texas cedar elm
Ulmus thomasii Sarg.	cork elm, rock elm

Grouped by genus

Group	Binomial name	Common/vernacular name
Acasia	***Acacia* spp.**	
	Acacia mangium Willd.	black wattle, forest mangrove, hickory wattle, mangium
	Acacia mangium × *auriculiformis*	acacia hybrid
Alder	***Alnus* spp.**	
	Alnus glutinosa L.	European alder, common alder, black alder
	Alnus incana (L.) Moench	grey alder, speckled alder
	Alnus rubra Bong.	red alder
	Alnus subcordata C.A. Mey.	Caucasian alder
Apple	***Malus* spp.**	
	Malus domestica Borkh.	apple
Ash	***Fraxinus* spp.**	
	Fraxinus americana L.	American ash, white ash
	Fraxinus angustifolia Vahl.	narrow-leaved ash
	Fraxinus excelsior L.	common ash, European ash
	Fraxinus nigra Marshall	black ash
	Fraxinus pennsylvanica Marshall	green ash, red ash
Beech	***Fagus* spp.**	
	Fagus crenata Blume	buna, Japanese beech, Siebold's beech
	Fagus grandifolia Ehrh.	American beech, North American beech
	Fagus moesiaca C.	Balkan beech
	Fagus orientalis Lipsky	Oriental beech
	Fagus sylvatica L.	common beech, European beech
Birch	***Betula* spp.**	
	Betula alleghaniensis Britt.	golden birch, yellow birch
	Betula lenta L.	black birch, cherry birch, mahogany birch, spice birch, sweet birch
	Betula papyrifera Marshall	American white birch, canoe birch, paper birch
	Betula pendula Roth.	East Asian white birch, silver birch, warty birch
	Betula platyphylla Sukaczev	Asian white birch, Japanese white birch, Siberian silver birch
	Betula pubescens Ehrh.	downy birch, European white birch, hairy birch, moor birch, white birch
Chestnut	***Castanea* spp.**	
	Castanea dentata (Marsh.) Borkh.	American chestnut
	Castanea sativa Mill.	sweet chestnut

Cypress	***Cupressus* spp.**	
	Cupressus nootkatensis D.Don	Alaska cedar, Alaska yellow cedar, Nootka cedar, yellow cedar
	Cupressus sempervirens L.	Italian cypress, Mediterranean cypress, pencil pine, Persian cypress, Tuscan cypress
Elm	***Ulmus* spp.**	
	Ulmus americana L.	American elm, water elm, white elm
	Ulmus crassifolia Nutt.	cedar elm, Texas cedar elm
	Ulmus thomasii Sarg.	cork elm, rock elm
Eucalyptus	***Eucalyptus* spp.**	
	Eucalyptus camaldulensis Dehnh.	river red gum
	Eucalyptus cloeziana F.Muell.	dead finish, Gympie messmate
	Eucalyptus delegatensis R.T.Baker	alpine ash
	Eucalyptus globulus Labill.	blue gum, southern blue gum
	Eucalyptus gomphocephala DC.	tuart
	Eucalyptus grandis W. Hill ex Maiden	flooded gum, red grandis, rose gum
	Eucalyptus macrorhyncha F.Muell. ex Benth.	red stringybark
	Eucalyptus marginata Donn ex Sm.	djarraly, jarrah, swan river mahogany
	Eucalyptus obliqua L'Hér.	brown top, brown top stringbark, messmate, messmate stringybark, Tasmanian oak
	Eucalyptus robusta Sm.	swamp mahogany, swamp messmate
	Eucalyptus viminalis Labill.	manna gum, ribbon gum, white gum
Fir	***Abies* spp.**	
	Abies alba Mill.	European silver fir, fir, silver fir
	Abies amabilis Douglas ex J.Forbes	Pacific silver fir
	Abies balsamea (L.) Mill.	balsam fir
	Abies concolor (Gordon) Lindley ex Hildebrand	white fir
	Abies grandis (Douglas ex D. Don) Lindley	giant fir, grand fir, great silver fir, lowland white fir, Oregon fir, Vancouver fir, western white fir
	Abies procera Rehder	Christmas tree, noble fir, red fir
Hazelnut	***Corylus* spp.**	
	Corylus colurna L.	Turkish filbert, Turkish hazel
Hemlock	***Tsuga* spp.**	
	Tsuga canadensis (L.) Carrière	Canadian hemlock, eastern hemlock, eastern hemlock-spruce, pruche du Canada
	Tsuga heterophylla (Raf.) Sarg.	western hemlock, western hemlock-spruce

	Tsuga heterophylla (Raf.) Sarg.	
Hickory	***Carya* spp.**	
	Carya aquatica (F.Michx.) Nutt.	bitter pecan, water hickory
	Carya cordiformis (Wangenh.) K.Koch	bitternut hickory
	Carya glabra Miller	broom hickory, coast pignut hickory, pignut, pignut hickory, smoothbark hickory, swamp hickory, sweet pignut
	Carya ovalis (Wangenh.) Sarg.	red hickory, sweet pignut hickory
	Carya pallida (Ashe) Engelm. & Graebn.	sand hickory
	Carya tomentosa Sarg.	bullnut, hognut, mockernut, mockernut hickory, white hickory, whiteheart hickory
Hornbeam	***Carpinus* spp.**	
	Carpinus betuls L.	common hornbeam, European hornbeam
Juniper	***Juniperus* spp.**	
	Juniperus communis L.	common juniper
	Juniperus virginiana L.	aromatic cedar, Baton Rouge, Carolina cedar, eastern juniper, eastern red cedar, eastern redcedar, pencil cedar, red cedar, red juniper, red savin, Virginian juniper
Larch	***Larix* spp.**	
	Larix laricina (Du Roi) K. Koch	American larch, black larch, eastern larch, hackmatack, red larch, tamarack
	Larix occidentalis Nutt.	western larch
	Larix olgensis A.Henry	Olga bay larch, Olgan larch
	Larix sibirica Ledeb.	Russian larch, Siberian larch
Linden	***Tilia* spp.**	
	Tilia americana L.	American basswood, American linden
	Tilia cordata Mill.	littleleaf linden, small-leaved lime, small-leaved linden
Maple	***Acer* spp.**	
	Acer platanoides L.	Norway maple
	Acer pseudoplatanus L.	sycamore, sycamore maple
	Acer saccharinum L.	creek maple, large maple, silver maple, silverleaf maple, soft maple, swamp maple, water maple, white maple
	Acer saccharum Marshall	rock maple, sugar maple
	Acer trautvetteri Medw.	red-bud maple
Merbau	***Intsia* spp.**	
	Intsia spp. (*I. bijuga*, *I. palembanica*)	Ipil, Kwila, merbau

Oak	***Quercus* spp.**	
	Quercus alba L.	white oak
	Quercus falcata Michx.	Spanish oak
	Quercus kelloggii Newberry	California black oak, Kellogg oak
	Quercus nigra L.	water oak
	Quercus petraea (Matt.) Lieb.	Cornish oak, durmast oak, sessile oak
	Quercus phellos L.	willow oak
	Quercus robur L.	common oak, English oak, European oak, pedunculate oak
	Quercus rubra L.	northern red oak, red oak, southern red oak
Pine	***Pinus* spp.**	
	A genus of more than 160 species	albizzia
	A number of conifer species which tend to grow in similar plant communities in USA and yield similar strong wood.	Southern yellow pine, yellow pine
	Pinus brutia Ten.	brutia pine, Calabrian pine, East Mediterranean pine, Turkish pine
	Pinus caribaea Morelet	Caribbean pine
	Pinus cembra L.	Arolla pine, Austrian stone pine, stone pine, Swiss pine, Swiss stone pine
	Pinus contorta Douglas	contorta pine, lodgepole pine, shore pine, twisted pine
	Pinus densiflora Siebold & Zucc.	Japanese pine, Japanese red pine, Korean red pine
	Pinus echinata Mill.	shortleaf pine (Southern yellow pine)
	Pinus elliottii Engelm.	slash pine
	Pinus halepensis Mill.	Aleppo pine
	Pinus lambertiana Douglas	sugar cone pine, sugar pine
	Pinus massoniana Lamb.	Masson's pine
	Pinus monticola Douglas ex D. Don	California mountain pine, silver pine, Western white pine
	Pinus nigra Arnold.	Austrian pine
	Pinus nigra var. maritima	Corsican pine
	Pinus palustris Mill.	longleaf pine, pitchpine
	Pinus pinaster Aiton	cluster pine, maritime pine
	Pinus ponderosa Douglas ex C.Lawson	blackjack pine, bull pine, filipinus pine, ponderosa pine, western yellow-pine
	Pinus radiata D.Don	insignis pine, Monterey pine, radiata pine
	Pinus resinosa Sol. ex Aiton	Norway pine, red pine
	Pinus strobus L.	eastern white pine, northern white pine, soft pine, Weymouth pine, white pine

	Pinus sylvestris L.	Baltic pine, Riga pine, Scots pine
	Pinus taeda L.	loblolly pine
Poplar	***Populus* spp.**	
	Populus balsamifera L.	balsam poplar, bam, bamtree, eastern balsam-poplar, hackmatack, tacamahac poplar, tacamahaca
	Populus cathayana Rehder	Cathay poplar, Mantsurian poplar
	Populus nigra L. (section *Aigeiros*)	cottonwood
	Populus nigra var. *pyramidalis* L.	black poplar
	Populus tomentosa Carr.	Chinese white poplar
	Populus tremula L.	aspen, common aspen, Eurasian aspen, European aspen, quaking aspen
	Populus tremuloides Michx.	American aspen, golden aspen, mountain aspen, quaking aspen, trembling aspen, trembling poplar, white poplar
	Populus ussuriensis Komarov	Ussuri poplar
	Populus ssp.	hybrid poplar
Rubberwood	***Hevea* spp.**	
	Hevea brasiliensis Müll. Arg.	Pará rubber tree, rubberwood, seringueira, sharinga tree
Spruce	***Picea* spp.**	
	Picea abies (L.) Karst.	European spruce, Norway spruce
	Picea engelmannii Parry ex Engelm.	Engelmann spruce, mountain spruce, silver spruce, white spruce
	Picea jezoensis (Siebold & Zucc.) Carr.	dark-bark spruce, ezo spruce, Ezomatsu, jezo spruce, yezo spruce
	Picea mariana (Mill.) Britton, Sterns & Poggenburg	black spruce
	Picea sitchensis (Bong.) Carr.	coast spruce, Sitka spruce, tidewater spruce
Thuja	***Thuja* spp.**	
	Thuja occidentalis L.	eastern arborvitae, eastern white cedar, northern white-cedar
	Thuja plicata Donn ex D.Don	giant arborvitae, giant cedar, Pacific red cedar, shinglewood, western arborvitae, western red cedar
Tupelo	***Nyssa* spp.**	
	Nyssa aquatica L.	cottongum, large tupelo, tupelo-gum, water tupelo, water-gum, wild olive
	Nyssa biflora Walter	swamp black-gum, swamp tupelo
Walnut	***Juglans* spp.**	
	Juglans nigra L.	black walnut, eastern American black walnut

	Juglans regia L.	Carpathian walnut, common walnut, English walnut, Madeira walnut, Persian walnut
Willow	***Salix* spp.**	
	Salix alba L.	white willow
	Salix spp.	osiers, sallows, willows
Others		
	Adansonia digitata L.	African baobab, boabab, cream of tartar tree, monkey-bread tree, upside-down tree
	Anthocephalus chinensis (Lamk) A. Rich. ex Walp. and *Anthocephalus macrophyllus* (Roxb.) Havil.	bur-flower tree, cadamba, common bur-flower tree, kadam, kelempayan, laran, Leichhardt pine
	Araucaria cunninghamii Mudie	colonial pine, Dorrigo pine, hoop pine, Moreton bay pine, Queensland pine, Richmond river pine
	Artemisia monosperma L.	wormwood
	Calocedrus decurrens (Torr.) Florin	California incense-cedar, incense cedar
	Celtis occidentalis L.	American hackberry,beaverwood, common hackberry, hackberry, nettletree, northern hackberry, sugarberry
	Chamaecyparis lawsoniana (A. Murray) Parl.	Port Orford-cedar
	Chamaecyparis obtuse (Siebold & Zucc.) Endl.	hinoki, hinoki cypress, Japanese cypress
	Citrus limon (L.) Osbeck	lemon tree
	Corymbia maculata (Hook.) K.D. Hill & L.A.S.Johnson	spotted gum
	Cryptomeria japonica (L.f.) D.Don	Japanese cedar, Japanese redwood, Japanese sugi, sugi
	Cunninghamia konishii Hayata	China-fir, Chinese fir, Cunninghamia
	Dendrocalamus asper (Schult.) Backer	bamboo (monocot tree)
	Dendrocalamus barbatus	giant bamboo (monocot tree)
	Dendrocalamus spp.	bamboo (monocot tree)
	Dicorynia guianensis Amshoff	Angelique, Angelique batard, Angelique gris, Barakaroeballi, Basralokus
	Distemonanthus benthamianus Baill.	Ayan, movingui, Nigerian Satinwood
	Elaeis guineensis Jacq. (monocot tree)	African oil palm, macaw-fat, oil palm
	Endospermum malaccense L.S.Sm.	cheesewood, sesendok, white milkwood, whitewood

Entandrophragma cylindricum Harms	sapele, sapelli
Gmelina arborea Roxb.	beechwood, gmelina, goomar teak, Kashmir tree, Malay beechwood, white teak, yemane
Grevillea robusta A.Cunn. ex R.Br.	Australian silver oak, silk oak, silky oak, silver oak, Southern silky oak
Intsia bijuga (Colebr.) Kuntze	Johnstone river teak, Pacific teak, scrub mahogany
Liquidambar styraciflua L.	alligatorwood, American storax, American sweetgum, bilsted, hazel pine, redgum, satin-walnut, star-leaved gum, sweetgum
Liriodendron tulipifera L.	American tulip tree, fiddletree, fiddletree, tulip poplar, tulip tree, tulipwood, whitewood, yellow-poplar
Lophira alata Banks ex Gaertn	azobé, ekki, red ironwood tree,
Magnolia spp.	magnolia
Melia azedarach L.	bead-tree, Cape lilac, chinaberry tree, Indian lilac, mindi, Persian lilac, Pride of India, syringa berrytree, white cedar
Mitragyna ciliata Aubrév. & Pellegr.	abura, bahia, M'Boy
Notholithocarpus densiflorus (Hook. & Arn.) Manos, Cannon & S.H.Oh	tanbark-oak, tanoak
Nyssa sylvatica Marshall	black gum, black tupelo, sour gum
Paraserienthes falcata Becker	albizzia
Parkia biglobosa (Jacq.) R.Br. ex G.Don	African locust bean, dodongba, iru, néré, netetou, sumbala
Paulownia elongata S.Y. Hu	paulownia
Pinaceae spp.	cedar
Platanus occidentalis L.	American planetree, American sycamore, buttonwood, occidental plane, water beech, western plane
Prioria copaifera Griseb.	cativo
Prunus serotina Ehrh.	black cherry
Pseudotsuga menziesii (Mirbel) Franco	Columbian pine, Douglas fir, Douglas-fir, Oregon pine
Pseudotsuga menziesii var. Glauca (Mayr) Franco	Rocky Mountain Douglas-fir
Pseudotsuga menziesii var. Lindleyana (Roezl) Carrière	Mexican Douglas fir
Pseudotsuga menziesii var. *menziesii*	coast Douglas-fir

Pterocarpus dalbergioides DC.	Andaman padauk, Andaman redwood, East Indian mahogany
Pterocarpus macrocarpus Kurz.	Burmese padauk
Pterocarpus soyauxii Taub.	African coralwood, African padauk
Pterocarpus spp.	padauk
Pyrus spp.	wild pear
Pyrus elaeagnifolia Pall.	oleaster-leafed pear
Robinia pseudoacacia L.	black locust, false acacia
Schinus molle L.	American pepper, anacahuita, California pepper tree, escobilla, false pepper, molle del Peru, pepper tree, peppercorn tree, pepperina, Peruvian pepper, Peruvian peppertree, pirul Peruvian mastic
Sequoia sempervirens (D.Don) Endl.	California redwood, coast redwood, coastal redwood, redwood
Shorea spp.	balau, bangkirai, lauan, lawaan, luan, meranti, Philippine mahogany, seraya
Sorbus aucuparia L.	mountain ash, rowan
Taxodium distichum (L.) Rich.	bald cypress, baldcypress, gulf cypress, Pondcypress, red cypress, Southern cypress, swamp cypress, tidewater red cypress, white cypress, yellow cypress
Tectona grandis L. f.	Burmese teak, Central Province teak (CP teak), Nagpur teak, teak
Terminalia superba Engl. & Diels	afara, African limba wood, frake, korina, limba
Triplochiton scleroxylon K.Schum.	abachi, African whitewood, ayous, obeche, sambawawa, wawa

Index